Lecture Notes in Computer Science   9631

Commenced Publication in 1973
Founding and Former Series Editors:
Gerhard Goos, Juris Hartmanis, and Jan van Leeuwen

More information about this series at http://www.springer.com/series/7411

Thomas Karagiannis
Xenofontas Dimitropoulos (Eds.)

Passive and Active Measurement

17th International Conference, PAM 2016
Heraklion, Greece, March 31 – April 1, 2016
Proceedings

 Springer

Editors
Thomas Karagiannis
Microsoft Research
Cambridge
UK

Xenofontas Dimitropoulos
FORTH-ICS
Heraklion
Greece

ISSN 0302-9743   ISSN 1611-3349 (electronic)
Lecture Notes in Computer Science
ISBN 978-3-319-30504-2   ISBN 978-3-319-30505-9 (eBook)
DOI 10.1007/978-3-319-30505-9

Library of Congress Control Number: 2016931998

LNCS Sublibrary: SL5 – Computer Communication Networks and Telecommunications

Printed on acid-free paper

This Springer imprint is published by SpringerNature
The registered company is Springer International Publishing AG Switzerland

Preface

Welcome to the proceedings of the 2016 Passive and Active Measurements (PAM) conference, which was held in Heraklion, Crete, in Greece. The conference took place from March 31 to April 1, and featured 30 papers spanning a wide spectrum of topics in the general area of Internet measurements. This was the 17th year of PAM, which continues the tradition of a conference publishing original, early academic work that fosters discussion and active participation from the attendees.

While PAM in the past focused on research and practical applications of network measurement at Layer-3, over the past few years, PAM has broadened its scope significantly to encompass measurements of networked applications, content distribution networks, online social networks, overlay networks, and more. Measurement technology is needed at all layers of the stack: for power profiling of hardware components; at the MAC/network/transport layers; as well as up the stack for application profiling and even to collect user feedback. Measurement technologies are being designed for the digital home, residential access networks, wireless and mobile access, enterprise, ISP, and data center networks.

Overall, PAM aims to understand the role that measurement techniques can play in networked environments and applications, across different layers, and how they can serve as critical building blocks for broader measurement needs. At the same time, PAM also continues with its original goal, to expand the techniques, tools, and practical uses of network measurement technology and to be open to works at their early stages.

This year PAM attracted 93 submissions from a variety of institutions in academia and industry all around the world – authors of submitted papers originated from 22 different counties representing 128 institutions! In all, 30 papers were selected for the conference by the Technical Program Committee (TPC) having a similar diverse geographical and institutional span (12 countries, 44 institutions). The TPC itself comprised experts across several areas so that the new, broadened scope of PAM is well represented. Most TCP members were selected from PAM participants and contributors in previous conferences.

Each paper received at least three reviews from TPC members, while papers were extensively discussed on-line by the TPC after the review round was over. A number of papers were selectively shepherded, as reviewers required a number of comments to be addressed before final publication. This year's program comprised high-quality papers covering a wide scope of topics ranging from security and privacy, studies on mobile, cellular, broadband and the Web, to more traditional PAM topic such as DNS, routing and measurement frameworks, and testbeds.

Before closing this preface, we would like to thank the Steering Committee for its guidance throughout the organization of the conference, and Antonis Papadogiannakis, who provided an excellent advertisement campaign of the conference as our publicity chair. We are further indebted to Pavlos Sermpezis for his tremendous support for HotCRP and in the overall organization of the conference. Last but not least, we would like to thank our local volunteers who made the conference possible.

March 2016

Thomas Karagiannis
Xenofontas Dimitropoulos

Organization

General Chair

Xenofontas Dimitropoulos   University of Crete/FORTH-ICS, Greece

Program Chair

Thomas Karagiannis   Microsoft Research, UK

Publicity Chair

Antonis Papadogiannakis   FORTH-ICS, Greece

Local Arrangements Chairs

Christos Liaskos   FORTH-ICS, Greece
Pavlos Sermpezis   FORTH-ICS, Greece

Steering Committee

Fabio Ricciato   University of Salento, Italy
George Riley   Georgia Institute of Technology, USA
Ian Graham   Endace, New Zealand
Neil Spring   University of Maryland, USA
Nevil Brownlee   The University of Auckland, New Zealand
Nina Taft   Google, USA
Matthew Roughan   University of Adelaide, Australia
Rocky K.C. Chang   The Hong Kong Polytechnic University, Hong Kong, SAR China

Program Committee

Alan Mislove   Northeastern University, USA
Aleksandar Kuzmanovic   Northwestern University, USA
Alessandro Finamore   Telefonica, Spain
Amogh Dhamdhere   CAIDA/UC San Diego, USA
Ben Zhao   University of California Santa Barbara, USA
Bozidar Radunovic   Microsoft Research, UK
Chadi Barakat   Inria, France
Christo Wilson   Northeastern University, USA
Constantine Dovrolis   Georgia Tech, USA

Costin Raiciu	Universitatea Politehnica Bucuresti, Romania
Dejan Kostic	KTH Royal Institute of Technology, Sweden
Elias Athanasopoulos	Vrije Universiteit Amsterdam, The Netherlands
Fahad Dogar	Tufts University, USA
Georgios Smaragdakis	MIT/TU Berlin, Germany
Gianluca Iannaccone	Facebook, USA
Harsha Madhyastha	University of Michigan, USA
Marco Mellia	Politecnico di Torino, Italy
Marina K. Mahesh	The University of Edinburgh, UK
Matthew Luckie	University of Waikato, New Zealand
Pietro Michiardi	Eurecom, France
Richard Mortier	University of Cambridge, UK
Robert Beverly	Naval Postgraduate School, USA
Rocky K.C. Chang	The Hong Kong Polytechnic University, Hong Kong, SAR China
Roya Ensafi	Princeton, USA
Simon Leinen	SWITCH, Switzerland
Srikanth Sundaresan	ICSI, USA

Sponsoring Institutions

Microsoft Research, UK

Contents

Testbeds and Frameworks

Web

DNS and Routing

IXPs and MPLS

Scheduling and Timing

Security and Privacy

Exploring Tor's Activity Through Long-Term Passive TLS Traffic Measurement

Johanna Amann[1(✉)] and Robin Sommer[1,2]

[1] International Computer Science Institute, Berkeley, USA
{johanna,robin}@icir.org
[2] Lawrence Berkeley National Laboratory, Berkeley, USA

Abstract. Tor constitutes one of the pillars of anonymous online communication. It allows its users to communicate while concealing from observers their location as well as the Internet resources they access. Since its first release in 2002, Tor has enjoyed an increasing level of popularity with now commonly more than 2,000,000 simultaneous active clients on the network. However, even though Tor is widely popular, there is only little understanding of the large-scale behavior of its network clients. In this paper, we present a longitudinal study of the Tor network based on passive analysis of TLS traffic at the Internet uplinks of four large universities inside and outside of the US. We show how Tor traffic can be identified by properties of its autogenerated certificates, and we use this knowledge to analyze characteristics and development of Tor's traffic over more than three years.

1   Introduction

Anonymous online communication has become a paramount interest for both researchers and the Internet community at large. Tor represents the most popular system to that end, allowing users to communicate with Internet servers while keeping their identity and location private. While many conceptual aspects of Tor's communication have been studied in the past, details about its network-level properties—such as, especially, the clients' behavior—remain scarce. Most of what the community knows about the Tor network comes from public *directory information*, which it uses to maintain the network. However, as Tor purposefully limits this knowledge, there is hardly any information about real-world usage patterns of Tor clients.

By default, Tor uses the SSL/TLS[1] protocol suite to establish encrypted connections between participating nodes, just as it is commonly used by web browsers, email clients, etc. In difference to other services using TLS, Tor does not partake in the global PKI with its trusted Certificate Authority system. Instead, Tor nodes automatically generate X.509 server certificates, which they rotate frequently. It turns out, however, that Tor's current certificate algorithm leaves them identifiable through pattern matching, enabling passive observers of the TLS data stream to distinguish Tor connections from other TLS connections.

---

[1] For the remainder of this paper, we will refer to either SSL or TLS as "TLS.".

© Springer International Publishing Switzerland 2016
T. Karagiannis and X. Dimitropoulos (Eds.): PAM 2016, LNCS 9631, pp. 3–15, 2016.
DOI: 10.1007/978-3-319-30505-9_1

In this paper, we exploit this characteristic to present a measurement study of the Tor network using passively collected TLS session information. We *(i)* identify Tor sessions; *(ii)* compare the connections against publicly available information from Tor directory authorities and; *(iii)* use metadata from the TLS protocol layer to infer properties of clients and servers.

Our data set consists of passively collected information of all outgoing TLS sessions from 4 university networks with, in total, more than 300,000 users, spanning a period of more than 3 years. Of the 138 billion total sessions in that set, Tor contributes more than 40 million.

We organize the remainder of this paper as follows: Sect. 2 gives a short overview of the related work. Section 3 summarizes the Tor protocol and introduces our data set. Section 4 discusses the methodology of our measurement study. Section 5 takes a look at the properties of outgoing Tor connections in our data set while Sect. 6 examines characteristics of Tor servers. Section 7 discusses our results and concludes this paper.

2   Related Work

There are a number of works that measure different parts of the Tor infrastructure. In 2009, McCoy et al. [17] measure the Tor network by joining in as exit and relay nodes. Their results show that non-interactive protocols consume a disproportionate amount of bandwidth; that substantial Tor communication involves clear-text protocols (including transmitting user passwords); and that at least one exit node examined the content of user payloads. In 2010, Chaabane et al. [5] perform a slightly different measurement using the same approach.

Loesing measures the relay as well as the client side of the Tor network using information from the Tor directory authorities [14,15], showing trends from 2006 to 2009. The studies examine the number, bandwidth and country distribution of relays and clients, and offer an estimate of the number of requests that the network transfers. Dhungel et al. [7] measure and examine delays introduced by guard relays using active probing.

While there is further a wealth of work examining anonymity in the Tor network [11,13,16], proposing updates to the Tor routing algorithms [20], and measuring specific details like underground marketplaces [6] and child pornography trafficking [12], to the best of our knowledge no prior effort has studied the encrypted traffic between Tor nodes.

3   Background

We begin our discussion by summarizing the background, starting with an overview of the inner working of Tor with a focus on its communication protocol. For this we first introduce Tor's different node types in Sect. 3.1, followed by an overview of their communication in Sect. 3.2. Finally, Sect. 3.3 introduces the data set from the ICSI Notary service that we use throughout this paper.

3.1 Tor Node Types

The Tor network consists of different types of nodes. Users run a *Tor client* that allows them to access the Tor network. They use a web browser, or other local software, to access the network via a proxy port that the Tor client opens on their machine. Clients connect to *relays*, which forward their information to other nodes or the Internet at large.

Information about all currently available relays is publically available from semi-trusted *directory authorities*, which the Tor client software hardcodes. At the time of writing, the Tor network offers 9 directory authorities. After retrieving relay information from a directory authority, clients connect to the network by connecting to typically three *guard relays*. The Tor network chooses guard relays through an automated process that favors stable and reliable nodes.[2] Clients keep connecting to the same set of guard relays for about 4 to 8 weeks— a design that protects against attackers controlling nodes only for shorter periods while aiming to correlate timing information [18].[3] Next, *exit relays* forward connections to the public Internet, with a relay's administrator deciding if the node may act in this role.

When a Tor client wants to connect to a host on the Internet, it picks a random path through the Tor network, starting at one of its guard relays. Neighboring relays on that path establish connections between each other, forming *circuits* that allow clients to reach the destination. The same circuit can be re-used by a client for several connections to the same target server. The time limit for a circuit's reuse depends on the Tor version, and tends to lie between 10 min and 2 h.[4] Finally, *bridges* represent a further class of relays. Their IP addresses remain private to allow clients from censored countries or networks to access the Tor network, even if those countries block all Tor relays listed by the public directory authorities. Bridge IP addresses can, e.g., be obtained via Tor's website, which enforces rate limits and uses captchas.

3.2 Tor Node Communication

Tor supports two ways of communication: *(i)* using the traditional Tor protocol; and *(ii)* using pluggable transports. When using the traditional Tor protocol [8], Tor nodes connect to each other using a TLS connection. Depending on the Tor protocol version, the way in which a node establishes the TLS connection varies slightly, but with all modern versions of Tor the server presents an automatically generated X.509 certificate. The nodes start using the Tor communication protocol after finishing the setup of the TLS connection.

The second way of connecting to the Tor network uses pluggable transports,[5] which enable tunneling Tor through other protocols. Tor supports several such

---

[2] https://blog.torproject.org/blog/lifecycle-of-a-new-relay.

[3] https://www.torproject.org/docs/faq.

[4] https://lists.torproject.org/pipermail/tor-dev/2015-March/008548.html.

[5] https://gitweb.torproject.org/torspec.git/tree/pt-spec.txt.

transport protocols, including obfs2 and obfs3[6] (protocol obfuscation layers for TCP protocols), WebSockets,[7] and Meek,[8] which uses domain fronting to hide inside innocuous-looking HTTP requests to CDNs.

For our study, we examine only Tor communication over TLS, not any pluggable transports.

3.3 The ICSI SSL Notary

For our study, we use data from the ICSI SSL Notary [1], which passively collects TLS session and certificate information from currently seven research and university networks, covering activity of approximately 390 thousand users in total. To date, the Notary has recorded more than 138 billion TLS connections, and more than 3 million unique certificates.[9] The first data providers started contributing data to the Notary in February 2012. Our data providers run the open-source Bro Network Monitoring System [4,19] on their gateway links. We provide them with a custom Bro analysis script that collects details from each outgoing SSL connection. For more details about the setup, we refer to [1]. For this paper, we use data from four of our seven data providers, choosing universities with large user populations that have been contributing consistently. Table 1 shows aggregate information about these four providers. This subset covers more than 300,000 users on two continents for a period of more than 3 years.

Table 1. Summary of data set properties from contributing sites. N = North America, X = rest of world. *Total* reflects the number of *unique* items across the sites. *Filt.* counts certificates after filtering Tor and Grid Computing certificates.

Site	Certificates		Connections		Time
Site	Users Filtered certs	Tor certs	Total conns	Tor conns	Days
N1	90 K 2.6 M	3.7 M	60 G	11 M	1,284
N2	50 K 1.1 M	9.5 M	22 G	29 M	1,022
N3	170 K 1.4 M	658 K	42 G	1,1 M	853
X1	12 K 233 K	258 K	3.1 G	252 K	1,003
Total 391 K 3.5 M		16 M	127 G	41 M	—

4   Methodology

In this section we introduce our measurement methodology, including our approach to identifying Tor certificates. We also present the features that we consider for each Tor connection.

---

[6] https://gitweb.torproject.org/pluggable-transports/obfsproxy.git.
[7] https://crypto.stanford.edu/flashproxy/.
[8] https://trac.torproject.org/projects/tor/wiki/doc/meek.
[9] Not counting Tor and Grid Computing certificates.

For studying Tor sessions, we need to distinguish traffic between Tor nodes from other TLS communication. Examining Tor's payload, as well as its TLS source code,[10] reveals that the certificates that Tor servers generate exhibit characteristics tha renders them unique. By default, both the issuer and the subject of the certificates use random Common Names consisting of the components www., a random 8 to 20 letter base-32 encoded domain name, and a .com or .net ending (e.g., www.4dpbq2neblawq7lbq.net, www.iqo3xm6iukfa4qf.com). The subject and issuer fields are generated independently and thus differ from each other. Neither subject nor the issuer fields contain further information that is commonly found in certificates (and mandated by Certificate Authorities), such as location or company names.

Table 2. Features collected by our TLS data collection. Shaded features are used in this study.

Collected Features		
Timestamp	TLS extension value lengths	Client EC curves
TLS Version	Client SNI (RFC6066)	DH parameter size
Server certificates	Server ticket lifetime (RFC5077)	Sent & Received bytes
No. client certificates	*Hash*(Client & Server session ID)	Connection Duration
Server IP & port	*Hash*(Client IP, Server IP, Salt)	Selected EC curve
Client available ciphers	*Hash*(Client IP, SNI, Salt)	TLS Alerts
Selected cipher	Client & Server ALPN (RFC7301)	Client EC point formats

These properties allow us to identify Tor connections by parsing the X.509 certificates in our data set and then matching a corresponding regular expression on their subject and the issuer fields. Through a set of semi-automated cross-checks, we verified that our data set contains no non-Tor TLS sessions with certificates matching this heuristic.

One potential pitfall of identifying Tor connections this way stems from TLS session resumption, which skips most of the TLS handshake, including the certificate exchange, for consecutive connections to the same TLS server. However, the Tor specification states that Tor clients and servers must not implement session resumption (Sect. 2.2 of [8]), hence avoiding that challenge.

Table 2 summarizes the features that our notary data set provides.[11] Most of the collected information concerns the TLS handshake, such as the supported cipher list a client sends, the server selected cipher or different TLS extensions. In addition to this, the Notary information also contains the IP address and port of the server. To retain anonymity of users at contributing sites, we hash client IP addresses with Server IP (and SNI if present), along with a site-specific secret salt unknown to us. This enables us to identify unique client/server pairs while keeping client IPs private.

---

[10] https://doxygen.torproject.org/tortls_8c_source.html#l01178.

[11] Since we have extended our data collection script over time, information about older connections does not contain all the listed attributes.

5   Tor Server Connections

As a first step in our exploration of the Tor network, we compare the passively collected data from our measuring points with publically available information from the Tor network. The Tor Project releases a set of statistics containing information about the relays and bridges in the network on its CollecTor webpage.[12]

5.1   Tor Consensus Information

For our subsequent analysis, we use CollecTor information about the Tor network status consensuses. These network status consensuses contain all the relays in the Tor network as agreed on by the semi-trusted Tor directory authorities (see Sect. 3.1). Among others, the data contains the IP addresses, ports, and Tor versions of all public relays, as well as the relay flags (like *guard* relay, *exit* relay, *stable*, *fast*). This data is available since the end of 2007 with hourly granularity.

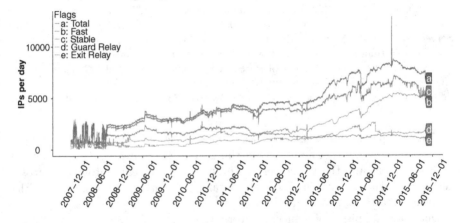

Fig. 1. Relay types derived from CollecTor data.

Figure 1 shows a plot of the consensus information showing all relays as well as specific subclasses of relays having the *exit*, *guard*, *stable* and *fast* status flags set. A single relay can hold several flags simultaneously to represent, e.g., both a guard and an exit node.

As the graph shows, the Tor network size has been rising slowly over the recent years. However, this is not true for all node types. While the average number of relays per day increased from 3,984 in 2011 to 7,524 in 2014 (i.e., 89% more), and the number of guard nodes increased from 793 to 1,911 (141%), the number of exit relays indeed decreased by 37% from 1,965 to 1,243 per day. We assume this corresponds to an increasing awareness that Tor exit node maintainers may find themselves facing legal challenges.[13] However, this also means that in 2014, each exit node routed a larger fraction of the traffic than in 2011—which

[12] https://collector.torproject.org/.
[13] https://www.torproject.org/eff/tor-legal-faq.html.en.

makes operating an exit node more interesting to malicious participants aiming
to examine outgoing traffic.

The *stable* flag signals that a node has remained reliable over time; it constitutes a requirement for becoming a guard node. Tor considers a relay stable
when either its mean time between failures (MTBF) is at least the median of
all known active relays or its weighted MTBF (definition in [22]) is more than
7 days [22]. The number of stable Tor relays has increased by 183 % from 2011
to 2014, from an average of 1,466 relays to 4,171. This might correlate with
permanent Internet connections becoming more available to end-users.

5.2 Connection Classification

Generally, in any large end-user network, we would expect most Tor nodes to
act as clients. Hence, most outgoing connections should connect to guard relays.
To check this, we match all outgoing connections to the Tor network consensus
information of CollecTor.

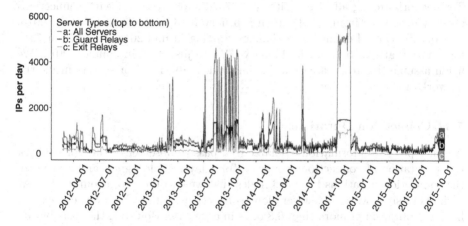

Fig. 2. Connections to differing node types at N1.

Figure 2 shows the total number of external relay IP addresses seen each day
at site N1, also indicating which of them act as guard and exit relays. Over the
time period of the measurement, 50 % of all connections (5,318,445 of 10,612,263)
terminated at guard nodes. Considering that the average number of guard nodes
in the Tor network is just 20 % (all-time; 25 % in 2014), this indicates that there
is a sizeable fraction of clients running at this institution.

The graph also contains several distinct peaks during which the ratio of guard
nodes per day is much lower. During these times, most connections terminate
at "normal" relay nodes on the Tor network that are neither exit nor guard
relays. We suspect that the peak between August and November of 2013 can
be attributed to the Mevade Botnet, which caused a massive global rise in the
number of active Tor users, going from approximately 1 million daily users to
nearly 6 million [10]. We are not aware of specific reasons for the other spikes,
the most notable spanning October to December 2014. However, as we do not see

similar artifacts at our other sites, and taking into account that most connections do not target guard servers, we speculate that a local user was running a Tor relay during these times, offering the university's excellent bandwidth to the Tor network. To verify that hypothesis, we analyze the TLS fingerprints of the connections from this site to the Tor network. In particular, we focus on two bits of information that each client sends in its TLS *client hello* message: the lists of cipher suites and TLS extensions that it supports, which both depend on the interplay between the versions of Tor and OpenSSL. This analysis reveals that the spikes in December 2014, the Mevade spike between August and November 2013, the spike in February 2014, and the spike in March 2013 all map to specific TLS fingerprints, indicating a single software responsible for each.

Looking at our other sites, site N3 and site X1 exhibit a generally low level of Tor connections (1,286 and 418 connections per day on average, respectively) in comparison to site N1 (9,366/day). Connections there mostly terminate at guard nodes in the Tor network (80 % and 75 % of connections respectively), suggesting client activity. Site N2 has the largest number of connections into the Tor network among all of our sites (21,675/day on average), with connections steadily increasing from 2,818/day in February 2013 to 88,666 in February 2015. The distribution of connections changes starting in mid-2014, going from 72 % terminating at guard nodes in January 2014 to just 38 % in January 2015. We again assume this to be a case of having well-established Tor servers inside the network of this university.

5.3 Connection Durations

Another piece of information available to a passive observer of the Tor network is the duration of connections going to Tor relays. Table 3 gives an overview of the connection durations to guard nodes that we encountered at our 4 sites. At each of our sites, we see a few very long connections, with at least one connection having a duration of more than 6.8 days in each case. However, the distribution of durations is highly skewed towards very short connections. Depending on the site, the median connection duration across the data set is between 3.0 and 6.3 min, with the mean being a bit higher at 7.3 to 19.5 min. Figure 3 shows a comparison of the *daily* mean and medium durations at site N1, illustrating that the mean remains stable over time while the median fluctuates more, potentially due to local user activity.

Table 3. Summary of guard relay connection durations for each site in minutes. Qu. = Quantile.

Site	1st Qu.	Median	Mean	3rd Qu.	Max
N1	3.0	3.0	9.6	10.1	9,839
N2	3.0	6.3	19.5	16.8	22,280
N3	1.5	3.0	7.3	3.2	16,370
X1	3.0	3.0	8.3	3.3	10,120

We find a partial explanation for this behavior by examining how Tor relays establish connections between each other. When two Tor relays set up a circuit, they keep the TLS session alive for up to three minutes to potentially reuse for followup requests; only if there are no further circuits going over this connection during that time, they will tear it down [2]. However, from the literature we could not identify an explanation for the even shorter duration that we see frequently as well. Their high number (17 %, 6.9 %, 34 % and 13 % of all connections for N1, N2, N3, and X1, respectively) points towards a systematic reason. Possible explanations include Tor clients using short-lived connections for internal house-keeping, independent of user activity (e.g. to update their relay lists); and implementation artifacts.

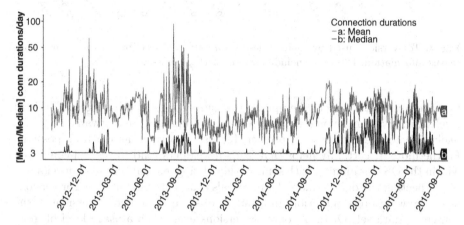

Fig. 3. Median and mean guard relay connection durations at site N1 in minutes. y-axis log-scale.

6 Server Characteristics

In this section, we take a look at the server side of the Tor, beginning with an examination of the server version changes in Sect. 6.1, followed by a look at the server-chosen cipher suites in Sect. 6.2.

6.1 Tor Server Versions

The Tor network consensus introduced in Sect. 5.1 provides the software versions for all running Tor relays. We extracted these and show their distribution over time in Fig. 4. While generally the uptake of new server versions is rather fast, we see a long tail of servers that remain on older releases for a significant period of time. From a deployment perspective, this makes sense; unlike for the Tor client software which, when used in form of the Tor Browser bundle, comes with an autoupdate functionality, administrators install Tor relay servers either manually or via the package management system of their operating system.

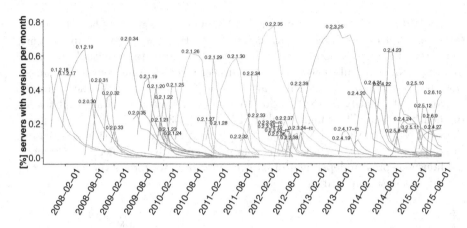

Fig. 4. Tor versions used by relay nodes, according to CollecTor network status consensus information. Does not include versions with peak usage < 10 %.

Considering this, we deem the update rate surprisingly good, suggesting a high level of motivation among server operators to update the software diligently, likely due to their interest to protect Tor users' privacy as much as possible. Furthermore, it certainly helps that Tor's developers tend to be well-connected within the OS community, with some of them being, e.g., also Debian developers.

Inspecting the data in more detail reveals that a large number of Tor versions never see widespread adoption. In total, we observe 325 different versions in the consensus data set. Of these, only 48 versions ever reach a usage level of more than 10 % of all relays. Of the 277 versions with a maximum usage level below 10 %, 257 are alpha or release candidate versions. As Fig. 4 shows, there are only 6 versions of Tor that exhibit a combined use of more than 60 % of all relay nodes. There is a repeating pattern of specific versions like, e.g., 0.2.2.36 to 0.2.2.38, do not see any widespread use, while their parent version keeps enjoying popularity (which however then ends rapidly eventually). This kind of behavior suggests that OS distributions may not include certain versions of the software, preventing it from seeing widespread adoption.

6.2   Server Cipher Suites

With this knowledge, we take a deeper look at the Notary data set. Another piece of information present in our data is the cipher suite that a server chooses in its TLS *server hello* message, which represents the encryption algorithm used for the remainder of the TLS session.

Figure 5 shows the main cipher suites that the outgoing connections at site N1 selected. It suggests a number of encouraging conclusions. Tor, in general, chooses secure cipher suites that use ephemeral keys and are thus perfectly forward secure. This indeed matches one of the original design goals of Tor, which also contributed to its choice to avoid session resumptions (see Sect. 4).

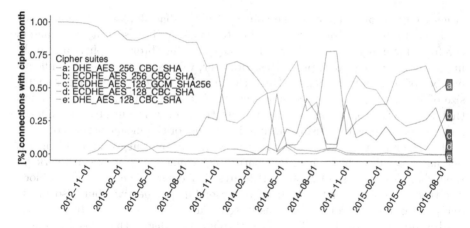

Fig. 5. TLS connection ciphers at site N1.

The plot also shows that Tor connections started to switch from Diffie-Hellman (DH) key exchange to Elliptic Curve Diffie-Hellman (ECDH) in December 2012. The process has proceeded only slowly and is still ongoing: more than 50 % of the connections still use DH. Examining the DH key exchange in more detail reveals that its parameter size is always 1024 bits; Tor apparently never uses larger parameters. We assume that the reason for the continuing use of DH key exchanges lies in the OpenSSL versions that are installed on Tor servers. Some operating system providers have excluded ECDH support from their OpenSSL libraries for a long time due to fears of patent claims [9], making DH key exchanges the only viable alternative for perfect forward secrecy. While 1024 bit keys are not yet considered insecure, their use is discouraged. Since a sizeable percentage of connections is still using DH key exchanges, Tor should consider switching the parameter size to 2048 bits.

For ECDH connections, we at first see an uptake of connections using AES-128 with SHA1 in cipher block chaining (CBC) mode, which in 2014 rapidly switches to either AES-256 with SHA1 and CBC, or AES-128 using Galois/Counter-Mode (GCM) and SHA-256. The reason for this is probably that OpenSSL only supports GCM starting with OpenSSL 1.0.1. Version 1.0.0, which is still maintained, cannot use this cipher mode. Since GCM is the preferential choice of cipher suites, we assume that Tor falls back to CBC if not available. EC connections almost exclusively use the secp256r1 curve, which also is the most commonly supported curve on web servers [3].

Taking a look at all other cipher suites that we observe, only a few thousand connections (<0.1 %) use non perfectly forward ciphers. We assume these are the result of non-Tor software trying to contact Tor servers.

7   Discussion and Conclusion

This paper presents a longitudinal measurement study of Tor's network-level activity, derived from passively collected TLS connection information at four large-scale network sites over the course of more than 3 years. Generally, our study confirms that Tor pays attention to choosing TLS security parameters carefully, including ensuring forward secrecy, avoiding broken ciphers and picking modern cryptographic primitives. However, we also notice that a significant number of servers keep using a Diffie-Hellman key exchange with a parameter size of 1024, which could become a security risk soon. Our analysis also shows that while server operators tend to update their software quickly, a significant long-tail of systems keep using outdated versions for significant periods of time.

For the reader not intricately familiar with Tor, one surprising result might be the ease with which one can identify Tor connections on the network by their characteristic use of X.509 certificates. For environments aiming to block Tor traffic—common not only from a censorship perspective, but also inside many enterprise environments—this suggests an alternative route to the standard approach of tracking Tor relays through blacklists, which need frequent updates. Interestingly, Tor switched to the current certificate scheme precisely to avoid such detection. As [21] discusses, earlier versions used "funny-looking certs [that] made Tor pretty easy to profile". With Tor 0.2.0.20, they switched to the current scheme to better blend in. However, as our study shows, detection remains an arms race, and an attacker with the ability to match regular expressions against certificates on the wire can easily identify Tor traffic today. Going forward, Tor could raise the bar further by avoiding the tell-tale signs that our detector picks up on. However, longer term, their strategy to rely on pluggable transports promises a better chance to render their users invisible again.

Acknowledgments. We thank Phillip Winter and David Fifield for their feedback during the writing of this paper. This work was supported by the National Science Foundation under grant numbers CNS-1528156 and ACI-1348077. Any opinions, findings, and conclusions or recommendations expressed in this material are those of the author(s) and do not necessarily reflect the views of the NSF.

References

1. Amann, J., Vallentin, M., Hall, S., Sommer, R.: Extracting Certificates from Live Traffic: A Near Real-Time SSL Notary Service. Technical report TR-12-014, International Computer Science Institute, November 2012
2. Biryukov, A., Pustogarov, I., Weinmann, R.-P.: TorScan: Tracing long-lived connections and differential scanning attacks. In: Foresti, S., Yung, M., Martinelli, F. (eds.) ESORICS 2012. LNCS, vol. 7459, pp. 469–486. Springer, Heidelberg (2012)
3. Bos, J.W., Halderman, J.A., Heninger, N., Moore, J., Naehrig, M., Wustrow, E.: Elliptic curve cryptography in practice. In: Christin, N., Safavi-Naini, R. (eds.) FC 2014. LNCS, vol. 8437, pp. 156–174. Springer, Heidelberg (2014)
4. Bro Network Monitoring System. https://www.bro.org
5. Chaabane, A., Manils, P., Kaafar, M.A.: Digging into anonymous traffic: a deep analysis of the tor anonymizing network. In: Proceedings of NSS (2010)
6. Christin, N.: Traveling the silk road: a measurement analysis of a large anonymous online marketplace. In: Proceedings of WWW (2013)

7. Dhungel, P., Steiner, M., Rimac, I., Hilt, V., Ross, K.: Waiting for anonymity: understanding delays in the tor overlay. In: Proceedings of P2P (2010)
8. Dingledine, R., Mathewson, N.: Tor Protocol Specification. https://gitweb. torproject.org/torspec.git/tree/tor-spec.txt
9. Enable Elliptical Curve Diffie-Hellman (ECDHE) in Linux, July 2013. https:// www.internetstaff.com/enable-elliptical-curve-diffie-hellman-ecdhe-linux/
10. Hopper, N.: Challenges in protecting tor hidden services from botnet abuse. In: Christin, N., Safavi-Naini, R. (eds.) FC 2014. LNCS, vol. 8437, pp. 312–321. Springer, Heidelberg (2014)
11. Hopper, N., Vasserman, E.Y., Chan-TIN, E.: How much anonymity does network latency leak? ACM Trans. Inf. Syst. Secur. **13**(2), 13: 1–13: 28 (2010)
12. Hurley, R., Prusty, S., Soroush, H., Walls, R.J., Albrecht, J., Cecchet, E., Levine, B.N., Liberatore, M., Lynn, B., Wolak, J.: Measurement and analysis of child pornography trafficking on P2P networks. In: Proceedings of WWW (2013)
13. Le Blond, S., Manils, P., Chaabane, A., Kaafar, M.A., Castelluccia, C., Legout, A., Dabbous, W.: One bad apple spoils the bunch: exploiting P2P applications to trace and profile tor users. In: Proceedings of LEET (2011)
14. Loesing, K.: Measuring the Tor Network, Evaluation of Client Requests to the Directories to Determine total Numbers and Countries of Users. Technical report 2009–06-002, The Tor Project, June 2009
15. Loesing, K.: Measuring the Tor Network from Public Directory Information. Technical report 2009–08-002, The Tor Project, August 2009
16. Manils, P., Abdelberi, C., Blond, S.L., Kâafar, M.A., Castelluccia, C., Legout, A., Dabbous, W.: Compromising Tor Anonymity Exploiting P2PInformation Leakage. CoRR abs/1004.1461 (2010). http://arxiv.org/abs/1004.1461
17. McCoy, D., Bauer, K., Grunwald, D., Kohno, T., Sicker, D.C.: Shining light in dark places: understanding the tor network. In: Borisov, N., Goldberg, I. (eds.) PETS 2008. LNCS, vol. 5134, pp. 63–76. Springer, Heidelberg (2008)
18. Overlier, L., Syverson, P.: Locating hidden servers. In: Proceedings of IEEE S&P (2006)
19. Paxson, V.: Bro: a system for detecting network intruders in real-time. Comput. Netw. **31**(23–24), 2435–2463 (1999)
20. Tang, C., Goldberg, I.: An improved algorithm for tor circuit scheduling. In: Proceedings of CCS (2010)
21. Tor Wiki – TLS History. https://trac.torproject.org/projects/tor/wiki/org/ projects/Tor/TLSHistory
22. Tor Directory Protocol, Version 3. https://gitweb.torproject.org/torspec.git/tree/ dir-spec.txt

Measuring the Latency and Pervasiveness of TLS Certificate Revocation

Liang Zhu[1(✉)], Johanna Amann[2], and John Heidemann[1]

[1] USC Information Sciences Institute, Marina del Rey, USA
liangzhu@usc.edu, johnh@isi.edu
[2] International Computer Science Institute, Berkeley, USA
johanna@icir.org

Abstract. Today, Transport-Layer Security (TLS) is the bedrock of Internet security for the web and web-derived applications. TLS depends on the X.509 Public Key Infrastructure (PKI) to authenticate endpoint identity. An essential part of a PKI is the ability to quickly revoke certificates, for example, after a key compromise. Today the Online Certificate Status Protocol (OCSP) is the most common way to quickly distribute revocation information. However, prior and current concerns about OCSP latency and privacy raise questions about its use. We examine OCSP using passive network monitoring of live traffic at the Internet uplink of a large research university and verify the results using active scans. Our measurements show that the median latency of OCSP queries is quite good: only 20 ms today, much less than the 291 ms observed in 2012. This improvement is because content delivery networks (CDNs) serve most OCSP traffic today; our measurements show 94 % of queries are served by CDNs. We also show that OCSP use is ubiquitous today: it is used by *all* popular web browsers, as well as important non-web applications such as MS-Windows code signing.

1 Introduction

Transport Layer Security (TLS), the successor to Secure Socket Layer (SSL) is one of the key building blocks of today's Internet security. It provides authentication through its underlying X.509 Public Key Infrastructure (PKI) as well as encryption for end-to-end communication over the Internet such as online banking and e-mail.

With the millions of certificates that are part X.509 PKI, it is inevitable that some private keys will be compromised by malicious third parties, lost, or corrupted. An attacker that manages to get access to a certificate's private key can impersonate its owner until the certificate's expiration date. Heartbleed is one example where the private keys of certificates were potentially exposed [9,24]. Even more risky than attacks on individual certificates and keys are attacks on the infrastructure of specific Certificate Authorities (CAs), which can issue certificates for any server (e.g. [5–7]).

Two primary mechanisms exist to revoke certificates: Certificate Revocation Lists (CRLs) [8] which provide downloadable lists of revoked certificates, and the

© Springer International Publishing Switzerland 2016
T. Karagiannis and X. Dimitropoulos (Eds.): PAM 2016, LNCS 9631, pp. 16–29, 2016.
DOI: 10.1007/978-3-319-30505-9_2

Online Certificate Status Protocol (OCSP) [18] which allows clients to check for revoked certificates by sending short HTTP requests to servers of the respective CA. Alternatively, OCSP stapling [17] allows revocation information to be sent by the server in the initial TLS handshake. Some in the security community question the usefulness and viability of these approaches, citing privacy, speed, and other concerns [11, 20].

Today, most major web browsers do not reliably check certificate revocation information [12], thus opening their users up to attacks.

In this work, we examine live traffic at the Internet uplink of the University of California at Berkeley (UCB) to check the pervasiveness and latency of OCSP, and then confirm our conclusions with active measurements from two sites.

The primary contribution of this paper is new measurements of OCSP that show that OCSP latency has improved significantly since 2012. We see a median latency of only 20 ms (Sect. 4), far lower than the 291 ms reported in previous studies [20]. We show that one reason for this improvement is that most OCSP traffic today is served by content delivery networks (CDNs). Our second contribution is a cost evaluation of OCSP connections. We identify that OCSP verification typically accounts for 10 % of the TLS setup time. OCSP will almost never delay TLS when being run in parallel with the TLS handshake, and it only adds a modest delay if run sequentially (Sect. 4.3). Our final contribution is examination of how OCSP is being used today: *all* popular web browsers and important non-web applications such as MS-Windows code signing (Sect. 3) use OCSP. Furthermore, 88 % of the IPv4 addresses that perform TLS queries during our measurement also perform OCSP queries.

2 Data Collection

Our study uses passive data collected from live Internet traffic to determine characteristics and features of OCSP use. We augment our passive data with information from active scans to verify our timing results and to check which OCSP servers use CDNs. We use passive measurements to study how OCSP is actually used on the Internet, and to evaluate the interplay between server and client software. These passive measurements are from a specific site (UCB), so our passive results depend on what sites that population visits. We take active probes from two sites, Berkeley and the University of Southern California. While this data source may bias our results, Berkeley has a large user population and we probe many observed sites, so our data reflects the real experiences of this population, and does not reflect outliers due to rarely used servers. Our active measurements are from two sites (to avoid some bias), but both are well connected and users with slower connectivity may experience higher latencies. We believe this dataset is informative and reflects the lookup performance of current OCSP servers and their use of CDNs, even if future work is needed to confirm the results from other viewpoints. These risks are common to many measurement studies that depend on data from large, real populations where multiple data sources are difficult to obtain due to privacy concerns around network measurement.

For our data collection, we extended the Bro Network Monitor [2,15] with the capability to parse OCSP requests and responses. Bro uses a file signature (expressed as a regular expression) to detect OCSP requests and replies. We correlate OCSP messages with TLS connections using IP addresses, certificate hashes and timing information (see Sect. 4.3). Our changes will be integrated in the next version of Bro.

Our passive measurements cover 56 days of data taken between 2015-07-28 to 2015-09-28 at the Internet uplink of the University of California at Berkeley (UCB). We record data for only 56 days of this 63-day period because of outages due to hardware failures, fire, and preemption by another study that required complete access to the hardware for about a week. We observed 1690 M TLS connections with certificates encountered and about 42 M OCSP requests over this period.

After processing the data we noticed that in 0.43 % of the OCSP connections, we have zero (or in a handful of cases negative) lookup times. We verified the correctness of our measurement manually against network traces and were not able to reproduce these error cases. We believe these impossible results are caused by interactions between packet retransmissions and Bro.

Table 1. OCSP applications (based on HTTP user agent) observed in 41.87 M OCSP HTTP requests. Date: 2015-07-28 to 2015-09-28.

Category		Application	Percent
Web browsers	32.10 %	Firefox	31.63 %
		Chrome	.21 %
		Pale moon	.06 %
		Opera	.06 %
		Rekonq, Bolt, Midori, Iceweasel, Seamonkey, Safari Sonkeror, IE, Camino, Epiphany, Konqueror	<.15 %
Library or daemon used by applications	66.87 %	ocspd	37.15 %
		Microsoft-CryptoAPI	23.74 %
		Securityd	4.74 %
		Java	1.24 %
		CFNetwork	<.0001 %
Email client	.32 %	Thunderbird	.30 %
		Postbox, Gomeza, Zdesktop, Eudora, Icedove	.02 %
Other applications	.33 %	Lightning	.31 %
		Zotero	.01 %
		Celtx, ppkhandler, Komodo, Dalvik, slimerjs, Unity Phoenix, Sunbird, Slurp, miniupnpc, googlebot Entrust entelligence security provider	<.0074 %
Unknown	.38 %	Unknown	.38 %

3   OCSP use in Applications and Hosts

We first want to understand how widely OCSP is used—how many applications and hosts make OCSP queries.

Applications: We evaluate which applications use OCSP by examining the user-agent header of the OCSP requests. Table 1 shows the resulting distribution of user-agents. The majority of the lookups are done by Firefox and system libraries and daemons: Microsoft-CryptoAPI (Windows) and ocspd (Mac OS).

To understand this distribution, we examine the behavior of common Internet Browsers (IE, Chrome, Firefox, Safari) and operating systems. We find that Firefox always uses its own user-agent, which is attributable to the fact that it uses its own encryption library [1]. Microsoft Internet Explorer and Safari use their respective operating system functionality for OCSP lookups, not directly revealing their user-agents. Google Chrome only uses OCSP for extended Validation certificates [11,12]. It uses the operating system functionality for OCSP lookups on Windows and Mac OS. On Linux, it performs OCSP requests with its own user-agent.

This use of libraries makes it difficult to distinguish the different browsers. This problem is exacerbated by the fact that a manual examination of OCSP requests revealed that Windows and Mac OS also perform OCSP requests for application signatures with the same user-agent. When we examine all unique OCSP requests (those for different certificates), we see that 81 % of these unique certificates account for nearly all (95 %) of total OCSP requests observed on the wire. Hence, the number of code-signing requests is at most the number of requests without matching certificates in traffic: 5 % of all OCSP requests and at 19 % of the unique requests encountered.

Application Comments: While examining the OCSP requests, we noticed a number of software bugs in different implementations. According to the respective standard, an OCSP request sent with HTTP GET will be base 64 and then URL-encoded. Some clients do not adhere to this standard, skipping the URL-encoding of requests. Servers still seem to accept these malformed requests. In our dataset, 99.9 % of these non-standard requests were caused by the Apple ocspd versions 1.0.1 and 1.0.2. The bug was apparently fixed in version 1.0.3, appearing in MacOS 10.10. We also encountered requests where the user-agent only contains the string representation of a memory address.

Clients can choose which hash algorithm they wish to use in an OCSP requests. During our monitoring effort, all clients used SHA1.

During a random day (2015-08-24), the median size of the OCSP requests and responses were 300 and 1900 bytes.

Use of OCSP by Hosts: To evaluate how many hosts send OCSP, we examine how many IP addresses send both OCSP and TLS traffic. We found that *88 % of IPv4 addresses using TLS also send OCSP*, suggesting widespread use of OCSP. We do not measure IPv6 addresses because hosts exchange web traffic via TLS on IPv6 but issue their OCSP request via IPv4. Underuse of IPv6 for OCSP is likely because of limited support of IPv6 in OCSP servers: only 45 % of the 304 unique OCSP servers we observe have an IPv6 address.

Please note that Network Address Translation may cause an overestimate of OCSP deployment. Ideally, one would want to determine the exact number of connections that use OCSP; however performing such measurements would require simulating the use of OCSP caching and is beyond the scope of this paper.

4 Latency of OCSP

Web browsing is very sensitive to latency, and there have been concerns that the latency introduced by OCSP is too high [11]. In this section, we study OCSP latency in three ways. First, we measure OCSP latency in live Internet traffic in Sect. 4.1. Then, we verify these results with active probes of OCSP servers in Sect. 4.2. Finally, we compare OCSP latency to the TLS connection setup latency in Sect. 4.3.

4.1 OCSP Delay in Network Traffic

As a first step, we use our passive dataset (Sect. 2), to analyze the distribution of OCSP latency.

Methodology: We define *OCSP lookup time* as the time from setting up a new TCP connection to getting the first OCSP response. When multiple OCSP responses are pipelined over a single TCP connection, we define the lookup time for subsequent requests from start of request to the end of the corresponding response. This definition reflects the amortization of connection setup time over several requests, but it may underrepresent the user-perceived time if requests arrived in a burst.

CDNs used in Traffic: We find that overall the *current* OCSP lookup is very quick with a median time of 19.25 ms (Fig. 1). Even when we include the connection setup times by considering only new HTTP connections, the median OCSP lookup time is still only 23.78 ms. Studies by Stark et al. in 2012 showed medians 14× larger [20] (291 ms compared to our 19 ms). Although most lookups are fast, the distribution of times has a long tail, with a very few (less than 0.1 %) taking 5 s to 8 min.

We believe the primary reason OCSP performance has improved since 2012 is that today most OCSP traffic is served by CDNs. To identify OCSP queries going to CDNs we mapped IP addresses in the traffic to hostnames and well known CDNs (like Akamai, Edgecast, and Google) or the presence of CDNs in the reverse hostname.

Table 2 shows the fraction of lookups (dynamic traffic) and servers (static OCSP sites) that we identify as being served or hosted by CDNs. While only 39 % of the servers that are accessed in our passive measurements are hosted by known CDNs, we see that these servers manage the popular certificates: *more*

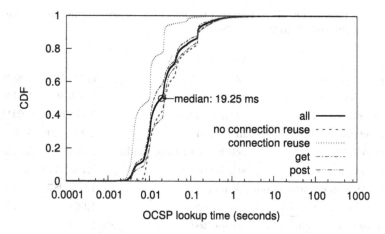

Fig. 1. Cumulative distribution of OCSP lookup time including the TCP handshake time for the first OCSP request in HTTP connection, over 41.12 M OCSP lookups. Date: 2015-07-28 to 2015-09-28

Table 2. CDN usage of 304 unique OCSP servers discovered in our passive monitoring over two months. Date: 2015-07-28 to 2015-09-28

	Query traffic		OCSP servers	
CDN	39,313,464	94 %	120	39 %
Other	2,526,338	6 %	184	61 %
Total	41,839,802	100 %	304	100 %

than nine-tenths of queries (94 %) are served by CDNs. Service is quite heavily skewed, with the 68 % of traffic serviced by the top 10 busiest OCSP servers (Table 3). All of them are handled by third party or internal CDNs.

CDNs seen on Servers: To get further evidence of the use of CDNs by CAs, we examine the certificates of an Internet-wide scan of TCP port 443 by Rapid7 Labs [3]. Using their scan of 2015-09-28, we extract a list of 455 unique OCSP servers. This list includes 57 % of the OCSP servers we discovered, but neither list subsumes the other. We evaluate this list for CDNs using the same method as before. We find that 29 % of the OCSP servers are invalid (non-existent domain), which is probably cased by misconfigurations, outdated, or internal certificates. Of all certificates with valid servers, 23 % are served by CDNs, confirming that many CAs use CDNs for their OCSP servers. It also shows that CDN use is more common in certificates of popularly used servers than in all certificates. We believe this skew to be caused by the fact that popular services keep their certificates updated better than the "average" TLS user. This result again shows the importance of studying dynamic traffic to differentiate typical OCSP performance from the worst case.

Table 3. Top 10 busy OCSP servers and their lookups discovered in our passive monitoring. Date: 2015-07-28 to 2015-09-28

Server	Observed CDN	Lookup	
ocsp.digicert.com	phicdn.net	6,205,125	14.83 %
clients1.google.com	self-hosted	4,859,409	11.61 %
sr.symcd.com	akamaiedge	3,778,672	9.03 %
ocsp.entrust.net	akamaiedge	2,421,420	5.79 %
ocsp.godaddy.com	self-hosted (using akadns)	2,399,931	5.74 %
ocsp.usertrust.com	self-hosted	2,248,577	5.37 %
vassg141.ocsp.omniroot.com	akamai	1,915,287	4.58 %
ss.symcd.com	akamaiedge	1,663,053	3.97 %
ocsp.comodoca.com	self-hosted	1,478,911	3.53 %
ocsp.verisign.com	akamaiedge	1,345,724	3.22 %
All 294 others		13,523,693	32.32 %
Total		41,839,802	100 %

We have two additional observations about OCSP latency. First, we see that GET requests are faster than POST requests (median 13.0 ms compared to 22.8 ms, Figure 1). The HTTP standards recommend GET for short requests, and we see about half of all OCSP requests using this method.

Finally, we see that it is not uncommon for OCSP requests to reuse an existing HTTP connection, avoiding connection setup latency. In our measurements, 24 % of all OCSP lookups reuse a connection. Examining random samples of OCSP requests that were reused reveals that connection reuse has several likely causes: webpages that include resources from several other pages that share the same OCSP servers, users accessing pages that share the same OCSP server quickly to each other, and checks for end-host and intermediate certificates that share the same OCSP server. Connection reuse reduces the overhead significantly: OCSP queries that reuse connections complete with a median of 10 ms; less than half that of those that start new connections (24 ms).

Our data includes OCSP requests for both intermediate certificates and leaf certificates. Our analysis reflects the overall lookup performance of OCSP servers; we do not study specific types of certificates.

4.2   OCSP Server Delay

Our passive study of OCSP traffic emphasizes the performance of the most commonly used servers. We next augment our study with observations of active probes to OCSP servers, to verify the results of our passive measurements and capturing a static picture of the time an application takes to verify the validity of certificates.

Methodology: We actively probe OCSP servers of the Alexa top-1000 from two different vantage points, UCB and USC. We perform an HTTPS connection attempt for each site (Fig. 2a). We discard 362 (USC: 364) sites with failing DNS lookups, where servers not answer to HTTPS requests or where we cannot obtain valid certificate chains. We obtain complete certificate chains for the remaining 638 (USC: 636) sites. We identify 508 (USC: 506) unique end host certificates, discarding 130 (USC: 130) duplicate certificates (typically by sites operated by the same company, such as youtube.com and google.com). We then query the OCSP servers to check each end certificate using a custom program that employs the `OpenSSL` library to send OCSP requests via HTTP POST. We record the query start and response times. We conducted this experiment on two well connected, capable machines (32-core with x86-64 Fedora 21 Linux 4.0.5 and 4-core with x86-64 Fedora 22 Linux 4.2.6). We repeat each query 20 times and report the median value to avoid outliers.

Our active probes show overall short latencies with a median of 22.28 ms at UCB (Fig. 2b), which is similar to the median of OCSP network delay measured by passively collected data (Sect. 4.1). It also shows that computational cost for generating OCSP request and parsing response is small; in our experiment, the time to generate an OCSP request is normally less than 0.5 ms. The latency of most OCSP requests is acceptable: at UCB, 77 % of the OCSP queries are completed within 50 ms, although there are also some tardy responses (22 %) taking more than 150 ms. This also confirms our passive measurements of network delay and reinforces that lookup time improved significantly compared to [20]. Our measurements from USC show a similar distribution of OCSP lookup performance, but with slightly smaller latency (median 6.6 ms). We think the difference is caused by fewer hops to CDNs from our vantage point at USC. The stepped pattern in Fig. 2b is caused by certificates sharing the same OCSP servers and the speed of the different CDNs.

sites	UCB	USC
considered	1000	1000
no IPv4	29	27
no TLS	308	310
TLS	663	663
no cert/chain	25	27
duplicates	130	130
unique certs	508	506
no ocsp url	2	2
complete	506	504

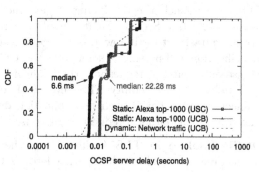

(a) Certificates retrieved.   (b) Cumulative distribution of OCSP delay.

Fig. 2. Evaluating OCSP across the Alexa top-1000 websites. Date: 2016-01-09.

4.3   OCSP Overhead in TLS

Our measurements show only modest OCSP delays. However, this cost needs to be put into the context of overhead it adds to the TLS connection setup. We now examine how OCSP affects TLS performance during session establishment, using our passive dataset (Sect. 2). We define *TLS delay* as the time between the *client hello* message and the first encrypted application data packet sent by client. During an OCSP query, the TLS handshake can either be interrupted until an OCSP response is received, or continue in parallel. In the parallel case, the client must not send its first request to the server until receiving a valid OCSP response.

Matching OCSP Requests to TLS Connections: To understand the overhead OCSP adds to TLS, we must map OCSP messages transmitted via HTTP to their corresponding TLS connections. We log all TLS connections and information about their certificates in addition to all OCSP requests and responses. We then match OCSP requests to TLS connections using the 4-tuple (*source ip, ocsp URL, issuer name hash, serial number*) from both flows and identify the TLS connection closest in time to the OCSP request. We identify and discard cases where the OCSP request precedes the TLS connection (an *early request*), and when it follows by more than 10 s (*a late request*).

Using the method above, we successfully correlate 52 % of the 41 M OCSP requests with TLS connections (*matched requests*). We discard 17 % as early requests, 1.8 % as late requests and are unable to match 30 % using the 4-tuple (*unmatched requests*).

Although we match the majority of requests, the high mismatch rate (including impossible early requests) stems from several challenges in matching. We believe a large number of mismatches are caused by dual-stack, IPv4/v6 hosts where TLS connections occur on IPv6 but where the OCSP servers only support IPv4. While 88 % of IPv4 addresses send both TLS and OCSP requests, 90 % of IPv6 addresses send no OCSP requests. OCSP requests caused by non-TLS services, such as code-signing [22] are another reason for unmatched OCSP requests [22] (see Sect. 3) Finally, while the reported packet-loss in our monitoring infrastructure is low (about 1 % of packets), it may still prevent the identification and parsing of some TLS and OCSP connections. To avoid errors, we use only matched requests in the following analysis.

Finally, we filter empty TLS and OCSP queries: we discard 11 % of TLS connections that have no client application data and 0.9 % of OCSP lookups that are missing either a request or response.

OCSP Lookup in TLS Delay: Using the paired OCSP queries and TLS connections, we evaluate how much latency the OCSP lookup adds to TLS connections in Fig. 3.

The key result is that *OCSP typically accounts for one-tenth of the total TLS delay*. We see a median TLS delay of 242 ms compared to a median OCSP lookup time of 15.8 ms. We compute the ratio of OCSP lookup time to TLS delay for each paired connection with a median of 0.0965. We see some outliers (1.2 %)

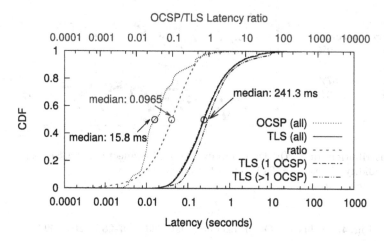

Fig. 3. Cumulative distribution of OCSP network latency and TLS delay for all matched pairs. Date: 2015-07-28 to 2015-09-28. The blue dotted line shows the cumulative distribution of the ratio of the sum of OCSP network latency to TLS delay for every matched pair.

where the OCSP lookup time exceeds the TLS delay; we expect these cases to be caused by timeouts.

The actual delay OCSP incurs to the user depends on the structure of the application. Many applications do OCSP validation in parallel with starting the TLS connection. Our evaluation shows that OCSP lookup time is only about 10 % of TLS delay overall, as shown by the median latency ratio, and the cost is typically 16 ms. This cost suggests that, *if OCSP is performed in parallel with TLS session setup, the OCSP delay is almost never visible.*

In summary, the OCSP lookup latencies we observe have improved significantly compared to prior reports [20]. OCSP lookup only adds modest delay to TLS setup, and potentially never adds latency when performed in parallel.

4.4 Effectiveness of OCSP Caching

A final component of OCSP latency is caching of OCSP responses. Our data does not provide an exact picture of caching, but we can use it to estimate the effectiveness of caching.

The potential of OCSP caching can be seen in the OCSP validity periods. Our passive dataset of OCSP traffic, Fig. 4a shows that most OCSP responses have a validity period of a week or more. 95 % are valid for at least one day.

To give some estimate of the effectiveness of caching we counted the aggregate number of OCSP requests relative to TLS connections. Figure 4b shows the number of TLS connections and OCSP requests per day, with a mean of 30 M TLS connections and only 0.7 M OCSP requests per day. Since we have shown that most browsers and most IPv4 addresses use OCSP (Sect. 3), this ratio of 1 OCSP request for 40 TLS connections suggests very effective caching. To

validity	percent
< 1 day	2%
1–6 days	38%
7–10 days	57%
> 10 days	3%

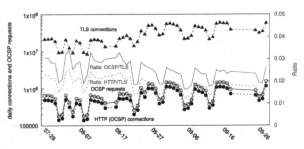

(a) Distribution of OCSP validity times for 290 k unique certificates.

(b) Daily number of TLS connections, OCSP requests and HTTP (OCSP) connections.

Fig. 4. Evaluating OCSP caching. Date: 2015-07-28 to 2015-09-28.

understand the exact impact of OCSP caching, future work must distinguish a cache hit from cases where browsers disable OCSP, and from TLS sessions are established by software that does not use TLS.

The potential of long-term OCSP caching is important because it significantly attenuates the information about end-user browsing that is visible to CAs. Since OCSP replies can be cached for at least one day, the information visible over this channel is quite limited.

5   OCSP in Action: Revoked Certificates

The point of OCSP is to revoke certificate that are no longer suitable for use, a condition that we expect to be very rare but still very important. OCSP is effective in practice—*we see a few examples of revoked certificates in our data.*

As expected, there are relatively few revoked certificates. We see OCSP replies for 2,180 unique revoked certificates in our passive dataset that contains OCSP replies for 1,418,315 unique certificates. Only 0.3 % of OCSP queries report a revoked certificate.

We manually examined the top 10 revoked certificates by number of OCSP requests to understand their use. Seven of these were expired code-signing certificates for software on the Windows platform. The rest were for subdomains of t-mobile.com, aol.com and lijit.com that were inaccessible in October 2015. We speculate that these revocations indicate deployed software that has not been updated and is trying to use discontinued services.

Finally, we observe a very few 638 (0.001 %) OCSP responses for 105 unique certificates with the status of "unknown". Searching for cases where the same OCSP responses also returned a different status revealed the cause for 72 of these requests for 12 unique certificates: The most common cause is certificates that have just been issued and are not known to the revocation server yet. For 4 certificates, the CA returned an unknown status, apparently without reason (certificate valid, later replies indicate "good" again). For 1 code-signing certificate, the CA apparently returns unknown after the certificate expired. For the remainder of the requests we could not identify a reason.

6   Related Work

There has been a wealth of work to measure different parts of the TLS and certificate ecosystem, including studies of details of the CA ecosystem [10], TLS errors [4] and certificates contained in root stores [16].

Prior work examined different aspects of TLS certificate revocation. After the 2008 Debian OpenSSL vulnerability and the Heartbleed bug, researchers studied the number of revocations, revocation patterns and patching behavior [9, 23, 24]. In difference to these studies which focus on certificate revocation patterns after a vulnerability, we study the performance impact of revocation in general. Researchers also proposed to use alternative approaches to certificate revocation like FM radio broadcasts for certificate revocation [19] as well as using short-lived certificates to make revocations unnecessary [21].

Most recently, Liu et al. use full IPv4 scans and compare them with blacklists [12]. They also study revocation checking behavior of web browsers and operating systems as well as Google's certificate revocation infrastructure. In difference to us, they do not study the actual use of OCSP on the Internet or its latency impact on the Internet.

Most related to our work, Stark et al. measured OCSP lookup latency [20]. Like their work, we use active and passive approach to understand OCSP latency. However, we collect network traffic at a university network with a broader coverage. Our data has a more diverse and much larger set of clients. Furthermore, we also compare the speed of OCSP connections to the remainder of the TLS handshake. Netcraft published OCSP performance surveys of major CAs [13, 14]. They use static sites to study OCSP latency and reliability. In contrast, our analysis uses live network traffic to understand current OCSP latency.

OCSP stapling [17] was proposed as an alternative. Examining the usage of OCSP stapling and its overhead is future work.

To the best of our knowledge, no previous work examined OCSP network traffic. Our analysis of actual traffic patterns provides insight into dynamic *traffic*, complementing these prior studies that focused on analysis of static sites.

7   Conclusion

Our measurements show that the speed of OCSP servers has increased tremendously. Due to the widespread use of CDNs OCSP almost never has any user-perceived performance cost when done in parallel with TLS setup, and adds only about 10 % additional latency if done sequentially (Sect. 4.1).

Privacy has been a second concern about OCSP—CAs running the OCSP servers can potentially deduce parts of a users browsing behavior. We have shown that OCSP caching means that queries most queries are sent weekly or at most daily, limiting this channel (Sect. 4.4).

A third concern about OCSP are problems with captive portals—web-pages that require a user to agree to terms and conditions before being able to use the Internet; some of these captive portals use HTTPS. In these cases, the OCSP servers cannot be contacted to verify that the site certificate has not yet been revoked. We leave addressing this problem to future work. One possible approach is to use OCSP stapling [17] for captive portals—in these cases, OCSP lookups would not be necessary. Alternatively, captive portals could allow HTTP connections to specific OCSP servers.

Finally, we have shown that while certificate revocations are quite rare (as expected), they do occur in practice (Sect. 5).

Ultimately, the data in our paper suggests that OCSP today is both important and viable—it adds minimal or no user-visible delay or privacy, and it provides an essential protection against certificate compromise.

Acknowledgments. This work was supported by the National Science Foundation (NSF) under grant numbers CNS-1528156 and ACI-1348077, by the Department of Homeland Security (DHS) Science and Technology Directorate, HSARPA, Cyber Security Division, via SPAWAR Systems Center Pacific (contract N66001-13-C-3001), and via BAA 11-01-RIKA and Air Force Research Laboratory, Information Directorate (agreements FA8750-12-2-0344 and FA8750-15-2-0224). The U.S. Government is authorized to make reprints for governmental purposes notwithstanding any copyright. The views contained herein are those of the authors and do not necessarily represent those of NSF, DHS or the U.S. Government.

References

1. Network security services. https://developer.mozilla.org/en-US/docs/Mozilla/Projects/NSS
2. The Bro network security monitor. https://www.bro.org
3. Project Sonar: IPv4 SSL certificates, August 2015. https://scans.io/study/sonar.ssl
4. Akhawe, D., Amann, J., Vallentin, M., Sommer, R.: Here's my cert, so trust me, maybe? Understanding TLS errors on the web. In: WWW, May 2013
5. Arthur, C.: DigiNotar SSL certificate hack amounts to cyberwar, saysexpert, September 2011. http://www.theguardian.com/technology/2011/sep/05/diginotar-certificate-hack-cyberwar
6. Bhat, S.: Gmail users in Iran hit by MITM attacks, August 2011. http://techie-buzz.com/tech-news/gmail-iran-hit-mitm.html
7. Comodo. Comodo fraud incident, March 2011. https://www.comodo.com/Comodo-Fraud-Incident-2011-03-23.html
8. Cooper, D., Santesson, S., Farrell, S., Boeyen, S., Housley, R., Polk, W.: Internet X.509 public key infrastructure certificate and certificate revocation list (CRL) profile. RFC 5280, May 2008
9. Durumeric, Z., Kasten, J., Adrian, D., Halderman, J.A., Bailey, M., Li, F., Weaver, N., Amann, J., Beekman, J., Payer, M., Paxson, V.: The matter of Heartbleed. In: ACM IMC (2014)

10. Holz, R., Braun, L., Kammenhuber, N., Carle, G.: The SSL landscape: a thorough analysis of the X.509 PKI using active and passive measurements. In: ACM SIGCOMM (2011)
11. Langley, A.: Revocation checking and Chrome's CRL, February 2012. https://www.imperialviolet.org/2012/02/05/crlsets.html
12. Liu, Y., Tome, W., Zhang, L., Choffnes, D., Levin, D., Maggs, B., Mislove, A., Schulman, A., Wilson, C.: An end-to-end measurement of certificate revocation in the web's PKI. In: ACM IMC (2015)
13. Netcraft. Certificate revocation and the performance of OCSP. http://news.netcraft.com/archives/2013/04/16/certificate-revocation-and-the-performance-of-ocsp.html
14. Netcraft. OCSP server performance in April 2013. http://news.netcraft.com/archives/2013/05/23/ocsp-server-performance-in-april-2013.html
15. Paxson, V.: Bro: a system for detecting network intruders in real-time. Comput. Netw. **31**(23–24), 2435–2463 (1999)
16. Perl, H., Fahl, S., Smith, M.: You wont be needing these any more: on removing unused certificates from trust stores. In: FC (2014)
17. Pettersen, Y.: The transport layer security (TLS) multiple certificate status request extension. RFC 6961 (2013)
18. Santesson, S., Myers, M., Ankney, R., Malpani, A., Galperin, S., Adams, C.: X.509 internet public key infrastructure online certificate status protocol - OCSP. RFC 6960, June 2013
19. Schulman, A., Levin, D., Spring, N.: RevCast: fast, private certificate revocation over FM radio. In: ACM CCS (2014)
20. Stark, E., Huang, L.-S., Israni, D., Jackson, C., Boneh, D.: The case for prefetching and prevalidating TLS server certificates. In: NDSS (2012)
21. Topalovic, E., Saeta, B., Huang, L.-S., Jackson, C., Boneh, D.: Towards short-lived certificates. In: W2SPP (2012)
22. Wikipedia. Code signing. https://en.wikipedia.org/wiki/Code_signing
23. Yilek, S., Rescorla, E., Shacham, H., Enright, B., Savage, S.: When private keys are public: results from the 2008 Debian OpenSSL vulnerability. In: ACM IMC (2009)
24. Zhang, L., Choffnes, D., Levin, D., Dumitras, T., Mislove, A., Schulman, A., Wilson, C.: Analysis of SSL certificate reissues and revocations in the wake of heartbleed. In: ACM IMC (2014)

Tracking Personal Identifiers Across the Web

Marjan Falahrastegar[1]([⊠]), Hamed Haddadi[1], Steve Uhlig[1],
and Richard Mortier[2]

[1] Queen Mary University of London, London, UK
marjan.falahrastegar@qmul.ac.uk
[2] University of Cambridge, Cambridge, UK

Abstract. User tracking has become de facto practice of the Web, however, our understanding of the scale and nature of this practice remains rudimentary. In this paper, we explore the connections amongst all parties of the Web, especially focusing on how trackers share user IDs. Using data collected from both browsing histories of 129 users and active experiments, we identify *user-specific IDs* that we suspect are used to track users. We find a significant amount of ID-sharing practices across different organisations providing various service categories. Our observations reveal that ID-sharing happens in a large scale regardless of the user profile size and profile condition such as logged-in and logged-out. We unexpectedly observe a higher number of ID-sharing domains when user is logged-out. We believe that our work reveals the huge gap between what is known about user tracking and what is done by this complex and important ecosystem.

1 Introduction

The rise in the use of personal data and the application of sophisticated algorithms to track and analyse our online browsing behaviour have caused an increase in the number of different tracking services. These services include third-party advertising and analytics services on the Internet and the mobile web [1–3]. User tracking services build a *user profile* by collecting, aggregating, and correlating an individual's browsing behaviour, demographics and interests. While these services are vital for the online economy, there are complex debates over privacy issues that are caused directly or indirectly by such services (e.g., misusing ad tracker cookies to identify individuals [4]).

These services are not only growing steadily in number [2], but are also evolving in terms of mechanisms and technologies. An example of this trend is the emergence of various user tracking mechanisms such as Flash cookies, ETags re-spawning [5] and canvas fingerprinting [6] in a relatively short period of time.

One of the very important phenomena of the Web ecosystem that has been less explored is the practice of sharing user-specific identifiers (IDs). A few works have highlighted the presence of this practice [2,7]. Moreover, the authors in [6] introduced a method to identify user-specific IDs. Although we are aware of the existence of this phenomenon, our understanding about the extent of this

T. Karagiannis and X. Dimitropoulos (Eds.): PAM 2016, LNCS 9631, pp. 30–41, 2016.
DOI: 10.1007/978-3-319-30505-9_3

practice and the nature of the parties involved in user-specific ID sharing is rudimentary.

In the rest of this paper, we explore the characteristics of user ID-sharing groups by analysing the organisational and categorical relation amongst the members of ID-sharing groups (Sect. 2). We then investigate the effect of user profile on the presence of ID-sharing groups. We show that users are being tracked regardless of their profile size (e.g., amount of their browsing history) and profile condition (logged-in or logged-out) (Sect. 3). After discussing the related work (Sect. 4), we provide our conclusions (Sect. 5).

2   User Tracking

We start our analysis by exploring the connections between domains when they are aimed to track users. User tracking is a practice by which a domain, either being directly visited by a user or indirectly through third-party trackers, assigns a unique identifier to the user, and shares this identifier with other domains. The parties participating in user tracking are able to aggregate the data collected by other parties in order to construct a comprehensive profile of users. In the rest of this section, we first describe our methodology and dataset, and subsequently explore the size and nature of a user ID-sharing group.

2.1   Methodology and Data Collection

We extended the Lightbeam Firefox plug-in to log all headers of HTTP requests and responses. The plug-in additionally records the country where the user is located (our modified version is available in [8]). The recorded data is delivered automatically to our server using an encrypted connection. While there are various Firefox plug-ins to visualize and block third-party trackers, we chose Lightbeam (Fig. 1) because of its interactive and easily understandable user interface. We asked our colleagues and friends to install our plug-in and use Firefox as their main browser for the minimum duration of two weeks. In order to preserve users' privacy we did not record any identifiable information such as the IP address, name or contact information. Additionally, we obtained ethics approval from QMUL ethics committee (code QMREC1416a) before performing our user studies. All our data were obtained between 20 February 2015 until 1 April 2015. In total we had 129 participants from 22 countries across the globe. Our participants have visited 4951 unique websites which include 6568 unique third-party trackers. Table 1 lists the number of our participants in each geographical region.

2.2   Nature of ID-Sharing Groups

To explore user tracking via sharing user-specific identifiers, we first need to determine the identifiers that are likely to be used as *user-specific IDs*: a unique identifier stored in a cookie or embedded as a parameter in a URL. For this purpose, we apply the following rules inspired by Acar *et al.* [6] on all items stored in the cookies and the URL parameters.

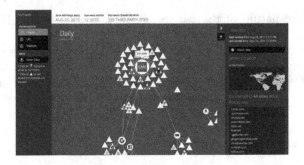

Fig. 1. Lightbeam presents the connection between websites with an interactive and easily understandable user interface.

Table 1. Number of participants per geographical location.

Region	Country	No. P
Europe	BE, CH, FE, DE, DK, ES, GB, GR, NL, FI	97
Middle East	BD, IR, QA	11
America	CA, MX, US	9
Oceania-East Asia	AU, CN, MY	8
Africa	SG, MR	3

- Extract (`key,value`) pairs using delimiters such as ampersand (`&`) and semi-colon (`;`). For instance, this string `id=ece53b2e-ea5c-4433-ad3d&ssid=02ba238451cec44ba88` contains two (key,value) pairs: (id,ece53b2e-ea5c-4433-ad3d) and (ssid,02ba238451cec44ba88).
- Exclude (key,value) pairs that are *inconsistent*: a (key,value) pair is inconsistent if there are multiple values for the same key belonging to a certain domain. For example these pairs (id,ece53b2e-ea5c-4433) and (id,ffc87j3o-gh11-3278) observed from `bbc.co.uk` are excluded.
- Exclude those value strings that are shared by multiple users.
- Only include those value strings that their length is longer than 7 characters. After applying the aforementioned rules on our dataset, we found that 96 % of user-specific IDs have a minimum length of 7 characters.

We applied the above-described method for each user. Table 2 shows sample URLs and their identified user-specific IDs with their associated keys. The identified IDs appear in various formats of which the most common are { xx..x}, { x-x-..-x} and { x|x|..|x} where x can be any combination of characters and numbers. We find 3,224 unique user IDs from 806 domains. To our surprise, the vast majority of these IDs (96 %) are being shared between at least two domains. We identify 769 domains that share unique user IDs with other domains. Extracting the user-specific IDs enables us to identify *user ID-sharing groups*: a set of domains that share user-specific IDs. We identify 660 unique

Table 2. Example of URLs and the identified user-specific IDs with their associated keys.

URL	User-Specific IDs	Key
http://ads.rubiconproject.com/ad/11078.js	65d39451-1f73-435a-bf39	put_2760
http://apex.go.sonobi.com/trinity.js	i736hcjtwb05natk	uin_bw
http://cm.adform.net/pixel	d4848|VOzy0|N1xas	adform_pc

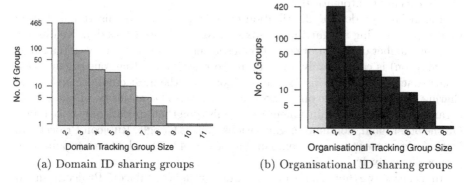

(a) Domain ID sharing groups   (b) Organisational ID sharing groups

Fig. 2. Size of ID sharing groups based on number of (a) domains and (b) organisations (Y-axis in both figures uses a logarithmic scale).

ID-sharing groups containing two to more than eight domains. Figure 2a provides the distribution of the number of different sharing groups (y-axis uses a logarithmic scale) across their group size (x-axis). From Fig. 2a, we observe that user IDs are mainly shared between two (467 unique groups, 2742 occurrences) or three (86 unique groups, 201 occurrences) domains. Moreover, the number of unique groups and their occurrences drop steadily as group size increases.

Organisational Sharing. User ID-sharing groups consist of multiple domains that may actually belong to the same organisation. Therefore, we broaden our approach from domains to organisations, resulting in *organisational sharing groups*. For example, the organisational sharing group for {google.com, youtube.com} is {Google}, and for this group: {youtube.com, scorecardresearch.com} is {Google, comScore}.

To identify the organisation behind a set of domains, we applied a combination of three methods. First, we used Collusion's dataset[1] to detect ID-sharing domains belonging to the same company. We manually inspected this dataset for any changes using websites and wiki pages of the companies involved. Second, we used the e-mail addresses of domains obtained by querying their SOA (Start of Authority) record. The email address, however, is unhelpful if it is a general account from a cloud, CDN or DNS service. For example, awsdns-

---

[1] http://collusion.toolness.org/.

hostmaster@amazon.com is the email address of all third-parties hosted on Amazon Web Services, and dns-admin@google.com is assigned to all services hosted on Google App Engine. We identified the unhelpful email addresses by their email domain name belonging to the known CDN and DNS services, or containing keywords indicating such services. For these cases we used the organization indicated in their whois records if available, or else we assumed the domain has no parent company. We are aware that there can be some cases with an outdated whois record or email addresses but we believe this is the best approach that can be executed automatically.

Figure 2b provides the distribution of the number of organisational sharing groups (again using a logarithmic y-axis) across their sizes (x-axis). We observe that the number of within-organisational sharing groups (sharing within a single organisation) is considerably lower than those with more than one organisation (sharing across different organisations). Moreover, the most cross-organisational sharing appears between only two organisations. The majority of these two-organisation groups contain a member organisation that appears only once (306). On the other hand, dominant organisations such as Google, Rubicon Project and Optimizely (a user targeting company) appear in 43, 40 and 33 two-organisation groups respectively.

In general, we find some organisations such as Rubicon Project (an ad exchange company) appears strongly in the cross-organisational sharing groups (112 groups) while large organisations such as Google appears in both cross-organisational and within-organisational sharing groups. Table 3 shows the top 15 most popular organisational sharing groups (in their frequency of occurrence) and the nature of their user-specific ID-sharing within the group, i.e., within an organisation (w-org) or cross organisations (c-org).

Cross Categories Sharing. To gain more insight into the nature of user ID-sharing, we analysed the ID-sharing groups with a different approach. We examined the categories of domains in each group. We first identified domain categories using the Trend Micro Site Safety Center categorization service[2]. The Trend Micro service contains 85 different interest categories. Moreover, we manually inspected those that were not available on Trend Micro. We find categories related to the ad ecosystem (e.g., ad networks, analytics, ad exchanges) have, expectedly, the highest presence. This strong presence is due to the employed advertising mechanisms (e.g., real-time bidding) that share user-specific IDs across different entities of the ad ecosystem.

We then compared the categories of domains in each group. For instance, in the following ID-sharing group {getclicky.com,ibtimes.co.uk} the categories of domains in the group are {Analytics, News}. Table 4 shows the top 15 categories of the sharing groups (in their frequency of occurrence) and the nature of their domain categories in the group, i.e., within a category (w-cat.) or cross categories (c-cat). We observe that the majority of ID-sharing in the groups happens across different categories. We find only 28 ID-sharing groups of which their

---

[2] http://global.sitesafety.trendmicro.com.

Table 3. Top 15 user ID-sharing groups ordered based on their frequency of occurrence. The Type column indicates the nature of organisational sharing within the group (within-organisation=w-org versus cross-organisation=c-org).

Sharing group	Type
google.com, googleadservices.com	w-org
google.com, youtube.com	w-org
flickr.com, yahoo.com, yahooapis.com	w-org
bbc.com, effectivemeasure.net	c-org
yahoo.com, www.yimg.com	w-org
bing.com, live.com	w-org
adxcore.com,cherryssp.net	c-org
rubiconproject.com, wtp101.com	c-org
rubiconproject.com, tapad.com	c-org
bing.com, live.com, msn.com	w-org
eyeviewads.com, rubiconproject.com	c-org
everesttech.net, rubiconproject.com	c-org
rubiconproject.com, w55c.net	c-org
sina.com.cn, weibo.com	w-org
rubiconproject.com, rundsp.com	c-org

members belong to the same category (within-category sharing). This number is considerably lower than 110 groups with members belonging to different categories (cross-categories sharing). We have also observed that sensitive domain categories such as health related ones participate in the ID-sharing with domains related to advertisement trackers and search engines (7 groups). For instance, webmd.com (a health information website) has shared user-specific IDs with gravity.com (an advertisement tracker). Looking at a sample HTTP request from webmd.com to gravity.com in Table 5, shows that gravity.com logs users' visited pages via *referrer* URL-parameter. This information enables gravity.com to create users' profiles based on their visited pages and searched terms on webmd.com. The presence of such domain categories within sharing groups raises serious privacy concerns since users' sensitive information can be exposed within sharing groups.

3   Effect of User Profile

In the previous section, we observed strong presence of user ID-sharing based on two-weeks online activities' logs of over 100 users. In this section, we further examine the potential intentions behind the ID-sharing by studying the effect of user profile on the presence of ID-sharing domains. For this purpose we run multiple crawls on sets of trained user profiles. In order to create the user profiles, we

Table 4. Top 15 categories of the sharing groups ordered based on their frequency of occurrence. The Type column indicates the nature of domain categories within the sharing group (within category=w-cat. versus cross category=c-cat.).

Sharing group	Type
Search engines, Web advertisements	c-cat
Search engines, Streaming media	c-cat
Ad-tracker	w-cat
Search engines	w-cat
Ad-tracker, Web advertisements	c-cat
Ad-tracker, Internet infrastructure	c-cat
Ad tracker, Photo searches, Search engines	c-cat
Media, News	c-cat
Ad tracker, News	c-cat
Web advertisements	w-cat
Ad-tracker, Business	c-cat
Health	w-cat
Internet infrastructure, Web advertisements	c-cat
Ad tracker, Search engines	c-cat

first created five artificial users with separate accounts on Google, Amazon, eBay and Twitter. We assigned three different profile sizes, in terms of the browsing histories, to our users: (1) Two users were given a browsing history consisting of Alexa's top 500 websites (*Profile-500*); (2) Two other users with smaller size of browsing history including Alexa's top 200 websites (*Profile-200*); (3) One user with an empty browsing history (*Profile-0*). To explore the effect of not having a user profile, we considered a user with an empty browsing history and without any accounts on the aforementioned websites (*noAcount*). We created the browsing history by crawling the corresponding Alexa's list of websites for five consecutive times while users were logged-in. The profile-training step was done on the Firefox browser installed on a separate Linux machine per user. After creating the user profiles, we installed the Firefox extension from the Sect. 2.1 on the Firefox browsers. Then, we executed the main step of the experiment by visiting Alexa's top 1000 websites for each user. We repeated this step for 20 iterations to expose as many as possible ID-sharing domains. We performed the main step identically under two conditions: user logged-in and user logged-out.

We applied the same rules as described in Sect. 2.2 to identify user-specific IDs. Consequently, we identified 4,104 unique user-specific IDs shared by 787 domains. Figure 3 illustrates the accumulated number of unique ID-sharing domains across the iterations per user and profile condition. We observe that the highest rise occurs between the first and second iteration (approximately 40 %), in comparison with subsequent iterations (Fig. 3). Moreover, we explored

Table 5. A sample HTTP request from webmd.com (a health information website) to gravity.com (an advertisement tracker). Gravity.com logs users' visited pages via *referrer* URL-parameter. Consequently, the searched terms by users on webmd.com are exposed to gravity.com (e.g. query=breast-cancer)

RequestURL:	http://rma-api.gravity.com/v1/beacons/log?action=beacon&user_guid=21737bfabd4416779f6&referrer=
	http://www.webmd.com/search/search_results/default.aspx?query=breast-cancer
Host:	rma-api.gravity.com
Referer:	http://www.webmd.com/breast-cancer/default.htm

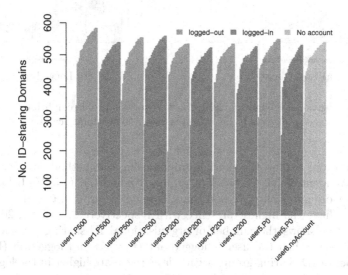

Fig. 3. Number of ID-sharing domains across the iterations. Each bar represents an iteration.

the number of ID-sharing domains across various profile sizes (browsing histories) and profile conditions (logged-in, logged-out, and noAcount). Table 6 shows the unique number of ID-sharing domains per profile size and condition. The results in Table 6 suggests that users with a larger profile (more browsing history) are tracked by a higher number of ID-sharing domains than those with smaller profile sizes. On the other hand, we find the number of ID-sharing domains, unexpectedly, higher in the logged-out condition than logged-in (Table 6b). In general, the comparable numbers of ID-sharing domains across various profile conditions and profile sizes suggest that the users are being tracked regardless of their profile condition and the amount of browsing history (Table 6).

Afterwards, we examined the presence of organisational ID-sharing groups across different profile conditions. We defined ID-sharing groups as sets of domains that share user-specific IDs (refer to Sect. 2.2). In addition, we identified

Table 6. Total number of unique ID-sharing domains for each (a) profile size and (b) profile condition.

Profile Size	#Domains
P-500	649
P-200	631
P-0	538

Profile Condition	#Domains
no-account	531
logged-in	599
logged-out	749

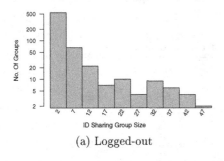

(a) Logged-out

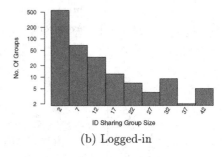

(b) Logged-in

Fig. 4. Organisational ID-sharing groups across various profile conditions: (a) logged-out and (b) logged-in (Y-axis in both figures uses a logarithmic scale).

the organisations behind the sharing groups using the method described in the Sect. 2.2. We identified 694 ID-sharing groups of which 357 (=51 %) belonging to two distinct organisations. We find that across these groups, Google and Rubicon Project have the highest presence with respectively 27 (=7 %), 20 (=5 %) cases. Figure 4 shows the number of organisational ID-sharing groups against their group size when the user is logged-out (Fig. 4a) and logged-in (Fig. 4b). The number of ID-sharing groups with a larger size are higher in the logged-out condition comparing to the logged-in condition. As an example, Fig. 5 shows the largest ID-sharing group for the logged-out mode. In this group, we find the Rubicon Project, Switch Concept (an ad. Network company) and StickyADStv (a video publisher company) as the most dominant ones in terms of organisational ID-sharing. We observe strong collaborations between specific organisations such as the Rubicon Project, Sovrn (an ad Network company), Google and StickyADStv.

This unexpected finding can be due to the fact that more domains have been collaborating with each other when the user was logged-out, to compensate for the lack of context about the user, and trying to create a more precise profile for that user—by gathering as much information as possible.

4   Related Work

A number of studies have analyzed trackers from different points of view. Krishnamurthy & Wills [2] showed the expansion of third-party trackers and the acquisitions of tracking companies from 2005 for a period of three years.

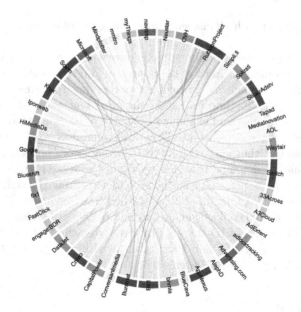

Fig. 5. The biggest organisational ID-sharing group in the logged-out mode. Link thickness represents the frequency of collaboration between two organisations. A Darker colored organisations are involved in higher number of cross-organisational ID-sharing.

In [9], they examined the access of web trackers to personal information based on the category of the first-party website in which they are embedded. They found that websites providing health and travel-related services disclose more information to trackers than other types of websites. Gill *et al.* [10] studied the amount of inferred information about users through tracking their visited websites by ad networks. Liu *et al.* [11] have looked at tracking personal data on the web using ISP travel from 2011, however the big shift away from using clear text in the web introduces a much more complicated user ID sharing ecosystem in the web today. They observed that ad networks are able to estimate users' interest with 50 % accuracy. These studies showed the possible access of trackers to the user personal information whereas we study the scale and nature of tracking ecosystem.

Roesner *et al.* [12] proposed a framework for classifying the behaviour of web trackers based on the scope of the browsing profile they produce. They show the spread of the identified classes amongst the top 500 websites in the world. Zarras *et al.* [13] studied the ecosystem of ad networks that serve malicious advertisement. Interestingly, they observed some ad networks which more than a third of their traffic belongs to malicious advertisement. Gomer *et al.* [14] focused on the network aspects of third-party trackers which appeared in the search results of three search engines. They show a consistent network structure of third-party trackers and high efficiency in exchanging information among third-parties.

Mayer *et al.* [15] surveyed different techniques which are used by web trackers to collect user information. Acar *et al.* [6] presented a thorough study of persistent user tracking mechanisms, particularly canvas fingerprinting and evercookies. They introduced a method for identifying persistent user IDs. They crawled top 3,000 Alexa domains, and examined the effect of blocking third-party cookies as well as advertisement opt-out. They observed a decrease in the number of shared IDs, however, they showed that such decrease does not affect the overall access of ID sharing domains to user's browsing history. The main purpose of this study is to explore persistent methods of user tracking through active measurements. Additionally, Olejnik *et al.* [7] studied cookie syncing. They observed the presence of over 100 cookie syncing across top 100 sites. While these studies highlighted the presence of ID-sharing practice across the Web, we focus on the nature of ID sharing groups and their relation with user information using a series of active and passive measurements.

5   Conclusion

In this paper, we explored the entangled connections between all parties of the Web ecosystem. In particular, we investigated the tracking groups that shared user specific identifiers. We recorded the browsing history of more than 100 users for more than two weeks. To our surprise, we find 660 ID-sharing groups in our data. We identify a significant amount of ID-sharing across different organisations. We identified Google and Rubicon Project (an ad. network company) as the most dominant companies that used ID-sharing. Similar to our observation at the organisational level, we observe a significant presence of domains from different categories within ID-sharing groups. We observe that sensitive domain categories such as health related ones participate in the ID-sharing with domains related to advertisement trackers and search engines (seven ID-sharing groups). Moreover, we examined the effect of user profile on the presence of ID-sharing domains. Interestingly, we observe that users are being tracked regardless of their profile condition (logged-in or logged-out) and the amount of browsing history. We unexpectedly observe that the number of ID-sharing domains are higher in the logged-out condition than logged-in. Our results suggest that more domains are collaborating with each other when the user is logged-out trying to create a more precise profile for that user. As a further work, we would like to examine whether this collaboration amongst ID-sharing domains in the logged-out mode aims to identify the user, or it is a side-effect of knowing less about the user, hence being more inclusive in potential advertising sources. Note that from our data we cannot directly observe whether domains use these IDs to merge collected data from different sources. However, considering the possibility of such practice, we believe it is important to get additional insight about what ID-sharing groups actually do through the user IDs.

References

1. Vallina-Rodriguez, N., Shah, J., Finamore, A., Grunenberger, Y., Papagiannaki, K., Haddadi, H., Crowcroft, J.: Breaking for commercials: characterizing mobile advertising. In: Proceedings of the ACM Internet Measurement Conference (2012)
2. Krishnamurthy, B., Wills, C.: Privacy diffusion on the web: a longitudinal perspective. In: Proceedings of the 18th International Conference on World Wide Web. ACM (2009)
3. Falahrastegar, M., Haddadi, H., Uhlig, S., Mortier, R.: The rise of panopticons: examining region-specific third-party web tracking. In: Dainotti, A., Mahanti, A., Uhlig, S. (eds.) TMA 2014. LNCS, vol. 8406, pp. 104–114. Springer, Heidelberg (2014)
4. NSA using Google's online ad tracking tools to spy on web users. http://threatpost.com/nsa-using-google-non-advertising-cookie-to-spy/
5. Ayenson, M., Wambach, D.J., Soltani, A., Good, N., Hoofnagle, C.J.: Flash Cookies and Privacy II: Now with HTML5 and ETag Respawning. Social Science Research Network Working Paper Series (2011)
6. Acar, G., Eubank, C., Englehardt, S., Juarez, M., Narayanan, A., Diaz, C.: The web never forgets: persistent tracking mechanisms in the wild. In: Proceedings of the 2014 ACM SIGSAC Conference on Computer and Communications Security, CCS 2014, pp. 674–689. ACM, New York (2014)
7. Ghosh, A., Roth, A.: Selling privacy at auction. In: Proceedings of the 12th ACM Conference on Electronic Commerce, EC 2011, pp. 199–208. ACM, New York (2011)
8. Findtracker. http://www.eecs.qmul.ac.uk/~marjan/repo/findtracker.zip
9. Krishnamurthy, B., Naryshkin, K., Wills, C.: Privacy leakage vs. protection measures: the growing disconnect. In: Proceedigs of the Web 2.0 Security and Privacy Workshopp (2011)
10. Gill, P., Erramilli, V., Chaintreau, A., Krishnamurthy, B., Papagiannaki, K., Rodriguez, P.: Follow the money: understanding economics of online aggregation and advertising. In: Proceedings of the Conference on Internet Measurement Conference, IMC 2013, pp. 141–148. ACM, New York (2013)
11. Liu, Y., Song, H.H., Bermudez, I., Mislove, A., Baldi, M., Tongaonkar, A.: Identifying personal information in internet traffic. In: Proceedings of the 3rd ACM Conference on Online Social Networks (COSN 2015), Palo Alto, November 2015
12. Roesner, F., Kohno, T., Wetherall, D.: Detecting and defending against third-party tracking on the web. In: USENIX Symposium on Networking Systems Design and Implementation (2012)
13. Apostolis, Z., Alexandros, K., Gianluca, S., Thorsten, H., Christopher, K., Giovanni, V.: The dark alleys of madison avenue: understanding malicious advertisements. In: Proceedings of the Conference on Internet Measurement Conference, IMC 2014, pp. 373–380. ACM, New York (2014)
14. Gomer, R., Rodrigues, E., Frayling, N.M., Schraefel, M.C.: Network analysis of third party tracking: user exposure to tracking cookies through search. In: Web Intelligence and Intelligent Agent Technology, vol. 1 (2013)
15. Mayer, J.R., Mitchell, J.C.: Third-party web tracking: policy and technology. In: Proceedings of the IEEE Symposium on Security and Privacy (2012)

Like a Pack of Wolves: Community Structure of Web Trackers

Vasiliki Kalavri[1]([✉]), Jeremy Blackburn[2], Matteo Varvello[2],
and Konstantina Papagiannaki[2]

[1] KTH Royal Institute of Technology, Stockholm, Sweden
kalavri@kth.se
[2] Telefonica Research, Barcelona, Spain

Abstract. Web trackers are services that monitor user behavior on the web. The information they collect is ostensibly used for customization and targeted advertising. Due to rising privacy concerns, users have started to install browser plugins that prevent tracking of their web usage. Such plugins tend to address tracking activity by means of crowdsourced filters. While these tools have been relatively effective in protecting users from privacy violations, their crowdsourced nature requires significant human effort, and provide no fundamental understanding of how trackers operate. In this paper, we leverage the insight that fundamental requirements for trackers' success can be used as discriminating features for tracker detection. We begin by using traces from a mobile web proxy to model user browsing behavior as a graph. We then perform a transformation on the extracted graph that reveals very well-connected communities of trackers. Next, after discovering that trackers' position in the transformed graph significantly differentiates them from "normal" vertices, we design an automated tracker detection mechanism using two simple algorithms. We find that both techniques for automated tracker detection are quite accurate (over 97 %) and robust (less than 2 % false positives). In conjunction with previous research, our findings can be used to build robust, fully automated online privacy preservation systems.

1 Introduction

The massive growth of the web has been funded almost entirely via advertisements shown to users. Web ads have proven superior to traditional advertisements for several reasons, the most prominent being the ability to show personally relevant ads. While the content of the web page the ad is being served on can help provide hints as to relevance, web advertisement agencies also rely on mechanisms to *uniquely identify* and *track* user behavior over time. Known as *trackers*, these systems are able to uniquely identify a user via a variety of methods and over time can build up enough information about a user to serve extremely targeted ads.

While ad agencies' use of trackers has enabled services to provide access to users free of charge, there is also a certain degree of "creepiness" in the way the

© Springer International Publishing Switzerland 2016
T. Karagiannis and X. Dimitropoulos (Eds.): PAM 2016, LNCS 9631, pp. 42–54, 2016.
DOI: 10.1007/978-3-319-30505-9_4

current ecosystem works that has also been highlighted in the US congress [12]. Recent work [5] has even shown that government agencies can easily exploit trackers to spy on people. Privacy concerns have led to the creation of client side applications that block trackers and ads. For example, AdBlock [1] blocks trackers by filtering requests through a set of crowdsourced rules. Unfortunately, such lists are mostly opaque: there is no straight forward way to understand why a tracker was added to the list or to get a sense as to how trackers work on an individual or group basis, and users can be left out in the cold as evidenced by the recent sale of AdBlock to an undisclosed buyer who immediately enabled opting in to the "Acceptable Ads" program [14].

In the research community, several strategies for detecting and defending against trackers have been introduced [7,10,13]. Overall, these works focus on understanding the methods that trackers use in order to define techniques for obfuscating a user's browsing behavior. However, these previous works are generally focused on lower level intricacies, e.g., how trackers fingerprint users or ensure that cookies persist even after users clean them.

In this paper, we take a different approach and attempt to characterize some more fundamental aspects of trackers. Our rationale is that user requests, e.g., accessing `google.com`, and requests to trackers, e.g., 3rd party request to `doubleclick.net`, can be represented as a bipartite graph from which we can derive unique tracker properties, allowing for the optimization and automation of the tracker detection problem.

This work makes several contributions.

1. We model user browsing as a 2-mode graph using 6 months (November 2014– April 2015) of traffic logs from an explicit web proxy. By analyzing this graph, we discover that trackers are very well connected: 94 % appear in the largest connected component of the graph.
2. We explore the communities trackers form by inducing a 1-mode projection of the 2-mode browsing graph. We find that trackers form very well-defined communities that distinguish them from regular URLs.
3. We show that the 1-mode projection graph is a useful tool to automatically classify trackers with high precision and very low false positive rate. More importantly, using the projection graph for tracker detection is very robust to evasion since it captures a fundamental necessity of the tracking ecosystem: presence of trackers on multiple sites, and presence of multiple trackers on the same site, which allows publishers to better monetize ad display through real time bidding. Changing such a behavior would limit the efficiency of tracking as a whole.

2 Background and Dataset

Trackers enable targeted advertising and personalization services by monitoring user behavior on the web. To understand web tracking, let us consider what happens in the browser when a user visits a URL. First, the browser issues an

HTTP request to the site to fetch the contents of the web page. The response contains the page resources, including HTML, and references to embedded objects like images and scripts. These references might then instruct the browser to make additional HTTP requests (e.g., for the image itself) until the page is fully loaded. Embedded objects can be hosted on different servers than the page content itself, in which case they are referred to as *third-party* objects. A fraction of these third-party objects open connections to trackers, e.g., the popular Facebook "like" button, at which point the users' online whereabouts are logged for targeting/personalization purposes.

2.1   Dataset

Our dataset is derived from 6 months (November 2014–April 2015) of traffic logs from an explicit web proxy. The proxy is operated by a major telecom located in a large European country. Our data is delivered to us in the form of augmented Apache logs. The logs include fields to identify the user that made the access, the URL that was requested, headers, performance information like latency and bytes delivered. We call this dataset the *proxy log*, and in total it represents 80 million accesses to 2 million individual sites. In the following section, we describe how we use the proxy log to model web tracking as a graph problem. We label URLs in our dataset as *tracker* or *other* based on ground truth derived from the EasyPrivacy list for AdBlock [3].

2.2   Web Tracking as a Graph Problem

A *2-mode graph* is a graph with two different modes (or classes) of vertices, where edges are only allowed between vertices belonging to different modes. The interactions between explicit user requests and background requests, both page content and third-party objects like web tracking services, can be naturally modeled as a 2-mode graph. The first mode of vertices in the graph are URLs that the user intentionally visits, while the second mode are URLs for objects that are embedded in the visited page.

More precisely, we represent the URLs that a browser accesses as a 2-mode graph $G = (U, V, E)$, where U are the URLs that the user explicitly visits, V are the URLs that are embedded within those pages, and E is the set of edges connecting vertices in U (explicitly visited URLs) to vertices in V (URLs embedded within visited pages). In this paper, we call vertices in U *referers*, vertices in V *hosts*, and G the *referer-hosts graph*.

In graph analysis, *communities* are groups of vertices that are well-connected internally, and sparsely connected with other groups of vertices. Vertices belonging to the same community are more likely to be similar with respect to connectivity and network position than vertices belonging to different communities. V contains both regular embedded objects and third-party objects potentially associated with trackers. We expect regular embedded objects to only appear on the hosting web page, while tracker objects need to appear on as many web pages as possible to enable successful tracking of users across websites.

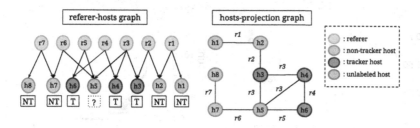

Fig. 1. Example of the hosts-projection graph transformation. Vertices prefixed with r are the pages the user explicitly visited while those prefixed with h were embedded within the r vertex they have an edge with. Note that additional information associated with the vertex (e.g., tracker/non-tracker/unknown label) is not affected by the transformation.

This implies that: (1) tracker vertices in V should be linked to many different vertices in U and (2) tracker vertices are members of well-defined communities in G.

Unfortunately, working with communities in 2-mode graphs like ours can be tricky. For example, the relationships between vertices in the same mode are only *inferred* from relationships that pass *through* vertices in the second mode, which can lead to unexpected results from standard community detection algorithms run on a raw 2-mode graph. This is especially a problem when the community structures of the two modes are different as we might expect in our case [9]. To avoid this problem, it is typical to extract and analyze 1-mode projections of 2-mode graphs.

Assuming that users do not intentionally visit tracker sites, U should not contain tracker URLs which are instead contained in V. Accordingly, we can project the 2-mode graph into a 1-mode graph that only contains the vertices in V, by creating the *hosts-projection graph* G'. In G', we create an edge between any two vertices in V that share a common neighbor in G. I.e., if two vertices, v and v' from V both share an edge with a vertex u from U, then there is an edge $e = (v, v')$ in G'. Figure 1 illustrates this transformation. This way, G' preserves much of the original graph's structural information and captures implicit connections between trackers through other sites.

3 Trackers' Position in the Graph

In this section we present an analysis on the referer-hosts graph and the hosts-projection graph. We are especially interested in discovering whether trackers have different properties than "normal" URLs in these graphs.

3.1 In the Referer-Hosts Graph

We first investigate trackers' degree centrality, or how well trackers are connected to other vertices in the graph. Although trackers are essentially required

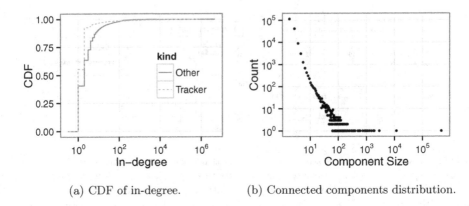

(a) CDF of in-degree.   (b) Connected components distribution.

Fig. 2. Basic analysis of referer-hosts graph.

to appear on many different pages to collect meaningful data, we are interested in quantifying this. We begin by plotting the in-degree of vertices in mode V of the referer-hosts graph, broken down into "trackers" and "others" in Fig. 2a. The figure can be thought of as illustrating the number of unique referers that tracker/non-tracker hosts are embedded within. Surprisingly, we find that trackers tend to have a slightly lower in-degree than other URLs, which contradicts our initial observation that trackers must appear on many different pages in order to work. When looking at things a bit closer, we discovered that this is due to the use of *user/page specific tracking URLs*, mostly from Google, such `unique-hash.metrics.gstatic.com`. It follows that simply assuming high in-degree vertices as characteristic of trackers is not suitable. As we will discuss later, the hosts-projection graph transformation can be used to shed additional light on this situation.

Next, to see how well connected trackers are *to each other* we extract connected components and plot the distribution of their sizes in Fig. 2b. A connected component is a subgraph in which there exists a path between any two of its vertices. As expected, there are many 2-vertex components (pages that were only visited once and that host no, or very uncommon 3rd party content) and one dominant component. This largest connected component (LCC) contains 500,000 vertices, *i.e.*, one fourth of the distinct URLs in our dataset, and 94 % of all trackers in our dataset (identified via EasyPrivacy list) are in the LCC. We will leverage this finding in Sect. 4 when showing how the community structure of trackers can be exploited for detection purposes.

3.2   In the Hosts-Projection Graph

We create the hosts-projection graph from the largest connected component in the referer-hosts graph. The projection has 80,000 vertices and 43 million edges. We note that the only substantive information lost in the projection graph is the number of unique pages a tracker appears on (i.e., the in-degree of the

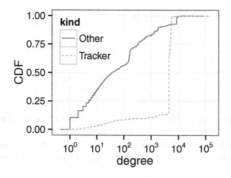

Fig. 3. CDF of degrees in the hosts-projection graph for trackers and others.

vertex within the referer-hosts graph). We first look at the degree distribution of trackers, and then examine the composition of their neighborhoods within the hosts-projection graph.

Trackers' Degree Distribution is a Distinguishing Factor. Figure 3 shows the degree distribution of trackers and other hosts in the hosts-projection graph. As opposed to the referer-hosts case, here we observe a clear difference between the degree distribution of trackers and other pages, noting that the low-degree skew of trackers has disappeared. This is due to the construction of the projection graph: while in the referer-hosts graph, trackers only have edges to the pages they are embedded within, in the projection graph, they are directly connected with any URL that co-appears on the same page. For example, if we have three trackers that are only embedded within a single page, they will each have an in-degree of 1 in the referer-hosts graph, however, they will all be connected in the projection graph, resulting in a degree of 2. In general, we note that a higher degree might imply that trackers are more "important" in the projected graph than other pages.

Figure 3 also illustrates another distinguishing factor of trackers. Their degree distribution skews extremely high, with about 80 % having a degree of over 3,000. The explanation for this is that URLs that point to content on sites (e.g., CDNs) tend to be unique, or at least tend to appear on only a few sites. On the other hand, trackers *must* appear on multiple sites to be effective, and thus co-appear with many other URLs (some tracker, some not).

Trackers are Mainly Connected to Other Trackers. Next, we examine trackers' neighborhoods more closely. Figure 4a shows the ratio of a vertex's neighbors that are trackers, distinguishing between tracker vertices and other. We observe that the vast majority of trackers' neighbors are other trackers. To further investigate how well-connected trackers are among them, we plot the ratio of a vertex's neighbors that are trackers over the total number of trackers in Fig. 4b and observe that *trackers tend to be direct neighbors with most of*

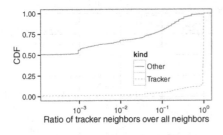 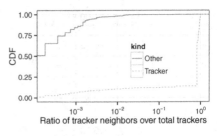

(a) Ratio of the projection graph vertices'   (b) Ratio of a node's tracker neighbors over
neighbors that are trackers.   the total number of trackers in the dataset.

Fig. 4. CDFs of neighborhood compositions for trackers and non-trackers.

Fig. 5. Tracker oriented visualization of the hosts-projection graph from April's logs. The visualization includes only edges where at least one end point is a tracker, resulting in 60 k vertices and 340 k edges. The darker a vertex's color, the higher its degree. The community on the right contains trackers and ad servers, where ad servers can be seen as having a slightly lighter color and being mostly clustered on the left edge of the community. The left cluster consists of normal webpages and a few popular trackers, distinguished by their larger size and darker color (Color figure online).

the other trackers in the graph. This result is likely an artifact of publishers' tendency to add multiple trackers on their websites in the hope of serving better targeted ads.

From a privacy standpoint, this result is worrying as it highlights the pervasiveness of passive "surveillance" on the web. Even completely blocking any particular tracker could be somewhat mitigated by collusion. We do note that because the hosts-projection graph flattens the referer-hosts graph, collusion would not be enough to regain information on visits to pages where it is uniquely present.

Our findings up until now suggest that trackers form a dense community in the hosts-projection graph. This dense community is quite clearly seen in Fig. 5, which visualizes the host-projection graph (from April's logs) focused around trackers' positions. We observe that the majority of low-degree trackers indeed

Table 1. New trackers per month

	Test records in LCC	Trackers in LCC	Total new trackers
February	13685	760	811
March	18313	740	774
April	40465	747	792

form a very dense and easily identifiable community (the cluster on the right). On the other hand, there exist a few *popular* trackers (the large dark nodes in the left cluster), which are connected to the majority of normal URLs and are also very well-connected among each other.

4 Classifying Trackers

Our findings suggest that trackers form a well-connected cluster in the hosts-projection graph, and are mostly connected to other trackers. In this section, we leverage these findings to automatically classify trackers. We show that even a simple assessment of vertices' neighbors in the hosts-projection graph can yield good classification results with two methods: (1) a rule-based classifier which analyzes the first-hop neighborhoods of each unlabeled vertex in the hosts-projection graph, and (2) an iterative label propagation method.

4.1 Classification via Neighborhood Analysis

This classification method analyzes the first-hop neighborhoods of each unlabeled node in the hosts-projection graph. For each unlabeled node, we count the number of trackers among its immediate neighbors and make a classification decision based on a configurable threshold. If the percentage of tracker neighbors is above the threshold, then the node is labeled as a tracker.

We evaluate our classifier using three subsets of our dataset. For every subset, we use all the hosts that appear in the last month as the test set and all the previous months as the training set. Thus, we use, e.g., the logs from November up to January in order to classify hosts seen in February logs. Hosts in the training set are labeled as "tracker" or "other" using the EasyPrivacy list as ground truth. Note that we also ensure that previously labeled vertices are not included in any future test sets. We use our classifier to tag each of the untagged nodes as *tracker* or *non-tracker* and measure precision, accuracy, false positive rate (FPR) and recall for each method. We assess classification stability, by randomly choosing test sets out of the complete dataset.

The number of test records and previously unseen trackers per month are shown in Table 1. We observe around 800 new trackers per month and this number is independent from the total number of requests to new pages over the

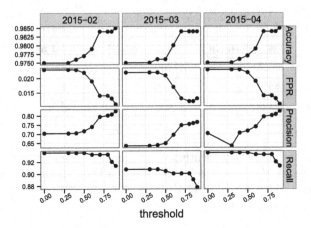

Fig. 6. Classifier performance for the neighborhood analysis method.

6 months of our dataset[1]. This indicates that there is enough diversity in the tracker "ecosystem" that users are constantly exposed to "new-to-them" trackers. In turn, this strengthens the need for an automated detection system to alleviate the load on crowdsourced approaches.

The classification results for February, March, and April are shown in Fig. 6. We assess the impact of threshold selection in the following ways: (a) Unlabeled nodes take the label of their neighbors' most common tag (threshold = 0.00), and (b) The tag appears on at least a given fraction of the vertex's neighbors.

In all cases, we achieve a classification precision that varies from 64 % up to 83 %. We observe that precision increases for higher thresholds: the more tracker neighbors a node has, the higher the probability that it is a tracker itself. Similarly, FPR and accuracy both improve for higher thresholds, but remain under 2 % and over 97 % in all cases. On the other hand, recall decreases as we increase the threshold, which means that we might miss a few trackers, but it is above 88 % in all cases.

4.2 Classification via Label Propagation

Label Propagation is a scalable iterative algorithm for community detection [11]. It exploits the graph structure to propagate labels and identify densely connected groups of vertices. Initially, vertices are assigned unique labels. Then, in an iterative fashion, vertices exchange labels with their neighbors. At each iteration, a vertex receives a list of labels of its immediate neighbors, adopting the most frequent label for itself. The algorithm converges when an iteration results in no label changes.

Figure 7 illustrates how we use this algorithm on the hosts-projection graph. First, vertices propagate labels until convergence (i=0:4 in Fig. 7a); next vertices

---

[1] We consider a tracker new if our users have not been exposed to it before. Note that we identify trackers by their unique URLs, without grouping them by domain.

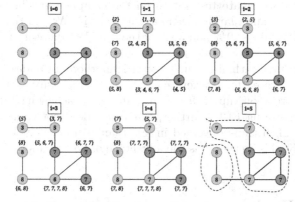

(a) Cluster identification with label propagation.

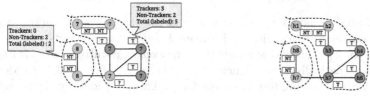

(b) Assigning tags to individual vertices.   (c) Super tag assignment to communities.

Fig. 7. Illustration of label propagation technique for tracker classification.

Table 2. Label propagation classification results

		Precision	FPR	Accuracy	Recall
Monthly test sets	February	0.934	0.004	0.993	0.932
	March	0.946	0.002	0.994	0.9
	April	0.922	0.001	0.997	0.872
Random test sets	5 %	0.923	0.004	0.994	0.958
	10 %	0.934	0.004	0.993	0.941
	20 %	0.941	0.003	0.994	0.948
	30 %	0.939	0.003	0.994	0.951

with the same label are grouped in the same community (i=5 in Fig. 7a). Then, we use the EasyPrivacy list to identify and *tag* known trackers inside the clusters, and tag as non-trackers white-listed vertices (Fig. 7b). Finally, we assign a super tag to each cluster by choosing the most popular tag among its cluster members (Fig. 7c). We classify unlabeled nodes by assigning them the super tag of the cluster in which they belong.

The results for the label propagation method are shown in Table 2. To assess classification stability, we evaluate the classification using random sets of test records of varying sizes. Instead of selecting the test set based on the timestamp of the log record, we create test sets from the complete graph, by randomly choosing log records and marking them as "untagged". We run this experiment for test sets of 5 %, 10 %, 20 % and 30 % of the complete dataset and repeat it 3 times.

By exploring further than the first-hop neighborhood of nodes, this method can successfully locate the trackers community and classify test items with extremely high precision, up to 94 %, in addition to achieving high accuracy and recall, and lowering FPR. Further, this result does not come at a performance cost: the algorithm converged in less than 10 iterations for all the test sets used. Finally, this method has the advantage of not needing a manually set threshold.

5   Related Work

A number of studies have empirically analyzed the ecosystem of trackers and third-parties on the web, focusing on behavioral and network aspects.

TrackAdvisor [8] is a tool that analyzes cookie exchange statistics from HTTP requests to automatically detect trackers. Similar to us, their goal is to identify trackers without having to rely on blacklists. They also identify third-party requests by looking at the referer field. Their dataset is created by visiting Alexa top 10 K pages (not real user data) and is an order of magnitude smaller than ours (500 k requests in total). Our method does not need to intercept cookie traffic. Our finding that a tracker appears in multiple pages agrees with their results. In conclusion, we could call the two methods complementary; they could be combined to produce a more powerful tool.

Roesner et al. provide a study of web tracking, classifying tracking behaviors and evaluating defense mechanisms [13] using web traces from AOL search logs to simulate real user behavior. They build a classification framework for distinguishing different types of trackers, based on their functionality. In contrast, our classification method distinguishes between trackers and non-trackers, while it is oblivious to the tracker mechanisms and functionality specifics.

Bau et al. propose a machine learning mechanism for detecting trackers [4]. They evaluate machine learning approaches and present results from a prototype implementation. They use DOM-like hierarchies from the crawl data HTTP content headers as the main features. While they achieve precision of 54 % for 1 % FPR, our methods achieve much better precision and lower FRP, while not relying on page content collection.

Gomer et al. investigate the graph structure of third-party tracking domains in [6] in the context of search engine results. They obtain their graph by using searching several popular search engines with a set of pre-defined queries as opposed to real browsing behavior as we do. Their focus is on how users are exposed to trackers via normal search behavior and they find a 99.5 % chance of being tracked by all major trackers within 30 clicks on search results. They further found that the graph structure was similar across geographic regions, which reduces the concern of bias in our dataset.

In agreement with our findings, most of the above works also find that a small number of trackers are able to capture the majority of user behavior. However, our work is, to the best of our knowledge, the first to show that using this community structure as an explicit feature can accurately predict whether an unknown URL is a tracker or not.

6 Conclusion

In this paper we explored the community structure of trackers using a large-scale dataset from an explicit web proxy. We transformed user requests into a 2-mode referer-hosts graph where vertices in the first mode represent pages the user visited and vertices in the second mode represent requests for objects embedded in those pages. We found that 94 % of trackers were in the largest connected component of this graph. In order to study how trackers relate to each other, we collapsed the referer-hosts graph into a 1-mode hosts-projection graph. From the hosts-projection graph we observed an extremely high degree of clustering, indicating the formation of tight communities. From this observation, we demonstrated the effectiveness of two tracker detection mechanisms: (1) a simple threshold based classifier that examines the number of tracker neighbors of unknown vertices and (2) a label propagation algorithm that makes implicit use of the communities trackers form. Both techniques achieved highly surprising accuracies (over 97 %) and low false positive rates (under 2 %).

We implemented the analysis and classification algorithms using Apache Flink [2]. In the future we intend to port them to a streaming version for deployment within our explicit web proxy, but even our initial implementations are quite fast. For example classification via the label propagation method was on the order of minutes when run on a commodity Mac laptop, indicating there are few scalability concerns for production deployment.

References

1. AdBlock. https://getadblock.com/
2. Apache Flink. http://www.flink.apache.org
3. EasyPrivacy list. https://hg.adblockplus.org/easylist/
4. Bau, J., Mayer, J., Paskov, H., Mitchell, J.C.: A promising direction for web tracking countermeasures. In: Web 2.0 Security and Privacy (2013)
5. Englehardt, S., Reisman, D., Eubank, C., Zimmerman, P., Mayer, J., Narayanan, A., Felten, E.W.: Cookies that give you away: the surveillance implications of web tracking. In: Proceedings of the 24th international conference on World Wide Web, WWW 2015 (2015)
6. Gomer, R., Rodrigues, E.M., Milic-Frayling, N., Schraefel, M.C.: Network analysis of third party tracking: user exposure to tracking cookies through search. In: Proceedings of the IEEE/WIC/ACM International Joint Conferences on Web Intelligence and Intelligent Agent Technologies, pp. 549–556 (2013)
7. Krishnamurthy, B., Wills, C.: Privacy diffusion on the web: a longitudinal perspective. In: Proceedings of the 18th International Conference on World Wide Web, WWW 2009, pp. 541–550 (2009)

8. Li, T.-C., Hang, H., Faloutsos, M., Efstathopoulos, P.: TrackAdvisor: taking back browsing privacy from third-party trackers. In: Mirkovic, J., Liu, Y. (eds.) PAM 2015. LNCS, vol. 8995, pp. 277–289. Springer, Heidelberg (2015)
9. Melamed, D.: Community structures in bipartite networks: a dual-projection approach. PLoS ONE **9**(5), e97823 (2014)
10. Papaodyssefs, F., Iordanou, C., Blackburn, J., Laoutaris, N., Papagiannaki, K.: Web identity translator: behavioral advertising and identity privacy with WIT. In: Proceedings of the 14th ACM Workshop on Hot Topics in Networks (to appear), HotNets 2015 (2011)
11. Raghavan, U.N., Albert, R., Kumara, S.: Near linear time algorithm to detect community structures in large-scale networks. Phys. Rev. E **76**(3), 036106 (2007)
12. Rockefeller, J.D.: Do-Not-Track online act of 2013. US Senate (2013)
13. Roesner, F., Kohno, T., Wetherall, D.: Detecting and defending against third-party tracking on the web. In: Proceedings of the 9th USENIX Conference on Networked Systems Design and Implementation, NSDI 2012 (2012)
14. Williams, O.: Adblock extension with 40 million users sells to mystery buyer, refuses to name new owner (2015). http://thenextweb.com/apps/2015/10/02/trust-us-we-block-ads/

Mobile and Cellular

A First Analysis of Multipath TCP on Smartphones

Quentin De Coninck[1]([✉]), Matthieu Baerts[2], Benjamin Hesmans[1], and Olivier Bonaventure[1]

[1] Université catholique de Louvain, Louvain-la-Neuve, Belgium
{quentin.deconinck,benjamin.hesmans,olivier.bonaventure}@uclouvain.be
[2] Tessares SA, Louvain-la-Neuve, Belgium
matthieu.baerts@tessares.net
http://smartphone.multipath-tcp.org

Abstract. Multipath TCP is a recent TCP extension that enables multihomed hosts like smartphones to send and receive data over multiple interfaces. Despite the growing interest in this new TCP extension, little is known about its behavior with real applications in wireless networks. This paper analyzes a trace from a SOCKS proxy serving smartphones using Multipath TCP. This first detailed study of real Multipath TCP smartphone traffic reveals several interesting points about its behavior in the wild. It confirms the heterogeneity of wireless and cellular networks which influences the scheduling of Multipath TCP. The analysis shows that most of the additional subflows are never used to send data. The amount of reinjections is also quantified and shows that they are not a major issue for the deployment of Multipath TCP. With our methodology to detect handovers, around a quarter of the connections using several subflows experience data handovers.

1 Introduction

TCP is the dominant transport protocol, both on the wired Internet and in wireless networks. Over the years, TCP has evolved and included various optimizations. Multipath TCP is the last major extension to TCP [9,20]. It enables a multihomed host to exchange data for a single connection over different interfaces.

Multipath TCP was standardized in early 2013. Although the extension is still young, it is already used to support several commercial services. In September 2013, Apple has deployed Multipath TCP on hundreds of millions of smartphones and tablets to improve the user experience for the Siri voice recognition application. In July 2015, Korean Telecom announced that they have enabled Multipath TCP on Android smartphones to bond WiFi and LTE together. These smartphones reach download speeds of 800 Mbps and more. In September 2015, OVH, a French ISP and hosting provider, announced their OverTheBox service that uses Multipath TCP to enable SMEs to bond several DSL over cable links together. Other use cases are being explored and it can be expected that Multipath TCP traffic will grow in the coming years.

© Springer International Publishing Switzerland 2016
T. Karagiannis and X. Dimitropoulos (Eds.): PAM 2016, LNCS 9631, pp. 57–69, 2016.
DOI: 10.1007/978-3-319-30505-9_5

Despite the important role that Multipath TCP could play on smartphones, little is known about its behavior with real applications. Most of the articles on Multipath TCP performance relied on lab measurements [15,19] or were carried out with test applications [1,7,8].

This paper provides the first detailed analysis of the operation of Multipath TCP on smartphones used by real users. Since Multipath TCP is not yet deployed on Internet and cloud servers, installing a Multipath TCP kernel is not sufficient to automatically generate Multipath TCP traffic. To benefit from Multipath TCP, a SOCKS proxy had to be installed on a server supporting Multipath TCP and the smartphones were configured to use the SOCKS server as their relay for all connections. This is the same setup as KT's commercial deployment. By sharing the studied trace, the measurement tools and the analysis, this paper improves our understanding of the dynamics of this new protocol.

This paper is organized as follows. It first provides a brief overview of Multipath TCP and discusses related work in Sect. 2. It describes the collected dataset in Sect. 3 and gives first characteristics in Sect. 4. In Sect. 5, it takes a closer look at the performances of Multipath TCP. It concludes in Sect. 6 with the main lessons that we learned from this first detailed analysis of Multipath TCP packet traces.

2   Multipath TCP and Related Work

Multipath TCP is a recent TCP extension that enables the transmission of the data belonging to one connection over different paths or interfaces [9]. A Multipath TCP connection is a logical association that provides a bytestream service. To understand its operation, let us see briefly an example on how a smartphone could use Multipath TCP. To request the utilization of Multipath TCP, the smartphone adds the MP_CAPABLE option in SYN segment sent over its cellular interface. This option contains some flags and a key [9]. If the server supports Multipath TCP, it includes its key in the MP_CAPABLE option sent in the SYN+ACK. According to the Multipath TCP terminology, this TCP connection is called the initial subflow [9]. The smartphone can use it to exchange data over the cellular interface. If the smartphone wants to also send data for this connection over its WiFi interface, it sends a new SYN segment with the MP_JOIN option over this interface. This option contains a token derived from the key announced by the server in the MP_CAPABLE option. This token identifies the Multipath TCP connection on the server side. The server replies with a SYN+ACK containing the MP_JOIN option and the second subflow is established. At this stage, the Multipath TCP connection contains two subflows, but this number is not fixed. The WiFi subflow can stop when the smartphone goes away from access point. At this point, the smartphone can advertise the proxy that it lost one address through a REMOVE_ADDR sent unreliably in TCP options. Another subflow can be created when another IP address is learned from a different access point. Multipath TCP sends data over any of the available subflows. Two levels of sequence numbers are used by Multipath TCP : the regular TCP sequence number and the Data Sequence Number (DSN). The DSN corresponds to the

Multipath TCP bytestream and when data is sent over a subflow, its DSN is mapped to the regular sequence numbers with the DSS option that also contains DSN acknowledgements. When losses occur, Multipath TCP can retransmit data over a different subflow. This operation is called a reinjection [20].

The operation of a Multipath TCP implementation depends on several algorithms that are not standardized by the IETF. First, the *path manager* defines the strategy used to create and delete subflows. The smartphones use the full-mesh path manager that creates one subflow over each pair of interfaces as soon as the initial subflow has been fully established or as soon as a new address has been learned. Second, the *packet scheduler* [16] selects, among the active subflows that have an open congestion window, the subflow that will be used to send the data. The smartphones and the proxy used the default Multipath TCP scheduler in the Linux kernel that prefers the subflow with the smallest RTT. Third, the *congestion controller*. Here, the standard one (LIA) was used.

Various researchers have analyzed the performance of Multipath TCP through measurements. Raiciu et al. [19] discuss how Multipath TCP can be used to support mobile devices and provide early measurement results. Paasch et al. [15] propose three modes for the operation of Multipath TCP in wireless networks and analyse measurements of handovers. Chen et al. [1] analyze the performance of Multipath TCP in WiFi/cellular networks by using bulk transfer applications running on laptops. Ferlin et al. [8] analyze how Multipath TCP reacts to bufferbloat and propose a mitigation technique. As of this writing, this mitigation technique has not been included in the Linux Multipath TCP implementation. Ferlin et al. [7] propose a probing technique to detect low performing paths and evaluates it in wireless networks. Deng et al. [4] compare the performance of single-path TCP over WiFi and LTE networks with Multipath TCP on multi-homed devices by using active measurements and replaying HTTP traffic observed on mobile applications. They show that Multipath TCP provides benefits for long flows but not for short ones, for which the selection of interface for the initial subflow is important from a performance viewpoint. Hesmans et al. [11] analyze a one week-long server trace supporting Multipath TCP.

3   Dataset

Although Multipath TCP is already used by hundred of millions of Apple smartphones to support the Siri voice recognition application, it is difficult to collect both WiFi and cellular traces without cooperation from an ISP. Instead, a Multipath TCP capable SOCKS proxy was set up (like KT) and this analysis focuses on the Multipath TCP implementation in the Linux kernel [14]. This implementation is distributed from http://multipath-tcp.org and can be integrated in Android.

The dataset covers the traffic produced by a dozen of users using Nexus 5 smartphones running Android 4.4 with a modified Linux kernel that includes Multipath TCP v0.89.5. These users were either professors, PhD or Master students at Université catholique de Louvain. While some of them used their device to go only on the Internet, others are still using them as their main phone.

However, installing Multipath TCP on the smartphones is not sufficient to use it for all connections established by applications. As of this writing, there are probably only a few dozens of Multipath TCP enabled servers on the Internet and these are rarely accessed by real smartphone applications. To force these applications to use Multipath TCP, ShadowSocks[1] was installed on each smartphone and configured to use a SOCKS server that supports Multipath TCP for all TCP connections. Note that since ShadowSocks does not support IPv6, this trace only contains IPv4 packets. The smartphones thus use Multipath TCP over their WiFi and cellular interfaces to reach the SOCKS server and this server uses regular TCP to interact with the final destinations. From the server side, all the connections from the dozen smartphones appear as coming from the SOCKS server. This implies that the external (cellular or WiFi) IP address of the smartphone is not visible to the servers that it contacts. This might affect the operation of some servers that adapt their behavior (e.g. the initial congestion window) in function of the client IP address. Moreover, note that the ShadowSocks client sends DNS requests over TCP.

A special Android application [3] managing the utilization of the cellular and WiFi interfaces was also installed on each smartphone. Smartphones with Android 4.4 assume that only one wireless interface is active at a time. When such a smartphone switches from cellular to WiFi, it automatically resets all existing TCP connections by using Android specific functions. This application enables the cellular and WiFi interfaces simultaneously. It also controls the routing tables and updates the policy routes that are required for Multipath TCP every time the smartphone connects to a wireless network. Thanks to this application, the modified Nexus 5 can be used by any user since it does not require any networking knowledge.

The SOCKS proxy ran tcpdump to collect all the packets exchanged with the smartphones. Measurements were performed in Belgium from March 8th to April 28th 2015. Over this period of 7 weeks, more than 71 millions Multipath TCP packets were collected for a total of 25.4 GBytes over 390,782 Multipath TCP connections.[2] To our knowledge, there is no equivalent public dataset. The analysis scripts are also open-sourced [2,3].

4 Characterization of the Trace

The main characteristics of the Multipath TCP connections in the dataset are first analyzed. The destination ports of the captured packets are not sufficient to identify the application level protocol. Since the smartphone connects through a SOCKS proxy, all the packets are sent towards the destination port used by the proxy (443 to prevent middlebox interferences). The real destination port is extracted from the SOCKS command sent by the ShadowSocks client at the beginning of each connection. As shown on Table 1, most of the connections and data bytes are related to Web traffic. Since ShadowSocks sends DNS requests

---

[1] Available at http://shadowsocks.org.

[2] Anonymized traces available: http://crawdad.org/uclouvain/mptcp_smartphone.

Table 1. Statistics about destination port fetched by smartphones.

Port	# connections	% connections	Bytes	% bytes
53	107,012	27.4	17.4 MB	< 0.1
80	103,597	26.5	14,943 MB	58.8
443	104,223	26.7	9,253 MB	36.4
4070	571	0.1	91.7 MB	0.4
5228	10,602	2.7	27.3 MB	0.1
8009	10,765	2.8	0.97 MB	< 0.1
Others	54,012	13.8	1,090 MB	4.3

over TCP, it is expected to have a large fraction of the connections using port 53. Among other popular port numbers, there are ports 4070 — e.g., used by Spotify —, Google Services (5228) and Google Chromecast (8009).

65 % of the observed connections last less than 10 s. In particular, 4.3 % are failed connections, i.e. the first SYN was received and answered by the proxy, but the third ACK was lost (or a RST occurred). 20.8 % of the connections last more than 100 s. Six of them last for more than one entire day (up to nearly two days).

Looking at the bytes carried by each connection, most (86.9 %) of them carry less than 10 KBytes. In particular, 3.1 % of the connections carry between 9 and 11 bytes. Actually, those are empty connections, since the SOCKS command are 7 bytes long, two bytes are consumed by the SYNs and the use of the remaining two bytes depend on how the connections were closed (RST or FIN). The longest connection in terms of bytes transported around 450 MBytes and was spread over five subflows.

5 Analysis

In the following, the analysis will focus on relevant subsets of the trace such as connections with at least two subflows, connections using at least two subflows or connections experiencing handover. Table 2 gives the characteristics of these subsets. They are used to analyze how Multipath TCP subflows are created (Sect. 5.1), study the heterogeneity of the available networks in terms of round-trip-times (Sect. 5.2), estimate the packet reordering of Multipath TCP (Sect. 5.3), study how subflows are used (Sect. 5.4), quantify the reinjection overhead (Sect. 5.5) and identify connections experiencing handovers (Sect. 5.6).

5.1 Establishment of the Subflows

With Multipath TCP, a smartphone can send data over various paths. The number of subflows that a smartphone creates depends on the number of active interfaces that it has and on the availability of the wireless networks.

Table 2. The different (sub)traces analyzed in this section.

Name	Description	# connections	Bytes to proxy	Bytes from proxy
T_0	Full trace	390,782	652 MB	24,771 MB
T_1	At least 2 established subflows	126,040	238 MB	13,496 MB
T_2	At least 2 used subflows	32,889	152 MB	11,856 MB
T_3	With handover	8,461	36.7 MB	4,626 MB

Table 3. Number of subflows per Multipath TCP connection.

Number of subflows	1	2	3	4	5	>5
Percentage of connections	67.75 %	29.96 %	1.07 %	0.48 %	0.26 %	0.48 %

Table 3 reports the number of (not necessarily concurrent) subflows that are observed in T_0. Most of the connections only have one subflow. On another side, 2.29 % of the connections have more than two subflows. Having more subflows than the number of network interfaces is a sign of mobility over different WiFi and/or cellular access points since IPv6 was not used. A connection establishing 42 different subflows was observed.

Another interesting point is the delay between the establishment of the connection (i.e. the first subflow) and the establishment of the other subflows. The smartphone tries to create subflows shortly after the creation of the Multipath TCP connection and as soon as a new interface gets an IP address. Late joins can mainly be expected when a smartphone moves from one network access point to another. To quantify this effect, Fig. 1 plots the CDF of the delays between the creation of each Multipath TCP connection and all the additional subflows that are linked to it. 57.4 % of all the additional subflows are established within 200 ms. This percentage increases to 72.2 % if this limit is set to one second. If the analysis is restricted to the first additional subflow, these percentages are respectively 61.7 % and 77.5 %. Joins can occur much after the connection is established. Indeed, 13.5 % of the additional subflows were established one minute after the establishment of the connection, and 1.5 % of them were added one hour later. The maximal observed delay is 134,563 s (more than 37 h) and this connection was related to the Google Services. Those late joins suggests network handovers, and late second subflow establishments can be explained by smartphones having one network interface unavailable.

5.2   Subflows Round-trip-times

From now, we focus on the subtrace T_1 that includes all the connections with at least two subflows. A subflow is established through a three-way handshake like a TCP connection. Thanks to this exchange, the communicating hosts agree on the sequence numbers, TCP options and also measure the initial value of the round-trip-time for the subflow. For the used Linux implementation of Multipath TCP,

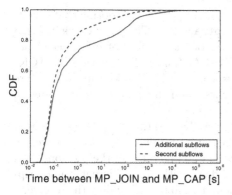

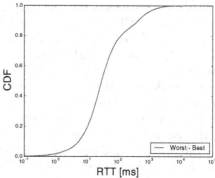

Fig. 1. Delay between the creation of the Multipath TCP connection and the establishment of a subflow.

Fig. 2. Difference of average RTT seen by the proxy between the worst and the best subflows with at least 3 RTT samples.

the round-trip-time measurement is an important performance metric because the default packet scheduler prefers the subflows having the lowest round-trip-times.

To evaluate the round-trip-time heterogeneity of the Multipath TCP connections, the analysis uses `tstat` [13] to compute the average round-trip-time over all the subflows that a connection contains. Then, it extracts for each connection the minimum and the maximum of these average round-trip-times. To have consistent values, it only takes into account the subflows having at least 3 RTT estimation samples. Figure 2 plots the CDF of the difference in the average RTT between the subflows having the largest and the smallest RTTs over all connections in T_1. Only 19.4 % of the connections are composed of subflows whose round-trip-times are within 10 ms or less whereas 77.9 % have RTTs within 100 ms or less. 3.9 % of the connections experience subflows having 1 s or more of difference in their average RTT. With such network heterogeneity, if a packet is sent on a low-bandwidth and high-delay subflow s_0 and following packets are sent on another high-bandwidth low-delay one s_1, the sender may encounter head-of-line blocking.

5.3   Multipath TCP Acknowledgements

As explained in Sect. 2, Multipath TCP uses two ACK levels: the regular TCP ACKs at the subflow level and the cumulative Multipath TCP ACKs at the connection level. It is possible to have some data acknowledged at TCP level but not at Multipath TCP one, typically if previous data was sent on another subflow but not yet acknowledged. Figure 3 plots in red-dotted curve the CDF of the number of bytes sent by the proxy that are acknowledged by non-duplicate TCP ACKs. This plot is a weighted CDF where the contribution of each ACK is weighted by the number of bytes that it acknowledges. In TCP, ACKs of 1428 bytes or less cover 50.7 % of all acknowledged bytes and considering ACKs of 20 KB or less the percentage is 91.1 %.

The same analysis is now performed by looking at the DSS option that carries the Multipath TCP Data ACKs with mptcptrace [10]. The green curve in Fig. 3 shows the weighted cumulative distribution of the number of bytes acked per Data ACK. Compared with the regular TCP ACKs, the Multipath TCP ACKs cover more bytes. Indeed, 51 % of all bytes acknowledged by Multipath TCP are covered with Data ACKs of 2856 bytes or less, and this percentage increases to 70.6 % considering Data ACKs of 20 KB or less.

The difference between the regular TCP ACKs and the Data ACKs is caused by the reordering that occurs when data is sent over different subflows. Since the Data ACKs are cumulative they can only be updated once all the previous data have been received on all subflows. If subflows with very different round-trip-times are used, it will cause reordering and data will possibly filling the receiver's window during a long period. This can also change the way applications read data which would be more by large bursts instead of small frequent reads. On mobile devices, such memory footprints should be minimized.

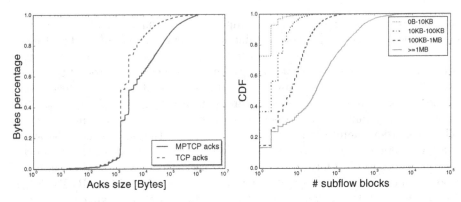

Fig. 3. Size of the Multipath TCP and TCP ACKs received by the proxy (Color figure online).

Fig. 4. Size of the subflow blocks from proxy to smartphones on T_1.

5.4 Utilization of the Subflows

The next question is how data is spread among the subflows. Does Multipath TCP alternates packets between the different subflows or does it send bursts of packets? Again, to be relevant, the subtrace T_1 is considered.

To quantify the spread of data, this paper introduces the notion of *subflow block*. Intuitively, a *subflow block* is a sequence of packets from a connection sent over a given subflow without any packet transmitted over another subflow. Consider a connection where a host sends N data packets. Number them as $0, ..., N - 1$ with 0 the first data packet sent and $N - 1$ the last one. Let f_i denote the subflow on which packet i was sent. The nth subflow blocks b_n is defined as $b_n = \{\max(b_{n-1}) + 1\} \cup \{i \mid i - 1 \in b_n \text{ and } f_i = f_{i-1}\}$, with $b_0 = \{-1\}$ and $f_{-1} = \perp$. As an example, if the proxy sends two data packets on s_0, then three on s_1, retransmits the second packet on s_0 and sends the last two packets on s_1, we will have $b_1 = \{0,1\}$, $b_2 = \{2,3,4\}$, $b_3 = \{5\}$ and $b_4 = \{6,7\}$. This notion is implemented in our analysis scripts [2]. A connection balancing the traffic with several subflows will produce lot of small subflow blocks whereas a connection sending all its data over one single subflow will have only one subflow block containing all the connection's packets. Figure 4 shows the number of subflow blocks that each connection contains. Each curve contains connections carrying their labeled amount of total bytes from proxy to smartphones. For most of the large connections, Multipath TCP balances well the packets over different subflows. In particular, 26.4 % of connections carrying more than 1 MB have more than 100 subflow blocks. As expected, the shorter the connection is, more the subflow blocks tend to contain most of the connection traffic. For short connections carrying less than 10 KBytes, 72.8 % of them contain only one subflow block, and therefore they only use one subflow. This number raises concerns about unused subflows. If connections having at least two subflows are considered, over their 276,133 subflows, 41.2 % of them are unused in both directions. It is worth noting that nearly all of these unused subflows are actually additional subflows, leading to 75.6 % of unused additional subflows. This is clearly an overhead, since creating subflows that are not used consumes bytes and energy [18] on smartphones since the interface over which these subflows are established is kept active.

There are three reasons that explain those unused subflows. Firstly, a subflow can become active after all the data has been exchanged. This happens frequently since 62.9 % of the connections carry less than 2000 bytes of data. In practice, for 21 % of the unused additional subflows the proxy received their third ACK after that it had finished to send data. Secondly, as suggested in Sect. 5.2, the difference in round-trip-times between the two available subflows can be so large that the subflow with the highest RTT is never selected by the packet scheduler. If the server does not transmit too much data, the congestion window on the lowest-RTT subflow remains open and the second subflow is not used. Though, 36.2 % of the unused additional subflows have a better RTT for the newly-established subflow than the other available one. However, 59.9 % of these subflows belong to connections carrying less than 1000 bytes (90.1 % less than 10 KBytes). Thirdly, a subflow can be established as a backup subflow [9]. Indeed, a user can set the cellular subflow as a backup one, e.g., for cost purpose. 2.1 % of the unused additional subflows were backup subflows.

5.5   Reinjections and Retransmissions

In addition to unused subflows, another Multipath TCP specific overhead is the reinjections. A *reinjection* [20] is the transmission of the same data over two or more subflows. Since by definition, reinjections can only occur on connections that use at least two subflows, this analysis considers the subtrace T_2. A reinjection can be detected by looking at the Multipath TCP Data Sequence Number (DSN). If a packet A with DSN x is sent first on the subflow 1 and after another packet B with the same DSN x is sent on the subflow 2, then B is a reinjection of A. `mptcptrace` [10] was extended to detect them. A reinjection can occur for several reasons: *(i)* handover, *(ii)* excessive losses over one subflow or *(iii)* the utilization of the Opportunistic Retransmission and Penalization (ORP) algorithm [17,20]. This phenomenon has been shown to limit the performance of Multipath TCP in some wireless networks [21]. Typically, Multipath TCP reinjections are closely coupled with regular TCP retransmissions. Figure 5 shows the CDF of the reinjections and retransmissions sent by the proxy. The number of retransmitted and reinjected bytes are normalized with the number of unique bytes sent by the proxy over each connection. 52.7 % of the connections using at least two subflows experience retransmissions on one of their subflows whereas reinjections occur on 29.3 % of them. This percentage of retransmissions tends to match previous analysis of TCP on smartphones [6,12]. 68.7 % of T_2 connections have less than 1 % of their unique bytes retransmitted, and 85 % less than 10 %. 79.7 % of the connections have less than 1 % of their unique bytes reinjected, and 89.8 % less than 10 %. Observing more retransmissions than reinjections is expected since retransmissions can trigger reinjections. In the studied trace, the impact of reinjections remains limited since over more than 11.8 GBytes of unique data sent by proxy, there are only 86.8 MB of retransmissions and 65 MB of reinjections. On some small connections, we observe more retransmitted and reinjected bytes than the unique bytes. This is because all the data sent over the connection was retransmitted several times. On Fig. 5 the thousand of connections having a fraction of retransmitted bytes over unique bytes greater or equal to 1 carried fewer than 10 KB of unique data, and 83.3 % of them fewer than 1 KB. Concerning the reinjections, the few hundred of connections in such case carried less than 14 KB, 63.4 % of them carried less than 1 KB and 76.1 % of them less than 1428 bytes.

5.6 Handovers

One of the main benefits of Multipath TCP is that it supports seamless handovers which enables mobility scenarios [9,15]. A handover is here defined as

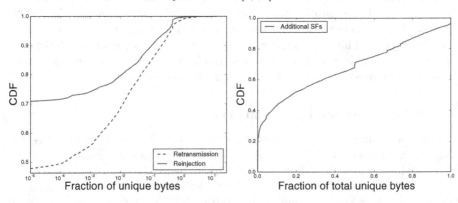

Fig. 5. Fraction of bytes that are reinjected/retransmitted by the proxy on T_2.

Fig. 6. Fraction of total data bytes on non-initial subflows sent by the proxy on T_3.

a recovery of a failed subflow by another one. A naive solution is to rely on REMOVE_ADDRs to detect handover. However, this TCP option is sent unreliably. Indeed, 22.1 % of the connections experiencing handover have no REMOVE_ADDR.

This paper proposes an alternative methodology implemented in [2] that relies on the TCP segments exchanged. Let LA_i be the time of the last (non-RST) ACK sent by the smartphone seen on subflow i (that was used to send data) and LP_j the time of the last (non-retransmitted) segment containing data on subflow j. If $\exists\ k, l\ |\ k \neq l$, no FIN seen from the smartphone on subflow k, $LA_l > LA_k$ and $LP_l > LA_k$, then the connection experiences handover. Notice that only handovers on the subflows carrying data are detected. Among the connections that use at least two subflows, 25.7 % experience handover. It has also the advantage to be implementation independent since it does not use the ADD_ADDRs or REMOVE_ADDRs options that are not supported by all implementations [5].

Based on the subtrace T_3, Fig. 6 shows the fraction of unique bytes that were sent by the proxy on the additional subflows on connections experiencing handover. This illustrates the connections that could not be possible if regular TCP was used on these mobile devices. Indeed, an handover is typically related to the mobility of the user who can go out of the reachability of a network. Notice that this methodology can also detect handover in the smartphone to proxy flow. Indeed, 20.4 % of connections experience handover with all data sent by the proxy on the initial subflow because the smartphone sent data on another subflow after having lost the initial one.

6   Conclusion

This work brings the first results about real Multipath TCP traffic on smartphones. In addition to analyzing the released trace, this paper proposes techniques to quantify the utilization of the subflows and presents a simple implementation independent methodology to detect handover. The analysis tools are also available for the community [2]. The results shows that Multipath TCP offers benefits for long connections, since it allows seamless handovers. However, with the default algorithms, the protocol brings some overheads, in particular with the establishment of unused subflows. This opens new areas of improvements to adapt Multipath TCP with the smartphone case, in particular the path manager.

Acknowledgements. This work was partially supported by the EC within the FP7 Trilogy2 project. We would like to thank Gregory Detal and Sébastien Barré for the port of the latest Multipath TCP Linux kernel on the Nexus 5 and Patrick Delcoigne and his team for the cellular measurements.

References

1. Chen, Y.-C., et al.: A measurement-based study of MultiPath TCP performance over wireless networks. In: IMC 2013, pp. 455–468. ACM, New York (2013). http://doi.acm.org/10.1145/2504730.2504751

2. De Coninck, Q., Baerts, M.: Analysis scripts (2015). http://github.com/multipath-tcp/mptcp-analysis-scripts

3. De Coninck, Q., et al.: Poster: evaluating android applications with Multipath TCP. In: MOBICOM 2015, pp. 230–232. ACM (2015). http://dx.doi.org/10.1145/2789168.2795165

4. Deng, S., et al.: WiFi, LTE, or both?: measuring multi-homed wireless internet performance. In: IMC 2014, pp. 181–194. ACM, New York (2014). http://doi.acm.org/10.1145/2663716.2663727

5. Eardley, P.: Survey of MPTCP Implementations. Internet-Draft draft-eardley-mptcp-implementations-survey-02, IETF Secretariat, July 2013. http://tools.ietf.org/html/draft-eardley-mptcp-implementations-survey-02

6. Falaki, H., et al.: A first look at traffic on smartphones. In: IMC 2010, pp. 281–287. ACM, Melbourne (2010). http://dx.doi.org/10.1145/1879141.1879176

7. Ferlin, S., Dreibholz, T., Alay, Ö.: Multi-path transport over heterogeneous wireless networks: does it really pay off? In: Proceedings of the IEEE GLOBECOM. IEEE, Austin, December 2014. http://dx.doi.org/10.1109/GLOCOM.2014.7037567

8. Ferlin-Oliveira, S., et al.: Tackling the challenge of bufferbloat in multi-path transport over heterogeneous wireless networks. In: 2014 IEEE 22nd International Symposium of Quality of Service (IWQoS), pp. 123–128, May 2014. http://dx.doi.org/10.1109/IWQoS.2014.6914310

9. Ford, A., Raiciu, C., Handley, M., Bonaventure, O.: TCP Extensions for Multipath Operation with Multiple Addresses. RFC 6824, January 2013. http://www.rfc-editor.org/rfc/rfc6824.txt

10. Hesmans, B., Bonaventure, O.: Tracing Multipath TCP connections. SIGCOMM Comput. Commun. Rev. **44**(4), 361–362 (2014). http://doi.acm.org/10.1145/2740070.2631453

11. Hesmans, B., Tran-Viet, H., Sadre, R., Bonaventure, O.: A first look at real multipath TCP traffic. In: Steiner, M., Barlet-Ros, P., Bonaventure, O. (eds.) TMA 2015. LNCS, vol. 9053, pp. 233–246. Springer, Heidelberg (2015). http://dx.doi.org/10.1007/978-3-319-17172-2_16

12. Huang, J., et al.: Anatomizing application performance differences on smartphones. In: MobiSys 2010, pp. 165–178. ACM (2010). http://dx.doi.org/10.1145/1814433.1814452

13. Mellia, M., Carpani, A., Cigno, R.L.: TStat: TCP statistic and analysis tool. In: Ajmone Marsan, M., Listanti, G.C.M., Roveri, A. (eds.) QoS-IP 2003. LNCS, vol. 2601, pp. 145–157. Springer, Heidelberg (2003). http://www.tlc-networks.polito.it/mellia/papers/Tstat_QoSIP.ps

14. Paasch, C., Barre, S., et al.: Multipath TCP in the Linux Kernel. http://www.multipath-tcp.org

15. Paasch, C., et al.: Exploring Mobile/WiFi handover with Multipath TCP. In: ACM SIGCOMM CellNet Workshop, pp. 31–36 (2012). http://doi.acm.org/10.1145/2342468.2342476

16. Paasch, C., et al.: Experimental evaluation of Multipath TCP schedulers. In: CSWS 2014, pp. 27–32. ACM, New York. http://doi.acm.org/10.1145/2630088.2631977

17. Paasch, C., et al.: On the benefits of applying experimental design to improve Multipath TCP. In: CoNEXT 2013, pp. 393–398. ACM, New York (2013). http://inl.info.ucl.ac.be/publications/benefits-applying-experimental-design-improve-multipath-tcp

18. Peng, Q., et al.: Energy efficient Multipath TCP for mobile devices. In: MobiHoc 2014, pp. 257–266. ACM, New York (2014). http://doi.acm.org/10.1145/2632951.2632971

19. Raiciu, C., et al.: Opportunistic mobility with Multipath TCP. In: MobiArch 2011, pp. 7–12. ACM, New York (2011). http://doi.acm.org/10.1145/1999916.1999919

20. Raiciu, C., et al.: How hard can it be? designing and implementing a deployable Multipath TCP. In: NSDI 2012, pp. 29–29. USENIX Assoc., Berkeley (2012). http://inl.info.ucl.ac.be/publications/how-hard-can-it-be-designing-and-implementing-deployable-multipath-tcp

21. Sup Lim, Y., et al.: Cross-layer path management in multi-path transport protocol for mobile devices. In: INFOCOM 2014, pp. 1815–1823. IEEE, April 2014. http://dx.doi.org/10.1109/INFOCOM.2014.6848120

Crowdsourcing Measurements of Mobile Network Performance and Mobility During a Large Scale Event

Alexander Frömmgen[1(✉)], Jens Heuschkel[2], Patrick Jahnke[3], Fabio Cuozzo[1],
Immanuel Schweizer[2], Patrick Eugster[3], Max Mühlhäuser[2],
and Alejandro Buchmann[1]

[1] Databases and Distributed Systems, TU Darmstadt, Darmstadt, Germany
`{froemmgen,cuozzo,buchmann}@dvs.tu-darmstadt.de`
[2] Telecooperation Lab, TU Darmstadt, Darmstadt, Germany
`{jens.heuschkel,schweizer,max}@tk.informatik.tu-darmstadt.de`
[3] Distributed Systems Programming, TU Darmstadt, Darmstadt, Germany
`{jahnke,peugster}@dsp.tu-darmstadt.de`

Abstract. Cellular infrastructure in urban areas is provisioned to easily cope with the usual daily demands. When facing shockingly high loads, e.g., due to large scale sport or music events, users complain about performance degradations of the mobile network. Analyzing the impact of large scale events on the mobile network infrastructure and how users perceive overload situations is essential to improve user experience. Therefore, a large data set is required to get a detailed understanding of the differences between providers, mobile devices, mobile network access technologies, and the mobility of people.

In this paper, we present experiences and results from a crowdsourcing measurement during a music festival in Germany with over 110,000 visitors per day. More than 1,000 visitors ran our crowdsourcing app to collect active and passive measurements of the mobile network and the user mobility. We show that there is significant performance degradation during the festival regarding DNS and HTTP failures as well as increased load times. Furthermore, we evaluate the impact of the carrier, the access technology, and the user mobility on the perceived performance.

1 Introduction

Network providers are facing rapidly increasing mobile data traffic [1]. Their cellular infrastructure is provisioned to easily cope with the usual daily demands. High demand peaks at events with thousands of users in a small area, however, are highly challenging for the infrastructure. Figure 1 shows the venue of a music festival, the *Schloßgrabenfest*[1], on a normal day and during the event. This paper investigates the question how the network performance of the user devices is affected by large scale events. Understanding how users perceives overload situations requires a large data set. Especially for a comparison between different

---

[1] The official website [German]: http://www.schlossgrabenfest.de/2015/.

© Springer International Publishing Switzerland 2016
T. Karagiannis and X. Dimitropoulos (Eds.): PAM 2016, LNCS 9631, pp. 70–82, 2016.
DOI: 10.1007/978-3-319-30505-9_6

(a) Normal day.   (b) During the festival.

Fig. 1. The *Schloßgrabenfest*, a music festival in the city center of *Darmstadt*.

network providers, mobile devices, and access technologies, a systematic study with actively controlled measurements on the user devices is required.

Based on these considerations, we developed a crowdsourcing app which actively measures network performance during events. The app measures the performance of different network protocols (e.g. HTTP and DNS), the network paths, the used network technologies, the signal strengths, and location data. As this app is executed on the user's device, the results represent the actual performance perceived by the user and are not limited to certain carriers. With this app, we took a large measurement during the *Schloßgrabenfest* 2015, a music festival with more than 110,000 visitors per day. More than 1,000 participants ran the crowdsourcing app, allowing detailed analysis of the event.

In this paper, we (i) present our crowdsourcing measurement app, (ii) provide a first look at the measurements[2] on end user devices during a large scale event, and (iii) investigate the impact of the high load on the network performance. We especially analyze how the HTTP and DNS performance suffers depending on the location, the time, and the network carrier. Furthermore, we briefly show insights from additionally measured data, such as Bluetooth beacons.

The remainder of this paper is structured as follows: Sect. 2 presents the crowdsourcing app, the venue, and a summary of the collected data. Based on a discussion of the location data in Sect. 3, we analyze the HTTP performance in Sect. 4 in detail. Section 5 briefly investigates the DNS performance, traceroute results, and traffic statistics. Section 6 presents related work. Finally, Sect. 7 concludes the paper and gives an overview of future work.

2 Methodology and Data Set

Venue: The *Schloßgrabenfest* is the biggest music festival in the state of Hesse in Germany. During the festival, the city center of *Darmstadt*, a city with approximately 150,000 inhabitants, is highly crowded (Fig. 1). The event takes four days (Thursday till Sunday) and has more than 110,000 visitors per day.

Crowdsourcing App: We advertised *Research4Refill*, our crowdsourcing app for Android smartphones, in local print media[3], local television, social media,

---

[2] Available at https://www.dvs.tu-darmstadt.de/research/sgf.

[3] http://www.echo-online.de/lokales/darmstadt/tu-informatiker-erforschen-per-app-die-handynetz-ueberlastung_15328733.htm.

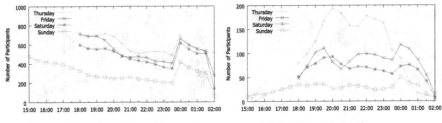

(a) Total number of participants.   (b) Participants at the venue.

Fig. 2. The number of participants running the crowdsourcing app.

the university campus, and on the video screen during the festival. In our advertisement, we stressed that users help us to understand their network problems.
As additional incentive, we offered a *free drink* for users who ran the app. We
found more than 1,000 users willing to give up some privacy for a free beer.

As we were focusing on a very large data set with as many participants as
possible, we limited the amount of collected data to preserve privacy and to avoid
scaring off potential participants. The app tracks the location (GPS, network,
and additional placed Bluetooth Beacons), the WiFi and cellular network state,
and actively executes HTTP, DNS, and traceroute measurements. Additionally,
we asked all users to fill in a short questionnaire. Thus, the app does not track
the actual transferred user data and requires minimal rights.

Data Set: The app automatically started on all devices at 18:00 and stopped at
02:00 (on Sunday, the app started earlier). Figure 2 shows the number of participating users during the festival. The number decreased per day. We assume that
this happens due to the higher energy consumption which drained the battery.
We concentrate our further analysis on Thursday, as this is the day with the
highest number of participants at the venue (at once up to 194). On Thursday,
the number of participants at the venue decreases earlier than on the other days,
as Friday was a workday. The feature to *continue measurements tomorrow* led
to an unintended increase of participants at midnight, as many devices suddenly
continued to measure. The feature should have continued tomorrow *evening*.

In total, 1,401 participants ran our app. According to GPS information, 740
of these were at least one time at the venue, and 410 participants were at the
venue on Thursday. We identified 252 additional smartphones at the venue due
to Bluetooth beacon signals, 135 of these users were at the venue on Thursday.
Thus, out of 110,000 visitors of the venue on Thursday, 545 ($\approx 0.5\%$) run our
app. Traditional counting of visitors can not track users and therefore sums
up the number of visitors per day. Officially, 500,000 people visited the event.
Summing up the number of app participants per day leads to 1562 users. Thus,
this method overestimates the number of unique participants by 592 (61 %).

86 % of the devices belonged to one of four leading brands running the
Android OS. Most devices had Android SDK 19 or 21 (58 %). The four German mobile carrier were represented with between 21.4 % and 28.3 %, which
does not reflect the distribution of all users in Germany.

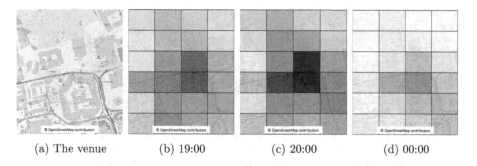

(a) The venue   (b) 19:00   (c) 20:00   (d) 00:00

Fig. 3. User density on Thursday (white: low density, black: high density).

Limitations: The data has to be interpreted carefully, as the collected data sample might not be representative. We assume that most participants are tech-savvy and students. The app might influence the participants, as they stayed longer to gain a free drink, or only installed the app if they planned to stay long. Additionally, the app induced network traffic and increased the energy consumption of the smartphone.

3   Active Measurement: Location

The location information of users is important to understand movement patterns and investigate possible mitigation strategies, such as ad hoc or delay tolerant networks. Out of 1,196,875 location measurements, 161,429 location samples are located in the area of the venue. We discarded location information outside of this area due to privacy concerns. The app used the network and the GPS location provider. As 276 devices only returned network locations, we assume that many users manually turned off GPS.

In this section, we discuss the distribution of the people, their movement patterns, the accuracy of the location provider reported by the operating system, and our experiences with Bluetooth Beacons for location tracking.

3.1   User Density and Movement

Figure 3 visualizes the distribution of the participants on Thursday evening. For this purpose, we divide the venue in areas and count the number of participants per area per hour. This implies that people moving between areas in one hour are counted multiple times. The user density rapidly increases at the beginning of the event and decreases at midnight. Figure 3 shows that the participants concentrate in a few areas, which are in front of the main stage of the music festival. Some participants were located in areas which were inaccessible during the event. Figure 4 illustrates the user movement. Dark arrows represent many area transitions, bright arrows a few. Thus, even though the user density in front of the main stage is high, people are constantly moving between areas. A more detailed analysis could evaluate the efficiency of delay tolerant networks and placement strategies for access points.

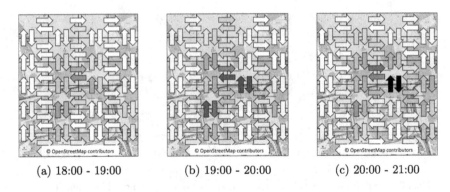

(a) 18:00 - 19:00   (b) 19:00 - 20:00   (c) 20:00 - 21:00

Fig. 4. User movement on Thursday evening.

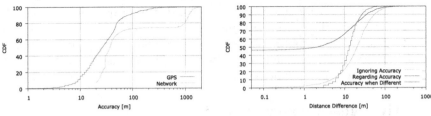

(a) Comparison of measured accuracy between GPS and network.

(b) Comparison of the difference between GPS and Beacon signal strength.

Fig. 5. Analysis of the location accuracy.

3.2   Location Accuracy and Bluetooth Beacons

As using GPS for location data is often discouraged due to the energy consumption, we investigate the measured accuracy of the samples. Figure 5a shows that nearly 40 % of all GPS results had an accuracy of less than 20 m, whereas the network never had such a high accuracy. The network accuracy rapidly decreases at about 70 %, thus 30 % of all network location samples could not benefit from seen WiFi access points but relied on cellular networks.

Beside the GPS and network location provider, the app regularly searches for Bluetooth *Beacons*. We placed 50 *Bluetooth Low Energy* Beacons[4] at the venue. We were surprised that most people turned off Bluetooth immediately and complained about this measurement. However, 250 devices saw at least 3 Beacons at the same time and can be located with the Beacon information. As we do not have the ground truth locations, we compare location measurements to investigate differences between GPS and the Beacons. We distinguish between the difference ignoring the reported GPS accuracy, and the difference after regarding the GPS accuracy. Figure 5b shows that nearly 50 % of all samples are equal regarding the GPS accuracy. Ignoring the accuracy, 50 % of all samples have a difference of less than 20 m (99 % less than 100 m). The Figure

---

[4] http://www.beaconinside.com/.

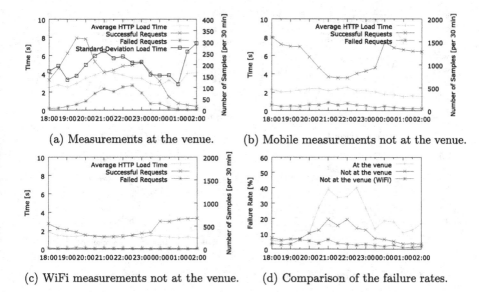

(a) Measurements at the venue.   (b) Mobile measurements not at the venue.

(c) WiFi measurements not at the venue.   (d) Comparison of the failure rates.

Fig. 6. Active HTTP measurements on Thursday.

shows the reported GPS accuracy for those measurements which are different regarding the accuracy. Most of these measurements have an accuracy of less than 20 m.

4   Active Measurement: HTTP Load Times

In this section, we investigate how the HTTP load time varied during the event. The app regularly triggered HTTP GET requests to different web pages, e.g., the front pages of Google, Wikipedia, and Facebook. We measured the load completion time, but canceled the request after 30 s. In the following, we analyze the general performance, investigate differences between carriers, web pages, and the used network type.

4.1   General Overview

Figure 6a shows the HTTP load time of all devices at the venue on Thursday evening. With the increasing number of users at the venue, the amount of samples per time increases. The successful requests increase till 20:00. Between 20:00 and 23:00, the number of failed requests increases rapidly. As there is only a limited amount of samples after half past midnight, these results are imprecise. The average HTTP load time and its standard deviation show the same pattern. To conclude, during the event, both the failure rate and the average load time increases significantly.

Nikravesh et al. [5] showed that network performance follows a daily pattern. To prove that the event caused a performance degradation, we compare the

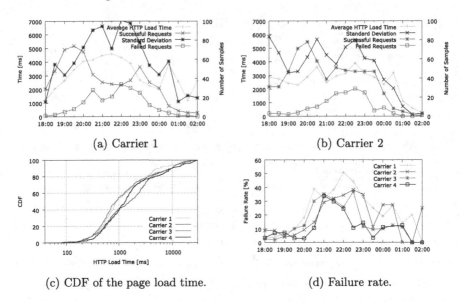

(a) Carrier 1　　　　　　　　　　　　　(b) Carrier 2

(c) CDF of the page load time.　　　　　　(d) Failure rate.

Fig. 7. Comparison of the carriers for the HTTP measurements on Thursday.

results with all devices which where not at the venue (Fig. 6b) and those which were not at the venue and were connected to WiFi (Fig. 6c). Here, the average load time and the number of failures are both rather stable. We were surprised that the number of successful requests dropped. We assume that many users who were not at the venue stopped our app after recognizing that it was running. Even before the performance at the venue decreases, the WiFi measurements show a significant lower average load time. This supports the results of existing measurements [7]. Regarding the failure rate, Fig. 6d shows a peak failure rate of nearly 40 % at the venue, whereas the WiFi measurements have a constantly low failure rate. The reasons for the increased failure rate for devices not at the venue require further investigation. The total number of requests increases after midnight due to the *continue tomorrow* feature. This is not reflected in Fig. 6a, as people left the venue earlier on Thursday.

To conclude, the comparison of the performance between participants at the venue and those who were not at the venue proves that the event caused a high performance degradation.

4.2 Carrier Analysis

Figure 7 shows the performance depending on the carrier on Thursday. The performance of all carriers decreases during the event. However, the load time distribution differs between the carriers (Fig. 7c). Even though Carrier 3 has the lowest load times for the first 50 % of all requests, it has a worse tail distribution than Carrier 1. Carrier 2 performs significantly worse. The failure rates, however, provide a different view on the performance (Fig. 7d). Here, Carrier 1

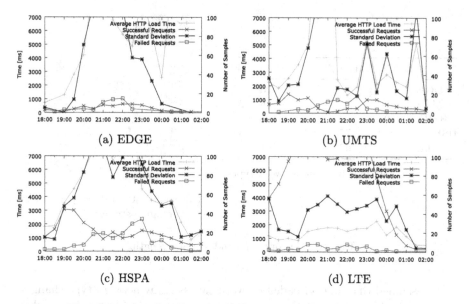

Fig. 8. Impact of the network type on the HTTP performance.

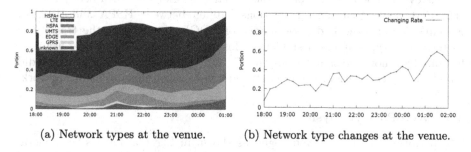

(a) Network types at the venue.   (b) Network type changes at the venue.

Fig. 9. Used network types at the area.

nearly always has the highest failure rate, whereas Carrier 4 nearly always has the lowest failure rate. Thus, the carrier with the lowest failure rate (Carrier 4) has the second worst load time, whereas the carrier with the worst failure rate (Carrier 1) has one of the best load times.

4.3 Network Type

Figure 8 shows the load times depending on the network type. As expected, the network type has a huge influence on the performance. The LTE requests have the lowest average load time and nearly no failed requests were reported. Between 20:00 and 22:30, however, the portion of participants using EDGE increased (Fig. 9a), whereas LTE decreased. Thus, the overall performance degradation might be partly caused by a lower portion of LTE connections.

	EDGE	UMTS	HSPA	HSPA+	LTE
EDGE				28	
UMTS	70			76	24
HSPA	21			198	58
HSPA+	52	75	293		34
LTE	45	67	70	101	

(a) Transitions between network types.

(b) Signal strength map (darker: higher signal strength).

Fig. 10. Network type and signal strength.

We assumed that an overloaded network causes many network type changes. However, Fig. 9b shows that the network type does not change more often during the event. The distribution of the actual transitions between network types (Fig. 10a) shows that most transitions happen between HSPA and HSPA+. Keeping in mind the bad performance of EDGE and UMTS, the transitions to these two types imply a sudden performance degradation for the users. A first analysis how the signal strength (Fig. 10b) influences the performance did not show any correlation. A more detailed investigation remains as future work.

4.4 Web Page Analysis

The performance of most web pages, as shown in Fig. 11a, follows the general pattern of Fig. 6a. This supports the assumption that the first network hops of the client devices are overloaded. However, the page load time of the venue's page shows a sudden increase between midnight and 2 (Fig. 11b). We assume that this is caused by the high load introduced by our measurements and the high number of users at midnight.

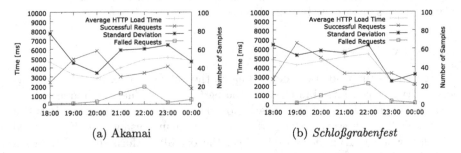

(a) Akamai

(b) *Schloßgrabenfest*

Fig. 11. Differences between web pages regarding the page load time.

5 Additional Measurements

5.1 Active Measurement: DNS Lookup

In addition to the HTTP measurements, we tested the performance of DNS during the event. Therefore, we actively executed 167,412 DNS lookups on the smartphones. We used both popular domains and randomly generated domains to investigate the impact of caching (mainly in the Android system). The randomly generated domains often resolved to *Navigation Help* pages of the carriers (e.g. *62.157.140.133* and *80.156.86.78*). Figure 12a shows a CDF of all executed DNS requests depending on the domain (*existing, not existing*) and the result (*successful, not successful*). The successful requests for not existing domains (*Navigation Help* resolutions) take at least 20 ms. Thus, 5 % of the not successful requests for not existing domains already failed due to network failures. Regarding the existing domains, it is surprising that even cached results take up to 20 ms. For existing domains, more than 50 % of all failed requests fail in the first 20 ms. However, the tail of the failed requests for not existing domains is the longest of all four. Figure 12b shows that the performance during the event follows the same pattern as the HTTP requests. To investigate the impact of the location on the performance, Fig. 13 shows the load time depending on the location and the time. Even though there are differences between the locations, we find that at 21:00 the performance suffers all over the area.

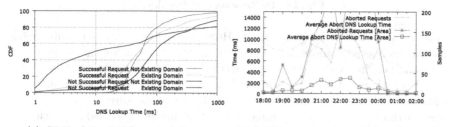

(a) CDF of the DNS request time.   (b) DNS request time during the event.

Fig. 12. DNS measurement results.

5.2 Active Measurement: Traceroute

To allow correlations between the network performance and the paths in the network, we executed 2202 trace routes to multiple domains. Figure 14a shows how the path length differs between the carriers. In our measurements, we observe a longest path of 23 hops (Carrier 1), which occurs one time. For future work, we will try to reenact results from other traceroute studies, such as Brownlee [2] and Luckie et al. [4].

5.3 Passive Measurement: Traffic Stats

Beside the active measurements, we passively collected traffic statistics provided by Android (Fig. 14). Except for the mobile received bytes, the metrics do not

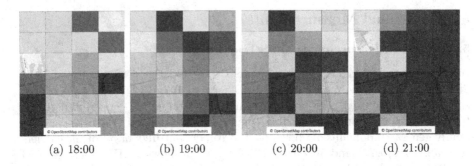

(a) 18:00   (b) 19:00   (c) 20:00   (d) 21:00

Fig. 13. DNS request time during the event (darker: slower)

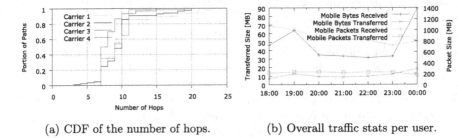

(a) CDF of the number of hops.   (b) Overall traffic stats per user.

Fig. 14. Traffic stats on Thursday.

significantly change during the event. However, it is unclear why this metric suddenly increases at midnight. In general, users downloaded 4 times more than uploaded. This fits with the average packet size, as transferred packets were not filled. Even though these statistics include the induced traffic of our measurements, these results do not correspond with recent measurements from other papers. Erman et al. [3], for example, found that people uploaded as much data as download during the Super Bowl event.

6   Related Work

Related work on large scale events concentrates on a single carrier or passive measurements of users in the network infrastructure. Erman et al. [3] analyzed the Super Bowl from AT&T's perspective and provided a detailed analysis of the performance and the user behavior. Shafiq et al. [6] describe provider observations of two crowded events. They present lower layer metrics, but provide only limited insights into the actual performance available at the end device. Additionally, they are restricted to the perspective of a few network operators.

Crowdsourcing approaches leverage users which support measurements. Thus, they have access to details on the end device and are not restricted to certain network operators. Nikravesh et al. [5], for example, evaluated a long time crowdsourcing measurement. With samples from all over the world, they provide valuable insights into the general network performance. Xu et al. [8] used crowdsourcing to investigate a cellular network in Singapore.

Our work is the first combining the benefits of extensive crowdsourcing with active measurements of a crowded event.

7   Discussion and Future Work

App-Based Crowdsourcing: Our measurement study shows that large crowdsourcing measurements are feasible. We convinced more than 1,000 users to participate in our study. We noticed that people liked the idea to help us to understand their performance issues. A small fraction of participants complained (e.g., in the play store) about the increased data transmission and higher energy consumption due to the app. Our measurement setup does not allow us to distinguish between the induced energy consumption of our app and a potentially increased consumption due to the overloaded network. Future crowdsourcing studies should explicitly consider this.

Measurement Results: The analysis of the movement patterns showed that users moved even during crowded times. The Bluetooth beacon based location service allowed us to trace users who did not provide GPS locations. We showed that there is significant performance degradation during the festival regarding DNS and HTTP failures as well as increased load times. The performance degradation differs between network operators, network types, and locations. Carriers with a low failure rate during the event had a higher average load time. We currently investigate the underlying causes for these differences.

Future Work: The large data set allows to retrieve detailed movement models for large scale events, analysis of dependencies between the signal strength and the user density, and the evaluation of new technologies to deal with crowded events. By making the data available to the community, we hope to encourage others to conduct similar analysis.

Acknowledgements. This work has been funded by the German Research Foundation (DFG) as part of projects A2, B2, B1 within the Collaborative Research Center (CRC) 1053 – MAKI.

References

1. Cisco visual networking index: global mobile data traffic forecast update 2014–2019 white paper (2015). http://www.cisco.com/c/en/us/solutions/collateral/service-provider/visual-networking-index-vni/white_paper_c11-520862.html
2. Brownlee, N.: On searching for patterns in traceroute responses. In: Faloutsos, M., Kuzmanovic, A. (eds.) PAM 2014. LNCS, vol. 8362, pp. 67–76. Springer, Heidelberg (2014)
3. Erman, J., Ramakrishnan, K.K.: Understanding the super-sized traffic of the super bowl. In: Proceedings of the 2013 Conference on Internet Measurement Conference, pp. 353–360. ACM (2013)

4. Luckie, M., et al.: A second look at detecting third-party addresses in traceroute traces with the IP timestamp option. In: Faloutsos, M., Kuzmanovic, A. (eds.) PAM 2014. LNCS, vol. 8362, pp. 46–55. Springer, Heidelberg (2014)

5. Nikravesh, A., Choffnes, D.R., Katz-Bassett, E., Mao, Z.M., Welsh, M.: Mobile network performance from user devices: a longitudinal, multidimensional analysis. In: Faloutsos, M., Kuzmanovic, A. (eds.) PAM 2014. LNCS, vol. 8362, pp. 12–22. Springer, Heidelberg (2014)

6. Shafiq, M.Z., Ji, L., Liu, A.X., Pang, J., Venkataraman, S., Wang, J.: A first look at cellular network performance during crowded events. In: ACM SIGMETRICS Performance Evaluation Review, vol. 41, pp. 17–28. ACM (2013)

7. Sommers, J., Barford, P.: Cell vs. Wifi: on the performance of metro area mobile connections. In: Proceedings of the 2012 ACM Conference on Internet Measurement Conference, IMC 2012, pp. 301–314. ACM, New York (2012)

8. Xu, Y., Wang, Z., Leong, W.K., Leong, B.: An end-to-end measurement study of modern cellular data networks. In: Faloutsos, M., Kuzmanovic, A. (eds.) PAM 2014. LNCS, vol. 8362, pp. 34–45. Springer, Heidelberg (2014)

A Study of MVNO Data Paths and Performance

Paul Schmitt$^{(\boxtimes)}$, Morgan Vigil, and Elizabeth Belding

University of California, Santa Barbara, USA
{pschmitt,mvigil,ebelding}@cs.ucsb.edu

Abstract. Characterization of mobile data traffic performance is diffi-cult given the inherent complexity and opacity of mobile networks, yet it is increasingly important as emerging wireless standards approach wireline-like latencies. Mobile virtual network operators (MVNOs) increase mobile network topology complexity due to additional infrastructure and net-work configurations. We collect and analyze traces on mobile carriers in the United States along with MVNO networks on each of the base carri-ers in order to discover differences in network performance and behavior. Ultimately, we find that traffic on MVNO networks takes more circuitous, less efficient paths to reach content servers compared to base operators. Factors such as location of the destination server as well as the provider network design are critical in better understanding behaviors and impli-cations on performance for each of the mobile carriers.

1 Introduction

What factors cause one mobile Internet provider to be faster than another, even if they share some common core infrastructure? Traditional metrics chosen to represent speed may not perfectly correlate with end-user performance and are heavily influenced by the design and behavior of the underlying mobile data network. The challenge of mobile network characterization is further extended with the rise in popularity of mobile network virtual operators (MVNOs). In this paper, we shed light on observable traffic behaviors exhibited by mobile networks that affect performance metrics and user experience. We examine mobile data network behavior when connecting to popular content delivery networks used to serve media. We are particularly interested in performance comparisons between the four major mobile carriers in the United States and MVNOs that license use of the underlying base carrier infrastructure. Ultimately, we want to explore network topology factors that affect traffic in mobile data networks.

Increasingly popular due to relaxed contract terms, MVNOs have quickly grown their market share in recent years [1–3]. They operate by leasing access to base mobile network operator (MNO) infrastructure, thus avoiding the high cost of building their own networks or licensing spectrum. Performance of MVNO data networks is often assumed to be inferior, but ultimately at least somewhat attributable to the underlying base carrier network. Previous work [4] has shown that is indeed the case; application performance suffers when using MVNO net-works compared to MNOs. We investigate MVNOs and MNOs, searching for

© Springer International Publishing Switzerland 2016
T. Karagiannis and X. Dimitropoulos (Eds.): PAM 2016, LNCS 9631, pp. 83–94, 2016.
DOI: 10.1007/978-3-319-30505-9_7

potential causes of degraded performance such as server resolution location and inefficient (e.g. excess hop counts and geographically indirect) paths.

We focus on traffic to content delivery networks (CDNs), which improve performance for end users by replicating identical content across geographically diverse locations [5]. CDNs are important factors in the user experience as they are typically responsible for delivering large web objects. The exact CDN server chosen by the client when browsing is typically dependent on DNS resolution with the expectation that the client is 'near' the DNS resolver. Unfortunately for most users, mobile data networks are strongly hierarchical and it has been shown that accurately localizing mobile users is a difficult challenge [6]. The localization problem illuminates a critical issue for mobile networks: the closest or best server depends on the mobile network core topology as well as peering arrangements between the content providers and mobile carriers. We study geographic paths taken by traffic on all of the mobile networks in order to better understand the obtained performance and routing behavior of the networks. Specifically, we are interested in the following questions:

- *Can we identify reasons behind MVNOs performing worse than MNOs?* We characterize network performance for all four major U.S. carriers as well as a single MVNO for each, discovering that performance appears to be dramatically affected by destination server location.
- *Can we find potential areas for improvement in order to reduce performance gaps between mobile carriers?* We find that MVNOs have more intermediate hops, which are also geographically inefficient in the case of full MVNOs we study. From our study we believe there is room for improvement with regards to mobile network topology.
- *Do we observe marked difference between full and light MVNOs?* We observe that a light MVNO closely resembles the underlying MNO, while traffic on full MVNOs differs, often exceptionally, compared to respective MNOs.

2   Background

CDNs and DNS. The use of CDNs to deliver content from distributed replica servers is commonplace in order to improve performance as Internet content has become increasingly heavy and media-rich. Client DNS requests resolve to particular replica server IP addresses when the clients browse the Internet. Ideally, the resolved servers are 'near' (e.g. lowest round trip time) the client relative to other potential servers in order to maximize application performance [7,8]. A challenge for mobile data networks is that the limited number of public-facing gateways in the cellular core network, as well as the location of cellular network DNS resolvers, make localizing clients from an outside perspective difficult. Peering arrangements, or lack thereof, between mobile providers and content providers also leads to inefficient traffic routes even with the presence of a nearby replica [9].

MVNOs. Recently, MVNOs have increased in popularity worldwide. MVNOs are virtual in the sense that they offer telecommunications services without owning all of the mobile infrastructure used by clients. Instead, MVNOs pay MNOs for the right to service user traffic using the underlying base carrier network. The rise in popularity of MVNOs is often attributed to relaxed contract terms such as pay-as-you-go and pre-paid plans compared to traditional base carriers in the U.S. which have traditionally operated using post-paid plans. MVNOs can be classified in one of two ways: **full** or **light**. Full MVNOs are carriers that license only the radio network of the base carrier. They implement their own core, including authentication and billing services (i.e. they distribute their own SIM cards). Light MVNOs, also called *resellers*, are re-branded versions of the base carrier, which means they can fully use the base carrier infrastructure. Mobile operators often create light MVNOs to target specific demographics or to lower consumer cost by cutting back on support services.

3 Data Collection

We collect data from eight mobile devices running on eight different carriers between March 6 and March 20, 2015. We conduct the experiment over two weeks to account for performance differences attributable to time-of-day patterns. All measurement phones are located in Santa Barbara, CA and left in a static location. All phones report 'good' or 'great' signal strength via the Android telephony API throughout the experiment. For simplicity, we focus on routes and performance associated with the popular social media sites Facebook and Instagram. These services are responsible for huge amounts of mobile Internet traffic, 19.43 % and 4.27 % respectively in North America [10], and are widely replicated across many well-known CDN data centers, which allows us to explore geographic differences between carriers. Measurements gathered across additional locations, carriers, and sites would be ideal; however, this study is an initial look at potential factors impacting MVNO network performance and we hope to motivate further, more in-depth research. The list of CDNs that we use as measurement points can be accessed on our project repository at https://github. com/schmittpaul/mobileCDNs. The list includes 108 servers: 72 associated with Facebook and 36 associated with Instagram. Some servers are location-specific, identified by location clues in the name. We include international servers in our study as through initial work we find that mobile traffic surprisingly resolves to such servers a significant portion of the time (>5 %) for multiple carriers.

3.1 Carriers and Phones

We collect data on all four of the major base carriers in the United States. We identify base carriers as A, B, C, and D. Carriers A and C are GSM networks while carriers B and D use CDMA technology. MVNO carriers are identified as A-1, B-1, C-1, and D-1, with their letters indicating the underlying base carrier. MVNO B-1 is a light MVNO, which means that it has full access to the infrastructure of carrier B. Carriers A-1, C-1, and D-1 are all branded as the same full MVNO with different SIM cards and contracts specifying the base carrier used. All phones run Android 4.4 and we leave them in a high-power state to avoid latency due to radios entering low-power states. All phones are attached to their carrier (i.e. not roaming). We choose to run all experiments while connected via 3G rather than 4G due to uneven 4G LTE coverage in our area between carriers. Recent work [9] has found that 3G and 4G mobile networks in the U.S. have few Internet ingress points, meaning 4G networks will exhibit similar behavior in terms of routes and CDN resolution as 3G networks.

3.2   Traceroute and Location Data

Each hour of the testing period, each device records a `traceroute` to each of the servers in the CDN server list, resulting in $14 \times 24 \times 8 \times 108 = 290,304$ records. We then use multiple techniques to estimate the location of each IP address in the traceroute records. We first employ the IP2Location DB5 database in order to map the traceroute IP addresses to latitude and longitude coordinates. Unfortunately, prior work has established that IP geolocation databases are often rather inaccurate [11]. We also verify through a manual sanity check of the IP-location mapping, where we find improbable location mappings. To fix inaccuracies we use two other sources to manually estimate location for 5,172 unique, routable IP addresses observed over the course of the experiment. We use `nslookup` to resolve the human-readable name of the IP address if it exists. We do this because routers and servers often include three or four character location clues in their names. Next, we use Internet looking glass servers, available through `traceroute.org` from multiple cities around the U.S., to traceroute to each IP address. Observing the paths taken and RTT values from geographically diverse vantage points enables us to further estimate location (e.g. RTT of a few milliseconds from a particular looking glass server and intermediate hops containing location identifying names). Overall, we find that out of the 5,172 unique IP addresses, we override 1,988 addresses (36.4 %) from the IP2Location database with our manual location estimate.

We run `whois` on each observed IP address to determine the associated Autonomous System (AS) number. With this information, we create a data set corresponding to each attempted traceroute that includes: the number of hops, the IP address associated with each hop, the geographic coordinates associated with each hop, the autonomous system number for each hop, and the observed RTTs associated with three traceroute probes.

4   Network Analysis

We measure traffic on the four major mobile network operator networks in the United States as well as MVNO carriers operating on each of them. We first look at network performance using standard metrics such as round trip times, hop counts, and autonomous system paths. We then combine geographic information and traceroute records to explore traffic route path characteristics.

4.1   Round Trip Times (RTT)

We begin by investigating RTTs for packets traversing the mobile networks to the 73 **non-location specific** servers specified in our CDN server list.

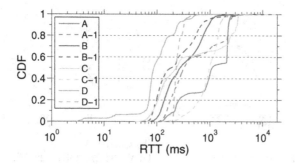

Fig. 1. RTT measurements for mobile carriers to non-location specific servers.

RTT is a critical metric in network performance as the majority of TCP variants rely on RTT to determine throughput [12]. Figure 1 shows a cumulative distribution function (CDF) plot of measured RTT values for all carriers in our study. We see considerable performance variance between the networks despite all measurements originating from the same location.

We also observe significant performance differences between base carriers and MVNO carriers operating on the corresponding base carrier infrastructure. For instance, in Fig. 1 we see a 772.03 ms difference between the median RTT values for carrier A and the MVNO carrier A-1. However, the most surprising results are that MVNO carriers A-1 and B-1 outperform their respective base carriers in terms of achieved RTTs, with the aforementioned 772 ms lower median value for A-1 and a 87.24 ms median difference between B and B-1. These results contradict the expectation that MVNOs universally offer inferior performance. Previous work has established the widespread use of transparent middleboxes on mobile networks [13], which could help explain why networks with better RTT performance do not necessarily outperform others as such middleboxes likely ignore our measurement traffic. In order to understand round trip performance more fully we must also consider the *locations* of servers to which client traffic is resolved, explored in the next section.

4.2 Location-Specific RTTs

We study performance by examining the data center locations to which carriers are most likely to resolve. We record the geographic location for the destination server in all of the traceroutes corresponding to non-location specific requests in the previous experiment and find that the vast majority of requests resolve to data centers in nine US cities and most carriers heavily favor relatively few server locations. We then measure RTT performance to all locations using our list of location-specific servers, which are identified using 3-character airport codes in server names (e.g. `scontent-a-lax.cdninstagram.com` corresponds to an Instagram server in Los Angeles). Figure 2 shows RTT CDFs for each of the data center locations and highlights each carrier's top three 'preferred' locations. We find location preference by calculating the percent of 'hits' at each location for all non-location specific requests.

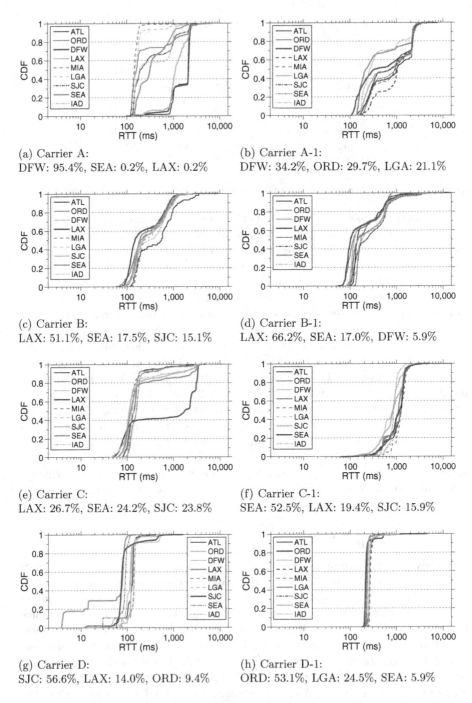

Fig. 2. RTT comparison for specific CDN locations identified by airport codes: Atlanta (ATL), Chicago (ORD), Dallas (DFW), Los Angeles (LAX), Miami (MIA), New York (LGA), San Jose (SJC), Seattle (SEA), Washington DC (IAD). Each carrier's top three preferred locations are indicated.

The figure illustrates large performance differences and unique behaviors between carriers. Some MVNOs appear to mimic the underlying base carrier, while others behave in drastically different ways. Perhaps the most interesting performance is seen on carriers A and A-1. Carrier A experiences vastly different round trip times between different CDN locations. Additionally, carrier A favors CDN sites (Dallas, Seattle, Los Angeles) that have the slowest median RTT compared to the other locations. The latency to Los Angeles servers is the second longest, despite Los Angeles being the data center nearest our measurement location of Santa Barbara. Carrier A-1 (Fig. 2(b)) displays the broadest range of RTT values across all CDN sites, and also favors servers located in Dallas, TX. However, carrier A-1's second and third most popular locations are Chicago and New York, respectively. We believe these results are due to A-1 being a full MVNO; thus, they employ their own core infrastructure and have service and peering arrangements independent from the base carrier A.

Carriers B and B-1 (Fig. 2(c) and (d)), on the other hand, perform more similarly in both latency measurements and preferred destinations. In fact, MVNO B-1 slightly outperforms the base MNO in terms of RTT in our experiments. Both carriers tend to route traffic toward Los Angeles. Los Angeles also tends to correspond to the lowest RTT values for both carriers. The striking similarity can be explained as carrier B-1 is a 'light MVNO,' thus B and B-1 use the same infrastructure to handle client traffic. In this regard, it stands to argue that customers considering carriers B and B-1 are essentially choosing between the same service when it comes to connecting to our specified CDN sites.

Carriers C and C-1 are quite different from one another in terms of performance even though they favor the same three data center locations. Interestingly, carrier C (Fig. 2(e)) routes the highest percentage of its traffic to servers in Los Angeles, which achieve highly variable RTT values (seemingly bimodal). We speculate that this result is due to the carrier load-balancing flows across dissimilar paths. Latency values on carrier C-1 (Fig. 2(f)) are rather consistent to all CDN locations, with higher RTTs overall compared with carrier C. Carrier D (Fig. 2(g)) experiences the lowest network latencies overall. This carrier tends to favor CDN servers located in San Jose, CA, which also has the lowest median RTT value for carrier D. MVNO carrier D-1 (Fig. 2(h)) shows the most consistent latency across all data center locations, but interestingly favors CDN servers in Chicago, 2,961 km away from San Jose. Similar to A-1, we believe this is likely due to D-1 being a full MVNO, with traffic traversing a different core network than the base MNO.

Overall, we observe that some MVNOs exhibit drastically different RTT performance from their MNO counterparts, while others are similar. While it seems that the light MVNO can be characterized as simply a re-branded version of the base MNO, our experiments using full MVNOs show unique latencies and resolutions between them and their MNOs. Thus, these carriers do not appear to simply reflect the performance of the MNO network on which they reside. Such behaviors will clearly impact network latency and throughput and may help to explain why MVNOs networks generally perform worse than MNOs.

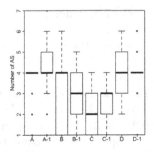
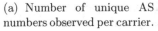
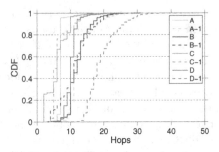

(a) Number of unique AS numbers observed per carrier.

(b) Number of hops observed per carrier.

Fig. 3. Path metrics for mobile networks. MNOs and MVNOs exhibit similar AS path lengths but differ in the number of hops taken to reach the destination.

4.3 Autonomous System Paths and Hop Counts

We next investigate traffic routes with respect to autonomous system (AS) paths in the traceroutes for each carrier to non-location specific servers. We use `whois` queries to map all IP addresses seen in carrier traceroutes to AS numbers. Figure 3(a) shows the number of unique AS numbers observed across the carriers, with the dark line indicating the mean. As shown, it appears as though MVNO behavior overall is similar to MNO networks. This result illustrates that MVNO networks are bound to some degree to the MNO network configuration. We study the actual AS numbers traversed by traffic between MNOs and MVNOs and find that they generally match, and as such omit this analysis for brevity. Interestingly, although carriers A-1, C-1, and D-1 all fall under the 'same' MVNO brand, traffic for each client behaves differently based on the underlying carrier. It appears that in terms of AS paths, MVNOs closely reflect the underlying MNO. These results lead us to investigate hop counts to help explain performance differences between MVNOs and MNOs.

We consider the total number of hops in traceroute records for traffic on each mobile network to non-location specific servers. We only consider records that reach the destination server. Figure 3(b) shows the results. As with other metrics, we observe considerable variability between carriers. Carriers A and D both use dramatically fewer hops to reach the server compared to their respective MVNOs, while carriers B and C closely resemble their respective MVNOs. The path length inflation seen on carriers A-1 and D-1 could help explain poorer RTT performance compared to the base carrier. We also observe that MVNOs A-1, C-1, and D-1, which are all marketed as the same carrier, experience very different length paths to reach the destination servers. We believe the variance may be attributable to the different preferred locations observed in Fig. 2.

4.4 Geographic Path Analysis

Lastly, we study the geographic paths taken by traffic on each mobile provider going to specific CDN locations. This analysis provides us visual insight into

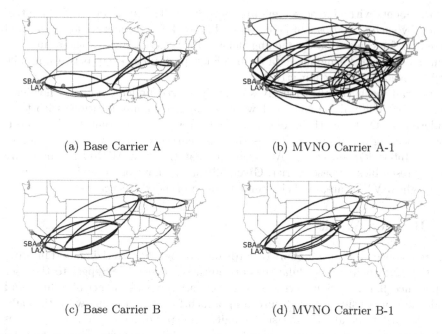

(a) Base Carrier A   (b) MVNO Carrier A-1

(c) Base Carrier B   (d) MVNO Carrier B-1

Fig. 4. Paths taken for each carrier to reach servers located in Los Angeles (LAX) from clients in Santa Barbara (SBA). Arc weight indicates the number of times a particular hop was taken. Clockwise arcs indicate direction of traffic between adjacent hops.

the carrier network behavior and performance. Figure 4 illustrates hops taken by traceroutes over our two-week experiment where the destination servers are located in Los Angeles, CA (140 km away from our location in Santa Barbara, CA). Due to space limitations, we only include plots for Los Angeles and four carriers, as it is representative for all locations observed and illustrates the contrast between full and light MVNOs. The figures indicate the differences in behavior between MVNOs and their base carriers. For instance, carrier A (Fig. 4(a)) clearly operates over different, more stable routes compared with its corresponding MVNO (Fig. 4(b)). This helps explain why there is such a marked difference in performance between the two when connecting to various data centers. Carriers B and B-1 (Fig. 4(c) and (d)), on the other hand, are quite similar to one another. This result depicts the difference between light and full MVNOs, where the light MVNO (B-1) routes traffic in the same way as the base MNO, while full MVNOs that implement their own core are influenced by outside factors and differ from their respective base carriers.

A curious finding is that many of the carriers, particularly the MVNOs, contain paths that pass through Los Angeles only to continue with subsequent hops in distant locations before finally returning to Los Angeles. This seems to indicate the lack of peering between the network that the earlier Los Angeles hop is within and the content provider located in Los Angeles. This behavior is interesting given that [9] found three of the four major US MNOs have peering arrangements with Google servers in Los Angeles. The propagation delay introduced by such scenarios can be considerable, without accounting for additional potential for congestion or queuing delays. Bottlenecks such as these must be removed in order for mobile data to shrink the performance gap between mobile and traditional wired connectivity.

Overall, path visualization gives us an increased understanding of how carriers differ. The full MVNOs that we measure share many locations with their underlying MNO, but their routes are more frenetic. This could be due to different peering arrangements versus the base carrier or simply due to different overall Internet connectivity. We also see that the light MVNO in our study closely resembles its base carrier. Given all that we have observed it seems clear that light MVNOs are, at their foundation, re-branded base carriers.

5   Related Work

There has been significant effort towards measuring, characterizing, and improving the performance of cellular network infrastructure with respect to the user experience [9,14,15]. Sommers et al. [14] compare the performance of cellular and WiFi networks using a crowdsourced approach for measuring network throughput. Nikrashev et al. [15] measure longitudinal performance from end-devices to uncover the prevalence of middleboxes in mobile networks. Zarifis et al. [9] use end-devices to identify latency caused by inflated routes and the relationships between user performance, Internet ingress points, and peering agreements. Similar to previous work, we use measurements from the end-user perspective to understand the impacts of network infrastructure on user experience.

Zarinni et al. [4] compare application performance over two major carriers and three MVNOs per carrier. Our work focuses on performance with respect to underlying network layers (e.g. latency and route paths) and considers all four major U.S. carriers and MVNOs operating on top of each.

As cellular networks become the primary mode of Internet connectivity, research efforts have focused on the analysis of the impact of content placement and network configuration on end-user experience [6,9]. Zarifis et al. [9] find that route inflation leads to increased RTT experienced by end users connecting from locations with limited infrastructure. Rula et al. [6] explores the relationship between cellular DNS infrastructure and the location of selected content replicas, finding that instability of cellular DNS resolvers significantly degrades the experience of mobile users. We find that locations of resolved content servers are not universally attributable to one single factor.

6   Discussion and Conclusion

Given the results of our measurement study, what are the overriding lessons?

Round Trip Times. We observe that round trip times vary significantly between MNOs as well as MVNOs. Additionally, we see that location of destination servers drastically affects RTTs, and resolved server locations do not appear to be logical in that they are often physically distant from the client location. Such behavior could be the result of mobile carrier peering arrangements, DNS infrastructure, and Internet ingress points. Future work should focus on making more efficient network topologies in order to close the performance gap between mobile carriers.

Route Paths. We find that MVNOs typically traverse the same autonomous systems as their MNO counterparts in their paths to reach servers. However, we often observe a higher number of hops on the MVNOs. The root cause of such path inflation needs more thorough investigation, as it could be attributable to multiple factors such as: Internet ingress points or middleboxes used for accounting or traffic shaping in the mobile core network. Given our geographic analysis, we believe that full MVNOs, which operate their own core networks, route traffic through seemingly inefficient paths. Perhaps increasing the number of ingress/egress points as well as replicating middlebox functionality across more geographic locations could improve the directness of mobile traffic on such networks.

MNOs vs MVNOs. With the exception of carrier B-1, we observe marked performance differences on MVNO networks compared with their underlying MNO networks. As carrier B-1 is a light MVNO, while the others are all full MVNOs, we can argue that consumers should expect a different user experience when connecting via full MVNOs compared with base carriers. The observed light MVNO leads us to conclude that its use is in essence the same as the base carrier. It remains to be seen whether the same is true for all light MVNOs. We find that full MVNOs tend to share some infrastructure with the MNO, but that they are less predictable in terms of routing paths. Latency differences are also considerable between MNOs and full MVNOs and some variability can be attributed to destination server location. It seems likely that MVNOs may have fewer peering agreements with content providers, evidenced by considerably longer, more circuitous paths taken.

We do not believe that MVNOs, by their nature, are bound to offer inferior performance compared to MNO carriers. There appears to be multiple avenues available to explore for MVNO carriers in order to maximize traffic efficiency. For researchers, this subject deserves more in-depth, longitudinal studies from many locations to fully understand performance of these networks. For consumers considering which MVNO or plan is the best option, there is currently no clear answer. Additionally, the 'best' carrier will likely vary based on what content the user intends to consume on the Internet. The inherent tradeoffs between carriers are worthy of future exploration using real-world user traffic.

Limitations. Our measurement study provides only a limited glimpse into the performance of mobile data networks given a single measurement location and targeting a small set of servers. A longitudinal, in-depth measurement campaign is required to fully understand the tradeoffs between mobile carriers and content delivery networks. Measurements also rely on the efficacy of the tools we use, such as `traceroute`, and the equal treatment of measurement traffic by the carrier core networks. A larger study must include more real world traffic.

Acknowledgements. This work was funded through NSF Network Science and Engineering (NetSE) Award CNS-1064821.

References

1. Kechiche, S.: M2M and MVNOs driving US connections growth.http://gsmainte lligence.com/research/2013/08/m2m-and-mvnos-driving-us-connections-growth/ 397/. Accessed 15 August 2013
2. Cricelli, L., Grimaldi, M., Ghiron, N.L.: The competition among mobile network operators in the telecommunication supply chain. Int. J. Prod. Econ. **131**(1), 22–29 (2011)
3. Shin, D.H., Bartolacci, M.: A study of MVNO diffusion and market structure in the EU, US, Hong Kong, and Singapore. Telematics Inform. **24**(2), 86–100 (2007)
4. Zarinni, F., Chakraborty, A., Sekar, V., Das, S.R., Gill, P.: A first look at performance in mobile virtual network operators. In: IMC 2014, Vancouver, BC, Canada, November 2014
5. Vakali, A., Pallis, G.: Content delivery networks: status and trends. IEEE Internet Comput. **7**(6), 68–74 (2003)
6. Rula, J.P., Bustamante, F.E.: Behind the curtain: cellular DNS and content replica selection. In: IMC 2014, Vancouver, BC, Canada, November 2014
7. Qureshi, A., Weber, R., Balakrishnan, H., Guttag, J., Maggs, B.: Cutting the electric bill for internet-scale systems. ACM SIGCOMM Comput. Commun. Rev. **39**(4), 123–134 (2009)
8. Alzoubi, H.A., Lee, S., Rabinovich, M., Spatscheck, O., Van der Merwe, J.: Anycast CDNS revisited. In: WWW 2008, Beijing, China, April 2008
9. Zarifis, K., et al.: Diagnosing path inflation of mobile client traffic. In: Faloutsos, M., Kuzmanovic, A. (eds.) PAM 2014. LNCS, vol. 8362, pp. 23–33. Springer, Switzerland (2014)
10. Sandvine: global internet Phenomena report: 2H 2014. https://www.sandvine. com/downloads/general/global-internet-phenomena/2014/2h-2014-global-internet-phenomena-report.pdf. Accessed 21 November 2014
11. Poese, I., Uhlig, S., Kaafar, M.A., Donnet, B., Gueye, B.: IP geolocation databases: unreliable? ACM SIGCOMM Comput. Commun. Rev. **41**(2), 53–56 (2011)
12. Jacobson, V.: Congestion avoidance and control. SIGCOMM Comput. Commun. Rev. **18**(4), 314–329 (1988)
13. Vallina-Rodriguez, N., Sundaresan, S., Kreibich, C., Weaver, N., Paxson, V.: Beyond the radio: illuminating the higher layers of mobile networks. In: Mobisys 15, Florence, Italy, June 2015
14. Sommers, J., Barford, P.: Cell vs. WiFi: on the performance of metro area mobile connections. In: IMC 2012, Boston, Massachusetts, USA, November 2012
15. Nikravesh, A., Choffnes, D.R., Katz-Bassett, E., Mao, Z.M., Welsh, M.: Mobile network performance from user devices: a longitudinal, multidimensional analysis. In: Faloutsos, M., Kuzmanovic, A. (eds.) PAM 2014. LNCS, vol. 8362, pp. 12–22. Springer, Switzerland (2014)

Detecting Cellular Middleboxes Using Passive Measurement Techniques

Utkarsh Goel[1]([✉]), Moritz Steiner[2], Mike P. Wittie[1], Martin Flack[2],
and Stephen Ludin[2]

[1] Department of Computer Science, Montana State University,
Bozeman, MT 59717, USA
utkarsh.goel@montana.edu, mwittie@cs.montana.edu
[2] Akamai Technologies, Inc., San Francisco, CA 94103, USA
{moritz,mflack,sludin}@akamai.com

Abstract. The Transmission Control Protocol (TCP) follows the end-to-end principle – when a client establishes a connection with a server, the connection is only shared by two physical machines, the client and the server. In current cellular networks, a myriad of middleboxes disregard the end-to-end principle to enable network operators to deploy services such as content caching, compression, and protocol optimization to improve end-to-end network performance. If server operators remain unaware of such middleboxes, TCP connections may not be optimized specifically for middleboxes and instead are optimized for mobile devices. We argue that without costly active measurement, it remains challenging for server operators to reliably detect the presence of middleboxes that split TCP connections. In this paper, we present three techniques (based on latency, loss, and characteristics of TCP SYN packets) for server operators **to passively identify Connection Terminating Proxies (CTPs) in cellular networks**, with the goal to optimize TCP connections for faster content delivery. Using TCP and HTTP logs recorded by Content Delivery Network (CDN) servers, we demonstrate that our passive techniques are as reliable and accurate as active techniques in detecting CTPs deployed in cellular networks worldwide.

Keywords: Cellular · Middleboxes · Split TCP · Network measurement

1 Introduction

The Transmission Control Protocol (TCP), Hyper Text Transport Protocol (HTTP) and secure HTTP (HTTPS) were originally designed with the assumption that clients communicate over end-to-end connections with servers. However, given the different types of networks involved in an end-to-end connection between cellular clients and servers (such as the radio network, the cellular backbone, and the public Internet), optimizing communication for each of these networks independently improves the overall performance of the end-to-end connections between clients and servers [5,10,11]. One of the techniques used by

© Springer International Publishing Switzerland 2016
T. Karagiannis and X. Dimitropoulos (Eds.): PAM 2016, LNCS 9631, pp. 95–107, 2016.
DOI: 10.1007/978-3-319-30505-9_8

cellular carriers to improve the communication performance in their networks is to deploy Connection Terminating Proxies (CTPs) that split TCP connections between clients and servers [9,13]. CTPs allow cellular carriers to speed up TCP transfers between devices and the cellular gateways to the Internet through TCP optimization, content caching, and bandwidth throttling.

Content Distribution Networks (CDNs), cloud providers, or other server providers on the Internet are mostly unaware of specific CTPs deployed by individual cellular carriers. As a result, servers may not optimize their connections for CTPs, but optimize connections for the mobile device instead. We believe that if server providers are made aware of the presence of CTPs, TCP configurations could be fine-tuned to improve content delivery to the middlebox and to the end-user [7]. However, without expensive active network measurements on mobile devices, it remains challenging for server operators to reliably detect the presence of CTPs and optimize connections accordingly [17].

In this study, we propose three techniques to **passively** detect the presence of CTPs in cellular networks, using TCP and HTTP logs recorded by Akamai's geographically distributed CDN servers. Our first technique compares **latency** estimated by clients and servers for TCP connections. The second technique compares the **packet loss** experienced by CDN servers for HTTP and HTTPS sessions. Our third technique analyzes characteristics of **TCP SYN** packets for connections to ports 80 (HTTP) and 443 (HTTPS). Although our evaluation is based on Akamai server logs, we argue that our techniques are not limited to CDN providers and also apply to other types of servers. The major contributions of this work are as follows:

- We perform the first large scale measurement study to passively detect the presence of CTPs deployed in cellular networks worldwide. Our study is based on data collected by Akamai CDN servers during January-July 2015. Our current dataset contains performance metrics from over a total of 14 million TCP connections from clients in different cellular networks.
- We propose three techniques for server operators to passively detect the presence of CTPs from TCP and HTTP server logs. Results from our measurements indicate that the use of CTPs is very popular among cellular carriers worldwide. In fact, carriers employ CTPs for splitting HTTPS sessions, in addition to splitting HTTP sessions.

Table 1. Comparison of results from our passive techniques with previous work [17] that uses active experiments, for cellular networks in the US.

Carrier	Latency	Packet Loss	TCP SYN	DH [16]
AT&T	✓	✓	✓	✓
Verizon W.	✓	✓	✓	✓
Sprint	✓	✓	✓	✓
T-Mobile	✓	✓	✓	✓

- Using the collected data, we demonstrate that our techniques are reliable in detecting CTPs deployed in cellular networks across several countries. In Table 1, we compare the results of our passive techniques with the **Delayed Handshake (DH)** active measurement technique of CTP detection for cellular carriers in the US [17]. The tickmarks in the table indicate the presence of CTPs. We show that despite the fact that our passive measurement techniques do not generate probing traffic, they correctly detect CTPs as detected by active experiments in DH [17].

The rest of the paper is organized as follows. In Sect. 2, we discuss related work on detecting cellular middleboxes. In Sect. 3, we present our methodology. In Sects. 4, 5, and 6, we discuss how server operators could detect CTPs by using latency estimated by clients and servers, packet loss observed on the server-side, and inspecting TCP SYN packets, respectively. In Sect. 7, we offer discussion of our results. Finally, we conclude in Sect. 8.

2   Related Work

Several studies have investigated the characteristics, performance benefits and deployment locations of CTPs in cellular networks. Weaver *et al.* and Xu *et al.* investigated the characteristics of transparent Web proxies in cellular networks using active experiments on mobile devices [16,17]. Other studies looked at the performance benefits of TCP splitting proxies to improve Web communications in cellular networks [6,9,13]. Ehsan *et al.* measured the performance gains of CTPs for Web caching and packet loss mitigation in satellite networks [8]. A study by Wang *et al.* characterized implications of cellular middleboxes on improving network security, device power consumption and application performance [15]. Our work, in contrast to these studies, focuses on detecting CTPs using passive measurement techniques, instead of active experiments.

3   Data Collection Methodology

To verify that our latency-based technique reliably detects CTPs in cellular networks worldwide, we used the webpage timing data collected by Akamai's Real User Monitoring system (RUM) [3], which leverages the Navigation Timing API on the client browser [1]. The data includes the time to establish TCP connections for both HTTP and HTTPS sessions. Akamai's RUM also records TCP latency estimated by CDN servers for HTTP and HTTPS session. To investigate whether our packet loss-based technique reliably detects CTPs, we used TCP logs recorded by CDN servers deployed worldwide and extracted the number of packets retransmitted by the server for both HTTP and HTTPS sessions. Finally, to investigate whether our TCP SYN-based technique detect CTPs, we collected TCP-dumps on CDN servers for several hours and captured SYN packets for connection requests to port 80 (HTTP) and 443 (HTTPS).

4   Detecting CTPs from Client and Server-Side Latency

When a CTP splits an end-to-end connection between clients and CDN servers, the latency estimated by clients should be higher than latency estimated by CDN servers. This is because the latency observed by the client will include the radio and cellular backbone latency (~tens of milliseconds [2]). Whereas the latency estimated by CDN servers would include the latency on the wired public Internet and is likely to be low (~5 ms), as CDNs have wide deployment of servers inside many cellular networks.

In this section we analyze the TCP latency estimated by clients and servers for TCP connections (both HTTP and HTTPS sessions) using two different methods. First, we compare the latency from both client and server endpoints to identify networks where the latency experienced by clients is significantly higher than latency experienced by servers – which indicates that a CTP is being used for a connection. Second, we compare the latency for HTTP and HTTPS sessions only from the server-side to identify networks where servers experience significantly different latencies for HTTP and HTTPS sessions – which indicates that a CTP is used for one type of connections.

Table 2. Distribution of TCP latency estimated by clients (Client RTT) and servers (Server RTT) for IPv4-based cellular networks in North America.

CC	Carrier	Protocol	Hits	Client RTT			Server RTT			Proxy?
				p25	p50	p75	p25	p50	p75	
US	AT&T	HTTP	1.7M	37	47	67	3	4	8	✓
US	AT&T	HTTPS	686K	45	60	89	52	75	114	X
US	Verizon W.	HTTP	1.9M	36	45	69	5	10	21	✓
US	Verizon W.	HTTPS	471K	44	60	87	48	65	87	X
US	T-Mobile	HTTP	2.1M	40	59	85	19	68	157	Limited
US	T-Mobile	HTTPS	459K	45	65	98	59	94	180	–
US	Sprint	HTTP	1.4M	39	52	78	3	12	28	✓
US	Sprint	HTTPS	275K	47	63	93	52	72	118	X
US	Clearwire	HTTP	96K	75	93	128	75	95	139	X
US	Clearwire	HTTPS	39K	75	92	137	82	100	143	X
CA	Bell Canada	HTTP	63K	38	50	69	49	78	151	–
CA	Bell Canada	HTTPS	17K	38	49	73	57	85	157	–
CA	Rogers	HTTP	97K	37	51	86	41	64	110	–
CA	Rogers	HTTPS	30K	37	52	87	48	72	119	–
CA	Telus	HTTP	65K	34	43	60	9	19	49	✓
CA	Telus	HTTPS	16K	43	58	83	47	66	104	X
CA	Sasktel	HTTP	10K	27	41	83	23	33	75	X
CA	Sasktel	HTTPS	2K	43	63	116	59	100	230	–
CA	Videotron	HTTP	7K	44	55	71	44	58	91	X
CA	Videotron	HTTPS	4K	46	58	86	50	70	120	X
MX	Uninet	HTTP	41 K	83	113	183	142	267	571	–
MX	Uninet	HTTPS	8 K	79	109	177	163	256	446	–

In Table 2, we show the distribution (25th, 50th, and 75th percentile) of network latency measured by the client (**Client RTT**) and by the server (**Server RTT**) for major cellular networks in North America. The column **CC** represents the country code of each network. Column **Hits** represents the number of unique TCP connections behind latency distributions. The column **Proxy?** indicates whether our techniques detect CTPs for a given cellular carrier. For example, for AT&T network in the US, the **Client RTT** for HTTP sessions is almost 10 times the **Server RTT**, which indicates that servers are communicating with a device only 4 ms away. Since 4 ms is too low for an end-to-end connection over a cellular network [2], we argue that servers communicate with CTPs deployed in AT&T network (as indicated by ✓ in the Proxy column). In the case of HTTPS sessions in AT&T, we observe that **Client RTT** and **Server RTT** are similar, which indicates that there is no CTP for HTTPS sessions in the AT&T network (as indicated by X in Proxy column). Further, when we look at only the **Server RTT** for HTTP and HTTPS sessions, we see that servers experience significantly higher latency for HTTPS sessions, which further confirms that AT&T does not employ CTPs for splitting HTTPS sessions. Tables 3, 4, and 5 show the application of the latency technique to detect CTPs in cellular networks in Asia, Europe, and Oceania and South America, respectively.

Table 3. Distribution of TCP latency estimated by clients (Client RTT) and servers (Server RTT) for cellular networks in Asia.

CC	Carrier	Protocol	Hits	Client RTT			Server RTT			Proxy?
				p25	p50	p75	p25	p50	p75	
CN	China Mobile	HTTP	85 K	34	61	101	46	77	128	X
CN	China Mobile	HTTPS	24 K	49	81	132	57	93	170	X
TW	HiNet	HTTP	53 K	33	48	70	35	50	91	X
TW	HiNet	HTTPS	18 K	33	48	77	38	58	103	X
CN	ChinaNet	HTTP	4 K	45	81	149	33	83	167	X
CN	ChinaNet	HTTPS	5 K	207	342	471	118	144	215	–
CN	China Unicom	HTTP	8 K	55	90	150	70	119	209	X
CN	China Unicom	HTTPS	4 K	70	109	187	82	127	213	X
HK	China Mobile	HTTP	9 K	32	53	93	34	60	110	X
HK	China Mobile	HTTPS	3 K	32	48	91	39	57	108	X
IN	Vodafone	HTTP	304 K	58	128	367	33	59	170	–
IN	Vodafone	HTTPS	191 K	80	131	349	102	244	553	–
KR	Korea Telecom	HTTP	28 K	29	35	43	30	40	51	X
KR	Korea Telecom	HTTPS	25 K	30	38	56	37	43	65	X
JP	SoftBank	HTTP	44 K	30	40	55	3	8	13	✓
JP	SoftBank	HTTPS	8 K	37	47	64	41	49	62	X
MY	TM Net	HTTP	13 K	57	75	120	65	113	397	X
MY	TM Net	HTTPS	3 K	60	82	129	83	136	380	X
AE	Eitc	HTTP	4 K	123	153	217	139	159	221	X
AE	Eitc	HTTPS	3 K	139	159	233	140	161	228	X
AE	Etisalat	HTTP	4 K	30	37	49	3	5	29	✓
AE	Etisalat	HTTPS	3 K	33	40	52	35	42	57	X

While employing our latency-based techniques to detect CTPs in cellular networks worldwide, we made five observations on the behavior of CTPs. First, we observe that for **p25** of HTTP sessions in T-Mobile USA network, the latency experienced by clients and servers is significantly different, which indicates a presence of CTPs HTTP sessions in T-Mobile network. However, for **p50** of the HTTP sessions, the two latencies are similar – indicating no presence of CTPs for HTTP sessions in T-Mobile network. To investigate this surprising behavior of T-Mobile network, we classified our data based on server locations and domain names. Table 6 shows the distribution **Client RTT** and **Server RTT** for HTTP sessions for different domain names across different locations in the US. We observe that for clients connecting to servers in CA and VA, CTPs are used on per domain basis. For example, the HTTP latency estimated by servers in CA to download webpages associated with a clothing website is significantly lower than latency estimated for a ticketing website. We see similar trends at other locations in the US and across several domain names. Next, we observe that T-Mobile employs CTPs for HTTP sessions only at a few locations in the US. For example, in Table 6 the latency experienced by clients connecting to servers in TX indicate that T-Mobile does not use a CTP for terminating HTTP sessions for any domain name. Thus we argue that T-Mobile's deployment of CTPs in the US is different across different locations and domain names. Based on these observations, we label the **Proxy?** column in Table 2 as 'Limited'.

The second observation we make is that cellular networks in the US use CTPs for TCP connections over their IPv4 networks, but not over their IPv6 networks. Since we did not observe statistically significant IPv6 traffic from cellular carriers deployed outside of the US, we restrict this observation to cellular carriers in the US only. In Table 7, we show the distribution of TCP latency for IPv6 networks deployed by major US carriers, estimated by clients and CDN servers. We observe that clients in Verizon Wireless connecting to CDNs over IPv6 network experience latency similar to that estimated at the server for HTTP sessions. However, from Table 2, we observe that Verizon clients connecting to CDN servers over its IPv4 network experience much higher latency than experienced by the CDN servers, for HTTP sessions – indicating the presence of CTP for HTTP sessions in its IPv4 network. Therefore, we argue that Verizon employs CTPs for HTTP sessions in its IPv4 network and not in its IPv6 network.

The third observation we make is that some networks use CTPs to split HTTPS sessions. Using our measurement data, we identified a cellular carrier in France that employs CTPs to split HTTPS sessions. In Table 4, we show that for France Telecom, the **Server RTT** for HTTPS sessions is significantly lower than the **Client RTT**, therefore we believe that France Telecom uses CTPs to split HTTPS sessions. Telefonica in Spain is another cellular carrier for which we observe that CTPs split HTTPS sessions, as the latency estimated by CDN servers is lower than latency estimated by clients. Further, Telefonica's recent design of mcTLS protocol indicates that ISPs work towards deploying CTPs for HTTPS sessions [12], likely to support content caching and connection optimization for secure connections [14].

Table 4. Distribution of TCP latency estimated by clients (Client RTT) and servers (Server RTT) for cellular networks in the Europe.

CC	Carrier	Protocol	Hits	Client RTT			Server RTT			Proxy?
				p25	p50	p75	p25	p50	p75	
DE	DTAG	HTTP	22K	39	50	75	5	8	14	✓
DE	DTAG	HTTPS	13K	53	79	125	34	46	93	–
DE	Vodafone	HTTP	57K	39	51	82	7	11	16	✓
DE	Vodafone	HTTPS	17K	49	64	100	53	70	128.5	X
ES	Telefonica	HTTP	65K	55	92	372	10	18	30	✓
ES	Telefonica	HTTPS	136K	108	149	218	14	22	35	Limited
ES	UNI2	HTTP	43K	41	57	96	38	62	141	X
ES	UNI2	HTTPS	121K	43	59	102	45	64	115	X
ES	Vodafone	HTTP	91K	30	43	72	6	15	30	✓
ES	Vodafone	HTTPS	223K	35	49	76	39	55	90	X
ES	Jazztel	HTTP	9K	56	75	127	61	90	233	X
ES	Jazztel	HTTPS	17K	56	73	109	66	87	147	X
FR	Bouygues	HTTP	75K	28	37	57	2	4	38	✓
FR	Bouygues	HTTPS	26K	30	39	59	35	47	79	X
FR	France Telecom	HTTP	37K	37	48	73	1	6	13	✓
FR	France Telecom	HTTPS	17K	40	56	94	1	7	39	✓
FR	SFR	HTTP	41K	37	50	82	3	7	33	✓
FR	SFR	HTTPS	15K	44	62	103	48	72	142	X
FR	Free	HTTP	23K	43	59	92	40	59	90	X
FR	Free	HTTPS	10K	45	63	116	26	42	71	–
GB	Telefonica	HTTP	186K	49	71	109	7	11	23	✓
GB	Telefonica	HTTPS	40K	59	85	150	48	72	115	X
GB	Vodafone	HTTP	115K	41	56	89	7	14	57	✓
GB	Vodafone	HTTPS	24K	49	68	111	54	76	145	X
IT	H3G	HTTP	49K	55	73	116	60	81	157	X
IT	H3G	HTTPS	14K	55	77	142	65	93	221	X
IT	Tim	HTTP	55K	39	57	94	6	12	41	✓
IT	Tim	HTTPS	13K	46	67	110	53	80	167	X
AT	France Telecom	HTTP	8K	41	57	80	59	97	210	–
AT	France Telecom	HTTPS	3K	43	59	87	66	101	219	–
AT	H3G	HTTP	9K	40	57	79	58	94	205	–
AT	H3G	HTTPS	4K	41	59	88	62	98	225	–
AT	T-Mobile	HTTP	10K	33	48	72	5	15	48	✓
AT	T-Mobile	HTTPS	3K	40	58	83	52	76	131	X
NL	Vodafone	HTTP	8K	33	39	61	2	2	16	✓
NL	Vodafone	HTTPS	2K	35	43	80	37	46	71	X
SE	Vodafone	HTTP	8K	37	45	59	62	97	175	–
SE	Vodafone	HTTPS	39K	37	46	58	65	89	142	–
TR	Turk Telecom	HTTP	34K	54	83	150	39	80	143	X
TR	Turk Telecom	HTTPS	9K	49	72	138	50	80	145	X
TR	Vodafone	HTTP	16K	40	59	116	9	51	85	Limited
TR	Vodafone	HTTPS	4K	55	92	128	64	102	152	X

Table 5. Distribution of TCP latency estimated by clients (Client RTT) and servers (Server RTT) for cellular networks in Oceania and South America.

CC	Carrier	Protocol	Hits	Client RTT			Server RTT			Proxy?
				p25	p50	p75	p25	p50	p75	
AU	Vodafone	HTTP	106 K	31	40	62	2	3	13	✓
AU	Vodafone	HTTPS	64 K	38	51	94	36	48	87	X
NZ	Vodafone	HTTP	7 K	30	49	71	2	11	27	✓
NZ	Vodafone	HTTPS	6 K	38	59	99	37	61	115	X
BR	Telefonica	HTTP	560 K	51	108	273	58	120	309	X
BR	Telefonica	HTTPS	63 K	40	78	165	51	100	212	X
PY	Telefonica	HTTP	13 K	180	217	289	186	237	430	X
PY	Telefonica	HTTPS	3 K	184	221	297	202	262	428	X

Table 6. Distribution of HTTP latency estimated by clients (Client RTT) and servers (Server RTT) for T-Mobile across different domains & locations.

State	Domain Type	Client RTT			Server RTT			Proxy?
		p25	p50	p75	p25	p50	p75	
CA	Clothing website	37	51	75	2	3	3	✓
CA	e-Commerce website	40	56	80	2	2	3	✓
CA	Health Care website	40	56	90	40	80	175	X
CA	Ticketing website	37	49	65	43	93	186	X
VA	Clothing website	39	57	80	2	2	2	✓
VA	e-Commerce website	46	68	89	2	2	2	✓
VA	Health Care website	44	64	90	27	63	121	X
TX	Clothing website	54	72	96	49	93	204	X
TX	Health Care website	56	75	97	61	107	211	X
TX	Ticketing website	50	70	90	33	67	111	X
TX	Movies website	56	71	91	88	156	301	X

The fourth observation we make is that for some carriers, the **p75** of **Server RTT** is similar to **p25** of **Client RTT**, when the **p25** and **p50** of **Server RTT** indicate the presence of CTPs in that carrier. For example, the **p75** of **Server RTT** for HTTP sessions in Etisalat network in Table 3, suggests that CTPs may not be used for splitting all HTTP sessions. We speculate that when CTPs get overloaded, client requests are likely not sent to CTPs and instead sent directly to servers. As a result servers occasionally experience (unproxied) latency of end-to-end connections to mobile devices. To deal with such occasional instances, TCP stacks of servers should interpret such connections as direct connections to mobile devices.

Finally, the fifth observation we make is that for a few cellular carriers the **Server RTT** is either higher or lower than **Client RTT** by at least 80 ms for **p75**. Specifically, if we observe **Server RTT** to be higher than **Client RTT**, we speculate that CTPs are deployed near the gateway and Internet egress points are

Table 7. Distribution of TCP latency estimated by clients (Client RTT) and servers (Server RTT) for IPv6 cellular networks in North America.

State	Domain Type	Client RTT			Server RTT			Proxy?
		p25	p50	p75	p25	p50	p75	
CA	Clothing website	37	51	75	2	3	3	✓
CA	e-Commerce website	40	56	80	2	2	3	✓
CA	Health Care website	40	56	90	40	80	175	X
CA	Ticketing website	37	49	65	43	93	186	X
VA	Clothing website	39	57	80	2	2	2	✓
VA	e-Commerce website	46	68	89	2	2	2	✓
VA	Health Care website	44	64	90	27	63	121	X
TX	Clothing website	54	72	96	49	93	204	X
TX	Health Care website	56	75	97	61	107	211	X
TX	Ticketing website	50	70	90	33	67	111	X
TX	Movies website	56	71	91	88	156	301	X

far from the gateway. If we observe **Server RTT** to be lower than **Client RTT**, we speculate that CTPs are near to both egress points and gateways but clients connect to gateways far in the network. For such cellular carriers we place a '-' in the **Proxy?** column in Tables 2, 3, 4, and 5. We argue that for such cellular carriers, passive techniques in the following sections may be used to detect the presence of CTPs.

5   Detecting CTPs from Packet Loss on the Server-Side

In previous section, we discussed how server operators could use latencies measurements by clients and servers to detect the presence of CTPs. In this section, we are interested in verifying another technique, based on packet loss, to passively detect CTPs across cellular networks worldwide using measurement data collected by Akamai CDN servers. Since we observe TCP latency estimated by CDN servers to CTPs is significantly low, we argue that CTPs and CDN servers are usually deployed within the same or nearby datacenters. Therefore, when a CTP is employed to split connections, the number of packets retransmitted by servers should be lower than packets retransmitted for connections where CTPs are not used. Following this assumption, in Fig. 1, we show the distribution of packet loss observed during our tests for thousands of HTTP and HTTPS sessions. Our first goal is to identify networks where packet loss observed by CDN servers is higher for one type of connections and not others. We also aim to determine whether results from using packet loss correlate with our CTP detection in the previous section. Due to space limitations, we show distribution of packet loss for only a few cellular carriers in North America and Europe.

In Fig. 1(a), we show the distribution of packet loss observed for HTTP and HTTPS sessions in four major cellular carriers in the US. Specifically, in the case

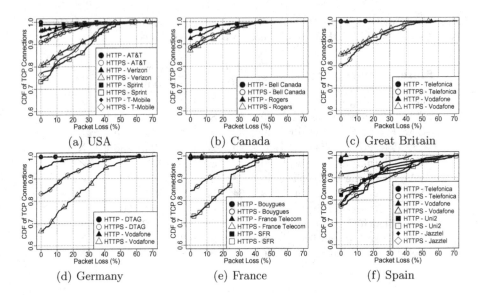

Fig. 1. Distribution of packet loss over HTTP and HTTPS sessions for cellular networks in different countries. For visibility, we reduced the number of symbols on each line.

of Verizon, AT&T, and Sprint networks, we observe that for HTTP sessions CDN servers experience low packet loss, whereas for HTTPS sessions CDN servers experience significantly higher packet loss – indicating the presence of CTPs for HTTP sessions. The results for these networks agree with our observations from using latency-based technique. However, in the case of T-Mobile, we see that the packet loss for HTTP sessions is slightly higher compared to other networks. We speculate that the packet loss for HTTP sessions in T-Mobile network are influenced by T-Mobile's policy to employ CTPs at only a few locations and domain names in the US (Table 6).

Next, we compare the packet loss observed for connections in a network where CTP is not employed, the Rogers network in Canada, as detected by our latency-based technique in Table 2, with a network where our latency-based technique could not detect the presence of CTPs, the Bell Canada network in Canada. In Fig. 1(b), we show that for both HTTP and HTTPS sessions in Bell Canada and Rogers networks, CDN servers observe similar packet loss. We speculate that either CTPs are not employed in the Bell Canada network or CTPs are present but CTPs experience same network conditions as Rogers network without CTPs.

We now extend our discussion and compare packet loss observed by CDN servers for connections in major cellular carriers in the UK, Germany, France, and Spain. Similarly to carriers in the US, in Fig. 1(c) and (d), we show that packet loss observed by servers for HTTP sessions is significantly lower than packet loss observed for HTTPS sessions – indicating the presence of CTPs for HTTP sessions, similar to our observations from using latency-based technique. For cellular carriers in France in Fig. 1(e), we observe that packet loss for

HTTPS sessions in France Telecom network is similar to packet loss for HTTP sessions, with both being almost zero. This indicates that CTPs are employed by France Telecom for splitting both HTTP and HTTPS sessions – validating our observations from using latency-based technique.

Finally, in Fig. 1(f), we show distribution of packet loss observed by CDN servers for major cellular carriers in Spain. We observe that for Vodafone and Telefonica networks, the packet loss for HTTP sessions is much lower than packet loss for HTTPS session – indicating the presence of CTPs for only HTTP connections, similar to our observations from using latency-based technique. For Uni2 and Jazztel, however, we observe that packet loss for both HTTP and HTTPS is similar. This indicates that CTPs are used for both HTTP and HTTPS sessions, similar to our observations from using latency-based technique. One exception to our results is for Telefonica. Using the latency technique we identified that Telefonica could be a potential carrier where CTPs are used to terminate HTTPS sessions. However, the high packet loss for HTTPS sessions indicates that CTPs are not used for splitting HTTPS sessions. To disambiguate the presence of CTPs, we propose another technique that relies on analyzing the characteristics of TCP SYN packets, which we discuss next.

6 Detecting CTPs from TCP SYN Characteristics

Our third technique is based on analyzing TCP SYN packets to detect the presence of CTPs in cellular networks. Our active experiments on understanding characteristics of TCP SYN packets generated by different types of mobile devices have revealed that the advertised Initial Congestion Window Size (ICWS), TCP Timestamp in the TCP options header, and Maximum Segment Size (MSS) values are different across different types of mobile devices. We also observed that these values are different even when the same device connects to Wi-Fi and cellular network. Based on this observation, our goal is to identify whether analyzing TCP SYN packets (captured passively for HTTP and HTTPS sessions) have the same ICWS, MSS, and an increasing TCP Timestamp value, which would indicate that SYN packets are likely being generated by a single machine (a CTP), instead of from multiple mobile devices with different hardware.

Results from our analysis of TCP SYN packets indicate that for all observed TCP SYN packets on port 80 from cellular carriers for which our latency and packet loss-based techniques suggest presence of CTP for HTTP sessions, the ICWS and MSS fields in the TCP SYN packets have the same value and the TCP Timestamp option have monotonically increasing values with a near constant skew – indicating the presence of CTPs for splitting HTTP sessions. For TCP SYN packets (generated from networks for which our latency and packet loss-based techniques suggest absence of CTPs for HTTPS sessions) to port 443 of CDN servers, we observed varying values of ICWS, MSS, and TCP Timestamp – indicating that the TCP SYN packets are likely generated by different mobile devices, instead of CTPs. We also verified our technique to be reliable for cellular carriers that employ CTPs for HTTPS sessions. For example, for France Telecom network in France we observed that the characteristics of all observed TCP SYN packets to port 443 were similar – indicating the presence of CTPs for HTTPS connections. For Telefonica in Spain, we did not observe similar characteristics of observed TCP SYN packets to port 443 – indicating absence of CTPs for splitting HTTPS sessions. Based on our findings on Telefonica's CTPs for HTTPS sessions from our latency, loss, and SYN-based techniques, we argue that active measurements may be needed to reliably detect CTPs. Finally, based on the data collected we did not find networks where ICWS and MSS values were similar but CTP was not detected using latency packet loss based techniques.

7 Discussion

We believe that one can leverage the use of our latency-based technique to identify the cellular latency offered by carriers where CTPs are present. We argue that for such carriers, **Client RTT** is a reliable indicator of the cellular latency, comprising of the sum of radio latency and latency within the cellular backbone. Specifically, if 4G is widely deployed by a cellular carrier, the latency offered by 4G would be reflected in both **p25** and **p75** of **Client RTT**. Further, if 3G is more widely deployed than 4G, then the latency offered by 4G would be reflected in the **p25** and latency offered by 3G would be reflected in **p75** of **Client RTT**. For example, for Telefonica in Spain, Sensorly's [4] signal strength data suggests a wide deployment of 3G, but little deployment of 4G. Therefore, in Table 4, the **p25** of **Client RTT** for HTTP sessions (55 ms) reflects Telefonica's latency over its 4G network, whereas the **p75** latency of 372 ms reflects its 3G latency. Further, the Etisalat network in AE (in Table 3) has wide deployment of 4G (based on Sensorly data), thus the HTTP latency shown in both **p25** (30 ms) and **p75** (49 ms) of **Client RTT** represents the latency offered by Etisalat's 4G network. For other cellular networks with CTPs also, we verified that using Sensorly's data and **Client RTT** together allows cellular latency estimation in a given carrier.

8 Conclusions

Connection Terminating Proxies (CTPs) have been a great area of interest for many cellular carriers in the past. These proxies allow for optimizing TCP connections between servers and client devices. In this paper, we propose three techniques to passively identify the presence of CTPs, based on latency, loss, and TCP SYN characteristics. We also conduct an extensive measurement study based on Akamai server logs to demonstrate that our techniques can reliably detect CTPs in cellular networks worldwide. Based on our measurement results, we argue that server operators could use our suggested techniques to detect CTPs using server logs only and optimize communications for different cellular networks with the goal of faster content delivery to end-users.

Acknowledgments. We thank Ruomei Gao, Chris Heller, Ajay Kumar Miyyapuram, and Kanika Shah for their invaluable insights on refining our data collection process. We also thank National Science Foundation for supporting this work through grant NSF CNS-1555591.

References

1. Navigation Timing, August 2015. http://w3c.github.io/navigation-timing/
2. NSF Workshop on Achieving Ultra-Low Latencies in Wireless Networks, March 2015. http://inlab.lab.asu.edu/nsf/files/WorkshopReport.pdf
3. Real User Monitoring, August 2015. https://www.akamai.com/us/en/resources/real-user-monitoring.jsp
4. Unbiased Wireless Network Information, August 2015. http://www.sensorly.com
5. Border, J., Kojo, M., Griner, J., Montenegro, G., Shelby, Z.: Performance Enhancing Proxies Intended to Mitigate Link-Related Degradations, June 2001. https://tools.ietf.org/html/rfc3135
6. Botta, A., Pescape, A.: Monitoring and measuring wireless network performance in the presence of middleboxes. In: Conference on Wireless On-Demand Network Systems and Services, January 2012
7. Dukkipati, N., Refice, T., Cheng, Y., Chu, J., Herbert, T., Agarwal, A., Jain, A., Sutin, N.: An argument for increasing TCP's initial congestion window. SIGCOMM CCR **40**(3), 26–33 (2010)
8. Ehsan, N., Liu, M., Ragland, R.J.: Evaluation of performance enhancing proxies in internet over satellite. Int. J. Commun. Syst. **16**(6), 513–534 (2003)
9. Farkas, V., Héder, B., Nováczki, S.: A split connection TCP proxy in LTE networks. In: Szabó, R., Vidács, A. (eds.) EUNICE 2012. LNCS, vol. 7479, pp. 263–274. Springer, Heidelberg (2012)
10. Gomez, C., Catalan, M., Viamonte, D., Paradells, J., Calveras, A.: Web browsing optimization over 2.5G and 3G: end-to-end mechanisms vs. usage of performance enhancing proxies. Wireless Commun. Mob. Comput. **8**, 213–230 (2008)
11. Ivanovich, M., Bickerdike, P., Li, J.: On TCP performance enhancing proxies in a wireless environment. IEEE Commun. Mag. **46**, 76–83 (2008)
12. Naylor, D., Schomp, K., Varvello, M., Leontiadis, I., Blackburn, J., Lopez, D., Papagiannaki, K., Rodriguez, P.R., Steenkiste, P.: Investigating transparent web proxies in cellular networks. In: ACM SIGCOMM, August 2015
13. Necker, M., Scharf, M., Weber, A.: Performance of different proxy concepts in UMTS networks. In: Wireless Systems and Mobility in Next Generation Internet, June 2004
14. Thomson, M.: Blind Proxy Caching, July 2015. https://httpworkshop.github.io/workshop/presentations/thomson-cache.pdf
15. Wang, Z., Qian, Z., Xu, Q., Mao, Z., Zhang, M.: An untold story of middleboxes in cellular networks. In: ACM SIGCOMM, August 2011
16. Weaver, N., Kreibich, C., Dam, M., Paxson, V.: Here be web proxies. In: Faloutsos, M., Kuzmanovic, A. (eds.) PAM 2014. LNCS, vol. 8362, pp. 183–192. Springer, Heidelberg (2014)
17. Xu, X., Jiang, Y., Flach, T., Katz-Bassett, E., Choffnes, D., Govindan, R.: Investigating transparent web proxies in cellular networks. In: Mirkovic, J., Liu, Y. (eds.) PAM 2015. LNCS, vol. 8995, pp. 262–276. Springer, Heidelberg (2015)

The Last Mile

Home Network or Access Link? Locating Last-Mile Downstream Throughput Bottlenecks

Srikanth Sundaresan[1][(✉)], Nick Feamster[2], and Renata Teixeira[3]

[1] ICSI, Berkeley, USA
srikanth@icsi.berkeley.edu
[2] Princeton University, Princeton, USA
[3] Inria, Lyon, France

Abstract. As home networks see increasingly faster downstream throughput speeds, a natural question is whether users are benefiting from these faster speeds or simply facing performance bottlenecks in their own home networks. In this paper, we ask whether downstream throughput bottlenecks occur more frequently in their home networks or in their access ISPs. We identify lightweight metrics that can accurately identify whether a throughput bottleneck lies inside or outside a user's home network and develop a detection algorithm that locates these bottlenecks. We validate this algorithm in controlled settings and report on two deployments, one of which included 2,652 homes across the United States. We find that wireless bottlenecks are more common than access-link bottlenecks—particularly for home networks with downstream throughput greater than 20 Mbps, where access-link bottlenecks are relatively rare.

Keywords: Bottleneck location · Wireless bottlenecks · Last-mile · Passive measurements

1 Introduction

Many countries around the world are investing heavily to increase the speeds of access network infrastructure. As the downstream throughput of access links increases, a natural question is whether users are reaping the benefits of these faster speeds. The downstream throughput they are experiencing may be limited by other factors, such as their home wireless networks, which may face performance problems due to a variety of factors (*e.g.*, a poorly placed access link, interference from competing networks or even devices on the same network). In light of these trends, we study a simple question: *Do users tend to see downstream throughput bottlenecks more often in their access ISPs or in their home wireless networks?* To study this question, we design and implement an algorithm, *HoA (Home or Access)*, that can accurately locate these downstream bottlenecks on commodity home routers. We deploy HoA in 2,652 home networks in the United States and characterize the throughput bottlenecks that we observe across this deployment.

© Springer International Publishing Switzerland 2016
T. Karagiannis and X. Dimitropoulos (Eds.): PAM 2016, LNCS 9631, pp. 111–123, 2016.
DOI: 10.1007/978-3-319-30505-9_9

Despite the importance and widespread interest in answering this question, both data and conclusions have proved to be elusive. Although throughput analysis and wireless diagnosis tools exist, each existing tool has some limitation that makes it unsuitable for studying this question—typically, these tools require performing measurements from multiple vantage points (which are hard to convince users to install in their home networks), performing active measurements (which can affect the performance of the wireless network), or custom hardware (which can hamper widespread deployment). (Section 4 explains how our work relates to previous throughput detection and analysis tools and why existing tools do not apply in our setting.) In contrast, we seek to develop a passive network measurement tool that can run from a low-cost, commodity home network router. This choice necessarily limits the extent of the data that we can collect (and, as a result, the conclusions that we can draw), but it also affords a relatively large-scale deployment. HoA's simplicity allowed us to implement it on a commodity Netgear router for two in-home deployments: A deployment of BISmark routers across 64 homes and 15 countries; and another deployment that was sponsored by the US Federal Communications Commission (FCC) and included 2,652 homes across the United States. These deployments allowed us to conduct a first-of-its-kind large-scale study of last-mile bottlenecks. Section 2.6 describes the deployments in more detail.

Realizing HoA required tackling several challenges. First, we needed to properly isolate performance problems in the home network versus outside of the home; capturing measurements at the home router offers a convenient solution to this challenge, since it lies between these two parts of the network. Next, we had to identify and validate metrics that were lightweight enough to capture on a low-cost home router, yet sufficient to accurately locate downstream throughput bottlenecks. We also wanted to use performance metrics from passive network traffic capture, to avoid introducing conditions that might either alter the state of the wireless network or disrupt network performance for home network users. Ultimately, we identified two features—the coefficient of variation of packet inter-arrival time and the round-trip time on the wireless LAN—that can be measured passively, are lightweight enough to be deployed on a commodity home gateway, and can identity last-mile bottlenecks in many circumstances. Section 2 incorporates these metrics into a complete identification algorithm.

We offer two important contributions: (1) the design of HoA, a lightweight tool that both accurately detects home access link and wireless network bottlenecks; (2) a detailed characterization of the nature and extent of throughput bottlenecks that commonly arise in many home networks using data from a large-scale prototype deployment of HoA in home routers. We do not determine *why* a particular bottleneck exists (*e.g.*, it cannot determine whether a wireless problem results from poor device placement, non-WiFi interference, or other causes), but rather only *where* the problem exists, to the granularity of whether the problem is inside or outside the home. Our study yields the following important findings:

- Access link bottlenecks rarely occur in home networks where downstream access throughput exceeds 20 Mbps. Rather, in these cases, throughput bottlenecks are often introduced by the home wireless network.

- Access link bottlenecks only tend to be common for users whose downstream access throughput is less than 10 Mbps.
- In homes with multiple devices where we detect a wireless bottleneck, it is equally likely that only a single device experiences the wireless bottleneck as it is that all devices in the home experience the bottleneck simultaneously.

Our results suggest that it is worth spending effort to improve home wireless network performance, in addition to the extensive attempts to optimize performance in other parts of the network and end hosts.

2   HoA: Design, Implementation, and Deployments

We describe the design, implementation, and deployment of HoA.

2.1   Design Choices

Our first design choice was to perform measurements from the home access point. Locating bottlenecks at the last mile becomes easier with a vantage point inside the home network. Although vantage points in the access ISP (such as in the DSLAM for a DSL ISP) can see all the home traffic, these locations outside the home obscure metrics that can provide important clues about whether the home wireless network is introducing a bottleneck. Inside the home, we can either instrument end-hosts or the access point itself. Client devices can observe wireless properties from their own traffic but may not be able to observe traffic properties of other clients. A device also cannot determine characteristics of the access link. End-host tools such as T-RAT [22] can monitor TCP properties such as congestion window or duplicate ACKs to identify the causes of throughput bottlenecks but cannot isolate the location of congestion.

Our second design choice was to use passive traffic measurements. While active probing may yield useful information about the state of the network, it also carries potential drawbacks. It risks introducing extra load on the network, thereby affecting the conditions that we are trying to measure; it may also disrupt the users who are hosting our measurement devices. Thus, we rely on passive measurements of *in situ* user traffic as the main source of information for detecting performance bottlenecks. We aim to do so without custom wireless drivers or anything that could adversely affect the performance of the networks we are measuring, so we look for features at the IP layer that can indicate performance problems. Possible metrics thus include flow timings and sizes, packet timings and sizes, and information that we can retrieve from TCP headers. We briefly discuss our choices.

2.2   Network Metrics

Packet arrival timings and TCP RTT are promising metrics particularly because our vantage point at the access point allows us to separately compute these

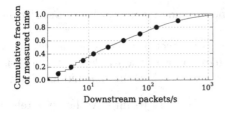
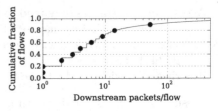

(a) *Cumulative distribution of the number of packets per second in FCC deployment.*

(b) *Cumulative distribution of the number of packets per flow in FCC deployment.*

Fig. 1. Properties of test samples from the FCC deployment

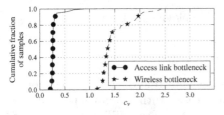
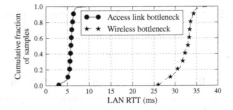

Fig. 2. Coefficient of variation of packet interarrival times. When the access link is a downstream throughput bottleneck, packet arrivals are smooth (*i.e.*, the variance on packet interarrival time is lower).

Fig. 3. TCP RTT between client and access point. When the wireless link is the throughput bottleneck, the TCP RTT between the device and the access point is significantly higher.

metrics for the WAN and LAN portions of the end-to-end path, potentially allowing us to disambiguate problems that occur on either side of the access point.

Packet Interarrival Time. We exploit an observation that is common to many bottleneck links: *packets traversing a bottlenecked link experience buffering immediately upstream of the link; as a result, they experience smoothed arrival patterns downstream of the bottleneck link.* To capture this effect, we use the coefficient of variation of packet interarrival times, c_v, which is the standard deviation of packet interarrival time divided by the mean packet interarrival time. In our example, when the access link is the bottleneck $c_v = 0.05$; whereas when the wireless is the bottleneck c_v is 0.88. In Fig. 2, the "access link bottleneck" curve presents the distribution of c_v for 100 experiments where we introduced a bottleneck at the access link; and the "wireless bottleneck" curve for 100 experiments where the bottleneck was on the wireless. There is no overlap between the two curves: c_v is lower when the access link is the bottleneck versus when it is not.

Wireless Round-Trip Time. The second effect is that devices in home networks are only one hop away from the access point, so the baseline latency between the access point and the device should be a few milliseconds (as we measured in our controlled experiments). We observe that the delays caused by buffering in the wireless network (*i.e.*, those caused by throughput bottlenecks) are significantly higher. We measure this effect by capturing the TCP RTT, τ, between the device and the access point. Figure 3 presents the LAN TCP RTT (the RTT over TCP between the access point and a device in the home network) for two downstream throughput bottleneck scenarios: an access network bottleneck and a wireless bottleneck. In both experiments, we established (through repeated experiments) the wireless network capacity to be about 40 Mbps. In the first case, the access link is 30 Mbps, so it is always the bottleneck. In the second case, the access link is 70 Mbps so that the wireless network becomes the bottleneck. When the access link is the bottleneck, the RTT is about 5 ms. In contrast, when the wireless is the bottleneck, packet buffering at the head of the wireless link (*i.e.*, the access point) increases RTTs to about 25–35 ms.

2.3 Detection Algorithm

For each device, d, we use two independent detectors. One detector uses a decision rule that determines whether an access-link bottleneck event, B, occurs, given a particular observed value of c_v. The other detector uses a decision rule that determines whether a wireless bottleneck event, W, occurs given a particular observed value of τ_d. We first compute likelihood functions $f(c_v|B)$ and $f(c_v|\overline{B})$ in a controlled setting, where we use our ability to control the throughput of the upstream link to introduce a bottleneck on the access link. We then define our decision rule in terms of the likelihood ratio:

$$\Lambda(c_v = v) = \frac{f(c_v = v|B)}{f(c_v = v|\overline{B})}$$

where v is the measured coefficient of variation of packet interarrival time for packets over the observation window. When Λ is greater than some threshold γ, the detector says that the access link is the bottleneck (*i.e.*, it is more likely than not, given the observation of $c_v = v$, that the prior is the event B). We can tune the detector by varying the value of γ; higher values will result in higher detection rates, but also higher false positive rates. We use a similar approach for W. The next section presents our choices of threshold.

We can only perform bottleneck detection if the network is sending enough traffic. We set a minimum number of packets per second, T_{pps}, and a minimum number of packets per flow, T_{pf}, for running HoA. Figure 1 shows the distribution of the number of packets per second and packets per flow observed across homes in the FCC deployment. In approximately 40 % of measured one-second intervals, we observe packet rates of less than 10 packets per second. We also tested T_{pps} values of 50, 100, and 150 packets per second, and T_{pf} values of 25, 50, and 75 packets per flow on real-world deployment data; none of these settings changed our conclusions.

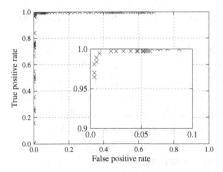 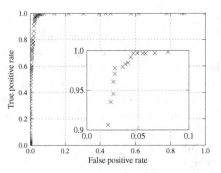

Fig. 4. Receiver operating characteristic for access link bottleneck detection using the coefficient of variation of
packet interarrival time.

Fig. 5. Receiver operating characteristic for wireless bottleneck detection
using the TCP RTT between the access
point and the client.

2.4 Calibration

We built a testbed to run controlled experiments to calibrate detection thresholds. The testbed has an access point, its LAN, a network traffic shaper upstream
of the access point, a well-provisioned university network, and servers in the
university network. The access point is a Netgear WNDR3800 router running
OpenWrt. To change the downstream throughput of the emulated access link,
we use `tc` and `netem` on a second WNDR3800 router running OpenWrt. We
run our tests against servers in the same well-provisioned university network to
avoid potential wide-area bottlenecks. We run two sets of experiments using the
testbed.

We use a traffic shaper to shape the link to different throughput levels while
keeping the wireless link constant. In this case, identifying the ground truth
is straightforward, as we know the capacities of both the wireless link and the
shaped access link. We use 802.11a and 802.11n for the wireless link with respective capacities of 21 Mbps and 80 Mbps over TCP. We generate 1,356 experiments
with 11 different emulated access links, with capacities varying from 3 Mbps to
more than 100 Mbps. To introduce wireless bottlenecks, we conduct two sets of
experiments. (1) Reduce capacity by degrading channel quality: we do this by
positioning the host at different distances from the access point, and with multiple obstructions, and also transient problems by human activity. (2) Reduce
the available capacity of the channel by creating contention with an interfering host that sends constant UDP traffic, with the interfering host close to the
access point. For each setting, we run a TCP throughput test using `iperf`. To
minimize interference that we do not introduce ourselves, we use the 5 GHz
spectrum, which is less congested than the 2.4 GHz range in our testbed. In our
repeated controlled experiments, we found that the wireless channel in our testbed delivers a TCP throughput of about 80 Mbps on 802.11n. We performed
1,356 experiments over many operating conditions.

Because there can only be one throughput bottleneck on an end-to-end path, by definition, the detectors should never detect bottlenecks simultaneously. Using the thresholds that we computed for each detector—as we describe for each case below—simultaneous detection occurs only 2 % of all time intervals, typically in cases where the throughput values for the home wireless network and the access link were similar (Fig. 5).

Packet Interarrival Time (T_{cv})**.** We use the results from the controlled experiments described above to compute the likelihood functions $f(c_v|B)$ and $f(c_v|\overline{B})$ to determine the detection threshold T_{cv}. We first evaluate the detection accuracy of the algorithm for different values of T_{cv}. Figure 4 shows the receiver operating characteristic for this detector. When T_{cv} is low (close to zero), the detector will always determine that the access link is not the bottleneck; when T_{cv} is high (close to one), the detector will always identify the access link as the bottleneck. Our results indicate that detection accuracy remains high for a wide range of threshold settings for T_{cv}, particularly between 0.7 and 0.9. Detection accuracy is very high in this range, with a true positive rate more than 95 % and a false positive rate less than 5 %. The range of good thresholds reinforces our confidence of its robustness as a detection metric. We use a threshold $T_{cv} = 0.8$, which offers the best tradeoff between the true positive and false positive rates, to declare the access link the bottleneck.

Wireless Round-Trip Time (T_τ)**.** We calibrate the thresholds for the likelihood functions $f(\tau_d|W)$ and $f(\tau_d|\overline{W})$ using a similar method. We choose a threshold $T_\tau = 15$ ms, which yields a detection rate of 95 % and a low false positive rate of less than 5 %. Similar to the T_{cv} parameter, T_τ is also robust; we get similarly high true positive rates and low false positive rates for values ranging from 12–17 ms. Higher LAN latencies in the wireless network can result from other wireless problems that may manifest as retransmissions or backoffs. We observe empirically that these wireless issues introduce up to 8–12 ms of delay, whereas delays caused by wireless throughput bottlenecks introduce more than 15 ms of extra delay, thresholds which yield a high detection and low false positive rate in our experiments.

2.5 Limitations

HoA has several limitations. First, because it relies on passive traffic analysis, the link must carry enough traffic to enable analysis. Section 2.3 how we determine minimum thresholds for detection, which are heuristics. Second, constant bit rate traffic could in some cases yield a low cv, thus causing HoA to mistakenly detect a throughput bottleneck on the access link; such cases may need to rely on other detection methods. With respect to bottlenecks, HoA cannot identify the root cause of bottlenecks, and it cannot identify bottlenecks far from the last mile, such as peering or server-side bottlenecks. HoA can only locate throughput bottlenecks where the link is work-conserving; because wireless links violate this assumption, HoA cannot detect upstream throughput bottlenecks.

Additionally, detection thresholds may be sensitive to certain settings and configurations: T_τ may depend on the wireless driver and hardware; in cable access networks, T_{cv} may depend on the channel bonding configuration of the DOCSIS modem. The calibration methods from Sect. 2.4 may help determine the appropriate thresholds in various settings. Finally, to reduce CPU load, HoA collects data periodically, which does not allow us to capture aspects of the network that vary over small timescales.

2.6   Deployments

Table 1 summarizes our two deployments, which we briefly describe below.

Table 1. Deployments of HoA, including locations and study durations. In addition to the larger FCC deployment, we also performed a pilot deployment of HoA on 100 homes in the FCC deployment from August 24–30, 2014.

	BISmark	FCC
Homes	64	2,652
Location	15 Countries	United States
Duration	March 6–April 6, 2013	November 4–5, 2014
Tests	52,252	73,193

BISmark Deployment. We deployed HoA on Netgear's WNDR3700/3800, which has an Atheros chipset with a 450 MHz processor, one 802.11bgn radio, and one 802.11an radio. The 3800 has 128 Mbytes of RAM, and the 3700 has 64 Mbytes of RAM. The devices run OpenWrt, with the ath9k wireless driver. The driver uses the Minstrel rate adaptation algorithm, with the default setting to a maximum bitrate of 130 Mbps. Every 5 min, HoA collects packet traces from the WAN port for 15 s and extracts timestamps and per-flow RTTs on either side of the access point, as well as the number of packets for each connection using tcptrace [21]. tcptrace tracks packets and the corresponding ACKs to compute the RTTs.

FCC Deployment. We use the FCC's deployment of Netgear WNR3500L, which has a Broadcom chipset and a 480 MHz processor, one 802.11bgn radio, and 64 Mbytes of RAM. The devices run a custom Netgear firmware based on OpenWRT. The resource constraints of the WNR3500L required two changes to our implementation. First, we imposed a packet limit and a time limit for every trace collection iteration. The collection runs for 10 s or until it has collected 10,000 packets, whichever comes first. We discard any trace for which the packet filters dropped at least 5 % of packets from our analysis. Additionally, due to resource constraints, we do not perform any processing on the device, except for anonymization. Instead, we offload the packet header traces for offline analysis. To avoid conflicts with FCC's Measuring Broadband America program, we could only perform our measurements three times per hour.

3 Results

This section explores our findings: (1) In home networks where downstream throughput exceeds 20 Mbps, the home wireless network is the primary cause of throughput bottlenecks. (2) Access link bottlenecks are prevalent in home networks where the downstream throughput is less than 10 Mbps. (3) In homes where HoA detects a wireless throughput bottleneck, it is about equally likely that the wireless throughput bottleneck is isolated to a single device or observed across all devices.

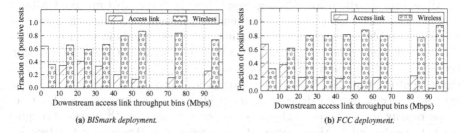

(a) BISmark deployment.   (b) FCC deployment.

Fig. 6. Prevalence of access link and wireless bottlenecks home networks the two deployments deployment. When downstream access-link throughput exceeds about 20 Mbps, only about 20 % of last-mile bottlenecks occur on the access link.

3.1 Prevalence of Last-Mile Bottlenecks

In this section, we explore the prevalence of downstream throughput bottlenecks in access links versus home wireless networks using HoA. Specifically, we study the fraction of tests for which HoA identifies downstream throughput bottlenecks, and to what extent these bottlenecks are caused by the access link versus the home wireless network.

We perform more than 50,000 tests over a wide range operating conditions in the field. HoA identifies downstream throughput bottlenecks in 55 % of tests in the BISmark deployment and 47 % of tests in the FCC deployment. When HoA does not detect a bottleneck, the underlying cause may be low demand or bottlenecks being elsewhere in the network (*e.g.*, at a peering point). As expected, homes with access-link throughput less than 10 Mbps experience the largest fraction of throughput bottlenecks; 55 % of tests detect a bottleneck. The fraction of tests where HoA detects a bottleneck, however, remains close to 40 % even for homes with access-link throughput above 90 Mbps. In the rest of this section, we further characterize the tests where HoA detects a downstream throughput bottleneck.

Figure 6a plots the fraction of downstream throughput bottlenecks in the BISmark deployment that are located either in the access link or in the home wireless network. We group home networks into bins of 10 Mbps according to the measured downstream throughput of their access links. The results show that many throughput bottlenecks in the BISmark deployment are due to the wireless network. Our analysis of the bottlenecks per home in the BISmark deployment shows that the fraction of wireless bottlenecks varies significantly across homes even for homes with similar access-link throughput. For example, homes with access-link throughput less than 20 Mbps had wireless bottlenecks in between 3–58 % of downstream throughput bottlenecks, and 11–83 % of downstream throughput bottlenecks. By default, we configured these home routers to use 802.11n, which can support significantly higher rates. The default 802.11n configuration supports frame rates of up to 130 Mbps (we observed about 85–90 Mbps over TCP), while 802.11 g supports only framerates up to 54 Mbps. The fact that these networks are experiencing throughput bottlenecks suggests persistent problems with home wireless network deployments in practice.

Figure 6b shows the same results for the FCC deployment. First, access-link bottlenecks only occur frequently for home networks with downstream access throughput less than 20 Mbps. Homes with access throughput less than 10 Mbps experience access-link bottlenecks in about 66 % of cases; however this fraction drops rapidly as access throughput increases: for homes with access throughput between 10 and 20 Mbps about 40 % of downstream throughput bottlenecks are due to access-link bottlenecks, whereas for homes with access links exceeding 20 Mbps access-link bottlenecks explain only about 20 % of downstream throughput bottlenecks. Conversely, wireless throughput bottlenecks become more prevalent in homes with higher access throughput: 33 % of downstream throughput bottlenecks for homes with throughput less than 10 Mbps are due to wireless bottlenecks; 40 % of the bottlenecks are in the wireless network for homes with 10–20 Mbps access throughput; and, nearly 80 % of the bottlenecks are in the wireless network when access throughput exceeds 20 Mbps. That wireless throughput bottlenecks occur even for access links with such low speeds is surprising: the FCC access points support 802.11n, with default frame bitrates of up to 130 Mbps and a maximum frame bitrate of 300 Mbps. Some users had configured their routers to 802.11g, and those users did experience lower throughput. Yet, 802.11g comprised only 10 % of all tests, so most of the problems that we observed occurred even with 802.11n.

In about 8 % of downstream throughput bottlenecks in homes with access-link throughput less than 10 Mbps, HoA indicates that both the wireless network and the access link are introducing throughput bottlenecks. In principle, this should not occur as, by definition, there can be only one bottleneck. The prevalence of this result for primarily low-throughput access links suggests that in these cases, at least one device in the home network may be experiencing poor wireless conditions in conjunction with an access-link bottleneck.

3.2   Wireless Bottlenecks Within a Home

The previous section demonstrated that wireless bottlenecks are common; in cases where wireless bottlenecks exist, at least one device in the home experiences a wireless throughput bottleneck during the tests. For about 75 % of tests when HoA detects a wireless bottleneck, we only observe traffic for one device in the home. For the remaining 25 % of tests with a wireless bottleneck, we investigate whether the active devices experience a downstream throughput bottleneck in the wireless network simultaneously. Simultaneous throughput bottlenecks in the wireless network to independent devices might indicate a more systemic problem (e.g., pervasive interference, poor signal from the access point, contention), whereas isolated throughput bottlenecks are more likely to indicate a problem with a particular device. About half of the cases we observed involve throughput bottlenecks that are isolated to a single device; in another 45 % of cases, all of the devices in the home simultaneously experience a throughput bottleneck.

4 Related Work

HoA draws inspiration from several previous diagnosis techniques. Zhang et al. developed T-RAT [22] to analyze TCP performance. T-RAT estimates TCP parameters such as maximum segment size, round-trip time, and loss to understand flow behavior. Katabi et al. [11], used entropy in packet interarrival time to estimate shared bottlenecks. Biaz et al. [3] used packet interarrival times for distinguishing between different kinds of losses. HoA is similar to some of the approaches used in these papers (e.g., it uses packet interarrival time as input to a detector for access link bottlenecks), but we tailor our approach so that it only relies on data that can be easily collected from a home router. Previous work has studied broadband access performance [4,8,9,20]. In particular, Sundaresan et al. [20] study residential access performance from home routers (also using the FCC Broadband America dataset). There have also been many previous approaches to diagnosing wireless networks. One approach is to deploy passive traffic monitors throughout the network to diagnose wireless pathologies [1,2,6,15,16] or to study wireless performance [14]. Kanuparthy et al. [10] developed a tool to detect common wireless pathologies (such as low signal-to-noise ratio, congestion, and hidden terminals) by using both active probes and an additional passive monitor deployed within the network. Kim et al. [12] analyze wireless metrics such as frame bitrates, frame ACKs and retransmission rates to identify root causes of wireless performance problems. Other approaches have monitored wireless networks with custom hardware [5,13,16–18]. Unfortunately, it is difficult to deploy multiple monitoring points or custom hardware in many home networks, since it requires deploying equipment beyond what a normal user is typically willing to install or have installed in their home. Other efforts have characterized home networks in terms of connected devices and usage [7,19]. None of these studies, however, have studied how often the home network constraint downstream throughput.

5 Conclusion

To identify performance bottlenecks in home networks, we developed an algorithm and tool, HoA, that passively observes traffic flows between the home network and the access network to determine the location of last-mile downstream throughput bottlenecks. Our prototype deployment of HoA in 2,652 home networks shed new light on the prevalence of downstream throughput bottlenecks in both home networks and access networks. We find that when the downstream throughput of a user's access link exceeds about 20 Mbps, a high fraction of throughput bottlenecks are caused by the user's home wireless network. This finding is significant in light of recent proposed regulations to change the definition of broadband Internet access to increasingly higher speeds. Our study opens several avenues for future work. First, we need methods to identify root causes that explain *why* various wireless performance problems exist in addition to where they are. Second, a follow-up to HoA could attribute problems that home network users experience to a more complete and more specific set of causes.

Acknowledgments. We thank the FCC and SamKnows for helping us develop and deploy HoA in the Measuring Broadband America (MBA) platform. We also acknowledge the participants of the MBA platform. We would like to thank our shepherd, Mahesh K. Marina, and the reviewers for their helpful comments. This work was supported by NSF awards CNS-1535796, CNS-1539906, and CNS-1213157, and the European Communitys Seventh Framework Programme (FP7/2007–2013) no. 611001 (User-Centric Networking).

References

1. Adya, A., Bahl, P., Chandra, R., Qiu, L.: Architecture and techniques for diagnosing faults in IEEE 802.11 infrastructure networks. In: MobiCom, pp. 30–44, Philadelphia, PA (2004)
2. Ahmed, N., Ismail, U., Keshav, S., Papagiannaki, K.: Online estimation of RF interference. In: ACM CoNEXT, Madrid, Spain, December 2008
3. Biaz, S., Vaidya, N.H.: Discriminating congestion losses from wireless losses using inter-arrival times at the receiver. In: IEEE Symposium on Application - Specific Systems and Software Engineering and Technology (ASSET), Washington, DC, USA (1999)
4. Canadi, I., Barford, P., Sommers, J.: Revisiting broadband performance. In: ACM SIGCOMM Internet Measurement Conference (IMC), October 2012
5. Cheng, Y., Bellardo, J., Benko, P., Snoeren, A.C., Voelker, G.M., Savage, S.: Jigsaw: solving the puzzle of enterprise 802.11 analysis. In: Proceedings of ACM SIGCOMM, Pisa, Italy, August 2006
6. Cheng, Y.C., Afanasyev, M., Verkaik, P., Benkö, P., Chiang, J., Snoeren, A.C., Savage, S., Voelker, G.M.: Automating cross-layer diagnosis of enterprise wireless networks. SIGCOMM Comput. Commun. Rev. **37**(4), 25–36 (2007)
7. Cioccio, L.D., Teixeira, R., Rosenberg, C.: Measuring home networks with HomeNet profiler. In: Roughan, M., Chang, R. (eds.) PAM 2013. LNCS, vol. 7799, pp. 176–186. Springer, Heidelberg (2013)
8. Croce, D., En-Najjary, T., Urvoy-Keller, G., Biersack, E.: Capacity estimation of ADSL links. In: Proceedings of CoNEXT, December 2008
9. Dischinger, M., Haeberlen, A., Gummadi, K.P., Saroiu, S.: Characterizing residential broadband networks. In: Proceedings of ACM SIGCOMM Internet Measurement Conference, San Diego, CA, USA, October 2007

10. Kanuparthy, P., Dovrolis, C., Papagiannaki, K., Seshan, S., Steenkiste, P.: Can user-level probing detect and diagnose common home-WLAN pathologies. SIG-COMM Comput. Commun. Rev. **42**(1), 7–15 (2012)

11. Katabi, D., Blake, C.: Inferring congestion sharing and path characteristics from packet interarrival times. Technical report MIT-LCS-TR-828, Massachusetts Institute of Technology (2002)

12. Kim, K.H., Nam, H., Schulzrinne, H.: WiSlow: a Wi-Fi network performance troubleshooting tool for end users. In: IEEE INFOCOM, pp. 862–870 (2014)

13. Lakshminarayanan, K., Sapra, S., Seshan, S., Steenkiste, P.: RFdump: an architecture for monitoring the wireless ether. In: Proceedings of the 5th International Conference on Emerging Networking Experiments and Technologies, CoNEXT 2009, pp. 253–264 (2009)

14. Mahajan, R., Rodrig, M., Wetherall, D., Zahorjan, J.: Analyzing the mac-level behavior of wireless networks in the wild. In: SIGCOMM 2006, pp. 75–86 (2006)

15. Niculescu, D.: Interference map for 802.11 networks. In: ACM SIGCOMM Internet Measurement Conference, pp. 339–350, San Diego, California, USA, October 2007

16. Rayanchu, S., Mishra, A., Agrawal, D., Saha, S., Banerjee, S.: Diagnosing wireless packet losses in 802.11: separating collision from weak signal. In: INFOCOM 2008, The 27th Conference on Computer Communications, April 2008, pp. 735–743. IEEE (2008)

17. Rayanchu, S., Patro, A., Banerjee, S.: Catching whales and minnows using WiFiNet: deconstructing non-WiFi interference using wifi hardware. In: USENIX NSDI, San Jose, CA

18. Rayanchu, S., Patro, A., Banerjee, S.: Airshark: detecting non-WiFi RF devices using commodity wifi hardware. In: ACM SIGCOMM Internet Measurement Conference, pp. 137–154, Berlin, Germany (2011)

19. Sánchez, M.A., Otto, J.S., Bischof, Z.S., Bustamante, F.E.: Trying broadband characterization at home. In: Roughan, M., Chang, R. (eds.) PAM 2013. LNCS, vol. 7799, pp. 198–207. Springer, Heidelberg (2013)

20. Sundaresan, S., de Donato, W., Feamster, N., Teixeira, R., Crawford, S., Pescapè, A.: Broadband internet performance: a view from the gateway. In: ACM SIGCOMM, Toronto, Ontario, Canada, August 2011

21. tcptrace: A TCP connection analysis tool. http://irg.cs.ohiou.edu/software/tcptrace/

22. Zhang, Y., Breslau, L., Paxson, V., Shenker, S.: On the characteristics and origins of internet flow rates. In: Proceedings of ACM SIGCOMM, Pittsburgh, PA, August 2002

A Case Study of Traffic Demand Response to Broadband Service-Plan Upgrades

Sarthak Grover[✉], Roya Ensafi, and Nick Feamster

Department of Computer Science, Princeton University, Princeton, USA
{sgrover,rensafi,feamster}@cs.princeton.edu

Abstract. Internet service providers are facing mounting pressure from regulatory agencies to increase the speed of their service offerings to consumers; some are beginning to deploy gigabit-per-second speeds in certain markets, as well. The race to deploy increasingly faster speeds begs the question of whether users are exhausting the capacity that is already available. Previous work has shown that users who are already maximizing their usage on a given access link will continue to do so when they are migrated to a higher service tier.

In a unique controlled experiment involving thousands of Comcast subscribers in the same city, we analyzed usage patterns of two groups: a control group (105 Mbps) and a randomly selected treatment group that was upgraded to 250 Mbps without their knowledge. We study how users who are already on service plans with high downstream throughput respond when they are upgraded to a higher service tier without their knowledge, as compared to a similar control group. To our surprise, the difference between traffic demands between both groups is higher for subscribers with moderate traffic demands, as compared to high-volume subscribers. We speculate that even though these users may not take advantage of the full available capacity, the service-tier increase generally improves performance, which causes them to use the Internet more than they otherwise would have.

1 Introduction

With the large impact of broadband Internet on our daily lives and its rapid increase in bandwidth-intensive services, policymakers and service providers (ISPs) are trying to determine how much bandwidth consumers need. With the proliferation of high quality video content, and the recent boom in Internet-enabled consumer device, it is worth studying—and continually re-evaluating—whether (and how) users consume the capacity that ISPs offer. Up to a certain point, users will exhaust available capacity, and they will also adapt when more capacity becomes available; this increased demand in turn drives provisioning. Above certain speeds, however, the typical user no longer exhausts the available capacity. At what speed does this inflection point occur? How do users adapt their demands when an ISP offers faster speed tiers? Answers to these questions will ultimately help inform policymakers and ISPs determine how to make investments in infrastructure, and when to make them.

T. Karagiannis and X. Dimitropoulos (Eds.): PAM 2016, LNCS 9631, pp. 124–135, 2016.
DOI: 10.1007/978-3-319-30505-9_10

In the United States, the Federal Communications Commission (FCC) is interested in the relationship between demand and capacity for several reasons. First, the FCC recognizes the need to define broadband benchmarks based on traffic demand and is considering doing so [9]. It has defined a "typical" household traffic demand to enable concurrent broadband use, such as video streaming, web browsing, and VoIP. The FCC has also asked for comments and suggestions on how to define such a demand-based benchmark for future planning [7,8]. Second, recent research shows that diurnal Internet usage patterns are correlated with GDP, Internet allocations, and the electrical consumption of a region [11], which makes the study of usage potentially relevant to the regulatory bodies responsible for development. Finally, the FCC is responsible for increasing broadband deployment throughout the US, and it recently decided to aggressively increase the broadband threshold benchmark to 25 Mbps downstream and 3 Mbps upstream. Yet, a survey conducted by NCTA (for the FCC) showed that the largest deterrent to deployment of faster speed tiers is that consumers do not *want* the faster speeds (the second largest deterrent is the price) [8]. Clearly, this question deserves both rigorous and continuous study.

Previous work discovered that users who are already maximizing their usage on a given access link will continue to do so when they are migrated to a higher service tier [1]. In this paper, we study how the traffic demands of subscribers who are *already* on service plans with high downstream throughput respond to an undisclosed service plan upgrade as part of a randomized control trial (RCT). This experiment offers the unique opportunity to explore the effects of a service-tier upgrade on user traffic demand, while mitigating the cognitive bias of the service-tier upgrade by withholding that information from subscribers. To the best of our knowledge, this is the first such comparative study of usage behavior in a controlled experiment to study responses to service upgrades.

Our study is based on data from the residential home gateways of Comcast subscribers in Salt Lake City, Utah. To measure traffic demand, Comcast collects aggregate byte counts every 15 min from two types of users: *control*, or users who pay and use a high capacity access link (105 Mbps); and *treatment*, or users who pay for 105 Mbps but were actually offered a 250 Mbps access link *without their knowledge*. We evaluate three months of traffic demand for more than 6,000 Comcast subscribers, 1,519 of whom were in the treatment group. We find that subscribers who are already using most of their available capacity at the 105 Mbps and the 250 Mbps service tiers do not show a significant difference in traffic demand. On the other hand, subscribers who exhibit moderate traffic demands in the both groups often exhibit a large relative difference in their traffic demands. This result suggests that even users who are not fully exhausting the available capacity at one service tier may increase usage at higher service tiers, perhaps because the improved performance at the higher tier may cause these subscribers to use the Internet more than they otherwise would. We also observed that the most significant difference in per-subscriber traffic demand occurred during non-prime-time hours on weekdays, suggesting that this demographic of consumer may disproportionately include users who work from home. Such a phenomenon is also consistent with our observation that traffic demands at these higher service tiers consistently rises throughout the course of the day, with no mid-afternoon drop in traffic volume, as is evident in other studies.

The rest of the paper is organized as follows. In Sect. 2 we overview some previous studies of traffic demand and service capacity. In Sect. 3, we offer details about our data, sanitization, and characterization. We then proceed by describing our evaluation criteria and analyze traffic demand in response to a service tier upgrade in Sect. 4. We summarize our findings in Sect. 5.

2   Related Work

The measurement community has produced a plethora of studies of broadband performance analysis, yet has performed relatively fewer studies of traffic demand in broadband access networks. The increasing availability of high-bandwidth Internet services and the FCC's recent interest in exploring traffic demand as a broadband benchmark [8] now calls for increased attention to the relationship between user traffic demand and broadband capacity.

Our work complements an earlier study by Bischof et al. [1], who used *natural* experiments to investigate causal relationships between the traffic demand (which they refer to as "user demand", or "usage" in their paper) and factors such as service capacity, performance, and price. Bischof et al. showed that demand increases with capacity, but "follows a law of diminishing returns"; in other words, increases in capacity for an already high tier results in a lower increase in demand. Our work presents complementary results from a large-scale *controlled* experiment and examines in particular a high service tier (105 Mbps) that has not been studied before. Our dataset mitigates the affect of price, performance, and other potential biases (such as regional [2,4], capped usage [3], and "geek-effect" [1]) by limiting the dataset to a large number of users selected randomly from the same service tier and location.

Zheleva et al. present a case study of the effects of an Internet service upgrade, from 256 kbps satellite to 2 Mbps terrestrial wireless, in rural Zambia [15]. This work observed that the stark change in traffic demand three months after the upgrade caused a performance bottleneck. In contrast, our case study focuses on traffic demands of subscribers from much higher service tiers who are not continuously bottlenecked by their access link; additionally, we study how users adjust their traffic demands without informing them of the upgrade, thus eliminating potential cognitive bias.

Other efforts such as [10,12] study the characteristics of residential broadband, and report the contributions of the most popular web applications to the total usage. The bi-annual Sandvine reports [13,14] provide an overview of overall Internet traffic demand from fixed lines and mobile carriers as well as an updated analysis of the most popular Internet applications. They showed that video accounts for 63 % of traffic usage overall, and traffic demand peaks during the peak evening hours, possibly due to increasing video content consumption. Our work does not concern with the applications responsible for most traffic, but only with the peak period during which an individual subscriber's traffic demand is high.

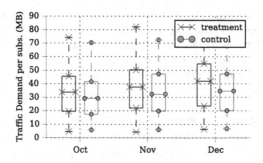

Fig. 1. Distribution of downstream demand averaged across subscribers in the *control* and *treatment* groups from October through December 2014.

3 Method and Data

We describe the design of our randomized control experiment and the dataset that we used for this experiment.

3.1 Method

In designing our controlled experiment, we follow the popular statistical convention of experimental designers to refer to the service upgrade as *factor*, the group of users without the upgrade as *control* and the upgraded users as *treatment* [5].

Controlled experiments are difficult to do on the Internet scale. Our work involves a randomized control experiment on the scale of a large urban city. This enables us to study the effect of just one factor, *the service plan upgrade*, while other factors, such as price, performance, or regional differences between users, are controlled. We believe the effects observed on this dataset will also be observed in others collected from urban cities and high tiers.

By examining a single ISP's high-capacity tier with an unannounced upgrade, our dataset mitigates several biases that previous studies may have suffered. Studying the behavior of users who opt for buying a higher service plan (unsatisfied subscribers) will naturally show an increase in demand on upgrading service [1]. Similarly users who have been offered an upgrade in service may change their behavior to utilize the upgraded capacity (cognitive bias) [15]. Studying datasets with these biases are prone to positive high correlation between demand and capacity.

3.2 Data

Our raw dataset consists of network usage byte counters reported every 15 min from October 1, 2014 to December 29, 2014 from about 20,000 Comcast residential broadband gateways in Salt Lake City, Utah. Each dataset contains the following fields: Device ID (household identifier), the 15-min time interval

Table 1. Overview of the *control* (4,845 subscribers) and *treatment* (1,519 subscribers) datasets for upstream and downstream traffic. The 95 percentile traffic is the peak of total demand. PT traffic is the average traffic demand per hour during prime-time hours. We normalize traffic for both groups to 1,000 subscribers for comparison. The daily demand is the average traffic demand per subscriber over a single day. All values are in gigabytes (GB).

Dataset	Hourly traffic per 1,000 subscribers (GB)				Per subscriber
	Total	95 % Traffic	PT	Non-PT	Daily demand (GB)
Control down	2.67×10^5	234.5	205.1	108.5	2.97
Treatment down	2.95×10^5	244.42	209.5	122.3	3.30
Control up	2.98×10^4	21.39	18.942	12.80	0.33
Treatment up	4.27×10^4	31.48	22.81	19.02	0.48

(end time), service direction ({downstream, upstream}), anonymized IP address, and the bytes transferred in each 15-min interval.

The data consisted of two groups: a *control* set, consisting of 18,354 households with a 105 Mbps access link; and a *treatment* set, consisting of 2,219 households that were paying for a 105 Mbps access link, yet were receiving 250 Mbps instead. Subscribers in the treatment group were selected randomly and were not told that their access bandwidth had been increased for the three months of our analysis. Our initial analysis of the data from more than 20,573 households showed that not all gateways were reporting their traffic counters every 15 min over the whole three-month period: 32 % of the *treatment* dataset and 72 % of the *control* dataset gateway devices were responsive less than 80 % of the time throughout the measurement period. For the analysis in Sect. 4, we present results based on the accepted group of subscribers that contributed to the three-month dataset more than 80 % during their lifetime. Our ultimate dataset consists of 4,845 subscribers in the *control* dataset and 1,519 subscribers in the *treatment* dataset.

Figure 1 shows the distribution of downstream traffic demand, averaged across subscribers (average bytes per 15-min sample period), for the three months in our measurement period for both groups. Table 1 compares the total demand for subscribers in the *control* and *treatment* datasets, scaled to a thousand households. The downlink 95th percentile traffic demand over an hour is 234.5 GB for the lower tier control group, and 244.42 GB for the higher tier treatment group. Table 1 also shows that an average subscriber in the control group would download 2.97 GB in a day, and 3.30 GB if they belonged to the treatment group. As for the uplink, an average subscriber would transfer 0.33 GB over a day in the control group, and 0.48 GB over a day in the treatment group.

4   Results

Table 2 shows the metrics that we use to evaluate how user demand responds to service-tier upgrades. The *traffic demand* for a subscriber is defined as the total bytes transferred, in upstream or downstream, during a single sample measurement (15 min). We use traffic demand to calculate the total demand per hour, and the average and 95th percentile peak demand over a day. To compare the total traffic of the control and treatment groups, we scale to a thousand subscribers wherever applicable. We define *prime time* as 8:00 p.m. to 12:00 a.m., when Internet usage tends to be highest. Indeed, we observed that the total daily traffic consistently falls within 90th percentile during this four-hour period. We define the *prime-time ratio* as the ratio of traffic during an average prime-time hour, to the average hourly traffic outside the prime-time hour. This ratio conveys the disparity between demand during the prime-time and the rest of the day. The rest of this section explores the effects of a service-tier upgrade on user traffic demand in the context of these metrics.

Table 2. Evaluation metrics

Parameter	Definition
Traffic Demand per Subscriber (Sect. 4.1)	$\dfrac{\text{total bytes transferred in measurement int.}}{\text{number of contributing subscribers}}$
Peak Demand (Sect. 4.1)	Daily 95th percentile of bytes transferred in any 15-min interval
Prime-Time Ratio (Sect. 4.2)	$\dfrac{\text{avg usage in peak (prime-time) hour}}{\text{avg usage in off-peak hour}}$
Peak-to-Average Ratio (Sect. 4.3)	$\dfrac{95\text{ \%-ile of daily traffic demand}}{\text{mean of daily traffic demand}}$

4.1   Traffic Demand Per Subscriber

We first explore how an upgrade to a higher service tier affected the average traffic demand per subscriber, for different times of the day and days of the week. Figure 2 shows the average downlink traffic demand across subscribers for a week, for both the treatment and control groups. We observe that subscriber behavior differs significantly on weekdays and weekends. The average per-subscriber demand over a weekday is 35.6 MB, and the 95th percentile peak demand is 61.12 MB for subscribers in the treatment group (Table 3). Over a weekend, the average demand is 40.1 MB, and the 95th percentile demand is 64.3 MB for treatment, but the median is 45.27 MB due to consistent use in the major part of the day. On weekdays, traffic demand increases monotonically from morning until prime-time hours in the evening. On weekends, we observed a sharp rise in demand in the early morning period, from 8:00 a.m. to 10:00 a.m. Then, the demand plateaued until the next rise before evening prime-time hours.

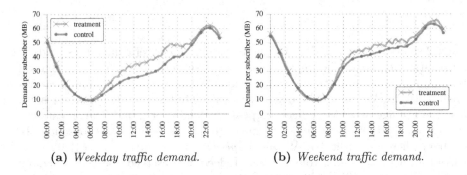

(a) *Weekday traffic demand.*   (b) *Weekend traffic demand.*

Fig. 2. Mean subscriber demand (bytes per 15-min interval).

Table 3. Weekday and weekend traffic demands (MB) per measurement window.

		Median	Mean	95 %
Weekday	Treatment	35.97	35.58	61.12
	control	28.06	31.12	58.78
Weekend	Treatment	45.27	40.10	64.27
	Control	41.15	37.66	62.23

Previous reports indicate that the aggregate traffic volume for US fixed access link providers usually troughs during mid-afternoon hours (between 2:00 p.m.– 6:00 p.m.) [13]. In contrast to these previous reports, we do not observe such troughs in subscriber demand.

Figure 3a shows the distribution of the 95th percentile downlink traffic demand over the three-month measurement period. The highest peak demand per 15-min interval amongst subscribers in the control group was 2.97 GB; in the treatment group, the highest peak demand was 3.0 GB. The average peak traffic demand was 169.8 MB for control and 186.6 MB for treatment. Given the 105 Mbps service-tier capacity, this means that users rarely utilize their links, even on averaging the 95th percentile demand (average utilization was 1.43 % for control and 1.5 % for treatment).

We suspected that the subscribers who downloaded most bytes in the higher service tier would be the ones causing the largest difference in mean demand, as previous studies have observed such a phenomenon. In fact, we observed that the more moderate (median) subscribers actually seemed to exhibit larger differences in traffic demand: The median peak demand was 66.7 MB for the lower service tier, and 98.4 MB for the higher tier. This result indicates that the more moderate subscribers who received a service-tier upgrade exhibit significantly higher peak demand than comparable users in the control group.

We also observed a significant difference in the mean peak demand was present in the 50 % of subscribers in the control group with the lowest traffic demand when compared to the same set of subscribers of the treatment group. (This disparity appears as a large gap under the 50 % tick in Fig. 3a.)

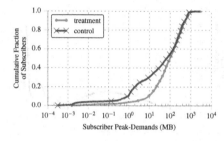 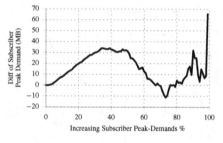

(a) *Peak (95%) traffic demand per sub-* (b) *Change in overall peak (95%) demand*
scriber. *per subscriber.*

Fig. 3. 95th percentile traffic demand (bytes per 15 min) per subscriber for the control
and treatment groups over the three-month measurement period. Subscribers were
considered at every 5 % in each group. The y-axis units are bytes transferred in the
peak 15-min interval, in MB.

Figure 3b shows another way of looking at this phenomenon: it explores the
difference between the distribution of users with particular traffic demands in the
control and treatment groups. For each group, we sort the subscribers according
to increasing demand. Then we compute the difference in peak demand for each
percentile in the group. For example, the plot shows the median user (50 % on the
x-axis) increased their peak demand by about 25 % in response to the service tier
upgrade. Comparing the 70 % subscribers of both groups with the least demand,
we see that peak demand in the treatment group is higher than the peak demand
in the control group, indicating that in fact even moderate users may increase their
demand as a result of the service-tier increase, even though they are not using the
full capacity in either case. When we combine this analysis with that in Fig. 3a, we
find that these subscribers who respond with increased usage have a peak demand
less than 200 MB. Naturally, the small number of users with the highest demand
(closer to 100 %) also show a substantially larger usage for the higher service-tier.

Further investigation revealed that users with moderate peak traffic demands
not only exhibit a large difference in their traffic demands in aggregate, but also
on a daily basis. Figure 4 shows that when subscribers on the lower tier had a
daily peak demand under 600 MB, 70 % of subscribers in the treatment group
had 15-min demands that were 5–20 MB higher. The ratio of the differences in
demand across percentiles also shows that the 40 % of subscribers with lowest
peak demands in the treatment group demonstrate more than double the daily
peak traffic demand of comparable users in the control group.

One possible explanation for why moderate users might increase their usage
in response to a service-tier upgrade is that the higher service tier not only
affords more capacity, but also a better user experience (*e.g.*, faster downloads).
Thus, even though users may not be exhausting the capacity of the higher service
tier, they nonetheless seem to respond to the service tier upgrade by using the
Internet more than they had before the service-tier upgrade.

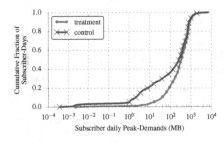 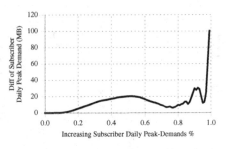

(a) *Daily peak (95%) traffic demand per subscriber.* (b) *Change in daily peak (95%) demand per subscriber.*

Fig. 4. 95th percentile traffic demand (bytes per 15 min) per day per subscriber for the control and treatment groups. Subscribers were considered at every 5 % in each group. y-axis units are bytes transferred in the peak 15-min interval, in MB.

4.2 Prime-Time Ratio

ISPs design networks to handle peak demand, which is usually observed during prime-time hours, when subscribers heavily consume real-time entertainment traffic, such as video. The FCC defines prime-time as the local time from 7:00–11:00 p.m. [6]. To measure the concentration of network usage during prime-time, we use Sandvine's definition of the *prime-time ratio*: the ratio of the average (hourly) traffic demand during prime-time hours to the average demand in non-prime-time hours [13,14]. We measured the prime-time ratio of the subscribers in the control and treatment groups considering each contiguous four-hour period in each day. Our experiment shows that, in fact, the evening hours with the largest prime-time ratio are 8:00 p.m.–12:00 a.m., so we use this time interval for our definition of prime time.

Table 1 shows that the average hourly prime-time downstream traffic per 1,000 subscribers is 209.5 GB for the treatment group, compared to 205.1 GB for the control group, which is about a 2 % difference. In contrast, during an average hour *outside* of prime time, the traffic per 1,000 subscribers is 122.3 GB for the treatment group, compared to 108.5 GB for the control group, amounting to about a 12 % difference. The more significant difference in demand during hours outside of the daily prime-time is also apparent from the weekly usage patterns in Fig. 2.

Table 4. Hourly traffic demand during (and outside) prime-time hours per subscriber, in MB. Prime-time traffic demand is defined as the average traffic demand during a prime-time hour.

		Hourly traffic in PT	Hourly traffic in Non-PT	Prime-time Ratio
Weekday	Treatment	233.12	124.18	1.88
	Control	225.40	104.30	2.16
Weekend	Treatment	246.93	143.08	1.73
	Control	238.15	133.16	1.79

We also calculated the prime-time ratio per day over weekends and weekdays, as shown in Table 4. On weekends, the prime-time ratios for the treatment and control groups are 1.73 and 1.79 respectively. On the weekdays, the prime-time ratio for the control group is 2.16 compared to 1.88 for the treatment group. In terms of absolute demand, the prime-time demand on weekdays in the treatment group is within 4 % of that in the control group. In contrast, the demand in *non-prime-time hours* is 19 % higher for the treatment group on weekdays, and only 7.5 % higher on weekends. The large difference in non-prime-time demand between the control and treatment groups on weekdays suggests that many of the users in the treatment group may in fact be subscribers who work from home may adjust their behavior during non-prime-time hours and weekdays in response to a higher service tier.

Although 6 % of the subscribers in both groups had a prime-time ratio over 100, we also observed that 9 % of the control group and 14 % of the treatment group had prime-time ratios *less than one*, indicating that these users actually had higher demand during the day than they did during prime time. Similarly, these users may be small home businesses or subscribers who work at home.

4.3 Peak-to-Average Ratio

In addition to examining traffic demands across the entire four-hour prime-time window, we also explored how subscribers in the treatment group exhibited different behavior for the 15-min interval of highest (95th percentile) demand in a day, regardless of prime-time hours. We measure the disparity between a subscriber's daily 95th percentile and the mean usage as the *peak-to-average ratio* (PAR). This standard metric shows the ratio of peak values to the effective value and extends those used in conventional studies of user traffic patterns, such as the Sandvine's peak traffic analysis [13].

Figure 5 shows the PAR for each subscriber in the treatment and control groups. The median PAR for subscribers from the treatment group is 4.64, compared to 4.51 for the control group. We found that 40 % of the subscribers in

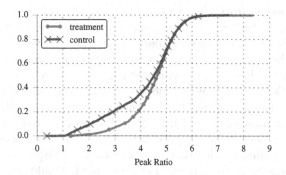

Fig. 5. Distribution of the daily peak-to-average ratio per subscriber, averaged for each subscriber over the measurement period in the treatment and control groups.

both groups have PAR greater than five; the PAR of subscribers in the treatment group is higher than those in the control group, perhaps indicating that users in both higher service tiers do in fact use the additional capacity for short periods of time. The notable difference occurs for peak-to-average ratios of less-than 5: as we observed in Sect. 4.1, subscribers with more moderate (median) traffic demands tend to increase their peak demand more in response to the increased service tier. Again, we believe these trends appear not because users are necessarily eager to fill the additional capacity of a higher service tier, but rather may be occurring because the upgrade results in better performance, and that this improved user experience in turn causes these subscribers to make more use of the Internet.

The lower prime-time ratio by volume, and a consistently higher peak-to-average ratio per subscriber indicates the following: subscribers in the treatment group have higher peak-to-average ratio than those in the control group. However, these subscribers tend to still have low absolute demand, so the relatively higher PAR for the treatment group does not significantly affect total traffic during prime-time and, when it is high, the demand tends to be in non-prime-time hours. Consistent with the results in Sect. 4.2, we also found that on weekdays, the peak-to-average ratios in the treatment group are higher than the control group, whereas on weekends peak-to-average ratios for both the control and treatment groups are similar.

5   Conclusion

In this paper, we study how subscribers respond to an increase in their ISP's service tier. To do so, we use a randomized control trial to compare per-subscriber traffic volumes between two groups of Comcast subscribers in the same city during the same time period: a control group, with Comcast's 105 Mbps service offering; and a treatment group of subscribers who were upgraded to the 250 Mbps service tier without their knowledge. We observed that subscribers with more moderate traffic demands exhibit a relatively higher usage for the upgraded service-tier as compared to subscribers who were already sending relatively high traffic volumes in both groups.

Initially, we were surprised by this result: after all, both intuition and previous work suggest that when users experience service-tier upgrades, they immediately exhaust the available capacity (particularly the high-volume subscribers). At higher tiers, however, we observe a completely different phenomenon: in general, users are not exhausting the available capacity, but a service tier upgrade may simply result in a better user experience that causes subscribers with more moderate traffic demands to use the Internet more than they otherwise would. The fact that the most significant difference that we observed between the two service-tier groups occurred during non-prime-time hours on weekdays also suggests that these higher service tiers may generally be disproportionately used by subscribers who work from home. Future research should aim to repeat our experiment for different cohorts (*i.e.*, different subscribers, geographies, service tiers, and ISPs), and could also strive to obtain more fine-grained traffic statistics to explore exactly which applications are responsible for the behavioral changes that we have observed.

Acknowledgments. This research was supported by the Comcast Tech Research Fund and by NSF Awards CNS-1539902 and CNS-1540066. We thank Jason Livingood and James Moon from Comcast for helpful discussions and access to the data that we used for this study.

References

1. Bischof, Z.S., Bustamante, F.E., Stanojevic, R.: Need, want, can afford: broadband markets and the behavior of users. In: Proceedings of the Conference on Internet Measurement Conference, IMC 2014, pp. 73–86. ACM, New York (2014)
2. Cardona, J.C., Stanojevic, R., Cuevas, R.: On weather and internet traffic demand. In: Roughan, M., Chang, R. (eds.) PAM 2013. LNCS, vol. 7799, pp. 260–263. Springer, Heidelberg (2013)
3. Chetty, M., Banks, R., Brush, A., Donner, J., Grinter, R.: You're capped: understanding the effects of bandwidth caps on broadband use in the home. In: Proceedings of the SIGCHI Conference on Human Factors in Computing Systems, CHI 2012, pp. 3021–3030. ACM, New York (2012)
4. Cho, K., Fukuda, K., Esaki, H., Kato, A.: The impact and implications of the growth in residential user-to-user traffic. In: Proceedings of the Conference on Applications, Technologies, Architectures, and Protocols for Computer Communications, SIGCOMM 2006, pp. 207–218. ACM, New York (2006)
5. Easton, V., McColl, J.: Statistics Glossary. STEPS (1997)
6. Federal Communications Commission. Measuring Broadband America - 2014, April 2014
7. Federal Communications Commission: Tenth Broadband Progress Report No 14-113, February 2014
8. Federal Communications Commission. Eleventh Broadband Progress Report No 15-10A1, February 2015
9. Federal Communications Commission. International Broadband Data Report (Fourth), February 2015
10. Grover, S., Park, M.S., Sundaresan, S., Burnett, S., Kim, H., Ravi, B., Feamster, N.: Peeking behind the nat: an empirical study of home networks. In: Proceedings of the Conference on Internet Measurement Conference, IMC 2013, pp. 377–390. ACM, New York (2013)
11. Quan, L., Heidemann, J., Pradkin, Y.: ANT Evaluation of the Diurnal Internet, October 2014
12. Maier, G., Feldmann, A., Paxson, V., Allman, M.: On dominant characteristics of residential broadband internet traffic. In: Proceedings of the 9th ACM SIGCOMM Conference on Internet Measurement Conference, IMC 2009, pp. 90–102. ACM, New York (2009)
13. Sandvine. Global Internet Phenomena Report - 1H, April 2014
14. Sandvine. Global Internet Phenomena Report - 2H, November 2014
15. Zheleva, M., Schmitt, P., Vigil, M., Belding, E.: The increased bandwidth fallacy: performance and usage in rural zambia. In: Annual Symposium on Computing for Development (DEV) (2013)

eXploring Xfinity

A First Look at Provider-Enabled Community Networks

Dipendra K. Jha, John P. Rula, and Fabián E. Bustamante[✉]

Northwestern University, Evanston, IL, USA
fabianb@eecs.northwestern.edu

Abstract. Several broadband providers have been offering community WiFi as an additional service for existing customers and paid subscribers. These community networks provide Internet connectivity on the go for mobile devices and a path to offload cellular traffic. Rather than deploying new infrastructure or relying on the resources of an organized community, these provider-enabled community WiFi services leverage the existing hardware and connections of their customers. The past few years have seen a significant growth in their popularity and coverage and some municipalities and institutions have started to consider them as the basis for public Internet access.

In this paper, we present the first characterization of one such service – the Xfinity Community WiFi network. Taking the perspectives of the home-router owner and the public hotspot user, we characterize the performance and availability of this service in urban and suburban settings, at different times, between September, 2014 and 2015. Our results highlight the challenges of providing these services in urban environments considering the tensions between coverage and interference, large obstructions and high population densities. Through a series of controlled experiments, we measure the impact to hosting customers, finding that in certain cases, the use of the public hotspot can degrade host network throughput by up-to 67 % under high traffic on the public hotspot.

1 Introduction

The impressive growth in the number of mobile devices and our dependance on them and the services they support have created a high demand for Internet connectivity on the go. Several large network providers including Comcast, Time Warner, British Telecom (UK), and Orange (France) have started addressing such demand by deploying millions of WiFi hotspots around the globe, as a free service to existing customers or as an additional source of revenue.

Rather than deploying new infrastructure or relying on the resources of an organized community [8], these provider-enabled community WiFi services leverage the existing hardware and connections of their customers for coverage. In these networks, residential and commercial customers' access points broadcast an additional public hotspot SSID to bootstrap coverage of the community WiFi network. Despite their rapid growth and extensive media coverage, we lack an

© Springer International Publishing Switzerland 2016
T. Karagiannis and X. Dimitropoulos (Eds.): PAM 2016, LNCS 9631, pp. 136–148, 2016.
DOI: 10.1007/978-3-319-30505-9_11

understanding of the effective value of these community network service for consumers, and the impact - if any - of their use on the residential customers they rely upon.

In this paper, we present the first characterization of a provider-enabled community WiFi network, focusing on the Xfinity Community WiFi. Xfinity WiFi is the largest of such networks available in the U.S. with over 10 million devices in July 2015 [24]. Taking the perspectives of both the home router owner and the public hotspot user, we characterize the coverage, availability, and performance of this service under various geographic and temporal contexts, over three weeks in 2014 and six weeks in 2015. We performed controlled experiments to measure the impact of concurrent access of both the home network and the public Xfinity WiFi hotspot. Our results highlight the challenges of providing these community WiFi services in urban and suburban settings considering the tensions between coverage and interference in high population densities.

Key Findings. First, we found significant growth in the Xfinity WiFi network in all areas measured during the period of our study. Much of this growth was in the number of from access points starting to broadcast in the 5 GHz band, particular in our urban environment where 45 % of access points use 5 GHz (compared to only 15 % in the measured suburban one). Second, despite the higher number of Xfinity WiFi access points, we found it challenging connecting to these access points for Internet connectivity. After examining the signal strength and interference in each environment, we found much lower signal strength and higher interference levels in our urban setting measurements, compared with the suburban ones, which partially explain the observed differences in connectivity and performance. Last, we found significant performance degradation of the hosting customer's home network with throughput reaching to half of the maximum attainable throughput for 4 Mbps traffic on public WiFi. This appear to be caused not by the additional traffic on the link, but rather because of the competition with the hosted public WiFi hotspot network for same radio device and spectrum.

2   Community Wifi Networks

There has been a growing interest in providing public WiFi access from the private sector, civil organizations and end users. As a notable example, the Electronic Frontier Foundation is one of the many sponsors of the Open Wireless Movement [13], aimed at creating a network of volunteer-supported free and open wireless Internet. Several router manufacturers are equipping routers with additional "Guest" WiFi access point, allowing public access while isolating public from home traffic. As another example, FON offers access to a virtually global WiFi network of "foneros" that support guest users in exchange for free roaming and/or revenue from paid users [15].

Several municipalities around the world, sometimes in cooperation with the private sector, have also begun providing free or fee-based access to city-wide wireless networks. Chicago is coming up with the Chicago Tech Plan to build a model for cities and technology for smart communities [22]. Other examples include early efforts such as the MIT RoofNet [4] and MadMesh [9], and the Google's public Wifi in Palo Alto, CA.

Recently, Internet service providers such as AT&T, Comcast, Time Warner, British Telecom (UK) and Orange (France) have also started to offer public WiFi hotspots for their existing customers. In the case of AT&T, for example, both existing cellular and broadband customers have access to a nationwide network of WiFi hotspots, labeled `attwifi`, located at AT&T retail locations, as well as partnered businesses.

2.1   Xfinity WiFi - a Provider-Enabled Community WiFi

On June 10th, 2013, Comcast announced its plans to create millions of WiFi AP available to its customers through a neighborhood hotspot initiative [10]. The company started to enable a second *xfinitywifi* SSID broadcast in their existing customer gateways to act as a publicly accessible hotspot. The uniqueness of this model comes from its customer-supported-and-provider-enabled approach, what we call *provider-enabled community WiFi*, that allowed Comcast to bootstrap hotspot coverage by leveraging the provided routers of existing commercial and residential customers.

Since then the service has grown to include over 10 million public hotspots in the US [24]. All Comcast users with XFINITY Internet Performance tier and above can connect to these hotspots for free[1], while non-Comcast customers can purchase an XFINITY WiFi Access Pass with different hourly, daily and weekly durations [11].

3   Characterization of Xfinity WiFi Network

To understand the challenges of providing community WiFi services in urban environments, we conducted a series of experiments in Chicago's central business district (*The Loop*) and in Evanston, one of its northern suburbs. We designed our experiments to capture the experience of public users, taking measurements from public areas surrounding Xfinity WiFi access points. In the following paragraphs, we use results from a series of such experiments conducted over the course of a year to discuss (*i*) the coverage of Xfinity WiFi, (*ii*) its availability as a usable Internet connection, and (*iii*) its performance to users. Motivated by the comparable poor connectivity and performance we observed in urban Chicago, we investigate possible causes including radio interference and signal strengths of deployed access points.

3.1   Data and Methodology

We measured the coverage, availability and performance of Xfinity WiFi using an instrumented Samsung Galaxy S4 to continuously scan for available APs,

---

[1] Before connecting, a Comcast user must be authenticated through an HTML form with their subscription credentials.

recording their signal strength, BSSIDs and channel, along with the device's current GPS location. When an available `xfinitywifi` SSID was found, the tool attempts to connect to the one with the strongest received signal strength (RSSI), and upon successful association and authentication, conducts network performance measurements using the Network Diagnostic Tool (NDT) [18][2].

We conducted our experiments in two geographic areas, one in the high-density urban environment of Chicago, IL and one in a mix of residential and low-density commercial in Evanston, IL. Each area covers a similar surface – 4 × 4 block area (0.13 sq. mi) and a 6 × 4 block area (0.15 sq. mi) in Evanston and Chicago respectively. We took our measurements at three separate times between 2014 and 2015: in September 2014, April 2015 and September 2015. In each instance, we canvassed each area, walking the same path in 2 h intervals both in the morning and evenings to capture peak and non-peak hours. Unless otherwise specified, the results presented for availability and network performance come from the September 2015 dataset.

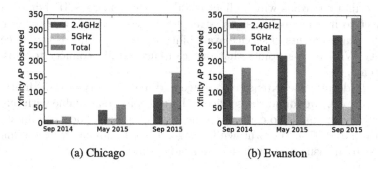

(a) Chicago   (b) Evanston

Fig. 1. Growth of Xfinity: Significant deployment of Xfinity WiFi APs in both areas, with more deployments using 5 GHz radio bands in urban Chicago compared to suburban Evanston.

3.2 Deployment and Coverage

We measured the growth in deployed Xfinity WiFi access points in both locations between September 2014 and September 2015, noticing a significant growth in both areas in the number of observed access points. We found that while Evanston gained more overall access points, Chicago saw a much larger relative increase. Between September 2014 and 2015, the number of Xfinity WiFi hotspots in urban Chicago has increased more than 7 times (from 22 to 164); during the same period, the number of hotspots in suburban Evanston has nearly doubled (from 181 to 342). Despite the large growth, we still observed twice as many access points in Evanston than in Chicago in our final measurement.

---

[2] While NDT results on network properties have been questioned, we believe that the gathered measurements should be consistent for comparisons between settings, and 2.4 GHz and 5 GHz bands [7].

Aside from the overall growth in the number of access points, we observed a higher proportion of new 5 GHz band deployments over the year. Similar to the results from total access points, we observed a much higher growth rate of 5 GHz hotspots in Chicago (around 45 %) compared with suburban Evanston (15 %). Deploying hotspots using 5 GHz radio band in urban environments may be driven by the assumption of lower radio interference.[3]

Geographic coverage is determined by dividing each measured area into a grid of cells - each cell an area of 0.001 degree latitude by 0.001 degree longitude - and searching for the presence of Xfinity WiFi access points in each. In September 2015, we found access points in over 70 % of areas in downtown Chicago, and over 90 % of areas in Evanston.

3.3 Availability

The utility of community WiFi networks depends not only on the presence of an access point, but in the ability of clients to successfully connect to them. There are many reasons why a client could see the service SSID but be unable to connect to it, such as low signal strength. In this section, we discuss results from our measurements of service availability which we define as the percentage of Xfinity WiFi access points that one can successfully connect to during an experiment.

Overall, despite the extensive coverage and high density of the Xfinity WiFi hotspot network, we found the service to be typically unavailable with our measurement device unable to connect to the large majority of access points – 56 % in Evanston and 87 % in downtown Chicago. Table 1 summarizes these findings, organized by measurement location and radio band.

Table 1. Xfinity WiFi APs statistics for urban Chicago and suburban Evanston, taken in September 2015.

Location	5 GHz				2 GHz			
	All	Xfinity	Attempted	Connected	All	Xfinity	Attempted	Connected
Chicago (urban)	3840	71	49	8 (16 %)	3688	97	75	10 (13 %)
Evanston (suburban)	442	56	39	13 (33 %)	2316	286	150	66 (44 %)

We find that the Xfinity WiFi in Evanston displayed much higher availability compared to downtown Chicago. Of 124 APs we attempted connection with in Chicago, we were only able to connect with 10 (13 %) 2.4 GHz and 8 (16 %) 5 GHz hotspots. In Evanston, we successfully connected to a significantly higher fraction of access points – 66 (44 %) 2.4 GHz and 13 (33 %) 5 GHz networks.

There can be many external factors which explain the poor connectivity in urban areas. We investigated how signal properties of these access points affected

---

[3] http://www.extremetech.com/computing/179344-how-to-boost-your-wifi-speed-by -choosing-the-right-channel.

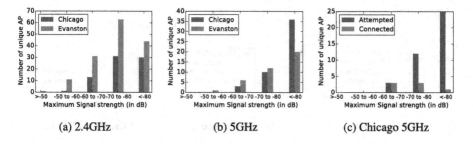

Fig. 2. Signal Strength in two areas. Chicago has poor wireless signal strength compared to suburban Evanston. APs with low signal strength suffer from very low connectivity rates.

our availability results, looking at the RSSI of devices we issued connect requests to Figs. 2a and b display the distribution of maximum signal strengths observed for the set of Xfinity WiFi access points found in each radio band.

We noted a higher presence of Xfinity WiFi hotspots with strong signal strength (broadcast RSSI) in suburban Evanston than in urban Chicago, which partially helps explain the higher service availability observed in Evanston. The impact of low signal strength on availability is clearly illustrated in Fig. 2c, which shows the number of successful connections compared to the total attempts for 5 GHz access points in Chicago at different signal strengths. The steep drop off of successful attempts with decreasing signal strength – including the 4 % success rate of 5 GHz APs with RSSI less than 80 – explains much of the low availability seen in this setting.

Investigating Wireless Properties. After observing the low availability of Xfinity WiFi access points in urban Chicago, we further investigated whether interference on Xfinity WiFi radio channel was contributing to the lack of connectivity. During our September 2015 measurements, we employed an instrumented Linux laptop equipped with an Atheros AR9820 802.11a/b/g/n chipset to measure interference on different WiFi channels by capturing channel busy time (CBT). CBT represents a more accurate picture of the radio channel than medium utilization as it also accounts for channel noise and packet collisions [2]. We continuously recorded the CBT from NIC registers exposed in Atheros radio. To normalize each CBT, we further calculated the Interference Factor (IF) for each channel, defined as the ratio of the observed busy time over the time spent on the channel [1].

A large source of interference for wireless 802.11 hotspots comes from other nearby access points. We found that the density of wireless access points in urban Chicago is significantly higher compared to our suburban setting. At median, we observed around 70 of 2.4 GHz and 90 of 5 GHz wireless APs per cell in Chicago compared to around 50 of 2.4 GHz and 5 of 5 GHz wireless APs per cell in Evanston as shown in Fig. 3a. The density of 2.4 GHz network is similar in both areas we measured, as well as, similar radio interference for 2.4 GHz.

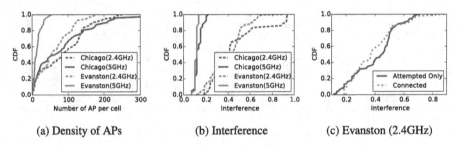

(a) Density of APs   (b) Interference   (c) Evanston (2.4GHz)

Fig. 3. Interference and Density of APs in two areas: Urban Chicago has slightly higher radio interference due to high density of wireless APs in both radio bands. 5 GHz networks have significantly less interference compared to 2.4 GHz band. However, we find small impact of interference on connectivity.

However, with an order of magnitude more 5 GHz radio networks in urban Chicago, we observed a very small but a clear separation in the interference graph of 5 GHz for the two areas (Fig. 3b). We found that interference in the 5 GHz radio band is much lower in both areas than the 2.4 GHz band with a median interference of 0.05 (compared to 0.4 for 2.4 GHz), for instance, in our urban environment.

Figure 3c illustrates the comparison of minimum channel interference observed for connected and attempted only access points, in the 2.4 GHz band in Evanston. In the median case, we see a difference of around 0.1 between the interference value for the access points we were able to connect and those we were not. For 5 GHz networks, which showed very low interference values, we did not noticed a significant impact of interference on connectivity.

3.4 Network Performance

We present the performance of Xfinity WiFi hotspots in both areas across download speed, upload speed and RTT, collected using NDT. We observed significant difference in network performance in between areas and radio bands, as well as

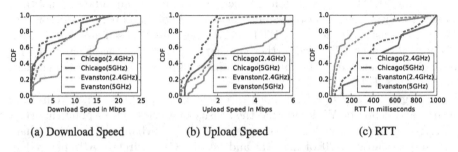

(a) Download Speed   (b) Upload Speed   (c) RTT

Fig. 4. Network performance measured at Xfinity WiFi hotspots by radio band and environment. Xfinity WiFi hotspots show lower performance in downtown Chicago across all metrics. 5 GHz band radios also performed better in both locations.

a large variation in performance of such networks within each area. The results are shown in Fig. 4.

We find a large performance differential between the two radio bands, with 5 GHz bands exhibiting higher throughput in both areas. Surprisingly though, these 5 GHz bands showed higher latencies in Chicago than 2.4 GHz bands. We believe this is likely due to the poor signal strength properties observed in Chicago rather than indicative of general performance. Sundaresan et al. [23] found similar performance results for home networks.

4   Cross Traffic Interference

Comcast is leveraging its customer's gateway routers as public hotspots for their *neighborhood xfinitywifi* service. To understand the impact of such sharing on customers' performance, we conducted controlled experiments for the case when both networks use same router with single radio band (and hence, share same radio channel). We generated cross traffic on a node connected to Xfinity WiFi network and measured the network performance on another node connected to home network. Since we started our study, Comcast has been moving toward double band routers now offering three new devices, two of them supporting dual band radio. However, one of these routers is currently only available in selected markets while the other one is provided only to customers with high-end Internet plans [12].

4.1   Methodology

We conducted our experiments over a continuous 24 h period to account for time-of-day patterns. Each set of tests consisted of injecting different amounts of downstream or upstream cross traffic (one direction at time) at different rates. We run experiments with downstream cross traffic at 0, 1, 2, 4, 8 and 16 Mbps and upstream cross traffic at 0, 1, 2 and 4 Mbps. Both upper bound limits were set based on our initial experiments. All experiments were run under controlled settings, with only one home device connecting to these gateways. We collected our measurements using a single Xfinity customer's ARRIS TG862 Gateway [5] which was actively broadcasting *xfinitywifi* SSID, in a home with a 25 Mbps subscription. Based on preliminary measurements, we believe that our key observations would apply to other single-radio-band devices and broadband subscriptions.

Cross traffic was generated on a separate node connected to the *xfinity-network* broadcasted from the same router. Upstream cross traffic was generated by running iPerf [16] utility to send upstream UDP packets at specific rates. Downstream traffic generation was generated using a python server hosted in university network that sent UDP packets at the requested rate to the *xfinity-network* node. These two processes of performance measurement on *home-network* and traffic generation on *xfinity-network* were coordinated and automated using a configuration/coordination server in our lab. We took all performance measurements using NDT [18] on a node connected to the *home-network*.[4] We took three measurements of download/upload rate and selected the maximum to handle small temporal variations.

4.2   Experimental Results

Figures 5a and c show the mean of the observed bandwidths along with the standard deviation for cross traffic. We observed significant performance degradation of the *home-network* WiFi due to cross traffic from *xfinity-network*. The impact of downstream cross traffic is significant starting at low values; for 2 Mbps cross traffic on *xfinity-network*, we observe the download speed of *home-network* drop from 15 Mbps to 10 Mbps, and drop by half (7.5 Mbps) for a cross traffic of 4 Mbps. Figure 5a illustrates this trend in decreasing performance as cross traffic is increased, with reduction in throughput as high as 67 % for 16 Mbps traffic on public WiFi.

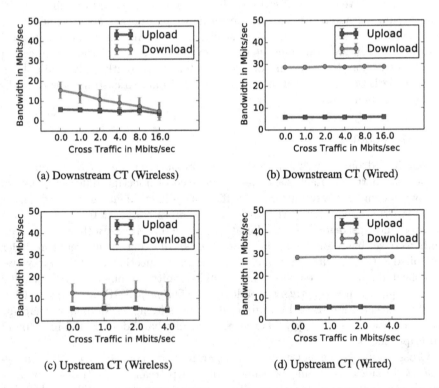

(a) Downstream CT (Wireless)   (b) Downstream CT (Wired)

(c) Upstream CT (Wireless)   (d) Upstream CT (Wired)

Fig. 5. Cross Traffic Impact of Public Hotspot on Hosting router's Personal Network. As the public and hosting WiFi share same radio spectrum, we observe significant performance degradation of hosting network.

---

[4] We refer to the public hotspot WiFi network as the *xfinity-network* and customer's personal network as the *home-network*.

As the upstream cross traffic is limited at 4 Mbps, it caused less wireless interference and has lower impact on download speed. The maximum upload speed we observed on the public hotspot was around 2 Mbps, and the impact on download speed and upload speed is not noticeable before 4 Mbps upstream cross traffic as seen in Fig. 5c. Hence, we don't observe any significant impact of upstream traffic from public hotspot network on the hosting network.

To isolate the cause of cross traffic interference, we performed the same series of experiments with the measurement node in *home-network* connected via Ethernet to the router in place of the wireless interface. Figures 5b and d show the home network performance for downstream and upstream cross traffic, respectively, for a client connected over the wired interface. The figures show that download and upload measured bandwidths of *home-network* remain constant for all values of cross traffic on *xfinity-network*, for both downstream and upstream cross traffic. With no cross traffic interference over the wired interface, we conclude that interference due to *xfinity-network* cross traffic originates solely from the two WiFi competing for same radio (device and spectrum) resulting in significant radio interferences with increase in network traffic.

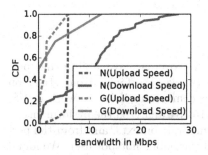
(a) Downstream Cross Traffic (10Mbps)

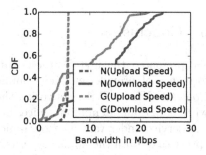
(b) Upstream Cross Traffic (2Mbps)

Fig. 6. Performance impact due to WiFi incompatibility of connected public hotspot user device. A public user with WiFi 802.11g device brings down the performance of 802.11n device in home network.

4.3 WiFi Compatibility Issues

The performance of the home-router owner could be impacted by a public hotspot user connecting with an old WiFi standard device. To evaluate the potential impact of this issue, we run experiments connecting a 802.11n device and a 802.11g device, one at a time, to *xfinity-network* and measuring the performance of a home user using a 802.11n device. We run our experiments using NDT, and during off-peak hours (2am–6am). Figures 6a and b present our results. We observed many NDT timeouts while measuring the impact of downstream cross traffic with the 802.11g device that lead to fewer data points. The 802.11g device has, as we expected, a significant impact on the home network and brings down the overall WiFi performance by a significance margin.

5   Related Work

Several projects have measured the performance characteristics of wireless networks, including Kotz et al. [17] study of campus-wide network and Aguayo et al. [4] report on link level characteristics of a rooftop based mesh network. Farshad et al. [14] used mobile crowdsourcing to characterize the Edinburgh WiFi. More closely to our work, Sathiaseelan et al. [21] focused on the technical and social context of providing Internet access by sharing existing broadband subscribers' connections deploying Public Access WiFi Systems in medium-sized British city. Mota et al. [19] recently evaluated the feasibility of offloading cellular data traffic through WiFi hotspots provided by the government and private WiFi access points in Paris. Robinson et al. [20] and Afanasyev et al. [3] studied the coverage properties of the Google WiFi mesh network around Mountain View, CA. Brik et al. [9] focused on a Mad Mesh network with 250 Mesh Access Points. Braem et al. [6] analyzed the end-to-end quality of Internet access in community networks. By contrast, our work focuses on characterizing a provider-enabled WiFi network in urban and suburban settings and from the perspectives of both the public user and the host network owner.

6   Conclusion

We presented the first characterization of the coverage, availability and performance of provider-enabled community networks. We focused our study on Comcast' Xfinity WiFi network - the largest community WiFi network in US, with more than ten million devices in July 2015. We analyzed the performance of this service under various geographic and temporal contexts, and from the perspectives of both the home router owner and the public hotspot user. We found that the connectivity and performance of these services in urban environment can be impacted by high signal attenuation from densely populated physical objects and radio interference from crowded wireless APs. Our results show a significant degradation on the performance of the hosting customer's home network with reductions in throughput as high as 67 % due to wireless interference. This preliminary study was focused on a single service in two limited geographic areas - downtown Chicago and Evanston, IL and we would like to expand this as part of our future work. We believe, however, that our findings and analysis should be applicable to other community WiFi networks and comparable urban and suburban environments.

Acknowledgments. We thank our shepherd Matthew Luckie and the anonymous reviewers for their invaluable feedback. Also, we thank Rishabh Gemawat and Sabita Acharya for helping with data collection. This work was supported in part by the National Science Foundation through Award CNS 1218287.

References

1. ACS (Automatic Channel Selection), May 2015. https://wireless.wiki.kernel.org/en/users/documentation/acs
2. Acharya, P.A.K., Sharma, A., Belding, E.M., Almeroth, K.C., Papagiannaki, K.: Congestion-aware rate adaptation in wireless networks: a measurement-driven approach. In: Proceedings of the IEEE SECON (2008)
3. Afanasyev, M., Chen, T., Voelker, G.M., Snoeren, A.C.: Analysis of a mixed-use urban wifi network: when metropolitan becomes neapolitan. In: Proceedings of the IMC (2008)
4. Aguayo, D., Bicket, J., Biswas, S., Judd, G., Morris, R.: Link-level measurements from an 802.11 b mesh network. In: Proceedings of the ACM SIGCOMM (2004)
5. ARRIS. ARRIS Touchstone® TG682 Telephony Gateway User's Guide. http://tinyurl.com/mw6gcgs
6. Bart Braem, C., Bergs, J.: Analysis of end-user qoe in community networks. In: Proceedings of the ACM DEV (2015)
7. Bauer, S., Clark, D.D., Lehr, W.: Understanding broadband speed measurements. TPRC (2010)
8. Braem, B., Blondia, C., Barz, C., Rogge, H., Freitag, F., Navarro, L., Bonicioli, J., Papathanasiou, S., Escrich, P., Viñas, R.B., Kaplan, A.L., i Balaguer, I.V., Tatum, B., Matson, M.: A case for research with and on community networks. In: SIGCOMM Computing Communication Reviews, July 2013
9. Brik, V., Rayanchu, S., Saha, S., Sen, S., Shivastava, V., Banerjee, S.: A measurement study of a commercial-grade urban wifi mesh. In: Proceedings of the IMC (2008)
10. Comcast. Comcast Unveils Plans for Millions of Xfinity WiFi Hotspots Through its Home-Based Neighborhood Hotspot Initiative. http://tinyurl.com/o23vvps
11. Comcast. Wireless Internet on the Go - XFINITY WiFi by Comcast. http://wifi.comcast.com
12. Comcast. The different wireless gateways for your home network (2016). http://customer.xfinity.com/help-and-support/internet/wireless-gateway-compare/
13. Electronic Frontier Foundation. Open Wireless Movement. https://openwireless.org/
14. Farshad, A., Marina, M., Garcia, F.: Urban WiFi characterization via mobile crowdsensing. In: Proceedings of the IEEE NOMS (2014)
15. Fon. How it Works — Fon. https://corp.fon.com/en/how-it-works
16. French forum for Iperf. Iperf - The TCP/UDP Bandwidth Measurement Tool. https://iperf.fr
17. Kotz, D., Essien, K.: Analysis of a campus-wide wireless network. In: Proceedings of MobiCom (2002)
18. M-Lab. NDT (Network Diagnostic Test). http://www.measurementlab.net/tools/ndt
19. Mota, V.F., Macedo, D.F., Ghamri-Doudane, Y., Nogueira, J.M.S.: On the feasibility of WiFi offloading in urban areas: the Paris case study. In: Proceedings of the IFIP (WD) (2013)
20. Robinson, J., Swaminathan, R., Knightly, E.: Assessment of urban-scale wireless networks with a small number of measurements. In: Proceedings of the MobiCom (2008)
21. Sathiaseelan, A., Mortier, R., Goulden, M., Greiffenhagen, C., Radenkovic, M., Crowcroft, J., McAuley, D.: A feasibility study of an in-the-wild experimental public access wifi network. In: Proceedings of the ACM DEV (2014)

22. Solutions, S.D.C.: The Chicago tech plan: building a model for cities and technology. http://tinyurl.com/p3zvanw
23. Sundaresan, S., Feamster, N., Teixeira, R.: Measuring the performance of user traffic in home wireless networks. In: Mirkovic, J., Liu, Y. (eds.) PAM 2015. LNCS, vol. 8995, pp. 305–317. Springer, Heidelberg (2015)
24. Voices, C.: 10 hidden wi-fi hotspots you never knew were there, July 2015. http://corporate.comcast.com/comcast-voices/free-wifi-hotspots-top-locations

NAT Revelio: Detecting NAT444 in the ISP

Andra Lutu[1]([⊠]), Marcelo Bagnulo[2], Amogh Dhamdhere[3], and K.C. Claffy[3]

[1] Simula Research Laboratory, Lysaker, Norway
andra@simula.no
[2] University Carlos III of Madrid, Getafe, Spain
[3] CAIDA/UC San Diego, San Diego, CA, USA

Abstract. In this paper, we propose *NAT Revelio*, a novel test suite and methodology for detecting NAT deployments beyond the home gateway, also known as NAT444 (e.g., Carrier Grade NAT). Since NAT444 solutions may impair performance for some users, understanding the extent of NAT444 deployment in the Internet is of interest to policymakers, ISPs, and users. We perform an initial validation of the NAT Revelio test suite within a controlled NAT444 trial environment involving operational residential lines managed by a large operator in the UK. We leverage access to a unique SamKnows deployment in the UK and collect information about the existence of NAT444 solutions from 2,000 homes and 26 ISPs. To demonstrate the flexibility of NAT Revelio, we also deployed it in project BISmark, an open platform for home broadband internet research. We analyze the results and discuss our findings.

1 Introduction

The Internet Assigned Numbers Authority (IANA) officially announced the depletion of IPv4 addresses in February 2011. But many Internet services and applications still require IPv4, motivating the standardization and deployment of protocols that support more aggressive, i.e., multi-level, sharing of IPv4 addresses [11], e.g., NAT444 within access ISP networks. NAT444 involves two phases of address translation, from a private IPv4 address block in the subscriber's network, to another local IPv4 address block in the provider's network, and finally to globally routable IPv4 addresses. NAT444 technology adds significant operational complexity that can impede performance or even break applications [6,8]. In particular, NAT444 removes the control that the residential user usually has to configure port forwarding over single-level NAT, e.g., for peer-to-peer gaming. NAT444 also limits the number of ports available per subscriber, threatening the availability of popular applications that use many ports, e.g., Google Maps [3]. Another complication of NAT444 is customer identification, since the subscriber no longer maps to a unique globally routable IP address. Finally, pervasive NAT444 deployment may slow down the transition to IPv6, promoting the likelihood of the Internet's fragmentation between the two protocols. With such potentially negative impacts of what seems a likely future scenario, it behooves policymakers, ISPs and Internet users to monitor the extent of NAT444 deployment in the Internet. But like many

© Springer International Publishing Switzerland 2016
T. Karagiannis and X. Dimitropoulos (Eds.): PAM 2016, LNCS 9631, pp. 149–161, 2016.
DOI: 10.1007/978-3-319-30505-9_12

aspects of Internet structure, systematic measurement and monitoring of NAT444 deployment in the wide area is challenging.

We propose *NAT Revelio*, a novel test suite methodology for detecting NAT444 deployments within the ISP access network. In order to detect NAT444 cases, the Revelio test suite aims to determine the location of the device translating to the globally routable public IP address that identifies the subscriber to the global Internet. If we find that the subscriber's home network is not hosting this device, we conclude that the ISP deploys NAT444. Our approach relies on detecting network configuration characteristics peculiar to NAT444 deployment in an access network. We design our solution to be highly versatile and not require prior knowledge of the setup that we are about to test. In particular, we target deployment of Revelio on large-scale measurement platforms deployed in subscriber homes, such as the SamKnows large scale measurements platform [14] and BISmark [16], an open platform for home broadband internet research.

2 Generic NAT444 Deployment Architecture

We design *NAT Revelio* [1] to detect a wide range of NAT444 solutions in various configurations in ISPs, without any prior knowledge on the environment we test. The *Revelio client* executes in a device deployed in the home network, such as a measurement device or a computer. The *Revelio client* performs six active tests against different elements, including one or more servers deployed in the public Internet. In the rest of this section we establish the terminology we use in this paper and give an overview of possible NAT444 deployment architectures. We use the latter to explain how we deploy NAT Revelio to detect NAT444 in the ISPs we test.

There are various NAT444 implementations. We describe next the NAT444 deployment architecture in the context of DSL access technology, although this maps cleanly to other access technologies, e.g., FTTx, cable. One type of NAT444 technology is *Carrier-Grade NATs* (CGN), also known as Large Scale NAT (LSN). DSL-based CGN devices are available in three configurations: (i) stand-alone, (ii) Broadband Remote Access Server (BRAS) insertion-card and (iii) Core Router (CR) insertion card. Also, NAT444 deployments can be distributed (at each BRAS) or centralized (at the CR). For simplicity of presentation, we describe a centralized deployment of stand-alone CGN directly connected to the CR in the ISP access network to explain our detection approach. Other NAT444 solutions are available [15].

In Fig. 1, we illustrate this NAT444 architecture in DSL networks using the terminology of the IETF's Large-Scale Measurement of Broadband Performance working group (LMAP WG) reference path [4]. The path elements include:

- **Subscriber Device:** which initiates and terminates communications over the IP network. In the context of our measurement experiment this is the *measurement device* inside the subscriber's home network that executes the *Revelio client*.

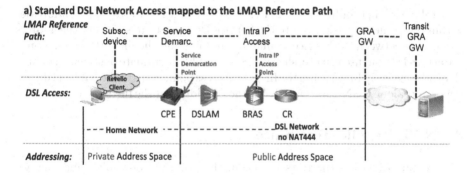

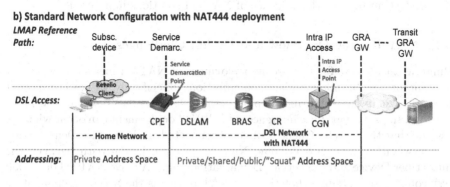

Fig. 1. Mapping between DSL access configuration and generic LMAP reference path (a) without NAT444 and (b) with NAT444 (in this case, a stand-alone CGN) in the access network.

- **Private Network:** a network of devices the subscriber operates in the home network, possibly using multiple layers of NAT, each operating different chunks of RFC1918 private address space.
- **Service Demarcation point:** where the ISP-managed service begins, usually the interface facing the public Internet on a residential gateway or modem.
- **Intra IP Access:** first point in the access network that uses a globally routable IP address.
- **Globally Routable Address Gateway (GRA GW):** the point of interconnection between ISP's administrative domain and the rest of the Internet.

Figure 1 illustrates the mapping between the LMAP reference path and a standard DSL network architecture, both (a) without NAT444 (but with traditional NAT), and (b) with NAT444 technology, using a stand-alone CGN device that connects to the CR. The customer premises equipment (CPE) usually performs the NAT function, translating private addresses in the home network to public addresses in the access network. The CPE is the Service Demarcation device; its Internet-facing interface is the Service Demarcation point. The BRAS is the Intra IP Access point – the first point *after the Service Demarcation point* that uses a globally routable IP address. The GRA corresponding to the subscriber maps to the IP address the ISP configures at the Service Demarcation point.

In the NAT444 configuration in Fig. 1(b) the subscriber uses private addresses within the home network, prior to the Service Demarcation point. For the address space used between the Service Demarcation point and the Intra IP Access point, the access ISP can use private, shared [18], or public (legitimate or stolen/"squat") IPv4 addresses [3]. In this case, the Intra IP Access point maps to the NAT444 device (the stand-alone CGN), and the GRA is the IP address at the Intra IP Access point.

3   NAT Revelio Test Suite

This section describes the tests we use in the proposed test suite, and how we interpret them to infer the presence of NAT444 solutions in access ISPs.

3.1   NAT Revelio Overview and Design Challenges

Building a test suite for large-scale deployment of NAT444 measurements must account for possible non-standard configurations. Specifically, we need to account for cases where the subscriber deploys several levels of NAT within the home network. In particular, false inferences of NAT444 deployment can occur when we assume that the Revelio Client is directly connected to the Service Demarcation device when, in fact, two in-home NAT devices are in the path between the Subscriber Device and the Service Demarcation point. A naive NAT444 detection test could falsely assume that the first NAT device is the Service Demarcation point, and falsely map the second in-home NAT device to an Intra IP Access point.

Thus, we design NAT Revelio to operate in two phases: (i) *Environment Characterization* and (ii) *NAT444 Detection*. In the first phase, Revelio aims to establish the location of the Revelio Client within the home network relative to the Service Demarcation point. In the second phase, Revelio tests for the presence of NAT444 solutions and interprets the measurement results using the environment information.

NAT Revelio performs active measurements from a device running the Revelio Client in the subscriber network (see Fig. 1). This step attempts to ascertain where the IPv4 address translation to the subscriber GRA occurs: in the subscriber home network (CPE) or in the ISP access network (a NAT444 device).

Figure 2 depicts a flow diagram of our test methodology. When deploying Revelio, we perform all the measurements in the test suite and merge their results to make an inference regarding the existence of NAT444 in the ISP.

3.2   Environment Characterization Phase

In the *Environment Characterization* phase Revelio runs three tests to determine the position of the Service Demarcation point relative to the Subscriber Device running the *Revelio client*. This step avoids false positive inferences of NAT444 and ensure accurate results over a wide range of in-home configurations. Figure 2 encloses the environment characterization tests in green rectangles. We use the

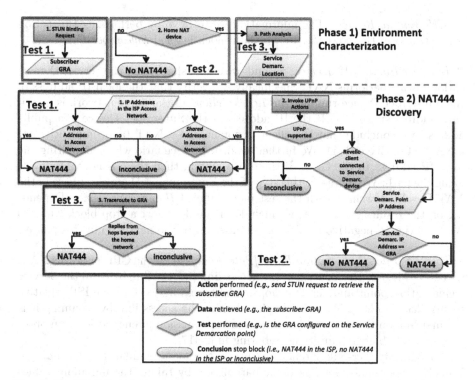

Fig. 2. The NAT Revelio test suite flowchart: measurement actions (sending/receiving packets) are in blue rectangles; measurement data is in green parallelograms; tests on retrieved data are in orange rhombuses. Inferences of NAT444 are in red stop blocks. We use the data we collect in phase 1 of environment characterization for all subsequent NAT detection test we run in phase 2 (Color figure online).

information we retrieve here to interpret the results of the tests we run in the subsequent NAT444 Detection phase. Additionally, this phase allows us to detect the IP addresses configured in the home network of the subscriber and the ones in the ISP access network.

1. Identify Subscriber's GRA. First, we use the Session Traversal Utilities for NAT (STUN) [13] protocol to discover the *Globally Routable Address (GRA)* that corresponds to the subscriber. STUN is a standard client-server protocol that allows a user behind a NAT to learn its public mapped address. We program the *Revelio client* to behave as a STUN client that queries an external STUN server (we use stun.stunprotocol.org), which replies with the GRA of the subscriber. If the ISP does not deploy NAT444 (Fig. 1(a)), this GRA corresponds to the address exposed at the Service Demarcation point. If the ISP deploys NAT444 using a topology similar to that of Fig. 1(b), this GRA corresponds to the public IP address exposed at the Intra IP Access point along the reference path. This step corresponds to the very first block of the Revelio flowchart in Fig. 2, labeled

STUN Binding Request. The information we retrieve by performing this action is illustrated in the flowchart by the data block labeled *Subscriber GRA*.

2. Discover Home NAT Device. Second, we establish whether the Service Demarcation device performs NAT. Specifically, we verify that the local IP address of the Subscriber Device running the *Revelio client* in the home network is in private address space [12]. If the IP address of the Subscriber Device is a public address, we conclude that the client is not behind a NAT (and, implicitly, not a NAT444 device either). We further confirm this scenario when comparing the local IP address to the GRA. If these two match, then there is no NAT device along the path. We represent this step of the Environment Discovery phase in the NAT Revelio flowchart with the test block labeled *Home NAT device*. Depending on the results of the test, we include in the flowchart a stop block with *No NAT444* (i.e., a negative result), or we move on to the next step in this phase.

3. Locate Service Demarcation Point [Path Analysis]. If the CPE performs NAT, we test to identify the location of the access link (i.e. the link between the Service Demarcation point and the first hop in the access network of the ISP) relative to the *Revelio client*. We heuristically identify the access link by assuming it is the first link on the outbound path with a transmission latency at least an order of magnitude higher than its neighboring links [17].

To quantify per-link latency we use a technique similar to *pathchar* [7]. Namely, we estimate per-link delay parameters by taking the minimum values of repeated Round Trip Time (RTT) measurements with different UDP packet sizes along a path, and assuming negligible queuing and processing delays (similar to [7]). To minimize the impact of these measurements on the subscriber's network, we gather the data by running traceroute hourly over a period of two days, using 21 different packet sizes varying from 120 bytes to 1,400 bytes, and using as a destination a high-availability IP address in Level 3's network. Limiting the number of packets to 21 per test allows us to complete one run of the NAT Revelio measurements in 30 s. Running Revelio once per hour for 2 days results in 48 RTT samples per TTL per packet size. We analyze these values to estimate per-link propagation delay, and infer that the first link with a ten times latency increase relative to its neighboring links is the access link. We use the pathchar result (labeled *Service Demarc. Location* in the flowchart) in the tests we perform in the second phase of NAT Revelio.

3.3   NAT444 Discovery Phase

This phase seeks to identify the location of the device performing NAT to the GRA mapped to the subscriber, namely before or after the Service Demarcation point. Figure 1(b) depicts the scenario with NAT444 (CGN) deployed in the DSL access ISP network, after the BRAS and the Core Router. When the ISP deploys NAT444, the location of the Intra IP Access point changes compared with the case where the ISP does not use NAT444 (Fig. 1(a)). In Fig. 2, we depict enclosed in red rectangles the three tests we run for NAT444 detection.

We perform all three tests and interpret the set of results we obtain together with the information we collect in the *Environment Characterization* phase to make an inference regarding NAT444 deployment in the ISP we measure. To increase the robustness of the test suite to non-standard architectures, e.g., when the ISP does not deploy NAT444, but configures private addresses in its access network, we assign a different confidence level to each test. One strength of Revelio lies in being able to compare the results of multiple tests for the same subscriber. To control against false positives, when test results conflict, we give priority to the negative result, concluding there is no NAT444 deployment in the ISP.

1. Identify Private/Shared Addresses in the ISP Access Network. The first method in the NAT444 Discovery phase detects the use of private or shared IP addresses in the access network, between the Service Demarcation point and the Intra IP Access point. Figure 1(b) depicts an ISP using special address domains (i.e., private or shared address space) in its access network when a NAT444 solution is in place. We characterize the path obtained by traceroutes in Phase (1), step 3, including inferring the position of the Service Demarcation point. We then check if private or shared addresses are configured along the path toward the public Internet target which is a router inside Level3, and if so, determine their location relative to the Service Demarcation point. This discovery helps us to establish if the private/shared addresses we identify are configured in the ISP access network. The information allows us to correctly distinguish cases of multiple levels of NAT in the home network, which can otherwise be easily confused with NAT444 deployment. The flowchart (Fig. 2) represents this step by including the data block labeled *IP Addresses in the Access Network* (which gets as input the location of the Service Demarcation point relative to the *Revelio client*) and the two following tests: *Private/Shared Addresses in Access Network.*

Note that we assign different confidence levels to these two tests. When we observe shared address space in the ISP, beyond the Service Demarcation point, we are *highly confident* of the presence of a NAT444 solution, given that these addresses are specifically for use in NAT444 deployment. However, when we observe RFC1918 private addresses beyond the Service Demarcation point, we give a *low confidence level* to our results, because the ISP might use private address space for its internal infrastructure without deploying NAT444. Moreover, in the case where NAT Revelio does *not* detect any private or shared addresses past the Service Demarcation point, the test suite cannot discard the possibility of a NAT444 deployment in the ISP. This case can occur when the ISP configures public addresses (legitimate or stolen "squat" address space) in the access network as part of a NAT444 deployment.[1]

2. Invoke UPnP Actions. NAT Revelio runs a series of tests that aim to infer the hop count between the Service Demarcation device and the device performing the final translation to the subscriber GRA. To check if the Service

---

[1] A common configuration is to assign private or shared address space only to the interface of the Service Demarcation point attached to the ISP network, while other elements of the ISP network use public addresses.

Demarcation device is the device translating to the subscriber GRA, we verify whether the address configured on the Service Demarcation point matches the subscriber's GRA.

If the *Revelio client* directly connects to the Service Demarcation device (Fig. 1), we leverage the Universal Plug and Play (UPnP) IGP protocol [2] if supported by the CPE. The *Revelio client* sends a UPnP client control message to the CPE that retrieves the IP Address of the WAN interface of the CPE, which, in this case, maps to the Service Demarcation point. In the case of a match, we infer that the ISP **does not** use NAT444. A mismatch between these addresses means that the ISP **does indeed** deploy NAT444. We give a *high level of confidence* to this result.

Otherwise, if the Subscriber Device running the *Revelio client* does not connect to the Service Demarcation device, we find ourselves in a non-standard configuration, where multiple NAT devices are present within the home network. In this case, we cannot draw any conclusion regarding the presence of NAT444 in the ISP from this test, since the UPnP test retrieves the IP address of the innermost CPE device within the home network, and not the IP address at the Service Demarcation point. The NAT Revelio flowchart includes this set of tests, following the *yes* branches both for the *UPnP Supported* and the *Revelio client connected to Service Demarcation device* tests, in the NAT444 Discovery phase in Fig. 2.

3. Traceroute to the Subscriber GRA. We also run traceroute from the *Revelio client* to the subscriber GRA to measure the hop count between them. Without NAT444, the GRA is at the Service Demarcation point (Fig. 1(a)), and all traceroute-responding hops are inside the home network. With NAT444 (Fig. 1(b)), the GRA is at the Intra IP Access point, which is past the Service Demarcation point. If we already know the location of the Service Demarcation point relative to the *Revelio client* (from the first phase), a UDP traceroute to the GRA distinguishes these two cases.

We assign to the *Traceroute to GRA* test a *high confidence level*, since it relies on no CPE-specific capabilities, nor on the assumption that the ISP configures private or shared IP addresses in the access network. Nonetheless, this test still may fail to determine the presence of NAT444 in the ISP, for example when the ISP actively blocks ICMP packets triggered by the traceroute. Thus, NAT Revelio cannot conclusively determine the presence of a NAT444 solution in the ISP. Figure 2 illustrates this possibility in the NAT Revelio flowchart with the purple *inconclusive* stop block.

4   Validation and Large-Scale *Revelio* Measurement Campaigns

4.1   Revelio Validation in Controlled Environment

With the help of a large UK ISP operator, we tested NAT Revelio on a controlled set of subscribers included in a trial deployment of a CGN implementation of

NAT444 within the ISP network. The trial environment consisted of operational DSL residential lines connected behind a stand-alone CGN NAT444 implementation. We ran the *Revelio client* on 6 Subscriber Devices, 2 of which were behind the NAT444 device. We found that *NAT Revelio* accurately detected the deployment configuration of all 6 devices. We explain details of the test results below.

After running the **Environment Discovery** (Sect. 3.2), we learned that all six Subscriber Devices running the Revelio Client connected directly to the Service Demarcation device within the home network.

For the two subscribers connected to the ISP behind a NAT444 solution, all tests in the **NAT444 Discovery** (Sect. 3.3) successfully indicated the presence of NAT444 within the access network. First, after retrieving the CPE's WAN IP address which corresponds to the Service Demarcation point address (as per the test we describe in Sect. 3.3.1), we identified it as shared address space, which is a clear symptom of NAT444 deployment. Second, we confirmed that the subscriber GRA did not match the Service Demarcation point address (as per the test we describe in Sect. 3.3.2), reinforcing evidence of NAT444 deployment. Third, when verifying how far from the Service Demarcation device the translation to GRA occurred (as per the test we describe in Sect. 3.3.3), we measured 6 hops between the Subscriber Devices and the device translating to the GRA. Only the first of these hops belonged to the home network, leaving 5 hops between the Service Demarcation device and the device performing translation to the GRA.

NAT Revelio successfully inferred that the other 4 Whiteboxes were not behind a NAT444 solution after *Invoking UPnP Actions* (Sect. 3.3.2) and concluding that the IP addresses at the Service Demarcation point matched the GRA of the subscriber.

To illustrate Revelio's robustness to non-standard configurations, we also tested our NAT444 detection approach on 24 residential DSL lines operated by a large Italian ISP that does not employ NAT444 solutions in its DSL network. However, in its access network configuration, the ISP does use private IP address space for its infrastructure. This is a non-standard configuration that can wrongly mimic the presence of a NAT444 solution in the ISP. Due to the fact that we consider multiple tests to detect NAT444 in the ISP, we were able to discard such cases on the basis of conflicting results. We found that the first test in NAT444 Discovery (Sect. 3.3.1) indicated the existence of a NAT444 solution in the ISP based on the detection of RFC1918 address space beyond the Service Demarcation point. Since the operator disabled UPnP on its home routers, we could not invoke any UPnP actions (Sect. 3.3.2). However, *traceroute to the subscriber GRA* (Sect. 3.3.3) showed that the GRA is, in fact, at the Service Demarcation point. As we mention in Sect. 3.3, when we have conflicting results from Revelio tests, we give priority to the negative test to avoid false negatives. Thus, we accurately concluded that the Italian ISP does not have any NAT444 deployment.

4.2 Large-Scale Measurement Campaigns

After the above validation exercise, we experimented with *NAT Revelio* on two different large-scale measurement platforms (SamKnows' UK deployment and BISmark), targeting multiple ISPs and potential NAT444 solutions.

SamKnows Deployment. We deployed the Revelio Client on a set of SamKnows Whiteboxes within home networks in the UK. A SamKnows Whitebox is a custom hardware device that residential users host voluntarily. We ran *NAT Revelio* from 2,000 Whiteboxes that allowed us to test 26 different ISPs for NAT444 solutions. We had no previous knowledge of the configuration of these ISPs. We collected results of tests of two different Revelio deployments that we performed 5 months apart, in June 2014 and October 2014. Although they did not cover the same subscribers, both campaigns yielded similar results, indicating that the NAT444 deployment did not expand during the five-month period.

The results of June 2014 campaign revealed that out of the approximately 2,000 residential lines we tested, we inferred that 10 different end-users connected behind a NAT444 solution. The 10 users were spread across 5 different ISPs. Thus, the proportion of end-users we inferred were behind a NAT444 solution was 0.5 % of all the residential lines we tested. We were able to validate these findings with the operators for only for one case.[2] The operator in question validated our inferences for the lines we found to be deployed behind a NAT444 solution.

Analyzing the results from the June 2014 campaign, we inferred that a total of 90 % of tested end-users were not connected through a NAT444 solution (no NAT444). The **Environment Characterization** phase of *NAT Revelio* helped us discard 60 % of the cases of in-home cascaded NATs that would have otherwise emerged as false positives.

In the **NAT444 Discovery** phase, the *Invoking UPnP Actions* test (Sect. 3.3.2) successfully ran on 82 % of the SamKnows Whiteboxes, further identifying 81.2 % of the tested customers as **not** configured to use a NAT444 solution. In the other 18 % of the cases, UPnP was not supported by the home gateway, so we could not run this test. Additionally, the *Traceroute to the GRA* (Sect. 3.3.3) independently classified approximately 50 % of the end-users we tested as not behind a NAT444 deployment. In 9.5 % of observed cases, we could not draw a conclusion because all tests included in the NAT444 Discovery phase gave **inconclusive** results.

The October 2014 deployment covered fewer subscribers (approximately 1,500 SK Whiteboxes) than the one in June 2014 (approximately 2,000 SK Whiteboxes). We found that 4 ISPs deployed NAT444 solutions. The results we obtained for 3 of the 5 ISPs were consistent with the results we inferred of the June 2014 campaign. We detected one additional ISP for which the Subscriber Device (Whitebox) connected directly to the Service Demarcation Device, but for which the Service Demarcation point address was a private (Sect. 3.3.2). We give high confidence to this result.[3]

---

[2] Attempting to validate our findings, we have contacted all the 5 ISPs, but we have yet to receive a reply from 4 of them.

[3] Attempting to validate this result, we found that several subscribers reported on the ISP's online customer support forum that they had identified the presence of the CGN by detecting the presence of shared address space in the ISP.

BISmark Deployment. Between 7–9 February 2015, we deployed NAT Revelio on 37 OpenWRT routers that are part of the BISmark measurement platform. Our BISmark experiment involved fewer vantage points than our SamKnows UK experiment, but they had much wider geographical distribution. We deployed the Revelio client in Subscriber Devices hosted in 24 different ISPs active in 13 countries distributed across the five Regional Internet Registries (RIRs). Using the Revelio test suite, we inferred the presence of NAT444 in three different ISPs: Vodafone for DSL customers in Italy, Embratel in Brasil and Comcast in the US. In all three cases, we inferred a NAT444 solution by establishing the presence of RFC1918 private addresses in the ISP access network (Sect. 3.3.1). The traceroute to the GRA (Sect. 3.3.3) gave inconclusive results in all three cases. Also, in the case of Embratel and Comcast, the Revelio client could not invoke UPnP actions (Sect. 3.3.2). Since an ISP may use RFC1918 addresses in the access network without deploying a NAT444 solution, we give low confidence to the latter two results, and mark them as potential false positives. In the case of the Subscriber Device connected to Vodafone Italia, the Revelio client could invoke UPnP actions and verify the presence of the NAT444 solution in the ISP. We give high confidence level to this result, where two Revelio tests detected NAT444 deployment.

5   Related Work

In recent years, detection of middleboxes, and characterization and assessment of their impact on the Internet, has become a topic of interest. In particular, researchers have studied how to identify the presence of middleboxes on the Internet path, including NAT444 solutions. A recent study proposed *NATAnalyzer* [10], an algorithm capable of discovering previously unknown cascaded NAT configurations. NATAnalyzer requires control of the client and server sides of the test, whereas *NAT Revelio* is a client-side discovery mechanism. NATAnalyzer determines the position of the NAT devices using repetitive traceroutes. First, the test establishes address mappings in NAT devices on the path by running a traceroute from the end-user side to the server. NATAnalyzer then relies on fixed NAT state timers to sequentially ensure that the per-hop mappings expire, while maintaining the rest of the mappings by sending traffic from the external server towards the client (a NAT configuration that represents a security risk and is not recommended). The algorithm does not account for timers that may differ for multiple NAT configurations across various networks. Revelio does not rely on any features of NAT devices, treating them as black boxes along the path.

The Netalyzr [9] tool, initially meant as a networking debugging tool, is continuously running a survey of the health of the Internet's edge by detecting anomalous configurations. This survey includes detection of NAT solutions. Unlike Revelio, Netalyzr is not specifically tailored to detecting NAT444 solutions, and might not be robust to non-standard configurations inside home networks.

Tracebox [5] is an extension to the widely used traceroute tool that detects various types of middlebox interference over an Internet path. The solution is prone to open issues affecting traceroute. Though this can also potentially impact Revelio, our test-suite also includes other tests which we can fallback on.

6   Conclusions and Future Work

Despite concerns about its performance impact, NAT444 is part of the technology landscape during this ongoing phase of transition from IPv4 to IPv6. In this paper, we proposed *NAT Revelio*, a novel methodology and test suite aimed at accurately detecting NAT444 deployments by running active tests from the home network. We validate the accuracy of our approach by evaluating the status of a control set of 6 residential lines tested in a NAT444 deployment trial within the network of a large UK operator. We tested the robustness of the test suite to a non-standard configuration by evaluating the status of 24 DSL residential lines connected to a large Italian ISP that does not deploy NAT444, but uses private addresses in its access network.

The large scale *NAT Revelio* distribution across the UK showed that NAT444 solutions are still in early stages of deployment in the UK. However, our results infer that operators are at least testing these solutions to potentially move them in production. Using the BISmark platform, we tested 24 additional ISPs active in 13 countries distributed across the five Regional Internet Registries (RIRs). We inferred the presence of NAT444 in three different ISPs and proved our solution to be highly versatile.

For future work, we will expand testing to other regions, where NAT444 solutions are more popular. In particular, we will deploy NAT Revelio in the SamKnows FCC Measuring Broadband America testbed in the US. We also plan to tackle the limitations of the proposed methodology, namely by designing other detection algorithms in the case when assumed CPE capabilities are not implemented or networks actively block ICMP packets.

Acknowledgments. This work has been partially funded by the European Community's Seventh Framework Program (FP7/2007-2013) grant no. 317647 (Leone). This work was supported by the U.S. NSF grants CNS-1513283 and CNS-1528148 and CNS-1111449. We would like to thank Sam Crawford and Andrea Soppera for their feedback and numerous discussions while designing NAT Revelio, as well as the support for the large-scale deployments of Revelio on the SamKnows UK panel. We also thank Guilherme Martins for his support during the BISmark deployment and Dario Ercole for his help validating NAT Revelio.

References

1. List of spells in Harry Potter. http://en.wikipedia.org/wiki/List_of_spells_in_Harry_Potter. Accessed 04 October 2015
2. UPnP Forum. Universal Plug and Play (UPnP) Internet Gateway Device (IGD) V 2.0, December 2010. http://upnp.org/specs/gw/igd2/. Accessed 15 June 2014

3. Aitken, B.: MC/159 Report on the Implications of Carrier Grade Network Address Translators. Final Report for Ofcom (2013)
4. Bagnulo, M., Burbridge, T., Crawford, S., Eardley, P., Morton, A.: A Reference Path and Measurement Points for Large-Scale Measurement of Broadband Performance. RFC 7398, February 2015
5. Detal, G., Hesmans, B., Bonaventure, O., Vanaubel, Y., Donnet, B.: Revealing middlebox interference with tracebox. In: Proceedings of the 2013 Conference on Internet Measurement Conference, pp. 1–8. ACM (2013)
6. Donley, C., Howard, L., Kuarsingh, V., Berg, J., Doshi, J.: Assessing the Impact of Carrier-Grade NAT on Network Applications. RFC 7021, September 2013
7. Downey, A.B.: Using pathchar to estimate internet link characteristics. In: Proceedings of the Conference on Applications, Technologies, Architectures, and Protocols for Computer Communication, SIGCOMM 1999 (1999)
8. Ford, M., Boucadair, M., Durand, A., Levis, P., Roberts, P.: Issues with IP Address Sharing. RFC 6269, June 2011
9. Kreibich, C., Weaver, N., Nechaev, B., Paxson, V.: Netalyzr: illuminating the edge network. In: Proceedings of the 10th ACM SIGCOMM Conference on Internet Measurement, pp. 246–259. ACM (2010)
10. Müller, A., Wohlfart, F., Carle, G.: Analysis and topology-based traversal of cascaded large scale NATs. In: Proceedings of the 2013 Workshop on Hot Topics in Middleboxes and Network Function Virtualization (2013)
11. Perreault, S., Yamagata, I., Miyakawa, S., Nakagawa, A., Ashida, H.: Common Requirements for Carrier-Grade NATs (CGNs). RFC 6888, April 2013
12. Rekhter, Y., Moskowitz, B., Karrenberg, D., de Groot, G., Lear, E.: Address Allocation for Private Internets. RFC 1918, February 1996
13. Rosenberg, J., Mahy, R., Matthews, P., Wing, D.: Session Traversal Utilities for NAT (STUN). RFC, October 2008
14. SamKnows^{TM}: Methodology and technical information relating to theSamKnows^{TM} testing platform - SQ301-002-EN (2012)
15. Skoberne, N., Maennel, O., Phillips, I., Bush, R., Zorz, J., Ciglaric, M.: IPv4 Address sharing mechanism classification and tradeoff analysis. IEEE/ACM Trans. Netw. 22(2), 391–404 (2014)
16. Sundaresan, S., Burnett, S., Feamster, N., De Donato, W.: Bismark: a testbed for deploying measurements and applications in broadband access networks. In: 2014 USENIX Conference on USENIX Annual Technical Conference (USENIX ATC 2014), pp. 383–394 (2014)
17. Sundaresan, S., De Donato, W., Feamster, N., Teixeira, R., Crawford, S., Pescapè, A.: Broadband internet performance: a view from the gateway. In: ACM SIGCOMM Computer Communication Review, vol. 41, pp. 134–145. ACM (2011)
18. Weil, J., Kuarsingh, V., Donley, C., Liljenstolpe, C., Azinger, M.: IANA-Reserved IPv4 Prefix for Shared Address Space. RFC 6598, April 2012

Testbeds and Frameworks

GPLMT: A Lightweight Experimentation and Testbed Management Framework

Matthias Wachs[1](✉), Nadine Herold[1], Stephan-A. Posselt[1], Florian Dold[2], and Georg Carle[1]

[1] Technical University of Munich (TUM), Boltzmannstr. 3, 85748 Garching, Germany
{wachs,herold,posselt,carle}@net.in.tum.de
https://www.net.in.tum.de
[2] Chair for Network Architectures and Services, Department for Informatics,
Technical University of Munich (TUM), Munich, Germany
dold@in.tum.de

Abstract. Conducting experiments in federated, distributed, and heterogeneous testbeds is a challenging task for researchers. Researchers have to take care of the whole experiment life cycle, ensure the reproducibility of each run, and the comparability of the results. We present GPLMT, a flexible and lightweight framework for managing testbeds and the experiment life cycle. GPLMT provides an intuitive way to formalize experiments. The resulting experiment description is portable across varying experimentation platforms. GPLMT enables researchers to manage and control networked testbeds and resources, and conduct experiments on large-scale, heterogeneous, and distributed testbeds. We state the requirements and the design of GPLMT, describe the challenges of developing and using such a tool, and present selected user studies along with their experience of using GPLMT in varying scenarios. GPLMT is free and open source software and can be obtained from the project's GitHub repository.

Keywords: Testbed management · Experimentation

1 Introduction

Network testbeds are an invaluable tool for researchers developing network protocols and networked systems to test a novel approach and existing, already deployed solutions "in the wild". A large variety of testbeds is available to researchers. Many of them focus on a specific domain (e.g. wireless experimentation, high-precision measurements, real-world network testbeds), and most of them use a non-standardized and domain-specific approach to how the testbed is designed, accessed, managed, and experiments are controlled, requiring manual adaptation for every experiment. When trying to transfer such an experiment to a different testbed, the experimenter has to adapt—and most of the time rewrite—the experiment to be able to transfer the experiment to a different platform. This makes it difficult to reproduce and confirm experiment results for both the researcher as well as the research community.

A testbed may be heterogeneous with respect to the hardware and the operating system, and may be physically distributed across more than one location.

© Springer International Publishing Switzerland 2016
T. Karagiannis and X. Dimitropoulos (Eds.): PAM 2016, LNCS 9631, pp. 165–176, 2016.
DOI: 10.1007/978-3-319-30505-9_13

This allows the researcher to evaluate reliability and portability under close to real-world conditions. However, an experiment is challenging to manage in a complex testbed. The life cycle of a network experiment comprises tasks such as testbed configuration, resource allocation, experiment definition, and deployment. Many testbed environments, for example PlanetLab, Emulab, or GENI, focus on testbed configuration and resource allocation but do not consider executing the experiment itself. The experiment's execution plan may require assigning different tasks to subsets of nodes in a precise timely manner to control the execution. At the end, the results need to be collected from all nodes. Monitoring and error handling also have to be considered, as resources may become unavailable, or a sub-task may fail. At worst, an experiment lasting several days has to be repeated.

Experiment runs often share similarities, but are still set up manually, or with the help of ad hoc scripts which are rarely reusable. Instead of implementing ad hoc solutions specific to our particular problems, we decided to realize a flexible and extensible testbed and experimentation tool, supporting us in our work and to make it available to the public.

With this work, we present GPLMT, a flexible, lightweight experimentation and testbed management tool. GPLMT provides an intuitive way for users to define experiments, supports the full experimentation life cycle, and allows experiments to be transferred between different testbeds and platforms, ensuring reproducibility and comparability of experiment results. GPLMT is free software and its source code is publicly available on the GPLMT website[1]. In the remainder of this paper we will give an overview of GPLMT, state the requirements and challenges for such a tool, and describe the design and implementation. We also describe the experiences of users working with GPLMT in various scenarios.

2 GPLMT Features

GPLMT is started on a control node and executes a user-supplied XML-based experiment description. GPLMT provides an experiment definition language to define the resources participating in the experiment, the tasks to execute and including specific order and parallelism, and to assign such tasks to resources. In addition, it allows the inclusion of files to reuse experiment definitions and to group resources. GPLMT connects to the nodes via SSH and can be extended with additional communication backends, runs tasks on the nodes, i.e. platform-specific binaries or executable scripts, and can transfer files between the controller and the nodes. To simplify the use of PlanetLab, GPLMT supports importing information about available and assigned nodes from the user's Planet-Lab account using the PlanetLab-API. Testbed specific functionality, e.g. setting link properties in the testbed, can be accessed in GPLMT using external scripts if the testbed provides an API. GPLMT offers additional features focusing on handling the intricacies of testbeds: the user can annotate commands with different modes of failure and register arbitrary cleanup actions to, for example, kill processes and delete temporary files.

---

[1] https://github.com/docmalloc/gplmt.

3   Requirements and Challenges

In this section, we highlight the requirements for the design of an experimentation and management tool realizing the features described in Sect. 2 and based on experiences obtained from conducting different types of experiments with various testbeds, exchange with the research community and an analysis of possible use cases varying from managing large scale and unreliable to small virtualization based testbeds.

Self-Containment. GPLMT is intended as a lightweight tool for researchers and experimenters. The tool should neither require a complex experimentation infrastructure, rely on client software like agents installed on testbed nodes nor have requirements for external services like a database server. The tool shall be realized as a portable, platform independent stand-alone tool.

Scalability is important for the experimentation tool to support large-scale testing and experimentation. When conducting experiments with many participants, orchestration and controlling of a large number of different nodes is a challenging task since large delays and setup times have to be prevented.

Resource Restrictions. Experimentation with GPLMT may be limited due to restrictions in the surrounding environment. Establishing a large number of connections to a large number of nodes has to be realized efficiently. Therefore, GPLMT has to be aware of resource restrictions in the host environment and reuse connections and provide rate limiting for new connections being established.

Heterogeneous Testbeds and Nodes. GPLMT has to make experimentation independent from the testbed platform and the participating nodes. Experiments have to be executable in heterogeneous environments with different operating systems and different versions of the operating system.

Fault Tolerance in Unreliable Environments. In real-world and large-scale network testbeds availability of resources cannot always ensured: not all assigned nodes and resources may be available or can fail during an experiment and become available again. GPLMT, therefore, has to cope with unreliable resources and has to provide automatic error handling and recovery transparent to the experiment.

High-level Experiment Definition. With GPLMT experiment definition shall be done on a high level of abstraction, to allow the experimenter to focus on essential aspects of experiment design and control flow without getting distracted by implementation details.

Experiment Reproducibility. Experiment reproducibility is essential for confirmability of experimental results. GPLMT has to support an experiment flow making execution independent from participants, resources, testbeds, external dependencies and state based on a high-level definition of experiments.

Experiment Portability, Reusability and Extensibility. Experiments shall be transferable to other testbeds infrastructures and allow researchers to share experiment definitions. Employing an abstraction over the testbed infrastructure and using a high-level description of an experiment allows an experiment definition to be reused and to be varied in different scenarios speeding up the testing process.

Grouping Entities in Experiments. In an experiment, tasks and resources may be assigned to different groups of nodes. GPLMT shall provide the functionality to group nodes and resources and to assign tasks to such a group.

Nested Task Execution and Synchronization. Within an experiment, tasks often have to be executed in a specific order or can be executed in parallel. GPLMT shall provide constructs to allow experimenters to specify the execution order of tasks. Tasks may also be nested and grouped in such sequential and parallel constructs. Additional synchronization barriers between the tasks have to be provided.

Repeatable, Periodic and Scheduled Tasks for Experiments. Often tasks inside an experiment have to be executed repeatedly or triggered periodically or at a certain point in time (e.g. for periodic measurements). GPLMT has to provide constructs to express a looping functionality and to schedule tasks to be executed at certain point in time or after a certain duration without adding high complexity.

Error Condition Handling in Experiments. In many cases the experiment control flow depends on successful or failed execution of tasks, making subsequent operations useless or the whole experiment fail. Therefore, GPLMT has to allow the experimenter to define the expected result of a task and how an error condition has to be handled. In addition, functionality to define a clean up and tear down task—executed before the experiment is terminated—is beneficial.

4   GPLMT Design and Implementation

GPLMT is designed as a stand-alone tool running on the so-called *GPLMT controller*. The GPLMT controller is responsible for orchestrating the whole experiment, i.e. scheduling tasks on the hosts of a testbed, from now on called *nodes*. GPLMT manages a connection from the controller to each node. GPLMT does not require any original services on the nodes, but relies on SSH, and possibly other protocols in the future. In addition, GPLMT can use the PlanetLab-API to obtain information about available nodes in the experimenter's PlanetLab slice. An experiment is conducted by passing an experiment description in a high-level description language to GPLMT. The description tells GPLMT which nodes to connect to, which files to exchange, and which tasks to run.

4.1   Resource Management

In large-scale experiments with many nodes, GPLMT will open a large number of connections. SSH is particularly resource-intense. The SSH connection setup is computationally expensive due to cryptography and may overload a low-powered controller or the physical host of a virtualized testbed. A high rate of connection attempts may stress IDS systems, and may trigger IDS alerts for alleged SSH scanning.

GPLMT offers two solutions to limit its resource usage: *connection reuse* and *rate limiting* of connection attempts. GPLMT will tunnel all commands to the same node through a single control connection, but will still try to reconnect when the connection is lost. GPLMT optionally delays connection attempts, including reconnects, to not exceed a configurable number of attempts per interval.

4.2 Implementation

The GPLMT controller is implemented in Python 3. Besides a few Python libraries and the Python interpreter itself, GPLMT only depends on the external tools which are needed to connect to nodes. Notably, GPLMT wraps OpenSSH, so all features of OpenSSH are available via a local OpenSSH configuration file. GPLMT directly uses OpenSSH's *control master* feature to reuse connections to the same node.

5 GPLMT's Experiment Definition Language

GPLMT provides a domain-specific language to describe the experiment setup and execution. Its syntax is defined in an *XML Schema* obtained from a *relax-ng* definition. Therefore, terms such as *element* and *attribute* refer to the respective XML objects.

The `experiment` root element may contain multiple `include`, `targets`, and `tasklist` elements and a single `steps` element. A `targets` element names the nodes and can also be used to group nodes. `tasklist` defines a set of commands to be run. Both definitions are tied together with the `steps` element, which states which tasklist is to be executed on which targets and at what time.

Target and tasklist definitions are optional and may also be imported from other documents. Targets and tasklists are distinguished and referenced by unique names.

5.1 Targets

A `target` element names a member node, and specifies how to access the node. The following types of targets are currently supported:

- `local` specifies execution on the GPLMT controller itself.
- `ssh` states that the nodes can be accessed using SSH. The child elements `username` and `password` may provide credentials.
- `planetlab` specifies a PlanetLab node and accepts the PlanetLab-API-URL, the slice, and the user name as attributes.
- `group` specifies a nested target definition, creating a set of nodes (and other groups) addressable as a single target.

To support parameterization per target, each target definition can contain multiple export-env elements, which declare an environment variable to be exported. The value of this variable is then available to tasks on the target.

5.2 Tasklists

The tasklist binds a list of *tasks* to a name. A *task* is one of the following predefined commands:

- get and put are used to exchange files between the controller and the targets.
- run accepts a command to be executed. When a target defines additional environment variables, those are passed to the command using export-env.
- The par and seq elements contain nested lists of tasks. seq will run those tasks in order, whereas par will immediately start all sub-tasks in parallel.
- call is used to reference a tasklist to be executed.

tasklist accepts the optional attributes cleanup, timeout, and error, controlling the tasklist's behavior in case of an error condition. cleanup references another tasklist to be executed after the current tasklist, even if the current tasklist aborts due to an error. This can be used to kill stale processes and delete temporary files or to save intermediate results. timeout specifies the maximum amount of time the tasklist is allowed to execute before it is aborted. This guarantees progress in case a command loops infinitely or dead-locks. on-error determines how GPLMT continues when a task fails. The following fail modes are available:

- abort-tasklist aborts the current tasklist and continues with the tasklist specified by the surrounding context.
- abort-step aborts the current *step* and continues with the next *step*. Steps are explained in Sect. 5.3.
- panic aborts the whole experiment.

5.3 Steps

The language requires exactly one steps element. It may contain multiple step, synchronize, register-teardown, and repeat elements.

The step element determines which tasklists run on which target. A start and a stop time can be added to schedule a task for later execution. Times are either relative to the start of the experiment or absolute wall clock times, allowing to defer a step until night-time when resources are available. Thus, step elements form the basic building block for orchestrating the experiment.

Consecutive step elements run in parallel. A synchronize element represents barrier synchronization, and execution can only continue after all currently running steps have finished.

register-teardown references a tasklist by name that is executed when steps finishes. This tasklist is always executed, even if errors lead to the abortion of the experiment. The registered tasklist is intended to contain cleanup tasks and to transfer experiment results to the controller. The `register-teardown` cleanup tasklist only needs to be registered right before the `step` that allocates the corresponding resources is issued.

GPLMT's experiment definition language offers basic loops within `steps`: The `repeat` element loops over the enclosed steps until at least one of the following conditions is satisfied:

- a given number of iterations (`iterations`)
- a given amount of time has passed (`during`)
- a given point in time was passed (`until`)

These are deliberately simple conditions that only allow for decidable loops, so it can be easily verified by manual inspection (or programmatically) whether a loop terminates.

5.4 Example

In this section, we present a brief example for a GPLMT experiment to illustrate how experiments are defined. In this experiment, we use GPLMT, running on the controller, to generate network traffic on two nodes and capture this traffic using a third monitoring node. Therefore, nodes A (IP 10.0.0.16) and B (IP 10.0.0.17) ping each other. The *monitor* collects all network traffic using *tcpdump*. At the end of the experiment, the resulting capture file is transferred to the controller. Listing 1.1 shows a (slightly abbreviated) description for this experiment.

First of all, an external experiment description containing teardown functionality is included (l. 4). Separating functionality in different files eases reuse of frequently used targets and tasklists.

The definition for the three nodes A and B and *monitor* is done in the `targets` element (ll. 6–23): nodes A and B are grouped into a target named `pingGroup`. To ping each other, these hosts have to know the partner's IP address which is provided in the environment variable `host`.

The experiment workflow is defined in the `steps` element (ll. 37–45). The different `step` elements reference tasklists from the `tasklists` element (ll. 25–35). The experiment starts with instructing the monitor node to capture network traffic using `tcpdump` (l. 38) using tasklist `createPCAP` (l. 26). To ensure `tcpdump` is terminated at the end of the experiment, the experiment registers tasklist `stopMonitoring` (l. 39), imported from a file (l. 4). Both tasklists, `createPCAP` and `stopMonitoring`, are executed in parallel.

The `synchronize` statement (l. 41) ensures monitoring is started before the nodes in group `pingGroup` (ll. 11–22) begin to ping each other (l. 42). Both nodes execute the same tasklist `doPing` (ll. 29–31). The shell on respective node expands the variable `host` (on l. 27) set to the other host's IP address (ll. 15,20).

The `synchronize` statement (l. 43) blocks until the `doPing` tasklists have finished (l. 30). The final step (l. 44) copies the captured traffic from the monitor node to the controller.

Listing 1.1. Example: Generate and Monitor Network Traffic with GPLMT

```
1   <?xml version="1.0" encoding="utf-8" ?>
2   <experiment>
3
4     <include file="include/teardowns.xml" />
5
6     <targets>
7       <target name="monitor" type="ssh">
8         <user>testaccount</user>
9         <host>monitor.example</host>
10      </target>
11      <target name="pingGroup" type="group">
12        <target name="A" type="ssh">
13          <user>testaccount</user>
14          <host>10.0.0.16</host>
15          <export-env var="host" value="10.0.0.17" />
16        </target>
17        <target name="B" type="ssh">
18          <user>testaccount</user>
19          <host>10.0.0.17</host>
20          <export-env var="host" value="10.0.0.16" />
21        </target>
22      </target>
23    </targets>
24
25    <tasklists>
26      <tasklist name="createPCAP">
27        <run>tcpdump -i eth0 -w testrun.pcap &</run>
28      </tasklist>
29      <tasklist name="doPing">
30        <run>ping $host -c 10</run>
31      </tasklist>
32      <tasklist name="getData">
33        <get>testrun.pcap</get>
34      </tasklist>
35    </tasklists>
36
37    <steps>
38      <step tasklist="createPCAP" targets="monitor" />
39      <register-teardown ref="stopMonitoring"
40        targets="monitor" />
41      <synchronize />
42      <step tasklist="doPing" targets="pingGroup" />
43      <synchronize />
44      <step tasklist="getData" targets="monitor" />
45    </steps>
46  </experiment>
```

6 User Studies

In the following section, we present an overview of projects using GPLMT to show the various different use cases and purposes GPLMT can be used for and highlight the challenges emerging with respect to both experimentation as well as using the GPLMT framework. Based on these experiences, we modified GPLMT in the current version to cope with this challenges.

6.1 The GNUnet Project - Large-Scale Software Deployment in Heterogeneous Testbeds

GNUnet[2] is a GNU free software project focusing on a future, decentralized Internet. GNUnet develops the GNUnet peer-to-peer (P2P) framework to allow developers to realize decentralized networking applications.

GNUnet employs GPLMT to deploy the GNUnet framework to a large number of PlanetLab nodes to be able to test the software under real-world conditions and to support bootstrapping of the network. GNUnet's requirement was to compile the latest GNUnet version on PlanetLab nodes directly.

GNUnet used GPLMT to provide the nodes with all software dependencies required. While running, GNUnet was monitored to analyze the behavior of the software and the P2P network and to obtain log files in case of a crash. With GPLMT detailed information for every node could be obtained.

For GNUnet, the major challenge was the unreliability and heterogeneity of the PlanetLab testbed. With a large number of nodes only a fraction were accessible and working correctly. PlanetLab nodes only provide outdated software and are very heterogeneous both with respect to versions of the operating system and version of software installed. Nodes also often get unavailable during operation.

6.2 OpenLab Eclectic - A Holistic Development Life Cycle for P2P Applications

The OpenLab Eclectic Project[3] focused on developing a holistic development life cycle for distributed systems by closing the gap between the testbed and the P2P community.

Eclectic used GPLMT to orchestrate, control and monitor networking, P2P testing, and experimentation on different testbeds. GPLMT's functionality to define experiments and to interact with testbeds using an abstraction layer allowed Eclectic to deploy distributed systems on local systems, HPC systems like the SuperMUC[4] and Internet testbeds like PlanetLab.

The main challenge for Eclectic was to define testbed independent experiments to be able to transfer experiments between different testbeds. GPLMT was

---

[2] https://gnunet.org.
[3] http://www.ict-openlab.eu/experiments-use-cases/experiments.html.
[4] https://www.lrz.de/services/compute/supermuc/.

also used to setup network nodes and collect experimental results. Within this project, GPLMT was integrated with the Zabbix[5] network monitoring solution to provide an integrated approach for infrastructure monitoring and experiment scheduling.

6.3 Testbed Management for Attack and Defense Scenarios

Datasets to train and test Intrusion Detection Systems (IDS) under realistic and reproducible conditions are hard to obtain and generate. Such datasets have to provide a high diversity of attacks with a high packet frequency but also have ensure reproducible results and provide a clear labeled information about the data flows.

At TUM's chair for network architectures and services, researchers used GPLMT to generate such datasets with different attack scenarios. To generate such datasets, a virtualized testbed environment with virtual machines grouped into attackers, victims and monitoring machines was used. These machines were used to execute attacks as well as provide defense mechanisms and obtain the generated network traffic. In addition, this testbed was used to evaluate the quality of port scanners and port scan detection tools with the results being collected and interpreted afterwards.

The main challenge was the grouping of the different entities, as well as the complex interaction and nesting of tasks assigned to the entities. Timing aspects as well as synchronization were crucial to this setting. The monitoring and generation of test datasets during the experiment executions was an additional challenge to be mastered.

6.4 Distributed Internet Security Analysis

In [1], security researchers developed a distributed, PlanetLab-based approach to conduct large-scale scans of today's TLS deployment in the wild. They used PlanetLab nodes to perform distributed scans of large IP ranges and analyzed the TLS certificates found on hosts. To conduct these scans, GPLMT was used to deploy the scanning tool used to the PlanetLab nodes, orchestrate the measurements, and obtain results from the nodes.

A major challenge in this use case was long lasting scan experiments in combination with the large number of parallel SSH connections established to PlanetLab nodes. The organization's intrusion detection system detected these connections as a malicious attack and blocked the control node as the source of these connections on the network as a consequence.

The main challenge was the large number of connections to the PlanetLab nodes. First, those connections had to be throttled during the experiment. Apart from this, the number of connections established had to be managed.

---

[5] http://www.zabbix.com/.

7 Related Work

Various different tools exist to manage and control network experiments. A rather extensive list can be found on the PlanetLab website[6]. [1] provides a comprehensive analysis with respect to quality and usability of such tools, finding most of them not usable or suitable to be used with respect to today's network experiments. Many of these tools are outdated and not available anymore (Plush, Nebula, Plman, AppManager) or were not even made publicly available at all (PLACS). Some of these tools provide rather basic functionality to invoke commands on remote nodes (pssh, pshell, vxargs) not supporting error conditions and error handling as well as orchestrating nodes to perform complex and synchronized operations. The Stork project[7] provides a deployment tool for PlanetLab nodes including configuration. This tool lacks fine-grained execution control to setup more complex experiments. Gush (GENI User Shell) [2] claims to be an execution management framework for the GENI testbed. Gush provides extensive methods to define resources but is limited regarding control flow aspects. Parallel or sequential execution is not possible in a straight forward manner. In addition, Gush is not longer supported[8].

Experimentation frameworks like NEPI [3] require the user to do rather complex adaptations in the source code to extend it with new functionalities and add support for new platforms. Approaches like OMF [4] focus on the management and operation of network testbed infrastructures and federation between infrastructures not focusing on the experiment part in the life cycle.

The COCOMA framework [5] focuses on providing an experimentation framework for cloud based services to control and execute tests for cloud based services in a controlled and reproducible manner and to study resource consumption of such services. [6] proposes an emulated testbed for the domain of cyber-physical systems. This work focuses more on the testbed implementation and less on the execution of experiments.

8 Future Work

For future versions, we plan to decouple the GPLMT controller from the experimenter's host and instead run GPLMT as a service on a dedicated control node. Users would then submit experiments to the *experiment queue* of a testbed, which is managed by GPLMT. This would ease the use of shared testbeds. Future versions of GPLMT may support target types other than SSH and PlanetLab, for example *mobile devices*. An intuitive user interface would ease experiment monitoring and control. This feature was provided based on Zabbix in an earlier version of GPLMT but is not available at the moment due to a recent refactoring of the code base.

---

[6] https://www.planet-lab.org/tools.

[7] http://www.cs.arizona.edu/stork/.

[8] http://gush.cs.williams.edu/trac/gush.

9   Conclusion

The focus of GPLMT is to provide a lightweight and convenient way for experimenters to conduct network experiments and manage testbed environments. Instead of using handcrafted onetime scripts for every experiment, we envision GPLMT to be flexible tool usable for different scenarios and use cases. Using a high-level description language GPLMT offers opportunities to share experiment descriptions among researchers and supports closer collaborations between experimenters. Moreover, GPLMT's language was designed to support error handling, nested execution flows and different timing aspects to provide a high level flexibility and adaptability. GPLMT is still under active development and will be extended in the future. With this work, we want to present GPLMT to the community and make it available for a broad audience. GPLMT is free software and can be obtained from the repository[9]. Both feedback as well as contributions from the community are highly appreciated.

Acknowledgments. This work has been supported by the German Federal Ministry of Education and Research (BMBF) under support code 16KIS0145, project SURF. The authors would like to thank Matthias Jaros, Oliver Gasser for their helpful feedback, Omar Tarabai for his work on GPLMT and the integration with Zabbix.

References

1. Jaros, M.: Distribution and orchestration of network measurements on the planetlab testbed. Bachelor's thesis, Technische Universität München, Chair for Network Architectures and Services, April 2015
2. Albrecht, J., Huang, D.Y.: Managing distributed applications using gush. In: Magedanz, T., Gavras, A., Thanh, N.H., Chase, J.S. (eds.) TridentCom 2010. LNICST, vol. 46, pp. 401–411. Springer, Heidelberg (2011)
3. Quereilhac, A., Lacage, M., Freire, C., Turletti, T., Dabbous, W.: Nepi: an integration framework for network experimentation. In: 19th International Conference on Software, Telecommunications and Computer Networks (SoftCOM), pp. 1–5, September 2011
4. Rakotoarivelo, T., Ott, M., Jourjon, G., Seskar, I.: OMF: a control and management framework for networking testbeds. ACM Oper. Syst. Rev. (OSR) **43**, 54–59 (2010)
5. Ragusa, C., Robinson, P., Svorobej, S.: A framework for modeling and execution of infrastructure contention experiments. In: 2nd Internation Workshop on Measurement-based Experimental Research, Methodology and Tools (2013)
6. Genge, B., Siaterlis, C., Fovino, I.N., Masera, M.: A cyber-physical experimentation environment for the security analysis of networked industrial control systems. Comput. Electr. Eng. **38**(5), 1146–1161 (2012). Special issue on Recent Advances in Security and Privacy in Distributed Communications and Image processing

---

[9] https://github.com/docmalloc/gplmt.

Periscope: Unifying Looking Glass Querying

Vasileios Giotsas[✉], Amogh Dhamdhere, and K.C. Claffy

CAIDA, UC San Diego, San Diego, USA
{vgiotsas,amogh,kc}@caida.org

Abstract. Looking glasses (LG) servers enhance our visibility into Internet connectivity and performance by offering a set of distributed vantage points that allow both data plane and control plane measurements. However, the lack of input and output standardization and limitations in querying frequency have hindered the development of automated measurement tools that would allow systematic use of LGs. In this paper we introduce *Periscope*, a publicly-accessible overlay that unifies LGs into a single platform and automates the discovery and use of LG capabilities. The system architecture combines crowd-sourced and cloud-hosted querying mechanisms to automate and scale the available querying resources. Periscope can handle large bursts of requests, with an intelligent controller coordinating multiple concurrent user queries without violating the various LG querying rate limitations. As of December 2015 Periscope has automatically extracted 1,691 LG nodes in 297 Autonomous Systems. We show that Periscope significantly extends our view of Internet topology obtained through RIPE Atlas and CAIDA's Ark, while the combination of traceroute and BGP measurements allows more sophisticated measurement studies.

1 Introduction

Measurement and monitoring tools are essential to many Internet research and engineering tasks, ranging from topology discovery to detection of security threats and network anomalies. However, the development of such tools is challenged by the decentralized nature of Internet infrastructure. For years, researchers have attributed measurement artifacts to the limited coverage of available measurement vantage points [14,17], which has motivated revision of Internet measurement practices. Large-scale distributed measurement projects either crowd-source the hosting of traceroute vantage points [1,7,27,28], or leverage cooperation from academic networks [25]. Network operators deploy their own monitoring infrastructure, including Looking Glass (LG) servers, which enable remote execution of non-privileged diagnostic tools, such as traceroute, ping or BGP commands, through a web interface. Although the primary purpose of LGs is operational, i.e., to debug connectivity and performance issues, LGs have also expanded researchers' cartographic and monitoring capabilities [15,19,20,23,29,30].

LGs have two characteristics that benefit Internet research. First, LGs often permit the execution of both traceroute and BGP queries, offering data and

© Springer International Publishing Switzerland 2016
T. Karagiannis and X. Dimitropoulos (Eds.): PAM 2016, LNCS 9631, pp. 177–189, 2016.
DOI: 10.1007/978-3-319-30505-9_14

control plane views from the same location. Second, in contrast to crowd-sourced traceroute monitors that are deployed at end-hosts (e.g. home clients), LGs are typically deployed near or at core and border routers. Despite these advantages, the use of LGs has been sporadic due to design features that limit their use for scientific studies that require systematic and repeatable measurement. First, LGs do not form a unified measurement network of homogeneous probes, such as the RIPE Atlas or Ark infrastructures. Each LG is independently owned and operated; there is no centralized index of available LGs, nor standardized querying or output formats. Furthermore, LG command sets change over time, there is attrition of LG infrastructure, and because LGs are generally intended for low-frequency (manual) querying, operators often configure query rate limits to mitigate the risk of DoS attacks against them (or using them).

In this paper we introduce *Periscope*, a platform that unifies the disparate LG interfaces into a standardized publicly-accessible querying API that supports on-demand measurements. The core of the Periscope architecture is a central controller that coordinates queries from multiple users to prevent concurrent requests to the same LG from violating rate limits configured by that LG. The controller dispatches LG requests to crowd-sourced and cloud-hosted querying instances, which scale as necessary to handle large bursts of queries. A parser transforms the LG results into a set of standardized output formats (JSON and iPlane), and aggregates them in a repository for future analysis. A daemon checks periodically for changes in the HTML interfaces of the LGs, and automatically extracts and updates the LG configurations. The Periscope API and the repository of raw data are publicly accessible to authenticated users.[1]

This paper describes the Periscope architecture and how each Periscope component tackles the challenges related to LG measurements. We compare Periscope's querying capabilities and coverage with those of two major measurement platforms (RIPE Atlas and Ark). Finally, we demonstrate the utility of having colocated BGP and traceroute vantage points with two case studies involving the validation of IP-to-AS mapping, and the geolocation of border router interfaces.

2 Architecture

We have four design goals to mitigate four key challenges related to using deployed LGs for systematic measurement:

- There is no authoritative list of active LGs. Periscope must automatically discover, extract and validate LG specifications from various sources.
- LGs are volatile, both in terms of availability and specification. Periscope must detect changes and automatically update LG specifications.
- There is no input/output standardization across LGs, so Periscope must translate query requests to the format supported by each individual LG and the output of individual LGs to a user-friendly format.

---

[1] A user requests access through email describing the intended use and we issue a unique security token which he/she uses to sign measurement requests.

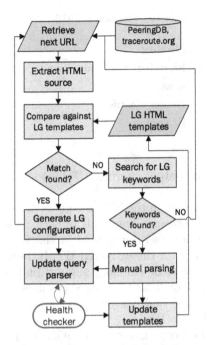

Fig. 1. End-to-end workflow to discover and extract looking glass specifications from web sources.

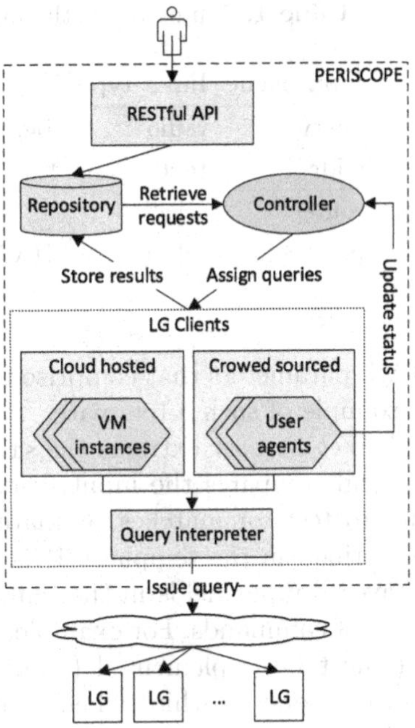

Fig. 2. The Periscope architecture, which sits on top of but does not itself include the LGs.

– LGs are intended for low-frequency querying and will block clients that exceed the configured querying rate limitations. Periscope should support multiple concurrent users without violating any LG limits.

2.1 Workflow of Periscope System

Figure 1 describes the Periscope workflow for integrating LGs into its querying system, which is repeated every month to update the list of supported LGs. The starting point of Periscope's workflow is the discovery of active LG servers, using public web sources that publish LG URLs, including PeeringDB [5] and `traceroute.org`. The system can easily integrate other listings of LG servers as they become available. Since these sources are non-authoritative, the published URLs may be stale or unresponsive. A **Web Crawler** visits each link and filters out pages that respond with HTTP errors.

To determine whether the collected URLs correspond to LGs, we attempt to automatically detect whether the HTML source contains web forms of LG interfaces. The automatic detection utilizes the fact that most LG deployments are based on open-source projects that determine the structure of the expected queries, the output format and the corresponding web interfaces [16]. We have processed seven popular open source projects [2,3,6,10–13] and created a template for each implementation, which describes the HTTP elements and the

Table 1. Template for the input parameters of the Version6 LG [12].

Input name	Input type	Expected values	Meaning
query	radio	[bgp, trace, ping]	[sh ip bgp, traceroute, ping]
addr	text	*	Query target
router	select	*	Router identifier
protocol	select	[IPv4,IPv6]	IP version

HTML parameters that comprise the input and output interfaces. Table 1 shows an example of such a template.

A *Web Scraper* extracts the `<form>` elements from the HTML code of active LGs and compares the input fields with the corresponding fields of each template to test for matches. A match occurs when each input field in the form is described in the template. It is not necessary for the extracted HTML form to have all input fields in the template, because some LGs may support only a subset of commands. For example, the template of Table 1 has three parameters that must be implemented (query, addr, router) and one optional parameter (protocol version) which when omitted defaults to IPv4.

When a form matches an LG template, Periscope generates a JSON configuration file that describes the interface of the LG, including the request HTTP method, the input parameters and their permissible values, the mapping of input combinations to network commands and the HTML elements that enclose the reply. The JSON configuration is used by the *Query Parser* to translate measurement requests to the format supported by each LG. When a form does not match with a template, the Web Scraper searches for LG-specific keywords (such as the name of network commands), to determine if the form contains LG inputs. If such keywords are found, we parse the form manually and update the LG templates as necessary to enable the automatic processing of similar forms in the future.

The final step of the workflow is to test the correctness of the auto-generated LG configurations. A *Health Checker* uses the Query Parser to issue measurement requests and process the replies. If the output is empty or if an HTTP error code is returned, the Health Checker will signal the error and mark that LG for manual inspection. The Health Checker runs these tests periodically to detect changes in LG templates, input parameters, or the response HTTP status.

2.2 Components of Periscope Architecture

Figure 2 illustrates how components of Periscope's architecture inter-operate to satisfy measurement requests. Periscope exposes a *RESTful API* that can be used to query the available LGs, request new measurements, and retrieve results. Every request is logged in the *Repository* which works as a broker between the API and the rest of the Periscope components.

An *LG Client* receives measurement requests submitted to the Repository and translates them to LG queries. The LG Client executes requests through

Selenium [9], a web browser automation suite[2] that interacts with the LGs through a headless (without screen) browser according to the JSON configuration file produced at the end of the Periscope workflow.

If LGs did not impose query rate limits, Periscope could transmit all measurement requests directly to LGs from a single LG client. But most LGs bound the number of requests a given client IP can submit during a given time interval. For example, the Telephone LG [11] software logs the time and IP address of queries in a database, and checks subsequent queries against the last query from the same IP address; if it is less than a configured timeout (e.g., 1 min), the LG drops the query. If Periscope had only a single LG Client (or multiple LG Clients behind the same public IP address), concurrent Periscope users would be limited to single-user querying frequencies. Although Periscope aims to prevent query rate violations, we also want to avoid very limited querying frequencies that would make Periscope impractical. For Periscope to scale to multiple users while being faithful to the per-user LG query rate, the system runs multiple LG client instances, using one IP address per end user.

Our first approach of assigning different public IPs to LG clients is by crowdsourcing their hosting as *User Agents* in end-user machines. As of December 2015 we had crowd-sourced 5 Periscope LG Clients. Because the Periscope client is software-based, we can extend coverage using cloud-hosted Virtual Machines (VMs), where each *VM instance* has a public IP address from the cloud provider's address space. Periscope uses two cloud platforms: Google Compute Cloud (GCC) and Amazon Web Services (AWS). Each VM Instance hosts a single LG Client. The elasticity of cloud resources allows Periscope to start VM instances only when needed to satisfy request volume, and terminate them when not in use. Periscope needs as many LG Clients as the maximum number of users that concurrently query a single LG. Periscope first attempts to satisfy the requests using the active crowd-sourced User Agents; if it needs more agents, it launches VM instances.

A central *Controller* assigns measurement requests to LG Clients; it has a global view of system resources and coordinates execution of LG queries so as to stay within the LG query limits. The controller manages the number of cloud-hosted instances, and every crowd-sourced instance sends a keep-alive message every 5 min to inform the Controller that they can still accept measurements. When Periscope receives a new measurement request, the Controller decides when to dispatch it and which Client instance will execute it. The Controller's logic is based on two LG-specific variables that restrict the maximum number of concurrent queries submitted to an LG[3]:

1. A *timeout* that expresses the minimum time interval between two consecutive LG queries by the same user

---

[2] Although most requests can be satisfied with simple HTTP requests, Selenium allows easier handling of HTTP sessions and cookies.

[3] We derived empirically conservative values for the timeout and number of slots for each LG.

Data: A set of measurement requests M for lg, and a set of active instances I
Result: Assignment of a client instance $i \in I' \supseteq I$ for each $m \in M$

```
1  for m ∈ M do
       /* Timestamp of next permitted user query                        */
2      m.ts ← lastQuery(m.user, lg) + lgTimeout(lg)
       /* Queue measurements in asceding m.ts order                      */
3      mQueue.add(m)
4  end
5  while mQueue ≠ ∅ do
6      measurement = mQueue.pop()
7      slots ← totalSlots(lg) - activeSlots(lg)
       /* Wait until the next measurement can be executed                */
8      while (now() < measurement.ts) || (slots < 1) do
9          wait()
10     end
11     assignedInstance ← false
12     for i ∈ I do
           /* Timestamp of next permitted instance query                 */
13         i.ts = lastQuery(i, lg) + lgTimeout(lg)
14         if i.ts > now() + lgTimeout(lg) then
15             assignedInstance ← i
16             break
17         end
18     end
19     if assignedInstance is false then
20         assignedInstance ← newCloudInstance()
21     end
22  end
```

Algorithm 1. The Controller's algorithm to assign concurrent measurement requests for an LG to the appropriate Client instances.

2. A number of *query slots* that indicate the maximum number of queries that Periscope will accept for an LG at any given moment.

Essentially, the timeout expresses a user-specific limit while the query slots impose a user-wide limit. If an LG has no available query slots it cannot be queried even if a user has not queried this LG for a period longer than the timeout. Algorithm 1 presents the Controller's decision process. For each query request the Controller calculates its execution time based on the timestamp of the last query from the same user toward the same LG, and the timeout of the LG (line 3). If the query does not conform to either of the two rate limits, it is queued inside the Controller (line 9) until the timeout expires and if at least one slot becomes available. When a query exits the queue, the Controller will choose an eligible Client instance to execute it. An instance is eligible if it has not executed a query to the same LG for a period longer than the timeout (line 15). If no active Client instance is eligible to execute the query, the Controller

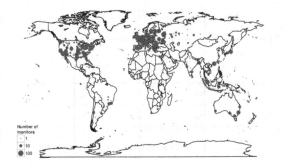

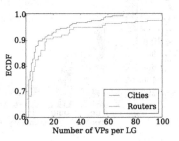

Fig. 3. Geographical distribution of LG VPs.

Fig. 4. CDF of router-level and city-level VPs per LG

will request a new cloud-hosted instance (line 21). The required number of active Client instances will therefore depend only on the number of concurrent queries to the same LG from different users, and not on the total number of active users or queried LGs.

3 Analysis

3.1 Coverage and Capabilities

As of December 2015 Periscope has extracted LGs for 297 Autonomous Systems. Periscope had automatically generated the configuration for 262 of these LGs; 35 LGs were not based on any of these initial templates and we parsed them manually. The LG-to-ASN mapping is not always readily available. In these cases we determined the IP address of the LG host and mapped it to an ASN using the longest prefix matching method. To get the IP address of the router that hosts each LG, we execute traceroutes against a machine under our control on which we run `tcpdump` to capture the incoming traceroute packets and extract the source address. We use the same technique to determine the traceroute protocol used by each LG. We found that 266 LGs use UDP probes, and 31 LGs use ICMP Echo Request probes. Whenever an LG supports both protocols, Periscope uses ICMP traceroute.

Each LG may allow the execution of its commands from different vantage points (VPs) inside the AS network, such as routers in different cities or routers that have different purposes (e.g. peering versus transit routers). We apply the same methodology we used for inferring the ASN of each LG, to geolocate an LG to a city whenever the LG interface does not reveal this information. After we determine the IP address of each vantage point, we map it to a city using NetAcuity's geolocation database [4]. Figure 3 shows the geographic distribution of LG vantage points that Periscope automatically parsed: 1,691 VPs distributed over 501 cities in 76 countries. As shown in Fig. 4, 40 % of the LGs have more than one city-level vantage point and 20 % of the LGs have ten or more VPs. Figure 5 shows how many VPs support each LG command extracted by Periscope.

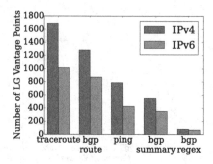
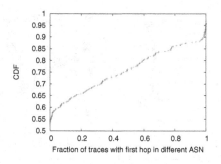

Fig. 5. Number of LG vantage points that support each command.

Fig. 6. CDF of fraction of traces with first hops (from LG VPs) that belong to a different AS, these LGs are likely deployed on border routers.

Over 75 % of the VPs offer both data and control plane measurements; 60 % of the VPs support IPv6 commands in addition to IPv4. To determine which of the LG VPs are located in border routers, we check whether the AS of the first hop is different from the AS of the LG host. We examine the 416 VPs that sourced at least 1000 traceroutes; of those, 222 had all traces going to an internal next hop, and 194 LGs had at least one trace that went directly to an IXP hop or a different ASN – these 194 are likely borders (Fig. 6).

3.2   Comparison of Topological Coverage from LGs and Atlas

To compare the topology visible from our set of LGs, Atlas, and Ark VPs, we executed a traceroute campaign from each platform toward 2,000 targets in October 2015. At the time of our measurements, Atlas had 7,292 public probes in 2,779 different ASes across 160 countries, while Ark hadf 107 probes in 71 ASes across 41 countries.

To get an unbiased set of targets, we first collected the IP addresses found in the iPlane dataset [25], and executed a *ZMap* scan to keep only IPs that responded to both UDP and ICMP probes. We mapped IP addresses to their owner AS, and for each AS we randomly selected one IP address until we had a target set of 2,000 IP addresses each in a different AS, and spanning 151 countries [4]. This small sample is not necessarily representative of the global Internet, but it is required due to the probing rate restrictions on LG and Atlas infrastructure. We executed measurements from all Atlas probes, more than 6 million traceroutes in 2 months, using an account with elevated probing quota. With the default rate limit, this probing would have taken five years [8].

We compared the number of ASes, AS links and IXPs (based on a list of IXP prefixes extracted from PeeringDB [5]) observed in each dataset. Traces from LG vantage points to the target destinations traversed 3109 ASes, 29525 AS links, and 167 IXPs. The traces from Atlas probes to the same targets traversed 3369 ASes, 55936 AS links, and 171 IXPs, while traces from Ark traversed 1608 ASes, 10237 AS links, and 136 IXPs. Table 2 shows the number of ASes,

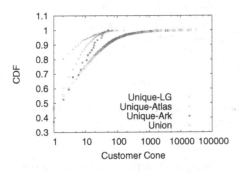

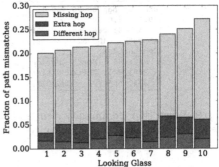

Fig. 7. CDF of the customer cones of ASes observed in LG, Atlas and Ark traces. The ASes uniquely observed in each dataset have significantly different customer cone sizes.

Fig. 8. Fraction of mismatches between traceroute and BGP paths, when longest prefix matching is used to map traceroute IP interfaces to ASes.

Table 2. Number of ASes, AS links and IXPs observed in LG, Atlas, and Ark traces. Many AS nodes and links are uniquely observed in the LG dataset.

Dataset	ASes		AS Links		IXPs	
	Observed	Unique	Observed	Unique	Observed	Unique
LG	3109	809	29525	13969	167	16
Atlas	3369	1464	55936	40620	171	21
Ark	1608	59	10237	1625	136	8
All	4657	-	73348	-	202	-

AS links and IXPs per dataset, including those uniquely observed in each dataset. Interestingly, close to half (47 %) of AS links seen in the LG traces (13,969 out of 29,525) did not appear in the Atlas or Ark traces, while 26 % (809 out of 3109) of ASes observed in the LG traces were not in Atlas or Ark traces. Finally, 16 IXPs observed in the LG traces were not observed in Atlas or Ark traces.

We compared ASes in each dataset using the *customer cone* as a metric of AS size. The customer cone is the number of ASes in the downstream path of a given AS, namely the number of ASes that can be reached through a customer, and it expresses the influence of an AS in the transit market [24]. Figure 7 shows the distribution of the customer cone sizes of ASes uniquely visible in the LG, Atlas and Ark datasets. ASes unique to each of the datasets significantly differ in cone size. LGs tend to capture more peripheral and stub ASes, while Ark and Atlas capture ASes with larger customer cones, due to the differences in the ASes that host the VPs of each platform. LGs are typically hosted in large transit providers that mainly access destination addresses through downstream paths. In contrast, Atlas and Ark VPs tend to be in eyeball ASes that traverse upstream paths to reach the same destinations. Comparison of topology visible from the LGs,

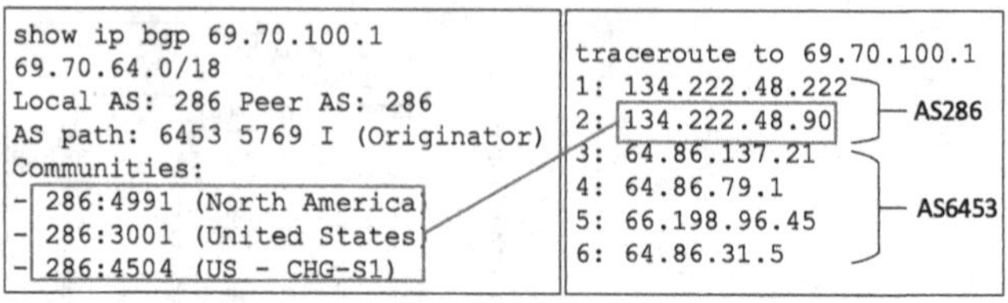

```
show ip bgp 69.70.100.1
69.70.64.0/18
Local AS: 286 Peer AS: 286
AS path: 6453 5769 I (Originator)
Communities:
- 286:4991 (North America)
- 286:3001 (United States)
- 286:4504 (US - CHG-S1)
```

```
traceroute to 69.70.100.1
1: 134.222.48.222 ┐
2: 134.222.48.90  ├─ AS286
3: 64.86.137.21   ┐
4: 64.86.79.1     │
5: 66.198.96.45   ├─ AS6453
6: 64.86.31.5     ┘
```

Fig. 9. When BGP community strings annotate the entry point of a route, combining them with traceroutes can enable city-level geolocation of IP interfaces.

Atlas VPs and Ark VPs reinforces our observation that the LG infrastructure provides a complementary view of topology compared to that visible from the existing Atlas and Ark infrastructures.

4 Case Studies

The ability to run BGP and traceroute measurements from the same LG VPs enables sophisticated studies that may not be feasible without combining control-plane and data-plane routing data.

4.1 Validation of IP-to-AS Mapping

Validation of IP-to-AS mapping techniques typically requires comparison of BGP and traceroute paths obtained from VPs inside the same AS [26]. However, even among the PoPs of one AS, intra-domain routing may induce different paths to the same destination. Having traceroute and BGP VPs as closely located as possible, minimizes this risk, and LGs often support both functions from the same router. To investigate this potential, we used Periscope to study the accuracy of IP-to-AS translation when using longest prefix match to map IP interfaces to ASNs. We randomly selected 500 addresses from the experiments in Sect. 3.1, and executed concurrent traceroute and `show ip bgp` measurements from 10 geographically diverse LGs. We sanitized the collected BGP paths by removing AS loops, private and reserved ASNs, and we discarded traceroute paths with unresponsive or unresolved interfaces. We compared the sanitized BGP and traceroute paths toward a given destination, ignoring IXP hops and repeated AS hops. Most path mismatches derived from traceroute missed the last AS-level hop that appears in the corresponding BGP path (Fig. 8), which typically happens when a router interface in a customer AS has an address from its provider's IP range [22].

4.2 Geolocation of IP Interfaces of Border Routers

Network operators often use the optional BGP communities attribute to tag a BGP route with the entry point where it was received by an external peer [18]. However, BGP communities provide only geographical location but not actual

IP interfaces of the border routers. Combining BGP communities with traceroute paths from the same VP allows us to associate the locations encoded in the communities values to router interfaces, by identifying the interface that corresponds to the border between two ASes (Fig. 9). We applied this technique for the AS286 LG, by executing simultaneous BGP and traceroute queries toward the same targets used in Sect. 4.1. We pinpointed 89 border interfaces, between AS286 and 58 of its AS-level neighbours, in 18 different cities. All of our inferences agreed with DNS-based geolocation [21], but only 66 of the interfaces had a corresponding hostname. In contrast, only 38 % of the locations derived from the communities agreed with the NetAcuity database. Through follow-up RTT measurements we confirmed the errors in the NetAcuity database.

5   Discussion and Future Work

We presented Periscope, a system that provides a unified interface to thousands of Looking Glass servers hosted by ISPs around the world. Periscope offers the capability for users to query any LG server without having to interact with individual LGs themselves, deal with timeouts and rate-limit issues, or develop code to automate issuing queries and parse LG responses. We showed that the topological view obtained from Periscope complements Atlas and Ark, serving as a valuable addition to the set of measurement platforms. Periscope respects the user-level limitations imposed by LGs, (a minimum time between successive queries by the same user to a given LG, and a maximum number of concurrent queries on the LG), and does not allow users to query at a rate faster than the LGs allow. Persicope distributes query instances, but measurements are dispatched through the API and a central Controller, which enforce LG rate limitations that cannot be overridden by querying instances. Preventing abuse is important, not only ethically but also because overwhelming the LGs would likely lead to their decommissioning from public use.

We plan to open Periscope for use by the research and operational community. We expect that allowing users into the system will be a (somewhat) manual process initially, mostly to prevent users from gaming the system by registering multiple user accounts. Beyond that we believe that the system can scale to many users, primarily because Periscope enforces the same per-user query quotas that the LGs themselves impose. Consequently, as long as Periscope can employ more LG clients than the typical number of query slots on a LG, the system can service user requests at the same rate offered by the LG. CAIDA's Archipelago [1] infrastructure already provides 132 active VPs that could be employed as LG clients. Cloud-hosted and crowdsourced LG clients can augment the set of clients, and reduce the querying load on each client. We provide documentation on how to obtain access and use the Periscope API at http://www.caida.org/tools/utilities/looking-glass-api/.

Acknowledgements. The work was funded by the DHS Science and Technology Directorate, Cyber Security Division (DHS S&T/CSD) BAA 11-02 and SPAWAR Systems Center Pacific via contract N66001-12-C-0130, and by Defence R&D Canada

(DRDC) pursuant to an Agreement between the U.S. and Canadian governments for Cooperation in Science and Technology for Critical Infrastructure Protection and Border Security. The work represents the position of the authors and not necessarily that of DHS or DRDC.

References

1. CAIDA Archipelago (Ark). http://www.caida.org/projects/ark/
2. Kewlio Looking Glass. http://sourceforge.net/projects/klg/
3. Multi-Router Looking Glass. http://mrlg.op-sec.us/
4. Netacuity. http://www.digitalelement.com/solutions/
5. PeeringDB. http://www.peeringdb.com
6. RANCID Loooking Glass. http://www.shrubbery.net/rancid/
7. RIPE Atlas. https://atlas.ripe.net/
8. RIPE Atlas rate limits. https://atlas.ripe.net/docs/udm/#rate-limits
9. Selenium browser automation suite. http://www.seleniumhq.org/
10. Stripes Looking Glass. https://www.gw.com/sw/stripes/
11. Telephone Looking Glass. https://github.com/telephone/LookingGlass
12. Version6 Loooking Glass. https://github.com/Cougar/lg
13. Vyatta. https://github.com/MerijntjeTak/vyattaLookingGlass
14. Achlioptas, D., Clauset, A., Kempe, D., Moore, C.: On the bias of traceroute sampling: or, power-law degree distributions in regular graphs. In: STOC (2005)
15. Augustin, B., Krishnamurthy, B., Willinger, W.: IXPs: mapped?. In: IMC 2009 (2009)
16. Bruno, L., Graziano, M., Balzarotti, D., Francillon, A.: Through the looking-glass, and what eve found there. In: WOOT (2014)
17. Cohen, R., Raz, D.: The internet dark matter - on the missing links in the AS connectivity map. In: IEEE INFOCOM 2006, April 2006
18. Donnet, B., Bonaventure, O.: On BGP communities. SIGCOMM Comput. Commun. Rev. **38**(2), 55–59 (2008)
19. Giotsas, V., Zhou, S., Luckie, M., Claffy, K.: Inferring multilateral peering. In: CoNEXT 2013 (2013)
20. He, Y., Siganos, G., Faloutsos, M., Krishnamurthy, S.: Lord of the links: a framework for discovering missing links in the internet topology. IEEE/ACM Trans. Network. **17**(2), 391–404 (2009)
21. Huffaker, B., Fomenkov, M., Claffy, K.: DRoP: DNS-based router positioning. SIGCOMM Comput. Commun. Rev. **44**(3), 5–13 (2014)
22. Huffaker, B., Dhamdhere, A., Fomenkov, M., Claffy, K.: Toward topology dualism: improving the accuracy of AS annotations for routers. In: Krishnamurthy, A., Plattner, B. (eds.) PAM 2010. LNCS, vol. 6032, pp. 101–110. Springer, Heidelberg (2010)
23. Khan, A., Kwon, T., Kim, H.c., Choi, Y.: AS-level topology collection through looking glass servers. In: IMC 2013 (2013)
24. Luckie, M., Huffaker, B., Claffy, K., Dhamdhere, A., Giotsas, V.: AS relationships, customer cones, and validation. In: ACM IMC 2013 (2013)
25. Madhyastha, H.V., Isdal, T., Piatek, M., Dixon, C., Anderson, T., Krishnamurthy, A., Venkataramani, A.: iPlane: an information plane for distributed services. In: USENIX NSDI 2006 (2016)
26. Mao, Z.M., Rexford, J., Wang, J., Katz, R.H.: Towards an accurate AS-level traceroute tool. In: ACM SIGCOMM 2003 (2003)

27. Sánchez, M.A., Otto, J.S., Bischof, Z.S., Choffnes, D.R., Bustamante, F.E., Krishnamurthy, B., Willinger, W.: Dasu: pushing experiments to the internet's edge. In: USENIX NSDI 2013, April 2013
28. Shavitt, Y., Shir, E.: DIMES: let the internet measure itself. SIGCOMM Comput. Commun. Rev. **35**(5), 71–74 (2005)
29. Shi, X., Xiang, Y., Wang, Z., Yin, X., Wu, J.: Detecting prefix hijackings in the internet with argus. In: IMC 2012 (2012)
30. Zhang, B., Liu, R., Massey, D., Zhang, L.: Collecting the internet AS-level topology. ACM SIGCOMM CCR **35**(1), 53–61 (2005)

Analyzing Locality of Mobile Messaging Traffic using the MATAdOR Framework

Quirin Scheitle$^{(\boxtimes)}$, Matthias Wachs, Johannes Zirngibl, and Georg Carle

Department of Informatics, Chair for Networking Services and Architectures,
Technical University of Munich (TUM), Munich, Germany
{scheitle,wachs,carle}@net.in.tum.de, zirngibl@in.tum.de

Abstract. Mobile messaging services have gained a large share in global telecommunications. Unlike conventional services like phone calls, text messages or email, they do not feature a standardized environment enabling a federated and potentially local service architecture. We present an extensive and large-scale analysis of communication patterns for four popular mobile messaging services between 28 countries and analyze the locality of communication and the resulting impact on user privacy. We show that server architectures for mobile messaging services are highly centralized in single countries. This forces messages to drastically deviate from a direct communication path, enabling hosting and transfer countries to potentially intercept and censor traffic. To conduct this work, we developed a measurement framework to analyze traffic of such mobile messaging services. It allows to carry out automated experiments with mobile messaging applications, is transparent to those applications and does not require any modifications to the applications.

Keywords: Mobile messaging · Security · WhatsApp · WeChat · Threema · TextSecure

1 Introduction

Mobile messaging services like WeChat or WhatsApp see a steady increase in both active users and messages sent, with a particular success in emerging markets like China, Brazil or Malaysia [18,30]. Some researchers predict a shift in communication paradigms with mobile messaging services eradicating classical forms of electronic communication like email or text messages. As an example, the number of text messages sent in Germany shrunk by 62 % from 2012 to 2014 [6], after it had been growing exponentially for over a decade.

Mobile messaging services and their design strongly differ from classic Internet communication services: established means of communication—like email, internet telephony or instant messaging—often rely on federated or decentralized architectures, with operators providing services to their customers and from within their domain.

Mobile messaging services tend to abandon established principles of openness and federation: messaging services are often realized in a closed, non-federated,

© Springer International Publishing Switzerland 2016
T. Karagiannis and X. Dimitropoulos (Eds.): PAM 2016, LNCS 9631, pp. 190–202, 2016.
DOI: 10.1007/978-3-319-30505-9_15

cloud-centric environment built upon proprietary communication and security protocols neither standardized nor disclosed to the public.

This paradigm shift puts at risk the user's freedom and access to secure, confidential and privacy-preserving communication. With such services, the user—relating to her social network through such applications—strongly depends on the service provider to not modify or restrict the service. The user's privacy also depends on the legislation the operating company is subject to: governments are often interested in controlling Internet services [14,31] and accessing messages [9] as well as metadata. The matters of security and privacy move along the same lines and generally involve a full trust into a closed system, a misleading assumption as we saw with WhatApp's announced *end-to-end-encryption*, which is supported on Android, but not Apple devices [1], without giving feedback on encryption status to the user. First attempts to analyze the security properties of mobile messaging services have for example been made by the EFF with its *Secure Messaging Scorecard* [4].

In this work, we analyze the implications of mobile messaging services on the users and their privacy. Similar to the discussion about a "nation-centric Internet" [32], we set out to understand the communication behavior and patterns of mobile messaging service by analyzing how *local* messaging traffic is from a geographic and legal point of view. We analyze how messaging traffic is routed through the Internet and which countries could therefore access this traffic. We compare this path with the direct communication path which could have been taken between communication partners to quantify the impact of mobile messaging services. For this analysis, we developed an analysis platform and testbed for mobile applications, called MATAdOR (Mobile Application Traffic Analysis plattfORm). We use MATAdOR to exchange messages between a large number of communication partners distributed over the world using different mobile messaging applications and automatically extract information about the network path the messages used.

Highlights of our results include: (a) Mobile messaging services largely distort traffic locality. (b) For Asian users (except Israel), Threema traffic is routed through the U.S. and hence 5 Eyes accessible. (c) Even South American internal traffic is routed through North America. (d) Europe-based users can reduce 5 Eyes access by routing messages through Threema's Switzerland servers. (e) Except WeChat, mobile messaging services showed globally uniform behavior.

2   Related Work

Several projects worked on analyzing the behavior and communication patterns of mobile messaging services and the challenges arising when conducting automated experiments with mobile devices and applications.

Fiadino et al. [7] investigated characteristics of WhatsApp communication based on a set of mobile network trace data from February 2014. In this set, they identified every DNS request to WhatsApp and resolved them in a distributed way through the RIPE Atlas service. They found the corresponding address to be exclusively located in the U.S. and focussed further on Quality of Experience analysis. Huang et al. [10] did similar work on WeChat, using network traces as well as controlled experiments. For the latter, they connected phones through WLAN, but relied on heavy manual work for message sending and traffic analysis. They do not mention a capability to proxy traffic out through remote nodes. On the collected data, they heavily focus on dissecting the protocol and architecture. Mueller et al. [16] researched security for a wide set of mobile messaging services and found many weaknesses, e.g. on the authentication bootstrapping process. They used a testbed similar to MATAdOR, but had to explicitly configure the mobile device's proxy settings. Frosch et al. [8] provided a detailed protocol analysis for TextSecure based on its source code. The life cycle of network experiments, automated experimentation and testbed management is in the focus of several related projects. The OpenLab Project[1] focuses on improving network experimentation for future distributed and federated testbeds and to provide tools to researchers. Various tools for supporting testbed setup and experimentation exist [19], but many are outdated or unavailable. None of these tools support experimentation with mobile devices or geographic diversion of network traffic.

[33] provides an extensive list of commercial platforms aiming to integrate functional mobile application testing in the software development cycle. Many platforms support the use of real devices and some even provide testing over mobile carrier networks to ensure functionality. Many solutions are only provided as a paid service.

3   Analyzing Communication of Mobile Messaging Applications

In order to analyze the impact of mobile messaging services on traffic locality, our approach is to compare the *network path*, defined as direct network path between communication partners obtained with forward path measurements, and the *application path*, defined as the forward path measurements from both partners to the mobile messaging service's backend infrastructure.

We use the MATAdOR testbed to send a large number of messages using different mobile messaging services between communication partners distributed all over the globe. To do so, we use MATAdOR equipped with two mobile devices and the mobile messaging application under test. MATAdOR tunnels the application traffic to PlanetLab nodes as depicted in Fig. 1. We intercept the applications' communication and extract the communication endpoints. Based on this information, we conduct forward path measurements to the mobile messaging service's backend servers to obtain the *application path* and between the nodes to obtain the *network path*.

We map the hops in both application path and network path to countries and analyze which jurisdictions and political frameworks the traffic traverses on

---

[1] http://www.ict-openlab.eu

its way between communication partners. As a result, we can give a qualified analysis how much the application path and the network path differ and if traffic is confined to a geographic region when both partners are located in this region.

3.1 Experimental Setup

The experimental setup of MATAdOR consists of a dedicated controller node, two WLAN routers, two Android mobile phones and the PlanetLab proxy nodes as depicted in Fig. 1. The controller node orchestrates the overall experimentation process, configures the WLAN routers, configures the Android devices and instruments them to send messages. Device instrumentation is realized using the Android Debug Bridge to configure network connections, start applications, and issue input events to the devices to automate message sending. The routers spawn two wireless networks and establish tunnels to the respective PlanetLab nodes. The router's task is to route, intercept and modify traffic as well as to automatically parse network traces and start path measurements to targets. To leverage PlanetLab for this experiment, we use a tool currently under development at our chair. This tool is able to transparently proxy traffic over PlanetLab nodes. It is currently in beta status and pending public release.

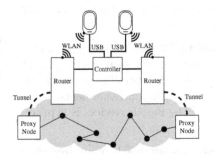

Fig. 1. Overall experiment design.

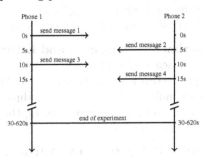

Fig. 2. Overview of messaging timers

Mobile Phone Configuration. To run the mobile messaging applications, we use two off-the-shelf, rooted Motorola Moto-E (2nd generation) smartphones running vanilla Android 5.0.2. For each device we created an individual Google Play account. To allow control through the Android Debug Bridge (ADB), devices are connected to the controller using USB. We use XPrivacy[2] to set the phone's location information according to the location of the specific PlanetLab node and `iptables` to restrict network communication to the specific mobile messaging application (based on its UID) under test. To prevent geolocation based on mobile network information, the phones were set to airplane mode with only WLAN enabled.

Router Configuration. Two GNU/Linux PCs, configured to act as WLAN access points, provide two dedicated WPA2-protected wireless networks, one to

---

[2] http://repo.xposed.info/module/biz.bokhorst.xprivacy

each mobile phone. Through DHCP, they provide a RFC 1918 private address and the PlanetLab node's DNS server to the phones. The routers use `tcpdump` to intercept traffic and `scapy` to automatically process network traces.

Measurement Orchestration. The measurements to conduct are defined as *experiments*. Within each experiment MATAdOR executes the respective set of commands. This involves setting up remote tunnels to two PlanetLab nodes, configuring the network settings on the routers according to the experiment, starting interception and manipulation software on the routers, configure the phone to use the wireless network, setting XPrivacy and firewall settings on the phone, capturing the phone's screen for later inspection, stepping through the experiment on the phones with ADB automation, parsing the network trace data automatically, and executing path measurements to all IP addresses found in the network trace.

Experiment Parametrization. To permit experimentation with different applications, all required experimental parameters are controlled through application-specific configuration files. This includes timers between the different steps of the experiment, blacklists of hosts not to include in path measurements (e.g. NTP or DNS servers), the text to send in the messages and how many messages to send with the application. Such messaging timers, depicted in Fig. 2, are controlled through these configuration files.

Experiment Monitoring and Error Handling. While running experiments, we have learned that using unaltered applications on physical devices in this complex setup is prone to errors. We therefore split the overall experiment into smaller junks to be able to reproduce missing or failing measurements. To be able to detect and analyze failures, the screen of the mobile devices is captured for each measurement.

Benefits Using the MATAdOR Testbed. Our approach minimizes effort and cost using common available off-the-shelf hardware. Since MATAdOR does not rely on device or run time emulation, simulated network connections, adapted applications, or the devices being otherwise modified in an unusual way (e.g. setting an application or device proxy), the testbed environment is transparent to both the phone and apps and looks like a "normal" wireless network. All steps within the experiment life cycle have been automated. This provides the possibility to efficiently scale the number of applications and experiments. MATAdOR provides functionality to easily and automatically intercept all network traffic. It can also transparently redirect network traffic through hosts at remote locations, appearing to outsiders and the application itself as if the phone was located at that place. When proxying the phone's traffic through a remote location, the phone's location services are manipulated accordingly.

3.2   Methodology

The goal of our experiment is to collect information about the path that messages take on the Internet when two communication partners communicate with each other using a mobile messaging application. In addition, we want to learn about the regions and countries a message traverses on its way. To do so, we have to analyze the network path between both communication partners and the messaging service infrastructure.

In our experiment, we use a set of four carefully selected mobile messaging services and use their respective applications to exchange messages between the two mobile phones in our testbed. In a single measurement, we use one specific mobile messaging application, connect to the mobile messaging service on both phones and exchange messages between both devices. By doing so, we can extract the communication endpoints for the mobile messaging service from the network traffic. We can then perform path measurements to these communication endpoints from both mobile phones to obtain the network path to the service provider infrastructure. To get a global view on communication, we tunnel traffic through 28 PlanetLab nodes. This way, we can learn the path messages take for example for a WhatsApp user in Australia communicating with a user in North America. In addition, we conduct direct path measurements between both respective PlanetLab nodes to obtain the direct network path.

For the path measurements, we use the standard `traceroute` tool provided with GNU/Linux. From the network traces, we extract the protocol (i.e. TCP or UDP) and port number (e.g. 443) the mobile messaging service uses and apply these settings to measure the network path to the mobile messaging service infrastructure. To obtain the path between nodes, we use `traceroute` with TCP and a random high port.

Selection of Applications. For this work, we carefully selected four different mobile messaging services based on different characteristics depicted in Table 1.

Based on their popularity, we picked WhatsApp and WeChat as the two mobile messaging services built for mobile chat. Due to its high rank in the EFF Scorecard with respect to security and privacy and being free software with its source code open to the public, we picked TextSecure as a third application for this experiment. We chose Threema for its promise of servers based in Switzerland and claim of strong privacy for the users. In addition, Threema is one of the few Europe-based providers. Since all of the previous solutions rely on a centralized client/server architecture, we select Bleep as a fifth candidate due to its decentralized peer-to-peer architecture. However, we could not enforce peer-to-peer behavior in our testbed and observed minute-long delays between messages. We concluded that peer-to-peer architectures require closer investigation including the use of NAT traversal techniques in our framework. For this reason, we excluded Bleep from the set of applications. We did not further pursue Firechat as it advertises peer-to-peer behavior only for local mesh networks.

Node Selection. To achieve a global view on messaging communication, we compiled a list of PlanetLab nodes providing a wide geographical distribution. The objective for this list was to cover as many regions and countries as possible. However, PlanetLab does not provide equal coverage in all regions and availability of nodes strongly differs across regions. When we conducted our experiment, PlanetLab featured nodes in 49 countries, but we only found 28 countries with at

Table 1. Properties of mobile messaging services and applications.

Application (Version)	Monthly active users[1] [22]	EFF Scorecard[2] Points [4]	Architecture	Server Distribution	Mobile First
WhatsApp (2.12.176)	800-900mn [12, 23] [27, p.23]	2	client-server	n/a	✓
WeChat (6.2.4)	400-600mn [27, p.22] [26, p.4]	n/a	client-server	n/a	✓
Facebook[3]	350-600mn [5], [27, p.22]	2	client-server	n/a	✗
Skype	300mn [15]	1	client-server	n/a	✗
QQ International	843mn [26, p.4]	2	client-server	n/a	✗
Viber	249mn [21]	1	client-server	n/a	✓
LINE	211mn [13]	n/a	client-server	n/a	✓
Kik	200mn[4] [25]	1	client-server	n/a	✓
Tango	70mn [24]	n/a	client-server	n/a	✓
KakaoTalk	48mn [2]	n/a	client-server	n/a	✓
Yahoo Messenger	n/a	1	client-server	n/a	✗
TextSecure (2.24.1)	>10mn[4] [17]	7	client-server	global	✓
Silent Text	n/a	7	client-server	n/a	✓
Telegram	30-50mn [27, p.22] [28]	4[5]	client-server	global	✓
Wickr	4mn[6] [20]	5	client-server	global	✓
Bleep (1.0.616)	n/a	n/a	P2P	n/a	✓
FireChat	n/a	n/a	mesh P2P	n/a	✓
Threema (2.41)	3mn[4] [29]	5	client-server	Switzerland	✓
SIMSme	1 mn[6]	n/a	client-server	Germany	✓

1: Around July 30, 2015, for exact date see app-specific source 2: EFF Secure Messaging Scorecard [4]
3: Stand-alone Facebook Messenger 4: Registered users 5: Score of 7 in secure chats 6: App Store Downloads

least one stable and responsive node, providing good coverage for North America, Europe, Asia and Oceania. For South America only a single node in Argentina and Brazil was provided, for Africa no nodes could be accessed at all.

For our experiment, we therefore used 4 nodes in the Americas (North America: 2, South America: 2), 7 nodes in Asia (Eastern Asia: 4, South-Eastern Asia: 2, Western Asia: 1), 16 nodes in Europe (Eastern Europe: 3, Northern Europe: 5, Southern Europe: 4, Western Europe: 4) and 2 nodes in Oceania.

Limitations. It is important to note that our path measurements only record a country as being part of a path if a hop from that country replies to path measurements. This can be biased by (a) nodes not answering those requests and (b) countries being passively traversed. Especially the latter is relevant, as intelligence services are known to also wiretap passively. For example, some measurements from Switzerland offer direct paths to Hong Kong or the U.S., but obviously more countries in between would have passive access to the cables in-between.

4 Postprocessing Experiment Results

Despite limiting application communication, the resulting network traces included some irrelevant flows. For this experiment, we solely want to evaluate traffic between the mobile messaging application and the mobile messaging service's backend. Therefore we had to classify network flows and assemble a black- and whitelist of network flows for exclusion or inclusion. Here, we went through several steps:

First, we limited background traffic by firewalling communication to only allow the specific mobile messaging application under test to access the network. Second, we conducted six measurements from America, Europe and Asia without the mobile messaging application running. This resulted in network traces containing "background noise" we could exclude after manual validation. Third, we manually inspected several dozens of traces per mobile messaging application to determine additional background traffic. The sources for this traffic were manually added to the filtering blacklist. Fourth, we separated authentication and other background traffic for every application from messaging traffic through temporal correlation with message timers.

For Threema, TextSecure and WhatsApp, we found all messaging servers to be resolved through DNS and to resolve uniformly across the globe, confirming the results of [7] for WhatsApp. We found WeChat to use both DNS requests and a custom-built DNS-over-HTTP protocol for name resolution, providing different name resolution when queried from within or from outside China. This DNS-over-HTTP uses a 30 min timeout and therefore "contaminates" our name resolution cache, which we flush after every experiment, typically lasting five to ten minutes. We therefore built the whitelist for WeChat analysis through manual analysis. The resulting detailed DNS table can be found online[3].

In a last step we automatically processed all traces and classified all addresses into this black- or whitelist. We manually classified all remaining addresses.

4.1 Mapping Path Measurements to Countries and Regions

To obtain the countries the traffic traverses, both the application path and the network path were processed to provide a geolocation of the IP addresses. With some manual corrections, we found the ip2location[4] country database to provide the most accurate results. To not overly rely on that database, we manually validated the mappings in at least one trace per target subnet and source country. With respect to known inaccuracies of both reverse DNS labels and geolocation databases, as described in [11,34], we paid special attention to round-trip times found in forward path measurements.

To analyze locality with respect to a specific geographic region, we used the United Nations geoscheme[5] to assign countries to regions and subregions. This scheme relies on 5 regions (Africa, Americas, Asia, Europe, Oceania) which are further divided into geographic subregions (e.g. for the Americas: Latin America and the Caribbean, Central America, South America, and Northern America).

---

[3] http://www.net.in.tum.de/pub/mobmes/dnstable.pdf
[4] http://www.ip2location.com
[5] http://millenniumindicators.un.org/unsd/methods/m49/m49regin.htm

4.2 Mapping Countries to Interest Groups

In addition to geographic locality, we analyzed the possibility of several juris-dictions and similar entities to access the network traffic. In this analysis, we defined several *interest groups* and checked for the different mobile messaging services if these interest groups can access the traffic. For this analysis we defined the following interest groups:

- *5 Eyes* consisting of: Great Britain, United States, New Zealand, Canada
- *European Union* consisting of: Austria, Belgium, Bulgaria, Croatia, Cyprus, Czech Republic, Denmark, Estonia, Finland, France, Germany, Greece, Hungary, Ireland, Italy, Latvia, Lithuania, Luxembourg, Malta, Nether-lands, Poland, Portugal, Romania, Slovakia, Slovenia, Spain, Sweden, United Kingdom
- *Arab League* consisting of: Algeria, Bahrain, Comoros, Djibouti, Egypt, Iraq, Jordan, Kuwait, Lebanon, Libya, Mauritania, Morocco, Oman, Palestine, Qatar, Saudi Arabia, Somalia, Sudan
- *Russia* with the only member Russia
- *China* with the only member China.

5 Results

With our experiments, running from Sep 30 2015 to Oct 12 2015, we conducted 406 measurements between the 28 PlanetLab nodes using the 4 selected mobile messaging services, resulting in 1624 measurements in total.

Table 2 shows the path comparisons between application path and network path. The first columns evaluate the direct measurements between nodes and show how many % of measurements failed to stay within the region. We found that all traffic from Israel to other Asian countries is being routed through Europe and the U.S. As we use seven nodes in Asia, six measurements from Israel fail to remain within region. Also, with two nodes in South America, the measurement between those two nodes leaves South America for routing through North America. As the two in-country measurements stay in the region, the 33 % understate the effect, caused by the low number of nodes. As a result we highlight that only Europe and North America feature at least one messenger that keeps traffic local. Asia traffic for WeChat does not remain local because of Israel's aforementioned routing and also because of traffic from Singapore and Thailand being routed to the Chinese WeChat servers through U.S. IXPs.

Table 3 shows how measurements from a specific region were subject to var-ious interest groups, both for the network path and for the specific application path:

Europe to Europe: 72 % of network path measurements within Europe were accessible to 5 Eyes (by routing through UK). 98 % of measurements were acces-sible to the European Union, with only measurements internal to Switzerland and Norway not being accessible. For application paths, Threema reduces the 5

Table 2. Mobile messaging services in almost all cases direct traffic out of region.

		Traffic leaving region					
		Network Path		Application Path			
Region	# Measurements	#	%	TextSecure	Threema	WeChat	WhatsApp
Europe	120	0	0%	100%	0%	100%	100%
Oceania	3	0	0%	100%	100%	100%	100%
Asia	28	6	21%	100%	100%	50%	100%
Americas	10	0	0%	0%	100%	100%	0%
South America	3	1	33%	100%	100%	100%	100%
Northern America	3	0	0%	0%	100%	100%	0%

Legend: > Network Path

Eyes access by 16 % as it effectively proxies traffic through Switzerland, which enforces continental routing for some routes (e.g. Poland - Switzerland - Spain as compared to Poland - UK - Spain). 99 % of WeChat measurements within Europe were accessible to 5 Eyes because of routing through the U.S. Only the Switzerland internal measurement offered a direct path to Hong Kong. As Switzerland has a direct path to the U.S. as well, this also explains the one case where EU can not access TextSecure messages. When using Threema within

Table 3. Mobile messaging services in most cases increase traffic accessibility for interest groups.

			Accessible for Interest Group											
	Interest		Network Path		TextSecure		Threema		WeChat		WhatsApp			
Region	Group	#Total	#	%	#	%	#	%	#	%	#	%		
Europe	5 Eyes	120	86	72%	120	100%	68	57%	119	99%	120	100%		
Europe	EU	120	118	98%	119	99%	119	99%	120	100%	120	100%		
Europe	China	120	0	0%	0	0%	0	0%	120	100%	0	0%		
Oceania	5 Eyes	3	3	100%	3	100%	3	100%	3	100%	3	100%		
Oceania	EU	3	0	0%	0	0%	3	100%	0	0%	0	0%		
Oceania	China	3	0	0%	0	0%	0	0%	3	100%	0	0%		
Asia	5 Eyes	28	6	21%	28	100%	21	75%	14	50%	28	100%		
Asia	EU	28	6	21%	7	25%	18	64%	7	25%	7	25%		
Asia	China	28	10	36%	7	25%	7	25%	28	100%	7	25%		
South America	5 Eyes	3	1	33%	3	100%	3	100%	3	100%	3	100%		
South America	EU	3	0	0%	0	0%	2	67%	0	0%	0	0%		
South America	China	3	0	0%	0	0%	0	0%	3	100%	0	0%		
North America	5 Eyes	3	3	100%	3	100%	3	100%	3	100%	3	100%		
North America	EU	3	0	0%	0	0%	2	67%	0	0%	0	0%		
North America	China	3	0	0%	0	0%	0	0%	3	100%	0	0%		

Legend: < Network Path; > Network Path

Switzerland, the application path remains in Switzerland as well, hence the EU cannot access those measurements.

Oceania to Oceania: As Australia and New Zealand are both members of 5 Eyes, obviously all measurements are accessible to the latter. It is remarkable that all WeChat traffic, e.g. generated by exile Chinese, is routed through China.

Asia to Asia: At a network level, both 5 Eyes, China and the European Union can access about 20 % to 40 % of traces sent within Asia. This is largely caused by the before mentioned Israel routing. 75 % of Threema traffic is 5 Eyes accessible by routing to Switzerland through the U.S. Also, a large portion of WeChat traffic (46 %) is accessible to 5 Eyes, both by Israel routing through the U.S. and by Singapore routing to WeChat's Chinese backend through an U.S. IXP.

North America to North America: As expected, 100 % of traffic is 5 Eyes accessible. For Threema, traffic from Canada to Switzerland was again routed through a direct hop from Miami to Zurich, resulting in two measurements seeming inaccessible to EU.

South America to South America: Measurements from Argentina were routed through a direct tunnel from Miami to Zurich and hence were not accessible for the EU in our metric. Hence only 2 out of 3 Threema measurements from South America are accessible for the EU. However, South America's communication is, independently of the mobile messaging service being used, always susceptible to 5 Eyes.

Russia and Arab League: None of the measurements did traverse Russia or the Arab League. We hence excluded those from the table.

6   Summary and Conclusion

We conducted traffic locality measurements between 28 countries for four mobile messaging services. We found those apps to heavily distort locality of traffic and hence drastically widen the set of actors able to access it. With a few notable exceptions, e.g. when using Threema in Switzerland, this has large negative impact on the users' privacy. This could be alleviated by decentralizing the mobile messaging services backend infrastructures or even the services themselves, using P2P techniques. With this being the first study on this particular topic, we hope to raise user and operator awareness for this problem. To conduct our measurements, we introduced the MATAdOR framework to analyze messaging traffic characteristics on mobile phones. A detailed overview over the MATAdOR framework can be found in [35]. We fully release both the MATAdOR framework and the dataset produced in our measurements through our website[6]. This enables future work to easily validate our results or do further analysis, such as deeper protocol analysis on the apps. Future work might also include analysis of WeChat's regional optimization within China, focus on peer-to-peer services

---

[6] http://net.in.tum.de/pub/mobmes/

like Bleep, or further dissect protocols of mobile messaging services. To improve quality of path measurement results, future work could use additional techniques such as fiber maps [3].

Acknowledgments. We thank Andreas Loibl for early access to his Measurement Proxy software.

References

1. Brandom, R.: WhatsApp rolls out end-to-end encryption using TextSecure code (2014). https://www.theverge.com/2014/11/18/7239221/whatsapp-rolls-out-end-to-end-encryption-with-textsecure. Accessed 14 September 2015
2. Kakao, D.: 2Q15 earnings report, August 2015. http://www.kakaocorp.com/upload_resources/ir/siljeok/siljeok_20150813080737.pdf. Accessed 23 September 2015
3. Durairajan, R., Barford, P., Sommers, J., Willinger, W.: InterTubes: a study of the US long-haul fiber-optic infrastructure. In: SIGCOMM 2015 (2015)
4. Electronic Frontier Foundation. Secure Messaging Scorecard (2014). https://www.eff.org/secure-messaging-scorecard. Accessed 14 September 2015
5. Facebook. Messenger at f8, March 2015. http://newsroom.fb.com/news/2015/03/messenger-at-f8/. Accessed 17 September 2015
6. Federal Network Agency for Electricity, Gas, Telecommunications Post and Railway. Annual report 2014, p. 81 (2014)
7. Fiadino, P., Schiavone, M., Casas, P.: Vivisecting WhatsApp in cellular networks: servers, flows, and quality of experience. In: Steiner, M., Barlet-Ros, P., Bonaventure, O. (eds.) TMA 2015. LNCS, vol. 9053, pp. 49–63. Springer, Heidelberg (2015)
8. Frosch, T., Mainka, C., et al.: How Secure is TextSecure? Technical report (2014)
9. Golson, J.: Apple fighting the US government over encrypted iMessages (2015). http://www.techrepublic.com/article/apple-fighting-the-us-government-on-turning-over-encrypted-imessages/. Accessed 14 September 2015
10. Huang, Q., Lee, P.P., et al.: Fine-grained dissection of WeChat in cellular networks. IWQoS (2015)
11. Huffaker, B., Fomenkov, M., Claffy, K.: DRoP: DNS-based router positioning. ACM SIGCOMM CCR **44**(3), 5–13 (2014)
12. Koum, J.: Whatsapp - now serving 900,000,000 monthly active users, September 2015. https://www.facebook.com/jan.koum/posts/10153580960970011. Accessed 23 September 2015
13. Line Corporation. LINE Corporation Announces 2015Q2 Earnings, July 2015. http://linecorp.com/en/pr/news/en/2015/1043. Accessed 17 September 2015
14. Marlinspike, M.: A Saudi Arabia telecom's surveillance pitch (2013). http://www.thoughtcrime.org/blog/saudi-surveillance/. Accessed 14 September 2015
15. McMurchy, L.: Skype connection hub ads provide increased scale for marketers, December 2014. http://advertising.microsoft.com/en/blog/29331/skype-connection-hub-ads-provide-increased-scale-for-marketers. Accessed 17 September 2015
16. Mueller, R., Schrittwieser, S., et al.: What's new with WhatsApp & Co.? Revisiting the security of smartphone messaging applications. In: iiWAS (2014)

17. Open Whisper Systems. Textsecure, now with 10 million more users, December 2013. https://whispersystems.org/blog/cyanogen-integration/. Accessed 23 September 2015
18. Pew Research Center. Mobile messaging and social media 2015 (2015). http://www.pewinternet.org/files/2015/08/Social-Media-Update-2015-FINAL2.pdf. Accessed 14 September 2015
19. PlanetLab Central. User tools. https://www.planet-lab.org/tools. Accessed 17 September 2015
20. Reader, R.: Wickr CEO Nico Sell: behind the glasses, January 2015. http://venturebeat.com/2015/01/13/wickr-ceo-nico-sell-behind-the-glasses/. Accessed 23 September 2015
21. Statista. Number of monthly active viber users, April 2015. http://www.statista.com/statistics/316423/. Accessed 23 September 2015
22. Statista. We are social. (n.d.). most popular global mobile messenger apps as of August 2015. http://www.statista.com/statistics/258749/. Accessed 23 September 2015
23. Statista. Number of monthly active WhatsApp users worldwide. http://www.statista.com/statistics/260819/number-of-monthly-active-whatsapp-users/. Accessed 23 September 2015
24. Tango. 200 million members!, March 2014. http://www.tango.me/blog/200-million-members. Accessed 17 September 2015
25. TechCrunch. Chat app kik hits 200m registered users, January 2015. http://techcrunch.com/2015/01/28/dont-expect-kik-maus/. Accessed 23 September 2015
26. Tencent. 2015Q2 results, August 2015. http://www.tencent.com/en-us/content/ir/news/2015/attachments/20150812.pdf. Accessed 23 September 2015
27. The European Commission. Case No COMP/M.7217 - FACEBOOK/ WHATSAPP (2014). http://ec.europa.eu/competition/mergers/cases/decisions/m7217_20141003_20310_3962132_EN.pdf
28. The Telegram Team. Telegram reaches 1 billion daily messages, December 2014. https://telegram.org/blog/billion. Accessed 17 September 2015
29. Threema. If you value security and privacy, September 2014. https://threema.ch/press-files/1_press_info/Press-Info_Threema_EN.pdf. Accessed 17 September 2015
30. TNS Global. The new social frontier: Instant messaging usage jumpps 12% (2015). http://www.tnsglobal.com/press-release/new-social-frontier-instant-messaging-usage-jumps. Accessed 7 October 2015
31. Vodafone. Law enforcement disclosure report 2015 (2015). https://www.vodafone.com/content/index/about/sustainability/law_enforcement.html. Accessed 14 September 2015
32. Wählisch, M., Schmidt, T.C., de Brün, M., Häberlen, T.: Exposing a nation-centric view on the German internet – A change in perspective on AS-level. In: Taft, N., Ricciato, F. (eds.) PAM 2012. LNCS, vol. 7192, pp. 200–210. Springer, Heidelberg (2012)
33. Wikipedia. Mobile application testing (2015). https://en.wikipedia.org/wiki/Mobile_application_testing#Some_Mobile_Application_Testing_Tools. Accessed 17 September 2015
34. Zhang, M., Ruan, Y., Pai, V.S., Rexford, J.: How DNS Misnaming Distorts Internet Topology Mapping. In: USENIX (2006)
35. Zirngibl, J.: Security Analysis of Mobile Messaging Traffic with an Automated Test Framework. Bachelor's thesis, Technische Universität München (2015)

Web

Scout: A Point of Presence Recommendation System Using Real User Monitoring Data

Yang Yang[✉], Liang Zhang, Ritesh Maheshwari, Zaid Ali Kahn,
Deepak Agarwal, and Sanjay Dubey

LinkedIn, 2029 Stierlin Court, Mountain View, CA 94043, USA
{yyang,lizhang,rmaheshw,zali,dagarwal,sdubey}@linkedin.com

Abstract. This paper describes, *Scout*, a statistical modeling driven approach to automatically recommend new Point of Presence (PoP) centers for web sites. PoPs help reduce a website's page download time dramatically. However, where to build the new PoP centers given the current assets of existing ones is a problem that has rarely been studied in a quantitative and principled way before; it was mainly done through empirical studies or through applying industry experience and intuitions. In this paper, we propose a novel approach that estimates the impact of the PoP centers by building a statistical model using the real user monitoring data collected by the web sites and recommend the next PoPs to build. We also consider the problem of recommending PoPs using other metrics such as user's number of page views. We show empirically that our approach works well, by experiments that use real data collected from millions of user visits in a major social network site.

1 Introduction

Most websites serve dynamic content (e.g. HTML and JSON) from their data centers and utilize Content Delivery Networks (CDN) for serving cacheable assets such as Cascading Style Sheets (CSS), JavaScripts, images etc. Reducing the download time of dynamic content is important to improve the experience of a typical user visiting the site. One commonly adopted strategy by web companies to accomplish this is to terminate user's TCP connection closer to the user by using Point of Presence centers (PoP).[1]

Point of Presence Centers, or PoPs, are "small scale data centers" usually with only a few racks. They act as TCP termination point of client requests for dynamic content. As shown in Fig. 1, data transfer over PoP to data center link happens in single round trip time (RTT) due to large congestion control windows between them. But the data transfer between clients and PoP can take multiple RTTs since that TCP connection is likely new with a small congestion control window and the dynamic content size is larger than what can fit in the smaller congestion window. For users with high RTTs to the data centers, early

---

[1] Another strategy is to use CDNs to deliver dynamic content, but it is less common due to security, privacy and cost concerns.

© Springer International Publishing Switzerland 2016
T. Karagiannis and X. Dimitropoulos (Eds.): PAM 2016, LNCS 9631, pp. 205–217, 2016.
DOI: 10.1007/978-3-319-30505-9_16

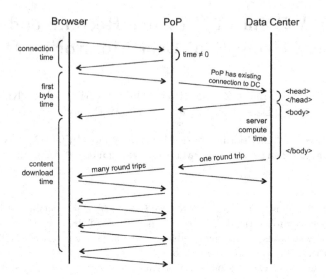

Fig. 1. An example illustration of how PoPs help in performance. In this paper, we focus on optimizing PoP location for page download time, which is defined as sum of first byte time and content download time.

TCP termination at PoPs help improve the overall download time by reducing the RTT between users and PoPs.

Our estimates (using historical costs from a major social network) show that building a PoP can be a costly affair: an initial investment of over 1 Million US dollars and a recurring cost of about US $720000 per year. An important question then arises: where should the next PoP be built? Note that the ideal location of the next PoP is dependent on many factors such as: (a) feasibility and cost of building a PoP in a given location; (b) potential performance improvement for end-users that will get impacted by the PoP; and (c) other business benefits to the company for the impacted regions like increased page views, engagement etc.

Traditionally, the selection of PoP locations is based on experience or intuition: web companies often follow their predecessor's paths to expand their PoP footprints, or study the network connection for the regions in which they want to expand businesses to propose new PoP locations. To the best of our knowledge, the problem of where to build the next PoPs has not been systematically studied in a quantitative and principled way before.

In this paper we propose *Scout*, a general purpose PoP recommendation system for web companies utilizing PoPs as end-user connection termination points. At a high level, Scout works as follows:

1. Scout takes as input a set of existing PoPs, a set of potential PoP candidates, passively collected real user monitoring (RUM) data from user visits to the website, and other relevant features such as user's geographical region, browser type, the size of the packets to be downloaded etc.

2. Scout uses the RUM data to train a statistical model to predict page download time using features such as distance between current PoP and end-user, end-user's network characteristics, PoP's network characteristics etc.
3. For each potential PoP in the candidate list, Scout then predicts page download time improvement for end-users who see a net positive gain if assigned to that PoP.
4. Scout calculates "impact score" for each candidate PoP, and outputs a sorted list of PoP candidate locations by the score. The impact score is defined to be either the improvement to the overall site performance, or the impact to some other business metrics such as total number of page views.

Real User Monitoring (RUM) Data. For the past few years, web companies have been able to collect client-side performance data for their end-users to analyze and detect performance issues using the Navigation timing API, which was recommended by the Web Performance working group of the World Wide Web Consortium (W3C) in 2012 and implemented by most of the major browsers. This technique of client-side monitoring is called Real User Monitoring, or RUM. In this paper, we use client IP address and page download time metrics from RUM to build our statistical models.

Related Work. We believe Scout is a novel approach to an age old problem faced by most web companies. Scout's design was motivated by a singular focus on using only readily available *passive* measurement data to deliver an end-to-end solution to PoP selection problem. This sets it apart from previous works [3,5,6,11] in the literature since most of them have used active measurement techniques and have tried to solve a piece of puzzle by only trying to estimate RTT. The essential metric for performance of a website is the total page download time. Our work estimates impact of building a PoP using metrics that impact the end-users' page download time which albeit includes RTT, but also includes many other important features, e.g. size of the webpage (which varies on a per-user basis), the potential PoP's peering density, concentration of the website's end-users around a given location, improvement in performance for end-users in a given location etc. Most works in literature have also evaluated their approaches in simulations or a small set of experimental data. In contrast, our approach uses millions of data samples from real users of a major social network site with > 400 million members and billions of page views per month. Finally, active measurement techniques require significant effort to collect data, whereas we use RUM data which is likely being already collected by most web companies. Other interesting works in this field that are orthogonal to our work but related are those (a) optimize how to assign users to PoPs (once built) [10,12], (b) use statistical modeling to correlate user request patterns with web server performance [8,15] and (c) study impact of web performance on user behavior [1,4,13,14].

2 Scout: A System for Recommending New PoP Centers

Assume a web company already has T number of existing PoP centers, denoted as $p_1, ..., p_T$. We would like to find the optimal location to build the next PoP p_{T+1}

from candidate set P, given p_1, ..., p_T. Since sometimes a fast-growing company may want to build multiple new PoPs at the same time, the problem can also be extended to finding an optimal set of PoP locations with pre-determined size L, p_{T+1}, ..., p_{T+L} from candidate set P, given p_1, ..., p_T.

PoP candidate set P is derived using the following constraints: availability of real estate to house a high density of power and proximity to metro region fiber, neutrality of PoP/data center operator, and closeness to Internet Exchange Points (IXP's) and interconnections. We start our list with the PeeringDB data [2] that contains about 1400 potential locations worldwide; we remove all IXP locations where number of ASNs peering at the IXP is below a certain threshold (e.g. 30). These locations are less desirable since they do not have as many potential peering partners. At the end our candidate list includes around 400 facilities where PoPs can be built for better performance. Others may use different selection criteria for PoP candidate list selection but our PoP recommendation system should still work in general.

At a high-level, our approach works as follows: (a) We build a statistical model to predict site speed when a user is allocated to a new candidate PoP center. (b) For a new candidate PoP center location, we measure the overall predicted improvement to site speed (impact score) obtained by hypothetically allocating a set of user visits to the new PoP. Note that only the user visits which are projected to benefit from the new PoP will be routed to it. We also assume that new PoPs are built with enough capacity so that load is not a factor. (c) When we have to recommend multiple PoP center locations simultaneously, we consider two strategies: a greedy strategy that computes impact score for each candidate PoP incrementally one at a time; a more computationally intensive strategy computes the impact score obtained by evaluating multiple PoPs simultaneously. We scale the computation for the latter by using Map-Reduce.

2.1   Site Speed Prediction Model Using RUM

We first describe our probabilistic statistical modeling approach of using a set of features to predict the **total page download time**, which equals the sum of connect time, first-byte time and content download time. The model is learned from the RUM data collected from user visits connecting to the current PoP centers. We consider three types of features here: (a) Context features of the user visit, e.g. time of the day, day of the week, the webpage that the users are visiting, through Secure Sockets Layer (SSL) or not, and so forth; (b) User-specific features, including user's geographical locations inferred from their IP addresses, operating systems, web browser types (e.g. Internet Explorer, or Mozilla Firefox, or Google Chrome) and versions, the size of packets to be downloaded from the server (or equivalent features), number of social network connections the user has, etc.; (c) PoP-specific features, including both the user distance to the PoP centers and the PoP center distance to the data centers. In this paper we use both the geographical distance and the network distance (which captures the number of hops it takes to connect from a user's original IP address to the PoP centers). The geographical distance between a user and the PoP center is obtained by calculating the straight line distance between the user's inferred geographical location (from their IP address) and the location of the PoP center. In order to calculate network distance between user's origin AS and PoP center, we obtained route server data for 70 IXP's globally from Packet Clearing House (PCH), which consist of all the possible routes from user's origin ASNs to the peering ASNs; an ASN connection map can be built such that given any potential PoP center location with a list of peered ASNs, the minimum number of hops it takes from the user's origin AS to connect to the PoP is obtained as the network distance to the PoP feature. For example, assume a user's origin ASN is 56203, and the ASN path to route to the current PoP is "56203 => 7545 => 174 => 10912". Then, the network distance feature is 3, since it takes 3 ASN hops to connect to the PoP's peering ASN 10912. Based on the data results, we find that the geographical distance makes the biggest contribution to the final prediction, but other features are also contributing.

Our Notations. For each user page view i and the PoP center p that the user is routed to, let $y_{i,p}$ be the observed total page download time, which is the sum of connection time, first byte time, and content download time. We also denote the corresponding feature set for observation i and PoP center p as $x_{i,p}$, a m-dim column vector. These features including context, user-specific and PoP-specific features, are used to predict site speed $y_{i,p}$ through a statistical model. Note that both the total page download time $y_{i,p}$ and the feature set $x_{i,p}$ depend on the location of the PoP center p. Hence, if the user visit i is routed to a new PoP center p' instead of p, the feature set would become $x_{i,p'}$, and the impact to the total page download time would be $y_{i,p'}$ instead of $y_{i,p}$.

The Model of Total Page Download Time. Given the feature set $x_{i,p}$, one simplest model to predict $y_{i,p}$ is linear regression upon the logarithm of the response $\log(y_{i,p}) \sim N(x'_{i,p}\beta, \sigma^2)$, where β is a m-dim column vector, and $x'_{i,p}\beta$ and σ^2 are respectively the mean and the variance of the Gaussian distribution. The logarithm transformation of $y_{i,p}$ is needed since the distribution of total page download time has a long tail towards the right. Here, we care about the estimate of β, which can be obtained by using the ordinary least square (OLS) method as

$$\hat{\beta}_{OLS} = \arg\min_{\beta} \sum_{i=1}^{N} (\log(y_{i,p_{obs}}) - x'_{i,p_{obs}}\beta)^2, \tag{1}$$

where p_{obs} means the PoP center that the users are routed to in the observed sample i, and N is the sample size. For feature vector $x_{i,p}$ where p can be any PoP center location, the expected total page download time can be predicted as $E[\log(y_{i,p})|x_{i,p}] = x'_{i,p}\hat{\beta}_{OLS}$.

Quantile Regression. Since the RUM data often include outliers and do not fit standard parametric distributions, it is customary to measure metrics such as total page download time through quantiles instead of the arithmetic mean. In such scenarios, since the model needs to be robust to outliers and the interest is to measure performance through quantiles such as median rather than the mean, using quantile regression (QR) [9] is a better approach. Assume the τ-th quantile of the total page download time $y_{i,p}$ is $y_{i,p}(\tau)$, i.e. $y_{i,p}(\tau) = \inf_t(P[y_{i,p} <= t] >= \tau)$. The corresponding coefficient vector can be solved by the loss function

$$\hat{\beta}_{QR}(\tau) = \arg\min_\beta \sum_{i=1}^{N} \rho_\tau(\log(y_{i,p_{obs}}) - x'_{i,p_{obs}}\beta), \tag{2}$$

where $\rho_\tau(z) = |z(\tau - I(z < 0))|$ for quantile $\tau \in (0,1)$, and $I(\cdot)$ is an indicator function. Given a set of features $x_{i,p}$, The predicted value of $y_{i,p}(\tau)$ is $\hat{y}_{i,p}(\tau) = \exp(x'_{i,p}\hat{\beta}_{QR}(\tau))$.

Better Feature Transformations. To model the potential non-linear relationship between the total page download time and some numerical features such as geographical distance, we apply piece-wise linear spline [7] on these features. For example, for the geographical distance d, given a set of knots $\{\xi_1, .., \xi_K\}$, the piece-wise linear spline is constructed by $K + 2$ number of basis functions as $h_1(d) = 1$, $h_2(d) = d$, $h_{k+2}(d) = (d - \xi_k)_+$, $k = 1, ..., K$, where $(x)_+ = x$ if $x > 0$, and 0 when $x <= 0$.

2.2   Recommend One PoP

In this section, we consider the problem of selecting the next PoP center candidate from the candidate set P, assuming we already have K number of PoP centers running. Our approach can be illustrated as follows:

1. Build a total page download time prediction model M based on the observed dataset $\{(x_{i,p_{obs}}, y_{i,p_{obs}}), i = 1, ..., N\}$. Note that M can be either linear regression or quantile regression. For linear regression with logarithm transformation of the response, $M(x_{i,p}) = \exp(x'_{i,p}\hat{\beta}_{OLS})$, and for quantile regression with logarithm transformation of the response, $M(x_{i,p}) = \exp(x'_{i,p}\hat{\beta}_{QR})$.
2. We predict the impact to the total page download time for record i if it is routed to PoP $p \in P$ instead of the current PoP center p_{obs}, by changing the feature set from $x_{i,p_{obs}}$ to $x_{i,p}$. The improvement of the total page download time can be calculated as $\Delta_i(p) = M(x_{i,p}) - M(x_{i,p_{obs}})$.
3. Since it may not be feasible to have personalized PoP center routing in practice, we group the users to segments by certain attributes, and route all users who belong to the same segment to the same PoP. The attributes to do such segmentation can be geographical regions or origin ASNs. For segment $\mathcal{I}$, we define

$$\Delta(p, \mathcal{I}) = \text{Median}\{M(x_{i,p}), i \in \mathcal{I}\} - \text{Median}\{M(x_{i,p_{obs}}), i \in \mathcal{I}\}, \tag{3}$$

and this is considered as the predicted impact on the median of the total page download time by routing to future PoP p for segment $\mathcal{I}$.

4. Calculate the impact score for each candidate PoP. Denote the probability of a page view request coming from segment $\mathcal{I}$ as $q_\mathcal{I}$, and $\sum_\mathcal{I} q_\mathcal{I} = 1$.

For each segment $\mathscr{I}$, if we route the traffic to PoP p, the predicted impact of site speed is $\Delta(p, \mathscr{I})$. However, if $\Delta(p, \mathscr{I}) < 0$, we would choose not to route to this new PoP given the projected gain is negative. Hence, the impact score $S(p)$ for PoP p can be defined as

$$S(p) = \sum_{\mathscr{I}} \max(0, \Delta(p, \mathscr{I})) q_{\mathscr{I}}. \tag{4}$$

And the best PoP candidate p_{opt} is $p_{opt} = \arg\max_{p \in P} S(p)$.

2.3 Recommend Multiple PoPs Simultaneously

Often we would like to have multiple new PoP recommendations at the same time, given the existing K number of PoPs. We can certainly run the approach described in Sect. 2.2 iteratively to obtain the list. However, this greedy approach may not be optimal; jointly considering the combinations of multiple PoP candidates at the same time can potentially give better impact scores overall. Assume we want to recommend L new PoPs out of the candidate set P, the problem to solve becomes

$$\max_{\{p_1,\dots,p_L\} \subset P} \sum_{\mathscr{I}} \max(0, \max_{p \in \{p_1,\dots,p_L\}} \Delta(p, \mathscr{I})) q_{\mathscr{I}} \tag{5}$$

The complexity of solving the optimization problem in (5) is $\binom{|P|}{L} L$, where $|P|$ is the number of PoP candidates. When $|P|$ and L are large, it will be computationally expensive to solve (5). However, note that the impact scores of all combinations of $\{p_1, \dots, p_L\}$ can be obtained in parallel. In this paper we use the Map-Reduce infrastructure for the parallelization, where the mappers generate all the possible combinations and the reducers compute the impact score for each combination, and finally another Map-Reduce step to sort and generate the top-K ranked list.

2.4 Recommending PoPs with Other Metrics

We have been using the total page download time improvement as the metric to recommend new PoPs; however, web sites often look at other downstream metrics impacted due to improvement in site speed, so sometimes it is desirable to recommend PoPs based on other business metrics, such as gains in user page views, engagement, or revenue. Here we illustrate the method by using the total number of user page views as an example. For each region $\mathscr{I}$, suppose from data analysis we can learn $f_{\mathscr{I}}(\Delta(p, \mathscr{I}))$, which is the rate of increase of the number of page views if median page download time improvement is $\Delta(p, \mathscr{I})$ for region $\mathscr{I}$, where $\Delta(p, \mathscr{I})$ is defined earlier in Eq. (3). Examples of such functions can be seen in Fig. 3. The impact to total number of page views on the site can then be defined as

$$PV(p) = \sum_{\mathscr{I}} f_{\mathscr{I}}(\Delta(p, \mathscr{I})) q_{\mathscr{I}}, \tag{6}$$

3   Experimental Results

In this section we show experimental results to measure predictive performance of our site speed models and the performance of our PoP recommendation algorithm. We also consider using business metrics such as number of page views on the site to recommend new PoPs, by studying the gains in such metrics given the predicted site speed improvements from our data.

Notes of Our Evaluation Strategy. An ideal evaluation approach to evaluate multiple PoP selection methods is to obtain top recommendations from each method and install PoPs at the recommended locations, and measure the site performance gain. However, installing a PoP just for experimentation is usually not practical and can be really expensive. Since the main challenge is to obtain an accurate site speed prediction model which can predict the performance gain after installing a PoP at a certain location, our evaluation mainly focuses on this aspect, which is described in Sect. 3.2. The PoP selection method described in Sects. 2.2 and 2.3 given the site speed performance model is quite straightforward, hence not much evaluation is needed there.

3.1   Our Data

We use a random sample of RUM data collected from a major social network site to train the site speed prediction model. The data set contains 4 million samples of user visits occurred during June 3, 2014 to June 9, 2014. We randomly do a 50:50 split of the data into training data and test sets. The models are estimated using training data and prediction accuracy is evaluated using test data.

Our candidate set for the new PoP recommendation includes around 400 facility names around of the world from peeringDB, each of which has a list of available peering ASNs. We use the same period of data that the site speed prediction model is trained with to recommend the new PoP facility locations.

In Sect. 2.4 we also consider using other user engagement metrics such as user's monthly number of page views for the PoP recommendation. To build the relationship between site speed and user page views (i.e. $f_{\mathscr{I}}(\Delta(p, \mathscr{I}))$), we used a random sample of the data in the entire month of June 2014.

3.2   Predictive Performance of Site Speed Model

We show the predictive performance of the total page download time for the statistical models described in Sect. 2, with the evaluation metric being the prediction error rate of the median page download time. Specifically, for each region $\mathscr{I}$ and PoP p,

$$error(\mathscr{I}, p) = \frac{|\text{Median}\{\hat{y}_{i,p}, \forall i \in \mathscr{I}\} - \text{Median}\{y_{i,p}, \forall i \in \mathscr{I}\}|}{\text{Median}\{y_{i,p}, \forall i \in \mathscr{I}\}} \qquad (7)$$

Quantile Regression vs. Ordinary Least Squares. To predict the median page download time, our experiments show that quantile regression is a better

choice versus linear regression using ordinary least squares. In Fig. 2 we show
the performance for both approaches in terms of the prediction error defined
in Eq. (7), where each circle indicates a geographical region, and the size of the
circle indicates the relative sample size of the region. The color of the circle
shows which PoP the region was routed to. There are in total 4 PoP at the
time of the analysis. It is clear that the prediction error of the median page
download time is significantly smaller in the case of quantile regression for the
major regions: all the big circles are above the $y = x$ line. This is mainly caused
by the fact that the distribution of total page download time still has a heavy
right tail even after taking logarithm transformation, so the mean prediction
tends to be noisier than the median prediction. Also note that the prediction
from the quantile regression model is often lower than 5 %, which provides a
good basis for our PoP recommendation algorithm to work well.

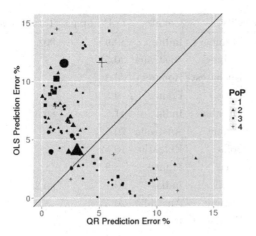

Fig. 2. Prediction error percentage of the median page download time comparing ordinary least square (OLS) and quantile regression (QR). The prediction error percentage
in both axises are defined in Eq. (7). Each circle indicates a geo region and the size
of the circle indicates the relative sample size of the region. The color of the circle
indicates which PoP the region is currently routed to. The black line is $y = x$.

3.3 PoP Recommendation Results

In this section we describe our experiments for recommending new PoPs, based
on the prediction model using quantile regression.

Recommending One PoP. We follow the approach described in Sect. 2.2 to
rank PoP candidates based on their impact scores, considering both the traffic
for each geographical region and the site speed improvement for such region.
Table 1 lists the top 8 recommended PoP facilities given the existing PoPs for
the social network site at the time the study was executed. It is interesting

Table 1. The top-ranked PoP recommendations if only one PoP is recommended.

IXP	City	Country	Impact score
TATA	Mumbai	India	47.1
TATA	Delhi	India	45.7
Netmagic	Chennai	India	41.2
UAE-IX	Dubai	UAE	38.3
INTERLAN	Bucharest	Romania	27.1
BIX.BG	Sofia	Bulgaria	26.2
UA-IX	Kiev	Ukraine	24.2
BiX	Bydapest	Hungary	23.6

Table 2. The top-ranked set of PoPs with each set containing 4 recommendations.

Rank	City	Country	PoP impact	Total impact
1	Mumbai	India	39.9	90.1
	Sydney	Australia	20.5	
	Bucharest	Romania	20.3	
	Paris	France	9.3	
2	Mumbai	India	41.6	89.5
	Sydney	Australia	20.5	
	Sofia	Bulgaria	18.52	
	Paris	France	8.9	
3	Delhi	India	40.1	89.2
	Sydney	Australia	20.5	
	Bucharest	Romania	19.2	
	Paris	France	9.4	

to see that the top 3 recommended facility locations are all in India, due to the fact that at the time this study was executed, no PoP existed in this region while its traffic to the site is quite high.

Recommending Multiple PoPs Simultaneously. Table 2 shows the top-ranked sets of PoP facilities that was obtained from applying the approach described in Sect. 2.3 with $L = 4$. It is interesting to observe that for all the three sets, the four locations now scatter around the world, with one in Asia, one in Oceanic, and two in Europe (Places such as Bucharest and Sofia are closer to Middle East while Paris mainly serve for Europe). It is also interesting to see that Sydney and Paris did not even show up in Table 1.

Recommending PoPs with Other Metrics. We first describe our approach to learn $f_{\mathscr{I}}(\Delta(p, \mathscr{I}))$, which is the rate of increase of the number of page views if median page download time improvement is $\Delta(p, \mathscr{I})$ for region $\mathscr{I}$. Note that

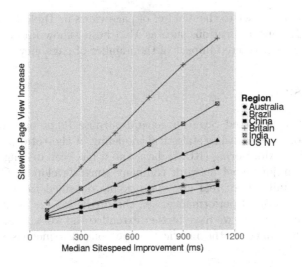

Fig. 3. Page download time improvement vs. increase rate of number of page views

Table 3. Top-ranked PoP recommendations from impact on user page views. The page view (PV) impact score is a rescaled number, proportional to $PV(p)$ in Eq. (6).

IXP	City	Country	PV impact
TATA	Mumbai	India	0.296
TATA	Delhi	India	0.296
UAE-IX	Dubai	UAE	0.255
Netmagic	Chennai	India	0.249
BNIX	Brussels	Belgium	0.241
France-IX	Paris	France	0.237
IXManchester	Manchester	UK	0.232
Edge-IX	UK	UK	0.232

naively looking at the marginal relationship between site speed and the number of page views can be misleading, since many confounding factors need to be adjusted. Hence we apply a stratification method to learn the relationship: (1) construct user segments based on confounding factors such as geographical region, number of connections etc., (2) for each user segment, estimate a smoothed curve of number of page views versus total page download time using locally weighted scatterplot smoothing (lowess), (3) an overall curve of page download time improvement versus increase of the number of page views is then obtained by aggregating the curves according to the traffic of each user segment. Figure 3 shows the learned relationship for several geographical regions. It is interesting to observe a significant difference in the slopes when we compare regions such as Great Britain and New York. We show the top-ranked PoPs from the perspective of impact to the number of page views in Table 3. Comparing to Table 1, more European locations such as Manchester show up in the list, since they have a higher predicted impact of the number of page views.

4 Conclusion

In this paper we proposed *Scout*, a general-purpose Point of Presence (PoP) recommendation system using statistical modeling of the total page download time on Real User Monitoring (RUM) data, and it has been driving the selection of PoPs for a major social network company since developed. Our empirical experiments on millions of real user data points obtained from a large social network show very good performance, i.e., the prediction errors are lower than 5 % for most regions, and we have further extended the work from purely using site speed performance as the metric to other business metrics such as total number of page views.

Acknowledgments. We are grateful to Samir R. Das for his valuable feedback on an earlier draft of this paper. We would also like to thank the anonymous reviewers for their insightful comments.

References

1. Brutlag, J.: Speed matters for google web search. Google, June 2009
2. www.peeringdb.com
3. Dabek, F., Cox, R., Kaashoek, F., Morris, R.: Vivaldi: a decentralized network coordinate system. In: ACM SIGCOMM Computer Communication Review, vol. 34, pp. 15–26. ACM (2004)
4. Dellaert, B.G., Kahn, B.E.: How tolerable is delay?: Consumers' evaluations of internet web sites after waiting. J. Interact. Mark. **13**(1), 41–54 (1999)
5. Francis, P., Jamin, S., Jin, C., Jin, Y., Raz, D., Shavitt, Y., Zhang, L.: Idmaps: a global internet host distance estimation service. IEEE/ACM Trans. Network. **9**(5), 525–540 (2001)
6. Gummadi, K.P., Saroiu, S., Gribble, S.D.: King: estimating latency between arbitrary internet end hosts. In: Proceedings of the 2nd ACM SIGCOMM Workshop on Internet Measurment, pp. 5–18. ACM (2002)
7. Hastie, T., Tibshirani, R., Friedman, J., Hastie, T., Friedman, J., Tibshirani, R.: The elements of statistical learning, vol. 2. Springer, New York (2009)
8. Iyengar, A.K., Squillante, M.S., Zhang, L.: Analysis and characterization of large-scale web server access patterns and performance. World Wide Web **2**(1–2), 85–100 (1999)
9. Koenker, R.: Quantile Regression. Cambridge University Press, Cambridge (2005)
10. Krishnan, R., Madhyastha, H.V., Srinivasan, S., Jain, S., Krishnamurthy, A., Anderson, T., Gao, J.: Moving beyond end-to-end path information to optimize cdn performance. In: Proceedings of the 9th ACM SIGCOMM Conference on Internet Measurement Conference, pp. 190–201. ACM (2009)

11. Madhyastha, H.V., Anderson, T., Krishnamurthy, A., Spring, N., Venkataramani, A.: A structural approach to latency prediction. In Proceedings of the 6th ACM SIGCOMM Conference on Internet Measurement, pp. 99–104. ACM (2006)
12. Maheshwari, R.: How LinkedIn used PoPs and RUM to make dynamic content download 25% faster. LinkedIn Engineering Blog (2014)
13. Ramsay, J., Barbesi, A., Preece, J.: A psychological investigation of long retrieval times on the world wide web. Interact. Comput. **10**(1), 77–86 (1998)
14. Sears, A., Jacko, J.A., Borella, M.S.: Internet delay effects: how users perceive quality, organization, and ease of use of information. In: CHI 1997 Extended Abstracts on Human Factors in Computing Systems, pp. 353–354. ACM (1997)
15. Squillante, M.S., Yao, D.D., Zhang, L.: Web traffic modeling and web server performance analysis. ACM SIGMETRICS Perform. Eval. Rev. **27**(3), 24–27 (1999). IBM TJ Watson Research Center

Is the Web HTTP/2 Yet?

Matteo Varvello[1]([⊠]), Kyle Schomp[2], David Naylor[3], Jeremy Blackburn[1],
Alessandro Finamore[1], and Konstantina Papagiannaki[1]

[1] Telefónica Research, Barcelona, Spain
matteo.varvello@telefonica.com
[2] Case Western Reserve University, Cleveland, USA
[3] Carnegie Mellon University, Pittsburgh, USA
http://isthewebhttp2yet.com/

Abstract. Version 2 of the Hypertext Transfer Protocol (HTTP/2) was
finalized in May 2015 as RFC 7540. It addresses well-known problems
with HTTP/1.1 (e.g., head of line blocking and redundant headers) and
introduces new features (e.g., server push and content priority). Though
HTTP/2 is designed to be the future of the web, it remains unclear
whether the web will—or should—hop on board. To shed light on this
question, we built a measurement platform that monitors HTTP/2 adoption and performance across the Alexa top 1 million websites on a daily
basis. Our system is live and up-to-date results can be viewed at [1].
In this paper, we report findings from an 11 month measurement campaign (November 2014 – October 2015). As of October 2015, we find
68,000 websites *reporting* HTTP/2 support, of which about 10,000 *actually* serve content with it. Unsurprisingly, popular sites are quicker to
adopt HTTP/2 and 31 % of the Alexa top 100 already support it. For
the most part, websites do not change as they move from HTTP/1.1
to HTTP/2; current web development practices like inlining and domain
sharding are still present. Contrary to previous results, we find that these
practices make HTTP/2 more resilient to losses and jitter. In all, we find
that 80 % of websites supporting HTTP/2 experience a decrease in page
load time compared with HTTP/1.1 and the decrease grows in mobile
networks.

1   Introduction

HTTP/2 (H2 for short) is the new version of HTTP, expected to replace version
1.1 (H1), which was standardized in 1999. H2 promises to make the web faster
and more efficient by compressing headers, introducing server push, fixing the
head of line blocking issue, and loading page elements in parallel over a single
TCP connection (cf. Sect. 2). Although the standard does not require encrypting
H2 connections with Transport Layer Security (TLS), the major browser vendors
currently only support encrypted H2 [19].

While on paper H2 represents the future of the web, it is unclear whether its
adoption will face a struggle similar to IPv6. As discussed in [5], the adoption of
a new protocol largely depends on the ratio between its benefits and its costs.

© Springer International Publishing Switzerland 2016
T. Karagiannis and X. Dimitropoulos (Eds.): PAM 2016, LNCS 9631, pp. 218–232, 2016.
DOI: 10.1007/978-3-319-30505-9_17

Modern websites are already designed to deal with H1's inefficiencies, employing hacks like spriting, inlining, and domain sharding [18]. While H2 would remove the need for such hacks, in theory simplifying web development, given their widespread use it is unclear how much H2 can improve performance over H1. Furthermore, it is unclear how these practices will affect H2 performance (which is crucial, since web developers cannot rebuild their sites overnight nor are they likely to maintain two versions until H1 disappears).

Motivated by these uncertainties, in this work we build a measurement platform that monitors the adoption and performance of H2. Using machines on PlanetLab [3] and in our labs in Spain and the U.S., we probe the top 1 million Alexa websites each day to see which support H2. For those that do, we note which features they use and measure performance with H1 and H2. Results are published daily at [1].

This paper reports findings from an 11-month measurement campaign, from November 2014 until October 2015 (cf. Sect. 4). As of October 2015, we find 68,000 websites *reporting* H2 support, of which only 10,000 *actually* serve website content over H2. NGINX, a popular web server implementation, currently powers 71.7 % of the working H2 websites, with LiteSpeed following at 13.7 % (in contrast to the 98 % they claim[1]). Our results also show that sites that have deployed H2 have not significantly altered their content; classic H1 hacks are still used in the H2 version. For example, inlining (putting CSS styles and JavaScript code directly in HTML) is still widely used, reducing caching benefits. The same is true of domain sharding (spreading web objects across multiple domains), causing H2 to use more TCP connections than necessary. In terms of page load time, for 80 % of the websites we measured an average reduction in page load time of 300 and 560 ms when accessed from a wired connection, respectively from Europe and the USA, 800 ms from a European 4G connection, and 1.6 s from a European 3G connection. The observed H2 benefits for mobile contradict previous studies; our analysis suggests that domain sharding, whether intentional or not, triggers the usage of several TCP connections, making H2 more resilient to losses and jitter typical of mobile networks.

2   Background and Related Work

H1 is an *ASCII* protocol that allows a client to request/submit content from/to a server. H1 is mostly used to fetch web pages, where clients request *objects* from a server and the resulting response is serialized over a persistent TCP connection. H1 provides pipelining to request multiple objects over the same TCP connection, but the benefits are limited since servers must respond to requests in order. Thus, an early request for a large object can delay all subsequent pipelined requests (*head of line blocking*). Clients mitigate this by opening several concurrent TCP connections to the server, which incurs additional overhead (TCP state on the server, TCP handshake latency, and TLS session setup

---

[1] https://www.litespeedtech.com/http2-ready—To their credit, another 27,000 websites powered by LiteSpeed redirect to an error page that loads over H2.

in the case of HTTPS [13]). Accordingly, browsers limit the number of simultaneous connections to each domain (e.g., 6 in Chrome and 15 in Firefox [22]). Web developers have responded to this limitation with *domain sharding*, where content is distributed across multiple domains, circumventing the per-domain connection limit. Finally, H1 requires the explicit transmission of headers on a per request/response basis. Therefore, common headers (e.g., server version) are retransmitted with each object—particularly wasteful for pages with many small objects.

SPDY and H2. SPDY is Google's update to H1. It is binary rather than ASCII, enabling efficient parsing, lighter network footprint, and reducing susceptibility to security issues caused by unsanitized input strings. SPDY opens a single TCP connection to a domain and *multiplexes* requests and responses, called *streams*, over that connection, which reduces the number of TCP/TLS handshakes and the CPU load at the server. SPDY also introduces content *priority* (clients can load important objects like CSS and JavaScript earlier), *server push* (the server can push objects before the client requests them), and *header compression* (reduces redundant header transmission). H2 builds on SPDY, making only relatively small changes. For example, H2 uses HPACK [16] for header compression, eliminating SPDY vulnerability to the "crime" attack [12].

NPN and ALPN. Since SPDY, H1, and H2 all use TLS over port 443, port number is no longer sufficient to indicate to web servers which application protocol the client wants to use. The Next Protocol Negotiation (NPN) [4] is a TLS extension developed by Google as part of its SPDY effort. During the TLS handshake, the server provides a list of supported application protocols; the client then chooses the protocol to use and communicates it to the server via an encrypted message. Application Layer Protocol Negotiation (ALPN) [20] is a revised version of NPN standardized by the IETF. In ALPN, the client sends which application protocols it supports to the server, ordered by priority. The server selects the protocol to use based on the protocols it supports and the client priority; next, it returns the selected protocol to the client via a plain text message.

Related Work. Previous work mostly investigate SPDY performance [8,10,11, 15]; to the best of our knowledge, [17] is the only work previous to ours focusing on H2. Although the results of these studies are mostly contradictory, they converge on reporting poor SPDY (and H2) performance on mobile networks.

Erman et al. [7] measure page load time for the top 20 Alexa websites via SPDY and H1 proxies in 3G. They find that SPDY performs poorly in mobile networks since TCP interprets cellular losses and jitter as congestion, causing unnecessary backoffs. Since SPDY uses fewer TCP connections than H1, its performance suffers more.

Xiao et al. [23] introduce new measurement techniques to provide a more robust characterization of SPDY. They show that, in absence of browser dependencies and computation, SPDY tends to outperform H1; however, the gains are reduced when dependencies and computation are factored back in (with the caveat that server push can squeeze additional performance gains from SPDY).

De Saxcè et al. extend this analysis to H2 [17]. Using the top 20 Alexa websites, they investigate H2 performance under various network delay, bandwidth, and loss using an open-source client and server. Their results confirm those for SPDY in [23]. Unfortunately, by serving clones of the websites from their own test server, they ignore the impact of important real-world website properties like domain sharding.

Our aim is to take the next step in characterizing H2 performance. Our measurements improve prior art in five ways: (1) we target more websites (1000 s as opposed to 10 s or 100 s); (2) we measure real servers from real networks (wired, 3G, and 4G); (3) we test real websites, not clones or synthetic traces; (4) we build on Chrome reliability to develop an accurate performance estimation tool; (5) we also study adoption and website structure trends.

3   Measurement Platform

This section describes our measurement platform. We start by summarizing a set of tools we have deployed, and then explain how we use them together to monitor H2 deployment and performance.

Prober is a lightweight bash script that identifies which application protocols a website announces. Prober uses OpenSSL [14] to attempt ALPN and NPN negotiations and returns either the list of protocols announced by the server or failure. Next, prober checks for H2 cleartext (H2C) support—that is, H2 without TLS—by including an UPGRADE header in an H1 request.

H2-lite is a lightweight client that attempts to download only the root object of a website using H2. H2-lite uses the Node.js [2] H2 library [9]. H2-lite follows HTTP redirects to obtain the root object and reports any protocol errors encountered along the way. H2-lite also identifies sites with certificate problems, e.g., self- signed certificates, mismatches between hostname and common name, or expired/revoked certificates.

Chrome-loader is a Python tool that loads pages using Chrome. It extracts object sizes and timing information using chrome-har-capturer [6]. Chrome-loader can instruct Chrome to use either H1 or SPDY/H2 (Chrome does not allow separate control over SPDY and H2). However, using Chrome's remote debugging protocol, chrome-loader reports which protocol was used to retrieve each individual object in a page.

We now describe our measurement platform in detail. It consists of a single *master* and many *workers*; the master issues crawl requests to the workers, which are deployed on both PlanetLab [3] and machines in our labs (U.S. and Spain). We use PlanetLab for simple measurements at a large scale and our lab machines for more complex measurements at a smaller scale and where machine reliability is important. The master constantly monitors PlanetLab to identify a pool of candidate machines (at least 500 MB of free memory, CPU load under 30 %, and no network connectivity issues). We collect measurements in three phases:

Phase I: It discovers, daily, which protocols are supported by the top 1 million Alexa websites. First, the master launches an instance of the `prober` on each PlanetLab worker. The worker is then assigned a unique 100-website list to probe. When it finishes, it reports results to the master and obtains a new list if one is available. This approach ensures load balancing among heterogeneous workers allowing faster workers to complete more tasks. To deal with slow workers, the master re-assigns uncompleted tasks to new workers after a timeout T (set to the average task completion time across workers). Phase I terminates when the tracker has a complete set of results.

Phase II: It verifies, daily, whether the sites that reported H2 support in Phase I *actually* serve content over H2. After Phase I, the master launches several instances of `h2-lite` and, as above, it dynamically assigns each 100 sites that reported H2 support in Phase I. Because the H2 library requires more up-to-date software than is available on PlanetLab, we run `h2-lite` on 4 machines under our control, 2 in Barcelona (Spain) and 2 in Cleveland (U.S.). When Phase II terminates, the master has a list of sites that *actually serve* content using H2.

Phase III: It fetches both the H1 and H2 version of websites that serve content via H2 using multiple network locations and access network types (e.g., fiber and 4G). The master is responsible for selecting the machines to be used and instructing them which websites to test. The master uses one of three strategies: (1) *regular*, where each network location with fiber access is weekly instructed to test all H2 websites identified by Phase II; (2) *lazy*, the same as the regular strategy but a website is tested only if one of these conditions is met: (a) it is a new website that recently adopted H2, (b) its content significantly changed from the last time it was tested, or (c) a timeout elapsed since the last test; (3) *mobile*, where only mobile-enabled locations are selected, and a subset of websites are tested based on their Alexa popularity.

To test a website, we fetch it 5 times with H1 and 5 times with either SPDY or H2 (as discussed above, Chrome does not provide fine-grained control between SPDY and H2). Fetches are run sequentially to limit the impact of network load. While testing a website, we run a background ping process to collect statistics about network latency and packet loss. For the mobile strategy, we force Chrome to report a mobile user-agent to the server, which may respond with a mobile version of the website. Before the five trials, an initial "primer" load is performed. This primer has a double purpose: (1) test whether a website significantly changed its content since the last time it was tested (used by the lazy strategy), and (2) ensure that DNS entries are cached at the ISP's DNS resolver before the first real trial (to prevent a cache miss on the first trial from skewing the load time results). Local content and DNS caches are disabled and each request carries a `cache-control` header instructing network caches not to respond.

We currently have Phase III workers in three different locations: Barcelona (Spain), Cleveland (USA), and Pittsburgh (USA). Each location consists of three machines with fiber connectivity. In addition, machines in Spain are connected to Android phones via USB tethering; each phone is configured to use either 3G or 4G. Because each SIM card has a 4 GB monthly limit, a maximum of about 200 websites—5 trials per protocol plus the primer—can be tested before exhausting the available plan. We ran Phase III with the regular strategy from November 2014 to September 2015, when the widespread deployment of H2 made it impossible to run Phase III weekly without additional machines. Thus, we switched to the lazy strategy. Finally, we ran Phase III with the mobile strategy only once in October 2015. We plan to run the mobile strategy once per month, as constrained by the mobile data plan.

4 Results

This section presents and analyzes the data collected using our measurement platform between November 10th, 2014 and October 16th, 2015. We invite the reader to access fresh data and analysis at [1].

4.1 Adoption

We recorded protocol support announced via ALPN/NPN for 11 months, during which time we saw support for 44 protocols (34 of which were versions of SPDY). Table 1 summarizes the evolution over time of the three most popular protocols, namely H1, SPDY 3.1, and H2; in addition, we also report NPN, ALPN, and H2C support when available. Each percentage is the maximum observed during the month; note that announce rates for H1 are underestimated since H1 sites are not required to use NPN/ALPN. The table also reports the total number of probed sites. From November 2014 to August 2015, we use the Alexa Top 1 Million list fetched on November 10th, 2014. Beginning in September 2015, we merge the current Alexa list with our own each day, constantly expanding the pool of sites we query (1.8 M as of October 16th 2015).

Overview. From November 2014 through August 2015, Table 1 shows mostly constant H1 and SPDY announce rates, with the exception of a large drop in May 2015 (2.2 and 2.5 percentage points respectively.[2]) By contrast, the H2 announce rate grows by 50 %—from 1.4 % to 2.2 %—with most of the growth occurring after May 2015, when H2 was standardized. As we start expanding the pool of sites that we probe (September 2015), H1 and SPDY announce rates grow slowly (SPDY grows from 5.1 % in July to 5.7 % in October), while H2 announce rates grow more quickly (2.2 % in July to 3.7 % in October). Interestingly, we measured a 0.1 % drop in SPDY in October (about 2,000 sites) and a 0.6 % increase in H2

---

[2] We did not find a public explanation of this drop, but we verified it was not measurement error.

Table 1. Protocol support from Nov. 2014–Oct. 2015 as percentage of top 1 million Alexa sites.

	Nov.	Dec.	Jan.	Feb.	Mar.	Apr.	May	Jun.	Jul.	Aug.	Sep.	Oct.
HTTP/1.1	9.8 %	10.2 %	10.5 %	10.8 %	11.2 %	11.3 %	9.1 %	9.7 %	10.8 %	11.4 %	12.1 %	12.1 %
SPDY/3.1	5.8 %	5.9 %	6.0 %	6.2 %	6.3 %	6.3 %	3.7 %	4.1 %	5.1 %	5.6 %	5.8 %	5.7 %
HTTP/2	1.4 %	1.4 %	1.3 %	1.3 %	1.3 %	1.3 %	1.2 %	1.4 %	2.2 %	2.7 %	3.0 %	3.6 %
NPN	9.8 %	10.2 %	10.5 %	10.8 %	11.2 %	11.3 %	9.1 %	9.7 %	10.8 %	11.4 %	12.1 %	12.1 %
ALPN	–	–	–	–	–	–	–	–	–	–	5.1 %	5.1 %
H2C	0 %	0 %	0 %	0 %	0 %	0.006 %	0.06 %	0.2 %	1.04 %	1.20 %	1.38 %	1.37 %
Tot. sites	1M	1M	1M	1M	1M	1M	1M	1M	1M	1.4M	1.7M	1.8M

(about 10,000 sites). If the trend continues, H2 support will overtake SPDY in the near future.

NPN, ALPN, and H2C. As of October 2015, 50 % of the sites supporting NPN also support ALPN. We added ALPN support to our measurement platform in September 2015; previous manual ALPN tests showed less than 0.5 % adoption. Although not shown in the table, as of October 2015 there are already 1,200 websites supporting ALPN but not NPN, 20 % more than in September. H2C announcement also grows quickly, reaching 1.37 % in October 2015 (about 22,000 sites). However, our UPGRADE header tests found only 20–30 sites that actually support H2C.

H2 Adoption. We now examine H2 adoption in detail. Figure 1(a) shows the evolution of the number of websites that (1) announce H2 support (H2-announce), (2) respond using H2, even just to return an error page or redirect (H2-partial), and (3) actually serve page content with H2 (H2-true, cf. Sect. 3).

Figure 1(a) shows the substantial growth of H2 adoption after its standardization (May 2015). The Figure also shows a large difference between "announced" (H2-announce) and "actual" H2 support (H2-partial and H2-true). However, while between November 2014 and May 2015 only 5 % of the websites announcing H2 support actually responded using H2 (H2-partial), this increases to 55 % as of October 2015. We also see that before May 2015, most websites serving content with H2 are well configured and properly working (i.e., the gap between H2-partial and H2-true is small). After May, the gap widens considerably: most new websites supporting H2 show some misconfiguration, like redirecting to an error page. This trend continues until October 2015 when the gap between H2-partial and H2-true is suddenly reduced.

Web Server Implementations. In order to further understand the different levels of H2 support noted above, Fig. 1(b) plots the popularity of the web server implementations powering the H2-true websites. Note that the resolution of this data is weekly until September 2015 and daily thereafter. For visibility, Fig. 1(b) shows only the 6 most popular web-server implementations (out of the 53 encountered). Figure 1(b) shows that, between October 2014 and May 2015, most H2-true websites are powered by Google web-servers (google_frontend, gws, gse and sffe). Then, in May 2015, two new H2 implementations debut: LiteSpeed and

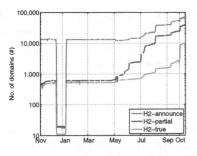

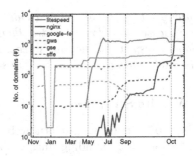

(a) H2-announce, H2-partial and H2-true.

(b) Web server implementations.

Fig. 1. H2 adoption over time. November 2014 – October 2015.

NGINX. Their adoption rates are very different; while LiteSpeed websites are quickly updated—LiteSpeed usage grows from 10 websites to 2,000 within two months—NGINX websites upgrade more slowly. The combination of fast adoption and the fact that most LiteSpeed websites are H2-partial and not H2-true suggests that LiteSpeed is used for virtual hosting more than NGINX. Despite lower overall numbers, NGINX currently powers more than 7,000 H2-true websites (71.7 % of all H2-true websites) compared to LiteSpeed's 1,300.

Notable Events. Figure 1(a) shows a few events that are worth noting. First, the number of servers supporting H2 drastically drops over a period of four days (December 14th–18th). This is because Google, the primary adopter of H2 at that time, disabled H2 support on their servers (cf. Fig. 1(b)) due to an issue with SDCH compressed content in Chromium.[3] It takes a month for the problem to be fixed, and H2 support is re-enabled again over four days (January 11th–15th), likely reflecting a specific roll-out policy for server configuration changes. The next interesting event happens between May and June 2015, when the number of H2-partial websites—though they are mostly error pages—doubles from 600 to 1,200. This spike is due to Hawk Host, a virtual web hosting provider, updating its servers with the latest version of LiteSpeed, which supports H2 (cf. Fig. 1(b)).[4] Figure 1(a) also shows a sudden increase in H2 support on October 3rd, caused by NGINX's footprint growing 40 % (from 25,000 to 35,000 websites) thanks to WordPress updating to the latest NGINX release.[5] Finally, note that the spikes in August and September are due to the extension of the pool of websites we query (cf. Table 1).

---

[3] https://lists.w3.org/Archives/Public/ietf-http-wg/2014OctDec/0960.html.

[4] http://blog.hawkhost.com/2015/07/13/http2-more-now-available-at-hawk-host-via-litespeed-5-0/.

[5] NGINX 1.9.5 (September 22nd) was sponsored by Automattic, the creators of WordPress. http://nginx.org/en/CHANGES.

Takeaway: *The H2 adoption trend reflects the broader Internet ecosystem, where most websites do not control their own technology stacks. There are a few big players responsible for the spread of new technologies; the average website owners might not even know they are serving content over H2.*

4.2   Website Structure

Number of Objects. Modern web pages are usually composed of several embedded objects, including images, JavaScripts, and style sheets. During our 11-month measurement campaign, we find no indication of a difference in the number of objects between pages served with H1 and H2 (cf. Fig. 2(a)). To verify this quantitatively, we compute the cosine similarity of the object counts for H1 and H2 every week and find values ranging from 0.96 to 0.98. Thus, at a macroscopic level, there is no difference in the content composition between the two protocols. Figure 2(a) also shows that from November 2014 to May 2015, pages served with H2 are mostly small pages, i.e., 50 % have 10 objects or less. After May 2015, more complex websites started to support H2; for example, in October 2015, 50 % of websites have about 60 objects, which is in line with the average number of objects per webpage reported in [21].

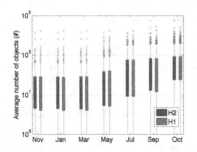
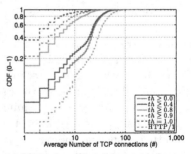

(a) Distribution of the number of objects per website. Nov. 2014-Oct. 2015   (b) CDF of number of connections per website as a function of th. Oct. 6th-13th

Fig. 2. Content analysis and delivery (Cleveland).

The objects embedded within a web page often reside on another webserver and the browser must open new TCP connections independent of the application protocol in use. In addition, the browser must renegotiate which application protocol to use for each new TCP connection. It follows that even if a website supports H2, it is possible that only a fraction of its objects are delivered using H2. Although not shown due to space limitations, we find that half of the websites actually serve about 50 % of their content using H2. Only 10 % of the websites serve 100 % of their objects using H2; these websites contain fewer objects and have an overall smaller size—400 KB on average compared to 1.5MB for all websites.

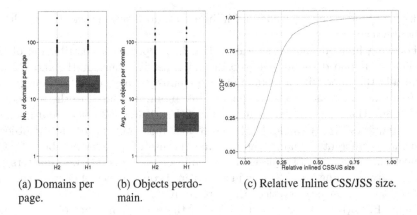

(a) Domains per page.   (b) Objects perdomain.   (c) Relative Inline CSS/JSS size.

Fig. 3. Content analysis and delivery.

Takeaway: There is no significant difference in object composition between the H1 and H2 versions of a website. Also, 90 % of the websites still leverage H1 to serve a portion of their content.

Number of Connections. We now investigate the number of TCP connections used to load a website using H1 versus H2. Motivated by the previous result, we differentiate websites based on how many of their objects are served with H2. Figure 2(b) shows the Cumulative Distribution Function (CDF) of the number of TCP connections per website as a function of th, or the fraction of the webpage's objects served with H2. In case of H1 we show a single curve as objects are always served with H1. The data for this plot was collected from our machines in Cleveland between October 6th–13th (8,492 distinct websites).

We first focus on the H1 curve and the H2 curve obtained with $th = 0$, where no websites are filtered. On average, H2 requires half as many TCP connections as H1; a few websites can even be served via a single TCP connection, but there are extreme cases where up to 100 connections might be required. As th increases, the required number of TCP connections decreases; this is intuitive since H1 and H2 cannot share the same TCP connection. For $th = 1$, all objects are served with H2, up to 40 % of the websites only need a single TCP connection indicating that the websites content is hosted entirely on a single webserver; still, the remaining 60 % need up to 20 TCP connections. This is a consequence of the way web content is organized today, where objects might reside on 3rd party domains. We further analyze this phenomenon next.

Takeaway: H2 does not currently succeed in serving a page using a single TCP connection: 50 % (4,300) of the websites using H2 today use at least 20 TCP connections.

Page Composition. Websites today try to optimize delivery using several techniques like *sharding, inlining, spriting* and *concatenation* (cf. Sect. 1 and [18]). We see no straightforward way to measure spriting and concatenation, so in this work we only focus on sharding and inlining. Figure 3 summarizes the results of this analysis.

Focusing first on domain sharding, Fig. 3(a) reports the distribution of the number of unique domains per website. The distributions for H1 and H2 are essentially the same with a median of 18 domains per page each, and outliers of ∼250 unique domains on a single page. This finding is related to the number of TCP connections opened per page (cf. Fig. 2(b)). While H2 allows multiplexing object requests over a single TCP connection, most web pages embed objects from many different domains, thus forcing the use of a larger number of TCP connections. There are two plausible explanations for this: (1) web masters are deliberately sharding, and (2) it is just a natural consequence of deep linking (as opposed to re- hosting) practices that are common across the web.

Next, Fig. 3(b) plots the distribution of the average number of objects per domain per website. We again find that there is no meaningful difference between H1 and H2: most domains are used for relatively few objects (median = {3.5, 3.5}, mean = {5.5, 5.4}, top 10th-percentile of {9.7, 9.6}, and a max of {179, 171} for H1 and H2 respectively). This *is* further evidence of sharding-esque behavior since web page objects are dispersed over a large number of domains.

Finally, Fig. 3(c) plots the size of inlined CSS/JS relative to the total size of the main HTML for each website; *i.e.*, what fraction of the total bytes making up an HTML document are from inlined CSS/JS. We find that there is a long tail where inlined CSS/JS makes up a considerable portion of the page: about 25 % of websites' page contents is more than 25 % inlined CSS/JS. With H1, inlining can help ensure the page loads faster by not requiring an extra TCP connection; however this is no longer an issue in H2, so these websites are potentially suffering a performance hit since inlined content cannot be cached separately by the client.

Takeaway: Most websites exhibit H1 practices like domain sharding and inlining in H2. Sharding causes H2 websites to use more TCP connections than necessary and inlining may reduce the utility of caching.

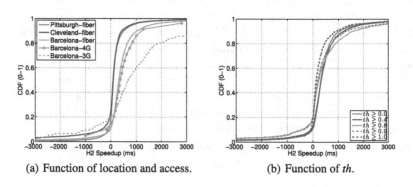

(a) Function of location and access.   (b) Function of *th*.

Fig. 4. CDFs of H2 speedup.

4.3 Performance

Comparison to H1. First, we investigate H2 performance by comparing a website's *page load time (PLT)* when using H1 and H2. There is no standardized definition of PLT; from a user perspective, it is the time from when the user enters a URL in the browser to when the page is displayed. Similar to other studies [7], we approximate PLT as the time from when Chrome starts fetching the page to the firing of the JavaScript "onLoad" event; this event occurs once the page's embedded resources have been downloaded, but possibly before all objects loaded via scripts are downloaded. We define "H2 speedup" as the difference in PLT between the H1 and H2 versions of a website; speedup values > 0 indicate websites that are delivered faster with H2 than H1.

For this analysis, we leverage the data collected from multiple locations and access networks in the second week of October. From fiber connections, we target 8,492 websites with verified H2 support (cf. Fig. 1(a)) using three network locations: Barcelona (Spain), Pittsburgh (U.S.), and Cleveland (U.S.). Experiments using 3G/4G connections are performed at a single location (Barcelona) and we restrict the list to the 200 most popular websites, as ranked by Alexa, that also support H2.

Figure 4(a) shows the CDF of H2 speedup at each location, and access network. We start by focusing on fiber access; the figure shows positive speedup values for 75–85% of the websites depending upon network location. While Pittsburgh and Cleveland show very similar H2 speedup values (decreasing the likelihood of this being an anomalous observation), speedup values measured from Barcelona are 10–15% higher. Our latency estimations coupled with the measurements (cf. Sect. 3) show that, on average, the Barcelona experiments suffer an additional 14 ms in RTT since most target websites are located in the U.S. Likely, the longer RTT negatively impacts H1 more than H2 due to the handshakes required by the additional TCP connections in H1 (cf. Sect. 4.2).

Next, we focus on a single location (Barcelona) and different network access, namely fiber, 4G, and 3G ordered by decreasing "speed." Figure 4(a) shows that as the access speed decreases, the benefit of adopting H2 also increases: the average speedup grows from 560 ms on fiber, up to respectively 800 ms on 4G and 1.6 s on 3G. Latency measurements show that the median RTT more than doubles from fiber to 4G (46 up to 105 ms), and it grows by an additional 10 % on 3G (117 ms). This additional latency again negatively impacts H1 more than H2. Figure 4(a) also shows that an additional 10 % of websites see a performance degradation, negative speedup, over 3G compared with 4G and fiber. This results is due to the fact that for 3G and 4G we target Alexa's 200 most popular websites that also support H2, which tend to be landing pages and are simpler than the average website. In this case, the application protocol used has little impact as PLT is dominated by RTT.

Takeaway: *80 % of the websites adopting H2 see an average page load time reduction of 500 ms (fiber) and 1.6 s (3G). The remaining 20 % see an average page load time increase of 1 s (fiber) and 1.4 s (3G).*

Partial Adoption. We now analyze the impact of the fraction of the webpage served with H2 (th) on H2 speedup (cf. Fig. 2(a)). For this analysis, we focus on a single location and access network (Cleveland, fiber) since no significant differences arise across locations and access types. We find that for $th < 1$ there is no statistically significant difference between the curves[6] and most websites benefit from even partial H2 adoption. On average, the speedup reduces by 10 % when we consider $th = 1$ which seems counter-intuitive. This again related to a simpler object composition of these websites for which H2 benefits result marginal.

Takeaway: Even partial H2 adoption improves PLT. In fact, the decrease in PLT for websites using both H1 and H2 is often greater than that for pure H2 websites (though this is likely an artifact of the small subset of websites that are fully H2, which tend to be very simple).

4.4 Discussion

In December 2015, a notable event shook our measurement infrastructure [1]. CloudFlare, a global CDN and DNS provider, enabled H2 for all its free customers.[7] This resulted in an additional 80,000 websites announcing H2 support (H2-announce) of which about 60,000 exhibit true support (H2-true). Note that CloudFlare uses an in- house version of NGINX, reported as cloudflare-nginx, which rapidly became the most popular web server implementation supporting H2.

Such rapid growth in H2-true websites affected Phase III's feasibility: at such scale, even the lazy strategy would require over a month to complete. Considering even further growth moving forward, we can either divide Phase III among our vantage points or sample the websites to test. We have temporarily suspended Phase III and are rethinking this component of our infrastructure. In addition, we are currently collaborating directly with CloudFlare to collect both server and client side measurements. We will soon report the outcome of an improved Phase III on [1] as well as in an extension of this work.

5 Conclusion

This work presents a measurement platform to monitor both adoption and performance of H2, the recently standardized update of H1. On a daily basis, our platform checks the top 1 million Alexa websites for which protocols they announce support. Next, it checks which websites *actually* support H2, and, once a week, tests their content structure and performance from multiple network locations. Once a month, a popular subset of these websites is also tested from 3G and 4G networks. Results are updated daily at [1]. In this paper, we report our initial findings from an 11 month measurement campaign, from November

---

[6] Two sample Kolmogorov-Smirnov tests provided no support to reject the null hypothesis.

[7] https://www.cloudflare.com/http2/.

2014 until October 2015. We find 68,000 websites already announcing H2 support, out of which 10,000 serve actual content, i.e., not an error page or redirect. An in-depth analysis of the content being served reveals that classic H1 hacks are still present with H2. In performance, we find that 80 % of the websites load faster with H2 than H1. The average decrease in page load time is 300–560 ms from multiple locations with a fiber access, and up to 1.6 s from a European 3G connection.

References

1. Is the Web HTTP/2 Yet?. http://isthewebhttp2yet.com
2. Node.js. https://nodejs.org/
3. Planetlab. http://planet-lab.org
4. Langley, A.: TLS Next Protocol Negotiation. https://technotes.googlecode.com/git/nextprotoneg.html
5. Akhshabi, S., Dovrolis, C.: The evolution of layered protocol stacks leads to an hourglass-shaped architecture. In: Proceedings of the ACM SIGCOMM, Toronto, Canada, August 2011
6. Cardaci, A.: Chrome har capturer. https://github.com/cyrus-and/chrome-har-capturer
7. Erman, J., Gopalakrishnan, V., Jana, R., Ramakrishnan, K.: Towards a SPDYier mobile web?. In: Proceedings of the ACM CoNEXT, Santa Barbara, CA, December 2013
8. White, G., Mule, J.-F., Rice, D.: Analysis of spdy and tcp initcwnd. https://tools.ietf.org/html/draft-white-httpbis-spdy-analysis-00
9. Molnár, G.: node-http2. https://github.com/molnarg/node-http2
10. Google: Spdy whitepaper. http://www.chromium.org/spdy/spdy-whitepaper
11. Podjarny, G.: Not as spdy as you thought. http://www.guypo.com/not-as-spdy-as-you-thought/
12. Rizzo, J., Duong, T.: The crime attack. In: Ekoparty (2012)
13. Naylor, D., Finamore, A., Leontiadis, I., Grunenberger, Y., Mellia, M., Munafò, M., Papagiannaki, K., Steenkiste, P.: The cost of the "S" in HTTPS. In: Proceedings of the ACM CoNEXT, Sydney, Australia, December 2014
14. OpenSSL: OpenSSL: The Open Source Toolkit for SSL/TLS. https://www.openssl.org/
15. Padhye, J., Nielsen, H.F.: A comparison of spdy and http performance. Technical report (2012)
16. Peon, R., Ruellan, H.: Hpack - header compression for http/2. https://tools.ietf.org/html/draft-ietf-httpbis-header-compression-12
17. Saxcè, H.D., Oprescu, I., ChenSaamer, Y.: Is HTTP/2 really faster than HTTP/1.1?. In: Proceedings ot he IEEE Global Internet Symposium (GI), Hong Kong, CH, April 2014
18. Stenberg, D.: HTTP2, background, the protocol, the implementations and the future. http://daniel.haxx.se/http2/http2-v1.9.pdf
19. Stenberg, D.: HTTP2 Explained. http://http2-explained.haxx.se/content/en/part5.html
20. Friedl, S., Popov, A., Langley, A., Stephan, E.: Transport layer security (tls) application-layer protocol negotiation extension. https://tools.ietf.org/html/rfc7301

21. The http archive: http://httparchive.org
22. Tuan, N.A.: Maximum concurrent connections to the same domain for browsers. http://sgdev-blog.blogspot.com.es/2014/01/maximum-concurrent-connection-to-same.html
23. Wang, X.S., Balasubramanian, A., Krishnamurthy, A., Wetherall, D.: How speedy is spdy. In: Proceedings of the NSDI, Seattle, WA, April 2014

Modeling HTTP/2 Speed from HTTP/1 Traces

Kyriakos Zarifis[1]([⊠]), Mark Holland[2], Manish Jain[2], Ethan Katz-Bassett[1],
and Ramesh Govindan[1]

[1] University of Southern California, Los Angeles, USA
kyriakos@usc.edu
[2] Akamai Technologies, Cambridge, USA

Abstract. With the standardization of HTTP/2, content providerswant
to understand the benefits and pitfalls of transitioning to the new standard. Using a large dataset of HTTP/1.1 resource timing data from production traffic on Akamai's CDN, and a model of HTTP/2 behavior, we
obtain the distribution of performance differences between the protocol
versions for nearly 280,000 downloads. We find that HTTP/2 provides
significant performanceimprovements in the tail, and, for websites for
which HTTP/2 does not improve median performance, we explore how
optimizations like prioritization and push can improve performance, and
how these improvements relate to page structure.

1 Introduction

HTTP/2 will soon supplant HTTP/1.1 as the IETF standard for the delivery
of web traffic and is already supported by major browsers and some content
providers [12]. The design of HTTP/2 has been motivated by concerns about
the performance of HTTP/1.1. The aspect of web performance most relevant
to end-users is page load time (PLT), which has been shown to correlate with
content provider revenue, so content providers have gone to great lengths to
optimize it. HTTP/2 is a step in that direction: it multiplexes objects on a
single TCP connection, permits clients to specify priorities, and allows servers
to push content speculatively.

Several prior studies have shown mixed results on the performance difference
between HTTP/1.1 and HTTP/2 [7,11,14]. The relative performance of these
two protocols has been hard to assess because modern web pages have complex
dependencies between objects, and can contain objects hosted on different sites.
Many of these prior studies are focused on lab environments, and some have not
used real browsers as test agents, which can restrict visibility into browser-side
tasks like resource parsing, execution or rendering time.

This has motivated us to study the performance of HTTP/2 using data
collected from live page views by real end-users. Our study uses HTTP/1.1
Resource Timing [2] data collected from a broad set of customers on a major
CDN (Akamai). The data we collect consists of detailed timing breakdowns for
the base page and each embedded resource on a small sample of all page views.

T. Karagiannis and X. Dimitropoulos (Eds.): PAM 2016, LNCS 9631, pp. 233–247, 2016.
DOI: 10.1007/978-3-319-30505-9_18

Contributions. The first contribution of this paper is a model, called RT-H2, that takes the resource timing data for a single HTTP/1.1 page view, and *estimates the difference in page load times* for that page view between HTTP/1.1 and HTTP/2. To do this, RT-H2 models four important components of HTTP/2: multiplexing, push, prioritization, and frame interleaving. RT-H2 also contains a model of TCP that is reasonably accurate for Web transfers.

Our second contribution is to explore the PLT differences between HTTP/1.1 and HTTP/2 from nearly 280,000 page views of customers of Akamai. Of these, we select 55 distinct websites which have a significant number of instrumented page views and explore the relative performance under zero packet loss. In this setting, page structure and the diversity of the client base (in terms of location, browser type, etc.) should determine performance. We found that roughly 60 % of the time HTTP/2 has smaller PLT and 28 % of the time it has negligible impact, but there are websites for which more often than others it leads to performance degradation. We explored two optimizations, prioritization and push. Push provided more improvement for cases where HTTP/2 was already beneficial, and both helped the cases that saw degradation with HTTP/2.

Taken together, our findings indicate that CDNs should start experimenting with HTTP/2 at scale, as it can have benefits for many clients of their customers.

2   Background and Approach

A typical web page consists of tens of resources fetched from many different servers. Many of these objects have dependencies between them. A base page HTML file is downloaded before sub-resources can be requested. Once sub-resources are downloaded and parsed, they can trigger the downloads of other resources. The user-perceived latency in loading a web page is a complex combination of the time taken to download, parse and render (if needed) its resources.

HTTP/1.1. The original HTTP/1.0 specification only allowed for one response-request stream to be transferred per TCP connection. HTTP/1.1 added the ability to re-use connections, but required that there be only one request in flight on a TCP channel at a time. It also added pipelining, which is rarely employed [1], so we ignore it in this paper.

Subsequent optimizations enabled parallel downloads by opening multiple concurrent connections to the server. Browsers typically limit themselves to six parallel connections per hostname. To leverage this to achieve faster downloads, *domain sharding*, is used to partition objects across different hostnames.

HTTP/2. HTTP/2 allows multiple, concurrent requests to be outstanding on the same TCP connection. This prevents the case where a resource that the browser is ready to load is forced to wait for an idle connection. It also allows for explicit *prioritization* of the delivery of resources. For example, when a server has received a request for both an image and a Javascript object, and it has both ready to deliver, the protocol allows (but does not mandate) that the Javascript be given priority for the connection. This prioritization facilitates parallelization of client processing and downloading. It also provides a mechanism for a server to *push* content to a client without receiving a request from it. While the standard does not specify best practices for pushing objects, the intent of this mechanism is to enable servers to keep the pipe to the client as busy as possible.

Page Load Time. Both HTTP/1.1 and HTTP/2 contain performance optimizations whose goal is to reduce PLT. Recent web performance studies have converged upon an operational definition of PLT [10], which is when the browser fires the *onLoad* event.

Understanding Relative Performance: Challenges. HTTP/2 contains several optimizations that should result in better performance than HTTP/1.*, but these performance benefits may not always be realized in practice. First, while mechanisms for prioritization and push are defined in the standard, actual performance improvements may depend upon the specific *policies* that Web servers implement for these optimizations. Second, interactions with TCP can limit the performance advantages of HTTP/2. Compared with when objects are retrieved over parallel connections, the congestion window on a single multiplexed channel grows more slowly. Moreover, parallel connections are more forgiving of loss: when a drop occurs in a stream, it will only trigger recovery on that stream.

Our Approach. We use Resource Timing [2] data collected using Javascript from a broad set of customers on Akamai's CDN. When enabled by a customer, Akamai servers insert a small body of Javascript into 1% of this customer's pages as they are delivered to end users. The script triggers the monitoring of per-resource timing information, which includes the start/end timestamps for: DNS lookup, TCP connection setup, TLS handshake if any, request sent to the server, and start and end from response from the server [2]. The script then encodes that information into a trie structure and delivers it to an Akamai back-end system. Over a selected one-week period we observed data for about 44,000 distinct base-page hostnames and 3.4 million distinct base-page URLs.

Unlike prior work [7,11,14], our data consists of detailed timing breakdowns for the base page and each embedded resource from real clients. From this information, we obtain realistic network delays and browser side processing and rendering delays for the complete set of resources in a page, and are able to assess PLTs as reported by browser onLoad events.

However, our dataset captures HTTP/1.* downloads, so the primary challenge we face in the paper is *how to predict the page load performance for this dataset under HTTP/2*. Using a real HTTP/2 deployment on the CDN is, at the moment, not an option, because of the complexity and scale of the endeavor. So, we resort to using a *model* of HTTP/2, as described in the next section.

3   The RT-H2 Model

Input. The input to RT-H2 is the Resource Timing (RT) data for a single HTTP/1.1 download of a website from a real client. The input can be visualized as a *waterfall*. Figure 1 (left) illustrates a simplified waterfall for a page

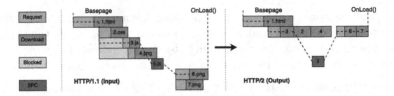

Fig. 1. Transformation of an HTTP/1.1 waterfall to an HTTP/2 waterfall (Color figure online).

downloaded via HTTP/1.1, containing seven objects: a base HTML page, one CSS file, 3 Javascript files and 3 images. The HTML file is downloaded first and it is parsed as it is being downloaded. So, even before 1.html completes, the browser has determined that 2.css, 3.js and 4.png need to be downloaded next. These three resources depend on 1.html, and that HTML page is said to be a *parent* of these resources. However, not all of these resources can be immediately downloaded: most browsers limit the number of parallel connections to a given website, and Fig. 1 (left) shows a simplified example with at most two parallel connections. Therefore, only the download of 2.css is initiated, and other objects are blocked until 1.html has downloaded.

The waterfall diagram also illustrates three other important features that can be gleaned from RT data. First, when 3.js completes, it triggers the download of 5.js. The time between the completion of 3.js's download and the request for 5.js represents the *processing time* for 3.js. The processing time for 5.js is also visible since that Javascript triggers the downloads of two images 6.png and 7.png. Second, 5.js is an example of *3rd-party content* (3PC). Examples of 3PC include ads, tags, analytics, and external JavaScript files that can trigger the download of other 3PC or origin content. Finally, the dashed line in Fig. 1 runs through objects that represent the *critical path* in the waterfall. The critical path of the waterfall demarcates objects whose download and processing times determine the PLT. The browser's OnLoad() event is triggered after 6.png is downloaded, so 6.png and its ancestors are on the critical path.

The waterfall also explicitly contains four kinds of download timing information. The blue boxes (*Request*), mark the time from when the object was requested by the client to the time when the first byte of the object was received. The red boxes (*Download*), mark the time from when the first byte of the object was received by the browser, to when the last byte of the object was received. The gray boxes (*Blocked*) represent the duration of time between when an object could have been retrieved and when the request was actually made. The green boxes (*3PC*) demarcate the retrieval of third-party content.

Real waterfalls have the same elements as in Fig. 1, but can be significantly more complex, with hundreds of objects, several levels of dependencies, and multiple sources of third-party content.

Output. The output of RT-H2 is a transformed version of the input waterfall produced by applying the features of HTTP/2 on a real HTTP/1.1 waterfall and the percentage change in PLT, which we denote Δ_{PLT}.

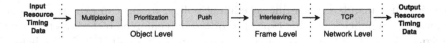

Fig. 2. RT-H2 Components

Components of RT-H2. Both HTTP protocol versions are complex, and HTTP/2 contains many optional features with unspecified policies or best practices. RT-H2 is designed to be able to explore *what-if* scenarios of different combinations of policies or optional features. It models HTTP/2 in a layered fashion and has several components, as shown in Fig. 2. We describe each of these below.

Multiplexing. In HTTP/2, a client maintains a single TCP channel with any one server, on which resources are multiplexed. RT-H2's multiplexing component, which operates at the object level, analyzes the input waterfall to determine which objects can be multiplexed. With HTTP/2, any resource with a URI covered by the certificate of the origin can reuse the same channel. RT-H2 parses resource URLs and looks for patterns resembling the base page URL. Because strict string matching does not cover all the cases (www.example.com and img.xmpl.com can in fact be the same origin), we also assume that any hostname that serves more than 5 resources in the same download must be origin content. The output of the multiplexing component is a collection of sets of objects that can be multiplexed by HTTP/2 because they come from the same server.

Browser-cached resources are not included in the multiplexer's output. RT data does not explicitly mark cached resources, so RT-H2 determines an object is cached if its retrieval time in the original waterfall is less than 10 ms. For cached objects, RT-H2 preserves the timing from the original waterfall. RT-H2 also preserves the duration of 3PC resources which are not on the origin connection.

Push. This component emulates the ability of an HTTP/2 server to proactively send resources to a client without the client having to request them. Push can keep the pipe to the client full. For example, in Fig. 1 (left), 2.css, 3.js and 4.png could be served by an HTTP/2 server as soon as 1.html is requested, rather than waiting for the client to request them.

While HTTP/2 specifies a push mechanism, it does not specify what *policies* to use for pushing. We have implemented a push policy, *ideal-push*, which assumes that the server can assess which objects the client might request after downloading the base HTML file. This is idealized, since there can be dynamic content, e.g. Javascript can be executed at the browser, and its output can at best be over-approximated by the server (for example, by static program analysis). However, *ideal-push* gives an upper bound on HTTP/2 push performance.

Prioritization. The last object-layer component of RT-H2 is a component that assigns *priorities* to objects. This prioritization represents a way for browsers to control the way a TCP channel is shared across multiplexed resources. As with push, the HTTP/2 specification defines the mechanism for assigning priorities, but does not mandate a specific scheduling policy; RT-H2 can explore different prioritization policies. A basic type of prioritization enforced by today's browsers assigns relative bandwidth resources to Javascript, CSS and HTML files before other file types since these files need to be processed by the browser and can trigger downloads of other objects. In this paper, we explore a prioritization policy which further preferentially prioritizes Javascript, CSS or HTML files that are on the critical path. In practice, browsers could guess this prioritization by extracting critical paths from historical traces of page downloads.

Interleaving. HTTP/2 permits interleaving of objects, and this component implements this capability. Among objects that can be multiplexed together at a given time, it interleaves 16K chunks (*frames*) of these objects in FIFO order.

TCP Module. The core of RT-H2 is a custom, discrete-event, TCP simulator which simulates TCP-CUBIC's congestion window growth [9]. When determining what data to transmit, the TCP module supplies the interleaving module with a desired number of bytes B that can be transmitted at each tick of the simulator. The latter, in turn, consults the multiplexing, prioritization, and push modules and determines which *frames* of which objects need to be served, such that the total size of the frames is less than B. This is repeated until all objects are served. The simulator clock ticks every RTT, changing the window appropriately. We assume that connections are not bandwidth-limited, based on the observation that for most (>90%) of the traces, the HTTP/2 multiplexed payload was small enough (<1 MB) to easily fit within several client-edge RTTs without exceeding the client's BW cap, assuming a 5 Mbps connection. In this paper, we only present results assuming no loss, to focus on the impact of page structure and other page characteristics on HTTP/2. As shown in previous work [14], loss affects HTTP/2 more negatively than HTTP/1.1 due to the single channel. We did extend our model to incorporate loss. Specifically, we give each packet an equal chance of getting dropped (1% or 2% in our experiments). If one or more packets within one window are dropped, we assess a 77% chance of causing a retransmission time-out [8] and increment the time counter appropriately. Our results were consistent with previous work [14], so we omit them for brevity.

Preprocessing the Input. The HTTP/1.1 waterfall input to RT-H2 was produced by a client running an unknown TCP stack version, and for which we know HTTP layer request latency, but not TCP characteristics like loss. To compare the two protocols on an even footing, we run the HTTP/1.1 waterfall through the TCP module, without any HTTP/2 features on, then *use the resulting waterfall as input to the HTTP/2 model*, and estimate Δ_{PLT} based on those two. This way, any inaccuracies in the TCP model impact both protocols equally. For the results presented here, the loss rate is always set to zero and the RTT is inferred from the download trace. Note that different client characteristics (TCP stack version, browser optimizations) could affect the actual download slightly differently. We do not try to infer all the client characteristics for each download. Instead we come up with a generic model that captures the most popular TCP stack and known client behaviors, and assume that implementation details do not affect the outcome significantly, especially in large numbers.

Other Details. RT data does not include object sizes. We use a separate dataset to obtain object sizes, and, for objects not listed in this dataset, we download them to obtain size. To compute the output waterfall, we need dependencies between objects: for this, we use techniques similar to those used in prior work [13].

Running a Waterfall Through RT-H2. Figure 1 shows how RT-H2 transforms an input waterfall to its HTTP/2 equivalent. 3.js is prioritized over 2.css. As a result, the simulation returns an earlier completion time for it than its original end time, and adjusts its dependent resources accordingly, shifting 5.js and its 2 children to the left. The request for 6.png and 7.png are requested on the same channel, maintaining their distance from the end of 5.js, which corresponds to processing time. The difference between the end times of the respective last resources is calculated, and the onLoad event is shifted accordingly. The Δ_{PLT} is defined as the % change between the times of the two onLoad events.

4   Validation

Methodology. In this section, we validate the RT-H2 model against PLT differences obtained from real traces for ground truth. The goal of validating RT-H2 is to understand whether the model's estimates for Δ_{PLT} are comparable to those observed in a realistic experiment. We set up an Akamai CDN server in a lab and configured it to serve 8 real websites both via HTTP/1.1 and HTTP/2. These 8 websites are the most popular ones in the CDN among those who have opted-in to resource timing monitoring and already use HTTPS.

We validate RT-H2 against those websites as follows: using Chrome, we download each web page through the CDN server 100 times via HTTP/1.1 and 100 times via HTTP/2. For each HTTP/1.1 download we generate a resource timing beacon that is used as input to our tool, generating 100 estimated HTTP/2 waterfalls, and we obtain the estimated Δ_{PLT} from those. We repeat this process for 3 RTT values (20 ms, 50 ms, 100 ms). This is the induced round-trip between the test client and the CDN edge server, which serves all of the pages' (cacheable) origin content. Since the base HTML file is not cached on the CDN because customers want to generate pages dynamically, the client request for that file is forwarded to the customer's origin server, the latency to which is variable.

Figure 3 shows an example of this process for one of the target web pages. There are 3 groups of 4 lines, each group representing a different RTT. Solid lines correspond to PLTs of real downloads, dashed lines correspond to their modeled equivalents. Blue lines are HTTP/1.1 and red lines are HTTP/2. Specifically, in each RTT group, the blue dashed line corresponds to the CDF of PLTs after passing the 100 waterfalls through the model but without applying the HTTP/2 features (so, simply passing them through our TCP model), and the red dashed lines corresponds to the CDF of estimated PLTs after applying HTTP/2. We

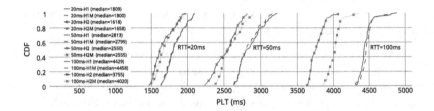

Fig. 3. Example of validation on a real page for 3 RTT values (Color figure online).

want the difference between the dashed lines (model) to be similar to that of the solid lines (ground truth), which means that the distribution transformation of the PLTs in our model after applying HTTP/2 was similar to the transformation of PLTs that the real downloads observed switching from HTTP/1.1 to HTTP/2. In this example, which corresponds to p1 in Table 1, the accuracy of the model is very good for RTTs of 20 ms and 50 ms, but slightly worse for 100 ms (predicted $\Delta_{PLT} = -18\%$, when in reality HTTP/2 reduced the PLT by 11% ($\Delta_{PLT} = -11\%$)).

Note that there is no 1-1 mapping between ground truth and experiment data points. HTTP/1.1 and HTTP/2 downloads were interleaved, to distribute network effects uniformly, but treating two adjacent HTTP/1.1 and HTTP/2 downloads as a pair has disadvantages: No two downloads are exactly equal, even if back-to-back, both because network characteristics are ephemeral, and because different resources (in numbers or variations, e.g. ads) can be downloaded each time. For this reason, we chose to look at aggregate distributions of sufficiently many samples rather than arbitrarily created pairs. The goal was not to validate exactly how one specific download would change via HTTP/2 and how accurately the model would predict that (because it is hard to produce exactly the same download for a live page over the real Internet), but rather to see how the distribution of PLTs of 100 downloads of a page changes via HTTP/2, and validate that the model tracks that distribution change fairly accurately.

Table 1 shows the ground truth and predicted Δ_{PLT} (%) for the 8 target pages. The values shown are the medians of each set of the 100 runs. The model estimates the overall impact of HTTP/2 on page load time of the test page very accurately for zero loss, upon which most of our results are based. For all estimations, the model always correctly estimates that the impact of HTTP/2 is positive, the difference between ground truth and estimated Δ_{PLT} is within 20% of the PLT, for 3/4 of them it is within 10%. The accuracy can decrease for higher RTTs (100 ms). However, we note that such high RTT values to Akamai's CDN edge are rarely observed. In the run with the lowest accuracy (p2, RTT = 50 ms), which has a median PLT of 2493 ms for HTTP1.1, the model predicted 2310.5 ms instead of the actual 2010 ms for HTTP/2. In this worst case the model is 200 ms off but still correctly predicts that HTTP/2 is faster. Given that this low accuracy happens less often for lower RTTs (which are more realistic) and considering the simplicity of the model, these validation results are encouraging for using the model to draw conclusions on larger scale data.

Table 1. Δ_{PLT} (%) prediction. For each page (p1-p8) and RTT value, "Real" indicates the ground truth PLT % change, and "Model" indicates the PLT % predicted by RT-H2.

RTT	Δ_{PLT}	p1	p2	p3	p4	p5	p6	p7	p8
20 ms	Real	−10.5	−12.0	−50.9	−2.6	−18.0	0.1	−15.4	−8.2
	Model	−7.8	−11.0	−53.2	−6.3	−11.8	−1.3	−2.3	−9.5
50 ms	Real	−9.3	−24.0	−97.7	−6.3	−23.5	−4.4	−11.4	−10.1
	Model	−8.7	−7.2	−84.0	−9.9	−18.1	−4.6	−2.4	−21.6
100 ms	Real	−15.2	−31.1	−104.4	−6.9	−32.7	−5.8	−14.6	−16.1
	Model	−9.8	−33.3	−92.6	−15.0	−19.2	−14.2	−6.1	−24.9

5 Results

5.1 Methodology

Dataset. The RT data contains page views sampled at 1 % from Akamai customers who have opted in this measurement. Each sample produces a waterfall. We run RT-H2 on two sets of waterfalls. The first is an *aggregate* dataset of 278,178 waterfalls spanning 56,851 unique URLs and 2,759 unique hostnames, corresponding to about 24 h worth of data. We then extracted a *per-website* dataset of 126,919 waterfalls drawn from the aggregate dataset. These waterfalls correspond to page views of 55 distinct websites. Each website has an average of 2,350 waterfall samples, with a minimum of 180 and a maximum of over 26,000. Intuitively, each website's collection of waterfalls represents a sample of the clients of that website, that use various browsers and devices, from geographically diverse locations. These 55 websites are the most popular of Akamai's customers that have opted in to the measurement and contain, on average, 111 objects per page, with the minimum and maximum being 5 and 500 respectively.

Metrics. Our primary metric is Δ_{PLT}. For the aggregate dataset, we are interested in the Δ_{PLT} distribution across all waterfalls. For the per-website dataset, we explore first-order statistics (min, max, mean, median and the top and bottom deciles). We focus particularly on the 90th percentile of the Δ_{PLT} distribution, since tail performance is increasingly important for content providers.

Experimental Settings. We first understand the performance of *basic HTTP/2*, and then explore the impact of two optimizations: prioritization and push.

The *prioritization* scenario was motivated by our observation that default HTTP/2 multiplexing can result in critical objects being downloaded later than they could, which can happen when many equal priority files are sent simultaneously. This what-if scenario asks: What would the Δ_{PLT} distribution look like if we knew how to prioritize objects that are on the critical path? This is somewhat hypothetical, since the browser or server would need to know the optimal order. We are exploring ways to make this possible, but this scenario gives us an upper bound on the performance improvement.

The *push* what-if scenario is based on our observation of the considerable idle network time until the base HTML file is available at the browser. This scenario asks: What would the Δ_{PLT} distribution look like if the server pushed content speculatively? *Ideal push* pushes all non-cached objects, and assumes an omniscient server which can predict what resources the client will need.

Network Conditions. Much prior attention has focused on the impact of network conditions on HTTP/2 [7,11,14]. Our evaluation of the impact of loss on HTTP/2 provided similar findings to previous work [14], so we omit it for brevity. Our primary evaluations, presented here, are under no loss settings, in which RT-H2's TCP module does not simulate loss. By removing loss as a factor, the Δ_{PLT} results are, to a large extent, impacted by page structure and its interplay with TCP window growth and RTT.

5.2   Evaluation

Basic HTTP/2, Aggregate Dataset. Figure 4 plots the distribution of Δ_{PLT}s across the aggregate dataset. Recall that this contains nearly 280K waterfalls. Of these, almost 60 % benefit from HTTP/2 (negative Δ_{PLT}). For another 28 % of the samples, the performance of the two protocols is identical, and HTTP/2 actually hurts performance for the rest. We discuss the possible reasons for some of these below, but these results paint a nuanced picture: HTTP/2 does improve performance for a majority of waterfalls, but despite better protocol design, web page PLTs can largely be determined by page structure and dependencies.

Basic HTTP/2, Per-Website Dataset. The aggregate dataset provides a macroscopic view of HTTP/2 performance, but looking at the per-website dataset provides more interesting insights. Figure 5 shows the fraction of times each website experienced a negative (green), positive (red), or zero (blue) Δ_{PLT}.

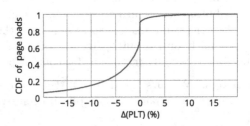

Fig. 4. Overall impact of HTTP/2 on PLTs over 280K input waterfalls at zero loss.

For a given website, each waterfall represents a page view by a client. This figure shows that different downloads of the same page may be impacted differently by HTTP/2. Several factors contribute to this: the RTT of a client, the variability of user agents, devices and processing times, and the impact of customizations and dynamic content mean that no two waterfalls are likely to be the same.

However, Fig. 5 hides the magnitude of the Δ_{PLT}s on each website, so we resort to a different view of this result. Figure 6 plots some first order statistics of the Δ_{PLT}s, for each website. The bottom and top whiskers indicate the 10th and 90th percentile respectively, the bottom and top of a bar indicates the 25th and 75th percentile, and the dark dot shows the median.

For all websites except 2, HTTP/2 improves PLT at the 75th percentile. In other words, for these websites, at least 75 % of the downloads would see a benefit by using HTTP/2. For nearly two-thirds of the websites, the 90th percentile of clients would see a benefit. For nearly half the websites (28 out of 55), the 10th percentile of clients see a Δ_{PLT} of 10 % or more. Taken together, these results present an interesting view of HTTP/2 performance: under no-loss conditions, the structure of most websites is such that multiplexing provides benefits.

But why is it that, for a third of the websites, the upper quartile of waterfalls are negatively impacted by HTTP/2? One hypothesis was that the clients of these websites had a qualitatively different RTT distribution than those of other websites (HTTP/2 is known to degrade with RTT [4]). However, plotting the distribution of RTTs (omitted for space) showed no obvious correlation between the distribution of first-order statistics of the RTTs and those of the Δ_{PLT}s.

Other potential reasons for performance differences across websites could be differences in macroscopic Web page characteristics such as total payload of resources in the waterfall, number, total payload and number of resources served from the origin domain (which get multiplexed), number of cached resources, number of 3PC resources, critical path length, number of 3PC resources on critical path, number of js/css/html files served from the origin (and thus get

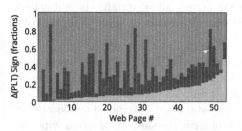

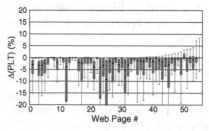

Fig. 5. Fraction of times a website experienced bad(red) / zero(blue) / good(green) PLT change (Color figure online)

Fig. 6. Δ_{PLT} distributions for each website at zero loss. Each candlestick shows 10/25/50/75/90th %ile.

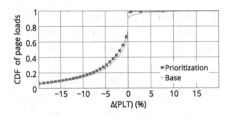 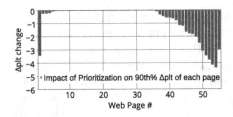

Fig. 7. Impact of Prioritization on the (i) Δ_{PLT} distribution across all samples of all pages (left) and (ii) 90th percentile of the Δ_{PLT} of each page (right).

prioritized in that channel) and device type. None of these seemed to directly correlate with the observed Δ_{PLT}s.

So, we resorted to a methodology that explores the impact of optimizations like prioritization and push, based on observed patterns in manually examined waterfalls, focusing on those that stood out in terms of HTTP/2 impact. Each optimization focuses on one aspect of page structure, and we wanted to see if negative HTTP/2 impact could be explained by some of these.

Prioritization, Per-Website Data. Figure 7 shows the results of the prioritization what-if scenario. Recall that this scenario was motivated by the observation that some pages download many critical objects (e.g. Javascripts), which in turn trigger many other downloads. Basic HTTP/2 does not prioritize these, so can delay the download of a resource that is on the critical path.

After applying prioritization, only 2 websites still see a negative impact from HTTP/2 at the 90 %th percentile (at most 10 % of the time). Figure 7 (right) shows *the increase or decrease in the 90th percentile*: for the third of the websites for which basic HTTP/2 can perform badly in the upper quartile, prioritization provides significant gains, improving the 90th percentile Δ_{PLT}s by up to 4 %. We notice that prioritization does not affect the 90th percentile of the websites in the middle of the figure, for which the impact of HTTP/2 was already almost always positive. Figure 7 (left) shows that across all waterfalls, prioritization slightly improves the Δ_{PLT} distribution but also removes the tail of negative impacts.

Push, Per-Website Data. Another reason why HTTP/2 performs worse than HTTP/1.1 is a structural one. We have found examples where HTTP/2 multiplexes 6 or fewer objects. In such cases, using parallel connections can be better, since each of those (up to 6 for most browsers) starts with an initial window of 10, whereas HTTP/2 uses a single TCP channel with the same congestion window. We have seen a similar effect with domain sharding. When a website is sharded across 3 domains and HTTP/2 multiplexes 18 objects or fewer, HTTP/1.1 wins. This indicates that these websites may have been optimized for HTTP/1.1.

Figure 8 shows performance using ideal push. As with prioritization, ideal push provides benefits at the 90th percentile except for 3 websites. However, relative to prioritization, it improves the median performance of each website significantly and only 7 out of 55 websites do *not* see more than 10 % gain for the top 10th percentile of samples. This more pervasive improvement is visible in the change in the aggregate CDF (Fig. 8 (left)), where now only 3–4% of waterfalls see a negative performance impact from HTTP/2.

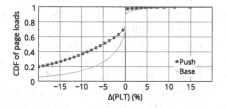 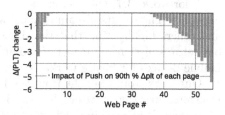

Fig. 8. Impact of Push on the (i) Δ_{PLT} distribution across all samples of all pages (left) and (ii) 90th percentile of the Δ_{PLT} of each page (right).

Putting it all Together. Figure 9 plots the overall impact of the optimizations on the aggregate dataset. This results in gains with HTTP/2 for nearly 70 % of the waterfalls, equal performance for most of the rest, and only about 1 % of the waterfalls seeing worse performance. The fraction of waterfalls with high performance gains is much higher, thanks in large part to push.

In summary, our results suggest that HTTP/2's features provide good performance gains for most of the websites. For about a third, the top quartile's PLT performance worsens with HTTP/2, but this can be fixed with a combination of prioritization and push. Prioritization addresses structural issues in the waterfall that cause this worse performance, and push does that too, but also increases the gains for HTTP/2 across the board by utilizing idle network time.

6   Related Work

Several prior studies have assessed the performance of SPDY [4–6], the precursor to HTTP/2. The approach of recording and replaying a website, used in many of those, misses out on unreplayable parts of a download, and does not expose the variability across many downloads of the same page due to personalization,

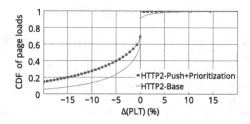

Fig. 9. Impact of HTTP/2 with optimizations on PLTs

localization and dynamic content [11,14]. Our work uses traces from real page views, so contains actual processing and rendering delays, and realistic client distributions. Furthermore, by using a model, we are able to explore several what-if scenarios on a very large dataset at fairly fast speed.

Prior work [3,7] has also focused on impact of SPDY specifically on cellular networks. The results are ambiguous, with some showing PLT decrease by 23% and others highlighting that the single channel suffers more often from spurious retransmissions. Our work is complementary, and we have left the focus on mobile devices for future work.

Our work would benefit from the help of a tool that calculates object relationships, like the browser plug-in wProf [13]. Unfortunately wProf calculates dependencies in real-time, which can not be used at the scale of traces that we are dealing with. A similar tool could be used to share structures and critical paths of targeted websites, which can inform optimal prioritization.

7   Conclusion

While HTTP/2 standardization is complete, the conditions under which HTTP/2 improves over the existing standard are not yet completely understood. Our work adds to this understanding by analyzing a large dataset of instrumented HTTP/1.1 page views using a model called RT-H2 that estimates Δ_{PLT} from this dataset. We find that HTTP/2's basic features can improve the 90th percentile Δ_{PLT} for nearly two thirds of the websites. Push and prioritization extend this further to cover all websites. Our work reveals aspects of page structure in our dataset that determine the efficacy of push and prioritization. Much work remains, however, including potentially enriching our model, exploring to what extent our estimated Δ_{PLT}s manifest themselves in CDNs, and finding methods to achieve the forms of prioritization and push we consider in this paper.

Acknowledgments. We thank our shepherd, Srikanth Sundaresan, and the reviewers for their helpful comments. Kyriakos Zarifis performed this work while employed temporarily at Akamai. This work was funded in part by the National Science Foundation (NSF) under grant number CNS-1413978.

References

1. HTTP Pipelining Not So Fast (Nor Slow!). http://www.guypo.com/http-pipelining-not-so-fast-nor-slow/
2. Resource Timing Specification. http://www.w3.org/TR/resource-timing/
3. SPDY Performance on Mobile Networks. https://developers.google.com/speed/articles/spdy-for-mobile
4. SPDY whitepaper. https://www.chromium.org/spdy/spdy-whitepaper
5. Cherif, W., Fablet, Y., Nassor, E., Taquet, J., Fujimori, Y.: Dash fast start using HTTP/2. In: NOSSDAV (2015)

6. El-Khatib, Y., Tyson, G., Welzl, M.: Can SPDY really make the web faster? In: IFIP Networking Conference (2014)

7. Erman, J., Gopalakrishnan, V., Jana, R., Ramakrishnan, K.K.: Towards a SPDY'ier mobile web? In: CoNEXT (2013)

8. Flach, T., Dukkipati, N., Terzis, A., Raghavan, B., Cardwell, N., Cheng, Y., Jain, A., Hao, S., Katz-Bassett, E., Govindan, R.: Reducing web latency: the virtue of gentle aggression. In: SIGCOMM (2013)

9. Ha, S., Rhee, I., Xu, L.: CUBIC: a new tcp-friendly high-speed TCP variant. Operating Syst. Rev. **42**, 64–74 (2008)

10. Meenan, P.: How fast is your web site? Commun. ACM **56**, 49–55 (2013)

11. Padhye, J., Nielsen, H.F.: A comparison of SPDY and HTTP performance. Technical report, July 2012

12. Varvello, M., Schomp, K., Naylor, D., Blackburn, J., Finamore, A., Papagiannaki, K.: To HTTP/2, or not to HTTP/2, that is the question. In: PAM (2016)

13. Wang, X.S., Balasubramanian, A., Krishnamurthy, A., Wetherall, D.: Demystifying page load performance with wprof. In: NSDI (2013)

14. Wang, X.S., Balasubramanian, A., Krishnamurthy, A., Wetherall, D.: How speedy is SPDY? In: NSDI (2014)

Behind Box-Office Sales: Understanding the Mechanics of Automation Spam in Classifieds

Andrew J. Kaizer[✉], Minaxi Gupta, Mejbaol Sajib, Anirban Acharjee, and Qatrunnada Ismail

School of Informatics and Computing, Indiana University, Bloomington, USA
akaizer@indiana.edu

Abstract. In spite of being detrimental to user experiences, the problem of automated messages on online classified websites is widespread due to a low barrier of entry and limited enforcement-of-rules against such messages. Many of these messages may appear legitimate, but turn into spam when they are posted redundantly. This behavior drowns out other legitimate users from having their voices heard. We label this problem as *automation spam* – legitimate messages that are posted at a rate that overwhelms normal posts. In this paper, we characterize automation on a popular classifieds website, Craigslist, and find that 2/3rd of the posts with URLs are automated. Automation is most prevalent in categories dominated by businesses, such as Tickets, Cars by Dealer, and Real Estate, with 67–92 % of the posts with URLs exhibiting automation. Even in categories with less automation, intermittent automation still overwhelms non-automated users, demonstrating that no category is safe.

1 Introduction

Various ills, including spam, malware, blackhat search engine optimization, and fraudulent product or video promotion, plague the modern web. While most of these issues receive the necessary attention from the research and operational communities, a lesser discussed ill is a special type of spam exemplified on online classified websites, forums, blogs, and online social networks (OSNs), etc. where legitimate content is forcefully pushed en masse onto users. While the content of these messages is reasonably related to the topic at hand, their spamminess is a result of the automation behind it which leads to a deluge that drowns out other users' posts. An example of this type of spam, referred to as *automation spam* subsequently, is an automated user posting a large number of advertisements of cars for sale in the automobile category of a classifieds website that drown posts of other legitimate users in that category. Even as a buyer finds the first automated post to be pertinent to their activity, their patience would wear thin

© Springer International Publishing Switzerland 2016
T. Karagiannis and X. Dimitropoulos (Eds.): PAM 2016, LNCS 9631, pp. 248–260, 2016.
DOI: 10.1007/978-3-319-30505-9_19

after the many such posts are presented to them – this makes automation spam a threat to the very utility of classifieds forums.

Automation spam is typically a result of software that allows a user to specify an advertisement(s) to post onto a website and then automatically post those messages, multiple times, on behalf of the user based on some posting criteria (number of times to post, when to post, etc.). These automation tools ultimately disrupt normal users from seeing content they want to see and as a result automation tools are strictly forbidden or strongly discouraged in the world of online classifieds due to its potential to turn into spam. Among the largest classified websites – Craigslist.org, eBayClassifieds.com, ClassifiedAds.com, and Backpage.com – the terms of service are clear in this regard. Craigslist, which commands an Alexa rank of 10 in the U.S., clearly states a no automation policy: *"It is expressly prohibited to post content to Craigslist using any automated means..."* [1]. Classifiedads.com has users agree not to use any form of automated device or computer program in their postings [2]. Even though automation is clearly restricted or forbidden, its use is still widespread because users often engage in this behavior to save time and effort while letting their posts be seen more often than competitors.

Given this unexplored category of spam, our key contribution in this paper is a characterization of automation spam in the context of a popular classifieds website, Craigslist. To this end, we collect all posts for 13 of the largest U.S. cities in 117 categories of Craigslist for a period of three weeks. Automation spam is then identified using a carefully chosen *post rate* threshold that identifies obvious circumvention of the post rate limit on Craigslist. Since Craigslist lacks public user accounts, we use URLs to group posts together into *automated spam campaigns* that share a common URL resource.

The key characteristic observations from applying our automation threshold to 2.4 million Craigslist posts with URLs are:

63 % of all Craigslist Posts Containing a URL are Automated. The most consistent automation appears in categories dominated by businesses. Examples include Tickets, Cars by Dealer, and Real Estate. In these categories, 67–92 % of posts with URLs are automation spam, drowning non-automated posts and creating a perverse incentive for more people to resort to automation to keep their posts visible and to overwhelm the competition.

While Automation is Low in Categories Dominated by individuals, such as Cars by Owner and Electronics, it Still Overwhelms These Categories Intermittently: 12–43 % of posts containing URLs are still automated in categories dominated by individuals.

Most of the Automated Posts Can be Grouped Under Campaigns and These Campaigns are Localized in Categories, but Span Multiple cities: Consequently, all the 13 cities in our data set witness similar levels of automation, in that 16–27 % posts (56–80 % of those containing URLs) are automated. For example, a campaign spanning cities might just focus on Cars by Dealer and Auto Parts categories.

Levels of Automation Range from Naive to Sophisticated: On the naive end are automators that allow campaigns where all posts contain URLs belonging to just one domain. On the sophisticated end are automators for campaigns that rotate through a large number of domains, use extensive redirections for accounting and hiding purposes, and provide templates so sellers can easily avail their automation services.

2 Data Collection

We collected posts from 117 of the Craigslist categories every fifteen minutes over three weeks using the RSS feeds provided by Craigslist. This includes categories under "community", "housing", "for sale", "services", "jobs", and "gigs". Furthermore, we focused on 13 major metropolitan regions in the United States, shown in Table 1 which describes the number of posts with URLs observed per city and the amount of automation observed. These locations were selected because they are among the most actively visited portions of the Craigslist website during data collection.

Table 1. Number of posts observed and the automation rates of posts with a URL over 21 days broken down by city.

City	Total posts	With URL	Automated-post % URL
Dallas	773,185	261,383	80.07 %
Boston	527,163	156,112	78.24 %
Chicago	564,744	185,749	73.88 %
Atlanta	527,671	158,838	72.57 %
Portland	561,809	147,880	71.79 %
Seattle	537,040	166,706	70.91 %
Washington D.C.	564,224	179,862	70.29 %
Phoenix	729,927	204,656	68.01 %
San Diego	710,381	175,380	67.93 %
New York	631,164	229,889	67.83 %
Las Vegas	218,937	71,371	63.74 %
San Francisco Bay	683,284	217,396	61.55 %
Los Angeles	889,433	256,723	56.97 %

For each post, we collect the following information: Craigslist URL for the post, post ID, post date and local time, post title, post body, and the Craigslist email handle which is unique to each post. Additionally, we know the category and city in which the post appeared. Each individual post collected is inserted into a database table if it meets the following criteria: the post ID, post time, and post title are unique. These criteria were selected as they allow ignoring duplicate posts while still capturing any new posts. Specifically, Craigslist allows *reposts*, so a post with the same post ID but different date or time is not a duplicate.

3 Identifying Automation Spam

In order to identify automation spam to be used in the characterization process, we first grouped all posts that shared a common external URL together, which we refer to as a *campaign*. Then, to identify automation spam, we applied a two step approach involving post rate and post count to ensure we focused only on automation spam and not on organic human posts. We discuss each aspect of identifying automation spam in more detail in each subsection.

3.1 Campaigns: Unpopular and Popular

We found that the external URLs used to identify campaigns fell into two broad categories that required different approaches to identify: Unpopular and popular domains. In the first category are URLs that lead to unpopular domains, where automators often rotated large numbers of such domains in an attempt to keep URLs unique and evade detection mechanisms related to URLs. Interestingly, irrespective of the number of domains, the IP addresses used to host them were most often just a single IP address. We refer to the IPs for one automation spam campaign as an *IP group* subsequently in the paper. Grouping IPs at a general prefix level could be used to try and catch a larger number of IPs into each campaign, but the campaigns we encountered would not benefit from this approach as they were concentrated on a single IP address.

The second category of external URLs include popular domains, including OSNs such as Facebook and image sharing websites. Here, the automated messages were often leading visitors to OSN pages of the business or using product pictures uploaded to image sharing websites. This category of URL is different from the unpopular domains in that the domain itself cannot be used to detect automation without the risk of false positives because the domain serves a wide variety of users with most users not using the popular service for automation. For this reason, our identification process uses the full URLs for all popular domains in the Alexa top 1 million to identify specific URLs that appear frequently in posts.

3.2 Identifying Automation: Post Rate and Post Volume

The **post rate** step inspects if a campaigns violated the *post rate limitations* in place for individual users that aims to prevent individual user spam. For the online classified site of Craigslist at the time of data collection, this limit was to allow a single account to post up to three times per minute, which was established as our minimum threshold.

The **post volume** step applies a more stringent filter to identify automation spam that violated the post rate step by focusing on particular behavior that impacts users the most. In particular, this paper only considers campaigns that posted an average of 24 times a day. This distinction ensures that our inspection of campaigns explores high volume campaigns that hurt a user's experience while also avoiding capturing posts from individual users.

4   Characterization of Automated Spam

Table 2 presents an overview of the collected data. Over the data collection period of three weeks between May 11th though June 1st, we observed 7,311,013 million

Table 2. 20 % of all posts (63 % of those with URLs) on Craigslist are automation spam

Post type	Count	Percentage (%)
No URL	4,898,618	67.01 %
Contains URL, is automated	1,517,500	20.75 %
Contains URL, is not automated	894,895	12.24 %

distinct post IDs, of which 2,412,395 (33 %) million had an external URL. Our algorithm classified 1,517,500 distinct post IDs as automation spam – almost 63 % of all posts with a URL present. We manually verified the classification of spam campaigns to ensure that we did not penalize any legitimate campaigns.

We identified 1109 automated campaigns. Of the automated campaigns, 760 belonged to popular domains and 349 to IP groups belonging to unpopular domains. The campaigns for popular domains had 494,063 – 20.48 % of posts with a URL – post IDs that were classified as automation spam with an average number of 895 posts per campaign and a median of 198. A total of 1,100,720 – 45.63 % of posts with a URL – posts were classified as automation spam using the IP group, with an average number of posts per campaign of 3,358 and a median of 1,249. This implies that *automation spam campaigns whose URLs led to unpopular domains post at a rate 3.9 times higher than those whose URLs lead to popular domains on an average.* Note that the total posts for automation spam campaigns whose URLs lead to popular and unpopular domains are greater than the total automation campaigns, albeit by a small amount. This is because a small percentage of automated posts contain URLs for both popular as well as unpopular domains.

4.1 Automation by Categories

Table 3 shows the top-10 Craigslist categories with most number of posts during our 3-week data collection period and the percentage automation in each. In general, the categories can be divided as *industry-based* versus *individual-based.* Industry-based categories are dominated by organizations or businesses that typically have an online presence, such as a website to sell products. Real Estate, Cars by Dealer, Tickets, and Apartments categories fall in this grouping. Specifically, Real Estate and Cars by Dealer are both organized and well established industries which have a large number of products with high values to be sold. The Apartments category has companies that have multiple properties with a revolving number of openings and there is an incentive to fill openings as quickly as possible. Finally, the Ticket resale business has been covered by the New York Times as a $4.5 billion industry that aggressively tries to sell their products [3].

Table 3. 10 largest Craigslist categories and their automation rates among all posts and only posts with a URL.

Category	Total posts	With URL	Automated post %URL
Cars by Dealer	1,075,163	619,037	77.08 %
Tickets	747,435	707,025	92.95 %
Furniture	599,052	114,967	43.30 %
Cars by Owner	410,130	31,726	11.92 %
Auto Parts	360,301	41,932	24.47 %
Apartments	336,680	202,650	66.89 %
General for Sale	269,752	25,886	17.24 %
Electronics	243,203	28,330	11.49 %
Real Estate	239,705	186,841	74.01 %
Mobile Phones	177,792	16,448	29.30 %

Three of these industry-based categories, Car by Dealer, Real Estate, and Apartments, already have a rich history of using paper classified ads and have recognized the utility of online classifieds. Unsurprisingly, all *industry-based categories have 40–88 % of all posts that are automation spam*. The number is even higher when considering automation in posts with URLs, with 67–92 % of posts with URLs being automated.

Individual-based categories are ones that have individuals selling items. Posting classifieds may not be their primary occupation. In fact, many rely on Craigslist directly and do not have a web presence or even use external URLs to sell their content, as such our algorithm would avoid grouping them due to a lack of an external URL, avoiding a false negative risk.

To understand the importance of the industry versus individual categories, consider the difference between Cars by Dealer and Cars by Owner categories. Cars sold through a dealer make heavy use of external URLs that link back to their website with more product details and, of course, more products to be viewed – this explains the high rate of external URLs and automation observed (44.38 %). Cars sold by their owner, however, are a one-time event; the owner has a single vehicle to sell and is not going to automate their one or two classified posts or create a website to sell this single vehicle. In this case, the individual is better served by using the features provided directly by Craigslist and leaving another avenue for potential buyers to contact them, such as providing a phone number or email address. Due to these reasons, we find much lower rates of automation in categories like Cars by Owner, General for Sale, Electronics, Mobile Phones, Auto Parts, and Furniture categories.

Even though there are fewer posts with a URL in the individual categories, this does not mean the rate of automation is equally low. Instead the percentage of all posts with a URL that was considered automation spam ranged from 12–43 %. This value is lower than the industry-based categories, but is still high enough that somewhere between 1 out of every 8 posts and 1 out of every 2.5 posts are automation spam if they contain a URL.

Intermittent Automation can Overwhelm Low Automation Categories: Interestingly, even in categories where the overall level of automation appears to be low, overwhelming automation can still occur. Consider the furniture category which has 8.31 % of its posts labeled as automation spam. If we break the result down by city to see the maximum amount of automation observed on the first page that has 100 posts – the page everyone sees when they look at a category – we observe an alarming amount of automation at certain times. For example, Boston's Furniture category had 95 of the top 100 posts automated, Dallas had 82 of 100, and of the rest of the cities we collected data on, only Washington D.C. had a maximum rate below 50, at 38. This phenomenon is widespread across most categories and strongly points to the fact that intermittent automation can overwhelm any category, even those that appear to have lower rates of automation.

Automation Drowns Human Posts in High Automation Categories: In categories where automation is high, automation can completely and consistently drown out posts made by humans. For example, the Tickets category is almost entirely automation spam posts, implying that an individual user who wants to sell tickets has little chance of being seen by a large audience. Similarly, auto dealerships or real estate offices that do not engage in automation risk their classifieds postings being drowned out by their competitors that use automators. In both of these cases 75 % of all posts with a URL in them were considered to be from an automation spam source. This provides a perverse incentive for more people to use automators to keep their posts visible, thereby leading to an exacerbation of the problem.

The following are a few other interesting facts about automation:

If automation in the Tickets and Cars by Dealer Categories were to be Curtailed, the Number of Posts we Observed Would have Plummeted by over 1.1. million, leaving only about 400,000 automation spam posts across every other category! This implies that *even a limited application of our algorithm to the higher traffic categories could alleviate most of the automation*, in turn allowing real human users' posts to be more fairly viewed.

The *Level of Automation Outside of the Top-10 Traffic Categories is Low,* Averaging 4.5 % with no Category Exceeding 23 %. We have found that this does not preclude users from being overwhelmed by negative automation, but rather that the automation that does exist is more bursty and erratic. However, no category is spared from having human users drowned out by automation at some point on a daily basis.

Most of the Automation Spam Campaigns are Localized into Related Categories, but Span Across Multiple Cities. For example, we found a campaign that occurred in two cities – Portland and Seattle – and was observed in the Car by Dealer, Auto Parts, and Car by Owner categories. Another campaign was observed in all cities but only the Ticket category. There appears to be very little automation common across all categories, but rather a wide variety of automation that targets particular categories.

4.2   Automation by Campaigns

As stated earlier, automation campaigns were rarely spread across many categories but instead focused on a handful of related categories, most often one. For example, if a campaign was observed in Tickets, it was unlikely to also be observed in the automotive categories. This observation makes it interesting to examine the behavior of top campaigns, the knowledge about which can be used to develop specialized solutions for specific tactics used by different campaigns. Indeed, we revealed different tactics and techniques employed by the various campaigns. Specifically, campaigns were of three types:

Table 4. Top-10 largest automation spam campaigns

Campaign	Category	Posts	% Automated
FrontPage Tickets	Tickets	144,918	100 %
Ticket Network	Tickets	90,486	99.98 %
TicketTrail	Tickets	81,846	92.36 %
Excellent Stubs	Tickets	40,054	100 %
.Info	Cars by Dealer	38,067	100 %
SimpleTicket Solutions	Tickets	31,640	100 %
Nondescript Domains	Cars by Dealer	31,095	100 %
CuttingEdge Tickets	Tickets	39,051	76.46 %
Market Leader	Real Estate	30,293	96.88 %
Moxie	Cars by Dealer	28,695	100 %

Bare-Bones: Bare-bones campaigns are those in which an automator was used that only makes automation spam easy by automatically posting ads to Craigslist. No additional features are present.

Middle-Man: Middle man campaigns are those that automatically post ads to Craigslist and allows a client to track which ads are being clicked on by having an intermediate URL that serves to redirect the user to their end destination. Before the redirection occurs, the middleman service records statistics about what URL was selected so the client can view how different ads are performing.

Full-Featured: A full-featured service is one where a client purchases a whole suite of services: Automated posting, URL tracking, web domain hosting, website templates, and other related services.

Table 4 details the ten largest automation spam campaigns observed in our data. Recall that our algorithm first groups posts with external URLs by IP group (for unpopular domains) and URLs (for popular domains) and then applies criteria for inferring automation. The campaigns in Tickets occupy six of the top-10 spots, with Cars by Dealer following with three spots. Next, we describe the biggest campaigns, one each in Tickets, Cars by Dealer, and Real Estate.

Campaign in Tickets: FrontPageTickets. This campaign was exclusive to the Tickets category and was tied to just one domain: frontpagetickets.com, which is a popular domain with an Alexa ranking of 517,000 globally and 100,000 in the United States. This campaign has two features that allowed our approach to easily link directly to the source of the automation and be certain of the judgment. The first feature is that external URL in the posts links directly to the service in question. The link does not redirect to another domain. A second feature is the consistent inclusion of links to the same three Facebook pages.

Hourly post rates for this campaign is shown in Fig. 1. The post rate is consistently sustained during all hours, even at night, with massive spikes occurring occasionally. The automation is confirmed by the volume of posts, which far exceed a human's ability to post, and the observation that the post rate did not slow or cease during night time - which would be expected due to the diurnal nature of human activity. Other facts about this campaign include:

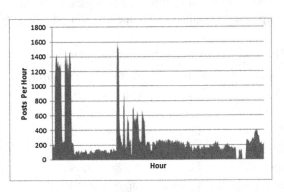

Fig. 1. Hourly post rate: FrontPageTickets campaign

This campaign appears **144,918** times in our data, accounting for **1.98 % of all posts observed over three weeks.**

The top-3 minute-by-minute post rates were: **51, 45, and 44.** This is almost one classified ad posted per second, which is not possible without automation.

Campaign in Cars by Dealer: .Info. This campaign relies on 38,067 unpopular *.info* domains that serve as a group of redirection services. A sample of the domains in this redirection campaign include flawcross.info, trailint.info, and catrating.info. The names of these domains do not appear to have any relationship to automotives and only served as redirects. The importance of grouping unpopular domains via IP Groups becomes apparent when we inspected this campaign: of the 38,067 posts classified as part of this IP group, we observed 38,067 FQDNs, implying that every classified post in this campaign used a unique domain name. If we had targeted automation only at URL granularity, we would have missed this campaign.

More generally, redirection style campaigns of this type operate by acting as a middle-man between the actual target and the source. Here, Craigslist is the source that links to the middleman automator which then redirects to the target URL(s). In this specific campaign each top-level domains has a unique subdomain that acts as the direction code – e.g. t4vg5b.flawcross.info. The use of redirection automators is clever: it allows tracking to identify which posts are producing actionable leads and allows the middle-man to defeat any frequency-based analysis Craigslist may be doing to identify automation by URL.

Where the FrontPageTickets campaign was described as consistent, this campaign was more erratic and bursty as shown in Fig. 2. It was rarely active during the overnight hours, often suddenly going dark between the hours of 00:00 and 06:00 local time, perhaps to mimic the human diurnal pattern. It would then ramp up again around 07:00AM for its most active hour, representing the majority of the higher spikes observed.

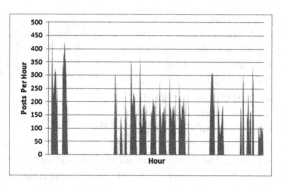

Fig. 2. Hourly post rate: .Info campaign

Other facts about this campaign include:

The 38,067 posts belonging to this campaign account for 0.52 % of *all* posts observed over three weeks.

The top three minute-by-minute post rates were: 26, 21, and 21. This is almost one classified posted every three seconds in a single minute, which is not possible for a human being.

Campaign in Real Estate: Market Leader. The real estate-based campaign observed in our data came from a variety of domains, both popular and unpopular. There were 833 distinct domains that appeared in this campaign. Investigating these 833 domains shows that they are hosted and managed through a single company called *Market Leader*. This company sells a unified management program for real estate websites and web services which includes a website template, lead generator (automator for Craigslist), and features related to management of the client's services [4].

By offering a full scale solution, this type of automator inadvertently allows their services to have too much homogeneity, making it easier to link the different domains together in two ways. The first is that the websites managed by the Market Leader service all appear on the same IP and therefore are part of the same IP group. Secondly, since the websites are provided via a template, they all share features that can be used to validate that the IP grouping our approach generates is correctly grouping domains from the exact same source together. The two most visible features are a common login/sign-up link at the top of the webpage and a "powered by market leader" notice on the footer of the webpage.

This campaign exhibited a nearly perfect diurnal pattern, as shown in Fig. 3. The posting rate is slower when the day begins, picks up until reaching a peak at the middle of the day, and then declines into the evening hours. The periods of time where there is a sharp spike in the posting rate is what leads our algorithm to consider 96 %

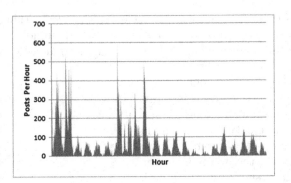

Fig. 3. Hourly post rate: Market Leader campaign

of the all posts from this campaign as suspected automation. These spikes are often in the early afternoon, but sometimes occurring as late as between 17:00–19:00 or as early as 10:00–12:00 local time. The spike behavior also stands out because it violates the normal behavior observed in aggregate for all posts observed on a majority of the days. Other facts about this campaign include:

The 29,348 posts from this campaign account for 0.40 % of *all* posts observed over three weeks.

The top three minute-by-minute post rates were: 46, 45, and 41. This is almost one classified posted every second in a single minute.

5   Related Work

Most research on classified websites has focused on the spam aspect of the specific categories rather than exploring the automation angle. Tran et al. focused on distinguishing between spam and advertising posts on Craigslist [5] and found that the traditional methods of spam detection failed due to a lack of linkage between posts. Instead they utilized domain knowledge of the categories the spam appeared in; e.g. information about automobile prices in the automotive category. Compared to Tran et al.'s domain specific application, our approach focused on all categories of Craigslist.

Other spam work has focused on dynamic spam URL detection on services. Research by [6,7] found that due to limited attacker resources, infrastructure would have to be reused in spam/malicious links on Twitter, especially for link redirection services. We extend this knowledge to the realm of non-malicious automated tools where automators would reuse the same domain infrastructure, but modify the subdomains in order to appear as if they were part of a different ad and not related to anyone else who used that automator's redirection service. Other research in identifying spam through Twitter users lack of web presence in the URLs they tweet achieved a 74 % level of fraudulent account detection [8]. We use a similar concept by using domain popularity in order to better establish if the website is popular enough to justify a high post volume.

An additional concern with most anti-spam solutions is their reliance on account information. For example, in the OSN space [9] used information related to message similarity, ratio of URLs in messages, number of friends, etc. to determine if an account is generating spam messages or is a real user. Likewise, [10] identified that many spam accounts on Twitter were generated in blocks and had nonsensical usernames. While our approach to identifying automation spam does not have access to accounts, due to the lack of publicly visible accounts, collaboration with providers could provide such details so that automated accounts can be identified more easily.

6 Conclusion

Our work in this paper shows that automation is widespread on Craigslist with 63 % of posts with URLs being automation spam. For occasional sellers or those users not resorting to automation, automation can become a nightmare if infringements of a website's terms of service are not properly dealt with. Overall, characterizing automation on Craigslist suggests that websites – especially those with a lower barrier of entry – will have to weigh the risks of automation and how to regulate it to protect their users. Ultimately, we have provided a first step towards identifying automation spam, which can be used help curtail these issues and improve user experience for everyone who uses these services.

Future work is still needed on two fronts: Identifying automation spam that does not contain a URL and creating a system that could be deployed to detect automation spam in real-time. Identifying automation spam without URLs would need to rely on content-based information: Phone numbers, email addresses, identifying common content by n-gram analysis, etc. This content-based approach could then be combined with our IP group based approach to provide a complementary set of features with which to identify automation spam with and without URLs. A real-time approach to detecting automation spam would then need to determine what specific IP group and content-based features provide the most coverage in identifying automation spam that could also be calculated in real-time.

Finally, a key research challenge in this line of research is the lack of readily accessible data sets to test and validate results. In order to develop a ground truth dataset, manual human effort was needed to label the posts as either automation spam or not-automation spam. We took this approach to verify our results, which is the same manual style approach that Jindal, et al. took in manually labeling reviews on Amazon as spam or non-spam for their spam analysis [11]. However, even after manual analysis of posts for automation behavior, there is still the fact to consider that our approach is only interested in capturing automation spam. As a result, other spam on Craigslist may exist that has characteristics we were not directly investigating, i.e. there could be traditional content spam in classified posts - e.g. illegal pharmaceutical companies.

The use of a system that does both IP grouping and content-based analysis, described above, would help to identify this traditional spam and automation spam. Using these complementary features would also help to identify spam that tries to evade IP group detection as IP group based approaches can be defeated if the *IP and URL* used are changed frequently enough to prevent creating groupings. Content-based features, however, are more likely to keep similarity between postings: The same or similar post content is likely to be used to describe the same product/service that is for sale. As a result, using both sets of features is likely to capture miscreants who try to evade either IP group or content-based approaches.

References

1. Craigslist TOU, "Craigslist terms of use" (2013). http://www.craigslist.org/about/terms.of.use
2. Classifiedads, "Terms and conditions" (2013). http://www.classifiedads.com/info.php?terms
3. Davidson, A.: The secret science of scalping tickets (2013). http://www.nytimes.com/2013/06/09/magazine/the-secret-science-of-scalping-tickets.html
4. MarketLeader, "One single, seamless real estate solution for your success | market leader", July 2013. http://www.marketleader.com/one-solution
5. Tran, H., Hornbeck, T., Ha-Thuc, V., Cremer, J., Srinivasan, P.: Spam detection in online classified advertisements. In: Workshop on Web Quality. ACM (2011)
6. Lee, S., Kim, J.: WarningBird: a near real-time detection system for suspicious URLs in twitter stream. IEEE Trans. Dependable Secure Comput. **10**, 183–195 (2013)
7. Thomas, K., Grier, C., Ma, J., Paxson, V., Song, D.: Design and evaluation of a real-time URL spam filtering service. In: IEEE Security and Privacy (2011)
8. Flores, M., Kuzmanovic, A.: Searching for spam: detecting fraudulent accounts via web search. In: Roughan, M., Chang, R. (eds.) PAM 2013. LNCS, vol. 7799, pp. 208–217. Springer, Heidelberg (2013)
9. Stringhini, G., Kruegel, C., Vigna, G.: Detecting spammers on social networks. In: Computer Security Applications. ACM (2010)
10. Verkamp, J.-P., Gupta, M.: Five incidents, one theme: twitter spam as a weapon to drown voices of protest. In: USENIX FOCI, vol. 22 (2014)
11. Jindal, N., Liu, B.: Opinion spam and analysis. In: International Conference on Web Search and Data Mining. ACM (2008)

DNS and Routing

Towards a Model of DNS Client Behavior

Kyle Schomp[1]([✉]), Michael Rabinovich[1], and Mark Allman[2]

[1] Case Western Reserve University, Cleveland, OH, USA
kyle.schomp@case.edu
[2] International Computer Science Institute, Berkeley, CA, USA

Abstract. The Domain Name System (DNS) is a critical component of the Internet infrastructure as it maps human-readable hostnames into the IP addresses the network uses to route traffic. Yet, the DNS behavior of individual clients is not well understood. In this paper, we present a characterization of DNS clients with an eye towards developing an analytical model of client interaction with the larger DNS ecosystem. While this is initial work and we do not arrive at a DNS workload model, we highlight a variety of behaviors and characteristics that enhance our mental models of how DNS operates and move us towards an analytical model of client-side DNS operation.

1 Introduction

The modern Internet relies on the Domain Name System (DNS) for two main functions. First, the DNS allows people to leverage human-friendly hostnames (e.g., www.cnn.com) instead of obtuse IP addresses to identify a host. Second, hostnames provide a layer of abstraction such that the IP address assigned to a hostname can vary over time. In particular, Content Distribution Networks (CDNs) employ this late binding to direct users to the best content replica. Previous work shows that DNS lookups precede over 60 % of TCP connections [14]. As a result, individual clients issue large numbers of DNS queries. Yet, our understanding of DNS query streams is largely based on aggregate populations of clients—e.g., at an organizational [6] or residential level [3]—leaving our knowledge of individual client behavior limited.

This paper represents an initial step towards understanding individual client DNS behavior. We monitor DNS transactions between a population of thousands of clients and their local resolver such that we are able to directly tie lookups to individual clients. Our ultimate goal is an analytical model of DNS client behavior that can be used for everything from workload generation to resource provisioning to anomaly detection. In this paper we provide a characterization of DNS behavior along the dimensions our model will ultimately cover and also anecdotally show promising modeling approaches.

Note, one view holds that DNS is a "side service" and should not be directly modeled, but rather can be well understood by deriving the DNS workload from

---

This work was funded in part by NSF grant CNS-1213157.

T. Karagiannis and X. Dimitropoulos (Eds.): PAM 2016, LNCS 9631, pp. 263–275, 2016.
DOI: 10.1007/978-3-319-30505-9_20

applications such as web browsing and email transmission. However, deriving a DNS workload from application behavior is at best difficult because (i) client caching policies impact what DNS queries are actually sent in response to an application event, (ii) some applications selectively use pre-fetching to lookup names before they are needed and (iii) such a derivation would entail understanding many applications to pull together a reasonable DNS workload. Therefore, we take the approach that focusing on the DNS traffic itself is the most tractable way to understand—and eventually model—name lookups.

To motivate the need for a model, we provide an exemplar from our previous work. In [14], we propose that clients should directly resolve hostnames instead of using a recursive resolver. Ideally, an evaluation of this end system-based mechanism would be conducted in the context of end systems themselves. However, the best data we could obtain was at the level of individual households—which we know to include multiple hosts behind a NAT. Therefore, the results of our trace-driven simulations are at best an approximation of the impact of the mechanism we were investigating. Our results would have been more precise had we been able to leverage a model of individual client DNS behavior.

Broadly, the remainder of this paper follows the contours of what a model would capture. We first focus on understanding the nature of the clients themselves in Sect. 3, finding that while most are traditional user-facing devices, there are others that interact with the DNS in distinct ways. Next we observe in Sect. 4 that DNS queries often occur closely-spaced in time—e.g., driven by loading objects for a single web page from disparate servers—and therefore we develop a method to gather together queries into clusters. We then assess the number and spacing of queries in Sect. 5 and finally tackle the patterns in what hostnames individual clients lookup in Sect. 6. We find that clients have fairly distinct "working sets" of names, and also that hostname popularity has power law properties.

2   Dataset

Our dataset comes from two packet taps at Case Western Reserve University (CWRU) that monitor the links connecting the two data centers that house all five of the University's DNS resolvers—i.e., between client devices and their recursive DNS resolvers. We collect full payload packet traces of all UDP traffic involving port 53 (the default DNS port). The campus wireless network situates client devices behind NATs and therefore we cannot isolate DNS traffic to individual clients. Hence, we do not consider this traffic in our study (although, future work remains to better understand DNS usage on mobile devices). The University Acceptable Use Policy prohibits the use of NAT on its wired networks while offering wireless access throughout the campus, and therefore we believe the traffic we capture from the wired network does represent individual clients. Our dataset includes all DNS traffic from two separate weeks and is partitioned by client location—in the residential or office portions of the network. Details of the datasets are given in Table 1 including the number of queries, the number of clients that issue those queries, and the number of hostnames queried.

Table 1. Details of the datasets used in this study.

Dataset	Dates	Queries	Clients	Hostnames
Feb:Residential	Feb. 26–Mar. 4	32.5 M	1359 (IPs)	652 K
Feb:Residential (filter)	Feb. 26–27, Mar. 2–4	16.4 M	1262 (MACs)	505 K
Feb:Residential:Users		15 M	1033	499 K
Feb:Residential:Others		1.11 M	229	7.94 K
Feb:Office	Feb. 26–Mar. 4	232 M	8770 (IPs)	1.98 M
Feb:Office (filter)	Feb. 26–27, Mar. 2–4	143 M	8690 (MACs)	1.87 M
Feb:Office:Users		118 M	5986	1.52 M
Feb:Office:Others		25.0 M	2704	158 K
Jun:Residential	Jun. 23–Jun. 29	11.7 M	345 (IPs)	140 K
Jun:Residential (filter)	Jun. 23–26, 29	6.22 M	334 (MACs)	120 K
Jun:Residential:Users		5.81 M	204	116 K
Jun:Residential:Others		408 K	130	4.13 K
Jun:Office	Jun. 23–Jun. 29	245 M	8335 (IPs)	1.61 M
Jun:Office (filter)	Jun. 23–26, 29	133 M	8286 (MACs)	1.52 M
Jun:Office:Users		108 M	5495	1.42 M
Jun:Office:Others		25.0 M	2791	63.1 K

Validation: During the February data collection, we collect query logs from the five campus DNS resolvers to validate our datasets[1]. Comparing the packet traces and logs we find a 0.6 % and 1.8 % loss rates in the Feb:Residential and Feb:Office datasets, respectively. We believe these losses are an artifact of our measurement apparatus given that the loss rate is correlated with traffic volume.

Tracking Clients: We aim to track individual clients in the face of dynamic address assignment. Simultaneously with the DNS packet trace, we gather logs from the University's three DHCP servers. Therefore, we can track DNS activity based on MAC addresses. Note, we could not map 1.3 % of the queries across our datasets to a MAC address because the source IP address in the query never appears in the DHCP logs. These likely represent static IP address allocations. Further, without any DHCP assignments we are confident that these IPs represent a single host.

Filtering Datasets: We find two anomalies that skew the data in ways that are not indicative of user behavior. First, we find roughly 25 % of the queries request the TXT record for debug.opendns.com (The next most popular record represents less than 1 % of the lookups!). We find this query is not in response to users' actions, but is automatically issued to determine whether the client is using the OpenDNS resolver (indicated in the answer) [1]. We observe 298 clients querying this record, which we assume use OpenDNS on other networks or used OpenDNS in the past. We remove these queries from further analysis. The second anomaly

---

[1] We prefer traces over logs due to the better timestamp resolution (msec vs. sec).

involves 18 clients whose prominent behavior is to query for debug.opendns.com and other domains repeatedly without evidence of accomplishing much work. The campus information technology department verified that these clients serve an operational purpose and are not user-facing devices. Therefore, we remove the 18 clients as they are likely unique to this network and do not represent users. We do not attempt to further filter misbehaving hosts—e.g., infected or misconfigured hosts—as we consider them part of the DNS workload (e.g., since a resolver would be required to cope with their requests).

Timeframe: To more directly compare residential and office settings we exclude Saturday and Sunday from our datasets.

Table 1 shows the magnitude of our filtering. We find commonality across the partitions of the data, so we focus on the Feb:Residential:Users dataset for conciseness and discuss how other datasets differ as appropriate.

Table 2. Feb:Residential clients that fit markers for general purpose devices.

Marker	Clients	%
All	1262	100 %
Google analytics	983	78 %
Search engine	1010	80 %
Google	1006	80 %
Any other	602	48 %
Gmail	881	70 %
LDAP login	840	66 %
Any	1033	82 %

3   Identifying Types of Clients

Since our focus is on characterizing general purpose user-facing devices, we aim to separate them from other types of end systems. We expect general-purpose systems are involved in tasks, such as (*i*) web browsing, (*ii*) accessing search engines, (*iii*) using email, and (*iv*) conducting institutional-specific tasks[2]. Therefore, we develop the following markers to identify general-purpose hosts:

Browsing: A large number of web sites embed Google Analytics [8] in their pages, thus there is a high likelihood that regular users will query for Google Analytics hostnames on occasion.

Searching: We detect web search activity via DNS queries for the largest search engines: Google, Yahoo, Bing, AOL, Ask, DuckDuckGo, Altavista, Baidu, Lycos, Excite, Naver, and Yandex.

---

[2] In our case, this is campus-life tasks, e.g., checking the course materials portal.

Email: CWRU uses Google to manage campus email and therefore we use queries for mail.google.com to indicate email use.

Institutional-Specific Tasks: CWRU uses a single sign-on system for authenticating users before they perform a variety of tasks and therefore we use queries for the corresponding hostname as indicative of user behavior.

Table 2 shows the breakdown of the clients in the Feb:Residential dataset. Of the 1,262 clients we identify 1,033 as user-facing based on at least one of the above markers. Intuitively we expect that multiple markers likely apply to most general purpose systems and in fact we find at least two markers apply to 991 of the clients in our dataset. Results for our other datasets are similar.

We next turn to the 229 clients ($\approx 18\,\%$) that do not match any of our markers for user-facing clients. To better understand these clients we aggregate them based on the vendor portion of their MAC addresses. First, we find a set of vendors and query streams that indicate special-purpose devices: (i) 48 Microsoft devices that query for names within the xboxlive.com domain, which we conclude are Xbox gaming consoles, (ii) 33 Sony devices that query for names within the playstation.net domain, which we conclude are Sony Playstation gaming consoles, (iii) 16 Apple devices that have an average of 11 K queries—representing 96 % of their lookups—for the apple.com domain, even though the average across all devices that lookup an apple.com name is 262 queries, which we conclude are Apple TV devices and (iv) 7 Linksys devices that issue queries for esuds.usatech.com, which we conclude are transaction systems attached to the laundry machines in the residence halls (!).

In addition to these, we find devices that we cannot pinpoint explicitly, but do not in fact seem to be general-purpose client systems. We find 41 Dell devices that differ from the larger population of hosts in that they query for more PTR records than A records. A potential explanation is that these devices are servers obtaining hostnames for clients that connect to them (e.g., as part of *sshd*'s verification steps or to log client connects). We also identify 12 Kyocera devices that issue queries for only the campus NTP and SMTP servers. We conclude that these are copy machines that also offer emailing of scanned documents.

For the IP addresses that do not appear in the DHCP logs (i.e., addresses statically configured on the hosts), we cannot obtain a vendor ID. However, we note that 97 % of the queries and 96 % of the unique domain names from these machines involve CWRU domains and therefore we conclude that they serve some administrative function and are not general purpose clients. The remaining 61 devices are distributed among 42 hardware vendors. In the remainder of the paper we will consider the general purpose clients (Users) and the special purpose clients (Others) separately, as we detail in Table 1. We find that our high-level observations hold across all of the Users datasets, and thus present results for the Feb:Residential:Users dataset only.

4   Query Clusters

Applications often call for multiple DNS queries in rapid succession—e.g., as part of loading all objects on a web page, or prefetching names for links users may click. In this section, we quantify this behavior using the DBSCAN algorithm [4] to construct clusters of DNS queries that likely share an application event. The DBSCAN algorithm uses two parameters to form clusters: a minimum cluster size M and a distance ε that controls the addition of samples to a cluster. We use the absolute difference in the query timestamps as the distance metric. Our first task is to choose suitable parameters. Our strategy is to start with a range of parameters and determine whether there is a point of convergence where the results of clustering do not change greatly with the parameters. Based on the strategy in [4], we start with an M range of 3–6 and an ε range of 0.5–5 s—note that $M = 2$ simplifies to threshold based clustering, but does not produce a point of convergence. We find that 96 % of the clusters we identify with $M = 6$ are exactly found when $M = 3$ and hence at $M = 3$ we have converged on a reasonably stable answer which we use in the subsequent analysis. Additionally, we find that for $\varepsilon \in [2.5, 5]$, the total number of clusters, the distribution of cluster sizes, and the assignment of queries to clusters remain similar irrespective of ε value and therefore use $\varepsilon = 2.5$ s in our analysis. We define the first DNS query per cluster as the *root* and all subsequent queries in the cluster as *dependents*. In the Feb:Residential:Users dataset, we find 1 M clusters that encompass 80 % of the roughly 15 M queries in the dataset.

To validate the clustering algorithm we first inspect the 67 K unique hostnames the algorithm labels as noise. We find a variety of hostnames with the most frequent being: WPAD [7] queries for discovering proxies, Google Mail and Google Docs, software update polling (e.g., McAfee and Symantec), heartbeat signals for gaming applications (e.g., Origin, Steam, Blizzard, Riot), video streaming (e.g., Netflix, YouTube, Twitch), and the Network Time Protocol (NTP). All of these names can intuitively come from applications that require only sporadic DNS queries, as they are either making quick checks every once in a while, or are using long-lived sessions that leverage DNS only when starting.

To validate the clusters themselves, we observe that there are frequently occurring roots. Indeed, the 1 M clusters have only 72 K unique roots, with the 100 most frequently occurring roots accounting for 395 K (40 %) of the clusters. Further, the 100 most popular roots include popular web sites (e.g., www.facebook.com, www.google.com). These are the type of names we would expect to be roots in the context of web browsing. Another common root is safebrowsing.google.com [9], a blacklist directory used by some web browsers to determine if a given web site is safe to retrieve. This is a distinctly different type of root than a popular web site because the root is not directly related to the dependents by the page content, but rather via a process running on the clients. This in some sense means SafeBrowsing-based clusters have two roots. While use of SafeBrowsing is fairly common in our dataset, we do not find additional prevalent cases of this "two roots" phenomenon. From a modeling standpoint

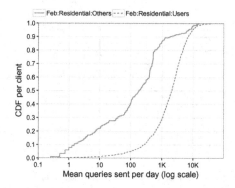

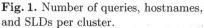

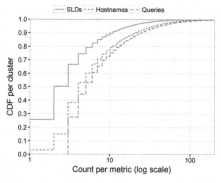

Fig. 1. Number of queries, hostnames, and SLDs per cluster.

Fig. 2. Queries issued by each client per day.

we have not yet determined whether "two roots" clusters would need special treatment.

Figure 1 shows the distribution of queries per cluster. While the majority of clusters are small, there are relatively few large clusters. We find that 90 % of clusters contain at most 26 queries for at most 22 hostnames. Additionally, we find 90 % of the clusters encompass at most 10 SLDs. The largest cluster spans 95 s and consists of 9,366 queries for names that match to the 3rd level label. The second largest cluster consists of 6,211 queries for myapps.developer.ubuntu.com—which is likely a Ubuntu bug.

5 Query Timing

Next we tackle the question of when and how many queries clients issue. We begin with the distribution of the average number of queries that clients issue per day, as given in Fig. 2. We find that clients in Users issue 2 K lookups per day at the median and 90 % of clients in Users issue less than 6.7 K queries per day. The Others datasets show greater variability where relatively few clients generate the lion's share of queries—i.e., the top 5 % of clients produce roughly as many total DNS queries per day as the bottom 95 % in the Feb:Residential:Others dataset.

A related metric is the time between subsequent queries from the same client, or inter-query times. Figure 3 shows the distribution of the inter-query times. The "Aggregate" line shows the distribution across all clients. The area "90 %" shows the range within which 90 % of the individual client inter-query time distributions fall. The majority of inter-query times are short, with 50 % of lookups occurring within 34 ms of the previous query. However, we also find a heavy tail, with 0.1 % of inter-query times being over 25 min. Intuitively, long inter-query times represent off periods when the client's user is away from the keyboard (e.g., asleep or at class). The Others datasets show wide ranging behavior suggesting that they are less amenable to succinct description in an aggregate model.

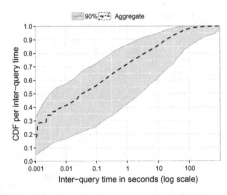

Fig. 3. Time between queries from the same client in aggregate and per client.

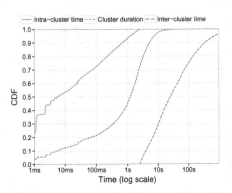

Fig. 4. Duration of clusters, inter-cluster query time and intra-cluster query time.

For the Users dataset, we are able to model the aggregate inter-query time distribution using the Weibull distribution for the body and the Pareto distribution for the heavy tail. We find that partitioning the data at an inter-query time of 22 s minimizes the mean squared error between the data and the two analytical distributions. Next, we fit the analytical distributions—split at 22 s—to each of the individual client inter-query time distributions. We find that while the parameters vary per client, the empirical data is well represented by the analytical models as the mean squared error for 90 % of clients is less than 0.0014. *Thus, parameters for a model of query inter-arrivals will vary per client, but the distribution is invariant.*

Next, we move from focusing on individual lookups to focusing on timing related to the 1 M lookup clusters that encompass 12 M (80 %) of the queries in our dataset (see Sect. 4). Figure 4 shows our results. The "Intra-cluster time" line shows the distribution of the time between successive queries within the same cluster. This time is bounded to $\varepsilon = 2.5$ s by construction, but over 90 % of the inter-arrivals are less than 1 s. On the other hand, the line "Inter-cluster time" shows the time between the last query of a cluster and the first query of the next cluster. Again, most clusters are separated from each other by much more than ε time, the minimum separation by construction. The line "Cluster duration" shows the time between the first and last query in each cluster. Most clusters are short, with 99 % less than 18 s. Additionally, we find that most of client DNS traffic occurs in short clusters: 50 % of clustered queries belong to clusters with duration less than 4.6 s and 90 % are in clusters with duration less than 20 s. For the Others datasets, a smaller percentage of DNS queries occur in clusters—e.g., 60 % in the Feb:Residential:Others dataset.

6   Query Targets

Finally, we tackle the queries themselves including relationships between queries.

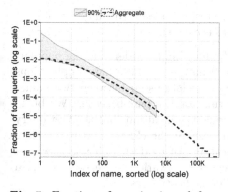

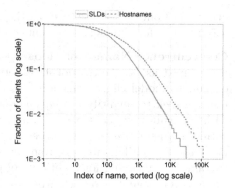

Fig. 5. Fraction of queries issued for each hostname per client.

Fig. 6. Fraction of clients issuing queries for each hostname and SLD.

Popularity of Names: We analyze the popularity of hostnames using two methods—how often the name is queried across the dataset and how many clients query for it. Figure 5 shows the fraction of queries for each hostname (with the hostnames sorted by decreasing popularity) in the Feb:Residential:Users dataset. Per Sect. 5, we plot the aggregate distribution and a range that encompasses 90 % of the individual client distributions. Of the 499 K unique hostnames within our dataset, 256 K (51 %) are looked up only once. Meanwhile, the top 100 hostnames account for 28 % of DNS queries. Figure 6 shows the fraction of clients that query for each name. We find that 77 % of hostnames are queried by only a single client. However, over 90 % of the clients look up the 14 most popular hostnames. Additionally, 13 of these hostnames are Google services and the remaining one is www.facebook.com. The plot shows similar results for second-level domains (SLDs), where 66 % of the SLDs are looked up by a single client.

The distributions of both queries per name and clients per name demonstrate power law behavior in the tail. Interestingly, the Pearson correlation between these two metrics—popularity by queries and popularity by clients—is only 0.54 indicating that a domain name with many queries is not necessarily queried by a large fraction of the client population and vice versa. As an example, updatekeepalive.mcafee.com is the 19th most queried hostname but is only queried by 8.1 % of the clients. At the same time, 55 % of the clients query for s2.symcb.com, but in terms of total queries this hostname ranks as only the 1215th most popular. This phenomenon may be partially explained by differences in TTL. The record for s2.symcb.com has a one hour TTL—limiting the query frequency. Meanwhile, updatekeepalive.mcafee.com has a 1 min TTL. Given this short TTL and that the name implies polling activity, the large numbers of queries from a given client is unsurprising. Thus, a model of DNS client behavior must account for the popularity of hostnames in terms of both queries and clients.

The heavy tails of the popularity distributions represent a large fraction of DNS transactions. However, we cannot disregard unpopular names—even those queried just once—because together they are responsible for the majority of DNS activity therefore impacting the entire DNS ecosystem (e.g., cache behavior).

Co-occurrence Name Relationships: In addition to understanding popularity, we next assess the relationships between names, as these have implications on how to model client behavior. The crucial relationship between two names that we seek to quantify is frequent querying for the pair together. We begin with the request clusters (Sect. 4) and leverage the intuition that the first query within a cluster triggers the subsequent queries in the cluster and is therefore the *root* lookup. This follows from the structure of modern web pages, with a container page calling for additional objects from a variety of servers—e.g., an average web page uses objects from 16 different hostnames [10].

Finding co-occurrence is complicated due to client caching. That is, we cannot expect to see the entire set of dependent lookups each time we observe some root lookup. Our methodology for detecting co-occurrence is as follows. First, we define $clusters(r)$ as the number of clusters with r as the root across our dataset and $pairs(r,d)$ as the number of clusters with root r that include dependent d. Second, we limit our analysis to the case when $clusters(r) \geq 10$ to reduce the potential for false positive relationships based on too few samples. In the Feb:Residential:Users dataset, we find 7.1 K (9.9 %) of the clusters meet these criteria. Within these clusters we find 7.5 M dependent queries and 2.2 M unique (r,d) pairs. Third, for each pair (r,d), we compute the co-occurrence as $C = pairs(r,d)/clusters(r)$—i.e., the fraction of the clusters with root r that include d. Co-occurrence of most pairs is low with 2.0 M (93 %) pairs having a C much less than 0.1. We focus on the 78 K pairs that have high C—greater than 0.2. These pairs include 98 % of the roots we identify, i.e., nearly all roots have at least one dependent with which they co-occur frequently. Also, these pairs comprise 28 % of the 7.5 M dependent queries we study.

We note that intuitively dependent names could be expected to share labels with their roots—e.g., www.facebook.com and star.c10r.facebook.com—and this could be a further way to assess co-occurrence. However, we find that only 27 % of the pairs within clusters with co-occurrence of at least 0.2 share the same SLD and 11 % share the 3rd level label as the cluster root. This suggests that while not rare, counting on co-occurring names to be from the same zone to build clusters is dubious. As an extreme example, Google Analytics is a dependent of 1,049 unique cluster roots, most of which are not Google names.

Finally, we cannot test the majority of the clusters and pairs for co-occurrence because of limited samples. However, we hypothesize that our results apply to all clusters. We note that the distribution of the number of queries per cluster in Fig. 1 is similar to the distribution of the number of dependents per root where the co-occurrence fraction is greater than 0.2. Combining our observations that 80 % of queries occur in clusters, 28 % of the dependent queries within clusters have high co-occurrence with the root, and the average cluster has 1 root and 10 dependents, we estimate that at a minimum $80 * 0.28 * 10/11 = 20$ % of DNS queries are driven by co-occurrence relationships. *We conclude that co-occurrence*

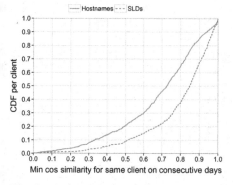

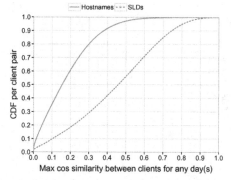

Fig. 7. Cosine similarity between the query vectors for the same client.

Fig. 8. Cosine similarity between the query vectors for different clients.

relationships are common, though the relationships do not always manifest as requests on the wire due to caching.

Temporal Locality: We next explore how the set of names a client queries changes over time. As a foundation, we construct a vector $V_{c,d}$ for each client c and each day d in our dataset, which represents the fraction of lookups for each name we observe in our dataset. Specifically, we start from an alphabetically ordered list of all hostnames looked up across all clients in our dataset, N. We initially set each $V_{c,d}$ to a vector of $|N|$ zeros. We then iterate through N and set the corresponding position in each $V_{c,d}$ as the total number of queries client c issues for name N_i on day d divided by the total number of queries c issues on day d. Thus, an example $V_{c,d}$ would be $< 0, 0.25, 0, 0.5, 0.25 >$ in the case where there are five total names in the dataset and on day d the client queries for the second name once, the fourth name twice and the fifth name once. We repeat this process using only the SLDs from each query, as well.

We first investigate whether clients' queries tend to remain stable across days in the dataset. For this, we compute the minimum cosine similarity of the query vectors for each client across all pairs of consecutive days. Figure 7 shows the distribution of minimum cosine similarity per client in the Feb:Residential:Users dataset. In general, the cosine similarity values are high—greater than 0.5 for 80 % of clients for unique hostnames—indicating that clients query for a similar set of names in similar relative frequencies across days. Given this result, it is unsurprising that the figure also shows high similarity across SLDs.

Next we assess whether different clients query for similar sets of names. We compute the cosine similarity across all pairs of clients and for all days of our dataset. Figure 8 shows the distribution of the maximum similarity per client pair from any day. When considering hostnames, we find lower similarity values than when focusing on a single client—with only 3 % showing similarity of at least 0.5—showing that each client queries for a fairly distinct set of hostnames. The similarity between clients is also low for sets of SLDs, with 55 % of the pairs showing a maximum similarity less than 0.5. Thus, clients query for different

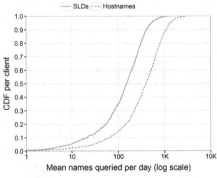
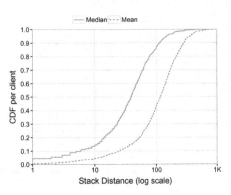

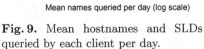

Fig. 9. Mean hostnames and SLDs queried by each client per day.

Fig. 10. Mean and median stack distance for each client.

specific hostnames and distinct sets of SLDs. *These results show that a client DNS model must ensure that (i) each client tends to stay similar across time and also that (ii) clients must be distinct from one another.*

A final aspect we explore is how quickly a client repeats a query. As we show in Fig. 2, 50 % of the clients send less than 2 K queries per day on average. Figure 9 shows the distribution of the average number of unique hostnames that clients query per day. The number of names is less than the overall number of lookups, indicating the presence of repeat queries. For instance, at the median, a client queries for 400 unique hostnames and 150 SLDs each day. To assess the temporal locality of re-queries, we compute the stack distance [12] for each query—the number of unique queries since the last query for the given name. Figure 10 shows the distributions of the mean and median stack distance per client. We find the stack distance to be relatively short in most cases—with over 85 % of the medians being less than 100. However, the longer means show that the re-use rate is not always short. *Our results show that variation in requerying behavior exists among clients, with some clients revisiting names frequently and others querying a larger set of names with less frequency.*

7   Related Work

Models of various protocols have been constructed for understanding, simulating and predicting traffic (e.g., [13] for a variety of traditional protocols and [2] as an example of HTTP modeling). Additionally, there is previous work on characterizing DNS traffic (e.g., [6,11]), which focuses on the aggregate traffic of a population of clients, in contrast to our focus on individual clients. Finally, we note—as we discuss in Sect. 1—that several recent studies involving DNS make assumptions about the behavior of individual clients or need to analyze data for specific information before proceeding. For instance, the authors of [5] model DNS hierarchical cache performance using an analytical arrival process, while in [14], the authors use simulation to explore changes to the resolution path. Both studies would benefit from a greater understanding of DNS client behavior.

8   Conclusion

This work is an initial step towards richly understanding individual DNS client behavior. We characterize client behavior in ways that will ultimately inform an analytical model. We find that different types of clients interact with the DNS in distinct ways. Further, DNS queries often occur in short clusters of related names. As a step towards an analytical model, we show that the client query arrival process is well modeled by a combination of the Weibull and Pareto distributions. In addition, we find that clients have a "working set" of names that is both fairly stable over time and fairly distinct from other clients. Finally, our high-level results hold across both time and qualitatively different user populations—student residential vs. University office. This is an initial indication that the broad properties we illuminate hold the promise to be invariants.

References

1. OpenDNS. http://www.opendns.com/
2. Barford, P., Crovella, M.: Generating representative web workloads for network and server performance evaluation. In ACM SIGMETRICS (1998)
3. Callahan, T., Allman, M., Rabinovich, M.: On modern DNS behavior and properties. ACM SIGCOMM Comput. Commun. Rev. **43**(3), 7–15 (2013)
4. Ester, M., Kriegel, H.-P., Sander, J., Xu, X.: A density-based algorithm for discovering clusters in large spatial databases with noise. In: AAAI International Conference on Knowledge Discovery and Data Mining (1996)
5. Fofack, N.C., Alouf, S.: Modeling modern DNS caches. In: ACM International Conference on Performance Evaluation Methodologies and Tools (2013)
6. Gao, H., Yegneswaran, V., Chen, Y., et al.: An empirical re-examination of global DNS behavior. In: ACM SIGCOMM (2013)
7. Gauthier, P., Cohen, J., Dunsmuir, M.: The web proxy auto-discovery protocol. IETF Internet Draft (work in progress) (1999). https://tools.ietf.org/html/draft-ietf-wrec-wpad-01
8. Websites using google analytics. http://trends.builtwith.com/analytics/Google-Analytics
9. Google safe browsing. https://developers.google.com/safe-browsing
10. HTTP archive. http://httparchive.org
11. Jung, J., Berger, A.W., Balakrishnan, H.: Modeling TTL-based internet caches. In: IEEE International Conference on Computer Communications (2003)
12. Mattson, R.L., Gecsei, J., Slutz, D.R., Traiger, I.L.: Evaluation techniques for storage hierarchies. IBM Syst. J. **9**(2), 78–117 (1970)
13. Paxson, V.: Empirically derived analytic models of wide-area TCP connections. IEEE/ACM Trans. Netw. **2**(4), 316–336 (1994)
14. Schomp, K., Allman, M., Rabinovich, M.: DNS resolvers considered harmful. In: ACM Workshop on Hot Topics in Networks (2014)

Detecting DNS Root Manipulation

Ben Jones[1]([✉]), Nick Feamster[1], Vern Paxson[2,3], Nicholas Weaver[2],
and Mark Allman[2]

[1] Princeton University, Princeton, USA
bj6@cs.princeton.edu
[2] International Computer Science Institute, Berkeley, USA
[3] University of California, Berkeley, USA

Abstract. We present techniques for detecting unauthorized DNS root
servers in the Internet using primarily endpoint-based measurements
from RIPE Atlas, supplemented with BGP routing announcements from
RouteViews and RIPE RIS. The first approach analyzes the latency to
the root server and the second approach looks for route hijacks. We
demonstrate the importance and validity of these techniques by measuring the only root server ("B") not widely distributed using anycast. Our
measurements establish the presence of several DNS proxies and a DNS
root mirror.

1 Introduction

The integrity and availability of many forms of Internet communication rely on
replies from the DNS root name servers. Entities operating unauthorized root
servers can completely control the entire Internet name space for any systems
within their sphere, including blocking access to sites by disrupting their name
resolution, or arbitrarily interposing on communication by redirecting through
man-in-the-middle proxies. In this paper, we present some techniques for assessing the prevalence of unauthorized root servers.

We develop techniques to detect several scenarios where clients cannot direct
queries to the authorized DNS root servers. We call this phenomenon *DNS root
manipulation*, regardless of whether correct DNS results are returned, because
such servers can provide adversarial responses. Countries such as China [3],
Pakistan [12,18], and Turkey [1] already manipulate DNS to impose censorship,
sometimes incidentally affecting DNS resolution for other countries [2,8]. We
are interested in similar cases where an attacker can control where DNS packets
are sent, thereby preventing access to the root. Given the size of this threat,
we focus on attackers who manipulate all DNS root-server replicas, rather than
those who subvert only a subset of them.

As deployed today, the DNS root comprises 13 server addresses run by
12 organizations, designated `a.root-servers.net` ... `m.root-servers.net`.
DNS resolvers have the IP addresses for these 13 logically distinct entities
hardwired into their configurations, grounding DNS resolution. All but one

© Springer International Publishing Switzerland 2016
T. Karagiannis and X. Dimitropoulos (Eds.): PAM 2016, LNCS 9631, pp. 276–288, 2016.
DOI: 10.1007/978-3-319-30505-9_21

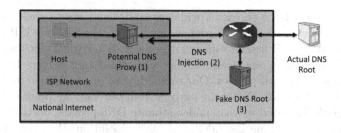

Fig. 1. Attackers can manipulate access to the DNS root with (1) an in-path DNS proxy, (2) DNS injection, or (3) changes to Internet routing to false DNS root servers.

of these servers uses anycast to route the corresponding IP address to multiple servers around the Internet. The number of topologically distinct replicas for each anycasted root server range from two (h.root-servers.net) to 150 (l.root-servers.net).

Threat Model. Figure 1 illustrates three ways that an attacker can implement DNS root manipulation. Although some malware has controlled DNS lookups directly on end-systems [10], that approach presumably presents difficult scaling issues to conduct in a widespread fashion. In this paper, we focus on network-based manipulation. The first method interposes a middlebox to intercept DNS traffic bound for root servers. For smaller networks, a transparent proxy achieves both control as well as potential performance improvements by caching queries. Transparent proxies are easy to implement because DNS operates over UDP, which is connectionless; thus, proxies do not need extensive state. Second, an attacker may observe DNS requests and inject responses before legitimate responses return. Finally, an attacker can compromise IP routing to redirect traffic for the DNS root servers to a false root replica—analogous to the anycast technology used for legitimate root replicas.

In all three cases, the attacker controls DNS responses, providing complete control over DNS. Due to the scale and complexity required to manipulate queries to the root servers, we assume that an entity seeking to subvert the DNS root servers would do so across all 13 logical servers to obtain unambiguous control. Additionally, our techniques assume that an in-path device does not selectively choose which DNS requests to manipulate.

Approach. As discussed in Sect. 3, our approach identifies some unauthorized root servers by examining side effects introduced by putting infrastructure in place to handle DNS root lookups. Specifically, we examine the latency and routing from various points around the Internet to the one non-anycasted root server, b.root-servers.net, which in the absence of unauthorized manipulation should reflect its singular location in Los Angeles, USA. We use the roughly 8,000-node RIPE Atlas [23] measurement platform for large-scale measurements. We complement our active probing with BGP routing table snapshots from RouteViews [26] and RIPE RIS [22].

We develop methods to cast a wide net and demonstrate their validity by finding several instances of DNS root manipulation. We find one ISP that redirects clients at the IP layer to an unauthorized root replica. Further, we find several ISPs prevent direct access to the authorized root servers by interposing on DNS lookup with proxies. Our methods give us confidence that we have detected most, if not all, DNS root mirrors from our vantage points, though we do not cover all ASes and we may underestimate DNS proxies. Section 2 sketches related work in examining the fidelity of DNS resolution. We then discuss our measurement approach in Sect. 3, and apply our approach in Sect. 4. We discuss future work in Sect. 5 and summarize in Sect. 6.

2   Related Work

Several previous efforts have explored DNS manipulation, measured DNS root servers, and looked for prefix hijacking.

DNS Manipulation. Dagon et al. found corrupt DNS resolvers by measuring open resolvers [10]. This effort focused on finding compromised hosts rather than DNS root manipulation and found that 2 % of resolvers provided incorrect queries and 0.4 % provided misleading answers. Closer to our work, Weaver et al. used the Netalyzr end-system network measurement platform to explore DNS manipulation [28] and characterize home network DNS resolution [13,27]. Between them, these two studies have characterized DNS manipulation from both the server and the client side but did not focus on root replicas.

DNS Root Measurement. Several studies of the DNS root infrastructure examine performance issues, particularly for anycast. Unfortunately, these works are often out of date (some over 10 years old) or measure from only a few vantage points [5,15,16,24,25]. Ballani et al. explored the DNS root anycast deployment using open resolver measurements, but made no attempt to find unauthorized roots [6]. Liang et al. also explored the DNS root, but focused on typical performance rather than exploring oddly low response times [14]. We also focus on using these measurements to find unauthorized roots, which Liang et al. mention but do not explore.

Prefix Hijacking. Several studies have explored prefix hijacking, theoretically and practically. Ballani et al. showed that ASes are theoretically capable of hijacking a large fraction of the IP space, especially if they are a tier-1 ISP [7]. Nordström et al. defined several potential attacks against BGP and suggested where new countermeasures were needed [19]. The past several years have also seen several studies of hijacking attacks in the wild, such as the Pakistani misconfiguration that prevented users around the world from accessing YouTube [20], and protecting important infrastructure, like the DNS root [9]. We use these methods to look for BGP attacks against the DNS root.

3   Measurement Method

To infer whether clients receive responses from an unauthorized root replica instead of the actual DNS root, we examine both *latency* (as evident from responses that return more quickly than they should, according to the distance to B root) and *server identity* (as evident from HOSTNAME.BIND replies, traceroutes, and BGP routes).

Table 1. Data sources used to investigate possible manipulation.

Measurements	Dates	Manipulation
RIPE Atlas		
Ping	July 6–13, 2014	Root mirrors
HOSTNAME.BIND	July 22, 2014	Proxies & Root mirrors
Traceroutes	July 6, 2014	Proxies & Root mirrors
BGP		
RIPE RIS	July 6–13, 2014	Root mirrors
RouteViews	July 7, 2014	Root mirrors

We use two different approaches to observe potential DNS root manipulation: (1) direct end-system measurements using RIPE's Atlas infrastructure (about 8,000 nodes in 2,755 distinct ASes over 189 countries); and (2) control-plane analysis via BGP monitoring. For each platform, Table 1 shows what measurements were collected, when they were collected, and the types of manipulation that can be detected from each measurement. We analyzed a week of measurements from the RIPE Atlas platform, spanning July 6–13, 2014. We received one HOSTNAME.BIND measurement from each of 6,135 Atlas probes and about 2,500 ping measurements from each of 6,546 Atlas probes. For reasons we could not determine, the dataset does not include all Atlas probes listed as currently deployed, but we use data from the 5,929 Atlas probes providing both measurements.

3.1   Anomalous Response-Time Latency

To look for transparent DNS proxies, we draw upon the ongoing ICMP ping measurements that by default the RIPE Atlas nodes make to each of the DNS roots every 240 s (four minutes) [21], analyzing in particular the ping times to the singular B root. Additionally, we time HOSTNAME.BIND DNS queries sent to B root. In the absence of a DNS proxy, we expect these response times to be similar. In the presence of a DNS proxy, we expect the DNS response time to be much lower because the DNS query will not go all the way to the authoritative B root DNS server. The latency difference would be evident in DNS injection and difficult for an attacker to mask. A strong attacker who can intercept DNS traffic could of course transform DNS replies instead of answering requests directly, and hence produce the expected latency from querying the corresponding authorized root servers.

3.2 Anomalous Server Identity

We next sketch three methods to establish the identity of the DNS root server and its position in the network.

HOSTNAME.BIND Queries. To identify anomalous server identities, we issue HOSTNAME.BIND queries from Atlas probes—special DNS queries that ask a DNS server to identify itself. HOSTNAME.BIND replies from the correct B root follow the pattern bx, where x ranges from 0 to 9. Invalid or null responses may indicate that the replies did not come from the actual root server. We also explored using the EDNS NSID extension [4], another DNS server identification protocol, but the extension does not provide additional information for our purposes, and is not supported by B root. It would be difficult for a DNS proxy to fake the HOSTNAME.BIND response because for responses to appear valid, they would need to be customized based on the root to which the original request was sent. This mode of operation would make the proxy more complex and is not supported by default software, making its use unlikely. A DNS root mirror might instead falsify the response of the singular B, but we did not observe such scenarios.

Traceroutes. We look for DNS root mirrors by analyzing the ongoing UDP traceroutes conducted from RIPE Atlas nodes to the B and L roots[1] every 1800 s (30 min) [21].[2] We use traceroutes to identify potential root mirrors by (1) checking the ASN on the penultimate hop before reaching B root and (2) comparing traceroutes from the Atlas probe to B and L roots. By checking the ASN on the penultimate hop, we can verify that the traffic left the Atlas probe's AS and that the probe's traffic took a valid route to B root. We assume that an attacker would have difficulty falsifying all of the traceroute hops to the root servers.

Similarly, we hypothesized that an attacker might use a single root mirror to serve multiple DNS roots to avoid replicating the same functionality. To detect root mirror reuse, we check how many hops match between traceroutes to B and L roots. (We again assume that an attacker would have difficulty falsifying all traceroute hops to the root servers.)

BGP Routing Tables and Updates. We also looked for evidence of manipulating routing to alter the topological location of the root servers. Private routes can occasionally leak to the public Internet, as when Pakistan censored YouTube [20]. Brown et al. found anecdotal evidence of DNS censorship in China affecting the DNS root for other countries [8].

---

[1] We L root selected solely for convenience.

[2] The UDP query packets are not DNS requests, nor do they use the DNS service port.

If a hijacked route propagates outside the targeted network, the announcement may appear in public BGP databases. To explore this possibility, we examine BGP data from University of Oregon's RouteViews project [26] and RIPE's Routing Information Service (RIS) [22] for the same time period as the RIPE Atlas data. Both RouteViews and RIS collect public peering data from exchange points around the world by pulling the data from route servers at regular intervals. We analyzed the data by checking RIBs for B root's prefix, and checking if the AS path or prefix differed from real announcements. We speculated that an AS might perform a hijacking attack (directed at either their internal BGP network or at other ASes) by interjecting themselves into the AS path or announcing a more specific prefix.

4   Results

We applied the techniques from Sect. 3 to look for evidence of DNS root manipulation. Analyzing anomalous latencies and HOSTNAME.BIND replies identified a modicum of DNS root manipulation; the routing and traceroute data did not yield any additional evidence of such manipulation.

4.1   In-Path DNS Proxies

We identified eleven HOSTNAME.BIND responses that did not match the expected bx pattern discussed in Sect. 3.2. One of these coincides with a DNS mirror in China, which we discuss in Sect. 4.2. We find that the other ten HOSTNAME.BIND responses from other root servers yielded identical results, suggesting that the Atlas probes reside behind a hidden DNS proxy. Only one ISP with such a DNS proxy hosted multiple Atlas probes, but three of the four Atlas probes on that network exhibited correct HOSTNAME.BIND responses, suggesting that the proxy may reflect user configuration rather than ISP deployment. For the other nine instances, the use of DNS proxies appears to reflect an intentional decision, because several HOSTNAME.BIND responses correspond to the name of the ISP. This manipulation may be used to improve performance. For example, an Atlas probe hosted by Wananchi, a Kenyan ISP, received a response purportedly from B root that identifies the server `dns3.wnanchi.com` in 14 ms—as opposed to 318 ms for ping measurements to B root.

Using the ping data, we looked for minimum ping times that were less than the minimum speed-of-light propagation delay from RIPE Atlas nodes to B root. These measurements should not be affected by any hidden DNS proxies because we base them on ICMP ping packets; they should also not reflect unrelated network failures (which can only increase latency, assuming we eventually receive a reply). To determine whether to deem a ping RTT as implausibly low, we geolocated each Atlas probe and restricted our analysis to low ping times from Atlas probes outside of North and South America. We compared Atlas's own geolocation information with MaxMind's [17] geolocation of the Atlas probe's externally visible IP address (as determined by Atlas's servers). This process yields only one source of geolocation for 1,388 Atlas probes (22.6 %); we find inconsistent location information for another 106 Atlas probes (1.7 %), which we do not use for our analysis.

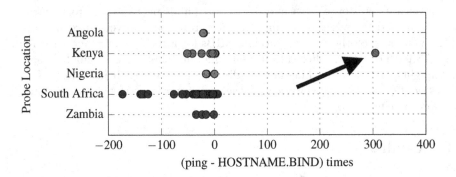

Fig. 2. Difference in response times between pings and HOSTNAME.BIND queries to B root. DNS response times significantly lower than ping times suggest the presence of a DNS proxy like the one the arrow points to.

These measurements detected the same ten DNS proxies as the HOST-NAME.BIND measurements we describe above by looking at the difference in response time between DNS queries and pings to B root. The fact that two independent techniques detected the same ten DNS proxies increases our confidence in the result.

Figure 2 shows the difference in response time between DNS queries and pings to B root for a representative sample of African countries. We observe a slightly smaller ping response time, except for the previously discussed DNS proxy in Kenya. These results are representative of the rest of our dataset; only eleven Atlas probes have DNS response times more than 50 ms faster than their ping and ten of these eleven Atlas probes are behind DNS proxies. The remaining Atlas device, which is not behind the root mirror, appears to reflect a network change between the ping and DNS measurements because both the ping and DNS query response time are over 350 ms. Our results are qualitatively consistent with those of Weaver et al. [27], which found that 1.4 % of Netalyzr clients resided behind hidden DNS proxies, although we observe one-tenth of that previously observed rate.

4.2 Rogue DNS Root Mirrors

One HOSTNAME.BIND response did not match the expected format from B root but did not appear to be a DNS proxy. We identified this response as an unauthorized DNS root replica in China and confirmed its presence with pings and traceroutes.

We explored the minimum response time to B root by continent, highlighting four clear outliers, one of which is shown in Fig. 3. As mentioned, one outlier was

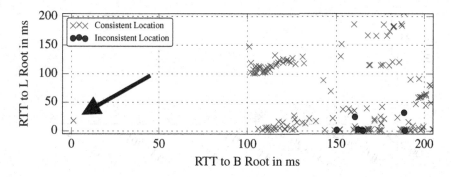

Fig. 3. Response times to B root (unicast from USA) and L root (150 anycast sites) from 184 RIPE Atlas probes geolocated to Asia. The arrow points to the DNS root mirror, a clear outlier.

a DNS root mirror, but the other three outliers were measurement errors. Despite these outliers, we are confident in our timing data because Fig. 3 demonstrates that the response times were generally consistent, even when geolocation was problematic (the plot also includes responses that were discarded for inaccurate geolocation). We continued exploring the outliers by validating our geolocation information with traceroutes. As a result of this validation, we discarded an Atlas probe in New York that erroneously geolocated to Switzerland. (The traceroute showed that the first hop was only a few milliseconds away and included "us" as part of the router name.)

When further analyzing the ping responses for the remaining outliers, we found that aside from the DNS root mirror itself, the other two outliers were measurement errors due to improper handling of ICMP error messages. For example, an Atlas probe in Belgium received many ping responses with a TTL of 255 and a response time around 5 ms followed by duplicate responses with a TTL of 44 and a response time around 168 ms. The TTL of 255 indicates that the first hop router sent an ICMP error message which the RIPE Atlas platform interpreted as an ICMP ECHO reply.

We determined that the fourth outlier was an unauthorized root mirror in the China Education and Research Network. The Atlas probe could ping B root in 1.2 ms and a HOSTNAME.BIND query produced an invalid response with a response time of 16 ms. The Atlas probe experienced infrequent network issues with 8 pings (0.11 %) over 100 ms, but Fig. 4 demonstrates that the pings were otherwise consistent. Both RIPE Atlas and MaxMind geolocated the Atlas device to China, and all hops on a traceroute to B root are in the same ASN. Additionally, the Atlas probe could directly communicate with a (non-root) authoritative DNS server under our control, so the Atlas probe does not appear to be behind a DNS proxy. The presence of so many measurements makes it more likely that this RIPE Atlas probe is behind a DNS root mirror.

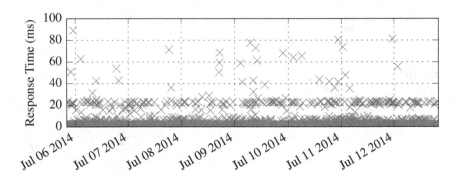

Fig. 4. 2,519 pings to B root from a Chinese Atlas probe are consistently, impossibly low, indicating a root mirror.

4.3   Traceroutes

We analyzed traceroutes to B and L roots and did not find any evidence of DNS root mirrors. We analyzed these traceroutes by noting the penultimate hop on the path to B root and comparing the traceroutes between B and L roots.

Validating Paths to B Root. To understand the penultimate router in the path to B root, we explored 4,333 traceroutes from 1,948 Atlas probes to B root. These totals do not include traceroutes that did not successfully complete or that contained any errors or packet drops. We found that the penultimate router for B root was in AS 226 (Los Nettos) for 1,647 Atlas probes (3,488 traceroutes), in AS 2153/2152 (California State University) for 295 Atlas probes (814 traceroutes), in AS 4 (ISI) for two Atlas probes (22 traceroutes), in AS 8121 (Layer 42) for 1 Atlas probe (5 traceroutes), in AS 34168 (Rostelecom) for one Atlas probe (2 traceroutes), and in AS 2914 (NTT Communication) for one Atlas probe (1 traceroute). The dataset included traceroutes from five Atlas probes identified as behind DNS proxies above, and in each case the Atlas probe transited through Los Nettos.

Los Nettos and California State University were the most prevalent routes and easily verified as legitimate given that Los Nettos is an advertised BGP neighbor of ISI (B root administrators) and ISI is located at the University of Southern California. The Layer 42 and NTT Communications cases can also be validated because they are different ASes than the ASes hosting the probes. Finally, the Atlas probe for Rostelecom is also hosted in Rostelecom, but the traceroute has 230 ms of latency, which suggests the Atlas probe is talking to the real root.

Comparing Paths Between B and L Roots. We hypothesized that if an attacker manipulated the DNS roots, they would likely redirect multiple roots to a single instance to avoid duplication. To evaluate this hypothesis, we analyzed 4,342 traceroute pairs to B and L roots from 1,292 Atlas probes. We removed all traceroutes that did not complete successfully or that contained an error or drop, then matched B and L root traceroutes that originated from the same Atlas probe within 30 min.

We compared traceroutes by iterating over each hop in the L root traceroutes, then checking if any IP at the hop appeared at any hop in the L root traceroute. If the L root traceroute IP appeared in the B root traceroute, we marked the hop as matching. After performing the measurements, computed the fraction of matching hops by dividing by the number of hops in the L root traceroute.

These methods revealed no evidence of root manipulation. The closest traceroute pair had a matching hop fraction of 0.85 (12/14 hops matched). If manipulation were taking place, we would have expected the traceroutes to match exactly. The dataset also included 5 Atlas probes previously marked as DNS proxies, and their highest matching hop fraction was 0.8 (12/15 matching hops). These results are consistent with the absence of DNS root mirrors.

4.4   BGP Routing Table Manipulation

We analyzed BGP routing table snapshots for B root and found no evidence of hijacked routes. We analyzed BGP data from 13 RIPE RIS route servers Internet exchange points (IXPs) as geographically diverse as London and Japan. We supplemented this with data from the University of Oregon's RouteView's route servers in an additional nine IXPs around the world. We did not observe any prefix hijacking of B root. Our analysis is consistent with the general expectation that unauthorized root replicas are quite rare, even though we are not guaranteed to see a prefix hijack of B root.

5   Future Work

We have enumerated a few methods for measuring DNS root manipulation, but future work could expand these measurements, as follows.

Anomalous Response Times. We could extend our anomalous response time measurements using open resolvers as our edge network vantage points, as well as accurate geolocation information to extend these techniques beyond B root. We could determine the likely closest anycast instance for each DNS root replica using the provided geolocation information [11] (accurate to the city level), but we would also need to accurately locate open resolvers. We could then force each open resolver to contact the root by querying a non-existent top level domain (TLD) and measuring the response time. If the client receives a response in less time than the speed-of-light propagation delay to the closest root instance, then we know that a root mirror or DNS proxy is in use. Unfortunately, we have already demonstrated that collecting such geolocation data is difficult and would be the primary challenge to extending our work.

Anomalous Server Identity. We could also extend techniques to identify anomalous server identities with server-side analysis. We could better identify DNS proxies by sending queries for a DNS zone we control and ensuring that

(1) the authoritative server receives the query and (2) the client receives the correct response. We could ensure that the queries always hit our server and are never cached by including a nonce and always returning the same value (*e.g.*, an A record for 1.1.1.1 or a SERVFAIL). We would also ideally also collect data from the vantage point of the roots and query for randomly generated, non-existent TLDs from Atlas probes and open resolvers. Such a configuration would reveal whether our measurement machines reached the root, providing strong conclusions about DNS root manipulation.

6   Summary

We extended earlier findings on hidden DNS proxies [27] and potential root-server manipulation [8] to develop a method for detecting DNS root manipulation. To do so, we used two measurement techniques. First, we use RIPE Atlas probes to conduct pings, HOSTNAME.BIND queries, and traceroute measurements. Second, we examine BGP routing table snapshots for evidence of route hijacks.

We cast a wide net to validate our methods—2,755 access networks in 189 countries and 22 IXPs—but we found only a modicum of tampering with access to B root. Our measurements located ten hidden DNS proxies, most likely deployed for performance purposes and self-identifying to an associated ISP, and one root replica in China. Even the latter is not widely deployed: only one out of the 24 RIPE Atlas probes in China encountered it. Although DNS root manipulation is rare, it is clearly important to detect it when it does occur. We have demonstrated that our methods can detect such manipulation. Given China's willingness to tamper with the DNS root [8], we expect that these methods will continue to be useful for detecting root manipulation.

Acknowledgments. This research was supported in part by NSF awards CNS-1540066, CNS-1602399, CNS-1223717, CNS-1237265, and CNS-1518918. Ben Jones is also partially supported by a senior research fellowship from the Open Technology Fund. Any opinions, findings, and conclusions or recommendations are those of the authors and do not necessarily reflect the views of the sponsors.

References

1. Anderson, C., Winter, P., Roya.: Global network interference detection over the RIPE atlas network. In: 4th USENIX Workshop on Free and Open Communications on the Internet (FOCI 2014). USENIX Association, San Diego, August 2014
2. Anonymous.: The Collateral Damage of Internet Censorship by DNS Injection. SIGCOMM Comput. Commun. Rev., 42(3), 21–27 (2012)
3. Anonymous.: Towards a comprehensive picture of the great firewall's DNS censorship. In: 4th USENIX Workshop on Free and Open Communications on the Internet (FOCI 2014). USENIX Association, San Diego, August 2014
4. Austein, R.: DNS Name Server Identifier (NSID) Option, August 2007. https://tools.ietf.org/html/rfc5001

5. Ballani, H., Francis, P.: Towards a global IP anycast service. In: Proceedings of the Conference on Applications, Technologies, Architectures, and Protocols for Computer Communications, SIGCOMM 2005, pp. 301–312. ACM, New York (2005)

6. Ballani, H., Francis, P., Ratnasamy, S.: A measurement-based deployment proposal for IP anycast. In: Proceedings of the 6th ACM SIGCOMM Conference on Internet Measurement, IMC 2006, pp. 231–244. ACM, New York (2006)

7. Ballani, H., Francis, P., Zhang, X.: A study of prefix hijacking and interception in the internet. In: Proceedings of the Conference on Applications, Technologies, Architectures, and Protocols for Computer Communications, SIGCOMM 2007, pp. 265–276. ACM, New York (2007)

8. Brown, M.A., Madory, D., Popescu, A., Zmijewski, E.: November 2010. http://research.dyn.com/wp-content/uploads/2014/07/DNS-Tampering-and-Root-Servers.pdf

9. Bush, R., Mankin, A., Massey, D., Pei, D., Wang, L., Wu, F., Zhang, L., Zhao, X.: Protecting the BGP routes to top level DNS servers, June 2002. https://www.nanog.org/meetings/nanog25/presentations/massey.ppt

10. Dagon, D., Lee, C., Lee, W., Provos, N.: Corrupted DNS resolution paths: the rise of a malicious resolution authority. In: Proceedings of 15th Network and Distributed System Security Symposium (NDSS), San Diego, CA (2008)

11. DNS Root Servers. root-servers.org (2015). http://root-servers.org/

12. Khattak, S., Javed, M., Khayam, S.A., Uzmi, Z.A., Paxson, V.: A look at the consequences of internet censorship through an ISP lens. In: Proceedings of the Conference on Internet Measurement Conference, IMC 2014, pp. 271–284. ACM, New York (2014)

13. Kreibich, C., Weaver, N., Nechaev, B., Paxson, V.: Netalyzr: illuminating the edge network. In: Proceedings of the 10th ACM SIGCOMM Conference on Internet Measurement, IMC 2010, pp. 246–259. ACM, New York (2010)

14. Liang, J., Jiang, J., Duan, H., Li, K., Wu, J.: Measuring query latency of top level DNS servers. In: Roughan, M., Chang, R. (eds.) PAM 2013. LNCS, vol. 7799, pp. 145–154. Springer, Heidelberg (2013)

15. Liston, R., Srinivasan, S., Zegura, E.: Diversity in DNS performance measures. In: Proceedings of the 2nd ACM SIGCOMM Workshop on Internet Measurment, IMW 2002, pp. 19–31. ACM, New York (2002)

16. Liu, Z., Huffaker, B., Fomenkov, M., Brownlee, N., Claffy, K.C.: Two days in the life of the DNS anycast root servers. In: Uhlig, S., Papagiannaki, K., Bonaventure, O. (eds.) PAM 2007. LNCS, vol. 4427, pp. 125–134. Springer, Heidelberg (2007)

17. MaxMind, Inc. GeoIP2 Country (2015). https://www.maxmind.com/en/geoip2-country-database

18. Nabi, Z.: The anatomy of web censorship in Pakistan. In: Presented as part of the 3rd USENIX Workshop on Free and Open Communications on the Internet. USENIX, Berkeley (2013)

19. Nordström, O., Dovrolis, C.: Beware of BGP attacks. SIGCOMM Comput. Commun. Rev. **34**(2), 1–8 (2004)

20. RIPE. YouTube Hijacking: A RIPE NCC RIS case study (2008). https://www.ripe.net/publications/news/industry-developments/youtube-hijacking-a-ripe-ncc-ris-case-study

21. RIPE. Built-In Measurements (2015). https://atlas.ripe.net/docs/built-in/

22. RIPE. Routing Information Service (RIS) (2015). https://www.ripe.net/data-tools/stats/ris

23. RIPE. What is RIPE Atlas? (2015). https://atlas.ripe.net/about/

24. Sarat, S., Pappas, V., Terzis, A.: On the use of anycast in DNS. In: Proceedings of 15th International Conference on Computer Communications and Networks, 2006, ICCCN 2006, pp. 71–78, October 2006
25. Sekiya, Y., Cho, K., Kato, A., Somegawa, R., Jinmei, T., Murai, J.: Root and ccTLD DNS server observation from worldwide locations. In: Proceedings of Passive and Active Measurement 2003, April 2003
26. University of Oregon. RouteViews Project (2015). http://www.routeviews.org/
27. Weaver, N., Kreibich, C., Nechaev, B., Paxson, V.: Implications of Netalyzrs DNS measurements. In: Proceedings of the First Workshop on Securing and Trusting Internet Names (SATIN), Teddington, United Kingdom (2011)
28. Weaver, N., Kreibich, C., Paxson, V.: Redirecting DNS for ads and profit. In: Presented as part of the 1st USENIX Workshop on Free and Open Communications on the Internet. USENIX (2011)

Behind IP Prefix Overlaps in the BGP Routing Table

Quentin Jacquemart[1]([✉]), Guillaume Urvoy-Keller[1], and Ernst Biersack[2]

[1] University of Nice Sophia Antipolis, CNRS, I3S, UMR 7271,
06900 Sophia Antipolis, France
{quentin.jacquemart,guillaume.urvoy-keller}@unice.fr
[2] Eurecom, Sophia Antipolis, France
erbi@e-biersack.eu

Abstract. The IP space has been divided and assigned as a set of IP prefixes. Due to the longest prefix match forwarding rule, a single assigned IP prefix can be further divided into multiple distinct IP spaces; resulting in a BGP routing table that contains over half a million distinct, but overlapping entries. Another side-effect of this forwarding rule is that any anomalous announcement can result in a denial of service for the prefix owner. It is thus essential to describe and clarify the use of these overlapping prefixes. In order to do this, we use Internet Routing Registries (IRR) databases as semantic data to group IP prefixes into *families of prefixes* that are owned by the same organization. We use BGP data in order to populate these families with prefixes that are announced on the Internet. We introduce several metrics which enable us to study how these families behave. With these metrics, we detail how organisations prefer to subdivide their IP space, underlining global trends in IP space management. We show that there is a large amount of information in the IRR that appears to be actively maintained by a number of ISPs.

1 Introduction

The IP space has been divided into a set of IP prefixes that are assigned to organizations by RIRs (Regional Internet Registries). These organizations can choose to further divide the IP prefixes they were assigned in smaller IP spaces that they can use as independent networks. This is possible because packets are routed according to the longest prefix match rule. In other words, any traffic will always be forwarded to the smallest IP space (i.e. the most specific prefix) containing the destination IP address. This can be useful in order to do traffic engineering, e.g. to make sure off-site servers are reachable from the global Internet. At the same time, the recent attack against Spamhaus demonstrated that announcing more specific prefixes is an effective DoS (Denial of Service) attack [12]. Even in the case of misconfigurations, large-scale repercussions can be disastrous [9].

The BGP (Border Gateway Protocol) routing table currently contains over half a million entries. With so many entries, it is improbable that there is no overlap among them. As a result, it is essential to describe and understand the

© Springer International Publishing Switzerland 2016
T. Karagiannis and X. Dimitropoulos (Eds.): PAM 2016, LNCS 9631, pp. 289–301, 2016.
DOI: 10.1007/978-3-319-30505-9_22

uses of overlapping prefixes from a BGP point of view. A way of doing this would be to create pairs of overlapping prefixes, and then compare them together. As an example, let us consider the three overlapping prefixes a/8, a.b/16, and a.b.c/24. How relevant is the study of the three pairs of these prefixes? If the organization to which the /8 has been assigned is an ISP, the /16 prefix might have been sold to one of its customer; and it is solely this customer who decided to create the /24 subnet. Hence, the comparison between the /8 and the /24 is not meaningful. Conversely, if the organization behind the /8 prefix is not an ISP, the /16 prefix is likely not a sub-allocation, but the result of network engineering.

Therefore, by trying to simply compare pairs of overlapping prefixes, we overlook assignment policies. Namely, IP blocks are assigned by RIRs to organizations. These organizations then use their IP space as they see fit. An ISP, for example, will most likely sell a part of its IP space to customers, who, in turn, will use the (sub) IP space as they see fit. As a result, simply comparing any pair composed of any overlapping prefix disregards the fact that different entities may administer the prefixes. In order to overcome this problem, we use the prefix assignment information included in IRR (Internet Routing Registry) databases in order to cluster overlapping BGP prefixes into *families of prefixes*. Prefixes inside these families are then guaranteed to be under the control of a single organization. Consequently, their comparison can be done without ambiguity.

In this paper, we present a method to group BGP prefixes into a set of prefix families with the help of the contents of the IRR databases. These families are composed of two types of prefixes: children prefixes, which are BGP announcements that are *not* included as-is in the IRR databases; and family fathers, which *are* included in the IRR databases. We define a set of metrics to analyse the behaviour of these families that shed light on how an organization sub-divides its own IP space into smaller networks for its own use. We look at a few real-world examples of families, and show that the behaviour inside groups of families of tier-1 ISPs, tier-3 ISPs, and private corporations, is comparable. At the same time, we investigate the distributions of prefixes inside BGP and inside the IRR databases, and offer possible reasons for their large size difference.

2   Data Sources

2.1   IRR Databases

We were able to secure access to the IRR databases of the five RIRs: AfriNIC, ARIN, APNIC, LACNIC, and RIPE. These databases contain information directly provided by network operators, on a voluntary basis, about their routing policies and announcements. They are composed of different objects that represent, among other things, people, IP address allocation, and AS numbers. We extract information from the `inetnum` objects, which contain "details of an allocation or assignment of IPv4 address space" [1].

Table 1 details the number of entries that we extracted from each database on August 1st, 2014. Because some RIRs include information about special-use IP space (e.g. the private IP space) for user friendliness, we discard 0.07 % of

Table 1. Number of CIDR IP prefixes extracted from IRR databases per RIR on August 1st, 2014

RIR	Parsed prefixes
AfriNIC	72,516
APNIC	1,432,154
ARIN	2,696,539
LACNIC	322,828
RIPE	3,846,706
Total	8,370,743
Filtered	8,364,909

Table 2. Quick guide to the metrics defined for the analysis

Name	Meaning
announced father	prefix is in IRR and BGP
unannounced father	prefix only in IRR
child	prefix only in BGP
announced family	at least the father or one child prefix is seen in BGP
nbr. children	nbr. of internal assignments (i.e. dividing IP space)
nbr. subfamilies	nbr. of external assignments (i.e. delegating IP space)
overlap ratio	fraction of father's IP space used by either children, or subfamilies

overall entries. Finally, we obtain 8,364,909 distinct IP prefixes from the IRR databases.

The accuracy of IRR databases is widely debated among the community. For example, [10] underlines the inconsistencies among the distributed content of the database, as well as the varying level of accuracy depending on the considered database and object. However, by comparing the origin AS inside the IRR with the one in BGP, [7] shows that around 90 % of autonomous systems register at least a subset of their BGP prefixes in the IRR database, making the information it contains valuable. In the end, even though IRR information needs to be considered with a grain of salt, we demonstrated in [13] that it provides a unique insight into BGP ground truth information.

2.2 BGP Data

Our source of BGP data is RIPE RIS [8]. We parse binary files that contain a dump of the BGP messages exchanged between the RIPE collector router and its BGP peers. We focus on **update** messages, that contain prefix announcements and withdrawals, as well as the AS path to the prefix. The AS path is an attribute that contains the list of ASNs (Autonomous System Numbers) which need to be crossed before reaching the destination. The last number in this list is known as the origin AS, i.e. the AS in which the prefix resides.

We process BGP **update** messages according to RFC4271. Namely, we maintain an adjacency table for each of our peers. A prefix is reachable if at least one of our peers has announced it; and is not reachable once every peer that had announced it has withdrawn it. In this way, we are able to build our own BGP routing table, which is dynamically updated as BGP messages flow between routers.

We selected RIPE's Amsterdam collector (rrc00) as our data feeder. It is the best-connected RIPE collector, with over 40 geographically diversified peers. The selected time window for the analysis was the whole month of August 2014, where we counted 629,595 distinct IP prefixes.

3   Methodology

3.1   Definitions

In Sect. 1, we stated why simply comparing overlapping prefixes together does not produce meaningful results. Instead, we use a combination of semantic data that we extract from the IRR database, and routing information that we get from BGP. In this section, we present how we group these elements into *families of prefixes* that are composed of a family *father*, of *children*, and of *subfamilies*.

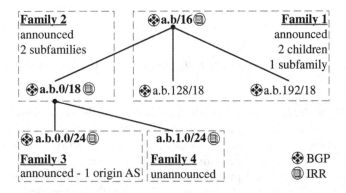

Fig. 1. Example of constitution of families and subfamilies

Each prefix included in the IRR database is *always* the **father of a family**. Consequently, we have as many distinct families as the number of filtered IRR prefixes (see Table 1). Because most of these prefixes overlap, some family fathers completely include some other family fathers. This situation leads to subfamilies. A **subfamily** is a family whose father is completely included in the IP space generated by another family's father.

For example, there are 4 distinct families in Fig. 1, because the prefixes a.b/16, a.b.0/18, a.b.0.0/24, and a.b.1.0/24 are included in the IRR database. Incidentally, these 4 prefixes are the fathers of their families. However, some of these fathers overlap. As a result, in Fig. 1, Family 2 is a subfamily of Family 1, because the father of Family 2 is more specific than the father of Family 1. Similarly, Family 3 and Family 4 are subfamilies of Family 2. However, neither Family 3 nor Family 4 is a subfamily of Family 1 because Family 2 "hides" them from Family 1. This accounts for the fact that a.b.0/18 has been delegated to another entity (because it has an IRR entry). In other words, the organization responsible for Family 2 is the one in charge to further subdivide this IP space.

Once the families have been put together, we populate them with BGP data. A prefix seen in BGP is either a family father, or a prefix more specific than a family father. In the first case, there is nothing left to do: a father already belongs to the family it defines. In the second case, the prefix is added to the family as a child prefix. A **child** is a prefix seen in BGP that is more specific than the family father, but not declared in the IRR database as having been assigned to another entity. The child is consequently managed by the organization linked with the IRR record of its family father.

Continuing with the example depicted in Fig. 1, three family fathers are announced in BGP: a.b/16, a.b.0/18, and a.b.0.0/24. Moreover, two non-IRR prefixes (a.b.128/18 and a.b.192/18) are also announced. Since they are both more specific than a.b/16, they are added as children in Family 1.

To summarize, we use the prefixes in the IRR database as a binding link between an organization in the real-world, and one or several BGP prefixes. An IRR prefix induces a family, which contains a certain number of children (BGP prefixes).

3.2 Metrics

In this section, we present the metrics that will be used in Sect. 4 to analyze prefix families.

The **number of children in a family** indicates the number of assignments that have been done internally in this family. In other words, this is the number of distinct IP zones that exist in this family, each possibly leading to different locations, but which should all be under the authority of the same organization. We put this number in relation with the **number of *aggregated* children in a family**, which is the number of prefixes resulting from an aggregation process on the children prefixes. Both sets of prefixes generate the exact same IP space, but the aggregated set does so with the minimal number of prefixes. Consequently, a difference in the number of children and the number of aggregated children indicates that internal assignments were done with contiguous IP blocks. For example, in Fig. 1, Family 1 has 2 children: a.b.128/18 and a.b.192/18. These prefixes define IP addresses that are contiguous, and they are aggregated as a.b.128/17. Thus, Family 1 has only 1 aggregated child.

The **number of subfamilies** in a family indicates the number of prefixes that have been delegated to other entities. This number is a constant in our method, because it results from the contents of the IRR database. We put this number in relation with the **number of *announced* subfamilies**, i.e. the number of subfamilies that were actually announced in BGP. We consider that **a family is announced** at time t if either the family father or one of the family child is announced in BGP at t. As an example, Fig. 1 depicts Family 2, which has 2 subfamilies. However, since a.b.1.0/24 is not announced in BGP (and has no child), it is marked as unannounced. Consequently, Family 2 only has 1 announced subfamily. Please note that we use the term "unannounced" to refer to the fact that a prefix is not seen as-is from the BGP control plane; it does not imply that the prefix is not used, or that no host is connected using an IP address included in this prefix. The prefix can be routed by a less specific announcement (resulting, for example, from a route aggregation).

The **children overlap ratio** is the ratio of the number of IP addresses available to family children divided by the number of IP addresses available to the family father. In the same fashion, the **subfamily overlap ratio** is the ratio of the number of IP addresses available to the *announced* subfamilies divided by the number of IP addresses available to the family father. For example, the children overlap ratio for Family 1 of Fig. 1 is 0.5, and the subfamily overlap ratio is 0.25.

Because the information contained in this section is quite dense, Table 2 provides a summary of the metrics that have been defined; and which can be used as a quick reference guide while going through the results presented in Sect. 4.

4   Results

4.1   BGP Vs IRR Database

In this section, we briefly compare the prefixes inside the IRR database and the prefixes announced in BGP.

In Sect. 2, we saw that we parsed over $8 \cdot 10^6$ IP prefixes from the IRR, and just a little less than 630 k from the BGP control plane. When we compared the distribution of the number of prefixes in both sources according to their mask length, we saw that the number of prefixes in both sources was comparable for /24's and larger prefixes. For smaller prefixes (i.e. prefixes with a mask length > /24), there is at least a factor 100 of difference in the number of entries. In other words, only 1 % of IRR prefixes were seen as-is from the BGP control plane, meaning that only 1 % of families whose father is more specific than a /24 prefix are *announced*. This phenomenon can be explained by two reasons. First, these prefixes have a long mask, and BGP good practices indicate that prefixes longer than /24 s should not be propagated [5], and confirming previous experiments on that topic [3]. Second, IRR database entries are not restricted to BGP users. Any assignment of IP blocks, for example by an ISP, is a potential entry in the IRR database, even though the ISP and its customer are not connected via BGP (but, for example, via DSL or cable). This also explains the high number of /32 entries in the IRR database (i.e. single IP addresses): these may be dedicated servers, and an entry in the IRR provides the rightful technical contact information. For unannounced families, there is a difference between the owner of the IRR prefix and the (BGP) manager of the prefix. The manager of the prefix is generally the ISP of the owner, the one that makes sure that the network is adequately connected. The owner of the prefix is the organization actually hosting machines on the IP addresses within the prefix, which is what the IRR entry specifies. For example, one of Eurecom's prefix is 193.55.113.0/24, which is announced from

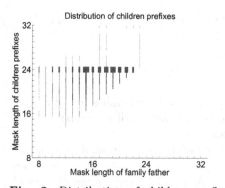

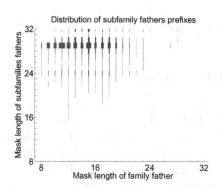

Fig. 2. Distribution of children prefix mask length depending on family father mask length

Fig. 3. Distribution of subfamily fathers prefix mask length depending on family father mask length

our provider, Renater, as an aggregated /15 prefix. However, the `inetnum` object for the prefix points to Eurecom, even though it is maintained by Renater.

We now focus on the relative size of children and subfamilies in a family. Figure 2 plots the distribution of the mask length of children prefixes according to the mask length of the family father. The x axis represents the mask length of the family father, and the y axis represents the mask length of the child. The plot data is the histogram of the distribution: the thicker the line is at a coordinate, the more prefixes there are of this size. As we can see, the bulk of the distribution is around children with a mask length of 24, regardless of the father. The fact that the distribution of children prefixes does not depend on the size of the father is surprising. Indeed, one would expect larger families to divide their IP space into bigger zones. The sparsity of available IPv4 addresses could explain this observation since RIRs and, consequently, ISPs prefer to distribute smaller blocks.

Figure 3 plots the distribution of the mask length of subfamily fathers prefixes according to the mask of the family father. Here, the bulk of the distribution is around /29, regardless of the mask length of the family father. This raises the question of why these assignments appear to be so popular. In our view, a /29 prefix contains 6 usable IP addresses, which, in today's Internet, is just enough for a small-to-medium size corporation: a couple of IP addresses for publicly accessible servers, plus a couple more for NAT gateways. As tier-3 ISPs typically offer Internet access to a number of SMEs, this could naturally result in a predominance of /29 assignments.

Finally, we have 194,465 families announced in BGP. This amounts to only 2.32 % of the total number of families from the IRR database. The results that we present now apply only to those announced prefixes; nothing else can be said about the other ones strictly from a BGP point of view. Moreover, the figures in the remainder of this section *always* plot the *time-weighted average* of the specified metrics. As a result, plots of discrete metrics show continuous values.

For example, a plot showing 0.1 child could mean that there was a single child, but 10 % of the time.

4.2   Children and Subfamilies

In this section we study the number of children and subfamilies a family has. We look at the IP space occupied by children and subfamilies; and we look at the correlation between children and subfamilies.

Figure 4 plots the number of children per family, and the number of aggregated children per family. It shows that only around 25 % of families have, on average one or more children, while the probability of having a large number of children decreases very rapidly. Comparing with the number of aggregated children, we see that in 16 % of cases, the families have one aggregated child. This means that, for 16 % of families, the IP space dedicated to children is contiguous. This indicates that prefix owners prefer to assign contiguous IP space in order to avoid fragmentation (which may lead to more complex and error-prone network configurations).

Figure 5 plots the number of subfamilies per family. The plot indicates that, in the IRR database, only 17 % of families have at least one subfamily. This can be explained by the rather large number of very-specific assignments (masks ≥ /29) in the IRR database: these prefixes are directly allocated to end networks, not to networks providers. On the other hand, only 6 % of *announced* families have at least a child, with 1 % of them having less than a child on average.

Figures 4 and 5 underline that the vast majority of announced families have neither children nor subfamilies. Table 3 shows the proportion of announced families, according to having children or subfamilies. 73 % of families do not have children or subfamilies. In other words, for 73 % of the announced families, the prefixes announced in BGP match the prefixes that were assigned, as shown in the IRR database. No further sub-allocation was done by the end-user, either internally (i.e. using child prefixes), or externally (i.e. subfamilies).

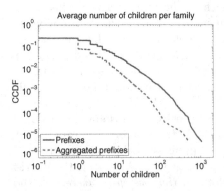

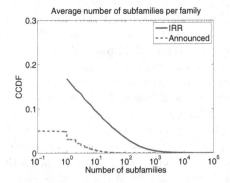

Fig. 4. Number of children per family   **Fig. 5.** Number of subfamilies per family

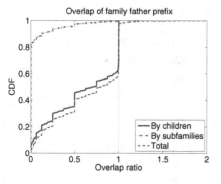

Fig. 6. Prefix overlap within a family

Table 3. Announced families

Child	Subfamily	Count	%
N	N	141,883	72.96%
N	Y	1,930	0.99%
Y	N	42,734	21.96%
Y	Y	7,918	4.07%
Announced families		194,465	100%

Furthermore, there is no correlation between the number of children and the number of subfamilies. The Pearson correlation coefficient, as well as the Spearman correlation coefficient have values between 0.14 and 0.25, depending on if we include or not families without any child or subfamily. In other words, a lot of children implies neither few, and neither a lot of subfamilies; and vice versa. We further study these two dimensions (number of children, and number of subfamilies) in Sect. 4.3, where we present case studies.

Because we study the relationships between overlapping prefixes, we must limit our analysis to the 27% of families that *do* have children, subfamilies, or both (see Table 3). Consequently, the results presented in the remainder of this section only apply to these 27% of (announced) families.

We now focus on the fraction of IP space of the family father that was allocated to children or to subfamilies. Figure 6 plots the children overlap ratio and the family overlap ratio. It shows that there is no overlap by subfamilies for about 80% families. This is because, as indicated in Table 3, in most cases, there is no subfamily when there are children. In contrast, children can occupy a much larger fraction of the family father IP space, up to 100% in 45% of the cases.

Figure 6 also plots the sum of both of these ratios for the families. Interestingly, this ratio exceeds 1 for a few cases. Effectively, this means that, for about 3% of families, children prefixes and subfamily prefixes overlap the family father more than once. Consequently, they also overlap each other. An example from the real world for this situation is the following one. The IRR database lists five prefixes: 5.102.0.0/19, 5.102.{0,8,16,24}.0/21. All these prefixes are also announced in BGP, plus two more: 5.102.{0,16}.0/20. As a result, the /19 family has four subfamilies that fully overlap the family father, and two children, which also fully overlap the family father. All prefixes are originated by a single AS, and belong to the same organization (a tier-3 ISP). It is worth noting that the time-weighted average values of these metrics were over 0.9 in both cases, indicating that this configuration was not transient.

Table 4. Real-world case studies

Business type	Name	#fathers	#children	#subfamilies
Tier-1 ISP	AT&T	64	363	582,863
	Cogent	39	87	1,416
	DeutscheTlkm	26	5	58,055
	NTT	152	466	2,744
	TeliaSonera	9	0	247
Tier-3 ISP	Belgacom	15	0	3,710
	Comcast	66	119	14,945
	Free	15	8	3,864
	Rogers	36	187	23,778
	Tele2	29	4	2,852
Private Corp.	Amazon	18	1	15
	Apple	2	196	1
	BBC	2	2	61
	DHL	2	21	0
	eBay	5	1	0
	HSBC	5	6	0
	Microsoft	40	86	3
	OVH	43	9	27,489
	Philips	8	0	0
	Sony	3	2	0
	Yandex	49	18	2,191

4.3   Real-World Case Studies

We consider in this section a few real-world cases to illustrate the typical relationship that can exist between the business of a company and the breakdown of its prefixes into subfamilies and children. We pick 21 companies – listed in Table 4 – that can be classified into three categories: tier-1, tier-3 and private corporations. The classification is approximate because companies acting as tier-1 providers can also run a tier-3 business at the same time, i.e. directly connecting end-users/small companies to the Internet. This is, for instance, the case of AT&T and Deutsche Telekom.

When looking at ISPs, and regardless of their size (i.e. tier-1 or tier-3), we observe a trend of having a large number of subfamilies and a comparatively smaller number of children. The sheer number of subfamilies suggests that ISPs routinely insert information about prefix delegation in the IRR database. This is in line with expectations: ISPs typically offer Internet access to other companies, and thus assign a set of IPs to its clients. Doing so, the ISPs choose to push this information into the IRR database, because it can be used for administrative purposes. We also observe again the trend that only a small fraction of these families are announced in BGP. This is because ISPs mostly provide Internet connectivity local businesses or home users, that would reap no benefit from the complexity and overload of running a BGP router.

For private corporations, the number of children is much higher than the number of subfamilies. We attribute this to corporations considering internal network policies as private information, thus not wanting to reveal additional company information it in the IRR database (e.g. branch office location). We see two noticeable exceptions: Yandex and OVH. Yandex operates the largest search engine in Russia, along with a number of additional services (cloud storage, etc.). The reason for the large number of subfamilies might be due to Yandex pushing up information concerning client companies (e.g. in the case of Web hosting service) in the IRR. The case of OVH is easier to diagnose: OVH offers PaaS and IaaS services, and reports in the IRR database the set of addresses assigned to each clients, just like an ISP would do.

5 Related Work

Previous work in this area can be divided into two categories: works that analyze the BGP routing table growth; and works that aim at validating BGP routing announcements using IRR data.

The evolution of the BGP routing table has been studied many times, most famously by [6], which reports on the growth of the routing table size from the mid 1990's to today. The analysis also includes AS number usage, average AS path length, and other typical BGP aspects. Other papers, such as [2], investigate the reasons behind this growth, and classify the prefixes inside the routing table depending on the reason for which they need to be announced. The methodology used by [4] to study the evolution of aggregation practices over time may bear some similarity to ours, but differs in several key aspects. Most notably, [4] provides limited prefix grouping methodology, where we make active use of the semantic information found in the IRR databases in order to group prefixes into families that are owned by the same organization. We consequently consider assignments made at the edge of the network by tier-2/tier-3 ISPs. We better illustrate and explain the relationships between the overlapping prefixes inside these families, whereas [4] focuses more on the dynamics of the BGP announcement and their consequences on BGP router processes. As a result, our methods are not directly comparable, even though the BGP-sides of the analyses exhibit similar global trends.

Validation of routing data based on IRR databases entries has been attempted to make the BGP infrastructure more robust. For example, [11] used IRR data to build a tool that informs network administrators of an anomaly that should be further investigated. More recently, [7] studied the validity of the association between a prefix and its origin AS in the IRR. The overall conclusion of this type of work is that the quality of the data inside IRR databases is highly dependent on the RIR. However, it also appears that more recent studies suggest that the IRR provides information that can be used in order to improve the security level of BGP.

6   Conclusion and Future Work

In this paper, we detailed how we use assignment data from the IRR database as semantic anchor points in order to cluster prefixes from the BGP routing table into families, inside of which we can non-ambiguously study the overlap among these prefixes.

We showed that the IRR database contains many times more prefixes than the BGP routing table. This is particularly true for prefixes with a mask length longer than 24. At the same time, we found that only 2.32 % of the families induced by these IRR entries were effectively seen from BGP. We attribute this difference to the fact that IRR entries are not restricted to BGP players, but can exist due to any IP assignment. For example, there are single IP addresses (i.e. /32 prefixes) with an IRR entry for administrative reasons.

We showed that 74 % of the announced families do not have children. This means that, for these families, only the prefix that was assigned is announced in BGP, which does not lead to (additional) routing table entries. It is also in accordance with the standard BGP good-practice of always announcing the assigned prefix. For about 15 % of all families – but about half of the families with children or subfamilies – this practice is not met, which means that these families are part of the *dormant* IP space, which appears to be more vulnerable to malicious prefix hijacking attacks, as demonstrated by [14].

A key take-away from our study is that a joint analysis of BGP and the IRR database sheds light on the way the IRR is used, and also enables to uncover different types of business practices. For instance ISPs (large, or small) are more likely to register their customer in the IRR database, leading to a greater number of subfamilies than children. Clients of ISPs being, most of the time, relatively small, the most popular flavour of subfamily is a prefix of mask length 29, which constitutes enough addresses for a small business. In our view, this implies that ISPs devote a lot of energy to populate and maintain their IRR entries. We argue that this is a proof that ISPs find the information in the IRR valuable. Consequently, even though IRR information is not perfect, it *cannot* be dismissed as entierly stale, inaccurate, and/or bogus. It provides a unique (administrative-level) insight into IP networks, and can help better understand a number of routing phenomenons, as we demonstrated in [13].

We see different possible ways of extending the scope of this work. First, we will study the AS-level relationship between father prefixes, their children, and between families and their subfamilies. Second, we would like to further study unannounced families. A first clue to know how much of that information is stale would be perform IP-level measurements, such as traceroutes, in order to see how the IP-level topology for addresses within the unannounced family differs from the topology inside the announced family. A complementary result from this experiment would be further validating the prefix/organization mappings that are available in the IRR.

References

1. APNIC: Using Whois: Quick Beginners Guide. http://www.apnic.net/apnic-info/whois_search/using-whois/guide
2. Bu, T., et al.: On characterizing BGP routing table growth. Comput. Netw. **45**, 45–54 (2004)
3. Bush, R., Hiebert, J., Maennel, O., Roughan, M., Uhlig, S.: Testing the reachability of (new) address space. In: Proceedings of the 2007 SIGCOMM Workshop on Internet Network Management, INM 2007, pp. 236–241 (2007)
4. Cittadini, L., Muhlbauer, W., Uhlig, S., Bush, R., Francois, P., Maennel, O.: Evolution of internet address space deaggregation: myths and reality. IEEE J. Sel. A. Commun. **28**(8), 1238–1249 (2010)
5. Hu, X., Mao, Z.: Accurate real-time identification of ip prefix hijacking. In: IEEE Symposium on Security and Privacy, May 2007
6. Huston, G.: BGP Reports. http://bgp.potaroo.net/
7. Khan, A., Kim, H., Kwon, T., Choi, Y.: A comparative study on IP prefixes and their origin ases in BGP and the IRR. Comput. Commun. Rev. **43**, 16–24 (2013)
8. Ripe, N.C.C.: Routing Information Service. http://www.ripe.net/ris/
9. Ripe, N.C.C.: YouTube Hijacking: A RIPE NCC RIS case study, March 2008. http://www.ripe.net/internet-coordination/news/industry-developments/youtube-hijacking-a-ripe-ncc-ris-case-study
10. Siganos, G., Faloutsos, M.: Analyzing bgp policies: methodology and tool. In: INFOCOM 2004, vol. 3, pp. 1640–1651, March 2004
11. Siganos, G., Faloutsos, M.: Neighborhood watch for internet routing: can we improve the robustness of internet routing today?. In: IEEE INFOCOM (2007)
12. Toonk, A.: Looking at the spamhaus DDOS from a BGP perspective, March 2013. http://www.bgpmon.net/looking-at-the-spamhouse-ddos-from-a-bgp-perspective/
13. Vervier, P.A., Jacquemart, Q., Schlamp, J., Thonnard, O., Carle, G., Urvoy Keller, G., Biersack, E., Dacier, M.: Malicious BGP hijacks: appearances can be deceiving. In: IEEE International Conference on Communications, ICC CISS 2014, Sydney, Australia, June 2014
14. Vervier, P.A., Thonnard, O., Dacier, M.: Mind your blocks: on the stealthiness of malicious BGP hijacks. In: Network and Distributed System Security Symposium, NDSS 2015, 8–11 February 2015, San Diego, California, USA, February 2015

Characterizing Rule Compression Mechanisms in Software-Defined Networks

Curtis Yu[1], Cristian Lumezanu[2](✉), Harsha V. Madhyastha[3], and Guofei Jiang[2]

[1] University of California, Riverside, USA
[2] NEC Labs America, Princeton, USA
lume@nec-labs.com
[3] University of Michigan, Ann Arbor, USA

Abstract. Software-defined networking (SDN) separates the network policy specification from its configuration and gives applications control over the forwarding rules that route traffic. On large networks that host several applications, the number of rules that network switches must handle can easily exceed tens of thousands. Most switches cannot handle rules of this volume because the complex rule matching in SDN (*e.g.*, wildcards, diverse match fields) requires switches to store rules on TCAM, which is expensive and limited in size.

We perform a measurement study using two real-world network traffic traces to understand the effectiveness and side-effects of manual and automatic rule compression techniques. Our results show that not using any rule management mechanism is likely to result in a rule set that does not fit on current OpenFlow switches. Using rule expiration timeouts reduces the configuration footprint on a switch without affecting rule semantics but at the expense of up to 40 % increase in control channel overhead. Other manual (*e.g.*, wildcards, limiting match fields) or automatic (*e.g.*, combining similar rules) mechanisms introduce negligible overhead but change the original configuration and may misdirect less than 1 % of the flows. Our work uncovers trade-offs critical to both operators and programmers writing network policies that must satisfy both infrastructure and application constraints.

1 Introduction

Software-defined networking (SDN) enables flexible and expressive network management by separating the policy specification from configuration. Applications and operators work with abstract network views [19] and specify policies using an API. A centralized controller program translates the high-level policies into low-level configurations—expressed as forwarding rules—and installs them into the switch memory using a specialized protocol, such as OpenFlow [16].

To maintain network performance, the set of forwarding rules installed at a switch must fit into the switch's memory. Two factors complicate this. First, as more applications adopt SDN, the number of rules required to express their

© Springer International Publishing Switzerland 2016
T. Karagiannis and X. Dimitropoulos (Eds.): PAM 2016, LNCS 9631, pp. 302–315, 2016.
DOI: 10.1007/978-3-319-30505-9_23

policies on every switch grows, similar to how BGP tables have grown with the spread of the Internet. Researchers have observed that an average top-of-rack (ToR) switch would have to hold around 78 K rules with the default expiration timeout [5,12]. Second, switches store wildcard rules in TCAM, which is expensive and limited in size. Most programmable switches can hold only a few thousand wildcard-based rules.

There are two general approaches to ensure that application policies do not result in too many rules: *compression* and *caching*. Network control programs can reduce the number of rules manually (by relying on programmers to employ OpenFlow constructs such as rule expiration timeouts or wildcards [5,27]) or automatically (by eliminating redundant rules or combining rules with related patterns). Compression may limit the expressivity of the configuration as it changes the original rule space. In addition, when rules are generated in response to traffic, it is difficult to predict how many rules we need *a priori* to tune the compression accordingly. Another approach is to cache the most popular rules in TCAM and rely on additional (software) switches or the controller to manage traffic not matching the cached rules [13]. This preserves the original configuration but may introduce additional devices and delay in the data plane of packets matching less popular rules.

In this paper, we use two sets of real world network traffic data to study the *effectiveness* and *side-effects* of manual and automatic rule compression. We seek to answer the following questions: *should SDN rely on programmers to employ mechanisms that reduce the number of rules installed on switches and if so, what are the most effective such mechanisms?* or *can SDN benefit from an automated rule reduction system that sits between the controller and switches and optimizes how rules are installed on switches?* Our work explores trade-offs critical to both operators and programmers writing network policies that must satisfy both infrastructure and application constraints.

First, we show how existing mechanisms that programmers and applications employ, such as reducing rule expiration timeout, using wildcards, or limiting the match fields, manage the rules on a switch (Sect. 4). Lowering rule timeouts can reduce the number of rules by 41–79 %, as compared to the default operation, but at the expense of increasing the utilization on the constrained controller-to-switch channel by up to 40 %. Even such high compression rates may be insufficient for most OpenFlow switches on the market. Using wildcards or limiting the match fields can further improve the configuration footprint but also limits the expressivity of the configuration as the original rule semantics change.

Second, we show that automatic rule compression can benefit SDN. We introduce and evaluate a simple mechanism that encodes rules using binary trees to identify and combine similar rules (Sect. 5). This reduces the configuration size on a switch by as much as 62 % compared to normal operation and at little change in network overhead. However, such benefit comes at a cost: aggressive automatic rule compression can also result in some flows (<1 %) being misdirected.

2 Motivation

In this section, we discuss how programmable switches store rules and implement rule matching. We also review related research work and potential solutions for reducing the number of rules. To keep the discussion simple, we consider Open-Flow as the de facto protocol for installing and managing switch configurations.

2.1 Rules and Memory

A network's configuration consists of the forwarding rules installed at the switches. Every rule consists of a bit string (with 0, 1, and * as characters) that specifies which packets match the rule, an action (to be performed by the switch on matched packets), and a set of counters (which collect statistics). Possible actions include "forward to physical port", "forward to controller", "drop", etc. Each rule has two expiration timeouts: a soft one, counted from the time of the last packet that matched the rule, and a hard one, from the time when the rule was installed.

Table 1. Several OpenFlow switches specify the maximum number of forwarding rules that they store. Each rule can contain any subset of the 12 fields specified in the OpenFlow v1.0 specification [22], which is used by most switches on the market. The HP 3800's fact sheet specifies the maximum number of routing, rather than OpenFlow, entries; a routing entry can be considered an OpenFlow entry with matches only on layer 3 fields.

Switch	Max # rules	Source
NEC PF5820	750	[1]
HP ProCurve 5406zl	1500	[5]
Pronto 3290	4000	[2]
HP 3800	10 k (routing)	[10]
NEC PF5240	64 k–160 k	[1]
IBM G8264	97 k	[11]

Implementation details of how rules are stored and matched is left to the discretion of each switch vendor [24]. A common approach is for switches to store wildcard rules in TCAM and exact match rules in SRAM. TCAM is fast and can support wildcards efficiently. However, since it is also expensive and power hungry, its size on switches is limited. On the other hand, SRAM is cheaper and is available in higher capacity, but has a higher lookup latency because it is often off-chip and uses search structures (*e.g.*, hash tables and tries) to locate entries.

Switch vendors do not advertise the details of their OpenFlow implementation. In addition, the number of OpenFlow rules that a switch can store in hardware is not always fixed and depends on how rules are formed (*e.g.*, whether they have wildcards, what fields they match on). We studied the public datasheets for six popular OpenFlow switches and compiled their published

OpenFlow table limits in Table 1. Unless otherwise noted, the numbers correspond to 12-tuple OpenFlow rules. Independent measurements and personal communication with vendors indicate that the values are representative for current OpenFlow switches [3,24]. Prior work [5,12] has observed that a typical ToR data center switch may store roughly 78 K rules, an order of magnitude larger than most switches in the table. Although architectural and algorithmic advances in switch design may extend the memory limits further (*e.g.*, by using memory other than TCAM or by making software lookups faster), reducing the configuration size to begin with is still essential to preserve flexibility and minimize the cost of lookups.

2.2 Managing Configuration Size

There are two types of solutions to manage configuration size: architectural-based and software-based. Architectural-based solutions seek to optimize the performance of a switch through various architectural design changes [2], but are slow to develop and integrate. Software-based methods seek to reduce the size of the configuration that can be stored on current architectures. We focus on software-based configuration size management and discuss the two main approaches: compressing the rule set and caching the more popular rules. In this paper, we study compression-based techniques.

Compression. Compression-based mechanisms are automatic (*i.e.*, without programmer involvement) or manual (*i.e.*, require actions from the programmer).

Manual. Personal communication with SDN operators and previous work [5, 27] indicate several OpenFlow-based mechanisms to reduce the flow table size on a switch. These methods limit the number of rules by *having existing rules cover more traffic* [5] (*e.g.*, using wildcards rather than exact matches, using fewer match fields) or *cover the same traffic for shorter periods of time* (*e.g.*, setting smaller rule expiration timeouts). However, this also results in a less expressive configuration because it reduces the ability to implement complex policies, such as multipathing [21]. Furthermore, wildcards and longer timeouts reduce visibility into the network as they increase the coarseness of the statistics that switches gather about flows.

Automatic. Rule management has been studied in the context of IP routing table compaction [25], with the goal of restricting the usage of TCAM [15,23]. While some of these methods (e.g., [15]) use binary trees to identify similar rules (like the approach we present later in Sect. 5), existing methods work on a "single IP to out port" action and are not easily applicable to OpenFlow rules, which may have as many as 12 different match fields to be aggregated at once. The TCAM Razor approach uses decision trees and multi-dimensional topological transformations to efficiently compress packet-classification rules [14,17], but cannot easily adapt to incremental rule changes. To the best of our knowledge, none of these methods have been implemented in an OpenFlow-based network.

Policy composition and arbitration frameworks such as Frenetic [7], Net-Core [18], and PANE [8] manage application policies to ensure that there are no conflicting or overlapping rules. vCRIB [20] intelligently places rules on differ-ent OpenFlow switches while being aware of the resources that the rules utilize. Although these systems can optimize the rules they place on switches (*e.g.*, by eliminating redundancies), their focus is on managing the policies installed across the network, rather than on reducing the configuration size on any single switch.

Caching. Rather than compressing the rule set, Katta *et al.* propose to keep only the more popular rules in TCAM and use additional (software) switches or the network controller to manage the traffic that does not match on the cached rules [13]. This approach preserves the semantics of the original rule space at the expense of additional devices or delay on the data path of a subset of the traffic.

3   Method and Data

We use two traces of real-world network traffic to characterize the effective-ness of manual and automatic rule compression techniques in reducing the flow table size.

Data. We use a packet trace from a campus network and a flow-level trace from a nation-wide research network. Our goal is to assess the *potential* of rule com-pression mechanisms *when regular network traffic traverses OpenFlow devices*. Thus, our traces are not collected from OpenFlow-based networks, whose traffic may already be adapted to the programmabile nature of the network. The first dataset, *Campus*, was collected by Benson *et al.* [4] at an edge switch of a large US campus network in Jan 2010 and contains 115 K flows over two hours. The second dataset, *Abilene*, contains 1 % sampled Netflow data from the Internet2 network, collected at the Washington, DC router in Feb 2013. The trace con-tains around 12 M flows over three hours. For anonymity, the IP addresses in the

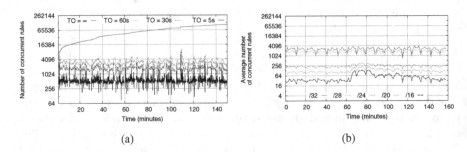

(a)   (b)

Fig. 1. (a) Maximum number of concurrent rules as we vary the timeout after which rules expire and (b) average number of rules over time as we vary the IP prefix size from /32 to /16.

Abilene trace have their last 11 bits zeroed out. These two datasets are typical for two important OpenFlow switch usage scenarios: at the edge and at the core of a network.

Rule Generation. Since neither of the two networks where the traces were collected is OpenFlow-enabled, we simulate the operation of an OpenFlow network to determine the set of rules that would be installed to handle the traffic. We first identify all five-tuple flows (src IP, dst IP, src port, dst port, protocol) in each dataset and assume that each flow must be handled by one rule (*i.e.*, with no wildcards). We create matches on five fields rather than all 12 supported by existing OpenFlow switches because these are the fields for which our traces include information. We assume a switch with a single flow table, conforming to OpenFlow v1.0, which is implemented on most switches on the market.

Table 2. Comparison of various rule management methods. For each method, we show for both datasets the maximum number of concurrent rules and the 95th percentile value (across minutes) of operations per second. Percentages for number of rules and ops/sec are in comparison to the default OpenFlow operation of using a 60 s timeout (for the manual techniques) and to the IP-only rules with 60 s timeout (for the automatic aggregation).

	Campus		Abilene	
	# rules	ops/sec	# rules	ops/sec
no mgmt. 60 s timeout	**115 K**	**46**	**12 M**	**1255**
	11 K	**176**	**100.5 K**	**2800**
Timeouts (Sect. 4.2)				
- 30 s	7,982 (−27 %)	200 (+14 %)	53 K (−47 %)	2,914 (+1.2 %)
- 10 s	6,757 (−39 %)	233 (+32 %)	29 K (−71 %)	3,214 (+12 %)
- 5 s	6,509 (−41 %)	247 (+40 %)	21 K (−79 %)	3,631 (+26 %)
Match fields (Sect. 4.3)				
- dest-only	7,052 (−36 %)	73 (−59 %)	75 K (−26 %)	1,949 (−32 %)
- IP-only	4,460 (−59 %)	125 (−29 %)	53 K (−47 %)	1,215 (−58 %)
Wildcard (IP granularity) (Sect. 4.4)				
- \24	8479 (−23 %)	69 (−61 %)	-	-
- \16	8225 (−25 %)	66 (−63 %)	100 K (−0 %)	2,784 (−3 %)
- \8	8218 (−25 %)	66 (−63 %)	99 K (−1.5 %)	2,752 (−4 %)
IP-only, 60 s	**4,460**	**125**	**53 K**	**1,215**
Simple aggregation (Sect. 5.1)				
$T = 100\%$	3,568 (−20 %)	121 (−3 %)	46 K (−13 %)	1,277 (+5 %)
Aggressive aggregation (Sect. 5.2)				
$T = 25\%$	1,695 (−62 %)	69 (−45 %)	40 K (−24 %)	1,189 (−2 %)
$T = 50\%$	2,676 (−40 %)	85 (−32 %)	43 K (−19 %)	1,234 (−1 %)
$T = 75\%$	3,122 (−30 %)	106 (−15 %)	45 K (−15 %)	1,265 (0 %)

As the data sets do not have any information about the actual out port number used for every flow, we use the following heuristics to determine the action of each rule. Since the *Abilene* dataset contains next-hop IP information, we associate every next-hop IP with a unique out port. For the *Campus* data set, we simulate a 24-port switch, where every flow is assigned to an out port based on its destination IP prefix. We assume a reactive OpenFlow deployment (*i.e.*, the installation of the rule corresponding to a flow is triggered by the first packet in the flow and its removal by the timeouts), as it offers a dynamic model for rule management and a worst case scenario for evaluation (because it maximizes the total number of rules that are generated).

Evaluation Metrics. To measure the effectiveness of rule reduction techniques, we use the maximum value across time of the *total number of rules installed on the switch* at any moment in time. To measure the side effects of reducing the number of rules, we measure the *rate of controller-to-switch operations* (to estimate overhead).

4   Manual Rule Management

In this section, we study manual solutions for reducing the number of rules on an OpenFlow switch. These are solutions that programmers must proactively use in their code. We derive them from personal communication with SDN operators and previous work [5,27]. These mechanisms limit *the time a rule stays on the switch* (through rule expiration timeouts), *the space occupied by a rule on the switch* (by reducing the number of fields to match on), or *the total number of rules* (by using wildcards).

4.1   Not Managing Rules

Figure 1(a) shows the number of concurrent rules that would have to be held on an OpenFlow switch that forwards the flows in the *Campus* dataset. We assume rules do not expire (TO = ∞) and contain exact matches on all five fields mentioned in Sect. 3. Since rules never expire, their number is continually increasing as new flows arrive, reaching a maximum of 115,323 rules at the end of the trace. We repeat the experiment for the *Abilene* data and find that it generates more than 12 M rules. Recall however that the *Abilene* IPs have their last 11 bits zeroed, therefore the rules are essentially wildcard rules; the number of exact match rules will be much higher. These numbers exceed the maximum number of flows supported by all but one of the OpenFlow switches described in Table 1.

4.2   Timeouts

We vary the soft timeout for each rule from 5 s to 60 s (the default timeout value in OpenFlow). Rules with short timeouts are expunged sooner and may need to be reinstalled if there are subsequent packets matching the rule. Large timeouts keep the rule in memory longer and are suited for long flows with lower packet arrival rates. Figure 1(a) and Table 2 show that, as the soft timeout becomes smaller, the number of concurrent rules decreases and the rate of operations increases. Current switches typically handle around 275 operations (*i.e.*, rule installations or deletions) a second [5] and could support the 95th percentile operation load in the *Campus* dataset but not in the *Abilene* trace.

4.3 Match Fields

Having fewer match fields should decrease the memory footprint of an Open-Flow rule. We consider two smaller matches: on IP-only (source and destination, no ports) and on destination-only (destination IP and port, no source). Table 2 shows that both destination-only and IP-only matches lower the number of concurrent rules by at least 26 %, as compared to 5-tuple rules with 60 s timeout. Though these rule savings are significant, the maximum number of concurrent rules with the *Abilene* trace is still quite high compared to the memory capacity of three of the OpenFlow switches in Table 1. While fewer rules result in a lower rate of operations on the switch, since the flow arrival is not uniform, the 95th percentile rate of operations per second in the *Abilene* trace is over 4x higher than the threshold of 275.

4.4 Wildcards

Wildcard-based rules cover a larger part of the flow-space and thus, fewer rules are necessary. However, they limit (1) the expressivity of the configuration because they cannot perform fine-grained matching (*e.g.*, for multipathing [21]), and (2) the application's visibility into the network because the controller cannot request statistics on the individual flows that match the rule.

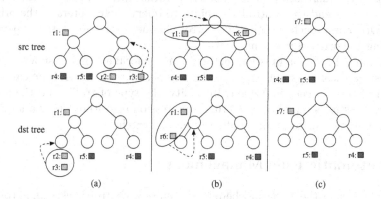

Fig. 2. Simple binary tree aggregation. For simplicity, we represent the subtrees corresponding to the last two bits of source and destination IPs. See Fig. 3 for example rules mapped on these subtrees (Color figure online).

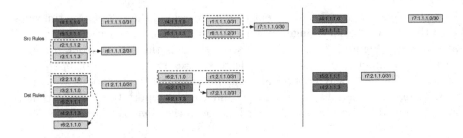

Fig. 3. Examples of rules mapping to the subtrees in Fig. 2 (Color figure online).

To evaluate the effect of wildcards on the flow table size, we consider the original 5-tuple rules, as well as the destination-only and IP-only rules. For each rule, we introduce wildcards in the rightmost bits of IP addresses, effectively reducing them to prefixes. Figure 1(b) and Table 2 show that the average number of rules over each minute decreases as we vary the IP prefix size from /32 to /16. The savings (23 % in the *Campus* data) come at the expense of more policy violations (30 % of packets are forwarded differently). Combining wildcards with fewer match fields further reduces the number of rules, but not always sufficiently enough to fit into the memory of all switches in Table 1. The reduction in number of rules is lesser in the *Abilene* data because it includes only /21 addresses. As with limiting the match fields, using wildcards reduces the expressivity of the installed configuration and our ability to retrieve information about the original rule set (*e.g.*, counters) as the rule semantics change.

4.5   Summary

The most consistently effective way to reduce the number of rules is by lowering rule expiration timeouts. Although it introduces a large network overhead because of the increased control channel operation rate, it preserves the original rule semantics and the controller's ability to query the counters of the original rules. Other approaches limit the control channel overhead at the expense of changing the original rule semantics.

No manual rule compression method is a panacea: as Table 2 shows, even in the best case compression scenario, the number of rules for *Abilene* cannot fit on half of the switches in Table 1. In reality, the type of traffic and the goal of network operators, in addition to rule compression algorithms, play a large role in determining how to fit the configuration on switches.

5   Automatic Rule Management

We now consider the scenario where the OpenFlow controller uses an automatic mechanism to reduce the number of rules. To the best of our knowledge there is no existing mechanism for rule space compression for SDN controllers. Existing rule compression approaches focus on IP routing table compaction [15,23] or minimizing packet classifiers in TCAM [6,17]. They use binary trees or decision trees to identify redundant and similar rules and focus on simple IP-based rules or on how to optimize ranges that cannot be stored as a simple prefix. Their applicability to OpenFlow is not clear yet as OpenFlow rules are more complex (up to 12 matching fields) [14]. Furthermore, IP-based rule management techniques cannot easily adapt to incremental rule changes.

To understand the potential of automatic rule compression, we propose a simple approach, based on the work of Liu [15], that uses binary trees to identify and aggregate related rules. In doing so, our goal is to provide a simple compression baseline. We do not seek to either introduce a novel OpenFlow table compaction method or to fully replicate and compare with previous rule aggregation methods built for IP-based rules. Evaluating these approaches within the scope of OpenFlow is subject to future work.

5.1 Simple Aggregation

To reduce the memory footprint of the configuration installed on a switch, we automatically aggregate *similar* rules into a single rule. A network controller can accomplish this by intercepting all OpenFlow control messages and storing the state of all switches in-memory. On a rule install to a switch, the controller adds the rule to its in-memory state for the switch and checks for aggregation. If aggregation is not possible, the controller simply installs the rule into the switch. Otherwise, it sends an aggregated rule and deletes all rules that are covered by it. Similarly, on a rule removal, the controller checks to see if it is part of any aggregated ruleset and appropriately reinserts rules as necessary.

To build a proof of concept implementation of rule reduction and demonstrate its effectiveness, we use binary trees [26] to store and aggregate rules on a particular switch. Because we use binary trees, we are limited to only IP-based rules. We are currently exploring other possibilities that can accommodate more header fields.

For every switch, we maintain two binary trees: one based on source IP addresses and the other based on destination IP addresses. Every node corresponds to a source or destination address prefix. When the controller wants to install a rule r to a switch, it adds the rule action to both the source and destination trees at the nodes corresponding to the source and destination prefix included in r.

Given this binary tree based representation of rules installed at a switch, we aggregate rules as follows. Consider a new rule r added at nodes s and d in the source and destination trees, respectively. We can potentially aggregate if r has the same action as another rule r' and if r' satisfies one of the following conditions in both the source and destination trees: (1) r and r' are at the same node in the tree, (2) r' is r's parent, or (3) r and r' are siblings. Moreover, in the case that r is aggregated up to its parent in either tree, we recursively continue checking upwards in the source and destination trees to see if further opportunities for aggregation exist.

Figures 2 and 3 show a three-level sub-tree representing the last two bits of the IP space, along with example rules. Different colors represent different rule actions. First, rules r_2 and r_3 are aggregated into r_6 because they (a) have the same associated action (blue), (b) are at the same node in the destination tree, and (c) are siblings in the source tree. Thereafter, recursive checks for aggregation find that r_1 and r_6 can be aggregated into r_7. On the other hand, though r_4 and r_5 have the same action (red) and are siblings in the source tree, they cannot be aggregated since they do not satisfy any one of criteria (1), (2), and (3) mentioned above.

5.2   Aggressive Aggregation

As described so far, we can aggregate a rule r up to its parent node only if there exists another rule with the same action at r's sibling. This limits the ability to aggregate similar rules when two rules are not at the same node or share a parent, but share a common ancestor. For example, in Fig. 2, although r_4 and r_5 could not be aggregated because they do not have a common parent in the destination tree, they could potentially be aggregated up to their common grandparent.

However, unless we place any restrictions, aggregating rules with common ancestors could result in the aggregation of very dissimilar rules. For example, two rules that are at the leftmost and rightmost nodes in either tree (as dissimilar as they can get), can be aggregated up to their common ancestor—the root. In such cases, the aggregated rule will span a very large part of the IP address space, and matched packets will be associated with an action that is perhaps not intended by the application policy.

To limit the aggressiveness of aggregation with common ancestors, we use a threshold T. We install an aggregated rule at a node in the source or destination tree only if the controller has already inserted rules that are associated with at least $T\%$ of the leaves in the subtree rooted at the node. For example, in Fig. 2, we could aggregate r_4 and r_5 into the root of the destination tree if $T \geq 50\%$.

One of the side-effects of aggressive aggregation is that it can violate application policies. When threshold-based aggregation is used, an aggregated rule may match packets that are not covered by rules previously installed by the controller. In the absence of the aggregated rule, these packets would trigger a PacketIn message sent to the controller, to which the controller may have chosen to insert a rule with a different action than the aggregated rule. Later, we evaluate the extent to which policy violations occur and the trade-offs involved in eliminating them.

5.3   Evaluation

Table 2 shows the results of our measurement.

Rule Savings of Simple Aggregation. Figure 4 shows how the rule savings vary with the use of wildcards $i.e.$, reducing the IP prefix size (ignore the lines

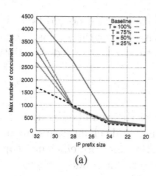
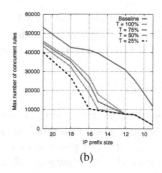

(a)   (b)

Fig. 4. Maximum number of concurrent rules needed to cover the (a) *Campus* and (b) *Abilene* flows, as we vary the value of T and use wildcards.

for $T < 100\%$ for now). In the *Abilene* dataset, as we decrease the prefix size, the potential for aggregation increases. Without aggregation, specifying rules at /16 granularity (rather than /21) reduces their number to only around 40 K (compared to slightly over 50 K). In contrast, when using aggregation, the maximum number of rules is further reduced by third (to around 25 K). The savings are even bigger for the *Campus* data set: up to 62 % savings when aggregating at /28 prefix).

Overhead of Simple Aggregation. Aggregation may increase the number of switch operations, because one rule addition or deletion performed by the controller can translate to several operations at the switch. This is reflected in the *Abilene* data where the operation rate increases slightly by 5 % (see Table 2). However, when we have many aggregations, we may also save operations because we delete an aggregated rule from the switch only when all rules it aggregates are deleted. Since the *Campus* data has more rule savings (and implicitly more higher-in-the-tree aggregations), the number of operations decreases slightly by 3 %.

Is Aggressive Aggregation Effective? Table 2 and Fig. 4 show that aggressive aggregation can reduce dramatically the number of rules (by 62 % for *Campus* and 24 % for *Abilene*) and the rate of switch operations (45 % for *Campus* and 2 % for *Abilene*). Using a threshold has only limited effect on the wildcarded *Campus* rules. When the prefix size is big, the savings are significant (up to 62 % with /28 prefix and 75 % threshold). However, because the IPs in the *Campus* data are more similar, most rules are already aggregated when the prefix size decreases enough (less than /24) and using a threshold cannot yield further savings.

We measure policy violations as the percentage of flows that are forwarded with a different action when we aggregate rules compared to a deployment where there is no aggregation. The fraction of flows for which rule aggregation leads to an incorrect output action is low. When the threshold is 25 % *i.e.*, we install an aggregate rule in a node even when only a quarter of the leafs in its subtree have an associated rule, less than 1 % of the *Abilene* flows could be misdirected. The number of policy violations decreases with higher thresholds. There are no violations for *Campus*, as the set of output actions is less varied than for *Abilene*.

5.4   Summary

Automatically aggregating similar rules reduces their number by up to 20 % compared to IP-only rules with 60 s timeout at negligible changes in control channel overhead. Operators or programmers can further increase efficiency (up to 62 % rule reduction) if they allow a small part of the traffic (under 1 %) to be directed to other destinations. While this is unacceptable for most applications, it may be a solution for dedicated network deployments where any of a set of destinations is acceptable (*e.g.*, load balancers, firewalls, anycast). As Table 2 shows, for many cases, it is more effective to use small timeouts than any automatic aggregation.

6   Conclusions and Future Work

Our real-world traces study shows that simple OpenFlow-based mechanisms, such as lowering rule expiration timeouts, are effective in managing the configuration size on OpenFlow switches although may increase (sometimes unacceptably) the utilization of the switch-to-controller channel. Other manual (using wildcards) or automatic (aggregating similar rules) mechanisms may reduce the size of the rule set even higher but curtail the expressiveness of the high-level policy and may, in a small number of cases, misdirect some packets. Understanding these trade-offs is important to SDN operators and programmers that must write network policies that satisfy both infrastructure and application constraints.

Our ongoing and future work spans two directions. On one hand, we are studying the adaptability of existing IP-based rule compression mechanisms [17] to OpenFlow. We are exploring the use of R-trees [9] to extend our ability to identify and aggregate rule similar in fields other than IP addresses (*e.g.*, protocol).

References

1. NEC OpenFlow switches. http://www.openflow.org/wp/switch-NEC/
2. Pronto OpenFlow switches. http://www.openflow.org/wp/switch-Pronto/
3. Appelman, M., Boer, M.D.: Performance analysis of OpenFlow hardware. Technical report, University of Amsterdam (2012)
4. Benson, T., Akella, A., Maltz, D.: Network traffic characteristics of data centers in the wild. In: IMC (2010)
5. Curtis, A.R., Mogul, J.C., Tourrilhes, J., Yalag, P., Sharma, P., Banerjee, S.: Devoflow: scaling flow management for high-performance networks. In: SIGCOMM (2011)
6. Dong, Q., Banerjee, S., Wang, J., Agrawal, D., Shukla, A.: Packet classifiers in ternary CAMs can be smaller. In: ACM Sigmetrics (2006)

7. Foster, N., Harrison, R., Freedman, M.J., Monsanto, C., Rexford, J., Story, A., Walker, D.: Frenetic: a netowrk programming language. In: ACM IFIP (2011)
8. Freguson, A.D., Guha, A., Liang, C., Fonseca, R., Krishnamurthi, S., Networking, P.: An API for application control in SDNs. In: SIGCOMM (2013)
9. Guttman, A.: R-trees: a dynamic index structure for spatial searching. In: SIG-MOD (1984)
10. HP 3800. http://h17007.www1.hp.com/us/en/networking/products/switches/HP_3800_Switch_Series/index.aspx
11. IBM OpenFlow switches. http://www.openflow.org/wp/ibm-switch/
12. Kandula, S., Sengupta, S., Greenberg, A., Patel, P., Chaiken, R.: The nature of datacenter traffic: measurement and analysis. In: IMC (2009)
13. Katta, N., Alipourfad, O., Rexford, J., Walker, D.: Infinite CacheFlow in software-defined networks. In: HotSDN (2014)
14. Kogan, K., Nikolenko, S., Culhane, W., Eugster, P., Ruan, E.: Towards efficient implementation of packet classifiers in SDN/OpenFlow. In: HotSDN (2013)
15. Liu, H.: Routing table compaction in ternary CAM. IEEE Micro 22(1), 55–64 (2002)
16. McKeown, N., Anderson, T., Balakrishnan, H., Parulkar, G., Peterson, L., Rexford, J., Shenker, S., Turner, J.: OpenFlow: enabling innovation in campus networks. ACM SIGCOMM CCR 38, 69–74 (2008)
17. Meiners, C.R., Liu, A.X., Torng, E., Razor, T.: A systematic approach towards minimizing packet classifiers in TCAMs. IEEE/ACM Trans. Netw. 18(2), 490–500 (2010)
18. Monsanto, C., Foster, N., Harrison, R., Walker, D.: A compiler and run-time system for network programs. In: ACM POPL (2012)
19. Monsanto, C., Reich, J., Foster, N., Rexford, J., Walker, D.: Composing software-defined networks. In: NSDI (2013)
20. Moshref, M., Yu, M., Sharma, A., Govindan, R.: Scalable rule management for data centers. In: NSDI (2013)
21. Openflow multipath proposal. http://www.openflow.org/wk/index.php/Multipath_Proposal
22. Openflow switch specification, 1.0.0. http://www.openflow.org/documents/open flow-spec-v1.0.0.pdf
23. Ravikumar, V.C., Mahapatra, R.N.: TCAM architecture for IP lookup using prefix properties. IEEE Micro 24(2), 60–69 (2004)
24. Rotsos, C., Sarrar, N., Uhlig, S., Sherwood, R., Moore, A.W.: OFLOPS: an open framework for OpenFlow switch evaluation. In: Taft, N., Ricciato, F. (eds.) PAM 2012. LNCS, vol. 7192, pp. 85–95. Springer, Heidelberg (2012)
25. Sarrar, N., Wuttke, R., Schmid, S., Bienkowski, M., Uhlig, S.: Leveraging locality for FIB aggregation. In: IEEE Globecom (2014)
26. Wang, R., Butnariu, D., Rexford, J.: OpenFlow-based server load balancing gone wild. In: Hot-ICE (2011)
27. Yu, M., Rexford, J., Freedman, M.J., Wang, J.: Scalable flow-based networking with DIFANE. In: ACM SIGCOMM (2010)

IXPs and MPLS

Blackholing at IXPs: On the Effectiveness of DDoS Mitigation in the Wild

Christoph Dietzel[1,2(✉)], Anja Feldmann[1], and Thomas King[2]

[1] TU Berlin, Berlin, Germany
christoph@inet.tu-berlin.de
[2] DE-CIX, Frankfurt, Germany

Abstract. DDoS attacks remain a serious threat not only to the edge of the Internet but also to the core peering links at Internet Exchange Points (IXPs). Currently, the main mitigation technique is to blackhole traffic to a specific IP prefix at upstream providers. Blackholing is an operational technique that allows a peer to announce a prefix via BGP to another peer, which then discards traffic destined for this prefix. However, as far as we know there is only anecdotal evidence of the success of blackholing.

Largely unnoticed by research communities, IXPs have deployed blackholing as a service for their members. In this first-of-its-kind study, we shed light on the extent to which blackholing is used by the IXP members and what effect it has on traffic.

Within a 12 week period we found that traffic to more than 7,864 distinct IP prefixes was blackholed by 75 ASes. The daily patterns emphasize that there are not only a highly variable number of new announcements every day but, surprisingly, there are a consistently high number of announcements (> 1000). Moreover, we highlight situations in which blackholing succeeds in reducing the DDoS attack traffic.

1 Introduction

Distributed Denial of Service (DDoS) attacks are and will continue to be a serious threat to the Internet. Indeed, the intensity and the dimension of such attacks is still rising, in particular due to amplification and reflection attacks [7,32,33]. DDoS attacks impact not only edge networks but can also overwhelm cloud services [36] or congest backbone peering links at Internet Exchange Points (IXP) [30]. Various DDoS detection and defense mechanisms strive to diminish the impact of attack traffic on the victim's infrastructure while minimizing the collateral damage to legitimate traffic. While there has been some progress towards limiting amplification [19], DDoS attacks remain a major security challenge as new protocol or implementation weaknesses are identified almost daily [38].

Various taxonomies [18,23,37] distinguish between proactive (preventive) and reactive techniques. Among the reactive defenses, we distinguish between *source-based*, *destination-based*, and *network-based* [39] mechanisms depending on where

© Springer International Publishing Switzerland 2016
T. Karagiannis and X. Dimitropoulos (Eds.): PAM 2016, LNCS 9631, pp. 319–332, 2016.
DOI: 10.1007/978-3-319-30505-9_24

they are deployed. In this paper, we focus on how *blackholing* – a network-based reactive defense mechanism – is used at IXPs.

The term blackhole originates in physics and describes an object with such a strong gravitation that nothing can escape from it. In networking it refers to situations where IP packets are silently discarded, often due to misconfiguration. Indeed, since the late-1980s, blackholing has been used – on a per device basis – to counter DDoS attacks [13]. In 2002, Greene [12] proposed to extend blackholing to routers within an Autonomous System (AS) via iBGP communities, see RFC 3882. In eBGP, an AS is able to communicate to another AS for which prefix the packets should be dropped via BGP communities [5]. In 2009, Kumari and McPherson extended the community ranges to include dropping by source addresses, see RFC 5635. Major Internet Service Providers (ISP), e.g., DT, NTT, and Hurricane Electric, use blackholing within their network and have been offering blackholing services since between 2005 and 2007 to their customers [9,15,27].

However, the use of eBGP blackholing services by a DDoS victim is not trivial as the victim has to contact its direct neighbors. The signaling has to be done on a per neighbor basis. IXPs simplify this by acting as a proxy. They offer a public peering infrastructure and the major IXPs have more than 500 member ASes. Due to this multiplication factor, IXPs are in principle convenient locations for blackholing. First ad hoc uses of blackholing occurred around 2010. The blackholing feature is now available at some major IXPs such as DE-CIX, MSK-IX, NETIX, NIX.CZ, and TPIX [8,25,26].

In this paper, we rely on three month's worth of routing and traffic measurements from one of the largest IXPs worldwide to examine the extent of blackholing usage and its effectiveness. We find a significant number of blackholes announced, mainly /32 but also less specific. Indeed, the usage considerably depends on the prefix length and the announcing member AS. Furthermore, we reveal that blackholing succeeds in reducing DDoS attack traffic.

2   Blackholing at IXPs

Blackholing is used as a DDoS mitigation strategy inside a single or between multiple ASes. Consequently, the victim AS announces the attacked destination IP prefix upstream network via BGP. Traffic towards these prefixes is discarded upstream, usually at the upstream AS ingress point. This reduces the amount of traffic not only for the destination network but also for all upstream ASes.

Historically, blackholing was implemented at the edge routers of an AS. However, over time it was moving from the edge (customer or provider networks) to the core of the Internet (ISPs and IXPs).

IXPs: IXPs are shared and settlement free peering platforms that operate a switching fabric to interconnect its members' networks. Among the member ASes that exchange traffic are typically a wide range of network types, e.g., Tier-1 ISPs, regional providers, hosters, content providers, CDNs, and even IXP resellers. Many IXPs offer route servers as a free value-added service [31].

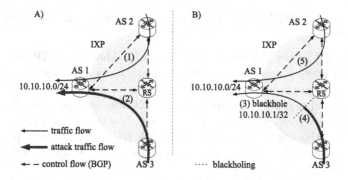

Fig. 1. DDoS attack at IXP member before/during blackholing.

It greatly simplifies the BGP session management for their connected members. Therefore, route servers collect routing information in a centralized manner and redistribute them to connected member routers.

If an IXP-connected network (AS) is hit by a massive DDoS attack that causes large amounts of ingress traffic over the IXP link, either the network itself or the network interconnection link is at risk of congestion. As a last resort, either operators of the targeted AS can trigger blackholing for its own prefixes or blackholing is triggered on the behalf of the prefix owner, e.g., through its upstream AS. Both scenarios render the attacked network unreachable for attackers and for everyone else.

Explanatory Example Scenario: Fig. 1 depicts the traffic flow process at an IXP prior (A) and after (B) the activation of blackholing. The initial situation is that a member (AS1) receives traffic from its peers and while AS2 sends solely legitimate traffic (1), AS3 traffic contains significant amounts of DDoS traffic (2). Now AS1's IXP-connected router advertises the attacked prefix – usually a more specific – for blackholing towards the route server (3). This can be done either explicitly, i.e., using a BGP next hop with a predefined blackholing IP address, or implicitly, i.e., via a well-known BGP community. The community is then translated to the next hop blackholing IP address at the route server. All connected members receive the BGP update, learn the new BGP next hop address for the announced prefix, choose it as best path since it is more specific, and send their traffic to the blackholing IP.

The IXP handles this IP address and resolves it by means of the ARP into a predefined blackholing MAC address. All Ethernet frames with this destination MAC are discarded via ACL at the IXP layer-2 ingress switch interfaces (4). Note, this process is non-transparent for the traffic source, e.g., attacker. All other announced prefixes remain unaffected (5), but may do not suffer from congestions anymore. In cases where the DDoS traffic is mainly coming from a certain member's networks, the so-called *policy control* feature of route servers can be used to limit blackholing only to those ASes. In general, policy control allows the definition of white- and blacklists for BGP announcements by a well-defined set of BGP communities. These communities are interpreted by the route server.

Blackholing Usage: The implementation of blackholing at IXPs is beneficial because: (i) route servers disentangle the configuration process for triggering blackholing. A single route update can address all members at once. (ii) The large number of networks that meet at the IXP also increase the effectiveness. (iii) Given the central position in the Internet, blackholing at IXPs allows the alleviation of the impact closer to the attack source. (iv) It can protect the intermediate networks on the path through the Internet, but it is far enough from the source to be efficient.

However, while blackholing at IXPs shields member networks and the links from congestions, it cannot distinguish between legitimate and malicious traffic. All packets destined for the defined IP prefix are dropped and, thus, it is not reachable from all upstream networks on the data path.

Moreover, after detecting a massive DDoS attack, the operator must trigger blackholing. This is a manual process where the router configuration must be adjusted in order to announce via BGP an IP prefix under attack. Typically, a more specific IP prefix is announced to limit the impact on benign traffic to the minimum. The triggering AS is not necessarily the owner of the IP prefix. Thus, the announcing member must register this prefix in the IRR database to be accepted by the IXP.

3 Data Sources

In this paper, we rely on the following datasets from one of the largest European IXPs [6]. This IXP serves around 600 members and peaks to over 4 Tbit/s in 2015.

We used 5-minute interval snapshots from a publicly accessible looking glass at the IXP route servers to gather the BGP announcements for long-term control plane analysis. The announcements for blackholing can be discriminated by means of a well-defined next hop IP. Due to the sampling frequency, only announced prefixes that were active at these moments can be captured. Short-term new and withdrawn announcements are not caught. If a previously active prefix was absent in one measurement we considered it as a new announcement when it reappears. The data covers a 3-month period from December 2014 onward. From this dataset we identify 22,994 blackholing BGP announcements (after excluding measurement and looking glass outages, etc.)

To understand the impact of blackholing on the traffic flow, we rely on IPFIX data from the IXPs switching fabric for the same period. IPFIX at the IXP is configured to randomly capture 1 out of 10,000 packets on every member link. The IPFIX data contains the MAC and IP addresses, IP protocol identifier, TCP/UDP port numbers, and length of the captured packets. For statements about traffic volumes we extrapolate from the sampled flows.

In addition we use route server and IPFIX data for policy control verification and a case study from July 2015.

4 Blackholing: A Usage Analysis

In this section, we elaborate on how blackholing is used in the wild from a control plane perspective. For the remainder of this paper the term *"announcement"* refers to BGP announcements that trigger blackholing. Additionally, all notations about IP prefixes refer to blackholed IP prefixes if not otherwise stated.

4.1 A Prefix View of Blackholing

The IXP's route server accepts BGP advertised blackholes with a prefix length n, with $/32 \leq n \leq /8$. We find that only prefixes $\geq /18$ are announced by the IXP members. Figure 2(a) shows the distribution of unique announcements (y-axis in log-scale) per prefix length. The mode on the far right indicates that mainly $/32$ prefixes are blackholed, indeed more than 97 % of all announcements. Another mode is between $/24$ and $/30$, which accounts for 2.5 %. Prefixes with the length of $\leq /23$ account for a very small fraction, namely 9 announcements (0.5 %). In summary, mostly host routes are used for blackholing.

Due to the employment of the policy control feature at the route server, prefixes are not necessarily announced to all peers. We randomly sampled the route server's RIB four times with a seven day interval. On average 25 % of all announcements carry a policy control community that limits its propagation.

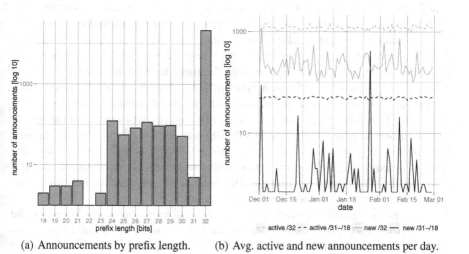

(a) Announcements by prefix length.   (b) Avg. active and new announcements per day.

Fig. 2. Prefix views of blackholing.

To understand if the blackholing usage changed over time, Fig. 2(b) shows the announcements per day, clustered by prefix length over a three-month period. We distinguish between new announcements per day and active on average per day. Unexpectedly, we find that the total number of active announcements is

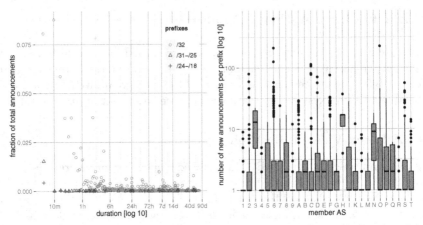

(a) Fraction of all announcement sperminutes binnedbyprefix.

(b) Announcement frequency perprefix [log 10].

Fig. 3. Prefix and AS view of blackholing.

almost stable. In particular, the /18 − /31 prefix cluster contains eight /24 announcements that are active over the entire measured period. Unfortunately, we did not get a response from the operator to fathom the intention for the long lasting announcements. For announcements between /25 − /30, we again see permanently announced prefixes that are active for a period of several weeks. Since the announcements with prefixes of the /18 - /31 are only short-lived, they do not impact the average number of active ones. In contrast, the most prevalent prefix class, the /32s, varies significantly. It ranges from an average minimum of 994 to a maximum of 1, 463 and a mean of 1, 195 for all active announcements.

The number of new announcements per day differ notably compared to the averages. They show significant variations. From no activities over several days to large numbers of new announcements during one day for all but the /32. Indeed, focusing on the peak on January 27th, we see a total of 415 newly announced unique prefixes. All prefixes are announced simultaneously by the same AS at 6 A.M. and last for about 10 minutes. The number of new announcements for the /32 prefixes varies between 102 and 1211.

Next, we consider the durations and remove all announcements where we did not capture either the beginning or the end. We cluster these announcements (100 %) by prefix length and show in Fig. 3(a) the histogram of announcement durations in minutes using log-scale. The majority of long announced prefixes are /32s. Altogether, the largest fraction (0.1 of all prefixes) is announced for about five minutes. The two clusters with the less specific prefixes (/18 − /24 fraction of 0.004 and /25 − /31 with 0.015) have few announcements longer than five minutes. Their longest announcements last for 57.39 days. The /32 prefixes are again more diverse. Notably, around 9 % of the announcements are active for about 10 minutes while 38.5 % last longer than 240 minutes.

Interestingly, multiples of 1 hour are more dominant. The longest duration we observe is 76.31 days.

The operational background for such observation is that the members' monitoring capabilities for blackholing are limited. As soon as a prefix is announced for blackholing, the announcing AS is not aware of the amount of traffic that is dropped. Hence, some members turn blackholing off and on within a short period of time in order to check whether the DDoS attack is still on-going.

4.2 An as View of Blackholing

To understand how the 75 different ASes (12 % of member ASes) use blackholing we take a closer look at the announcements from a member AS perspective. These ASes are categorized according to Peering DB: Network Service Providers (NSP) 50 %, Cable/DSL/ISP 25 %, and Content Providers 19 %. The NSPs are overrepresented compared to IXP-wide 42 %, while the latter two accord to those.

The ASes announced 7,864 unique prefixes, of which 10 % were announced once and around 15 % between two and three times. 47 ASes announced fewer than 50 prefixes in total and were excluded to focus on the blackholing-heavy ASes. We then focus on the remaining 28 ASes. The mean of all announcements for the same prefixes across all remaining ASes is 3.13 with a median of only 1. Figure 3(b) shows the number of announcements per unique prefix by AS in a boxplot. Overall, the median is almost always lower than 10. Looking at the details we find that, despite the prevailing low announcing frequencies, there are also AS-wide high frequencies. Surprisingly, outliers spread from 10 to 100. The observed maximum number of a unique announced prefix is 623. This observation may provide further evidence for an operational procedure where blackholing is switched on and off many times for the very same IP prefix within a short time frame.

To check if the frequently announced prefixes have an impact over the total time span that they are active, we accumulate the duration for all unique prefixes of our selected ASes. Figure 4(a) shows these values at the y-axis with the same ASes as in Fig. 3(b). We find that the majority of ASes announce prefixes for a duration longer than 1 hour but less than 7 days. Nevertheless, we observe some ASes that either announce their prefixes primarily over a short or long period of time.

Figures 3(b) and 4(a) expose no clear correlation between frequency and duration of announcements for the same AS. On the one hand some ASes announce the same prefix frequently for short times, and on the other hand some ASes announce blackholing only once for a short duration. However, also the contrary can be observed: frequent and once for a longer duration. This indicates that there is no common operational procedure for triggering blackholing. This is not surprising as DDoS attacks often differ from attack to attack. Thus, operators respond to each attack individually.

Nevertheless, we want to see if there are operational patterns: one would expect either more announcements during daytime working hours, or during peak hours. Neither is the case and the behavior differs by AS. For some, we

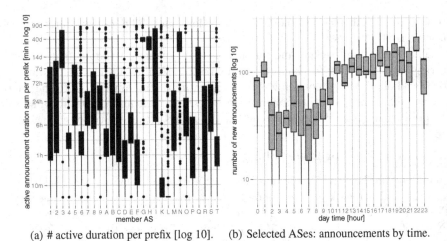

(a) # active duration per prefix [log 10].   (b) Selected ASes: announcements by time.

Fig. 4. AS views of blackholing.

see clear patterns, e.g., see Fig. 4(b). Here, the number of new announcements is substantially smaller but the variance is higher at night.

5   Blackholing Impact on Traffic

To study the effectiveness of blackholing on the data plane, we correlate the actual traffic with the BGP announcements on the control plane. Figure 5(a) depicts the bit rates of the blackholed traffic at the IXP during our three month observation period. It shows per day the hourly maximum and hourly average in Mbit/s. The per day maximum varies from 50 to 1,000 Mbit/s with a peak at 2,100 Mbit/s. At first glance, this may seem small especially when compared to the average traffic rates at this IXP. However, keep in mind that this is the traffic that is discarded and should only effect short time-scale DDoS attacks. Moreover, as soon as the blackhole is in effect, this regulates traffic volume. For TCP, blackholing disables connections and for UDP the sender might notice the blackhole and therefore throttle the attack. Another reason is what we plot: the average across a full hour. Indeed, the daily averages (dashed line) are up to 10 times smaller than the daily maxima (solid line).

Given the large number of blackholing announcements, see Sect. 4, we next determine how many of these prefixes actually receive traffic. We find that in those hours with more than 1 Mbit/s average blackhole traffic, a mean of 81 and a maximum of 871 IPs receive traffic. Thus, we conclude that typically only a small number of IPs receive a substantial amount of blackholed traffic.

To assess the impact of blackholing we next examine the temporal correlation of blackhole announcements with traffic. We focus on two case studies: (Case Study I) an event that lasted a relatively short time period and (Case Study II) one lasting longer and involving a larger traffic volume.

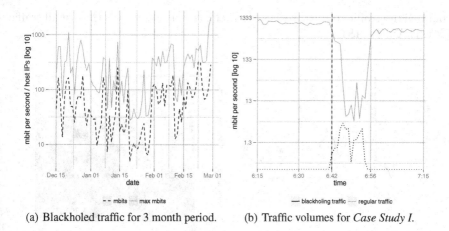

(a) Blackholed traffic for 3 month period.   (b) Traffic volumes for *Case Study I*.

Fig. 5. Traffic volumes over time.

Case Study I: Fig. 5(b) is an example where the blackholed prefixes are in the range /19 – /29. This AS (AS k in Figs. 3(b) and 4(a)) announced 415 prefixes for blackholing — all at the same time. Overall, the blackhole was active for roughly 10 min (dashed vertical line). Figure 5(b) shows the traffic volume as received by the AS for all these blackholed prefixes for 60 minutes, namely, ~30 min before the first blackhole announcement, during the blackhole, and ~20 min afterwards. In addition, we show the traffic for the same prefixes that is discarded, as well as the times when the blackhole announcements are made (vertical line). Right after the blackhole is announced the traffic that the AS receives drops by roughly a factor of 100. The blackholed traffic (dotted lines) is smaller than the "missing" traffic due to the reasons mentioned above. After the blackhole is deactivated the traffic volume rises to a level that is close to the previous one. The difference is roughly 300 Mbit/s. We also conclude that the objective of the blackhole was achieved as there were no further blackhole announcements for these prefixes by this AS.

One could expect that the amount of traffic that is blackholed is the same as the reduction of the regular traffic. This is not the case and explanations are: (i) Depending on the BGP router configuration, it cannot be guaranteed that a particular peer accepts more specific prefixes than /24. (ii) The AS under attack may take other corrective actions besides blackholing at IXPs. For instance, blackholing at upstreams, moving traffic from peering to transit, or activating DDoS traffic filtering services (e.g., CloudFlare or Prolexic). (iii) If the blackholed traffic contains a large fraction of TCP traffic and these TCP connections are broken by the blackhole, this can reduce the data traffic drastically.

Case Study II: Fig. 6(a) shows the same data but for another AS for a six day period from 26th of July 2015 onwards. We picked this case study as it involved substantial amounts of traffic, an interesting application (port) mix, and a single IP — a /32 prefix (*to bh*/32 and *to* /32 legend in Fig. 6(a)). In addition, the plot contains the traffic to the covering /16 prefix (*to* /16) as well as the overall traffic for this AS (*to AS*).

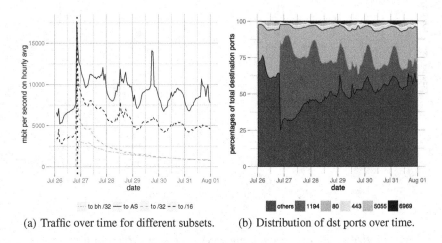

(a) Traffic over time for different subsets.   (b) Distribution of dst ports over time.

Fig. 6. Traffic and port mix for *Case Study II.*

Notice the radical increase in traffic shortly before the blackhole announcement. The traffic to the AS spikes from roughly 6 Gbit/s to 17.6 for an AS with an aggregated port capacity of 20 Gbit/s. The plot highlights that the root cause is in the non-blackholed /16 and in particular in the /32 that is then blackholed. The blackhole announcement for this /32 is highly effective as the regular traffic for the IP as well as for the /16 and the AS drops significantly immediately after the announcement. Note, that we can still see traffic to the /32 because not necessarily all peers accept more specific announcements than /24. We also notice the peak in the blackholed traffic for the /32, which increases to 3.2 Gbit/s. Thus, the blackhole reduces the traffic to the AS and the prefixes by about one third. Over the next days the traffic to the IP gradually decreases while the non-blackholed traffic to the /16 and /32 shows clear daily patterns. We captured several updates for the blackholed prefix. The blackhole is not revoked, but just updated with different communities which are not honored by the IXP's route server.

To understand why the blackhole is effective, we plot in Fig. 6(b) the relative transport TCP/UDP port distribution for the traffic to the AS. Over the whole period port 80 (http), 1194 (OpenVPN), 443 (https), 5055, 6969 (BitTorrent) are the most prominent ports. Accordingly, the plot is a stacked barplot with these ports and other ports at the bottom.

Initially, the traffic share of http is ∼ 30 %. But with the blackhole trigger event the OpenVPN traffic drastically increases. Indeed, it constitutes about 50 % of all traffic to this AS. As time passes and the blackhole takes effect the port mix slowly converges to the initial distribution. The dominance of OpenVPN is also reflected in the blackholed traffic for the blackholed IP. 99.9 % of the traffic is UDP and involves port 1194. Thus, this change of ports is also reflected in the distribution of transport protocols.

We find that blackholing is effective in numerous situations. However, the observed volumes of traffic depend on numerous factors, e.g., prefix length, announcement duration, general traffic utilization, attack pattern, and/or policy control settings. We also highlight that the traffic mix can vary significantly between non-blackholed and blackholed traffic.

6   Related Work

While this work focuses on blackholing, a network-based reactive measure to diminish massive DDoS attacks in the core of the Internet, this section summarizes other reactive DDoS defense mechanisms and highlights other measurement studies.

Source-based defense techniques are deployed near the source of an attack and aim to impede service of intermediate and destination networks. Common mechanisms are IP source address filtering and heuristics on ingress/egress traffic flows [1,10,22].

Alternatively, destination-based DDoS mitigation attempts to combat attacks near the victim-end of the Internet. Common places for their deployment are edge routers or access routers of the destined AS. Proposed mechanisms include adaptive rate limiting [16,21], network reconfiguration [3,4,35], and traceback [2,34]. Additionally, a multitude of filtering techniques such as time-based [14], history-based [29], and hop count-based [17] have been introduced.

Whereas source-based DDoS defense often suffers from its limited scope and the lack of a representative fraction of the attack traffic to be efficient, destination-based approaches come in too late on the path through the Internet. Thus, they jeopardize the destination AS or even intermediate networks. Network-based approaches seek to overcome these drawbacks and are deployed inside intermediate networks. They mainly incorporate distributed or trust-based detection and already presented reconfiguration or filtering mechanisms, e.g., [11,24,28].

Despite the large body of available approaches, effective reactive techniques that are deployed in practice are rare. Thus, there is a demand for defense techniques which are efficient, easy and quick to apply, and which ensure the continuing availability of the services, system, or network. However, none of the mentioned taxonomies for DDoS defense techniques [18,23,37] takes blackholing into consideration.

Although blackholing has not been examined to date, other recent measurement studies focus on attack amplification potential [7,20,32,33,38] and on progress towards diminishing their impact [19].

7   Summary and Future Work

In this paper, we perform a first study on the usage of blackholing at an IXP in the wild. We find that not only is blackholing frequently used with about 23, 000 announced blackholes over our measured period of 3 months, but also that they have a considerable prefix size — up to /18. While short-lived blackholes are prevalent, we also spot others that lasted for months. Moreover, we observe an apparently stable number of active blackholing announcements (about 1200).

The frequent usage of blackholing on the control plane correlates with significant amounts of blackholed traffic on the data plane. Using two case studies we show that blackholing successfully reduces the amount of traffic. This emphasises that blackholing at IXPs can be a very useful tool to diminish massive DDoS attacks. Indeed, our analysis of the application (port) mix of one of the blackhole incidents indicates that blackholing is successful in reducing unusual OpenVPN traffic, likely a DDoS attack.

In general, IXPs are great locations for countering DDoS attacks via blackholing, as the IXP infrastructure is a multiplication factor. Still, blackholing is a relatively new feature and there is room for increased efficacy, e.g., effective monitoring and reporting, partially retracting blackholing, as well as common operation practices at the ASes (acceptance of more specific than /24 prefixes), and transitive blackholing. Moreover, the blackholed data can be used to better mitigate attacks in the Internet.

Acknowledgments. We thank all our colleagues for their feedback, and the reviewers for their suggestions. This work is supported by European Unions Horizon 2020 research and innovation programme under the ENDEAVOUR project (grant agreement 644960) and by the German Federal Ministry of Education and Research (BMBF Grant 01IS14009D BDSec).

References

1. Abdelsayed, S., Glimsholt, D., Leckie, C., Ryan, S., Shami, S.: An efficient filter for denial-of-service bandwidth attacks. In: GOLBECOM (2003)
2. Adler, M.: Trade-offs in probabilistic packet marking for IP traceback. JACM **52**(2), 217–244 (2005)
3. Agarwal, S., Dawson, T., Tryfonas, C.: DDoS Mitigation via Regional Cleaning Centers. Technical report, Sprint ATL Research Report (2003)
4. Andersen, D., Balakrishnan, H., Kaashoek, F., Morris, R.: Resilient overlay networks. In: ACM SOSP (2001)
5. Battles, T., McPherson, D., Morrow, C.: Customer-triggered real-time blackholes. In: NANOG 30 (2004)
6. Chatzis, N., Smaragdakis, G., Böttger, J., Krenc, T., Feldmann, A.: On the benefits of using a large IXP as an internet vantage point. In: ACM IMC (2013)
7. Czyz, J., Kallitsis, M., Gharaibeh, M., Papadopoulos, C., Bailey, M., Karir, M.: Taming the 800 pound gorilla: the rise and decline of NTP DDoS attacks. In: ACM IMC (2014)

8. DE-CIX: DE-CIX Blackholing Support. www.de-cix.net/products-services/de-cix-frankfurt/blackholing/
9. Deutsche Telekom: AS3320 BGP Communities, August 2005. www.onesc.net/communities/as3320/AS3320_BGP_Communities_v1.1.pdf
10. Gil, T.M., Poletto, M.: MULTOPS: A data-structure for bandwidth attack detection. In: USENIX Security Symposium (2001)
11. Gonzalez, J.M., Anwar, M., Joshi, J.: A trust-based approach against ip-spoofing attacks. In: IEEE PST (2011)
12. Greene, B.R.: Remote triggering black hole filtering. Cisco Systems (2002)
13. Greene, B.R., Smith, P.: Cisco ISP Essentials. Cisco Press, Indianapolis (2002)
14. Hu, Y., Choi, H., Choi, H.-A.: Packet filtering to defend flooding-based DDoS attacks. In: Advances in Wired and Wireless Communication (2004)
15. Hurricane Electric: Customer Blackhole Community (2006). www.he.net/adm/blackhole.html
16. Ioannidis, J., Bellovin, S.M.: Implementing Pushback: Router-Based Defense Against DDoS Attacks. Columbia University Academic Commons (2002)
17. Jin, C., Wang, H., Shin, K.G.: Hop-count filtering: an effective defense against spoofed DDoS traffic. In: ACM CCS (2003)
18. Keshariya, A., Foukia, N.: DDoS defense mechanisms: a new taxonomy. In: Garcia-Alfaro, J., Navarro-Arribas, G., Cuppens-Boulahia, N., Roudier, Y. (eds.) DPM 2009. LNCS, vol. 5939, pp. 222–236. Springer, Heidelberg (2010)
19. Kührer, M., Hupperich, T., Rossow, C., Holz, T.: Exit from hell? reducing the impact of amplification DDoS attacks. In: USENIX Security Symposium (2001)
20. MacFarland, D.C., Shue, C.A., Kalafut, A.J.: Characterizing optimal DNS amplification attacks and effective mitigation. In: Mirkovic, J., Liu, Y. (eds.) PAM 2015. LNCS, vol. 8995, pp. 15–27. Springer, Heidelberg (2015)
21. Mahajan, R., Bellovin, S.M., Floyd, S., Ioannidis, J., Paxson, V., Shenker, S.: Controlling high bandwidth aggregates in the network. ACM SIGCOMM CCR (2002)
22. Mirkovic, J., Prier, G., Reiher, P.: Source-end DDoS defense. In: IEEE NCA (2003)
23. Mirkovic, J., Reiher, P.: A taxonomy of DDoS attack and DDoS defense mechanisms. In: ACM SIGCOMM CCR (2004)
24. Mizrak, A.T., Savage, S., Marzullo, K.: Detecting compromised routers via packet forwarding behavior. IEEE Netw. $22(2)$, 34–39 (2008)
25. MSK-IX: Protection against DDoS-attacks by blackholing. www.msk-ix.ru/eng/routeserver.html#blackhole
26. NETIX: Blackholing. www.netix.net/services/14/NetIX-Blackholing
27. NTT Communications: Terms and conditions for use of global IP network services, August 2007. http://www.ntt.net/english/library/pdf/terms.pdf
28. Park, K., Lee, H.: On the effectiveness of route-based packet filtering for distributed DoS attack prevention in power-law internets. In: ACM SIGCOMM CCR (2001)
29. Peng, T., Leckie, C., Ramamohanarao, K.: Protection from distributed denial of service attacks using history-based IP filtering. In: IEEE ICC (2003)
30. Prince, M.: The DDoS that almost broke the internet, March 2013. www.blog.cloudflare.com/the-ddos-that-almost-broke-the-internet/
31. Richter, P., Smaragdakis, G., Feldmann, A., Chatzis, N., Boettger, J., Willinger, W.: Peering at peerings: on the role of IXP route servers. In: ACM IMC (2014)
32. Rossow, C.: Amplification hell: revisiting network protocols for DDoS abuse. In: NDSS (2014)

33. Ryba, F., Orlinski, M., Wählisch, M., Rossow, C., Schmidt, T.: Amplification and DRDoS Attack Defense - A Survey and New Perspectives. arXiv preprint (2015). arxiv:1505.07892

34. Savage, S., Wetherall, D., Karlin, A., Anderson, T.: Network support for IP traceback. IEEE/ACM Trans. Netw. **9**(3), 226–237 (2001)

35. Shi, E., Stoica, I., Andersen, D.G., Perrig, A.: OverDoSe: A Generic DDoS Protection Service Using an Overlay Network. Computer Science Department (2006)

36. Sipgate: The Sipgate DDoS Story, October 2014. https://medium.com/@sipgate/ddos-attacke-auf-sipgate-a7d18bf08c03

37. Specht, S.M., Lee, R.B.: Distributed denial of service: taxonomies of attacks, tools, and countermeasures. In: ISCA PDCS, pp. 543–550 (2004)

38. van Rijswijk-Deij, R., Sperotto, A., Pras, A.: DNSSEC and its potential for DDoS attacks: a comprehensive measurement study. In: ACM IMC (2014)

39. Zargar, S.T., Joshi, J., Tipper, D.: A survey of defense mechanisms against distributed denial of service (DDoS) flooding attacks. IEEE Com. Surv. Tutorials **15**(4), 2046–2069 (2013)

Dissecting the Largest National Ecosystem of Public Internet eXchange Points in Brazil

Samuel Henrique Bucke Brito[✉], Mateus A.S. Santos,
Ramon dos Reis Fontes, Danny A. Lachos Perez,
and Christian Esteve Rothenberg

Information and Networking Technologies Research
and Innovation Group (INTRIG), School of Electrical and Computer Engineering,
University of Campinas (UNICAMP), Sao Paulo, Brazil
{shbbrito,msantos,ramonrf,dlachosp,chesteve}@dca.fee.unicamp.br

Abstract. Many efforts are devoted to increase the understanding
of the complex and evolving Internet ecosystem. Internet eXchange
Points (IXP) are shared infrastructures where Autonomous Systems (AS)
implement peering agreements for their traffic exchange. In recent years,
IXPs have become an increasing research target since they represent an
interesting microcosm of the Internet diversity and a strategic vantage
point to deliver end-user services. In this paper, we analyze the largest set
of public IXPs in a single country, namely the IX.br project in Brazil. Our
in-depth analyses are based on BGP data from all looking glass servers
and provide insights into the peering ecosystem per IXP and from a
nation-wide perspective. We propose a novel peering affinity metric well-
suited to measure the connectivity between different types of ASes. We
found lower values of peering density in IX.br compared to more mature
ecosystems, such as AMS-IX, DE-CIX, LINX, and MSK-IX. Our final
contribution is sharing the 15 GB dataset along all supporting code.

Keywords: IXP · BGP · Autonomous system · Inter-domain routing

1 Introduction

Internet eXchange Points (IXP) are a relevant approach to promoting the Internet development in terms of connectivity and performance. IXP facilities, located
at strategic places throughout nations, allow dozens or hundreds of Autonomous
Systems (AS) to interconnect and agree on their traffic exchange. The increased
participation of ASes at IXPs is contributing to the critical role of IXPs as tacti-
cal infrastructures in the overall Internet ecosystem [3]. The motivation of ASes
to peer at IXPs is mainly due to cost savings and performance benefits [13].
With video traffic representing 50 % (and growing) of the total Internet traffic, peering at IXPs allows a better distribution of content closer to end users
and reducing transit costs. During the 2014 Soccer World Cup[1], Brazilian IXPs

---

[1] https://labs.ripe.net/Members/emileaben/internet-traffic-during-the-world-cup-
2014.

© Springer International Publishing Switzerland 2016
T. Karagiannis and X. Dimitropoulos (Eds.): PAM 2016, LNCS 9631, pp. 333–345, 2016.
DOI: 10.1007/978-3-319-30505-9_25

Table 1. Traffic of some of the world's largest public IXPs (August 28, 2015).

IXP	Country	Members	Maximum Throughput (Gbps)			Average Throughput (Gbps)		
			Daily	Monthly	Yearly	Daily	Monthly	Yearly
(01) DE-CIX	Germany	600+	3,603.10	3,854.80	3,875.10	2,375.90	2,299.20	1,964.90
(02) AMS-IX	Netherlands	731	3,620.00	-	3,872.00	2,358.00	-	2,013.00
(03) LINX	United Kingdom	630	2,472.00	2,530.00	2,575.00	1,844.00	1,631.00	1,507.00
(04) MSK-IX	Russia	384	1,409.26	1,417.01	1,569.64	924.73	788.26	778.82
(05) NL-ix	Netherlands	527	1,080.00	-	-	871.56	-	-
(06) IX.br	Brazil	715	989.90	1,070.00	653.51	656.67	610.85	451.27
(07) HKIX	Hong Kong	225	436.43	468.12	485.18	305.02	302.84	245.51
(08) SIX	USA, Canada	200	398.68	411.22	411.22	304.89	288.53	239.61
(09) JPIX	Japan	138	315.54	-	-	200.00	-	-
(10) JINX	South Africa	24	15.90	20.80	11.10	8.60	8.30	6.00

(01) http://www.de-cix.net/about/statistics/   (02) https://ams-ix.net/technical/statistics
(03) https://www.linx.net/pubtools/trafficstats.html   (04) http://www.msk-ix.ru/network/traffic.html
(05) https://www.nl-ix.net/network/traffic/   (06) http://ix.br/cgi-bin/all
(07) http://www.hkix.net/hkix/stat/aggt/hkix-aggregate.html   (08) http://www.seattleix.net/agg.htm
(09) http://www.jpix.ad.jp/en/technical/traffic.html   (10) http://stats.jinx.net.za/showtotal.php

played a critical role in delivering the traffic and are expected to be again an important infrastructural piece during the 2016 Olympic Games.

The nature and services of an IXP largely depend on its business and operational model, i.e., the entity owning/operating an IXP may have different vision, incentives, regulatory and commercial considerations. Following the approximate classification of [3], we can distinguish "for-profit" and "non-profit" IXPs, which can be further divided into "cooperative" and "managed" non-profit IXPs (e.g., DE-CIX, AMS-IX, LINX). The latter, mainly found in Europe, are considered among the most vibrant and innovative IXPs [3]. In the US, the predominant business model of IXPs is private, for profit.

The case of Brazil, which leads Latin America by operating more than half of the IXPs in the region, follows an interesting approach that may inspire other countries, especially developing regions. Brazilian IXPs are part of an overarching project called IX.br (also known as PTTMetro) and adopt a non-profit business model managed and fully funded by NIC.br, the Brazilian Internet Steering Committee that takes care of DNS registry services, IP allocation, in addition to government-funded Internet development activities. Since 2006, Brazil has grown from 4 IXPs to the current 25 in operation –with 16 new locations under evaluation[2], especially in the north, west and central regions where there is a concerning deficit of rich Internet connectivity compared to the south, southeast, and northeast. The IX.br expansion plan aims at attracting ISPs (access providers) to those isolated areas with poor connectivity by offering IXP incentives (fee free usage). As shown in Table 1, IX.br is among the world's top ten IXPs in terms of traffic. PTT-SP (in Sao Paulo) alone is among the top five largest in terms of number of members (700+)[3].

In this paper, we present the first empirical analysis of the Brazilian IXP ecosystem and bring out an extensive data collection and analysis work considering all public IXPs operating in Brazil. After classifying all AS participants,

---

[2] According to NIC.br, there are currently 45 candidates interested in hosting the new IXPs. Interested entities, be it commercial or not, are only requested to operate neutrally and free of fees to IXP participants.

[3] http://ix.br/particip/sp.

we generate AS-level connectivity graphs (per IXP and nation-wide) to sustain the analytic studies on the observed topologies, shedding light on the peering density, advertised routes (AS-PATH), average vertices' degree, path depth, and traffic engineering practices based on AS-Prepend.

Another contribution is proposing *peering affinity* as a metric to evaluate the peering density between different types of ASes. Our publicly available[4] dataset –currently the largest one in the context of the Latin America IXPs– has more than 15 GB of data and the information from all 25 Brazilian public IXPs, including the member classification, IPv4/v6 BGP tables, supporting spreadsheets, connectivity matrices, as well as all coding and supporting tools (e.g. scripts, gnuplot, Neo4j, NetworkX) we use.

2   Methodology: Data In, Knowledge Out

Our workflow to gather data and generate outputs (knowledge) is as follows. The first step is to access every Brazilian IXP via telnet to its publicly accessible LG (`lg.<code>.ptt.br`) that mirrors the route server. Once connected by telnet at each IXP LG, the second step is to query BGP to collect the following data: (*i*) BGP tables (both IPv4 and IPv6), (*ii*) list of BGP AS-PATH, and (*iii*) community codes. The raw dataset with the output of these BGP queries is first stored locally as simple text files (step 3), and then parsed/pre-processed (step 4). Finally, the datasets go through a set of analytic functions (steps 5 and 6) implemented with two different graph-oriented tools. The manual and time-consuming task described in steps 1, 2 and 3 were automated through the developed framework consisting of a set of scripts to automatically access every Brazilian IXP by telnet and save the outputs from the different BGP queries in the corresponding text files.

Our analytic framework uses two different tools for the job of generating and dissecting the AS-level graphs based on the input BGP data: (1) NetworkX[5] software for complex networks, and (2) Neo4j[6] graph-oriented database. As inputs to both tools we used the adjacency matrices generated from the files extracted from each IXP LG. We generated an AS-level connectivity graph for each IXP and a nation-wide graph based on interconnecting all IXPs through their common AS members. In all graphs, nodes (vertices) are ASes as observed in the BGP AS-PATH attribute and edges represent the BGP connectivity.

3   Analyses and Discussion of the Results

Due to space limitations, we focus our analysis mainly on the nation-wide graph (column called "Brazil") and four representative IXPs: (*i*) small IXP (PTT-DF) located in the capital Brasilia, (*ii*) medium (PTT-MG), (*iii*) medium-to-large

---

[4] https://github.com/intrig-unicamp/ixp-ptt-br.

[5] https://networkx.github.io/.

[6] http://neo4j.com/.

Table 2. Profile of ASes at Brazilian IXPs as of March 25, 2015. The Brazil column includes absolute numbers whereas individual IXPs reflect only percentiles.

Classification	Brazil (a)		DF	MG	RJ	RS	SP
1. Internet provider	743	(65.1 % ± 20 %)	37.5 %	55.9 %	51.9 %	68.0 %	73.1 %
1.1 Transit provider	98	(8.6 % ± 09 %)	20.8 %	14.7 %	19.2 %	5.0 %	5.6 %
1.2 Access provider	645	(56.5 % ± 21 %)	16.7 %	41.2 %	32.7 %	63.0 %	67.5 %
2. Services provider	115	(10.1 % ± 07 %)	8.3 %	8.8 %	17.3 %	5.0 %	12.5 %
2.1 Content provider	37	(3.2 % ± 06 %)	0.0 %	2.9 %	5.8 %	3.0 %	4.7 %
2.2 Hosting provider	78	(6.8 % ± 05 %)	8.3 %	5.9 %	11.5 %	2.0 %	7.8 %
3. Public organization	140	(12.3 % ± 21 %)	37.5 %	20.6 %	15.4 %	11.0 %	4.4 %
3.1 Public university	20	(1.8 % ± 19 %)	0.0 %	0.0 %	0.0 %	2.0 %	1.1 %
3.2 Government	100	(8.8 % ± 13 %)	33.3 %	17.6 %	13.5 %	8.0 %	2.2 %
3.3 Other	20	(1.8 % ± 03 %)	4.2 %	2.9 %	1.9 %	1.0 %	1.1 %
4. Private organization	144	(12.6 % ± 09 %)	16.7 %	14.7 %	15.4 %	16.0 %	10.0 %
4.1 Private university	8	(0.7 % ± 03 %)	0.0 %	2.9 %	0.0 %	4.0 %	0.0 %
4.2 Private company	119	(10.4 % ± 09 %)	16.7 %	8.8 %	15.4 %	10.0 %	8.9 %
4.3 Other	17	(1.5 % ± 09 %)	0.0 %	2.9 %	0.0 %	2.0 %	1.1 %

(a) Average of ALL 25 Brazilian IXPs.

(PTT-RJ), and (*iv*) large (PTT-RS). However, raw data and results for every IXP are available in the public repository.

One noteworthy observation is the validity of the results of two IXPs, namely PTT-SP and PTT-PR. BGP data collected from both IXP LGs revealed that filters are being applied to the exported routing tables, a fact confirmed by IX.br representatives due to performance and scalability issues of the LG servers in operation. For this reason, most of the analyses do not include these IXPs.

3.1 Members Classification: Who Is Who?

A first effort to organize our dissection was manually classifying all 1,142 ASes at IX.br. Actually there are 715 unique members registered at IX.br, but there are 1,142 ASes considering the overlap of members peered at multiple IXPs[7]. Our "ground truth" attempt to classify the type of ASes present at IXPs is relevant for an accurate view on the current profile of the members interested in peering in every region of Brazil. The classification task was executed following a manual approach by members of our research group and included individual cross-validation actions. In addition to *whois* services of both NIC.br (Brazil) and LACNIC (Latin America), content from the AS Web sites was used to sort each AS into the categories presented in Table 2. Again, the complete dataset with the individual classification of all ASes can be found in our public repository.

The tables ahead include a column called "Brazil" with the average and confidence intervals of the results considering all IX.br IXPs. The high values of

---

[7] Although IX.br is a national project, we highlight that a member peered at one IXP of IX.br is not connected to the members of other IXPs.

the Brazil-wide standard deviation confirm the heterogeneity of IXPs, as their sizes end up being a relevant factor for many of the observed metrics.

Access Providers Dominate. Looking at the AS type profiling in Table 2, despite some variations in the percentile values, we observe that the majority of IXPs members are access providers of local coverage. This is an expected result given the economic incentives of access providers to exchange the maximum amount of traffic as possible through multilateral agreements at IXPs, thereby reducing the transit costs of upstream links. The increasing presence of smaller access providers at IXPs has a positive impact on the prices ISPs apply to their downstream customers, contributing to a scenario of local competition between multiple access providers. Like in most developing countries, the average quality of Internet connectivity in Brazil is still low compared to developed nations. The public IXP initiative is contributing to revert this situation by keeping traffic regionalized and reducing the distance between endpoints, and may be more importantly providing an incentive-rich environment for innovation and healthy IP connectivity market practices. These seem to be the factor behind ISPs, mostly access providers, extending their reach to include locations with poor connectivity options. Without the cost-attractive infrastructure of the IXPs, access providers would need to rely on transit providers, resulting in higher costs and fewer competition in the access provider arena –arguably the most interested type of AS in open peering.

In the Capital Things are Different. The only exception to the dominance of access providers happens at PTT-DF IXP where the presence of government and public organizations is high, a regional particularity at the federal capital of Brazil. Among the PTT-DF members we can highlight the Federal Senate, Federal Police, Serpro, Dataprev, Telebras, and others.

Few but Heavy Content Providers. A relative low participation of content providers was observed at IXPs of different Brazilian regions, such as newspapers, magazines, radio and television stations, etc. The majority of content providers are companies that operate Content Delivery Networks (CDN) responsible for a large fraction of the traffic. This result highlights the fact that few Brazilian content providers are exploring the benefits of IXP peering due to cost savings and reduced hop distance to eyeball ISPs. We recognize as a plausible reason the common practice of content providers relying on CDN providers to deliver their content closer to the users of a wider geographical span (including internationally), as opposed to IXPs that bring more localized benefits.

Low Presence of Private Companies. This fact can be explained by the main motivation of private companies to increase their redundancy through multihomed connections with larger ASes (telcos). These telcos can reach the whole Internet in contrast to IXPs with more restricted reachability towards their local region. While the amount of private companies at IXPs is low, the observed peering density (amount of open peering with all types of ASes) is relatively high, according to the results to be presented in Sect. 3.2.

Majority Incentives Lead to the Predominance of Open Peering. Based on the IX.br records, currently, 97.72 % of ASes opt for open peering through multilateral agreement –a high fraction in harmony with the spirit and efforts on public, open policies conducted by NIC.br. Only 2.28 %, mainly transit providers, choose private peering based on bilateral agreements, once large telcos sell transit to local access providers and hence lack economic incentives to openly exchange traffic except with ASes of similar size and nature. Small, regional ISPs are mostly customers that already buy transit somewhere else, recalling that one requirement of IX.br free usage of their IXPs is that ASes are not allowed to rely on the IXP connectivity as the only Internet access. Despite 97.72 % of members opted for multilateral peering in IX.br official records, this high percentage reflects just a contractual term. In practice this does not mean that an AS will effectively exchange traffic with all other members of an IXP, which explains the low peering density we found in our analyses. Considering the experiences from more mature IXPs in Europe, we may conjecture that the current high fraction of open peering is due to IX.br ASes still being in a "learning" phase seeking peering relationships with a very open approach.

Low AS Presence at Multiple IXPs. The broad majority (83.68 %) of ASes (759 of 907) are peered to only one IXP. This result can be expected because ASes choose to peer at IXPs mostly to benefit only from local traffic, so they are commonly multi-homed through at least one transit or access ISP to reach the entire Internet. The set of ASes peering at more than one IXP is mostly composed of access providers that sell services in more than one region. Again, the access providers motivation in exploiting open peering as much as possible is clear: cost savings by avoiding transit links sold by big telecommunication operators. Large ASes can be identified by their simultaneously peering practices in over half of all IXPs (14 to 23) and are predominantly two big telecom operators that we consider transit providers in the national landscape, namely NET and GVT, in addition to public organizations managing the DNS root servers (ICANN), a national Internet performance measurement service (NIC.br), and RNP.

Table 3. Peering density at IX.br (Brazil) and European more mature IXPs.

Description	Brazil (a)	DF	MG	RJ	RS	DE-CIX	MSK-IX
Peering links	126	57	79	271	1,952	-	-
Density (%)	44.2 % ± 23 %	20.7 %	34.2 %	21.3 %	63.4 %	79 %	95 %

(a) Average of 23 Brazilian IXPs without filters, that is, excluding PTT-PR and PTT-SP.

3.2   Peering Density: How Much Peering?

We consider density of peering as the ratio between the quantity of active BGP connections (peering links) of the n ASes at an IXP and the sum of all possible peers ($n*(n-1)/2$). The observed peering density (Table 3) shows wide dispersion in different regions and peering density below 50 % points to the potential to expand direct traffic exchange between current IXP members.

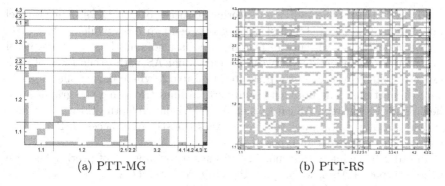

(a) PTT-MG   (b) PTT-RS

Fig. 1. Peering Matrices indicating the level of connectivity between ASes sorted by category: (a) PTT-MG is a medium size IXP and (b) PTT-RS is a large size IXP.

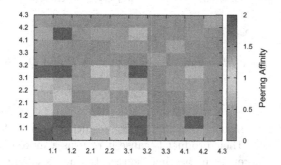

Fig. 2. Peering Affinity (PA): matrix of all Brazilian IXPs, where the amount of peering follows a color scale and both axes are grouped in a symmetrical fashion by AS type.

We find lower values of peering density in IX.br compared to those presented in previous works regarding other more mature ecosystem of IXPs, such as AMS-IX, DE-CIX, LINX and MSK-IX. While the average percentage of peering density in IX.br is around 40 %, more mature IXPs exhibit an average peering density between 79–95 % [6]. This study confirms our observation that there is a relevant empty space for peering between ASes exchanging traffic at IX.br. One possible explanation to the lower peering density is that IX.br is still young compared to more mature IXPs such as the above-mentioned European IXPs. While IX.br started its first IXP (PTT-SP) in 2004, the peering initiative in Europe started in the early 90 s –the oldest IXP of IX.br has only half the lifetime of the largest European IXPs. Another fact could be the relatively limited market that national ASes get through IX.br given that the traffic patterns in Brazil show strong international components.

Who Peers with Whom? Tell me Your AS Type... To analyze the inter-AS connectivity, we generated a peering matrix for every IXP in the spirit of an adjacency matrix, where x and y axis contain all IXP members (ASes) in a symmetrical fashion. We also considered a unified matrix with all the IXPs to provide a wider view on the nature of peering in the national landscape, i.e., integrating all individual IXPs.

Figure 1 depicts the individual peering matrices of two IXPs. A gray pixel (bit 1) indicates the existence of peering between two ASes while a white pixel (bit 0) indicates the absence of peering. The last column illustrates a scale of the amount of connections between an individual AS with other ASes of each respective category previously presented in Table 2, where darker shades mean more connections. The horizontal and vertical lines traversing the graphics are the boundaries between AS categories. We can visually identify through the long vertical and horizontal lines that some ASes (mostly from access ISP 1.2 cat.) tend to peer more with all types of ASes.

In order to quantify (and not just visualize) the amount of peering between different types of ASes, we propose **Peering Affinity (PA)** as a cross-AS-type peering metric defined as follows. Let P and Q be sets of ASes such that each set represents a single profile, including the case in which both sets are the same. Let $c(AS_i, AS_j)$, such that $AS_i \in P$ and $AS_j \in Q$, be the *connection function*:

$$c(AS_i, AS_j) = \begin{cases} 1 & \text{if } AS_i \text{ and } A_j \text{ are peers} \\ 0 & \text{otherwise} \end{cases}$$

Then, the *peering affinity* function in respect to P and Q, $\mathbb{PA}(P, Q)$, is:

$$\mathbb{PA}(P, Q) = \frac{\sum_{AS_i \in P} \sum_{AS_j \in Q} c(AS_i, AS_j)}{|P| + |Q|}$$

We opt to divide by the sum of vertices resulting in a scale from 0 to 2 instead of dividing by their product because it returns a more convenient scale to highlight the differences in peering degree. Taking as example the peering affinity between members of categories 1.2 (Access Providers) and 2.1 (Content Providers), the amount of connections between all peered ASes of categories 1.2 and 2.1 totals 98, divided by the number of vertices of both categories (236), returns 0.42 as the cross-AS-type peering affinity metric.

Figure 2 presents the result of the nation-wide analysis regarding peering affinity with the color scale being a function of the ratio between the sum of connections (peering between ASes) and the number of vertices of both crossed categories. We can observe a relatively high density of peering between ISPs, either transit or access providers. We also observe high density between public organizations, more specifically from the government. The availability of PTT-DF in the federal capital is certainly an enabler to the increased connectivity between many government agencies.

To the best of our knowledge, our peering density analysis is the first one that considers a set of peering matrices where ASes are grouped together by their type. When crossing the peering matrices in Fig. 1 with the numbers of Table 3, we find coherent results that reinforce our methodology.

3.3   Vertice Degree: How Many Peers?

We now turn our attention to the vertices' degree (both distribution and average values) in each IXP graph. By doing so, we aim at revealing and understanding the behavior of the ASes in terms of the amount of neighboring peers.

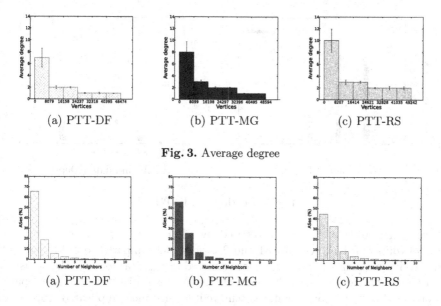

(a) PTT-DF   (b) PTT-MG   (c) PTT-RS

Fig. 3. Average degree

(a) PTT-DF   (b) PTT-MG   (c) PTT-RS

Fig. 4. Degree distribution

Figures 3 and 4 show the vertices' degree of the following IXPs graphs: PTT-DF (small size), PTT-MG (medium size), and PTT-RS (large size). Figure 4 plots the degree distribution for all ASes. Since the amount of vertices is large and diverse on an individual AS granularity, Fig. 3 sorts ASN in the x axis in a growing fashion and presents the average degree for a group of ASes in bins of 8,000 ASN along the 95% confidence interval. In sought of connectivity patterns, we discovered that nodes with higher degrees tend to correspond to older ASes based on the incremental assignment of AS numbers (ASN). This approach suggests that ASes registered for longer time (smaller ASN) exhibit higher connectivity, a coherent result considering that vertices with higher degrees commonly correspond to telecommunications operators with more adjacencies because of the nature of their transit business and their longer time in operation.

3.4 Depth/Diameter: How Far Are You?

As advertised prefixes traverse BGP domains, ASNs are added to the list of ASes (AS-PATH) to avoid routing loops. By counting the ASN that exist on every AS-PATH announce we can quantify the amount of AS-level hops to reach an advertised prefix from every IXP.

Figure 5(a) shows the observed depth from routes advertised by IXPs members based on the AS-PATH attribute. Depth values equal to 1 mean the AS-PATH is composed of only one AS, i.e., ASes directly connected to IXPs and advertising their own prefixes. The remaining routes –with depth higher than 1– correspond to those learned by IXP members from other ASes, which means

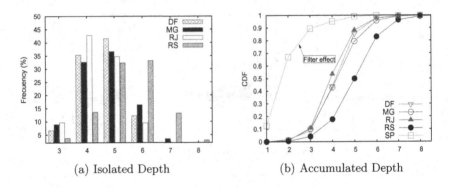

(a) Isolated Depth   (b) Accumulated Depth

Fig. 5. Depth of AS-PATH

these routes are not directly advertised by adjacent IXP members. The fraction of routes of depth equal to 1 and 2 is very low compared to the remaining route advertisements and are therefore omitted in Fig. 5(a) for the sake of visual clarity. To provide an accurate view on the AS-level distances (i.e., real path depth), redundant information was removed, for instance, duplicated ASNs due to AS-Prepend practices (further discussed in Sect. 3.5) were filtered.

By observing all IXPs together, we found that average depth of all routes advertised at IXPs varies between 4 and 6, with the higher concentration of routes being of depth equal to 5. We can conclude that 8 is the highest meaningful depth, that is, the most distant sources of AS announcements reaching IXPs are 8 AS hops far away, recalling that each hop means an entire AS –not a single router as `traceroute` would reveal. Prior studies regarding the Internet topology found an almost constant path length of 4 hops [4], while in our analysis we found an average diameter of 4–6 (majority equals to 5). Regarding this difference we recall that many routes have to leave the country toward international content, as already observed to happens in Africa [8].

As mentioned earlier, the results of PTT-SP and PTT-PR shall be carefully considered due to filtering practices. We include PTT-SP in Fig. 5(b) precisely to illustrate the effect of route filtering and how the resulting *out of the curve* observations may compromise this kind of Internet measurement research.

3.5   Traffic Engineering with AS-Prepend

The default behavior of BGP is preferring shorter routes, i.e., prefixes advertised with less ASNs in the AS-PATH attribute. A common "traffic engineering" practice referred to as AS-Prepend consists of ASes adding their own ASN multiple times to turn the resulting AS-PATH attribute less attractive (larger depth) regarding the reachability to a given prefix [2]. AS-Prepend is regarded as a BGP "knob" for inbound traffic engineering, often criticized and even considered harmful because it may compromise the integrity of routing information[8].

---

[8] https://www.ripe.net/ripe/meetings/regional-meetings/manama-2006/BGPBCP. pdf.

Table 4. Statistics on AS-prepend viewed through IXPs.

Metric description	Brazil (a)	DF	MG	RJ	RS
Routes	832,989	559,159	434,264	1,150,905	1,947,453
Routes with AS-Prepend	295,909	127,184	245,129	294,663	1,710,070
AS-Prepend X Routes (%)	30.8 % ± 22 %	22.7 %	56.4 %	25.6 %	87.8 %
ASes at Graph	43,333	47,176	46,939	47,632	48,351
ASes with AS-Prepend	7,305	6,206	8,629	8,890	10,803
AS-Prepend X ASes (%)	16.1 % ± 04 %	13.2 %	18.4 %	18.7 %	22.3 %
Members Advertising	18	24	22	51	79
Members Advertising with AS-Prepend	6	7	6	19	36
AS-Prepend X Members (%)	22.5 % ± 19 %	29.2 %	27.3 %	37.3 %	45.6 %

(a) Average of 23 Brazilian IXPs without filters, that is, excluding PTT-PR and PTT-SP.

The results of Table 4 show that AS-Prepend also is commonly used at IXPs as it is used in Internet. Note that while the second set of rows in the table refers to all ASes (be them IXP members or not) observed from IXPs' graphs, the last set of rows reflects only prepend practices from IXP members. We observe a larger amount of AS-Prepend practices per AS at IXPs, a fact pointing to the traffic engineering needs of IXP peering links.

When looking at the numbers in Table 4 it is worth to recall the difference between two distinct concepts present in BGP tables: (i) number of routes, and (ii) number of prefixes. While the full BGP table currently features around 512,000 prefixes, it is usual to find at IXPs BGP tables with millions of entries due to the advertisement of multiple routes towards the same prefix.

4 Related Work

Many efforts have been devoted towards a better understanding of the complex Internet ecosystem and IXPs have become attractive research targets because they represent a relevant microcosm of Internet diversity [1,5,9–12,14].

Closest to our work is a recent study characterizing the nature of Internet connectivity in Africa [7], specifically focused on JINX (Johannesburg) and KIXP (Nairobi), two major IXPs in Africa. The authors measured the presence of local ISPs in various African IXPs and which of them chose to interconnect at these exchanges. An interesting result was finding that 66.8 % of the paths between residential users and Google leave the continent, mainly because local ISPs are not present at these IXPs or because they are not peered between each other. The individual peering matrices for JINX and KIXP inspired our peering density analysis (Sect. 3.2), which lead to our proposed peering affinity metric based on a peering matrix grouped by AS types applied to individual IXPs and to the national-wide public IXP ecosystem.

5   Conclusion and Future Work

This paper presents the first effort to comprehend the peering ecosystem of the largest set of public IXPs in a single country, which happens to be in Brazil. We developed a analytics framework that allows scalable in-depth analyses of all Brazilian IXPs BGP data. Our studies move beyond traditional sets of individual peering matrices to include a single national-wide AS graph. Sorting ASes by their category, we propose a novel metric called *peering affinity* to quantify the amount of peering between different types of ASes.

Equally important to the analysis effort presented in this paper is to recognize some limitations of research work when building AS-level topologies [9]. It is important to highlight that information collected from public servers do not represent the totality of traffic exchange, but only a fraction of everything that can be publicly observed, specifically the multilateral peering at IXPs.

Our ongoing extensions of this work include a temporal analysis based on datasets over a longer period (different snapshots) that will allow a deeper understanding of the dynamic aspects and evolution of the IX.br ecosystem.

Acknowledgements. This work was supported by the Innovation Center of Ericsson, Brazil. The authors would like to thank Antonio Moreiras (NIC.br) and Antonio Galvao Filho (IX.br) for their help in accessing all LGs. We also thank Giovanni Comarela and Steve Uhlig for their insightful comments on earlier versions of the paper.

References

1. Ager, B., Chatzis, N., Feldmann, A., Sarrar, N., Uhlig, S., Willinger, W.: Anatomy of a large european IXP. In: sIGCOMM 2012, Helsinki, Filand, 13–17 August 2012
2. Caesar, M., Rexford, J.: BGP routing policies in ISP networks. IEEE Netw. **19**(6), 5–11 (2005). ISSN 0890–8044
3. Chatzis, N., Smaragdakis, G., Feldmann, A., Willinger, W.: On the importance of internet eXchange points for today's internet ecosystem. In: ACM SIGCOMM Computer Communications Review (CCR) (2013)
4. Dhamdhere, A., Dovrolis, C.: Ten years in the evolution of the internet ecosystem. In: iMC 2008, Vouliagmeni, Greece, 20–22 October 2008
5. Durairajan, R., Sommers, J., Barford, P.: Layer1-informed internet topology measurement. In: iMC 2014, Vancouver, BC, Canada, 05–07 November 2014
6. Giotsas, V., Zhou, S., Luckie, M., Claffy, K.: Inferring multilateral peering. In: coNEXT 2013, Santa Barbara, California, USA, 9–12 December 2013
7. Gupta, A., Calder, M., Feamster, N., Chetty, M., Calandro, E., Katz-Bassett, E.: Peering at the internet's frontier: a first look at ISP interconnectivity in africa. In: Faloutsos, M., Kuzmanovic, A. (eds.) PAM 2014. LNCS, vol. 8362, pp. 204–213. Springer, Heidelberg (2014)
8. Gupta, A., et al.: SDX - a software defined internet exchange. In: sIGCOMM 2014, Chicago, USA (2014)
9. Haddadi, H., Bonaventure, O.: Recent advances in networking. In: ACM SIGCOMM eBook Chapter 1: Internet Topology Research Redux, Vol. 1, August 2013

10. Khan, A., et al.: AS-level topology collection through looking glass servers. In: iMC 2013, Barcelona, Spain, 23–25 October 2013
11. Lodhi, A., Larson, N., Dhamdhere, A., Dovrolis, C., Claffy, K.: Using peeringDB to understand the peering ecosystem. In: ACM SIGCOMM CCR, April 2014
12. Luckie, M., et al.: AS relationships, customer cones, and validation. In: iMC 2013, Barcelona, Spain, 23–25 October 2013
13. Norton, W.B.: The Internet Peering Playbook: Connecting to the Core of the Internet. drPeering Press, USA (2014)
14. Richter, P., Smaragdakis, G., Feldmann, A., Chatzis, N., Boettger, J., Willinger, W.: Peering at peerings: on the role of IXP route servers. In: iMC 2014, Vancouver, BC, Canada, 05–07 November 2014

traIXroute: Detecting IXPs in traceroute paths

George Nomikos[✉] and Xenofontas Dimitropoulos

Foundation of Research and Technology Hellas (FORTH), Heraklion, Greece
{gnomikos,fontas}@ics.forth.gr

Abstract. Internet eXchange Points (IXP) are critical components of the Internet infrastructure that affect its performance, evolution, security and economics. In this work, we introduce techniques to augment the well-known traceroute tool with the capability of identifying if and where exactly IXPs are crossed in end-to-end paths. Knowing this information can help end-users have more transparency over how their traffic flows in the Internet. Our tool, called traIXroute, exploits data from the PeeringDB (PDB) and the Packet Clearing House (PCH) about IXP IP addresses of BGP routers, IXP members, and IXP prefixes. We show that the used data are both rich, i.e., we find 12,716 IP addresses of BGP routers in 460 IXPs, and mostly accurate, i.e., our validation shows 92–93 % accuracy. In addition, 78.2 % of the detected IXPs in our data are based on multiple diverse evidence and therefore help have higher confidence on the detected IXPs than when relying solely on IXP prefixes. To demonstrate the utility of our tool, we use it to show that one out of five paths in our data cross an IXP and that paths do not normally cross more than a single IXP, as it is expected based on the valley-free model about Internet policies. Furthermore, although the top IXPs both in terms of paths and members are located in Europe, US IXPs attract many more paths than their number of members indicates.

1 Introduction

A few hundred IXPs worldwide host more than one hundred thousand interconnections between Autonomous Systems (ASes) [10,14,20]. As critical components of the Internet infrastructure, IXPs influence its expansion [16], performance [11], and security [7]. However, their centralized nature is also a limitation that can be exploited for mass surveillance of Internet users or for targeted attacks. Although IXPs exist since the early days of the Internet, they have recently attracted intense interest from the academic community in part because the last decade the Internet topology is flattening [16,18,21,23], which implies an even more central role for IXPs.

In this work we extend the well-known and widely-used traceroute tool with the capability of inferring if and where an IXP was crossed. This is useful not only for end-users in having more transparency over where their traffic goes, but also for operators in troubleshooting end-to-end paths and for researchers

T. Karagiannis and X. Dimitropoulos (Eds.): PAM 2016, LNCS 9631, pp. 346–358, 2016.
DOI: 10.1007/978-3-319-30505-9_26

in understanding the evolving IXP ecosystem. Our tool, called traIXroute, detects IXPs based on data from the PeeringDB (PDB) and the Packet Clearing House (PCH). In particular, it uses the (i) exact IP addresses of BGP routers connected to IXP subnets; (ii) IXP member ASes; (iii) IXP prefixes; and (iv) IP addresses to AS mappings; and combines multiple information to detect IXPs with higher confidence than simply relying on IXP prefixes.

Our second contribution is that we evaluate the coverage and accuracy of the IXP router IP addresses, which we denote with a triplet $\{IP\ address \longrightarrow IXP, AS\}$, in PDB and PCH. We find in total 12,716 triplets for 460 IXPs worldwide. Using the exact router IXP addresses along with checking the IXP membership of the two adjacent ASes, we classify 78.2 % of the IXP paths. Therefore, in most cases we can detect an IXP with strong evidence. In addition, we find that 92–93 % of the triplets $\{IP\ address \longrightarrow IXP, AS\}$ extracted from PDB and PCH are consistent with the corresponding information extracted from live BGP sessions of route collectors at IXPs.

Third, to illustrate how traIXroute can be useful, in particular for researchers in Internet measurement studies, we use it to answer the following questions: (i) how often paths cross IXPs? (ii) which IXPs attract most paths? and (iii) how many IXPs are encountered per path? We apply traIXroute on 31.8 million traceroute probes collected from the ark measurement infrastructure [1]. We find that approximately one out of five paths crossed an IXP and that IXP-paths normally cross no more than a single IXP. The IXP hop is located on average near the 6th hop at the middle of the route. Finally, we show that the top IXPs in terms of paths differ in part from the top IXPs in terms of AS members.

The rest of this paper is structured as follows. In the next section, we discuss the related work and provide background into the problem of detecting IXPs in traceroute paths. Next, in Sect. 3 we describe traIXroute and its IXP detection techniques. In Sect. 4, we evaluate the coverage and accuracy of the data used by traIXroute and discuss the hit rate of its detection rules. Finally, in Sect. 5 we outline our IXP measurement study using traIXroute and in Sect. 6 we conclude.

2   Related Work and Background

Previous studies have examined the problem of mapping traceroute paths to AS-level paths [15,25]. Mapping IP addresses to ASes is not straightforward because routers can reply with source IP addresses numbered from a third-party AS. These studies ignore hops with IXP IP addresses. These addresses are used to number BGP router interfaces connected to the IXP subnet and it is hard to identify to which AS they belong.

Besides, a group of previous studies, starting with Xu *et al.* [27] and then followed by He *et al.* [22] and Augustin *et al.* [13], focus on inferring participating ASes and peerings at IXPs from *targeted* traceroute measurements. Compared to these studies, our goal is different: we build a general-purpose traceroute tool, while they aim at discovering as many peering links as possible. The basic methodology developed in [27] and then significantly extended in [13,22] detects IXPs based on assigned IP address prefixes and uses various heuristics to infer peering ASes. The seminal work of Augustin *et al.* [13] exploited also data for BGP routers at IXP, but by querying 1.1K BGP Looking Glass servers, which had significant processing cost. In contrast, we extract corresponding data from PDB and PCH, with low processing cost, and show that they are both rich and mostly accurate.

Recently, Giotsas *et al.* [19] introduced techniques to identify the physical facility where ASes interconnect using targeted traceroute measurements and a combination of publicly available facility and IXP based information.

Our starting point in this work is that **observing an IP address from an IXP prefix is not sufficient evidence to conclude that the IXP was crossed**. This happens for multiple reasons: (i) the available IXP IP address prefix data may be inaccurate; (ii) IXPs could use allocated addresses not only in the IXP subnet but also in other operational subnets; and (iii) third-party IP addresses from IXP subnets. To illustrate the latter consider the following example (cf. Fig. 1). A router connected to the IXP fabric could reply to traceroute probes using a source IP address from any of its interfaces, including the interface on the IXP subnet. Traceroute paths that do not cross the IXP, like the dotted one in Fig. 1, can include a reply with a source IP address from the IXP subnet. Therefore, the path appears to have an IP address from an IXP subnet, even if the IXP is not crossed. Our goal is to detect paths that cross the IXP fabric, like the dashed one in Fig. 1.

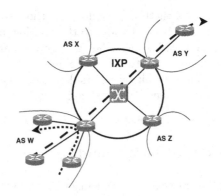

Fig. 1. Example IXP connected to four ASes. The dotted traceroute path could include a reply with an IXP IP address, even if the IXP is not crossed. Our goal is to identify paths that cross the IXP, like the dashed one.

To be more confident that an IXP is crossed, we exploit specific information about the IP addresses of BGP router interfaces connected to the IXP subnet. This data enable us also to associate IP addresses to ASes and IXPs. Furthermore, we check if the ASes before and after the IXP IP address are members of the candidate IXP based on the IXP membership data from PCH and PDB, which have not been explored in the previous studies for this purpose.

3   traIXroute Design and Heuristics

In this section, we first outline the design of traIXroute and then its IXP detection heuristics.

3.1   traIXroute Design

traIXroute is written in python and operates like traceroute. It can be configured to use either the standard traceroute tool in the background or the scamper tool [24], which implements the Paris traceroute technique [12]. It has a modular design and can be easily extended with new IXP data and detection rules. An example of the output of traIXroute is shown in Fig. 2. In this example the Vienna IX is detected between hops 5 and 6. The tool also prints the AS that corresponds to each hop based on simple origin AS lookups. traIXroute exploits three datasets to identify IXPs in traceroute paths which can be updated automatically from the command line:

1. **IXP Memberships Dataset:** We use IXP membership data from the PEERINGDB (PDB) [4] and the PACKET CLEARING HOUSE (PCH) [3]. They provide: (1) exact IP addresses of router interfaces connected to the IXP network; and (2) the ASes which these routers belong to. Therefore, this dataset provides an association from IXP IP addresses to ASes and IXPs, i.e., a triplet of the form {*IP address* ⟶ *IXP, AS*}, which we mainly exploit in our heuristics.

2. **IXP IP Address Prefixes Dataset:** We use, in addition, two datasets of IPv4 address prefixes assigned to IXPs. The first is provided by PDB, while we extract the second from PCH. These addresses are typically used to number the interfaces of the BGP routers connected to the IXP subnet. We organize the dataset in the form {*IP prefix* ⟶ *IXP*} to map IP addresses to IXPs.

```
$ traIXroute de-cix.net
traIXroute to de-cix.net (80.81.196.█), 30 hops max, 60 byte packets
 1  AS8522      139.91.68.253 (139.91.68.█)   0.564 ms  0.544 ms  0.579 ms
 2  AS8522      139.91.34.85 (139.91.34.█)   0.478 ms  0.545 ms  0.627 ms
 3  AS5408      forth-her-4-gw.eier.access-link.grnet.gr (62.217.98.█)   7.028 ms  7.037 ms  7.027 ms
 4  AS20965     grnet.mx2.ath.gr.geant.net (62.40.124.█)   7.061 ms  7.061 ms  7.049 ms
 5  AS20965     ae8.mx1.vie.at.geant.net (62.40.112.█)   37.316 ms  37.324 ms  37.312 ms
 6  Vienna IX->AS6939   10gigabitethernet1-3.core1.vie1.he.net (193.203.0.█)   43.740 ms  41.824 ms  41.898 ms
 7  AS6939      10ge1-4.core1.prg1.he.net (184.105.222.█)   50.897 ms  49.737 ms  49.754 ms
 8  AS6939      100ge8-1.core1.fra1.he.net (184.105.213.█)   79.408 ms  75.336 ms  75.328 ms
 9  AS6939      sgw2-te-0-0-2-0-v1210.fra.de-cix.net (216.66.80.█)   50.939 ms  51.273 ms  50.928 ms
10  AS51531     fw-ext-v190.fra.de-cix.net (46.31.120.█)   50.443 ms  50.322 ms  50.312 ms
11  AS51531     web1.de-cix.net (80.81.196.█)   50.767 ms  50.462 ms  50.479 ms
IXP hop detected:
1) 62.40.112.█->193.203.0.█, hop 5->6
```

Fig. 2. Example output of traIXroute.

3. **Routeviews Prefix to AS mappings Dataset:** We use IP address prefix
to AS mappings, i.e., $\{IP\ prefix \longrightarrow AS\}$, provided by CAIDA [5] based on
data from RouteViews [9], to associate IP addresses to ASes. Also, we filter
the IANA reserved IP addresses, which should not be announced to BGP,
to protect from route leaks and other misconfigurations. When encountering multi-origin-as [28] IP addresses, we check the IXP membership of all
the ASes.

PCH and PDB do not use consistent identifiers for IXPs and therefore if one
naively matched the IXP identifiers would introduce artifacts. For this reason, we
merge the two datasets by matching the IXP IP addresses, prefixes and names.
We ignore matched records that include inconsistent attributes. In addition, we
filter data for IXPs marked as inactive.

3.2   IXP Detection

Next, we describe our methodology to detect and identify at which hop we cross
an IXP in traceroute paths. When observing an IP address from an IXP subnet,
we ask what information we know, based on our data, for this and the adjacent
IP addresses. In particular, to infer an IXP crossing we follow three steps:

**(Step 1) - Does the IP Address Match an Exact BGP Router IP
Address from an IXP Subnet?** In this case, we have a specific triplet $\{IP$
$address \longrightarrow IXP, AS\}$, which gives us also additional information about the
AS of the router on the IXP. If an exact router IP address is not matched,
then we check if an IXP prefix is matched, like in previous works [13,22]. However, in this case we do not have any information about the AS that owns
the router. If an IP address in the k-th hop of a traceroute path IP_k belongs
to the interface of a router connected to the IXP subnet, then we denote this
with $IP_k \xrightarrow{inf} IXP, AS_k$, where IXP is the IXP and AS_k the AS of the router.
Otherwise, if we can associate IP_k only with an IXP IP prefix, then we denote
this with $IP_k \xrightarrow{prf} IXP$.

(Step 2) - Are the Adjacent ASes Members of the IXP? We map the IP
addresses 1-hop adjacent to the observed IXP IP address to ASes and, considering also the AS of the IXP IP address (if this information is available), we check
the IXP membership of the ASes. We distinguish four possible cases: (i) both
ASes are members, (ii)-(iii) only the AS in the left or right of the IXP IP address
is a member; and (iv) none of the ASes is an IXP member. Our assessment is
based on the available data about the ASes from triplets and from mapping IP
addresses to ASes using the Routeviews Prefix to AS mappings Dataset. Such
mappings could be wrong [25], therefore we do not consider this evidence alone
conclusive. In addition, if AS_k is a member of the IXP based on IXP membership data then we denote this with $AS_k \in IXP$.

**(Step 3) - Is the IXP Link Crossed Before or After the IXP IP
Address?** We check this when sufficient information about the ASes is available.

Table 1. IXP detection rules for a single IXP IP address, based either on IXP interface (inf) or prefix-level (prf) data, between two non-IXP addresses. The rows give the data attributes per hop to check in order to detect an IXP. Rules 1.1 to 1.3 use stronger evidence than Rules 1.4 to 1.7.

Rules	One IXP IP Address between two non-IXP IP addresses			Assessment	Hit Rate
	Hop Window				
	$@IP_k \xrightarrow{bgp} AS_k$	$@IP_{k+1}$	$@IP_{k+2} \xrightarrow{bgp} AS_{k+2}$		
	a		b		
1.1	$AS_k \in IXP$	$IP_{k+1} \xrightarrow{inf} IXP, AS_{k+1}$ $AS_{k+1} = AS_{k+2} \neq AS_k$	$AS_{k+2} \in IXP$	$a \to IXP$	65.57%
1.2	$AS_k \in IXP$	$IP_{k+1} \xrightarrow{inf} IXP, AS_{k+1}$ $AS_{k+1} \neq AS_k \neq AS_{k+2}$	$AS_{k+2} \notin IXP$	$a \to IXP$	8.79%
1.3	$AS_k \in IXP$	$IP_{k+1} \xrightarrow{inf} IXP, AS_{k+1}$ $AS_{k+1} \neq AS_k \neq AS_{k+2}$	$AS_{k+2} \in IXP$	a or $b \to IXP$	2.5%
1.4	$AS_k \in IXP$	$IP_{k+1} \xrightarrow{prf} IXP$	$AS_{k+2} \notin IXP$	$a \to IXP$	7.7%
1.5	$AS_k \notin IXP$	$IP_{k+1} \xrightarrow{prf} IXP$	$AS_{k+2} \in IXP$	$b \to IXP$	5.55%
1.6	$AS_k \notin IXP$	$IP_{k+1} \xrightarrow{inf} IXP, AS_{k+1}$ $AS_{k+1} = AS_{k+2} \neq AS_k$	$AS_{k+2} \in IXP$	$b \to IXP$	4.56%
1.7	$AS_k \notin IXP$	$IP_{k+1} \xrightarrow{inf} IXP, AS_{k+1}$ $AS_k \neq AS_{k+1} \neq AS_{k+2}$	$AS_{k+2} \notin IXP$	a or $b \to IXP$	1.21%

Table 2. IXP detection rule for two subsequent IXP IP addresses based on IXP interface (inf) data. The rows give the data attributes per hop which are checked to deduce an IXP.

Rules	Two Consecutive IXP IP Addresses		Assessment	Hit Rate
	Hop Window			
	$@IP_k$	$@IP_{k+1}$		
	a			
2.0	$IP_k \xrightarrow{inf} IXP, AS_k$	$IP_{k+1} \xrightarrow{inf} IXP, AS_{k+1}$ $AS_{k+1} \neq AS_k$	$a \to IXP$	1.36%

Our heuristics are applied on a traceroute path in a sliding window fashion, where the length of the window is three. By carefully reasoning about all possible combinations of evidence from Steps 1 and 2 that exist for three subsequent hops, we formulated 16 cases. Each case corresponds to a detection rule. For brevity, we next discuss only the cases (8 in total) that appeared with frequency higher than 1% in the matched IXP paths. The remaining cases are still supported in traIXroute. In Table 1 we show our detection rules for the most typical scenario, when we observe a single IXP IP address between two non-IXP IP addresses. We also consider the special case, shown in Table 2, when we observe two adjacent IP addresses from an IXP subnet. In most cases, we can deduce the exact link where the IXP was crossed, which we denote in Tables 1 and 2 as a or b. We split the rules into *strong* and *weak* evidence rules and order them based on their frequency, as shown in the last column of the tables (cf. Sect. 4).

Table 3. Various statistics about the PDB and PCH IXP datasets.

Statistics	PDB	PCH
# of IXPs	509	466
# of IXP address prefixes	312	343
# of IXP membership triplets	12,323	3,580
# of IXPs with membership data	448 (88 %)	343 (74 %)
% of IXPs in top-50 with membership data	100 %	62 %
# of IXPs with IP prefix data	272 (53 %)	299 (64 %)
% of IXPs in top-50 with IP prefix data	92 %	96 %

Rules 1.1 to 1.3 match the IP addresses of routers on the IXP subnet, extract information about the adjacent ASes, and find that both ASes are members of the IXP. In the Rules 1.1 and 1.2 the IXP is crossed in the first hop. The Rule 1.2 is otherwise the same with the Rule 1.1, but without information for AS_{k+2}. Finally, the Rule 1.3 is also identical otherwise, but with $AS_{k+2} \neq AS_{k+1}$. These three rules check multiple criteria and exploit data about triplets, which give also an association from IP addresses to ASes with high accuracy (cf. Sect. 4.2). We therefore consider that these rules rely on stronger evidence than the Rules 1.4 to 1.7.

The Rules 1.4 and 1.5 do not match a triplet, but only an IXP prefix. In addition, we find that one of the two adjacent ASes is a member of the IXP. Based on this evidence, we consider that an IXP may have been crossed. However, we have much weaker evidence than when Rules 1.1-1.3 hold. traIXroute marks these cases as potential IXP crossing. Similarly, the Rules 1.6 and 1.7 match an IP address from a triplet, however only one or none of the adjacent ASes is a member of the IXP. We also have weaker evidence in these detections.

Finally, the Rule 2 in Table 2 finds two consecutive IP addresses that match triplets from the same IXP. The ASes in the triplets are also found members of the IXP. We consider this also as strong evidence for IXP detection, since multiple evidence indicate so. This is a particularly interesting case, as it indicates that the IXP fabric may have been crossed twice. In other words, we observe in few cases a type of "ping pong" routing over the IXP fabric.

4   Evaluation

In this section, we evaluate and validate our methodology. We downloaded the IXP Memberships Dataset and the IXP IP Address Prefixes Dataset from PDB and PCH on January, the 10th 2015. Our Routeviews Prefix to AS mappings Dataset was downloaded from CAIDA on January, the 20th 2015.

4.1   Data Coverage and Hit Rates

PDB includes membership data for 448 (88 %) out of the 509 IXPs in the database. Similarly, PCH provides membership data for 343 (74 %) out of the 466

IXPs it includes. PDB and PCH provide membership data for 100 % and 62 %, accordingly, out of the top-50 IXPs (sorted by the number of their AS members). Besides, 312 of the IXPs in PDB and 343 of the IXPs in PCH provide IXP IP address prefixes. After merging, the combined dataset has 475 address prefixes for 417 IXPs and a total of 12,716 IXP membership triplets $\{IP\ address \longrightarrow IXP,\ AS\}$ for 460 IXPs, i.e., an increase of 38.5 % and 3.2 %, correspondingly, with respect to the largest individual dataset. These statistics along with other details are summarized in Table 3. For comparison, the April 2009 experiment reported by Augustin et al. [13] found triplets for 119 IXPs by querying 1.1 K BGP Looking Glass servers.

We then discuss the hit rate of the rules in Tables 1 and 2 in our traIXroute probes to shed more light onto the methodology. The strong evidence Rules 1.1 to 1.3 collectively account for 76.86 % of the detected IXPs, which shows that in most cases we can detect IXPs, while satisfying multiple criteria: (i) we observe an exact IP address of a BGP router on the IXP subnet; and (ii) we find that both ASes are members of the candidate IXP. Rule 1.1 is by far the most frequent as it matches 65.57 % of the detected IXPs. This indicates that the available datasets from PDB and PCH about exact IXP router addresses are rich enough to match most IXP addresses observed in traceroute measurements.

Rules 1.4 to 1.7 collectively account for 19.02 % of the matches. These rules rely on weaker evidence. The Rules 1.4 and 1.5, in particular, which rely on IXP prefixes match 13.25 % of the cases. We observe that IXP prefixes add a moderate amount of weak evidence matches compared to the IXP membership data.

Rule 2 hits in 1.36 % of the detected IXPs. This illustrates that in a few cases, the IXP fabric maybe crossed twice. This points to inefficient routing due to the BGP path selection process that relies on AS-level paths and ignores layer-2 topologies. In this case, the layer-2 IXP fabric is likely crossed back and forth, consuming resources.

Besides, we explored a number of other rules, which we do not show in Tables 1 and 2 because they matched in less than 1 % of the cases. From these rules, we confirmed (as expected) that the IXP link is almost always before the observed IXP address. This is because routers typically reply with the IP address of the inbound interface. In just 0.71 % of the cases we observed the IP address, which matched an IXP triplet, to belong to the same AS with the preceding IP address. Another interesting observation is that when an IP address matches an IXP prefix, but not an IXP triplet, then in only 2.98 % of the matches both of the

Table 4. Consistency of IXP router IP addresses in PDB and PCH with data from 87 BGP Route Collectors located at IXPs

Statistics	PDB	PCH
# of (*IXP-AS*) tuples in intersection with BGP	4,655	3,073
% of tuples (*IXP-AS*) with consistent IP addresses	93.4 %	92.1 %

adjacent ASes are members of the IXP. In contrast, the corresponding number for matched IXP triplets is 81.79 %. This supports further the point that triplets help to detect IXPs more reliably than IXP prefixes.

4.2   Data Accuracy and Validation

The data in PDB are primarily self-reported by IXP and ISP operators, while the data in PCH are based primarily on live BGP Route Collectors that PCH operates in multiple IXP sites, where it is an IXP member and peers with other ASes. The PDB data are often used by network operators for checking and configuring their routers. A recent study [26] showed that 99 % of the valid (i.e., that conform to the correct format) IP addresses reported in PDB matched the IP addresses used by BGP routers, based on a sample submitted by network operators for 256 routers. We validate further the accuracy of the used PDB and PCH IXP membership data based on BGP feeds from the Route Collectors of PCH.

We parse BGP routing table dumps downloaded on January, the 31st 2015 from 87 Route Collectors operated by PCH. Route Collectors on IXPs peer with members of the IXP to provide a live view of their routing announcements. They are therefore an excellent reference for validation because their attributes, e.g. IP addresses and AS numbers, are used in live BGP sessions. For each routing table entry, we extract the next hop IP address and the first AS in the AS path. We then compare the extracted data with the corresponding information from PDB and PCH. We find that 93.4 % of the 4,655 $\{IXP\text{-}AS\}$ tuples, which are common between PDB and BGP, have consistent IP addresses. Accordingly, 92.1 % of the 3,073 $\{IXP\text{-}AS\}$ tuples, which are common between PCH and BGP, have consistent IP addresses. This data is summarized in Table 4. This high degree of consistency shows that triplets $\{IP\ address \longrightarrow IXP,\ AS\}$ from PDB and PCH are a valid source of information for detecting IXPs in traceroute paths. The inconsistent part could result from stale or incomplete information in PDB and PCH. Triplets with stale IP addresses will not help, but will not also introduce problems in detecting IXPs with our methodology. Finally, we note that although the triplets we exploit have a reasonable level of accuracy, their completeness is hard to assess. This is a limitation for our work. However, our analysis is encouraging because we find 12,716 triplets for 460 IXPs after merging the PDB and PCH data.

Finally, as an extra validation step we cross-checked the Routeviews Prefix to AS mappings Dataset from CAIDA with the IP to ASN mapping service of Team Cymru [6] and found that the two mappings were fully consistent.

5   Use Case: IXPs in Traceroute Paths

Having evaluated and validated our approach, we next do a preliminary analysis of what we can learn about IXPs using an IXP-informed traceroute tool. We use traceroute paths collected from CAIDA's Ark measurement infrastructure [8],

Table 5. Statistics about IXPs in 27.85 million probed traceroute paths. The results are grouped into teams to show the consistency of the computed statistics across vantage points.

Statistics	Team 1	Team 2	Team 3
%Paths with IXPs	17.65 %	17.44 %	23.64 %
Avg. # of IXPs per IXP path	1.02	1	1.05
Avg. # of hops per path	14.77	14.37	14.06
Avg. IXP hop	6.68	6.35	5.40
Avg. # of ASes per path	4.48	4.17	4.33

which at the time of our experiments had 107 monitors distributed around the globe (split into three teams of similar size). The monitors rely on the scamper tool [24] configured with the Paris traceroute technique [12] to mitigate artifacts due to load balancing. We use one full cycle of measurements collected on January, the 20th 2015, which includes an ICMP-paris probe to each globally routed /24 block. Each probe is assigned to a team. We process the output of scamper with traIXroute to detect IXPs. We repeat our experiments with data from the three teams to check for the consistency of our results across different vantage points. In addition, we process the collected paths to remove probes without any reply or with loops. The number of probes after pre-processing dropped from to 31.8 million to 27.8 million probes.

In Table 5 we first report the fraction of traceroute paths which go through an IXP. The monitors are located in a mix of academic and corporate institutions [2]. We first observe that the fraction of paths that cross an IXP is 17.44 %, 17.65 % and 23.64 % in the three teams. We observe a slightly larger fraction in the 3rd team, because one of the monitors in this team is located in an IXP (AMS-IX). Despite this, our results are mostly consistent across the three teams: Approximately one out of five paths in our datasets go through an IXP. Furthermore, in paths that go through an IXP we observe 1 to 1.05 IXPs per path. This is interesting because it confirms the expectation based on the valley-free model [17] that up to one peering link, and therefore one IXP[1], is crossed in an end-to-end path. Even if BGP allows much more complex policies and the Internet IXP ecosystem evolves continuously, Internet paths in our measurements largely conform to the well-known valley-free model. Furthermore, we observe that paths cross on average between 14.06 to 14.77 hops, and the IXP hop is located near the middle, i.e., on average between hop 5.4 and 6.68 for the different teams. For completeness, we also compute the number of ASes the paths cross, which ranges between 4.17 and 4.48 ASes.

Top IXPs in Terms of Paths. We next analyze which IXPs attract most paths and how the number of paths an IXP attracts compares with the number of their member ASes. In Table 6 we show the top-10 IXPs in terms of paths,

---

[1] IXPs links are typically used for settlement-free peering relationships.

Table 6. Top IXPs sorted by the number of paths that cross them. For each IXP, we show the minimum and maximum number of paths that cross it over the three probing teams; and the number of AS members.

IXP name	Min-max # of paths over teams	# of member ASes
1. AMS-IX	277 K – 570 K	630
2. LINX	182 K – 234 K	526
3. DE-CIX Frankfurt	133 K – 215 K	520
4. Equinix Palo Alto	119 K – 134 K	116
5. Equinix Chicago	73 K – 80 K	145
6. Equinix Ashburn	43 K – 91 K	217
7. NAP of The Americas	45 K – 90 K	112
8. Equinix Los Angeles	37 K – 60 K	76
9. CoreSite - California	30 K – 58 K	195
10. Netnod Stockholm	33 K – 44 K	104

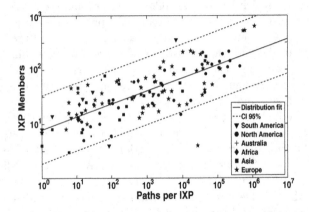

Fig. 3. Scatterplot of number of AS members vs. number of paths per IXP along with fitted line and 95 % confidence intervals (CI). IXPs are grouped by continent. The correlation is 0.8.

the min and max numbers of paths over the three teams, and number of their members. We first observe that the top-3 IXPs, namely AMS-IX, LINX, and DE-CIX, are the same both in terms of paths and members. These IXPs are located in Europe; 5 of the following IXPs are located in the US and 4 of these are run by Equinix, i.e., the largest IXP corporation in the US. Finally, one IXP in South America and one more European close the top-10. We note that in Table 6 the 570 K paths that cross the AMS-IX, is an outlier due to a single ark monitor located in AMS-IX. Despite this, the ranking does not change if we only consider the other teams of monitors.

Besides, below the top-3 IXPs we observe significant variance between the number of IXP members and the number of IXP paths. Figure 3 illustrates how the number of IXP members correlates with the number of paths. The overall correlation coefficient is 0.8. We observe that the top-3 IXPs are close to the 95-percentile confidence intervals, which means that compared to the average they have more members than paths. In contrast, many US IXPs have more paths than their number of members indicates. Notably, Equinix Palo Alto is in the 4th position with a small difference in terms of paths from DE-CIX, although the latter has 520 members and the former only 116.

6   Conclusions

Internet users, network operators, and researchers would benefit if they were able to know from which IXPs packets go through. To help towards this goal, in this paper we introduce a tool that extends the commonly used traceroute with techniques to detect IXPs. Our techniques rely on data about the exact IP addresses of BGP router interfaces connected to the IXP subnet, i.e., triplets {IP address ⟶ IXP, AS}, extracted from the PEERINGDB and the PACKET CLEARING HOUSE. This data has not been previously explored for identifying IXPs. We show that they are both rich, i.e., we find 12,716 triplets for 460 IXPs, and accurate, i.e., our validation shows 92–93 % accuracy. We also incorporate in our heuristics an IXP membership check for the adjacent ASes to have stronger evidence that an IXP was crossed. To demonstrate the utility of traIXroute, we use it to show that approximately one out of five paths cross an IXP in our data. In addition, in most cases, we observe not more than one IXP per path, which is located near the middle. Furthermore, we observe that although the top IXPs both in terms of paths and members are located in Europe, US IXPs attract many more paths than their number of members indicates. In the future, we plan to investigate how traIXroute could help Internet users to have more control over their paths.

Acknowledgements. This work has been funded by the European Research Council Grant Agreement no. 338402. We would like to thank Pavlos Sermpezis, Laurent Vanbever, Michalis Bamiedakis and the anonymous reviewers for their helpful comments.

References

1. Archipelago Measurement Infrastructure. http://www.caida.org/projects/ark/
2. CAIDA Monitors: The Archipelago Measurement Infrastructure. http://www.caida.org/data/monitors/monitor-map-ark.xml
3. Packet Clearing House - Internet Exchange Directory. https://prefix.pch.net
4. PeeringDB. http://www.peeringdb.com
5. Routeviews Prefix to AS mappings Dataset (pfx2as) for IPv4. http://www.caida.org/data/routing/routeviews-prefix2as.xml
6. Team Cymru, IP to ASN mapping. http://www.team-cymru.org/IP-ASN-mapping.html

7. The DDoS That Almost Broke The Internet. http://blog.cloudflare.com/the-ddos-that-almost-broke-the-internet

8. The IPv4 Routed /24 Topology Dataset. http://www.caida.org/data/active/ipv4_routed_24_topology_dataset.xml

9. The Route Views Project. www.routeviews.org

10. Ager, B., Chatzis, N., Feldmann, A., Sarrar, N., Uhlig, S., Willinger, W.: Anatomy of a large european ixp. In: Proceedings of ACM SIGCOMM (2012)

11. Ahmad, M.Z., Guha, R.: Studying the effect of internet exchange points on internet link delays. In: Proceedings of Spring Simulation Multiconference (2010)

12. Augustin, B., Friedman, T., Teixeira, R.: Multipath tracing with paris traceroute. In: Proceedings of IEEE End-to-End Monitoring Techniques and Services Workshop (2007)

13. Augustin, B., Krishnamurthy, B., Willinger, W.: Ixps: mapped?. In: Proceedings of ACM IMC (2009)

14. Chatzis, N., Smaragdakis, G., Feldmann, A., Willinger, W.: There is more to ixps than meets the eye. In: Proceedings of SIGCOMM CCR (2013)

15. Chen, K., Choffnes, D.R., Potharaju, R., Chen, Y., Bustamante, F.E., Pei, D., Zhao, Y.: Where the sidewalk ends: extending the internet as graph using traceroutes from p2p users. In: Proceedings of ACM SIGCOMM CoNEXT (2009)

16. Dhamdhere, A., Dovrolis, C.: The internet is flat: modeling the transition from a transit hierarchy to a peering mesh. In: Proceedings of ACM ICPS (2010)

17. Gao, L., Rexford, J.: Stable internet routing without global coordination. In: Proceeidngs of ACM SIGMETRICS (2000)

18. Gill, P., Arlitt, M., Li, Z., Mahanti, A.: The flattening internet topology: natural evolution, unsightly barnacles or contrived collapse? In: Claypool, M., Uhlig, S. (eds.) PAM 2008. LNCS, vol. 4979, pp. 1–10. Springer, Heidelberg (2008)

19. Giotsas, V., Smaragdakis, G., Huffaker, B., Luckie, M., Claffy, K.: Mapping peering interconnections to a facility. In: Proceedings of ACM SIGCOMM CoNEXT (2015)

20. Giotsas, V., Zhou, S., Luckie, M., Claffy, K.: Inferring multilateral peering. In: Proceedings of ACM SIGCOMM CoNEXT (2013)

21. Gregori, E., Improta, A., Lenzini, L., Orsini, C.: The impact of IXPs on the AS-level topology structure of the internet. Comput. Commun. 34, 68–82 (2011)

22. He, Y., Siganos, G., Faloutsos, M., Krishnamurthy, S.: Lord of the links: a framework for discovering missing links in the internet topology. IEEE/ACM ToN 17, 391–404 (2009)

23. Labovitz, C., Iekel-Johnson, S., McPherson, D., Oberheide, J., Jahanian, F.: Internet inter-domain traffic. In: ACM SIGCOMM CCR (2011)

24. Luckie, M.: Scamper: a scalable and extensible packet prober for active measurement of the internet. In: Proceedings of ACM IMC (2010)

25. Mao, Z.M., Rexford, J., Wang, J., Katz, R.H.: Towards an accurate as-level traceroute tool. In: Proceedings of ACM SIGCOMM (2003)

26. Snijders, J.: PeeringDB Accuracy: Is blind faith reasonable? NANOG 58 (2013)

27. Xu, K., Duan, Z., Zhang, Z.-L., Chandrashekar, J.: On properties of internet exchange points and their impact on AS topology and relationship. In: Mitrou, N.M., Kontovasilis, K., Rouskas, G.N., Iliadis, I., Merakos, L. (eds.) NETWORKING 2004. LNCS, vol. 3042, pp. 284–295. Springer, Heidelberg (2004)

28. Zhao, X., Pei, D., Wang, L., Massey, D., Mankin, A., Wu, S.F., Zhang, L.: An analysis of bgp multiple origin as (moas) conflicts. In: Proceedings of ACM SIGCOMM Internet Measurement Workshop (2001)

A Brief History of MPLS Usage in IPv6

Yves Vanaubel[1][✉], Pascal Mérindol[2], Jean-Jacques Pansiot[2],
and Benoit Donnet[1]

[1] Université de Liège, Liège, Belgium
yves.vanaubel@ulg.ac.be
[2] Université de Strasbourg, Strasbourg, France

Abstract. Recent researches have stated the fast deployment of IPv6.
It has been demonstrated that IPv6 grows much faster, being so more
and more adopted by both Internet service providers but also by servers
and end-hosts. In parallel, researches have been conducted to discover
and assess the usage of MPLS tunnels. Indeed, recent developments in
the ICMP protocol make certain categories of MPLS tunnels transparent
to traceroute probing. However, these studies focus only on IPv4, where
MPLS is strongly deployed.

In this paper, we provide a first look at how MPLS is used under IPv6
networks using traceroute data collected by CAIDA. At first glance,
we observe that the MPLS deployment and usage seem to greatly differ
between IPv4 and IPv6, in particular in the way MPLS label stacks are
used. While label stacks with at least two labels are marginal in IPv4 (and
mostly correspond to a VPN usage), they are prevalent in IPv6. After a
deeper analysis of the label stack typical content in IPv6, we show that
such tunnels result from the use of 6PE. This is not really surprising
since this mechanism was specifically designed to forward IPv6 traffic
using MPLS tunnels through networks that are not fully IPv6 compliant.
However, we show that it does not result from non dual-stack routers
but rather from the absence of native IPv6 MPLS signaling protocols.
Finally, we investigate a large Tier-1 network, Cogent, that stands out
with an original set-up.

Keywords: IPv6 · 6PE · Network discovery · MPLS · LDP · RSVP-
TE · Traceroute

1 Introduction

During the last years, IPv6 has drawn the attention of the research community.
For instance, Dhamdere et al. [1] showed that IPv6 is differently deployed over
the world (IPv6 is more present in Europe than in the USA), while the routing
dynamics and the path performance are largely identical between IPv4 and IPv6.
More recently, Czyz et al. [2] showed that IPv6 networks are becoming mature

B. Donnet—This work is partially funded by the European Commission funded
mPlane ICT-318627 project.

T. Karagiannis and X. Dimitropoulos (Eds.): PAM 2016, LNCS 9631, pp. 359–370, 2016.
DOI: 10.1007/978-3-319-30505-9_27

and entering now a production mode. Further, on September, 24th, 2015, the
ARIN IPv4 free pool reached zero, effectively triggering full IPv4 depletion. The
ARIN is now unable to provide any IPv4 block except for those requiring a small
block in order to ease the IPv6 transition [3]. We believe this should accelerate
the global IPv6 adoption.

In parallel to this IPv6 interest, MPLS has been more and more investigated
by the research community. For instance, Sommers et al. [4] examined the characteristics of MPLS deployments that are explicitly identified using RFC4950
extensions. Donnet et al. [5] provided algorithms for detecting MPLS tunnels
depending on the way MPLS routers react to the `ttl-propagate` and RFC4950
options. Others looked at the MPLS usage. Pathak et al. [6] quantified the additional delay caused by MPLS when used for traffic engineering (TE) reasons.
More recently, Vanaubel et al. [7] evaluated the MPLS usage in the light of transit path diversity, showing that the basic usage for scalability purpose (e.g., with
LDP) seems predominant, with or without path diversity and that TE is well
represented in a subset of specific ASes. None of those works investigated MPLS
under IPv6.

As the deployment of IPv6 is growing and the interest in MPLS is stronger,
we aim, in this paper, to investigate the state of MPLS deployment under IPv6.
In particular, we are interested in knowing how operators are using MPLS in
IPv6 and whether this usage differs from the one in IPv4. To achieve this goal,
we rely on an IPv6 `traceroute` dataset collected by CAIDA between 2009 and
2015. From this dataset, we extract tunnels [5] and show that, in parallel to
an increase in the IPv6 deployment, there is, along the time, an increase in the
MPLS usage in IPv6. This usage, as we show it latter in the paper, is essentially
oriented for 6PE purpose (i.e., either for connecting IPv6 islands together or
using LDP for IPv4 to build tunnels carrying both IPv6 and IPv4 traffic on dual
stack MPLS routers). We also investigate the particular case of Cogent, a large
Tier-1 ISP having both a very prominent position in the dataset and a very
particular behavior in regards to 6PE.

The remainder of this paper is organized as follows: Sect. 2 provides the
required background for this paper. Section 3 presents our findings. Finally,
Sect. 4 concludes this paper by summarizing its main achievements.

2   Background

2.1   MPLS Overview

The *Multiprotocol Label Switching* (MPLS) [8] was originally designed to speed
up the forwarding process. In practice, this was done with one or more 32 bits
label stack entries (LSE) inserted between the frame header (Data-link layer)
and the IP packet (Network layer). A given packet may carry out several LSEs
at the same time. In this case, the packet is said having a *stack of labels*. Each
LSE is made of four fields: a 20-bit label value used for forwarding the packet to
the next router, a 3-bit Traffic Class field for quality of service (QoS), priority,
and Explicit Congestion Notification (ECN) [9], a 1-bit bottom of stack flag

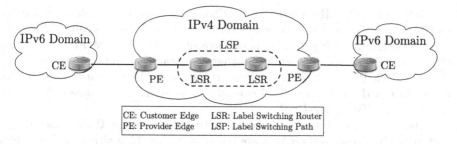

Fig. 1. 6PE usage of MPLS. PE routers are dual-stack, while LSRs are IPv4 only routers.

(when set the current label is the last in the stack [10]), and an 8-bit time-to-live (LSE-TTL) field having the same purpose as the IP-TTL field [11].

MPLS routers, called *Label Switching Routers* (LSRs), exchange labelled packets over *Label Switched Paths* (LSPs). The first MPLS router (*Ingress Label Edge Router*, or Ingress LER, i.e., the tunnel entry point) adds the label stack, while the last MPLS router (*Egress Label Edge Router*, or Egress LER, i.e., the tunnel exit point) removes the label stack. In some cases, and in particular with Cisco routers, the LSE stack may be removed by the penultimate MPLS router (*penultimate hop popping*, PHP) to reduce the MPLS overhead. The Egress LER then performs a classic IP lookup and forwards the traffic, reducing so the load on the Egress LER (especially if the Egress LER is shared among several LSPs). This means that, when using PHP, technically speaking, the MPLS tunnel exit is one hop before the Egress LER. In its most basic operation, LSPs are constructed along best effort routes using the *Label Distribution Protocol* (LDP [12]). More specific LSPs may be constructed for Traffic Engineering purposes, using an extension of the RSVP protocol, *RSVP-TE* [13]. In these two cases, the label stack contains only one LSE. A more complex usage is for Virtual Private Networks (VPN [14]), where LSPs are constructed using either LDP or RSVP-TE, and an additional LSE at the bottom of the label stack is used to specify a Virtual Routing Table at the Egress. In this case, the bottom of the stack is constant along an LSP, while the top of the stack is modified at each hop, as in the previous cases.

2.2   MPLS in IPv6

MPLS can be used in IPv6-only networks in the same way as it is used in IPv4 networks (see George and Pignataro [15] for a discussion on gaps remaining between IPv4 and IPv6). Indeed most routing protocols and label distribution protocols [16,17] have now their IPv6 version. However this has not always been the case. Moreover, providers do not activate IPv6 capabilities even when they are available in their hardware and software. Therefore, specific mechanisms have been devised to deliver IPv6 traffic across networks where there is either no IPv6 routing (IPv4 only networks) or where some mechanisms are not IPv6-aware such as LDP [12,16].

Thus, one of the MPLS usage under IPv6 is to connect IPv6 islands through an IPv4 core network that is unaware of IPv6. This mechanism is called *6PE* [18] and is illustrated in Fig. 1. This is done through the usage of *Provider Edge* (PE) routers that are dual-stack and that are located at the edge of the IPv4 domain. Each PE router receives IPv6 prefixes from the *Customer Edge* (CE) router in the IPv6 domain. IPv6 reachability is exchanged between 6PEs via multiprotocol-iBGP, MP-BGP.

When 6PE was released, the main objective was to ensure IPv6 connectivity on top of MPLS core routers that are not IPv6-aware. That situation drove the need for two labels in the data plane (due to the potential usage of PHP in particular): (*i*), the top label is the transport label, which is assigned hop-by-hop [12,13] and, (*ii*), the bottom label is a label assigned by BGP and advertised by iBGP between the PE routers. Quoting RFC4798 [18], "This label advertised by the egress 6PE Router with MP-BGP MAY be an arbitrary label value, which identifies an IPv6 routing context or outgoing interface to send the packet to, or MAY be the IPv6 Explicit Null Label". This last label has a value of 2 [10].

In that context, the PE routers that perform 6PE are the Ingress and Egress LERs. Note that today, now that global IPv6 deployment is more common, 6PE is also interesting for core LSRs with dual-stack routers and IPv6 connectivity. This is useful to build LSP for IPv6 without using an IPv6 label distribution protocol (LDP for IPv6 [16] has been finalized only recently), and/or for sharing the same LSP for IPv4 and IPv6 traffic, reducing so the control plane churn. Our analysis will show that this specific behavior is the most common in practice.

2.3   Revealing MPLS Tunnels

MPLS routers may send ICMP `time-exceeded` messages when the LSE-TTL expires (in both IPv4 and IPv6). In order to debug networks where MPLS is deployed, routers may also implement RFC4950 [19], an extension to ICMP allowing a router to embed an MPLS LSE in an ICMP `time-exceeded` message. In that case, the router simply quotes the MPLS LSE (or the LSE stack) of the received packet in the ICMP `time-exceeded` message. RFC4950 is particularly useful for operators as it allows them to verify the correctness of their MPLS tunnels and TE policy.

If the Ingress LER copies the IP-TTL value to the LSE-TTL field rather than setting the LSE-TTL to an arbitrary value such as 255, LSRs along the LSP will reveal themselves when using traceroute via ICMP messages even if they do not implement RFC4950. Operators can configure this action using the `ttl-propagate` option provided by the router manufacturer [11] (while, to the best of our knowledge, the RFC4950 is just a matter of implementation and cannot be deactivated on recent routers supporting it). These mechanisms are identical for IPv4 and IPv6.

In this paper we focus on *explicit MPLS tunnels*, i.e., tunnels that can be fully revealed via `traceroute` as they implement both TTL propagation (they are seen in traces) and RFC4950 (they are seen as LSRs providing their LSE). Note that in the case of 6PE, if the TTL of a `traceroute` packet expires inside

Table 1. Raw IPv6 statistics and deployment over 7 years of data (January, 1st of each year), where "VPs" gives the number of probing monitors, "Traces" the amount of `traceroute` performed, "prefixes" the number of probed prefixes, "ASes" the amount of different ASes in the dataset, "Addresses" the number of pure IPv6 addresses, IPv4-mapped IPv6 addresses and addresses involved in MPLS IPv6 tunnels, and "Tunnels" provides the number of unique MPLS tunnels encountered (note that "Complete Tunnels" refer to tunnels where all LSRs responded to `traceroute` probes).

Year	Probing				Addresses			Tunnels	
	VPs	Traces	Prefixes	ASes	v6	v4 map'd v6	MPLS	Raw	Complete
2009	5	7,765	2,128	988	4,009	0	14	47	68 %
2010	8	17,472	3,550	1,363	6,331	21	48	59	52 %
2011	13	51,636	8,347	2,365	12,307	211	199	1,235	22 %
2012	21	154,791	18,589	3,918	23,225	704	680	2,783	42 %
2013	25	256,725	25,891	4,992	33,239	370	1,468	14,366	45 %
2014	29	772,461	32,391	6,224	43,309	719	2,526	49,232	77 %
2015	29	1,181,139	38,901	8,181	58,150	420	3,098	50,805	85 %

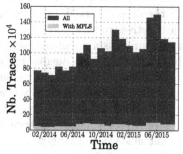

Fig. 2. Raw number of IPv6 traces traversing at least one MPLS tunnel.

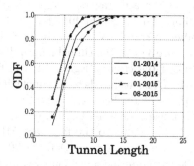

Fig. 3. IPv6 MPLS tunnels length distribution

the IPv4 core, the IPv4 router may be unable to send an ICMPv6 error message. In this case, the `traceroute` will be incomplete and the non-responding hop will be replaced by a *. If the router has no IPv6 connectivity but is IPv6-aware, it may send an ICMPv6 message, using a so-called IPv4-mapped IPv6 address [20] as source address. The error message is then propagated towards the Egress LER using MPLS, and then propagated through IPv6 routing.

3   Evaluation

3.1   Dataset

For evaluating the deployment of MPLS under IPv6, we use the IPv6 Archipe-lago dataset [21]. The data is collected by performing ICMP-based ParisTraceroute measurements [22], using scamper [23]. Each vantage point probes all announced IPv6 prefixes (/48 or shorter) once every 48 h by targeting a single random destination in each prefix. Some vantage points might, in addition, probe the first address (i.e., ::1) in a prefix.

Table 1 provides raw statistics about the IPv6 dataset. We collected the probing campaign made every January 1st since 2009. From this dataset, we extracted the various traces, explicit MPLS tunnels, and performed an IP2AS mapping using Team Cymru.[1] As already stated by others [1,2], we observe a slow deployment of IPv6 between 2009 and 2013, compensated by a fast increase between 2014 and 2015. MPLS deployment in IPv6 follows that tendency, the peak of MPLS tunnels being reached in 2014 and 2015. In the following subsection, we will focus on data collected between January, 1st 2014 and August, 1st 2015. For that period of time, we take into account the first measurement snapshot of each month, leading to 20 measurement cycles.

Figures 2 and 3 provide basic statistics about MPLS deployment in IPv6. In particular, Fig. 2 gives the raw number of traceroute (between January, 1st 2014 and August, 1st 2015) that traverses at least one MPLS tunnel. If the quantity of traces increases over time, on the contrary, the amount of traces involved in an MPLS tunnel remains quite stable. Compared to IPv4 [4,5,7], traceroute are traversing much less MPLS tunnels: on the order of 7–8% in IPv6 against (at least) 40 % for IPv4. Note that the drop observed, in terms of number of traces seen, in early 2015, is due to less active vantage points.

Figure 3 gives the tunnel length distribution for four measurement snapshots, including Ingress and Egress LER in the length distribution. This means that a length of 3 corresponds to a tunnel with a single LSR. We observe that the tunnel length oscillates between 3 and 21. More interestingly, the tunnel length seems to decrease over time, i.e., tunnels observed in 2015 are shorter than tunnels in 2014. This is due to the fact that MPLS tunnels of AS174 (Cogent) disappear from the dataset around October 2014, and Cogent made use of long tunnels.[2] While encountering a few longer tunnels, MPLS IPv6 tunnels length distribution follows observations made in IPv4 [4,5].

3.2 Label Stack Size Distribution

In this section, we study the characteristics of IPv6 MPLS tunnels compared to IPv4 ones. First, we are interested in the typical LSE size used by both data planes (i.e., the number of MPLS labels contained at each single LSR). The methodology we follow is quite simple: for each LSR of each tunnel, we count the number of labels contained in the stack and, on this basis, we map each tunnel to the maximum number of labels revealed by each of its LSRs. For short MPLS tunnels, it allows for mapping them to their most likely usage. For instance, and for IPv4 data plane, a short tunnel made of three LSRs such that we find the sequence 1,2,1 (in term of LSE sizes) we claim that such a tunnel

---

[1] http://www.team-cymru.org/.

[2] The impact of AS174 in IPv6 has already been discussed in the past [24,25].

is likely to be used for VPN purposes so that we retain the maximum value of two to map it to a 2-label LSP. Note that, in such a case, the bottom label is constant (i.e., the same from end-to-end) in order to denote the outgoing VRF (Virtual Routing and Forwarding) to use at the Egress LER.

Figure 4 shows the LSE size distribution over time, between January, 1st, 2014 and August, 1st, 2015. Globally speaking, we observe a different behavior between IPv4 (Fig. 4(a)) and IPv6 (Fig. 4(b)). Indeed, under IPv4, the majority of tunnels (around 80 %) exhibits a single LSE (this results is aligned with Sommers et al. observations [4]) while, in IPv6, the majority of tunnels (around 80 % also during the first half of the considered period) exhibits at least two labels.[3] This result may appear really surprising since there is no obvious reason that justifies a more extensive use of VPN in IPv6 than in IPv4.

Figure 5 deeper investigates the LSE typical content in IPv6. In particular, it looks at the label value at the bottom of the stack. As explained in Sect. 1, if the value is 2, it suggests a usage of 6PE where core LSRs are dual-stack capable.

Figure 5 clearly depicts a shift around October 2014. Before that date, tunnels with a label stack are observed almost as often with a bottom label 2 as with another bottom label. After October 2014, things are crystal clear: the majority of tunnels (more than 80 %) having a LSE stack use a bottom label of 2, meaning the usage of this type of 6PE is prevalent.

For tunnels with bottom label 2, we remove this bottom label, and compare the series of remaining labels with series of labels from tunnels found in IPv4 MPLS traces (in the same period).[4] We find out that a match is present in more than 40 % of the cases meaning that the same IPv4 LSP is used for IPv6 traffic reinforcing so our assumption about the 6PE usage.

The radical behavior change depicted in Fig. 5 is very surprising at the first glance. To explain it, we investigate the different ASes we encountered in the dataset around this date. Before October 2014, around 50 % of the tunnels belong to AS174 (Cogent). In November 2014, this AS disappears from the MPLS dataset while it remains visible through numerous non MPLS IPs. Almost all tunnels belonging to this Tier-1 network have a 2-label stack, but never use the bottom label 2. This is the reason why we have such a behavior modification in Fig. 5. The usage of label stack for Cogent is investigated in details in Sect. 3.3 since it is almost only specific to this AS.

Figure 6 looks at the architecture of the network core in case of dual-stack 6PE usage (i.e., bottom label 2). We observe a tiny proportion of 6PE tunnels that map IPv4 addresses into IPv6 ones (black region in Fig. 6). We understand this as a case where core LSRs are IPv6 aware (i.e., they are dual-stack) but do not have public IPv6 addresses. In order to be able to reply to probes (i.e., generating ICMP time-exceeded messages), they map their IPv4 address in a "fake" IPv6 one.

Most dual-stack 6PE tunnels we observed in the dataset have an IPv6 core (LSRs are dual-stack and have public IPv6 addresses). However, this 6PE usage

---

[3] The drop around October 2014 in IPv6 is due to the drastic decrease of MPLS usage by Cogent in the dataset. We show in details in Sect. 3.3 that Cogent has been a heavy user of LSE stacks but then got rid of MPLS.

[4] These IPv4 MPLS traces were also downloaded from the Archipelago dataset.

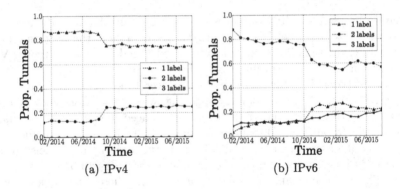

Fig. 4. LSE stack size distribution over time.

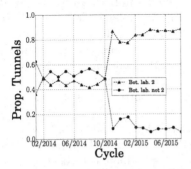

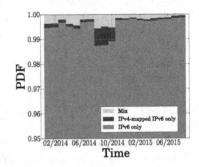

Fig. 5. Distribution of the value in the bottom stack LSE in IPv6.

Fig. 6. 6PE core architecture.

corresponds to the case where LSPs are deployed with LDPv4. That is, the same LSPv4 generally built with LDP and attached to a given IPv4 loopback destination on the Egress LER is used for both IPv4/v6 traffics. The bottom label 2 indicates to the Egress LER that the traffic is made of IPv6 packets rather than IPv4 ones (where the LSP is made of the same series of top labels without the bottom label). However, note that in practice and at the origin, 6PE has been used to ensure connectivity between IPv6 islands with a tunnel having a pure IPv4 core. In this case, LSRs are not IPv6 aware (no dual-stack and no IPv6 addresses). In such an architecture, IPv4 LSRs will not respond to IPv6 probes of `traceroute`, and the traces in our dataset are incomplete (several * appear between 6PEs). Unfortunately, we are not able to differentiate such a behavior from IPv6 nodes that simply not respond to the probes. The proportion of this type of 6PE tunnels is therefore underestimated in this paper.

3.3 The Cogent Case

The Cogent case is particularly interesting and quite intriguing. It has both a very prominent position in the dataset (Cogent is one of the largest Tier-1, in particular it has the second highest AS rank according to CAIDA[5]) and,

---

[5] See http://as-rank.caida.org/.

most of all, an MPLS IPv6 behavior completely different from other ASes we observed. This can be seen in Fig. 5 where around October 2014 Cogent more or less disappears from CAIDA MPLS traces and at the same time the proportion of stacks with bottom label 2 rises sharply.

First, the fact that MPLS traces are almost absent from Cogent after this date may either be due to a change in the configuration of its routers or, more simply, that the operator gets rid of MPLS. We conduct some tests to understand whether Cogent removes `ttl-propagate` at Ingress LERs to make MPLS tunnels invisible or not. This type of phenomenon has already been observed for IPv4 MPLS (look at Vanaubel et al. [7] and the specific study on Level3). For this purpose, we pick a subset of MPLS traces obtained before October 2014 and try to find similar pure IP traces after this date (i.e., we check whether the same sequence of IP addresses between Ingress and Egress LER exists before and after that date or if the two edge routers seem directly connected after). As a result, we find equivalent traces before and after, the only difference being that MPLS labels disappear after October 2014. We can conclude that Cogent just gets rid of MPLS (as they did in IPv4 two years before). To verify this conclusion, we contacted a Cogent network administrator who confirmed this first result.

The second, and most interesting fact is that, although most of its LSPs have a stack size greater or equal than 2, they never use a bottom label of 2 (the default value for 6PE), on the contrary to the dominant usage in other ASes (see Sect. 3.2). Note that RFC4798 [18] does not mandate the use of label 2 as bottom label but that BGP at the Egress router associates a label to each IPv6 prefix and announces it to its iBGP peers. Therefore, a 6PE implementation could choose any other arbitrary label for 6PE, or choose a different label for each prefix or set of prefixes.

After the analysis of Cogent stacks, it appears that the bottom label is not fixed (Cogent does not simply use another arbitrary value than 2) but varies greatly. In fact numerous different bottom labels can be found on LSPs connecting the same (Ingress, Egress) pair. For instance, we find one case where 38 distinct bottom labels are in use for a given pair. In theory, this could be 38 distinct VPNs or, more probably, the Egress could be using a distinct bottom label for each (group of) IPv6 prefix. Hopefully, our Cogent contact helped us to eliminate the VPN case (indeed, considering only the measurements perspective, nothing distinguishes VPN from 6PE, the general principle of using a bottom label being the same): Cogent simply did not use this technology but only 6PE before shutting down MPLS for IPv6 in October 2014.

One purpose of distinct bottom labels may be load sharing: in a network using Equal Cost Multipath (ECMP), packets arriving at a router with two equal cost routes for the destination are distributed along these routes according to a packet header hash. In a network using MPLS and ECMP, LSPs constructed by LDP signaling may make use of multiple paths, building several LSPs between the same pair of LSRs. In the case of Cogent, it is apparent that ECMP is in use in the core network. For example in the case of the Egress router having 38 distinct bottom labels, after removing the bottom label, there still exists 8 distinct LSPs between this pair of routers (considering IP addresses and top labels).

For IPv4 packets, the hash function considers at least the IP addresses in order to guarantee the same route for all packets of the same flow (avoiding so ordering issues with TCP). The same can be done with IPv6 packets, but it is more costly due to the IPv6 addresses length. Moreover in the case of 6PE, routers in the core may be totally IPv6 ignorant. In this case using the bottom label to split the load makes sense (this usage is for example mentioned in Cisco documentation [26]). Note that the conjunction of many routes (ECMP), hence top labels and many distinct 6PE bottom labels result in a large number of distinct LSPs when taking into account the full label stack. This partially explains why Cogent is so prevalent in terms of unique IPv6 MPLS tunnels in the dataset we consider besides its shere size. Several mechanisms have been proposed to allow MPLS networks to benefit from the use of multiple paths, such as Kompella et al. [27]. There have been also proposals to allow RSVP-TE to make a direct use of multiple ECMP paths [28].

Table 2. LPR [7] applied to some Cogent IPv6 2014 data.

	09/2014	10/2014	11/2014
Mono-LSP	23.1 %	30.8 %	0 %
Multi-FEC	3.4 %	2.7 %	0 %
Mono-FEC	58.6 %	52.3 %	0 %
Unclassified	14.9 %	14.2 %	0 %

To investigate further and retrieve the root cause of this variety of label stacks, we apply the Label Pattern Recognition (LPR) algorithm [7] on top labels of the Cogent IPv6 MPLS traces to quantify the usage of LDP (for IGP-BGP scalability purposes – *Mono-FEC* in Table 2) and/or RSVP-TE (for traffic engineering purposes – *Multi-FEC* in Table 2). To distinguish LSPs built through LDP and RSVP-TE, LPR analyses LSPs going through the same Ingress-Egress pair. If two LSPs have been built through LDP, the incoming top labels should be identical at converging routers. On the contrary, the incoming top labels should be different if these LSPs have been built through RSVP-TE. There is also the possibility that both protocols are used, building different LSPs according to the intended service. Our analysis (already apparent in the case of the Egress with 38 distinct LSPs), shows that the top-label is mostly generated by LDP (Mono-FEC line in Table 2). Therefore our interpretation is that the bottom-label is assigned by the Egress-router on a per IPv6 prefix basis using a variant of 6PE, in order to make a more efficient use of ECMP, while the top-label (i.e. the LSP itself) is built using LDP for IPv4.

4   Conclusion

The recent years have seen an increasing deployment and usage of IPv6. With the recent IPv4 depletion, this increase is going faster and we expect to see more and more IPv6 networks in a near future. In this paper, we focused on a specific aspect of the IPv6 deployment related to MPLS: how is MPLS deployed and used under IPv6? Is its usage strongly different from the one in IPv4? Based on traceroute collected by CAIDA, we tried to answer these questions.

Our first observations pointed out that the MPLS technical usage seems to strongly differ between IPv4 and IPv6. In particular, in the way label stacks are used, we discovered that under IPv4, stacks of more than one label are not that frequent while they are the norm under IPv6. However, we showed that this difference is not due to an increase in VPN BGP MPLS usage. Indeed, we explained that IPv6 MPLS mostly uses 6PE tunnels that are built using an IPv4 signaling protocol (in particular LDP for IPv4). This allows one to deploy MPLS for IPv6 across a network where some routers are not dual-stack, or where LDP is not available for IPv6 (the IPv6 version was only recently released). Therefore this can be seen as a transition mechanism, and it will be interesting to see the evolution of this usage as more and more networks become fully IPv6 compliant. The special case of the Cogent network also brought some light on the use of ECMP multipath in conjunction with MPLS. We argued that this network uses a specific form of 6PE to ease the way that IPv6 routers select their outgoing interfaces.

References

1. Dhamdhere, A., Luckie, M., Huffaker, B., Claffy, K., ELmokashfi, A., Aben, E.: Measuring the deployment of IPv6: topology, routing, and performance. In: Proceedings of ACM Internet Measurement Conference (IMC), November 2012
2. Czyz, J., Allman, M., Zhang, J., Iekel-Johnson, S., Osterweil, E., Bailey, M.: Measuring IPv6 adoption. In: Proceedings of ACM SIGCOMM, August 2014
3. American Registry for Internet Numbers (ARIN): IPv4 depletion, September 2015. https://www.arin.net/resources/request/ipv4_countdown.html
4. Sommers, J., Eriksson, B., Barford, P.: On the prevalence and characteristics of MPLS deployments in the open Internet. In: Proceedings of ACM Internet Measurement Conference (IMC), November 2011
5. Donnet, B., Luckie, M., Mérindol, P., Pansiot, J.J.: Revealing MPLS tunnels obscured by traceroute. ACM SIGCOMM Comput. Commun. Rev. **42**(2), 87–93 (2012)
6. Pathak, A., Zhang, M., Hu, Y.C., Mahajan, R., Maltz, D.: Latency inflation with MPLS-based traffic engineering. In: Proceedings of ACM Internet Measurement Conference (IMC), November 2011
7. Vanaubel, Y., Mérindol, P., Pansiot, J.J., Donnet, B.: MPLS under the microscope: revealing actual transit path diversity. In: Proceedings of ACM Internet Measurement Conference (IMC), October 2015
8. Rosen, E., Visanathan, A., Callon, R.: Multiprotocol label switching architecture. RFC 3031, Internet Engineering Task Force, January 2001
9. Andersson, L., Asati, R.: Multiprocotol label switching (MPLS) label stack entry: EXP field renamed to traffic class field. RFC 5462, Internet Engineering Task Force, February 2009

10. Rosen, E., Tappan, D., Fedorkow, G., Rekhter, Y., Farinacci, D., Li, T., Conta, A.: MPLS label stack encoding. RFC 3032, Internet Engineering Task Force, January 2001

11. Agarwal, P., Akyol, B.: Time-to-live (TTL) processing in multiprotocol label switching (MPLS) networks. RFC 3443, Internet Engineering Task Force, January 2003

12. Andersson, L., Minei, I., Thomas, T.: LDP specifications. RFC 5036, Internet Engineering Task Force, October 2007

13. Awduche, D., Berger, L., Gan, D., Li, T., Srinivasan, V., Swallow, G.: RSVP-TE: extensions to RSVP for LSP tunnels. RFC 3209, Internet Engineering Task Force, December 2001

14. Muthukrishnan, K., Malis, A.: A core MPLS IP VPN architecture. RFC 2917, Internet Engineering Task Force, September 2000

15. George, W., Pignataro, C.: Gap analysis for operating IPv6-only MPLS networks. RFC 7439, Internet Engineering Task Force, January 2015

16. Asati, R., Pignataro, C., Raza, K., Manral, V., Papneja, R.: Updates to LDP for IPv6. RFC 7552, Internet Engineering Task Force, June 2015

17. De Clercq, J., Ooms, D., Carugi, M., Le Faucheur, F.: BGP-MPLS IP virtual private network (VPN) extension for IPv6 VPN. RFC 4659, Internet Engineering Task Force, September 2006

18. De Clercq, J., Ooms, D., Prevost, S., Le Faucheur, F.: Connecting IPv6 islands over IPv4 MPLS using IPv6 provider edge routers (6PE). RFC 4798, Internet Engineering Task Force, February 2007

19. Bonica, R., Gan, D., Tappan, D., Pignataro, C.: ICMP extensions for multiprotocol label switching. RFC 4950, Internet Engineering Task Force, August 2007

20. Hinden, R., Deering, S.: IP version 6 addressing architecture. RFC 4291, Internet Engineering Task Force, February 2006

21. CAIDA: The CAIDA UCSD IPv6 topology dataset, September 2015. http://www.caida.org/data/active/ipv6_allpref_topology_dataset.xml

22. Augustin, B., Cuvellier, X., Orgogozo, B., Viger, F., Friedman, T., Latapy, M., Magnien, C., Teixeira, R.: Avoiding traceroute anomalies with Paris traceroute. In: Proceedings of ACM Internet Measurement Conference (IMC), October 2006

23. Luckie, M.: Scamper: a scalable and extensible packet prober for active measurement of the Internet. In: Proceedings of ACM Internet Measurement Conference, November 2010

24. Giotsas, V., Luckie, M., Huffaker, B., Claffy, K.: IPv6 AS relationships,clique, and congruence. In: Proceedings of Passive and Active Measurement Conference (PAM), March 2015

25. Leber, M.: IPv6 Internet broken, Cogent/Telia/Hurricane not peering, October 2009. Nanog Mailing-list. http://mailman.nanog.org/pipermail/nanog/2009-October/014017.html

26. Cisco: Cisco IOS IPv6 provider edge router (6PE) over MPLS, October 2015. http://www.cisco.com/en/US/products/sw/iosswrel/ps1835/products_data_sheet09186a008052edd3.html#wp39913

27. Kompella, K., Drake, J., Amante, S., Henderickx, W., Yong, L.: The use of entropy labels in MPLS forwarding. RFC 6790, Internet Engineering Task Force, November 2012

28. Kompella, K., Hellers, M., Singh, R.: Multi-path label switched paths signaled using RSVP-TE. Internet Draft (Work in Progress) draft-kompella-mpls-rsvp-ecmp-06, Internet Engineering Task Force, March 2015

Scheduling and Timing

An Empirical Study of Android Alarm Usage
for Application Scheduling

Mario Almeida[1]([✉]), Muhammad Bilal[1], Jeremy Blackburn[2],
and Konstantina Papagiannaki[2]

[1] Universitat Politecnica de Catalunya, Barcelona, Spain
mario.almeida@est.fib.upc.edu
[2] Telefonica Research, Barcelona, Spain

Abstract. Android applications often rely on alarms to schedule
background tasks. Since Android KitKat, applications can opt-in for
deferrable alarms, which allows the OS to perform alarm batching to
reduce device awake time and increase the chances of network traffic
being generated simultaneously by different applications. This mechanism can result in significant battery savings if appropriately adopted.

In this paper we perform a large scale study of the 22,695 most popular
free applications in the Google Play Market to quantify whether expectations of more energy efficient background app execution are indeed
warranted. We identify a significant chasm between the way application
developers build their apps and Android's attempt to address energy
inefficiencies of background app execution. We find that close to half of
the applications using alarms do not benefit from alarm batching capabilities. The reasons behind this is that (i) they tend to target Android
SDKs lagging behind by more than 18 months, and (ii) they tend to
feature third party libraries that are using non-deferrable alarms.

1 Introduction

Todays mobile devices support a diverse set of functionality, much of which is
not dependent on active user interaction. Many tasks are performed in the background, which has very clear impact on battery life and mobile data usage [4].
The impact is substantial enough that reducing and mitigating it has been the
focus of a significant amount of research and development.

A promising set of solutions aim to shape applications' traffic [3,5,8,9,12,16],
but suffer from severe limitations. These techniques ignore application-protocol
interactions and lack integration with applications and OSes, often *increasing*
energy consumption due to retransmissions and/or signaling issues [17] in real-
world scenarios. Other works [4,14,15,17] highlight the need for better application knowledge and/or integration with OS/platforms.

Alarms are Android's integrated application execution scheduling mechanism
(used, e.g., for background network activity) and are a primary vehicle for executing the traffic shaping techniques. Alarms are so critical to the functionality

T. Karagiannis and X. Dimitropoulos (Eds.): PAM 2016, LNCS 9631, pp. 373–384, 2016.
DOI: 10.1007/978-3-319-30505-9_28

of Android that they have been a hot topic at the last two Google IO conferences and a popular target for energy concerns[1,2]. One way Android mitigates Alarms' negative impact is *batching*, which can reduce total device awake time while increasing the chance that traffic from different applications can occur simultaneously. As of KitKat, developers can opt-in to have their alarms be *deferrable* which makes batching by the OS easier.

Unfortunately, the success of batching depends on the correct usage of alarm APIs by applications: apps themselves determine the deferrability, trigger time, and repetition interval of alarms. This leads to the situation Park et al. [13] discovered in their study of 15 Android applications: alarms are often unnecessarily set as non-deferrable. However, it is totally unclear how widespread such a practice is and thus its impact on the efficacy of alarm scheduling is unknown.

Since there is no indication that alarms will cease to be the preferred application level scheduling mechanism within Android, future design and development should be informed with an understanding of how developers use the current alarm APIs. Thus, in this paper we perform a large-scale study of 22,695 real applications from the Google Play Market (to the best of our knowledge, the largest such study to date) in order to find evidence of alarm API adoption delays and their impact on the performance of the Android OS; more specifically, the effectiveness of alarm batching in Android. We investigate how many apps use alarms, what type of alarms they use, differences in alarm usage by application category, and whether alarms are being used by apps themselves or by 3rd party libraries. We find that a shocking 46 % of apps with alarms do not take advantage of Android alarm scheduling capabilities due to either targeting old SDK versions or their use of 3rd party libraries. We further discuss and analyze the problems behind Android SDK adoption and propose possible directions for improving alarm batching across applications.

2   Android Alarms

Alarms are the primary mechanism Android provides to allow applications to schedule background activities. Alarms come in two flavors: (1) time critical alarms, and (2) non-time critical. The first type is called an *exact* alarm, and the second is known as an *inexact* or *deferrable* alarm. The OS is expected to execute exact alarms on schedule, but can delay the execution of deferrable alarms. Deferrable alarms are particularly interesting due to the manner in which Android can leverage them to improve power efficiency. For example, batching alarms to multiplex network activity of multiple applications can reduce the wake up frequency of the device's radio.

Decisions related to what type of alarms to use are left to the application developers since, in theory, only they have the insight necessary to assess the impact a delayed alarm will have on their app. Unfortunately, developers will often optimize for profit (e.g., ensuring fresh ads are retrieved/displayed as often

---

[1] GIO'15, Doze - http://goo.gl/KEJURc.

[2] GIO'14, Project Volta - https://goo.gl/aebnwF.

Table 1. Behavior of alarms based on the Target SDK level. We note that although our dataset was collected before SDK 23 was available, the continuing effort put into the alarm API highlights the critical nature of Android Alarms.

Alarm API	SDK < 19	SDK = 19–22	SDK = 23
set	Exact	Inexact	Inexact
setRepeating	Exact	Inexact	Inexact
setInexactRepeating	Inexact	Inexact	Inexact
setExact	NA	Exact	Exact
setWindow	NA	Inexact	Inexact
setAndAllowWhileIdle	NA	NA	Inexact
setExactAndAllowWhileIdle	NA	NA	Exact

as possible) and usability rather than energy efficiency. A second wrinkle with alarm types is that developers are free to define what Android SDK their app targets. If the device the application is installed on has a different SDK than the targeted one, a compatibility mode applies which in some cases can alter the app's behavior. This can have interesting consequences for alarms because the default functionality for a given Alarm API call might differ between SDK versions (see Table 1). E.g., if the targeted SDK version is less than 19, all API calls but setInexactRepeating create exact alarms. For SDK 19+, a new call to explicitly create exact alarms is introduced, and the behavior for the previously existing calls is changed to create inexact alarms.

Therefore, applications with exact alarms are those which: (1) have target SDK lower then 19 *and* use set or setRepeating calls or (2) use setExact.

Applications with inexact alarms are those which: (1) target ≥ SDK 19 *and* use set or setRepeating calls or (2) use setInexactRepeating *or* setWindow calls. It is important to note, however, that despite being able to create inexact alarms for SDK < 19, alarm batching across applications is only available for devices with Android KitKat (SDK 19) or higher [1].

Alternatively, Android apps can also use a new alternative designed to facilitate correct implementation of alarms and to reduce alarm occurrences based on app requirements: the JobInfo API. The JobInfo API provides new triggering conditions based on, for example, network (metered/unmetered) and device state (e.g., idle/charging), backed by more sophisticated retry mechanisms to avoid unnecessary execution, in turn allowing tuning apps with respect to battery consumption. The JobInfo APIs were introduced 6 months prior to our experiments (SDK 21), however, *none* of the apps in our dataset made use of them.

3 Results

3.1 Dataset

To understand the use of alarms in Android apps, we crawl Google Play and download up to 564 of the most popular free apps for each Google Play category.

Removing duplicates we are left with 22,695 unique apps. Although studying the most popular apps is clearly biased, it is justified for two reasons. First, these apps are more likely to be optimized than the least popular apps due to their associated revenues. Second, since these apps account for the majority of downloads, they are more representative of what users actually have on their mobile devices. This is evidenced by Viennot et al. [18] who found that the top 1 % of most downloaded apps account for over 81 % of the total downloads in November 30, 2013. To the best of our knowledge, our dataset (May 2015) should account for around 1.5 % of the total apps of the market in 2015 (AppBrain[3] claims around 1.5 Million apps in the first quarter of 2015).

For each of the 22,695 apps, we extract their manifest; an XML file that contains application meta-data, such as the application package name, components, permissions, etc. Three of the properties listed in the manifest are the minimum, maximum, and target SDK. The target SDK is the Android API level (e.g., Android 4.4 Kitkat has an API level of 19) that the application was developed for, and, as discussed earlier, determines the types of alarms available to the developer. By default, apps that do not define a target SDK have their target default to the minimum SDK.

3.2   Static Analysis

Since the focus of this study is understanding how alarms are being used by apps, we perform static analysis on the apps we crawled. We first decompile each of the apps, which provides us with assembly-like code (smali). We then statically analyze the smali code to locate occurrences of Android Alarm API calls. In our database, each occurrence of an alarm/jobinfo API call is registered along with the respective application, alarm API, smali file name, line and annotations to the method where it occurs. Since some free apps are likely to have ads [6], opposed to their paid version, we can analyze the API call location and correlate it with the ad libraries (Sect. 3.5). Annotations are useful since specific methods can use the `TargetAPI` annotation to denote that they want to execute the method in compatibility mode. For apps, the meta-data (target SDK, internet usage, category) is registered. In particular, we are interested in correlating target Android SDKs with the number of alarm API calls and their usage within different apps and app categories.

3.3   Impact of Target SDK on Alarms

As mentioned previously, the target SDK of an application can significantly affect the behavior of its alarms. As a first step towards understanding the impact of the chosen target SDK, we plot the distribution of SDK targets from our dataset in Fig. 1. It shows that despite the efforts of Google to promote the use of their newer SDKs (e.g., Google IO conferences, extensive documentation and application design guidelines), the majority of the popular apps target SDKs

---

[3] http://www.appbrain.com/stats/number-of-android-apps.

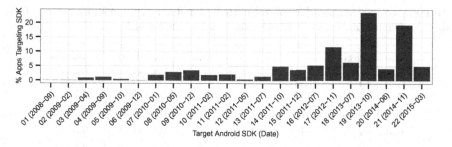

Fig. 1. Percentage of apps that define each Android SDK as the target SDK in their manifests. NB: We were unable to extract the target SDK from 1.5 % of apps in our dataset.

Table 2. Fraction of apps with exact and inexact alarms grouped by SDK version. Dates represent the release dates of each Android SDK. Note that an application can make use of both exact and inexact alarms.

Alarm type	SDK < 19	SDK >= 19
AlarmInexact	8.49 %	52.91 %
AlarmExact	44.05 %	2.31 %
Alarm	46.06 %	53.49 %

that were released more than 18 months ago (up to and including SDK 19, represent 71.6 %). Close to half (48 %) the apps target SDKs lagging behind by more than 21 months.

From the perspective of alarms, we note that 47.23 % of apps have a target SDK lower than 19; i.e., they are still going to use the older alarm API behavior with defaults oriented towards exact alarms. Out of the 22+K apps in our dataset, 47.25 % use alarms. Of the apps that use alarms, we see that 53.49 % have target SDK versions above 19, while 46.06 % target older SDKs (Table 2). As annotations can affect the targeted APIs on a per method basis, we confirmed that only 2 % of the apps with SDK < 19 had occurrences of the TargetAPI annotation in methods containing alarm calls.

The major apparent difference between SDK < 19 apps and SDK ≥ 19 apps is the flip-flop in usage of exact and inexact alarms: only 2.31 % of apps targeting SDKs ≥ 19 define exact alarms in contrast to the 44.05 % of apps targeting < 19. We note that this change might not necessarily be the result of developers being aware of the impact of exact alarms, but rather an end result of targeting newer SDKs.

The reason behind Android being so conservative with maintaining the previous alarm behavior even in newer versions of Android is to avoid apps from becoming unstable when updating. Since only 2.31 % of the apps targeting SDKs ≥ 19 use the exact alarm API call, if we would consider the hypothesis that apps with target SDK ≥ 19 updated from an older SDK, it is probable that either most apps did not have exact time constraints after all or that the ones that

Table 3. Example of popular and regularly updated apps with more than one million downloads and with target SDK older than 19 months (as of May 2015).

Application	SDK	Downloads	Version
es.lacaixa.mobile.android.newwapicon	17	1M-5M	2.0.17
com.cg.tennis	14	10 M–50 M	1.6.0
com.linkedin.android	15	10 M–50 M	3.4.8
com.rovio.angrybirds	18	100 M–500 M	5.0.2
com.cleanmaster.security	17	100 M–500 M	2.5.1
com.shazam.android	16	100 M–500 M	5.3.4
com.instagram.android	16	500 M–1000 M	6.20.2

do willingly avoided updating their SDKs. If the first is true, then Android is being very conservative with their approach regarding alarms batching behavior, which has a big impact on the power consumption of devices. Although we did not study apps update rates, it would have been interesting to determine if the second case holds by, for example, determining how many of these apps were updated after the release of Android API level 19. Our intuition is that even regularly updated apps often do not update their SDK. As an example, in Table 3, we show a few well known apps which, by the time of our study, had target SDKs lower than 19. Which means that these apps are unable to utilize the new energy efficient alarm APIs provided by the latest Android SDKs.

Even if the device is supported and up-to-date, apps can target old versions of the Android SDKs, which can have a negative impact on the overall performance of the device. Our results clearly demonstrate that there is slow adoption of new SDK versions by application developers. More importantly, we see that despite the efforts to make Android more energy efficient with respect to alarm handling (e.g., through JobInfo and the introduction of inexact alarms), backwards compatibility (a necessary evil at this point due to fragmentation), lack of developer awareness about new SDK benefits, and misuse of alarms by developers makes it hard to succeed.

3.4   Type of Alarms Depending on App Category

Considering the conservative behavior of Android regarding non-deferrable alarms, we now wonder which type of apps require exact alarms. To this end, we explore how different categories (as retrieved from Google Play) of apps make use of alarms (Fig. 2).

Surprisingly, categories of apps such as widgets (80 %), wallpapers (63 %) and personalization (60 %) have a bigger fraction of apps with alarms than communication (59 %) and social categories (55 %). While having more alarm definitions does not necessarily mean that there will be more alarm occurrences during runtime, we found that, for example, there are 308 widget apps defining repeating alarms (`setRepeating` and `setInexactRepeating`) (in Sect. 3.6 we

Category	Alarm	AlarmExact	AlarmInexact
WEATHER	53.9	35	25
TRAVEL_AND_LOCAL	43.9	19	28.1
TRANSPORTATION	33.7	11.9	25
TOOLS	45.2	17.5	31.5
SPORTS	50	21.6	30.9
SOCIAL	55.1	17.8	41.7
SHOPPING	50.6	22.7	32.6
PRODUCTIVITY	54.3	27.1	34.2
PHOTOGRAPHY	45.6	14.4	33.6
PERSONALIZATION	60.3	30.4	33.7
NEWS_AND_MAGAZINES	67.2	29.1	42.6
MUSIC_AND_AUDIO	38.9	14.7	30.7
MEDICAL	36.1	19.6	20
MEDIA_AND_VIDEO	38.8	15.1	26.1
LIFESTYLE	53.9	22.7	36.1
LIBRARIES_AND_DEMO	17.6	9.9	7.9
HEALTH_AND_FITNESS	56.4	26.2	35.5
GAME	48.4	23.5	28.1
FINANCE	44.2	18	28.8
ENTERTAINMENT	46.8	21.7	31.9
EDUCATION	38.8	18.5	23.5
COMMUNICATION	59.5	32.1	33
COMICS	33.8	15.6	20.4
BUSINESS	40.5	17.9	27.1
BOOKS_AND_REFERENCE	35.4	19.1	19.1
APP_WIDGETS	80	30.3	63.7
APP_WALLPAPER	62.9	24.5	45.1

Category	Alarm	AlarmExact	AlarmInexact
GAME_WORD	39.6	19.6	25.4
GAME_TRIVIA	37.7	19.8	22.8
GAME_STRATEGY	63.4	26.4	38.5
GAME_SPORTS	53.5	22.9	32.6
GAME_SIMULATION	45.6	18.2	30.1
GAME_ROLE_PLAYING	64.7	31.8	35
GAME_RACING	48.8	20.3	30.2
GAME_PUZZLE	46.5	18.9	29.8
GAME_MUSIC	32.7	15.6	17.3
GAME_FAMILY	52.6	32.5	22.5
GAME_EDUCATIONAL	44.3	25.6	23
GAME_CASUAL	38.2	17.7	23.8
GAME_CASINO	68.3	37.9	37.5
GAME_CARD	43.1	23	25.3
GAME_BOARD	38	17.1	22.2
GAME_ARCADE	49.7	25.1	27
GAME_ADVENTURE	48.6	23.7	26.9
GAME_ACTION	59.9	24.7	41.2

(a) All categories   (b) Game apps

Fig. 2. Percentage of apps per category (avg. 523 apps) that have any kind of alarms, have exact alarms and inexact alarms. Due to the high amount of Game categories, (a) groups this categories into GAME. Note that an application can make use of both exact and inexact alarms.

manually analyze some of these apps). Regarding time critical alarms, the five application categories with most apps with exact alarms are respectively: casino games (37.9 %), weather (35 %), family games (32.5 %), communication (32.1 %) and role-playing games (31.8 %). Finally, the average number of alarms defined by apps per category is shown in Fig. 3.

The widgets category not only has the largest number of apps with alarms and one of the highest time critical alarms usage (30.3 %), but also it also has the highest average number of alarms (4.9) defined within an application. The analyzed apps had up to 70 alarm definitions[4], e.g., Whatsapp defines 28 alarms, Instagram 11 and Facebook only 2. Again, we point that although Facebook has only 2 alarm definitions, its alarms are actually very frequent during runtime (Sect. 3.6).

---

[4] com.ecare.android.womenhealthdiary.

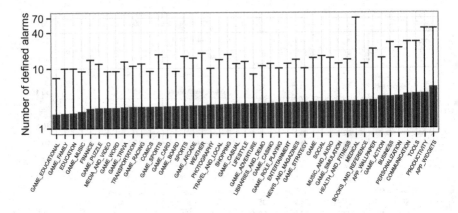

Fig. 3. Average number of alarms per application for each Google Play category. Error bars depict the maximum number of alarms for each category.

3.5   The Impact of 3rd Party Libraries

From our experience while studying apps, we have also seen that many apps have a big proportion of 3rd-party content. For example, consider Skype, only about 36.4 % of its code is actually Skype-specific functionality, while 31.8 % accounts for 3rd-party SDKs (e.g., roboguice, jess, qik, android support) and 32.8 % belongs to ads/analytics (e.g., flurry, Microsoft ads).

Hence one important aspect to check is whether defined alarms are native to the application itself or if they originate from 3rd party libraries. We analyzed the package names of the files where the alarms were detected and compared them to 93 ads and analytics libraries available for Android, retrieved from a public list provided by AppBrain[5]. The library package names and matches were manually confirmed to eliminate false positives.

Figure 4 shows the number of apps where alarms defined by these ads/analytics libraries were found. Alarms of ads/analytics libraries found in less than 10 apps are omitted (e.g., cellfish, inmobi, mopub). Although our approach might not cover all possible ads/analytics libraries, we were able to detect that 10.65 % of the unique apps (22.55 % of apps with alarms) have alarms defined by third-party ads/analytics, and around 10.42 % of all alarm API calls found belong to these libraries.

Finally, considering the number of alarms defined across all apps, we have discovered that 31.5 % of all alarms are repeating, while nearly 40.5 % of alarms are non-deferrable. Regarding 3rd-party ads and analytics libraries, their alarms account for 10.4 % of all alarm occurrences. From these occurrences, 72.6 % of them are repeating and 22.3 % of them are non-deferrable. Even though we only explored ads/analytics, given the large coverage of these 3rd-party libraries, optimizing their resource consumption and having them use inexact alarms

---

[5] http://www.appbrain.com/stats/libraries/ad.

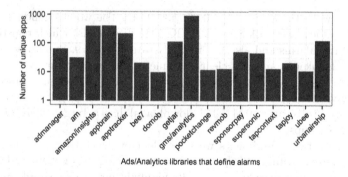

Fig. 4. Number of apps with alarms defined by third-party ads/analytic libraries.

(e.g., using `TargetAPI` annotation) would certainly lead to appreciable gains in terms of energy consumption.

3.6   Occurrence of Alarms at Execution Time

To confirm the impact of alarms on Android KitKat (SDK 19), the first to introduce batching by default, we perform two experiments. The experiments use two different sets of 30 apps. The first set is the top 30 most popular free apps of the Google Play market. The second set is the 30 apps with the largest number of `setRepeating` alarm definitions that also target SDK lower than 19. The latter was chosen since these alarms should be deferred if the target SDKs were set to $\geq$ 19 and notably includes apps with >1 K to >500 M downloads.

For each experiment we flash a new Android firmware (KitKat), install the 30 apps and create new accounts with no contacts/friends when needed (e.g., Gmail, Facebook, Twitter, etc.). All apps were started once to ensure Android gives them permission to execute on reboot if required, and then the phone is left on for around 30 min. We then reboot the phone, turn off its screen, and let it run for around 3 h. Finally, we gather the alarm and wakeup counts as reported by Android Dumpsys (`adb shell dumpsys alarm`) for the installed apps. Both experiments were repeated to confirm the patterns we observed.

There were a total of 261 alarms registered by the apps in our first experiment. Only 53 (20 %) caused the device to wakeup and we found no significant correlation between the number of registered alarms and the number of alarms that woke the device ($r = 0.11$, $p = 0.55$). That said, we were quite surprised to find that the two Facebook apps (messenger and the regular app) were responsible for the majority of wakeups (15 per hour). Upon closer examination, we determined that they were waking the phone to maintain a connection to a message queue, even though the accounts used had literally zero social activity.

A total of 1,041 alarms were registered by apps in our second experiment. Of these, 636 (61 %) woke up the device and we found a strong and significant correlation between the number of registered alarms and the number of alarms that woke the device ($r = 0.86$, $p < 0.01$). The worst offending application was the social network Spoora (10 K–50 K downloads) which registers *only* setRepeating alarms and also has its SDK target set to 9. Spoora was responsible for 372 wakeups and is a clear example of the negative impact of careless alarm usage which could be easily mitigated by simply targeting a newer SDK. Interestingly, this type of scenario is not unique to less popular apps: Norton Security and Antivirus (10 M–50 M downloads) has a target SDK of 17 and caused 141 wakeups.

From these two experiments we have clear evidence that poor alarm API usage can cause substantial impact on the device, and it is not limited to small time developers. In particular, our results highlight how even a simple misconfiguration (i.e., setting a target SDK too low) can have significant negative impacts in execution behavior. In the future, we intend to run similar experiments on a larger scale, taking direct battery measurements, manually modifying the target SDK to quantify exactly how the impact on battery consumption changes between target SDKs, and more closely examining the relationship between alarm type declaration and registration/wakeups.

4   Discussion and Conclusion

Research on energy efficiency in mobile devices tends to propose solutions focused on batching activity to amortize the cost of waking up the mobile device and its radio. The efficiency of such solutions depends on the ability of the operating system to schedule background activity at the most appropriate time. In Android, alarms are a popular mechanism to schedule background activities. To understand apps' usage of alarms, we crawled the Google Play store and downloaded over 22 thousand of the most popular apps.

We found that nearly 50 % of apps define their alarms to be *non-deferrable* by the operating system, thus hamstringing Android's ability to optimize scheduling at all. When examining the prevalence of alarms, we found that they existed across all categories of apps with some having up to 70 alarms declared. For apps with alarms, 22.5 % have them defined by 3rd party ads/analytics libraries they use, and these libraries account for at least 10.4 % of all declared alarms. We also showed the inefficiencies of alarms by manually analyzing 60 apps at runtime, finding apps waking up the device an inordinate number of times.

While Android fragmentation has been studied in the past [7,10,11], it generally approached from the perspective of the wide distribution of Android versions, heterogeneous hardware, and lack of updates. In this work we have revealed another facet of this problem: even if the device is supported and up-to-date, apps often target old versions of the Android SDKs, which can have a negative impact on the overall performance of the device. Via static analysis, we discovered that a substantial number of apps' alarms are non-deferrable due to targeting older versions of the Android SDK and that by simply changing the target SDK to > 19 these apps would likely benefit from advanced OS alarm scheduling mechanisms. Furthermore, while previous work [10] which studied a much smaller set of 10 open-source apps found that 28 % of method calls were outdated with a median lag time of 16 months, we also show that in the case of alarms, close to half the API calls are outdated by more than 18 months.

Ads and analytics are a particularly interesting subject of study since they have been shown to have a big impact on energy consumption [6]. We found that the majority of alarms related to ads and analytics are repeating, meaning that they most likely result in background operations that might have no real end-user benefit. This seems to be a problem that is core to Android in particular, since iOS does not have a direct analogue to alarms and has an extremely limited background execution environment [2]. Since from our experience a large pro-portion of Android apps make use of third-party code, future large-scale studies of energy consumption, optimization, and alarm usage should focus on common third-party libraries.

When we examined alarm usage at runtime we discovered that the implica-tions of the static analysis held true for the most part. The apps with the highest number of defined alarms were in fact executing the alarms at an exceedingly high rate. In one egregious case, a single application was responsible for 372 wakeups in a 3 h period.

This work serves as an initial large-scale look into alarms and their impact. Overall, our findings indicate that research on energy efficiency on mobile devices needs to incorporate an understanding around the use of alarms. Deeper exam-inations into the use and abuse of Android alarms should provide more fruitful insight and solutions, leading to increased energy efficiency and device perfor-mance.

References

1. Alarmmanager. http://goo.gl/ncrGaO
2. iOS Developer Library: Background execution. https://goo.gl/xZd16w
3. Athivarapu, P.K., Bhagwan, R., Guha, S., Navda, V., Ramjee, R., Arora, D., Padmanabhan, V.N., Varghese, G.: RadioJockey: mining program execution to optimize cellular radio usage. In: Proceedings of the 18th Annual International Conference on Mobile Computing and Networking (2012)
4. Aucinas, A., Vallina-Rodriguez, N., Grunenberger, Y., Erramilli, V., Papagiannaki, K., Crowcroft, J., Wetherall, D.: Staying online while mobile: the hidden costs. In: Proceedings of the Ninth ACM Conference on Emerging Networking Experiments and Technologies (2013)
5. Balasubramanian, N., Balasubramanian, A., Venkataramani, A.: Energy consumption in mobile phones: a measurement study and implications for network applications. In: Proceedings of the 9th ACM SIGCOMM Conference on Internet Measurement Conference (2009)
6. Gui, J., Mcilroy, S., Nagappan, M., Halfond, W.G.: Truth in advertising: the hidden cost of mobile ads for software developers. In: Proceedings of the 37th International Conference on Software Engineering (2015)
7. Han, D., Zhang, C., Fan, X., Hindle, A., Wong, K., Stroulia, E.: Understanding android fragmentation with topic analysis of vendor-specific bugs. In: 19th Working Conference on Reverse Engineering (2012)

8. Higgins, B.D., Reda, A., Alperovich, T., Flinn, J., Giuli, T.J., Noble, B., Watson, D.: Intentional networking: opportunistic exploitation of mobile network diversity. In: Proceedings of the Sixteenth Annual International Conference on Mobile Computing and Networking (2010)

9. Liu, H., Zhang, Y., Zhou, Y.: TailTheft: leveraging the wasted time for saving energy in cellular communications. In: Proceedings of the Sixth International Workshop on MobiArch (2011)

10. McDonnell, T., Ray, B., Kim, M.: An empirical study of API stability and adoption in the android ecosystem. In: Proceedings of the 2013 IEEE International Conference on Software Maintenance (2013)

11. Mulliner, C., Oberheide, J., Robertson, W., Kirda, E.: PatchDroid: scalable third-party security patches for android devices. In: Proceedings of the 29th Annual Computer Security Applications Conference (2013)

12. Nguyen, N.T., Wang, Y., Liu, X., Zheng, R., Han, Z.: A nonparametric bayesian approach for opportunistic data transfer in cellular networks. In: Wang, X., Zheng, R., Jing, T., Xing, K. (eds.) WASA 2012. LNCS, vol. 7405, pp. 88–99. Springer, Heidelberg (2012)

13. Park, S., Kim, D., Cha, H.: Reducing energy consumption of alarm-induced wake-ups on android smartphones. In: Proceedings of the 16th International Workshop on Mobile Computing Systems and Applications (2015)

14. Qian, F., Wang, Z., Gao, Y., Huang, J., Gerber, A., Mao, Z., Sen, S., Spatscheck, O.: Periodic transfers in mobile applications: network-wide origin, impact, and optimization. In: Proceedings of the 21st International Conference on World Wide Web (2012)

15. Shi, C., Joshi, K., Panta, R.K., Ammar, M.H., Zegura, E.W.: CoAST: collaborative application-aware scheduling of last-mile cellular traffic. In: Proceedings of the 12th Annual International Conference on Mobile Systems, Applications, and Services (2014)

16. Vergara, E.J., Nadjm-Tehrani, S.: Energy-aware cross-layer burst buffering for wireless communication. In: Proceedings of the 3rd International Conference on Future Energy Systems: Where Energy, Computing and Communication Meet (2012)

17. Vergara, E.J., Sanjuan, J., Nadjm-Tehrani, S.: Kernel level energy-efficient 3g background traffic shaper for android smartphones. In: Proceedings of the 9th International Wireless Communications and Mobile Computing Conference (2013)

18. Viennot, N., Garcia, E., Nieh, J.: A measurement study of google play. In: The 2014 ACM International Conference on Measurement and Modeling of Computer Systems (2014)

Network Timing and the 2015 Leap Second

Darryl Veitch[1]([✉]) and Kanthaiah Vijayalayan[2]

[1] Faculty of Engineering and IT, University of Technology Sydney, Ultimo, Australia
Darryl.Veitch@uts.edu.au
[2] Melbourne School of Engineering, University of Melbourne, Melbourne, Australia

Abstract. Using a testbed with reference timestamping, we collected timing data from public Stratum-1 NTP servers during the leap second event of end-June 2015. We found a wide variety of anomalous server-side behaviors, both at the NTP protocol level and in the server clocks themselves, which can last days or even weeks after the event. Out of 176 servers, only 61% had no erroneous behavior related to the leap second event that we could detect.

Keywords: Leap second · NTP · Stratum-1 server · Network measurement · LI bits · UTC

1   Introduction

Timekeeping is central to network measurement. It is a service typically provided by a computer operating system, whose *system clock* is synchronized, through timestamp exchange over the Network Time Protocol (NTP), to a remote reference. In the timeserver hierarchy, a *Stratum-s* timeserver synchronizes to a *Stratum s−1*. Anchoring the system are the *Stratum-1* servers, which have local access to reference hardware such as a GPS receiver or atomic clock. These roots of the timing forest 'hierarchy' can be PCs, or dedicated network appliances.

Network timing distributes *Coordinated Universal Time* (UTC). This is a discontinuous time standard: jumps known as *leap seconds* are inserted (roughly every two years) in order to keep the timescale in step with the solar day. Leap seconds are propagated through the server hierarchy, but it is well known to system administrators and others that this process is far from perfect, and can cause havoc with system clocks and the host systems themselves.

In this paper we examine the behavior of a set of public Stratum-1 servers during the leap second event of end-June 2015. Our objective is to determine which servers perform as expected, both from the server-clock accuracy and protocol points of view, and to characterise the deviations. We find that behavior which is far from ideal is quite common, and there are many examples of extremely poor behavior, for example servers which never incorporate the leap second, or never inform their clients of it. Ideal behavior, as far as we can measure it given the resolution of our dataset, occurs in only 61% of the servers we study. Given their role in the foundation of the timing system, these Stratum-1 findings are bad news for the public timing system as a whole.

© Springer International Publishing Switzerland 2016
T. Karagiannis and X. Dimitropoulos (Eds.): PAM 2016, LNCS 9631, pp. 385–396, 2016.
DOI: 10.1007/978-3-319-30505-9_29

Our conclusions are based on measurements using reference timestamps from a GPS synchronized DAG packet capture card, and an analysis methodology capable of disambiguating network events from server behavior. Although it has limitations, most notably the fact that we are only capturing a subset of all public Stratum-1's, we know of no prior study of leap second events which has the detail or precision of what we present here. We intend to make our data available to the community.

The paper is organized as follows. Section 2 provides background on time standards, leap seconds and NTP, and discusses prior work. Section 3 describes our testbed, the selection of servers, what the datasets are and how they were collected. Section 5 outlines the analysis procedure we employed to characterize the nature of the leap second behavior of the servers, even in the face of significant noise. Our results are detailed in Sect. 5, and finally, Sect. 6 discusses the import of our findings.

2   Background

2.1   Time Standards and Leap Seconds

The primary international time standard is the *Temps Atomique International* (TAI). It is based on combining the (relativistically corrected) outputs of high precision atomic clocks in over 300 National Laboratories, including the USA's National Institute for Standards and Technology (NIST), and Australia's National Measurement Institute (NMI). The TAI is a continuous time scale, with each second a standard SI second, and with epoch (origin) at HH:MM:SS = 00:00:10, 1st January 1972. It is best to think of TAI as a real number, in units of seconds, since that epoch. *Universal Time* (UT1) is a descendant of Greenwich Mean Time, a continuous time scale whose unequal seconds allow synchronization to the solar day. Because the Earth's rotation is slowing, UT1 is falling progressively further behind TAI.

The primary time standard used for general timekeeping is *Coordinated Universal Time* (UTC). This is a discontinuous time scale with epoch at $t_{\mathrm{TAI}} = -10\,\mathrm{s}$, best thought of as TAI to which jumps of exactly 1 s have been infrequently applied in order to keep UTC close (within 0.9 s) to UT1. Within UTC, a positive leap second manifests as a downward jump, slowing the clock down with respect to TAI. Leap seconds, when needed, are added at the end of the last minute of a month, typically June or December. Negative leap seconds are defined but have never been used.

Realizations of both TAI and UTC are maintained by the *Bureau international des poids et mesures* (BIPM). The timing standards body is the International Telecommunications Union (ITU), but it is the *International Earth Rotation and Reference Systems Service* (IERS) that decides on leap seconds, and announces them months in advance via its biannual "Bulletin C".

In this paper we focus on the leap second added at the end of June 30, 2015. The leap event was completed at 00:00:00 July 1st UTC when TAI was $t_{\mathrm{TAI}}^{*} = 1435708836\,\mathrm{sec}$, and $t_{\mathrm{UTC}}^{*} = t_{\mathrm{TAI}}^{*} - 36$. For convenience, we plot all timeseries against a timescale "t", which is t_{TAI} with its origin reset to t_{TAI}^{*}.

2.2   Leap Seconds and NTP

The NTP hierarchy distributes UTC. Stratum-1 servers learn of leap seconds through various mechanisms depending on the reference time source. The most common is GPS, which supports UTC and makes complete leap second information available. A commonly used alternative, used for example by many UNIX operating systems, is to include a 'leap-seconds' text file as part of NTP configuration. This file, which lists leap second event times as well as an expiry date, is maintained by NIST and is available from [1].

The main mechanism by which servers of higher strata learn of leap seconds is via their server (or peer). The NTP packet header has a 2-bit *Leap Indicator* (LI) field. RFC 5905 (NTP version 4), specifies that servers set LI = 01 in response packets when a (positive) leap second is scheduled *in the last minute of the current month*. Obsoleted RFCs 1305 (NTP v3) and 4330 (SNTP v4) instead state .. *in the last minute of the current day*. The language in the RFCs is ambiguous, as it confuses describing under what circumstances LI should be set (to 01), with how far in advance to do so. A consistent reading across RFC 5905 and RFC 4330/1305 is that LI should be set in each server response packet during the entire month (5905) or day (4330/1305) of a scheduled leap. Alternatively, there may have been no intention to specify how far in advance to set it. Most informal sources state that warnings are issued in the prior 24 h in common implementations. We discuss this further below.

The fact that UTC jumps backwards is inherently problematic. It is complex and confusing, may break software reliant on monotonic time, and is fertile ground for bugs. This is exacerbated by the fact that the detail of how time should be kept *during* leap second events is not standardized: approaches vary by operating system, OS version, and NTP version. Note that by 'leap second event' here we mean the entire second just before the jump itself, since over this interval clock software must do something non-standard to account for the leap, including allowing the corresponding minute to have 61 s. A useful reference here is [2]. As described in [3], using the *ntpd* daemon (the incumbent clock synchronization algorithm for client system clocks developed by David Mills [4]) with the -*x* option disables the sudden leap second adjustment and so avoids a number of problems, but results in convergence times to post-leap UTC of the order of 10's of hours.

2.3   Prior Work

There are many informal reports available on-line detailing implementation issues with leap seconds, describing bad behavior of client systems, related operating system bugs and configuration problems, and providing recommendations for system administrators. For example contemporary issues in Linux (including recommendations to simply shutdown NTP and restart around leap second events) can be found in [3,5,6]. RFC 7164 provides an overview of implementation issues in relation to POSIX. A recent paper by Burnicki [2] (see also the related presentation [7]) gives a useful description of how leap seconds are disseminated, and alternative proposals for how to deal with them in end systems, including several 'slewing' variants, where a sudden jump is replaced by a period of modified clock rate. This includes the slewing scheme included in NTP for Windows, and that proposed recently by Google.

There is very little peer-reviewed work on Stratum-1 server behavior, and still less on leap-seconds. The closest work appears to be that of Malone [8], a web page which gives two graphs looking at LI values, of a similar set of servers to ours, about the 2015, 2012, 2008 and 2005 leap second events. While informative, the results are coarse grained, with scant methodological detail, and do not extend to the server clocks themselves.

3   The Experiment: Testbed, Server List, and Data Set

The experiment ran over 22.3 days from June 29 to July 21, 2015. In it a single host ran multiple independent RADclock [9] daemon instances. RADclock is an alternative clock synchronization algorithm with high accuracy and robustness [10]. Each instance emitted an NTP timing request packet every $\tau = 64\,$s to its chosen server. Packets were timestamped to 200ns precision or better by a DAG3.7GP capture card [11] via a passive tap just outside the host, synchronized to a roof-mounted Trimble Acutime 2000 GPS receiver.

For an NTP packet i which completes its round-trip from the client to server and back, and is successfully matched on return, we obtain a 4-tuple *stamp* of UTC timestamps $\{T_{a,i}, T_{b,i}, T_{e,i}, T_{f,i}\}$. Here $T_{b,i}, T_{e,i}$ are made by the server and are extracted from the returning NTP packet, as are the LI bits and the server Stratum field from the NTP header. For this experiment the configuration was such that the DAG timestamps $T_{a,i}, T_{f,i}$ **ignore the leap second**, and so are on a continuous timescale ('pre-leap UTC') over the experiment.

Our server list is based on the public Stratum-1 url list maintained at *ntp.org*, and contains 176 servers. Of these, 156 were listed as OpenAccess at *ntp.org* at some time between Sep. 2011 and June 2015, and resolved to a unique IP address which responded to NTP requests, during the experiment. To this we added 9 public and 6 private (3 from NMI and 3 in our lab) Australian Stratum-1 servers, and 5 used by CAIDA Ark monitors [12].

4   Methodology

From the timestamp data we estimate, for each server, the time series of round-trip time $R_i = T_{f,i} - T_{a,i}$, *server change*: $C_i = (D_i^\uparrow - D_i^\downarrow)/2$, and *server error* $E_i = C_i + L_i$. Here $D_i^\uparrow = T_{b,i} - T_{a,i}$ and $D_i^\downarrow = T_{f,i} - T_{e,i}$ are the estimated outgoing and incoming delays, and $L_i = L(T_{e,i})$, where $L(t)$ is a step function rising from 0 to 1 at $t = t_{\mathrm{TAI}}^*$. The series C_i (resp. E_i) consists of errors in the server clock with respect to the DAG timescale (resp. UTC), together with 'noise' due to path routing changes and congestion. We use R_i, which is *entirely independent of server timestamps and of the leap second event*, to judge path conditions independently of server behavior.

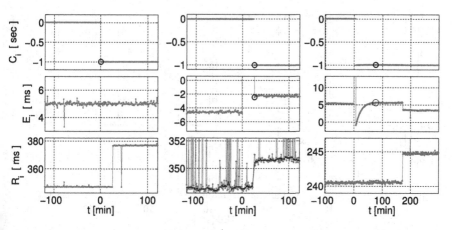

Fig. 1. Introduction to server behavior and the methodology for TEB determination. Left column: Good server; Middle: Bad server due to delayed leap; Right: Bad server with delayed leap plus post-leap instability resulting in a much larger TEB.

We illustrate our methodology through the examples appearing in Fig. 1. The server assigned the left column is well behaved, and so the top plot shows the leap behavior in C_i one would expect. More precisely, the detected leap position (black circle) at $t = 51.7\,\text{s}$ is at the first stamp past $t = 0$, and the previous stamp was at $t = -13.5$, before $t = 0$ as required. These values were determined through inspecting E_i (middle plot), whose variability is steady about $t = 0$ in a sub-ms band, showing no evidence of perturbations about the leap. Note that E_i is centred about 5.2 ms rather than zero due to path asymmetry, not server error. The level shift event in R_i at around 26 min does not appear in E_i as it results from a symmetric path change.

The middle column exhibits a server where the leap occurs neatly, but is $t = 26.2\,\text{min}$ late. We call this delay the *Time to Expected Behavior* (TEB). After the leap E_i is 2 ms higher than it was before $t = 0$, however inspection of R_i (and its median-filtered version, the black curve) in this zone reveals it to be due to a path change affecting path asymmetry, rather than additional leap-induced server errors. Hence the naive TEB value associated to the main jump is taken as the final value.

The right column shows a server where not only is the initial leap late, but there are additional errors beyond it of a few ms in amplitude (visible in E_i but hidden in C_i) resulting in TEB $= 75.8\,\text{min}$. The R_i plot confirms that this 'monotonic recovery' event in E_i does not result from path effects but is associated with the leap event at the server.

Each server was closely examined using the above approach to determine a TEB value which genuinely reflected recovery from the leap second event, rather than any other cause. More precisely, for each server the TEB was set to correspond to the earliest time at which the variations in E_i following a leap fell below the magnitude of the path noise as revealed by R_i. The precise stamp

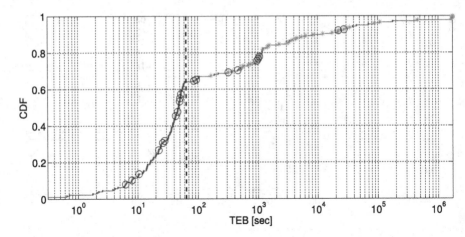

Fig. 2. A cumulative distribution function of TEB across all servers. Red stars denote Bad servers. All servers with TEB < 64 s (left of dashed line), are Good. The black circles are LI-Bad, that is Bad with respect to LI behavior (see Sect. 5.2.)

at which this occurs was selected 'by eye' taking into account the degree of short term variability of each time series. In a small number of cases, the nature and/or amplitude of the variability due either to path changes, congestion, or server errors unrelated to the leap event, make the exact value of TEB hard to evaluate, however we are confident that the resulting error is of the order of a few percent even in these cases.

5   Results

5.1   Server Clock Behavior

We label a server clock as 'Good' (else 'Bad'), with respect to its leap second response, when there is no hard evidence of incorrect behavior. That is when E_i is constant for all stamps both before and after $t = 0$, up to the observed variability as calibrated by R_i. The value of this constant reflects path asymmetry, and is close to zero relative to minimum RTT. Since the per-server periodic packet flows have random phase with respect to each other, for such servers we expect to find TEB values uniformly distributed in $[0, \tau]$. A consequence is that actual detection resolutions can be both higher or lower than the (unfortunately low) $\tau/2 = 32$ s average case. Note that lower values of τ would have run the risk of appearing as an attack on the server.

Figure 2 records the distribution of TEB values over servers in the form of the empirical $F(x) = \Pr(\text{TEB} \leq x)$. The values require a log scale as they are spread over the entire 22 day experiment duration, including 2 cases where the leap never occurred (TEB set to trace duration). A single server jumped early, at $t = -0.164$ s, and could not be plotted. All 112 servers with TEB $\in [0, \tau]$ (left

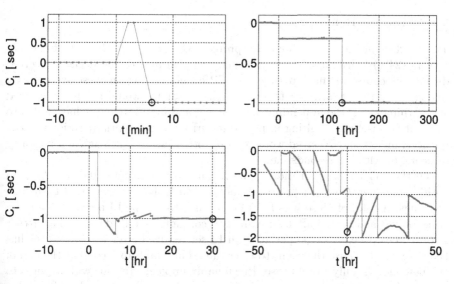

Fig. 3. Examples of Bad servers with more extreme behavior (black circle = TEB). We show C_i plots, as these have a range over 1 second and are thus well suited to contextualize extreme errors. Note that correctness of the displayed TEB values cannot be ascertained from this view. For that we require a zoomed view, such as E_i provides.

of the dashed vertical line in plot) are, not surprisingly, Good, and inspection in a linear plot showed they are uniformly distributed as expected, the smallest being TEB = 0.13 s. However, of the 131 Good servers, 19 have larger TEB values because the server did not respond for an interval extending beyond $[0, \tau]$. Although values a little beyond $t = \tau$ could indicate congestion losses or server overload, larger values imply a problem. Thus, for example, whereas TEB = 20 s for a Good server is consistent with a sampling resolution of $\tau = 64$ s and does not imply in any way that the server failed to leap for 20 s, TEB = 100 s for a Good server suggests that the server was not behaving ideally (perhaps offline as part of leap second management or failure), over this entire period.

The 45 Bad servers display a wide variety of behaviors. The 'delayed but otherwise clean' leap behavior encountered in the middle column of Fig. 1 is found in 15 cases, with a median delay at TEB = 22 min. For 5 other servers an initial delay was accompanied by a significant period where the server did not respond, but nothing more complex. The final 25 cases displayed more extreme behavior including multiple jumps, failure to jump, and post-leap instability occuring over periods ranging from hours to weeks. Figure 3 displays the C_i plots for a number of these. The bottom right plot deserves special mention. It shows a server whose delayed but clean leap at TEB = 9.0 s occurs in the context of persistent and severe underlying server errors, which in fact are present throughout the entire experiment. A number of both Good and Bad servers display server errors unrelated to their performance during the leap event. A detailed analysis of broader server anomalies is beyond the scope of this paper. In [13] we perform such a study based on different and longer datasets from a subset of the servers studied here.

5.2   Protocol Behavior

The most significant fact about the protocol compliance is that 41 of the 176 servers (24%) failed to set the LI bits correctly in **any** of the packets received during the course of the experiment. NTP clients relying on these servers as a reference, and their own clients lower in the hierarchy, would not have received the warning about the impending leap second, and would therefore have failed to insert it themselves, resulting in persistent errors and potentially serious consequences, unless they received word by some other means (such as via a majority of peers, or the leap-seconds file).

Of the 135 servers that did set the LI bits correctly, many did not do so in an ideal manner. Consider first the times at which the servers ceased their leap warnings. A total of 18 servers (13%) continued to set the LI bit after $t = 0$. Of these only 8 had ceased after an hour, two continued for 12 days! and a further 2 for a week. Even a single packet with LI set received after $t = 0$ however has the potential to cause the client to insert an additional leap second at the end of the new month, July in this case. Presumably implementations will attempt to disregard warnings received just after leap events to allow for delays in packet arrival from the server(s), however they may not succeed, in particular if the warnings continue indefinitely.

Now consider the times when the servers *began* to send warnings. As pointed out earlier, it is not clear from the NTP standard when warnings should in fact begin, however 24 h seems to be commonly used/supposed, in particular in SNTPv4 implementations (RFC 4330) which are still very common. In fact in 6 out of the 135 cases we found that warnings began exactly 6 months in advance! (We know this thanks to a complementary dataset we collected at that time. Interestingly, this happens to correspond to 00:00:00 Jan 1st, the other common time when leap seconds can be scheduled.). These extreme cases aside, the warning start times of the remaining $135 - 6 = 129$ servers do cluster about 24hrs, as shown in the histogram of Fig. 4. We see that in most cases ample warning is given, provided the systems in question are up. There is no evidence of warnings beginning a month in advance as, perhaps, suggested by RFC 5905.

Our results are consistent with the findings of Malone [8] for the same 2015 leap second event, who also reports that most leap second warnings begin close to 24 h in advance, and that around 60% to 80% of servers set the bits to the right value, namely LI = 01, for a positive leap second. He also comments that most servers had ceased their warnings by an hour after the event, in agreement with our findings here.

5.3   Overall Behavior

A natural question to ask is, how many servers are 'perfect'? meaning that there is no evidence of errors of any kind with respect to the expected leap second behavior, neither in the accuracy of the server clock timestamps, nor in the protocol compliance.

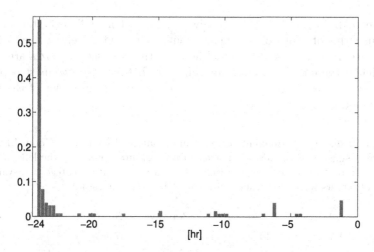

Fig. 4. Histogram of LI warning start times relative to $t = 0$ (excluding the 6 cases where warnings began exactly 6 months in advance).

To answer this question we must first define more precisely what we mean by protocol compliance. We define the warning start time to be Good if it falls in the interval $[-24 \times 3600, -3072]$ s. Here we assume that a client is using the maximum polling period to its server of $\tau = 1024$ s, and allow for 2 consecutive packet losses ($3 \times 1024 = 3072$) in order to define the last safe time at which a server should begin delivering warnings. In terms of the warning end time, we define behavior to be Good when no warnings are received after $t = 3$ s, to allow for worst case delay of a packet sent from the server at $t = 0^-$ to the client. Finally, we consider that a server is 'LI-Good' if it sends LI warnings in a way which is Good in each of the above two respects.

In Sect. 5.1 we reported that there were 131 Good servers, and using the above definition we find that there are 115 LI-Good servers. The intersection of these, the 'Perfect' servers, is 108 strong, or 61% of the total of 176 in the list. Note that of the Perfect servers, 97 (90%) are among the servers with TEB < 64 s from Fig. 2. Finally, we should not forget that Perfect should not be taken literally. It actually means that we found no hard evidence of failure in our sampled data. In fact, as explained earlier, a number of Good servers have suspiciously large TEB values indicative of a server with poor availability, which is not ideal server behavior, and of course our sampling resolution prevents us from detecting servers with errors that were corrected quickly.

Although we have assembled our server list from sources either known to be Stratum-1, or claiming to be through their presence on the list at *ntp.org*, it turns out that not all of them are. In fact a considerable number drop their Stratum-1 status every now and again (the S-varying group), and a small number were never Stratum-1 over the duration of the experiment. Table 1 gives a breakdown, and shows, for each stratum grouping separately, what percentages fall into the Good, LI-Good, and Perfect performance categories. The differences are smaller than one might imagine, with the S1-always servers doing a little better than the others in terms of protocol compliance, but, counterintuitively, worse in terms of clock accuracy. It should be noted however that the samples sizes are small. In particular there is not a significant difference between the two most populous and closely related categories, S1-always and S-varying, in either of the Good and LI-Good groups.

Table 1. Breakdown of different server groups that set LI bits into Good, LI-Good, and Perfect subsets. Four measured stratum-level groups appear on the left, and two National Laboratory groups on the right. The varying stratum category (S-varying) consists of servers which are usually Stratum-1 but sometimes not.

	S1-always	S2-always	S3-always	S-varying	NMI	NIST
Size	122	14	3	37	3	10
Good	72%	86%	67%	76%	100%	80%
LI-Good	66%	50%	67%	65%	100%	100%
Perfect	64%	50%	67%	54%	100%	80%

A breakdown of two National Laboratory groups is also given in Table 1 on the right hand side. This is interesting as we expect them to have the highest standards, and in the case of NIST, a large client base. For NMI on the other hand only registered clients are allowed – these are not public servers. Though both NMI and NIST servers showed excellent protocol compliance, 2 of 10 NIST servers in the list fell down on clock performance. Moreover, most of the NIST servers exhibited server anomalies unrelated to the leap second event, whereas none of the NMI servers did. This is in agreement with our findings in [13].

5.4   System Dependence

Information on the hardware and software platforms underlying the servers on the list is available at *ntp.org*, however it is incomplete, potentially out of date, and far from uniform. We are in the process of seeking out and contacting the server administrators in order to obtain a more complete picture of variables such as the nature of the reference timing source, the origin of the server hardware (commercial appliance or commodity), and operating system (proprietary, Linux or BSD), and NTP version and configuration. It is not possible to report on this in detail here, however it seems clear that, in agreement with the observations of Nelson in 1999 [14], that by far the most common reference source is GPS. We also find that NTPv4 is more prevalent than NTPv3, and that both commerical and commodity servers are well represented. The administrators and their organisations span a broad range, from National Laboratories in the US, Australia, Sweden, Russia and elsewhere, to time enthusiasts making servers available out of personal interest. Many of the servers on the list participate in the public *ntppool*.

6   Discussion

It is difficult to say how much influence the servers in our list have on public network based timekeeping, in particular since the advent, since late 2013, of NTP amplified reflection attacks [15], have caused administrators to block the server query commands that would have made a crawl of their clients and peers possible. Certainly they are only a minority of the total number of publicly accessible servers, given that Minar's 1999 survey discovered 957 Stratum-1 servers [14]. On the other hand our list contains several servers from National Laboratories, notably NIST, that can be expected to be well known with sizable client bases, as well as many others which participate in the widely used *ntppool*. We believe that it reasonable to claim that the deficiencies we have detailed in the paper, where only 61% of servers are behaving (as far as we can tell) correctly, and many behave in a very damaging way, can have a considerable impact.

Responding to leap seconds reliably is a complex affair, as it is a function of many interactions of software and hardware of different generations and provenance. The fact that in 2015 there are still so many issues, even in Stratum-1 servers, is a testament to this fact. For this reason it has been debated for some time within the ITU whether leap seconds should be abandoned entirely. In fact the ITU considered this question at the World Radiocommunication Conference (WRC-15) meeting in November 2015 (after this paper was submitted to PAM 2016). The outcome was that more study was needed, and a report on future time scales, including the fate of the leap second, will be considered by WRC-23 in 2023. The approach of this paper can be used as the basis of a broader study of future leap second events leading up to 2023, as well as to track the health of network timing infrastructure more generally.

Acknowledgment. Partially supported by Australian Research Council's Linkage Projects funding scheme #LP120100073, in partnership with Symmetricom (now Microsemi).

References

1. NIST. ftp://time.nist.gov/pub/leap-seconds.3629404800
2. Burnicki, M.: Technical aspects of leap second propagation and evaluation. In: Requirements for UTC and Civil Timekeeping on Earth Colloquium. Science and Technology Series, vol. 115. Univelt Inc., San Diego (2015)
3. Lichvar, M.: Five different ways to handle leap seconds with NTP. http://developerblog.redhat.com/2015/06/01/five-different-ways-handle-leap-seconds-ntp/
4. Mills, D.L.: Computer Network Time Synchronization: The Network Time Protocol. CRC Press Inc., Boca Raton (2006)
5. Elsins, M.: HANDLING THE LEAP SECOND - LINUX. http://www.pythian.com/blog/handling-the-leap-second-linux/
6. redhat, How to clear the Leap Second Insertion flag after it has been received?. https://access.redhat.com/articles/199563/

7. Burnicki, M.: Technical aspects of leap second propagation and evaluation. In: FOSDEM (2015). http://nwtime.org/leap-second-resources/
8. Malone, D.: Leap Second (2015). http://www.maths.tcd.ie/~dwmalone/time/leap2015/
9. RADclock Project webpage. http://www.synclab.org/radclock/
10. Veitch, D., Ridoux, J., Korada, S.B.: Robust synchronization of absolute and difference clocks over networks. IEEE/ACM Trans. Netw. **17**, 417–430 (2009)
11. Endace, Endace Measurement Systems. DAG series PCI and PCI-X cards. http://www.endace.com/networkMCards.htm
12. Archipelago monitor locations. http://www.caida.org/projects/ark/locations/
13. Vijayalayan, K., Veitch, D.: Rot at the roots? Examining public timing infrastructure. In: Proceedings of IEEE INFOCOM 2016, San Francisco, CA, USA, 10–15 April 2016
14. Minar, N.: A Survey of the NTP Network (1999). http://alumni.media.mit.edu/~nelson/research/ntp-survey99/html/
15. Czyz, J., Kallitsis, M., Gharaibeh, M., Papadopoulos, C., Bailey, M., Karir, M.: Taming the 800 pound gorilla: the rise and decline of NTP DDoS attacks. In: Proceedings of IMC 2014, IMC 2014, pp. 435–448. ACM, New York (2014)

Can Machine Learning Benefit Bandwidth Estimation at Ultra-high Speeds?

Qianwen Yin[✉] and Jasleen Kaur

University of North Carolina at Chapel Hill, Chapel Hill, USA
qianwen@cs.unc.edu

Abstract. Tools for estimating end-to-end available bandwidth (AB) send out a train of packets and observe how inter-packet gaps change over a given network path. In ultra-high speed networks, the fine inter-packet gaps are fairly susceptible to noise introduced by transient queuing and bursty cross-traffic. Past work uses smoothing heuristics to alleviate the impact of noise, but at the cost of requiring large packet trains. In this paper, we consider a machine-learning approach for learning the AB from noisy inter-packet gaps. We conduct extensive experimental evaluations on a 10 Gbps testbed, and find that supervised learning can help realize ultra-high speed bandwidth estimation with more accuracy and smaller packet trains than the state of the art. Further, we find that when training is based on: (i) more bursty cross-traffic, (ii) extreme configurations of interrupt coalescence, a machine learning framework is fairly robust to the cross-traffic, NIC platform, and configuration of NIC parameters.

1 Introduction

End-to-end available bandwidth (AB) is important in many application domains including server selection [1], video-streaming [2], and congestion control [3]. Consequently, the last decade has witnessed a rapid growth in the design of AB estimation techniques [4–6]. Unfortunately, these techniques do not scale well to upcoming ultra-high speed networks [7][1]. This is because small inter-packet gaps are needed for probing higher bandwidth —such fine-scale gaps are fairly susceptible to being distorted by noise introduced by small-scale buffering.

Several approaches have been proposed to reduce the impact of noise [8–10], most of which apply smoothing techniques to "average-out" distortions. Due to the complex noise signatures that can occur at fine timescales, these techniques need to average out inter-packet gaps over a large number of probing packets— this impacts the overhead and timeliness of these techniques.

In this paper, we ask: can supervised machine learning be used to automatically learn suitable models for mapping noise-afflicted packet gaps to AB estimates? We design a learning framework in which the sender and receiver side inter-packet gaps are used as input features, and an AB estimate is the output. Extensive evaluations are conducted, and find that a machine learning

---

[1] We focus on 10 Gbps speed in this paper, and use jumbo frames of MTU=9000B.

© Springer International Publishing Switzerland 2016
T. Karagiannis and X. Dimitropoulos (Eds.): PAM 2016, LNCS 9631, pp. 397–411, 2016.
DOI: 10.1007/978-3-319-30505-9_30

framework can indeed be trained to provide robust bandwidth estimates, with much higher accuracy and using much smaller number of probing packets than the state of the art.

In the rest of this paper, we describe the challenges of AB estimation at ultra high-speed, and the state-of-art in Sect. 2. We introduce our machine learning framework in Sect. 3, and our data collection methodology in Sect. 4. In Sect. 5, we experimentally evaluate our approach, and conclude in Sect. 6.

2   State of the Art

2.1   Background: Available Bandwidth Estimation

Main-stream bandwidth estimation tools adopt the *probing rate model* [11], which sends out streams of probe packets (referred to as **pstreams**) at a desired probing rate, by controlling the inter-packet send gaps as: $g_i^s = \frac{p_i}{r_i}$, where g_i^s is the send gap between the ith and $i\text{-}1$th packets, r_i is the intended probing rate, and p_i is the size of ith packet. The estimation logic is based on the principle of *self-induced congestion*— if $r_i > AB$, then $q_i > q_{i-1}$, where q_i is the queuing delay experienced by the ith packet at the bottleneck link, and AB is the bottleneck available bandwidth. Assuming fixed routes and constant processing delays, this translates to $g_i^r > g_i^s$, where g_i^r is the receive gap between the ith and $i\text{-}1$th packets. Most tools send out multiple packets (N_p) at each probing rate, and check whether or not the receive gaps are consistently higher than the send gaps. They try out several probing rates and search for the highest rate r_{max} that does *not* cause self-induced congestion. There are two dominant strategies for searching for r_{max}:

Feedback-Based Single-Rate Probing: The sender relies on iterative feedback-based binary search. The sender sends all packets within a pstream at the same probing rate, and waits for receiver feedback on whether the receive gaps increased or not. It then either halves or doubles the probing rate for the next stream accordingly. Pathload is the most prominent of such tools [4].

Multi-rate Probing: The sender uses **multi-rate** probing without relying on receiver feedback—each pstream includes $N = N_r \times N_p$ packets, where N_r is the

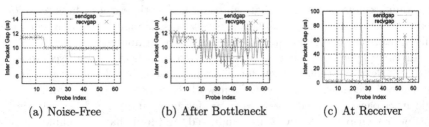

(a) Noise-Free   (b) After Bottleneck   (c) At Receiver

Fig. 1. Inter-Packet Gaps $N_r = 4, N_p = 16$

number of probing rates tried out. The sender then looks for the highest probing rate that did not result in self-congestion. Figure 1(a) illustrates a multi-rate pstream with $N_r = 4, N_p = 16$. The receive gaps are consistently larger than the send gaps since the third probing rate, so the second probing rate (r_{max}) is taken as an estimate of the AB. Multi-rate probing facilitates the design of light-weight and quick tools [7]. Pathchirp is the most prominent of such tools [5].

2.2   Challenge: Noise in Ultra High Speed Networks

End-to-end bandwidth estimation tools face three major challenges at ultra high-speed: accurately creating fine-scale inter-packet gaps at the sender, dealing with the presence of noise along the path, and precisely timestamping packet arrival at the receiver.[2] To address the first challenge, we use the framework described in [10], in which appropriate-sized IEEE 802.3x PAUSE frames — "dummy" frames that get dropped by the first switch on the path, are inserted for creating fine-scale inter-packet gaps. We focus on the remaining two challenges in this paper.

Any resource that is shared can be temporarily unavailable, even if it is not a bottleneck resource over larger timescales—a packet may have to wait in a transient queue at such a resource. In ultra-high speed networks, the magnitude of distortions created by queuing-induced noise are comparable to (or even larger than) the changes in inter-packet gaps that need to be detected for bandwidth estimation. [10] identifies two main noise sources:

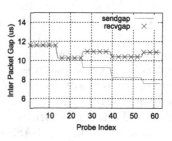

Fig. 2. BASS-denoised gaps

Bursty Cross-Traffic at Bottleneck Resources. If the cross-traffic that shares a bottleneck queue varies significantly at short timescales, then all packets sent at a given probing rate may not consistently show an increase in receive gaps. For instance, Fig. 1(b) plots the inter-packet gaps observed right after the bottleneck queue, for the same pstream as in Fig. 1(a). Due to the bursty cross-traffic, the receive gaps are consistently larger than the send gaps only for the 4th probing rate (resulting in an over-estimation of AB).

Transient Queuing at Non-bottleneck Resources. Even though a resource may not be a network bottleneck, it can certainly induce short-scale transient queues when it is temporarily unavailable while serving competing processes or traffic. *Interrupt Coalescence* is a notable source of such noise [8,14]. It is turned on by default at receivers, forcing packets to wait at the NIC before being handed to OS for timestamping, even if the CPU is available—the waiting time (a.k.a

---

[2] The first and third can be well addressed with specialized NICs [12], or with recent advances in fast packet I/O frameworks such as netmap [13]. In this study, however, we focus on end systems with standard OSes and commodify network hardwares.

interrupt delay) can be significant compared to the fine-scale gaps needed in ultra high-speed networks. Figure 1(c) plots the inter-packet gaps observed at the receiver (g_i^r) for the pstream in Fig. 1(a). We find that these gaps are dominated by a **"spike-dips"** pattern—each spike corresponds to the first packet that arrives after an interrupt and is queued up till the next interrupt (thus experiencing the longest queuing delay). The dips correspond to the following packets buffered in the same batch. With the "spike-dips" pattern, an consistently increasing trend of queuing delays will not be observed in any pstream, leading to persistent over-estimation of AB.

2.3 State of the Art: Smoothing Out Noise

Several approaches have been proposed to deal with the impact of noise on bandwidth estimation [4,8–10]. In general, all of these approaches employ *denoising techniques* for smoothing out inter-packet receive gaps, before feeding them to the bandwidth estimation logic. The recently-proposed Buffering-aware Spike Smoothing (BASS) [10] has been shown to outperform the others on 10 Gbps networks with shorter streams, and is summarized below.

BASS works by detecting boundaries of "buffering events" in recvgaps— each "spike" and the following dips correspond to packets within the *same* buffering event. Based on the observation that the average receiving rate within a buffering event is the same as that observed before the buffering was encountered, BASS recovers this quantity by carefully identifying buffering events and smoothing out both sendgaps and recvgaps within each. The smoothed gaps are then fed into an AB estimation logic. Figure 1(c) plots the BASS-smoothed gaps for the pstream in Fig. 2. In [10], BASS was used within both single-rate and multi-rate probing frameworks. For single-rate probing, BASS helped achieve bandwidth estimation accuracy within 10 %, by using pstreams with at least 64 packets. For multi-rate probing, BASS-smoothed gaps were fed to a variant of the Pathchirp bandwidth estimation logic, and estimation accuracy of mostly within $+/-10\%$ was achieved using multi-rate pstreams with N=96 packets and 50 % probing range[3].

For many applications of bandwidth estimation, that need to probe for bandwidth regularly and frequently, large probe streams pose a significant issue in terms of timeliness, overhead and responsiveness— both the duration for which each pstream overloads the network, and the total time needed to collect AB estimates, increase linearly with N (when N_r is fixed). Even a 96-packet pstream can last several milliseconds in a gigabit network—such a duration is too long in the context of ultra-high speed congestion control [3].

3   A Learning Framework for Bandwidth Estimation

It is important to note that noise can distort gaps within a pstream with several different signatures, each with its own magnitude of gap-distortion, and each

---

[3] Probing range is given by: $\frac{r_N}{r_1} - 1$.

with its own timescale and frequency at which it manifests itself (as exemplified in Fig. 1(b) and (c)). When simple smoothing heuristics are used by the state of the art for dealing with such diversity in noise, they result in an *underfit* model—expectedly, these techniques need to smooth over a *large* number of probe packets in order to be robust. The main hypothesis of this work is that machine learning (ML) can improve our understanding of the noise signature in gaps, with even shorter probe streams than the state of the art.

In this paper, we propose to use supervised learning to automatically derive an algorithm that estimates AB from the inter-packet send and receive gaps of each pstream. Such an algorithm is referred to as a learned "model". We envision that the model is learned *offline*, and then can be incorporated in other AB estimation processes. Below, we briefly summarize the key components of this framework.

Input Feature Vector. The input feature vector for a pstream is constructed from the set of send gaps and receive gaps, $\{g_i^s\}$ and $\{g_i^r\}$. Fourier transforms are commonly used in ML applications, when the input may contain information at multiple frequencies [15,16]—as discussed before, this certainly holds for the different sources of noise on a network path. Hence, we use as a feature vector, the fourier-transformed sequence of send and receive gaps for a pstream of length N: $x = FFT(g_1^s, ..., g_N^s, g_1^r, ..., g_N^r)$.

Output. The output, y, of the ML framework is the AB evaluation. For *single-rate* pstreams, the AB estimation can be formulated as a classification problem: $y = 1$ if the probing rate exceeds AB, otherwise $y = 0$. For *multi-rate* pstreams, it can be formulated as a regression problem, in which $y = AB$.

Learning Techniques. We consider the following ML algorithms—ElasticNet [17], which assumes a polynomial relationship between x and y; RandomForest [18], AdaBoost [19] and GradientBoost [20], which ensemble multiple weak models into a single stronger one; Support Vector Machine(SVM) [21], which maps x into a high dimensional feature space and constructs hyperplanes separating y values in the training set.[4]

Training-and-Testing. The success of any ML framework depends heavily on good data collection—data that is accurate as well as representative. Section 4 describes our methodology for generating hundreds of thousands of pstreams under a diverse set of conditions—it also describes how we collect the ground-truth of AB, AB_{gt}, for each pstream. The knowledge of AB_{gt} allows us to compute an expected value, y_{exp}, of the output of the ML framework—both for single-rate as well as multi-rate pstreams.

---

[4] Our evaluations revealed that models trained with ElasticNet and SVM result in considerable inaccuracy. For brevity, we don't present their results.

We use data from the above pstreams to "train" each of the learning techniques, and then "test" them on pstreams not included in the training set. In each experiment in Sect. 5, we generate more than 20000 pstreams, of which 10000 are used for training and the remaining for testing.[5]

Metrics. Each "test" that is run on a pstream, yields an estimate of the output, y. For single-rate pstream, the accuracy of the model is quantified by the *decision error rate*, which is the percentage of pstreams, for which: $y \neq y_{exp}$. For multi-rate pstream, we quantify *relative estimation error* as: $e = \frac{y - AB_{gt}}{AB_{gt}}$.

4   Data Collection

The success of a ML framework depends on its ability to work with a diverse and representative set on input data. We use a carefully-designed experimental methodology for obtaining such data. A salient feature of our methodology is that all evaluations are performed on a 10 Gbps testbed.

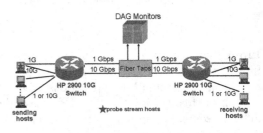

Fig. 3. Testbed topology

Testbed. We use the dedicated network illustrated in Fig. 3 in this study. The switch-to-switch path is a 10 Gbps fiber path. The two end hosts involved in bandwidth estimation are connected to either side of the switches using 10 Gbps Ethernet. The testbed includes an additional 10 pairs of hosts, each equipped with a 1 Gbps NIC, that are used to generate cross traffic sharing the switch-to-switch link. For each experiment, we collect packet traces on the switch-to-switch link using fiber splitters attached to an Endace DAG monitoring NIC which provides timestamps at 10 ns accuracy.

Pstream Generation. We use the Linux kernel modules implemented in [10] for sending and receiving pstreams. An *iperf* client is first used to generate data segments with an MTU size of 9000 bytes. A sender-side Linux Qdisc scheduler then turns the stream of these data segments into pstreams of a specified size and average probing rate. Inter-packet sendgaps are enforced by inserting appropriately-sized Ethernet PAUSE frames sent at link speed. [10] shows that these modules ensure gap accuracy within 1 μs, even when probing at 10 Gbps. At the receiver, packet arrival timestamps are recorded in an ingress Qdisc with microsecond precision. In each experiment summarized in Sect. 5, more than 20000 pstreams are generated, with their average probing rate ranging from 5 Gbps to 10 Gbps.

---

[5] In our Python implementation with scikit-learn [22] library, we use its automatic parameter *tuning* feature for all ML methods, and use 5-fold cross-validation to validate our results.

Calculating. AB_{gt} The first and last packet from every pstream are located in the packet trace, the bytes of cross traffic between those two packets are counted and then cross traffic throughput is computed. AB_{gt}, the groundtruth of AB for that pstream is calculated by subtracting cross traffic throughput from the bottleneck capacity.

Cross Traffic Generation: Incorporating Diversity in Burstiness. One major source of noise considered in this paper is fine-timescale burstiness in cross-traffic encountered at the bottleneck. In order to incorporate *diversity* in such burstiness in our data set, we generate serveral cross-traffic models.

BCT: We first ran a modified version of SURGE [23] program to produce bursty and synthetic web traffic between each pair of cross-traffic generators. An important consideration is that to study the impact of other factors, cross traffic should be consistently repeated across experiments. Thus, we record packet traces from each of the SURGE senders, and then *replay* these in all experiments on the same host using tcpreplay [24]. We denote the aggregate traffic of the replayed traces as "BCT". The average load of BCT is 2.4 Gbps.

SCT: We then generate a smoother version of BCT by running a token bucket Qdisc on each sending host. The resultant aggregate is referred to as **"SCT"**.

CBR: To obtain the least bursty cross-traffic (constant bit-rate, CBR) on the switch-to-switch link, we use iperf to create UDP flows between host pairs. We experiment with CBR traffic generated at 50 different rates, ranging from 1 Gbps to 5 Gbps.

UNC1-3: We also use three 5 min traces collected at different times on a 1 Gbps egress link of the UNC campus network. For each trace, we run a corresponding experiment in our testbed, in which the trace is replayed concurrently by 10 cross-traffic senders (with random jitter in their start times). We label the resultant aggregate traffic aggregates as UNC1, UNC2, and UNC3, respectively. The average load of UNC1 is 3.10 Gbps, UNC2 is 2.75 Gbps, and UNC3 is 3.28 Gbps.

Table 1. Cross traffic burstiness

Label	Burstiness 5–95 % Gbps
BCT	1.15–3.94
SCT	1.78–3.31
UDP	range ~ 0.51
UNC1	2.23–4.05
UNC2	1.84–3.77
UNC3	2.31–4.29

Table 1 quantifies the burstiness of each of the above traffic aggregates, by listing the 5th and 95th percentile load offered by each on the bottleneck link. In most experiments reported in Sect. 5, we use BCT as the cross-traffic—Sect. 5.2 considers the others too.[6]

---

[6] Note that replayed traffic retains the burstiness of original traffic aggregate, but does not retain responsiveness of individual TCP flows. However, the focus of this paper is to evaluate denoising techniques for accurate AB estimation —this metric is not impacted by the responsiveness of cross traffic, but only by its burstiness.

Incorporating Diversity in Interrupt Coalescence. Section 5 describes how we also experiment with diversity in the other major source of noise—receiver-side interrupt coalescence. We rely on two different NIC platforms in this evaluation: *NIC1*, a PCI Express x8 Myricom 10 Gbps copper NIC with the myri10ge driver, and *NIC2*, an Intel 82599ES 10 Gbps fiber NIC.

5 Evaluation

The two major sources of noise considered in this study are cross-traffic bursti-ness and receiver-side interrupt coalescence. In this section, we first present experiments conducted under conditions (BCT cross-traffic, and default con-figuration of interrupt coalescence on NIC1) similar to those used to evaluate BASS. Later, we explicitly control for, and consider the impact of cross-traffic burstiness and interrupt coalescence.

5.1 Performance with BCT, and Default Interrupt Coalescence

BASS has been shown to yield good bandwidth estimates on 10 Gbps networks, when used with single-rate pstreams of length $N = 64$, and multi-rate pstreams with $N = 96, N_r = 4$ [10]. In this section, we first evaluate our ML model under similar conditions, and then consider even *shorter* pstreams.

Single-Rate Probing: We first train models of dif-ferent ML algorithms with $N = 64$, and test them on pstreams probing at 9 discrete rates, ranging from 5–9 Gbps (with BCT, the average AB is around 7.6 Gbps). The bandwidth-decision errors observed at each rate are plotted in

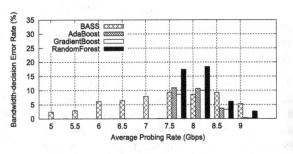

Fig. 4. Model Accuracy (single-rate, N=64)

Fig. 4. We find that (unlike BASS) each of the three ensemble methods leads to negligible error when probing rate is far below or above avail-bw. When prob-ing rates are close to the AB, both BASS and the ML models encounter more ambiguity. AdaBoost and GradientBoost perform comparable to BASS. Ran-domForest performs worse than the two boosting methods, which agrees with the findings in [25].[7] In the rest of the paper we focus our discussion on *Gradi-entBoost*.

---

[7] Each weak model in RandomForest is learned on a different subset of training data. The final prediction is the average result of all models. AdaBoost and GradientBoost follow a boosting approach, where each model is built to emphasize the training instances that previous models do not handle well. The boosting methods are known to be more robust than RandomForest [25], when the data has few outliers.

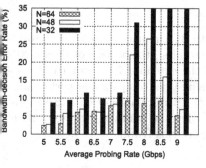

Fig. 5. BASS (single-rate)

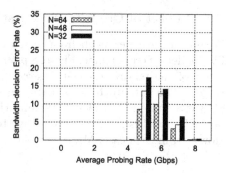

Fig. 6. GradientBoost (single-rate)

We then consider shorter pstreams by reducing N to 48 and 32, respectively, and compare the accuracy in Figs. 5 and 6. We find that the performance of BASS degrades drastically with reduced N: for $N = 32$ error rate can exceed 50 % when the probing rate is higher than 8 Gbps! Although GradientBoost also yields more errors with smaller N, the error rate is limited to within 20 % even with $N = 32$.

Multi-rate Bandwidth Estimation. We next train models with multi-rate pstreams of $N = 96, N_r = 4$ and probing range 50 %. Figure 7 plots the distributions of relative estimation error using BASS and the learned GradientBoost model—ML significantly outperforms BASS by limiting error within 10 % for over 95 % pstreams! We further reduce N to 48 and 32, and find that $N = 48$ maintains similar accuracy as $N = 96$, while $N = 32$ leads to some over-estimation of bandwidth.

Based on our experiments so far, we conclude that *our ML framework is capable of estimating bandwidth with higher accuracy and small pstreams than the state of the art, both with single-rate as well as multi-rate probing techniques.* In what follows, we focus on multi-rate probing with $N = 48$ and $N_r = 4$.

We next consider the impact of prominent sources of noise, namely, cross-traffic burstiness, and receiver-side interrupt coalescence. It is worth noting that the literature is lacking in

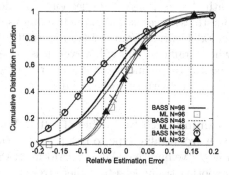

Fig. 7. Multi-rate: estimation error

controlling for and studying the following factors, each of which is a significant one for ultra-high-speed bandwidth estimation—this is a novelty of our evaluation approach.

5.2   Impact of Cross-Traffic Burstiness

We repeat the experiments from Sect. 5.1, with BCT replaced by each of the other five models of cross-traffic. Figure 8 plots the results—the boxes plot the 10–90 % range of the relative estimation error, and the extended bars plot the 5–95 % ranges. The left two bars for each cross-traffic type compare the performance of BASS and our ML model. We find that the performance of both BASS and our ML model is relatively insensitive to the level of burstiness in cross-traffic. However, in each case, ML consistently outperforms BASS.

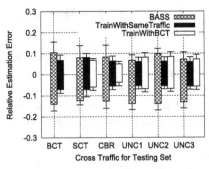

Fig. 8. Test with Same/Smoother traffic

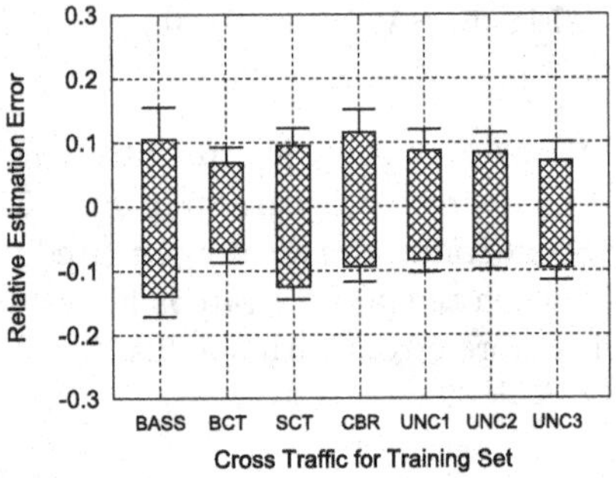

Fig. 9. Train with Smoother traffic

In the above experiments, the ML model was trained and tested using pstreams that encounter the *same* type of cross-traffic model. In practice, it is not possible to always predict the cross-traffic burstiness on a given network path. We next ask the question: how does our ML framework perform when burstiness encountered in the training vs testing phases are different? Intuitively, a model learned from bursty cross-traffic is more likely to handle real-world cases where traffic is bursty; however, it is more subjective to overfitting — the model may try to "memorize" the noisy training data, leading to poor performance for conditions with smoother traffic.

Training with Smoother Traffic. We next employ the models trained with each cross-traffic type to test pstreams that encounter the more bursty BCT in Fig. 9. We find that, ML outperforms BASS in all cases; but models learned with smoother traffic lead to higher errors than the one learned with BCT. This is to be expected—bursty traffic introduces a higher degree of noise. We conclude that it is *preferable to train an ML model with highly bursty cross-traffic, to prepare it for traffic occurring in the wild.*

Testing with Smoother Traffic. We use the model trained with BCT, to predict AB for pstreams that encounter other types of cross-traffic. In Fig. 8, we find that the BCT-derived model gives comparable accuracy as the one trained with the same cross-traffic type as the testing set. Thus, *a model learned from more bursty cross traffic is robust* to testing cases where cross traffic is less bursty.

5.3   Impact of Interrupt Coalescence Parameter

Interrupt coalescence by a NIC platform is typically configured using two types of parameters (*ICparam*): "rx-usecs", the minimum time delay between interrupts, and/or "rx-frames", the number of packets coalesced before NIC generates an interrupt. By default, NICs are configured to use some combination of both of these parameters—our experiments presented so far use the default configuration on NIC1, which roughly boils down to a typical interrupt delay of about 120 μs.

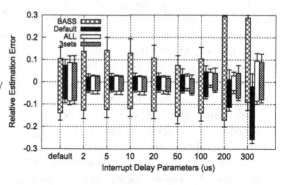

Fig. 10. Impact of ICparams in training set

Different *ICparam* lead to different "spike-dips" patterns in the receive gaps, in terms of the heights of the spikes, as well as the distances between neighboring spikes. We next study the impact of having different *ICparam* in the training vs testing data sets—a model learned with one parameter may fail on pstreams that encounter another. We first apply the previously learned ML model (with *ICparam=default*) to testing scenarios when rx-usecs is set to a specific value—ranging from 2 μs to 300 μs. Figure 10 compares the estimation accuracy of BASS and the ML model (left two bars in each group). The box plots the 10 %–90 % relative error, and the extended bar plots the 5 %–95 % error. We find that BASS severely over-estimates AB when interrupt delay is significant (rx-usecs ≥ 200 μs), while the ML model yields better accuracy. This highlights the model of carefully studying the impact of *ICparam*—this factor was not considered in the BASS evaluations in [10]. We also find that the ML model consistently under-estimates AB when rx-usecs=300 μs.

Machine learning performs best when the training set is representative of conditions encountered during testing. To achieve this, we create a training set that for each *ICparam*, include 5000 pstream samples that encounter it—we denote this as "ALL-set". As shown in Fig. 10, the model learned from "ALL-set" reduces error to within 10 % for most pstreams that encounter extreme rx-usecs values. In practice, however, *all* possible configurations of *ICparam* at a receiver NIC may not be known. We next ask: does there exist a model, which is trained with only a limited set of *ICparams*, but which manages to apply to all configurations? To study this, we minimize the training set to only include two extreme values (2 us and 300 us), in addition to the default setting. We refer to this set as "3sets". Figure 10 shows that "3sets" is sufficient to train an accurate ML model, which provides similar accuracy as "ALL-set".

5.4   Robustness and Portability Across NICs

Different NIC platforms may interpret and implement interrupt coalescence differently. For instance, NIC-2 relies an adaptive interrupt behavior, even though it allows us to specify "rx-usecs" and "rx-frames". Figure 11 illustrates that on this NIC by plotting the distribution of number of frames coalesced per interrupt—we find that "rx-frames" takes no effect when rx-usecs $\leq 12\mu s$. But "rx-usecs" is not respected once it exceeds 12 µs; the distribution mainly depends on rx-frames.

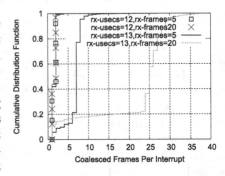

Fig. 11. Interrupting Behavior on NIC2

This unpredictability is quite different from what we observed on NIC1—we next study if our ML framework will work on such a NIC as well.

We repeat the experiments of Sect. 5.3, but use NIC2 instead of NIC1 for collecting both the training and testing data. We consider the following $ICparams$ for NIC-2: rx-usecs from 2 to 10 µs, and rx-frames from 2 to 20 (rx-usecs=100). Models are learned from training sets consisting of different combinations of $ICparams$ in training scenarios, namely,

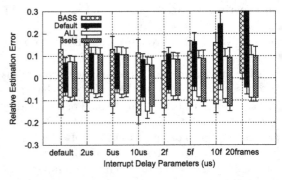

Fig. 12. Impact of ICparams on NIC-2

the "Default", "All-set", and the "3sets"(default,rx-frames=2 and rx-frames=20). Figure 12 plots the estimation errors for these three environments. We find that compared with Fig. 10, the estimation error is generally higher on NIC-2 than NIC-1, presumably due to greater unpredictability in its interrupting behavior. As before, the "3sets" on NIC-2 outperforms BASS significantly, and gives comparable accuracy as "All-set"—which agrees with our observation with NIC-1.

Cross-NIC Validation. To investigate the portability of a learned model across NICs, we next perform a cross-NIC validation: the model trained with data collected using one NIC is tested on data collected on a different NIC. We use only $ICparam=3sets$, and plot the results in Fig. 13(a) and (b). In general, we find that the cross-NIC models generally give comparable accuracy as models trained on the NIC itself. The notable exceptions occur for extreme values of $ICparam$— rx-$usecs$=$300\,\mu s$ on NIC1 and rx-$frames$=20 in NIC2.

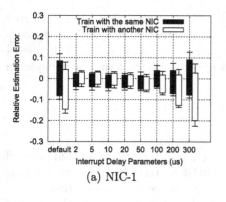

(a) NIC-1

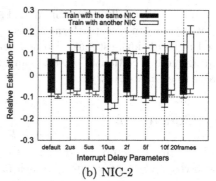

(b) NIC-2

Fig. 13. Cross-NIC evaluation

5.5   Implementation Overhead

The benefits of our ML framework are achieved at the cost of system overhead in the testing phase[8]—the whole model has to be loaded into memory, resulting in more memory usage; also, the estimation time in testing phase increases with model complexity. Table 2 lists the memory and CPU cost incurred by different models

Table 2. Per-pstream evaluation overhead

Single-rate N=48	BASS	Random forest	AdaBoost	Gradient boost
CPU Time(s)	1.7e-6	2.1e-6	1.0e-4	7.7e-6
Memory	-	3.8 MB	3.3 MB	248 KB
Multirate N=48	BASS	Random forest	AdaBoost	Gradient boost
CPU time(s)	8.1e-6	2.5e-5	6.3e-5	7.2e-6
Memory	-	237 MB	2.5 MB	260 KB

trained with *ICparam=3sets*, for generating a single estimate. The memory usuage shown is the relative increment compared with BASS. We find that GradientBoost reports similar costs for both single-rate and multi-rate probing frameworks. For multi-rate probing, it takes comparable CPU usuage as BASS, and only 260 KB more memory, which is negligible for modern end hosts with gigabits of RAM.

Although the above numbers are implementation-specific, it is important to understand the implementation complexity. In our evaluations, the offline-learned GradientBoost model consists of 100 base estimators, each with a decision tree with height less than 3— the memory cost of maintaining 100 small trees, as well as the time complexity in tree-search (upper-bounded by 300 comparisons), are both affordable in modern end-systems, in both user and kernel space. In practice, network operators can program the training process with any preferred ML library and store the learned model. The stored model contains

---

[8] Since models are trained off-line, the training overhead is not of concern.

parameters that fully define the model structure —thus, it can be easily ported to other development platforms. Even a Linux kernel module, such as the ones used in bandwidth-estimation based congestion-control [3], can load the model during module initialization, and can faithfully reconstruct the entire model in order to estimate AB.

6   Conclusion

In this paper we apply ML techniques to estimate bandwidth in ultra-high speed networks, and evaluate our approach in a 10 Gbps testbed. We find that supervised learning helps to improve estimation accuracy for both single-rate and multi-rate probing frameworks, and enable shorter pstreams than the state of the art. Further experiments show that: (i) a model trained with more bursty cross traffic is robust to traffic burstiness; (ii) the ML approach is robust to interrupt coalescence parameters, if default and extreme configurations are included in training; and (iii) the ML framework is portable across different NIC platforms. In further work, we intend to conduct evaluations with more NICs from different vendors, and investigate the practical issues of generating training traffic in different networks.

References

1. Dykes, S.G., et al.: An empirical evaluation of client-side server selection algorithms. In: INFOCOM 2000 (2000)
2. Aboobaker, N., Chanady, D., Gerla, M., Sanadidi, M.Y.: Streaming media congestion control using bandwidth estimation. In: Almeroth, K.C., Hasan, M. (eds.) MMNS 2002. LNCS, vol. 2496, pp. 89–100. Springer, Heidelberg (2002)
3. Konda, K.: RAPID: shrinking the congestion-control timescale. In: INFOCOM. IEEE (2009)
4. Jain, D.: Pathload: a measurement tool for end-to-end available bandwidth. In: PAM (2002)
5. Ribeiro, V., et al.: pathchirp: Efficient available bandwidth estimation for network paths. In: PAM, vol. 4 (2003)
6. Cabellos-Aparicio, A., et al.: A novel available bandwidth estimation and tracking algorithm. In: NOMS. IEEE (2008)
7. Shriram, A., Kaur, J.: Empirical evaluation of techniques for measuring available bandwidth. In: INFOCOM. IEEE (2007)
8. Kang, S.-R., Loguinov, D.: IMR-pathload: robust available bandwidth estimation under end-host interrupt delay. In: Claypool, M., Uhlig, S. (eds.) PAM 2008. LNCS, vol. 4979, pp. 172–181. Springer, Heidelberg (2008)
9. Kang, S.R., Loguinov, D.: Characterizing tight-link bandwidth of multi-hop paths using probing response curves. In: IWQoS. IEEE (2010)
10. Yin, Q., et al.: Can bandwidth estimation tackle noise at ultra-high speeds?. In: ICNP. IEEE (2014)
11. Strauss, J., et al.: A measurement study of available bandwidth estimation tools. In: The 3rd ACM SIGCOMM Conference on Internet Measurement (2003)

12. Lee, K.-S.: SoNIC: precise realtime software access and control of wired networks. In: NSDI (2013)
13. Rizzo, L.: netmap: A novel framework for fast packet I/O. In: USENIX Annual Technical Conference, pp. 101–112 (2012)
14. Prasad, R., Jain, M., Dovrolis, C.: Effects of interrupt coalescence on network measurements. In: Barakat, C., Pratt, I. (eds.) PAM 2004. LNCS, vol. 3015, pp. 247–256. Springer, Heidelberg (2004)
15. Dietterich, T.G.: Machine-learning research (1997)
16. Nguyen, T.T., et al.: A survey of techniques for internet traffic classification using machine learning. Commun. Surv. Tutor. 10(4), 56–76 (2008)
17. Zou, H., et al.: Regularization, variable selection via the elastic net. J. R. Stat. Soc.: Ser. B (Stat. Methodol.) 67(2), 301–320 (2005)
18. Liaw, A., et al.: Classification and regression by randomforest. R News 2(3), 18–22 (2002)
19. Freund, Y., et al.: A decision-theoretic generalization of on-line learning and an application to boosting. J. Comput. Syst. Sci. 55(1), 119–139 (1997)
20. Friedman, J.H.: Greedy function approximation: a gradient boosting machine. Ann. Stat. 29(5), 1189–1232 (2001)
21. Cortes, C., et al.: Support-vector networks. Mach. Learn. 20(3), 273–297 (1995)
22. Pedrogosa, F., et al.: Scikit-learn: machine learning in python. J. Mach. Learn. Res. 12, 2825–2830 (2011)
23. Barford, P., Crovella, M.: Generating representative web workloads for network and server performance evaluation. ACM SIGMETRICS Perform. Eval. Rev. 26(1), 151–160 (1998)
24. Turner, A.A., Bing, M.: Tcpreplay (2005)
25. Dietterich, T.: An experimental comparison of three methods for constructing ensembles of decision trees: bagging, boosting, and randomization. Mach. Learn. 40(2), 139–157 (2000)

Author Index

Printed in the United States
By Bookmasters